PRAISE FOR DENISE DONLON AND
FEARLESS AS POSSIBLE (UNDER THE CIRCUMSTANCES)

"A backstage view of the Canadian and international music scene over the last thirty years: MuchMusic glory days, Sony during the Napster collapse, CBC Radio. Readable, engaging, fascinating even for those who know spit about music, such as me. Lotsa gossip by one who was there (plus being female and about 6 feet tall)." — Margaret Atwood on Reco and Twitter

"Denise Donlon is the First Lady of the Canadian music business. *Fearless as Possible (Under the Circumstances)* is a funny and fascinating journey of a woman who has smashed every glass ceiling to smithereens and somehow has done it in the loveliest way. She also toured with Whitesnake. That alone makes it a must read." — Alan Doyle, Musician, Actor, and Author of *Where I Belong*

"What a ride. From the fly-by-the-seat-of-your-pants origins of MuchMusic — sowing the seeds that grew into the Canadian music scene we know today — to fundraising for the Clinton Giustra Enterprise Partnership, this woman has done it all. Denise Donlon relates her tale with honesty and humour, and with a fair sprinkling of Canadian humility. She is a treasure and we are all lucky to have her at the wheel for so many of our critical cultural events." — Jim Cuddy, Musician and Songwriter

"Denise Donlon isn't just a Canadian media trailblazer, she is a fierce feminist, a sharp intellectual, and one of our country's brightest beams of light. Reading *Fearless as Possible* is like sitting at the table of the greatest dinner party Canada's ever had." — Joseph Boyden, Scotiabank Giller Prize–Winning Author

"A beautiful, poignant, hilarious memoir from Canada's best-known music journalist. *Fearless as Possible* is an honest and deeply personal account from the ultimate woman-on-the-inside who has turned the microphone on everyone, from rock scions to world leaders. Want to know what it's like to go into labour taping a live MuchMusic special with the Cowboy Junkies? Travel with rock stars to conflict zones? Survive an artistic tussle with Leonard Cohen? Denise Donlon writes about it all. And in the process, she offers the kind of advice every underdog needs from the best friend we all wish for." — Samantha Nutt, Founder of War Child and Author of *Damned Nations*

"*Fearless as Possible* is an essential book, an amazing cultural, musical, and historical journey chronicling Denise Donlon's private and professional lives. She digs deep through her own history and shows how it has had an impact on ours. This book reminds us again, in case we'd forgotten, how boldly creative and artistic energy has helped shape the Canadian cultural landscape." — Gordon Pinsent, Actor, Screenwriter, Director, and Playwright

"Denise Donlon is unstoppable. She lit the fire under a whole television station, rallying everyone who worked at MuchMusic to donate time, energy, and expertise, turning Kumbaya into the first and largest ever artist-driven Canadian fundraiser and educator for people living with AIDS/HIV. It just would not have happened without her. If you are looking to get into the culture business in Canada, and when you get there you want to use your power for good, then this is the book for you." — Molly Johnson, Musician and Songwriter

FEARLESS

AS POSSIBLE

(Under the Circumstances)

A MEMOIR

DENISE DONLON

ANANSI

Published in Canada in 2016 by House of Anansi Press Inc.
www.houseofanansi.com

House of Anansi Press is committed to protecting our natural environment. As part of our efforts, the interior of this book is printed on paper that contains 100% post-consumer recycled fibres, is acid-free, and is processed chlorine-free.

20 19 18 17 16   1 2 3 4 5

Library and Archives Canada Cataloguing in Publication

Donlon, Denise, author
Fearless as possible (under the circumstances) / Denise Donlon.

Issued in print and electronic formats.
ISBN 978-1-4870-0002-8 (hardback).—ISBN 978-1-4870-0003-5 (html)

1. Donlon, Denise. 2. Sound recording executives and producers—Canada—Biography. 3. Canadian Broadcasting Corporation—Officials and employees—Biography. 4. Sony of Canada Ltd.—Biography. 5. Women television personalities—Canada—Biography. 6. Music trade—Canada. I. Title.

ML429.D66A3 2016   781.64092   C2016-900842-8
                          C2016-900843-6

Jacket design and typesetting: Alysia Shewchuk
Cover image: ©1988 Derek von Essen

 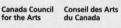

We acknowledge for their financial support of our publishing program the Canada Council for the Arts, the Ontario Arts Council, and the Government of Canada through the Canada Book Fund.

Printed and bound in Canada

This is dedicated to all the ladies in the house:

"Feel the fear. Then do it anyway."
— Gloria Steinem

CONTENTS

AUTHOR'S NOTE

IN 1972, PETER GZOWSKI decided Canada needed a national simile. He was host of CBC's *This Country in the Morning*, and he asked his radio audience, "What would be the Canadian equivalent of the phrase, 'As American as apple pie?'" It was the show's first contest and his listeners rushed to engage, phoning, faxing, and snail-mailing in their suggestions for weeks. Canadians are an enthusiastic bunch and excellent at letter writing.

"As Canadian as maple syrup," "As Canadian as Diefenbaker," and "As Canadian as hockey!" were some of the most commonly referenced submissions. It was a deceptively simple question that became an amusing way to consider our national identity and was hotly debated on the radio.

The winning phrase was from seventeen-year-old Heather Scott from Sarnia, who wrote, "As Canadian as possible under the circumstances." That so appealed to Peter, he had it framed and put on the wall. At the end of every season, everything stuck to the bulletin board came down — except that.

I expect that neither Heather nor Peter will mind that I've appropriated the phrase. Peter was a dear friend and Heather (who died in 1990) may very well be near him now, somewhere soft and sweet, still musing on what it means to be Canadian.

"Fearless as possible under the circumstances" started as a goofy turn of phrase that began to resonate as I wrote this book. I think it captures both my love of Canada and my curious tendency to dive into the deep end, in spite of grinding insecurities. Pollyanna in the shark pool.

(1)

BE A DONLON!

"I had a normal childhood but I managed to overcome it."
— T-SHIRT SLOGAN

IT WAS APRIL 8, 2009. I was standing on a grassy knoll outside the CBC station in Sydney, Nova Scotia, with a bullhorn in my hand. The wind was whipping my hair around my face and cutting through my cotton coat. In front of me was a crowd of about a hundred people chanting and waving placards that read "Save the CBC," "No More Job Cuts," and "We need CBC." The protesters were surrounded by cars and trucks lining the street. There was an ambulance and a fire truck, their red-and-white emergency lights popping against the cold, grey sky. The CBC staff were milling about behind me, more in body than in spirit. I knew some of them would have much rather been standing with the protesters, and against the head of CBC Radio—me.

The moment I felt the weight of the bullhorn in my hand, I remembered the last time I'd addressed a crowd with one. I was in the CityTV/ MuchMusic parking lot, standing on a stage in the pouring rain in front of a seething Smashing Pumpkins crowd. In between thunder rolls and streaks of lightning, I was trying to calm them, promising that the Pumpkins would take the stage as soon as the storm was over. The soggy mob had been waiting for hours and were now chanting, "Bullshit! Bullshit! Bullshit!"

Hopefully this moment would be different.

3

As I drew a slow breath, I thought about all the times I've had to face fear in an ugly situation, exuding a confidence I didn't have. This was a critical juncture for the CBC (one of many unfortunately), and I found myself in the middle of the maelstrom. I reminded myself how fortunate I was to be in a position of authority in the first place. As I stood there I remembered what my "orphan" mother would often say to me: "The world is your oyster, my dear." And she always made me believe it. My father would say: "Stop whining and be a Donlon!" He made me stand tall.

I have been guided by both of these outlooks my whole life — to grasp opportunity when it arises and to be tough when I need to be.

THE STORY OF MY mother's childhood is positively Dickensian. Born in 1927 in the south of Wales, Mavis May Churchill grew up just outside of London at a "ragged school" for homeless and destitute children — despite the fact that her father was still alive. When Mum was four or five, you see, her mother disappeared.

It was 1932, during the Great Depression, when my grandmother suddenly vanished. No warning. No one knew (or admitted to knowing) what happened. Murder? Suicide? She couldn't have simply walked away. Her shoes were found placed neatly side by side on the banks of the River Rhondda, near to where she'd lived with her husband and four young children in an impoverished coal-mining town in Wales.

All Mum remembers of the event is a stout, stern Salvation Army matron appearing at the door. She bundled Mum and her three brothers into a car and off they went to the train station, never to return to Wales. Mum was sent to the Esher Place Shaftesbury Home school for girls in Surrey, while her brothers ended up being shuffled through various foster homes. It would be eight years before she saw any of them again. And the circumstances of her mother's death would remain a dark mystery forever.

Mum remembers her years as a "ragged girl" as a miserable existence. She was a small, shy child, vulnerable to the cruelty of the older, stronger girls. When she tells me grisly stories of her childhood, I picture her as Jane Eyre in that old 1944 black-and-white movie, where Jane is standing, thin and trembling, on a stool and being harshly berated by the headmaster. She grew up feeling frightened, abandoned, and unloved in that bleak place where food was hard to come by but discipline was generously doled out. Still, of the four children, hers was the comparatively better life — one of her brothers committed suicide. When she left the institution at age fourteen, she was well-schooled in the domestic arts and had developed what would be a lifelong appreciation for classical literature and music, as well as a fierce devotion for anyone who showed tenderness toward her — especially, as it turned out, my dad.

To say that my father was good-looking is, even for a naturally biased daughter, an understatement. He could easily have graced film marquees. He'd trained as a boxer at the knee of his father, an Irish prize fighter who died of dropsy (edema, as we know it now), no doubt caused from being hit in the ring. Dad was an able worker, an animated storyteller, and a fine singer, but his real gift was his charm. His easy smile and cheeky wink opened more doors for him than any secret password ever could.

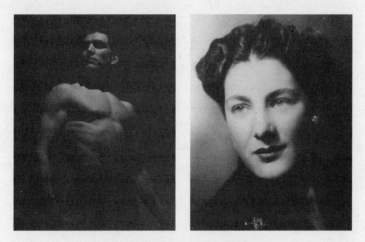

Ronald Donlon and Mavis May Churchill.

Yet despite his natural graces, his own unlucky childhood makes it rather remarkable that my father would eventually make his living very much on the right side of the law. Like Mum, he too was born in 1927, but grew up on the mean streets of Liverpool. Unemployment was high and many children suffered from malnourishment, rickets, and tuberculosis. People did what they had to do to get by. When Dad was a young teen — not even sixteen — he was arrested for petty theft. Instead of a reprimand, he was sent to serve time at Borstal Reformatory for young offenders in the

U.K. I'm sure his education there was in something other than bricklaying.

Once he was released, his mother told him to "never darken our door-step again." He was left to fend for himself, and he did. I expect the disdain for authority he'd acquired as a guest of the Crown, combined with his boxing prowess, was a one-two combination certain to be in conflict for him in the regimentation of army life.

Mavis May Churchill met Ronald Donlon in 1947, just after the end of the Second World War. They were both eighteen. She was a young patriot who had joined the Navy, Army, and Air Force Institutes (NAAFI), a British organization created to support the troops. He was a corporal in the Royal Army Service Corps. They were both stationed in Hoek Van Holland, a town in the southwestern corner of the Netherlands. The area had been occupied by the Germans during the war but later became a major embarkation port for Allied troops returning home.

My father wooed my mother aggressively. She used to joke that she had to marry my father out of compassion for her other suitors. He was a commanding presence and good with his fists, and he would literally scare off the competition, keeping an eye out while they walked her home, then suggesting that she was already taken.

It never occurred to me that his courtship might be considered stalking; it was just...romantic. Mum admits to having been a little afraid of my father, but she was enthralled with him at the same time. He was handsome, he made her laugh, and he doted on her. She felt she had a protector for the first time in her life.

While they were both stationed in Holland, Dad was a driver for the camp major, and the availability of a vehicle in the off-hours gave him access to the black market. He was the guy who always had a packet of cigarettes for a friend, or a bar of chocolate for the ladies.

I can't ask Dad for any more details to fill out these stories; he passed away in 1997. But as my mum tells it, his time in the army was capped by an extended sojourn in the brig, where he was treated brutally. He was jailed for having punched a sergeant major, a mistake that followed him through to the very last of his army days.

The sergeant major was known as "the Beast of the Camp" and roundly disliked by the enlisted men. One night, Dad saw him beating a drunk young soldier who was being held down by two others. Dad stepped in and knocked the sergeant major out cold. Dad wasn't arrested that night—apparently the Beast didn't want it known that he'd been bested with one punch—but word got out. Dad didn't buy a drink on base for weeks, while the sergeant waited for an opportunity for revenge.

On my father's last day in the army, he and Mum said a tearful goodbye before his boat sailed away for London. My mother confided to me later that she'd felt relieved he was leaving. She thought the time away from each other would be a good test of their relationship. But the separation was short-lived. A fight broke out on the boat; the military police broke it up and, upon searching my father, found illegal ration cards. Dad insisted that the fight was instigated by the sergeant major and that the ration cards were planted, but to no avail. He was returned by patrol boat to the camp in handcuffs.

While Dad was incarcerated, Mum finished her service in the NAAFI and returned to London, where she found work at Bourne and Hollingsworth, a high-end department store on Oxford Street. She was a counter clerk, but also occasionally worked as a model, a job that gave her self-confidence a huge lift. She also leaned on her last name, Churchill, to cover the scent of her orphanage upbringing. She'd whisper to me when I was growing up, "We're Churchills, but we were from the bastard side of the family, I'm afraid, darling."

Mum learned to approximate elegance on a shoestring, wearing her one good black suit to work every day. At night, she joined the lineup for the cheap theatre seats "in the gods." Surrounded by culture, fashion, and her new independence, her circle soon broadened and she began dating a soft-spoken Scottish aeronautical engineer working on a sleek new plane known as the de Havilland Comet.

I might have grown up with Gaelic as a second language had my father not resurfaced. He knew his rough ways were tough for my mum, so he worked hard to remake himself. He learned to affect a more posh English accent and before long was cutting a dashing figure on the London scene with his studied refinements and new suit. She fell for him all over again.

Their wedding photograph is of storybook beauty: Mum in her pearly tiara and veil, draped around her starched white eyelet dress; Dad handsome with sleek black hair, a dark tailored suit, and a smile like the cat who'd caught the canary. In the photo they're about to climb into their rented car and depart for their honeymoon. It looks like they have the world on a string. Sadly, the life in store for them wasn't as idyllic as that picture seemed to portend.

MY PARENTS EMIGRATED TO Canada in 1954. Dad had left a few months before Mum to look for work and find accommodations. Mum left three months later with my six-month-old brother John in her arms, travelling aboard a ship called the *Atlantic* on a journey that was rocked by storms.

Mum had worked hard to convince Dad to leave England, and I count my lucky stars that she was successful. She wanted a new start for them as a married couple and the chance at a better life for her son. Postwar London was a dreary, grasping place, with rationing still in effect and the country pulling its bootstraps out of the muck of the war. Dad resisted the move at first, but the Great Smog of December 1952 was the break my mother was looking for. Londoners were used to "pea soupers," as the coal-induced fogs were called, but this one, more concentrated due to unusual weather, caused thousands of fatalities. It preyed on the old, the very young, and those whose health was compromised by war-time injuries. Mum argued that they needed to leave for the sake of the baby, but she had another motive in mind: to get my father out of the country. She was worried that he might fall in with the wrong set in London.

Dad got off to a rocky start in Canada. Like many immigrants, he arrived with no connections and took any job he could get. He worked at a dry cleaner's, where he made five cents a shirt, hardly enough to support a family; then as a venetian blind salesman, which ended abruptly when he confronted the foreman for not paying him the overtime he was due. While Mum was crossing the Atlantic, he was working as a pest controller.

Mum arrived in Canada on October 13, 1954, fresh off a heaving boat that made most of the passengers seasick the whole way. Her flight from Halifax to Toronto to meet Dad was no better, encountering freakish turbulence as they neared the city. Hurricane Hazel hit the city the next day. The infamous storm devastated parts of Toronto, leaving in its wake the chaos of flooding, downed trees, broken bridges, and infrastructure destruction amounting to what would be over a billion dollars in today's money.

They barely recognized each other at the terminal. Mum remembers Dad looking about as bad as she felt. She was exhausted from the trip and had cut off her shiny auburn hair (I still have her braid), thinking short hair would be easier to manage with the baby on a ship. He was gaunt and dishevelled, and anxious about what Mum might think of the dingy basement apartment he'd managed to rent. Dingy or no, their residency in the basement was short. They were evicted by the landlady, who was bothered by their sick and crying baby. At the time there was a polio scare, and Mum was frantic that John might have contracted the disease, but he was a strong baby and eventually thrived.

Luckily, Dad's employment options were about to change. Dad was coming out of an apartment block, having finished a spray job, to find a policeman putting a ticket under the wiper of the pest control company's truck. The vehicle was in bad shape, rusty and with a shattered windshield. The officer gave him forty-eight hours to get the truck fixed or it would be impounded. The next day, when Dad went to the police station to plead for more time, the sergeant, a Liverpudlian, asked him to consider becoming a policeman. "We need good men," he said, and Dad promptly applied. Good thing they didn't check his record in the U.K., because his time at the Borstal would surely have shuttered the opportunity.

Dad was accepted into the police academy and soon became a motorcycle ticketing officer with a decent wage and benefits, even if the nature of the job meant he wasn't inclined to meet the happiest people around town.

Mum insisted they supplement his pay by taking on janitorial duties in the building in which they now lived. It was another "shite hole," as Dad put it, in the northwest end of Toronto. They shared responsibility for collecting the rents, fixing leaky taps, washing the floors, and fielding complaints for the landlord, who was never quick to respond. Mum took an instant dislike to the man, a rotund, uncouth, greasy fellow who often had a wet, shredded cigar hanging from the corner of his mouth. Dad's feelings toward him weren't much better—a barely contained seethe.

As the story goes, one day, while my dad was mopping, the landlord strode in, purposefully walking over the freshly cleaned floors. It was a classic power-play move certain to infuriate my father, which it did. Dad gave him a cuff around the head with the dirty mop, and that was the end of that job and that apartment.

It was another unwelcome move, and in the next apartment their janitorial duties included stoking the furnace. Once again Mum joined in, taking in washing, collecting the rents, and shovelling coal, the tasks becoming increasingly less manageable as she worked around her growing belly.

IN FEBRUARY 1956, I joined the family.

Apparently I was a horrible, colicky baby and no amount of nursing, gripe water, or walking around the block would calm me down. I was *that* kid.

Mum says now that she's glad she resisted throttling me. But I seemed quite willing to try and shorten my lifespan anyway, putting anything within reach into my mouth. No one minded much. Antiseptic sanitary wipes weren't even a pipe dream in those days. Dropped pacifier? Pick it up and pop it back in. Dirty face? Spit on a hanky and wipe. Scraped knee? Let the air get to it. Neighbour's kid's got the chicken pox? Hand the child over the fence, let's get it over with.

Apparently I was game to eat anything—pennies, buttons, dirt—but I'm told my singular favourite was creepy crawlies. There were lots of live bugs to choose from, a culinary predilection I apparently pursued like a flabby-tongued iguana.

One morning, the family woke up to a swarm of June bugs. We were in a first-floor apartment, and a small window had been left open during the night. Mum had opened the bedroom door to find the living room covered with flying, crawling, shiny brown bugs the size of fifty-cent pieces. One of my very first memories of my mother is watching her sweeping up huge piles of June bugs, deftly opening the door to cast them out, then slamming it quickly to prevent as many from flying back in.

I, meanwhile, had been placed for safekeeping in the middle of the round thrift-store rug. As Mum whirled about the room, I was sitting calmly, investigating the possibility of breakfast. By the time Mum looked over to see how I was doing, I had a big, juicy June bug in my mouth, its crunchy hind legs wiggling between my lips. Before she could react, I swallowed it down. Mum was horrified, but I was unharmed. She claims that I beamed at her as if I wanted more.

As the family grew, Mum continued to be penny-wise and pound-smart, her "ragged school" domestic skills and wartime rationing experience paying off. She was a champion of the cheap and cheerful meal. A wholesome lentil soup could last for days; one chicken could fuel a roast/stew/soup combination that would last even longer. She squirrelled away every spare dime, and eventually my parents scraped together enough money to put a down payment on our first house in Canada. Total cost? $11,000. It was a white wooden bungalow on Ellesmere Road in Highland Creek on the eastern outskirts of Scarborough—or, as we called it, "Scarberia." It had a living room with a fireplace, two bedrooms, a den, and a fenced backyard. We were going to need the room. Two years after me, there was another child on the way, my brother Paul, and two years after that would come my youngest brother, Peter.

Peter, Paul, me, and John.

That house was an oasis, surrounded by fields, forests, and fresh air, and only a half-hour or so by car to Dad's police division downtown. We had mature trees for manic kids to climb, a school within walking distance, and the first of three boxer dogs. We named them Prince, Prince, and Prince. It was a naming pattern broken only years later when we got a miniature white poodle, who we named Alfie. He was cuter and meaner than all of them.

Like most other kids in the neighbourhood, we ran around like feral creatures. Told to "Be home when the street lights come on" or—Dad's favourite—"Go play on the 401!" we ran amuck, getting into and out of trouble and somehow surviving without helicopter moms, cell phones, or subcutaneous tracking devices. Despite some minor mishaps, our free-range habits—and what today would probably be called, with some disapproval, my parents' "free-parenting" style"—resulted in us growing up energetic, reedy, and able to entertain ourselves without shrink-wrapping or screens of any size.

That said, it does surprise me a *bit* that none of us were Darwin Award winners.

Mum was largely unfazed by blood—by this time she was working in the emergency admitting department at Centenary Hospital—but we did our best to surprise her by amassing an impressive collection of cuts and concussions, broken bones, stitches, and occasional puzzling rashes.

There were burnt fingers and singed hair from setting insulation on fire in an abandoned barn and then hurling the flaming goo at each other. John got shot with BB pellets ("You'll shoot your eye out!"), which had to be artfully removed with tweezers. A rabies shot was considered when I got bit deeply on the ass by a neighbour's St. Bernard. A tetanus shot was delivered when I sliced my foot on broken glass jumping off a bridge into the muddy waters of Highland Creek on a dare. I was promised a quarter!

That creek would later be the scene of a daring rescue of my younger brothers Peter and Paul from a sudden flood. They thought they'd "shoot the rapids" in a broken canoe they'd found lying around somewhere. They abandoned the battered vessel when it started to sink, but Peter got stuck near the riverbank when his oversized rubber boots—borrowed from Dad— filled up with rushing water and mud. Firemen arrived to pull them out, but there was no way Peter was leaving Dad's boots behind. He was more afraid of our father than he was of drowning.

In the rare cases when anyone sustained a serious injury, there was always great excitement in the 'hood. We spent one afternoon on hands and knees in the front yard across the street, searching for the bloody toes of a kid who had chopped three of them off while mowing the lawn in his bare feet ("If we find them and put them on ice they can sew them back on!"). Only one toe was found, too mangled to save.

One year, Mum and Dad got enough cash together to go to England for a week's visit. There wasn't enough money for everyone, so they took the eldest children — John and me — and left Peter and Paul at home with "friends." In London we stayed with family on both sides, Mum and Dad doing their best to look flash and successful, even though Mum's finery was courtesy of the Extoggery, the East Toronto thrift store. Their attempts at being well turned-out caused resentment among some branches of the family, who sniffed at their "toffee-nosed" attitude and thought we were putting on airs. ("Gettin' a bit big for our britches, are we?") Not that John and I noticed at the time. We were happy to be cajoled into our Sunday second-hand best with bribes of lollies and crisps and promises of tea and biscuits, trays of which would appear when we arrived at a relative's door. I loved London.

John, Dad, Mum, and me (already adjusting for height . . .)

We returned home to Canada to find that the couple Mum and Dad had hired to look after Peter and Paul were nowhere to be found. Toys scattered around, dishes in the sink, flies a' buzzin' around the diaper pail; Where was everybody? After a moment's panic, the boys were found safe in the backyard, tied by the waist to the clothesline. I'm not sure they really minded the bondage; they had free run of the yard, after all, even if it was just enough to go back and forth. My parents located the couple eventually, when they came by for payment. Thank heavens no one had Children's Aid on speed dial in those days.

THERE WAS LOTS OF joy in our childhood too. Especially around Christmas.

Mum always made a *huge* deal out of Christmas. Our joke was that if you stood still long enough, she'd hang ornaments from your ears. Christmas had been the one day she'd treasured at the girls' school, the day when she'd get a present donated by someone in the village, plus, at the foot of her dorm-room cot, a stocking filled with nuts, toffees, black licorice, and — far down in the toe, the heaviest and most coveted gift of all — a big, fragrant navel orange. She's often described making that orange last for days, savouring it slowly, eating every last bit: pips, pith, and peel. She'd fill our stockings the way she remembered hers, though we were less enamoured with the nuts and citrus than with what might be under the tree.

Our Christmas videos, transferred over from Super-8 film one year by my dad, might prove interesting fodder for child psychologists. Take the silent-movie footage of a Christmas morning when I was about six years old. We four kids have our arms up to shield our eyes from the bank of hot camera lights as we dive under the tree. Like many families in our neighbourhood, our presents were from the Sally Ann or the Goodwill, repaired and repainted by Mum. No one cared that they weren't new. That year there was a set of junior boxing gloves for eight-year-old John. John donned the right-hand glove and gave the left hand to four-year-old Paul. In no time, they were whaling on each other with one hand each, roundhousing away in a festive fight club. I got into it too, and from the looks of the video I held my own.

Paul's gift that year was a plastic steering wheel. There's no toy car in sight, just the wheel. It was an insightful present, as his habit that year was to turn endlessly around in circles on the spot, his left thumb in his mouth, his right hand holding Mum's underwear while twirling his hair with his index finger. Apparently I too was a twirler. Later in the film there's a shot of me spinning, arms open wide, with a football the size of my head planted in my mouth.

My youngest brother Peter can be seen riding back and forth across the camera frame, bashing into furniture on his new used tricycle. Peter seemed to crave the feeling of impact at high speeds, curiously immune to pain even at three years old. If you look closely you can see there's a sizeable egg on his head, caused by his own bizarre nightly machinations. He'd grab both sides of the crib and rock himself back and forth, his head hitting the end and propelling the crib forward until finally it came to rest against the bedroom door. My parents would move the crib back into place and soothe him back to sleep, but he'd just wake up a few hours later and do it again. Eventually they just left him to his own devices, assuming he'd get over it one day. He was a happy, mischievous kid otherwise, and eventually outgrew both the practice and the little bald patch on top of his forehead.

I should note that there were no lasting effects from the twirling or the head injuries, nor are there abandonment issues caused by the free-parenting styles of the day. All three of my brothers are family men with fabulous kids. Paul's an accomplished mechanic, Peter is a successful realtor and facilities manager, and John is a long-distance trucker, no doubt enjoying the solitude of the road.

My present that year was a black baby doll in a shiny pink dress (in the original box!). I thought she was awesome. I doubt there was any conscious diversity instruction going on—she was simply what was available at the Goodwill that year. I also received a jewellery box with a wind-up ballerina that spun in tight circles to a tinkly Tchaikovsky tune. My own ballet aspirations were later to be dashed by a bun-headed madam who rightly proclaimed that I would grow too tall. "Zeyah vill be no vun who vill dahnce viss you," she pronounced. She was right. Best to know early.

Life on Ellesmere Road was good. It was a fine little house, save for that curious scrabbling sound under the floor. We tried to ignore the noises— "Go to sleep dear, it's just a tree branch against the window"—but one night, while Mum was in the bath, up through a hole in the wall beside the toilet bowl appeared a wet, whiskery snout with two long white teeth under black shiny eyes. A rat! Suddenly there was a blood-curdling sound that no one could mistake.

Our little bungalow had no basement. There was a distance of about a foot and a half between the sandy ground and the floorboards, the ground broken by a series of two-foot-wide culverts that often had about four feet of water in them.

There was a trap door in the floor of a closet that was intended to provide access to the plumbing in case things froze or fouled, and it was through that door that Dad laid out the rat poison. After that we all held our breath, listening for the tell-tale squeaky sounds and the rustle of the furry backs on the undersides of the floorboards. It took only a few days until everything was quiet on the southern front. There was a collective sigh of relief: the enemy was conquered. But the drama wasn't over. A week later, there was a noticeable pong wafting up from below, which got worse day by day. The rats were dead, but their corpses remained, floating bloated in the water and slowly rotting under the house.

Paul was elected to retrieve them. He was the only one small enough to fit under there. I think he was about five. I remember thinking it was a good thing he had a buzz cut — there was less chance of spiders collecting in his hair.

Dad lowered the kid into his high rubber boots, attached construction gloves to his hands, and tied a rope around his waist to secure him. (Mum had insisted on some guarantee that we wouldn't lose him under the house.) Paul seemed totally up for the adventure and happy for the attention — until it was time to go into the hole. His eyes became as watery as his destination.

"Don't worry, kid. You won't be down there for long and you'll get a quarter for every rat you bring up." Now you're talking — we Donlons would do a lot for a quarter.

Off he went down into the hole and soon enough he'd got one in his hands. It was a heavy, sodden thing, rounded with bloat, easily eight or nine inches long — and that's not counting the tail. Paul thrust it up through the hole like a professional weightlifter shuddering over his limit.

"Good boy. Be careful. Don't puncture them. Any more?"

Paul hoisted half a dozen rotting rats up through the hole, Dad putting them into a green garbage bag. Dad thought there might be more, but

Paul had had enough. He was spooked and teary. Dad pulled Paul up and gave him a big manly hug. High praise, indeed! Then he walked the heavy green plastic bag down the hall, out the front door, and into the garage, dripping all the way.

It was scary for Paul for sure, but sometimes we kids liked to be scared—Mum would read us fiendish stories she'd written about the wicked girls in her school (more fact than fiction, I'll wager), and we relished fairy tales in which trolls lived under bridges, witches ate children, and mermaids walked on knives. One night I watched a crude black-and-white Bela Lugosi vampire movie with my brothers and went to bed imagining that a vampire was coming to suck my blood. I dragged out the scenario, making the approach last forever—He's getting closer, closer . . .—until his teeth were hovering over my neck and I'd SCREAM! for someone to save me.

For some reason, I repeated this demented pantomime night after night, addicted to my awesome ability to scare myself silly. My brothers got into the act and started hiding in the closet and leaping out after dark with neon superballs in their eyes. It got to the point where I insisted I could only get to sleep if the hall light was on and I was allowed to wear one of Prince's two-inch studded leather collars. That particular element of the routine lasted only one night; the pillow was shredded and the dog needed his collar. The hall light lasted a few days longer, until my father sharply shut it off. "You think we're bloody made of money?"

Money *was* scarce. Mom bought day-old bread and discounted meat and a four-year supply of blue-ish powdered skim milk because she got a free standing mixer with it. If you didn't eat your liver at dinner, you might wake up to it at breakfast. (I still can't abide organ meat to this day. My husband Murray gets his fix while he's on the road—he loves his truck-stop liver and onions—careful not to come home with liver on his breath.)

There were two luxuries in the house, both off-limits to children. A small box of British Cadbury orange chocolate fingers was kept in the freezer, rationed for my father, and NO ONE but him was allowed to touch them. The other luxury was cheese. Cheese was strictly for grown-ups.

One morning while Mum and Dad were still in bed, I remember standing in front of the open fridge door, mesmerized by the forbidden cheddar cheese. Giving into temptation, I grabbed it, unwrapped it, and took a big bite. Wow. Cheese was amazing. I wrapped it up tight and put it back.

I soon realized the seriousness of my crime. What to do? Blame it on my brothers, of course. I took the cheese out of the fridge and walked it down to my parents' bedroom.

Knock, knock.

"Go away!" shouted Dad.

"Mum?" I whispered. "I've got something to show you. Please?"

"Oh, all right, come in," she said.

I walked over to the bed and held out my hand, Exhibit A pointedly on display. "Look. Somebody took a big bite out of the cheese!"

My father sat up in bed, took one look at me, then the cheese, and said, "Bring it here."

He picked it up, examined the bite mark, and said, "Open your mouth."

"But why?" I asked, then did as I was told.

"*Somebody* ate the cheese?" he said, fitting the perfectly formed tooth marks in the brick to my teeth: an exact match.

My father became an exceptional detective for a reason. Under his surveillance I learned a lot about the importance of honesty, the downside of duplicity, and being a law-abiding citizen.

Little Miss Innocent.

DAD WAS A CHARMING, complex man. He did the best he could to navigate a world that had set him up early for emotional hardship. It wasn't only the Borstal experience; like many men of his generation who went to war, he considered showing signs of sentimentality unmanly. He excelled at police work because he was a decent guy with a strong sense of justice, but with the work came a gruff, authoritarian exterior that I know hid an awkward tenderness. He was quick to laugh, always ready with a salty joke or a song. But he also had a very real temper.

Because Dad worked shifts, we'd tiptoe around, afraid to wake him. Our neighbourhood friends were wary too, seldom congregating at our house.

"C'mon over!"

"Is your dad home?"

"Yes."

"Nah, Let's go to my house."

I've certainly inherited a piece of the Donlon disposition. In times when I've shrunk from standing up for myself, Murray will remind me to "Be a Donlon!" But he doesn't mean I should let my temper out for a trot.

Dad's temper was a kind of rolling wrath that, once out of the bottle, was almost impossible to put back in until it had run its course. It was like watching a thundercloud build: his face reddening, veins thickening, spit flying. There was no running away. You had to just stand there and take it, without flinching if you could. The anger, the heat, the names. He'd call me a "slovenly bitch" or a "clumsy clod," and I believed I was those things. I became dogged about self-improvement. But the other side of the coin was that I also became skilled in negative reinforcement, calling myself names, dwelling on my failures.

My brother John remembers holding the ladder while Dad was soldering something on the roof. Drops of molten metal were falling down and landing on his shoulder. He flinched and Dad yelled at him to "Stop moving and keep that fucking ladder still." John did as he was told, even as the hot drops of solder landed on his bare arm.

In the face of rage, I learned to detach.

Be still.

Be cold.

Say nothing.

Breathe.

I knew that if I could stay still and bear it long enough, he would eventually storm out of the room. He *could* control it. He never hit me.

As I grew older, I was able to catch a glimpse of the needy boy underneath. I don't remember the exact moment when that happened, but it helped turn my fear into compassion. I suppose if I spent enough time on someone's couch I might understand it better, but I know for sure I don't ever want to feel like a victim again.

I came to hate any expression of anger, from road rage to bullying. I've met my father's kind of fury more than once in my career and it's thanks to him that I'm better armed to find the strength to stand up to it and, just as importantly, to recognize when I can't defeat it and find a way to remove myself from it. Ultimately I don't see rage as something to be scared of; I see it as a sign of weakness.

The entertainment business is rife with power-hungry arrogance. I've known bullies in the form of record company presidents, artist managers, tour managers, and broadcasters. Yellers and screamers and blowhards. But the words don't have to be loud to be hurtful. There's a more insidious approach that can be equally oppressive: delivered in a whisper, intended to make you feel stupid and humiliated.

I learned resilience. And I know it's because of my dad, too, that I've striven to be a pleaser. I may hate confrontation, but the avoidance of it has helped me build skills in negotiation. And, like him, I instinctively want to defend the powerless—it may be why I've been motivated to travel to conflict zones. I think that like many women in business, I find it easier to advocate for the rights of others—negotiating raises, titles, positions for the deserving—before fighting for myself. That said, I will rise to my full height when I have to.

My father did his best and I know he had a soft spot for me. He used to take me to the gun range and I became a pretty good shot, but one of my favourite memories of quality one-on-one Dad time is captured in another home movie—this one of the two of us working in the front yard. I'm about five, wearing a dress and rubber boots, smoothing cement with a plasterer's trowel on our new sidewalk. Prince is in the background and Dad's looking on, smoking and smiling, nodding in approval. A priceless memory of me learning a trade. It's always good to have something to fall back on.

Donlon family death match.

We may have had to tread lightly around him, but all us kids competed for Dad's attention. We loved to wrestle with him, and my MO was to try to make him laugh by telling him dumb kid jokes, the comic effect magnified by a childhood speech impediment. I had a lisp, made more pronounced by protruding front teeth. I was a dedicated thumb sucker. My parents tried to deter me from the habit with plastic gloves, boxing gloves, and wool mittens that were taped to my wrists, but I could always Houdini them off. Popular at the time was a nasty finger-painting remedy suggested by the druggist. They'd paint my thumb with the bitter red substance, but I'd persevere through the odious taste, my thumb soon back to normal: white, wet, and wrinkly with use.

My lisp was a real crowd-pleaser, though. I remember being roused from sleep and led, blinking, into the living room, where my dad would be enjoying a beverage with his friends.

"Say 'sausages'!"

I'd shake my head, mouth firmly clasped around my thumb.

"C'mon, honey. Say 'sausages.' I'll give you a quarter."

"Thaawthaajezzz," I'd sputter, and they'd all laugh.

"Say it again!" and again I'd mumble the word, until I had a warm coin in my hand and was allowed to go back to bed. I didn't mind. I was grateful for the attention, and the cash.

Everyone thought I'd grow out of it, but by grade three I was still a sibilant mess. And so, once a week, a little folded card bearing my name and a round clock-face would appear on the chalkboard rail at the front of the classroom for the kids to mock. I'd slink out of class at the appointed time and for forty-five minutes the speech therapist and I would play "Repeat after me."

"She sells sea shells by the sea shore. She sells sea shells by the sea shore."

I was eventually cured and stopped sucking my thumb, but a lisp will sneak back in whenever I'm nervous, especially when I'm on live television. "Months" is still a word I avoid.

My father died suddenly of an aortic aneurysm at the age of sixty-nine. He had just retired from the Toronto Police Service after a thirty-year career as a detective in Homicide and Holdup and then on the Emergency Task Force. I delivered the eulogy at his memorial, speaking to a crowd of mostly policemen who laughed when I told of my Dad coming around, just a few days before he died, to the house Murray and I had bought. It wasn't a palace. Dad looked at the basement window and said, "You better put bars on that before some thieving swine robs you blind." I spoke about the fun talks we'd have when I'd come home from university. He'd be hanging out with the ETF guys on the back porch. They'd be heavily armed in their blue jumpsuits, telling war stories; I'd be in my bell-bottoms campaigning for Greenpeace and the legalization of marijuana. I spoke about his colourful turns of phrase, his humour, his sweet singing voice, and his strong sense of morality. And I spoke about how much of our fathers we carry in ourselves. He'd built a tough exterior, having seen much ugliness in his world; but I knew his heart. He was building the strength to share his tenderness later in life, though it was a journey he didn't get to finish.

WHILE DAD WAS THE authoritarian in the house, Mum did her best to ensure we had a well-rounded cultural upbringing. When Dad was at work, she'd play classical music at full volume, singing along with her favourite operas — partly, I think, to drown out her rambunctious children. She insisted that John and I take piano lessons and found an old piano in the Classifieds. It was an imposing piece of furniture but a poor instrument, a square, heavyweight American Grand with massive carved feet and a cracked soundboard. It did the trick for a few years, until a short young man took it away, intending to strip it of its strings and use it as a bed.

Miss P. is the piano teacher I remember best. She was certainly the most bizarre. She was a short, round lady with a big bosom, dark red lips and nails, and a black beehive hairdo. She looked remarkably like the wide witch on Bugs Bunny, the one whose hairpins flew behind her whenever she mounted her broom.

She'd come to the house on Wednesdays after school, clipping across the living-room floor in her tiny stiletto heels. Those heels left pockmarks in the linoleum that built up over time, creating an indelible trail from the door to the piano. She was much too imperious to be asked to remove her shoes.

Miss P.'s lessons were an exercise in fear management. Her first move was always to set the metronome ticking; she'd then proceed to conduct us with a ruler that would snap out if we made a mistake. Once, when I'd made the same clunker in the same spot in an arpeggio one time too many, she grabbed my hand in frustration, stabbing my index finger repeatedly into the correct key—"This one! This one! This one!" That was one sharp red fingernail.

I found no joy playing the piano. I took years of Conservatory lessons, but without an inspirational teacher, it was a rote exercise, like math: the notes on the page bound by the staves, the signatures becoming music only if transcribed precisely, exactly. Happily, I learned to play other instruments by ear, and later, when I taught music to beginner students after high school, I went about it in a different way. It had to be fun.

Mum could see we were losing our enthusiasm, let alone the floor finishing, and eventually asked Miss P. not to return. She found us another teacher, a woman who lived just a few streets over, close enough that John and I could walk there. That was a shame, because now Mum could no longer listen in on the lessons (she'd been doing an impressive job teaching herself to play the piano, the value of a free lesson not lost on her), and besides, the new teacher was not much of an improvement. She was ancient, frail, and very bent, and she lived in a dark, musty house that we couldn't wait to escape the moment we walked through the door. I started to fake injuries so I didn't have to go, arriving home from school with a soiled tensor bandage wrapped around my arm (Fell off the monkey bars!), with a clumsily bound finger (Slammed it in a door!), or with my arm in a sling (Sprained it at volleyball!). I was careful to wrap a different body part every week, but the jig was up quickly. Mum told me to quit play-acting and get to the lesson. "Practice your left hand, then," she'd say. "It needs work."

Mum worked hard to raise us well and give us opportunities she never had. Higher education was something she herself had been denied. In her last year at the girl's school, she'd won a scholarship to go to art college, but was not allowed to pursue it. The day of her graduation was the moment when her absentee father suddenly stepped back into her life. The dashing hero she'd dreamed would rescue her turned out to be a coarse man with a thick Welsh accent. He promptly put her to work as a laundress so she could contribute to his new family. What she lost—choice and opportunity—she hoped for me. She would say, "The world is your oyster, my dear."

My higher education would be recompense for the life my mother was denied; but first, I had to get through primary school.

(2)

TALL, FLAT, AND BULLIED

"If you're going through hell, keep going."
— WINSTON CHURCHILL

BY THE TIME I was eleven, I was towering above most of the kids at Meadowvale Public School. At an alarming 5'10" tall (I plateaued at 6'1"), I was competitive, angular, and flat as a board. Given my family of brothers, girlfriends were achingly important to me, and it was against my friends Susan and Lee that I held myself up for comparison.

Susan was the exotic, athletic one, always the red-ribbon winner at the school track meets — her long-jump records are probably still standing. Susan's parents were from Germany and her mum was a wonderful home-maker. She'd greet Susan and her little sister at the end of the school day with a freshly baked poppyseed cake or a tray of creamy pastries sprinkled with sugar. Susan's family had a television in their wood-panelled basement rec room, and after school we'd race to her house to flop onto the nubby orange couch, sticky hands reaching for the channel knob to tune in to our favourite shows. Mine was *Hogan's Heroes*. Susan's father was a gentle soul but would be cross if he caught us watching it, offended by the way Colonel Klink and Sergeant Schultz made the Germans look ridiculous. I was too dumb to figure out why — the show's appeal for us was handsome Hogan. (My own father wasn't pleased that I hung out at Susan's after school. It always led to an awkward "Don't mention the war" moment.)

Lee was independent and fashion forward. Her hair was cut in a stylish bob and she had gorgeous thick bangs that were artfully set off with blue eye shadow and pearl pink lipstick. She and Susan were so cool. They both acquired white go-go boots, which I coveted dearly, but those weren't about to show up at the thrift store anytime soon.

Going to Lee's house was a different experience altogether. It was usually empty after school because her mother, like mine, worked outside the home. Mrs. Perkins always seemed more tired than her bright mod clothing let on. She was a curvy woman and a colourful dresser in a groovy, *Rowan & Martin's Laugh-In* kind of way. And she was missing a thumb on one hand, which made her very mysterious indeed.

Given her mum's buxom physique, it should have been no surprise that of the three of us, Lee was the first to develop and was the first girl in our class to acquire a bra. That bra was a thing of wonder to me. I was clueless about puberty and Mum wasn't the kind to leave her underthings around in the bathroom.

Lee had no such qualms. She made a huge stick-sketch of a brassiere in a dirt patch in the schoolyard, grandly sweeping the stick in half-circles on the ground in order to demonstrate the architectural wonders of sturdy underwiring. But then she made another sketch: this one a benign-looking rectangle that she claimed was something called a "sanitary napkin"—a device I had not only never seen, I'd never even heard of it. What could it possibly be for?

"Impossible!" I snorted when she told me. "That's insane. Women don't bleed down there. You're stupid."

I got good marks in school; I naturally thought that if anyone would have first knowledge of something as extreme as monthly bleeding, it would be me.

(I recognized myself years later in the movie *Coal Miner's Daughter*, when Loretta Lynn said, "I may be ignorant, but I ain't stupid!")

"What happens to the boys, then?" I said.

"Nothing."

Susan nodded. "Nothing."

"*Nothing?*" It was my first inkling that the world might just be unfair to girls.

After school, I waited impatiently by the door until my mum walked in from work and then fiercely demanded the truth. Loudly. In front of my brothers.

Mum spun me round and marched me into the bathroom. Course, she had to calm me down before she could provide any real detail because I was SHOCKED and MORTIFIED and needed someone to blame for being made to look stupid in front of my friends. So I stood there, cross-armed and furious, while she admitted that yes, dear, it was all true. My own period was years away, something she'd probably been able to predict from my scabby-kneed boyish development. Still, she apologized for not telling me sooner.

Once she started in on the details, it all became fact-based and scientific and therefore much easier to bear. But I was still suspicious. I couldn't get past the fact that this travesty happened only to girls. Surely there was some monstrosity in store for boys? Evidently not. Not even *men*opause was for them.

The girls in my class started to blossom. They huddled in cliques to whisper about boys and makeup and commiserate with each other about cramps (what fresh hell was that?), instead of hanging upside down on the monkey bars with me. My underdevelopment had become a burden, making me feel like a loser. I begged my mother for a training bra and even tried stuffing it for a while, but that was a sad, bumpy exercise in futility. I might get the volume right (too big? too small? same as yesterday?) but stability was a problem; I was constantly on guard for an errant wad of tissue that might escape and — *ta da!* — present itself to the schoolyard. Once they knew you stuffed you were a goner.

I wanted breasts so badly I'd lie on my back in bed at night with my elbows dug into the mattress in order to keep the covers off my chest, believing that if the sheets were held high all night, there'd be less weight on my chest, and I would wake up magically endowed with a pair of A-cups. I'd have been happy with AA martini-glass cups. Hell, I would have been happy with squished plum nubs at that point.

While I waited for a miracle, my beanpole stature was making it hell to get to school. I wasn't alone; everyone in my neighbourhood was teased, pink-bellied, or wedgied, and schoolyard punch-ups were pretty normal. My own daily rite of passage was the walk past a gauntlet of jeering boys — occasionally spearheaded by my own brothers. Head down, hunched over, books clutched to my chest, I tried to walk as fast as I could without running, while they heckled and hollered. The boys took to taking their shirts off, rubbing their nipples fast and hard, supposedly emulating me and my so-far futile efforts to stimulate growth.

There was no way of avoiding them—there was only one road that led to the school from my house, aside from a dangerous detour across the field and past Mrs. Chadwick's farmhouse. Everyone knew she kept a loaded salt gun handy for trespassers. Her aim was true, as evidenced by my brother Paul and his friend Gary, who she caught raiding her vegetable garden. For years afterward Gary laid claim to salt-shot pockmarks on his ass, despite his mom's best efforts to pick it all out.

It's hardly surprising that I started to slouch. "Stand up straight!" my mother would admonish me, "or you'll stay like that." She'd commiserate by telling me her own woeful stories, thinking that if I knew she'd had it worse, my harassment might be easier to bear.

When the little brats called me Alice the Goon and Olive Oyl after the two towering gals in the Popeye cartoons, Mum said, "Names will never hurt you."

"Not true," thought I, wishing hard for a spinach-fuelled sailor to come and beat the snot out of all of them.

Of course, once I made it past the gauntlet I'd imagine everything I wished I'd done but hadn't. I should have yelled FUCK YOU, ASSHOLES! and attacked them in a girl-fight tornado of kicking and punching and hair-ripping. I grew up with those boys, after all; I could run and build forts and throw rocks as well as they could. But they were brave in a pack. In hindsight, I should have been more strategic, hunting them down one by one, lying in wait in the trees and then pelting them with a torrent of apples and stones and cow pies. I could have been Pippi Longstocking and thrown my horse at them! Then they'd have been sorry.

But none of that happened. My self-consciousness robbed me of my righteous tomboy power.

IT'S HARD TO FIT in when you stick out. For me it was being freak-ishly tall, but as any young girl knows, adolescence can be a minefield of self-esteem issues as we navigate periods, pimples, hormones, and boy-friends. Or lack thereof. I distracted myself with books and sports. I iden-tified with the brave Laura Ingalls, and borrowed the *Little House on the*

Prairie books so often, the librarian gave me the old set when she had to replace them. I was also morbidly obsessed with the worst of history—slave ships and concentration camps. I was developing a strong sense of injustice. As for sports, I wasn't a great athlete, but I was "misheightened" enough to make membership on high school teams an inevitability. "Do you play basketball?" is always the second question any tall girl is asked, right after "How tall are you?" My height gave me enough advantage to approximate athleticism in basketball, volleyball, and, of course, the high jump, which was a risky sport in those days.

In high jump we had to clear the metal pole and land in a pit filled with nothing but sand and a sprinkle of wood shavings. Though when the Fosbury Flop (a technique where you curl almost backwards over the bar—at the cost of having to land on your back in the pit) became all the rage, our school caved in and bought a foam rubber mattress so we wouldn't break our necks.

Here's me winning (my only) first place in high jump at regionals. I thought it was a big deal at the time, but judging from the lineup for the podium, it may have been the beginning of the "everyone gets a badge for showing up" movement.

Rescue from peer pressure came in my last year of public school, when we moved from Highland Creek to West Hill—closer to Toronto but still firmly in Scarberia. I was desperate to get away from Meadowvale Public

School, but it didn't make sense to transfer to a new school in the middle of grade eight, so I walked the four miles there and back every day (yes, I can hear you—"barefoot in the snow, uphill both ways..."). All that walking gave me lots of time to stomp out my self-absorption, and at the end of the year graduation intervened to offer some hope that I just might turn out okay.

My final semester was a cheery hat trick of achievement: our senior volleyball team won the regional championships, I was chosen as class valedictorian, and on graduation night I was awarded the Robert Elsie General Proficiency Award, which was presented to "the grade eight pupil showing the greatest proficiency in all fields of endeavour." Whoa! That was a shocker. I remember walking onto the stage feeling like the Scarecrow in *The Wizard of Oz*, this piece of parchment completely at odds with my own self-assessment, yet hard evidence that my brothers' nickname for me—"Dunce"—wasn't true after all.

As the year ended, I began to look forward to what would surely be a total rebirth at my new school. I had an entire summer to stop growing *up* and start growing *out*. And no, it didn't happen magically over that summer, no matter how high I grew or how high I held the covers. But even if my physical nirvana was not meant to be, soon enough I didn't care so much. In high school I found new things to obsess about: music, waitressing, and boys.

(3)

MILLIE'S, MUSIC, AND MARIJUANA

"The ass will not kick itself."
— SHELLEY AMBROSE

OUR NEW HOUSE ON Manse Road in West Hill was three blocks from Millie's 24-Hour Restaurant, where I soon had a summer job waitressing, short-order cooking, bussing tables, and, on occasion, bouncing unruly customers. I was fourteen and logged every hour I could get. I was saving up for a car. I bought my first beater—an unreliable used Austin 1100—when I was fifteen, even before I had a licence. The day I turned sixteen, I was at the Ministry of Transportation, writing my learner's permit test. On the way home from passing the actual driver's licence test, I got my first speeding ticket. It was twelve dollars. As I handed my pristine licence to the officer, he peered at the date, then at me, and said, "Doing well, aren't we?" Helpful fellow.

I know the ticket was twelve dollars because I recorded it in my diary:

JULY 27: "What a day!!! I am so happy!!! Got my licence but stopped by cop. $12 speeding ticket!!!!!

Apparently I never met an exclamation mark I didn't love!!! Other entries include gems such as:

JANUARY 12, 1972: I'm going to fail my piano exam, maybe I'll break a finger.

JANUARY 30, 1972: Peter got kicked out of school for stink
bombs!!!!

FEBRUARY 22, 1972 (MY BIRTHDAY): I don't really know who I
am or why.

It's curious to read that last line now. Especially because, more than
four decades later, I'm not sure I'm any closer to the answer. At the time
it seemed easier to figure out not *who* or *why*, but *what* I was—and that
could easily have been a career waitress. Plus, if there's ever a job that will
help give you clue about who *other* people are, it's waitressing.

As kids, we were expected to contribute to the household finances—the
sooner the better. It wasn't that my parents condoned child labour; they
wanted us to learn some responsibility and the value of a dollar. Besides
babysitting, my first job was at the age of twelve, delivering a local weekly
paper. I felt very grown-up handing over a bit of my earnings to Mum
and Dad.

At the end of grade seven, I was working at a short-order restaurant
in Highland Creek Village. The owner was a friend of my dad's and a
fellow Mason. I didn't know what a Mason was then, and I'm still vague
about it now, but I knew it was a secret club. I once glanced through a
slim handbook my dad had forgotten in the bathroom called *The Book of
Constitutions*. I was flipping idly through the pages—perhaps assuming
it was about daily constitution*als*—when there was a sudden pounding
on the door.

"Is there a book in there?" my father bellowed.

"Um, yes," I said, startled.

"Are you reading it?"

"Um, yes."

"DROP IT! RIGHT NOW! Hand it here!"

I slid the scary thing under the door, wondering why I was suddenly
in trouble. Surely there was nothing dangerous about a few diagrams of
medieval-looking shields and medals and stuff. I expected it had something
to do with the weird powder-blue apron with the silver jangly bits Dad
wore over his pants on his way out some nights. He stopped going to the
meetings after a while; but years later, when CTV bought and renovated

the former Masonic Temple at Yonge and Davenport in Toronto, I, like many, scoured the papers for details. There were whispers of thrones and ritualistic goat sacrifices in secret rooms, but from what I could gather the secrets went out the window with the muzzy carpets.

At the short-order restaurant, because I was underage, I was mostly in the kitchen washing dishes and peeling potatoes. The peeler was from another age — a huge cast-iron barrel into which I'd heave a massive bag of potatoes. The potatoes spun around in water, the peels grinding off against the sides. I'd then dig out any remaining eyes or black bits before positioning the potatoes in the French fry press — another heavy contraption, with a handle much like a water pump. I thought I was pretty good. I could go through a twenty-five-pound bag and make a mountain of French fries in about thirty minutes, but the owner was ever impatient, yelling from the cash register, "Hurry up! Get the dishes!"

One day he called me out front to watch six breakfast sausages on the grill while he went out back to take a delivery. All of a sudden the place got very busy; people started arriving in packs, sitting at dirty tables as I rushed to clear them. Sure enough, in no time there was a cloud of smoke coming from the grill. (What *is* it with me and sausages?) I had the presence of mind to smother them with a lid and put out the fire. But just as I'd put another set on the grill, my dad's Masonic friend returned.

"How could you be so fucking useless! You're paying for those, you fucking idiot!"

Another rolling rager. The first time I saw Twisted Sister's "We're Not Gonna Take It" video, I did a double take — the resemblance to my spittle-flying restaurant boss was spot-on. It was becoming my version of normal. "You're useless and weak!" Happily, Mum came by one day and caught the tail end of one of his furies and hauled me outta there.

The summer I was thirteen I moved on to pumping gas. It was a two-pump station owned by a family friend on Highway 2. No more than a shack, really, with a few shelves displaying oil and pine-tree air fresheners and a big red Coca-Cola vending machine outside the door. I filled 'er up, checked the oil, topped up windshield-washer fluid, and cleaned the bugs off the windows. People would tip gas station servers in those days, and I got very precise and theatrical at windshield washing. I knew how to work a gratuity.

Mostly it wasn't that busy, so I'd pass the time listening to the radio and practising my guitar, a cheap gut string that responded well to oily fingers.

I was alone much of the day and didn't give a thought to the idea that a young girl might be vulnerable in such a situation, especially with a cash register full of money. Turns out it wasn't robbery I should have been wary of.

One hot summer day, a blue Ford Falcon pulled in. I remember the car because the gas nozzle was on the rear. As I removed the gas cap I hollered to the driver and asked him how much he wanted. He turned his head and said, "Five bucks." It was weird that the car was jiggling a bit.

"You want your oil checked too, Mister?" I said. But there was no answer; he seemed to be busy with something under the dash. I replaced the nozzle on the pump and went round to his window. As I leaned in, I remember noticing the air in the car was kinda stale—hotter and more humid even than outside. The man was grimacing and shaking. As I looked from his sweaty face into his lap, thinking he was looking for his wallet, I saw that he was holding his penis in his hand. It was sticking out from under his gut, the patchy red hair making a dry scratchy sound as he rubbed it hard. I was frozen for a moment, mostly dumbstruck by the audacity of it all, before I said something like, "Uhhh, that'll be five bucks, Mister," and backed away from the window.

The whole episode didn't feel scary so much as pathetic, especially reduced now to a lame transaction, his dick waggling around as he dug for the bills. At the time, I thought the grossest part was touching the money, but it remains one of those memories that can return in precise detail if I let it.

Did I tell anyone? No. I'd been warned about "bad" men. I just thought he was one of them. And I liked my job too much to worry anyone. Anyway, he peeled away quickly enough.

I learned about sexual assault a year later, when something a lot worse happened. Though "learned" might not be the best word, because as it turned out, I wouldn't consciously deal with that episode until much later, when my childhood was well behind me. Maybe some lessons can only be learned in their own good time.

BY THE TIME I was fourteen, I was thinking I might have a future in the service industry. It was then that I began my most formative job, at Millie's Restaurant on Old Kingston Road. Millie's was a twenty-four-hour family restaurant favoured by truckers and owned by a Slovenian immigrant entrepreneur named Joan Rahonc. It was located in between a pool hall and a motel, across the street from the local watering hole, the West Hill House.

Joan was a great Canadian rags-to-riches story. She arrived in Canada in 1957, a widow who spoke almost no English and with her daughter Millie in tow. Joan found a job in a hospital kitchen and worked and saved until eventually she came to own both the restaurant and the pool hall across the street, over which she lived.

I've never seen anyone work harder than Joan. She practically lived in her white restaurant-supply uniform; everyone assumed she worked twenty-three of the twenty-four hours that Millie's was open. She made an exception for Sundays when, barely recognizable in street clothes, her hair washed and curled and her handbag on her arm, she'd go to church, followed by a few hours at the track. She loved horses and studied the listings like a medical student. Every now and then she'd return to the restaurant with a few bucks for me. "Your horse won!" she'd announce, bending over and slapping her knees with both hands, thrilled with her luck. I suspect I was "tipped" more than the horse won, a nod to being trustworthy enough that she could escape.

Joan was a force to be reckoned with. She was a broad woman with a large chest, flat feet, dry, bleached blonde hair kept mostly in place with little combs stuck hither and yon, and a willful set of dentures that would often go missing. Those usually turned up in her pocket or her purse, though once they were found in the old tin can in the cooler that acted as her bank. She kept folded bills in that can so the till never looked too full when it was open in full view.

Joan wasn't exactly the picture of composed, gourmet hospitality. She sometimes talked to herself, stomping around and shaking her hands, muttering in her first language. She could look a little crazy to first-time customers, but Joan was all there — shrewd when she needed to be and fierce because she had to be.

There's a story about three young guys who tried to rob her one night. As they advanced on her she stormed back at them so aggressively that two of them just ran away. The last one allegedly had a gun. Joan didn't flinch. She grabbed the coffee pot by the handle and flung its boiling contents at him. As the gunman bolted, she yelled after him, *"You no come my place again!"* (That was something she said a lot, along with "Hoo-DEECH!" furiously judo-chopping the air with her arms if she was angry with a customer. I'm not sure what it meant, but it was definitely not a compliment. Sometimes she shouted at customers who stayed too long nursing a coffee. "Five meenute for one coffee. Five MEENOOTE!")

There were always cops around Millie's, and apparently they soon caught up with the three would-be robbers and asked Joan to come to the station to ID them. She knew who one of them was but didn't say so to the officers. She chose instead to go and visit the young man's parents. She believed in second chances. A few years later, that same kid showed up in an army officer's uniform to thank Joan for giving him a break.

Millie's Restaurant

Millie's was in a prime location on the corner of Old Kingston Road and (new) Kingston Road in Scarborough. It was a classic diner, with Formica counters circling the cash register, spinning stools, a milkshake machine, and a pie station. It was a compact operation; at capacity, it could hold maybe fifty people. There were three black Naugahyde-covered booths and two family tables in the back, though we didn't get a lot of families in that "family" restaurant; it was really a truck stop. The rigs had plenty of room to park across the street in the pool hall lot.

In the early days, we weren't licensed for alcohol; people actually came for the food. Not that it was anything fancy: hot turkey, beef, or hamburger sandwiches; grilled cheese; toasted westerns; burgers; fries; homemade (not really) pies; our 25-cent toasted Danish (a local favourite); soda fountain milkshakes; and, of course, the daily specials. But the real Millie's specialty was the foot-long hot dog, which you could get with any combo of four trimmings — exotic for those days — mustard, relish, ketchup, *and* raw onions. People drove from miles around, and customers were often drunk, staggering in with complicated orders. Well, complicated for them.

There's nothing quite like standing behind the counter in a jammed restaurant, notepad ready, trying to focus on one drunk customer while a roiling mass of humanity jostles for position around him. Some are trying to eat, some trying to order, some trying to pay, some trying to leave without paying, all while some bleary-eyed dude is weaving back and forth in front of you, his brain machinery clearly smoking and grinding with the effort of remembering his friends' takeout order.

"I'll have seven foot longs. Three with everything, one with no mustard, two with no relish. One with…ummm. Shit, no…Hang on. I'll start again. Seven foot longs. Right…Three with everything, one JUST mustard, two with…Aw, fuck. Just gimme everything, they can scrape it off. An' a carton of Exports. To go."

I would come to admire the "No Coke, Pepsi. No fries, chips!" singularity of *Saturday Night Live*'s Olympia Café.

I worked at Millie's after school and on weekends, taking as many shifts as I could. I did whatever was required, cooking and cleaning and serving and cashiering, often alone but never lonely. But on the weekends when it was always busy, I worked with Maria (who spoke the same first language as Joan) or with my friend Glenn. And later, when they were old enough, with my two younger brothers, Peter and Paul.

In the summers I'd often work the midnight-to-noon shift. It was a circus, especially around "lush hour," when people stumbled over for a bite after last call at the West Hill House, sometimes bringing their grudges in with them. "Fights outside!" we'd yell. Such a pain in the ass cleaning up when food was involved. (Though it was worse when patrons were ejected before they paid their bill.) By 3 a.m. it would calm down and then cops and cabbies and all-night truckers would start to dribble in. Dawn was a bit of a culture clash, with the arriving posties and construction guys stepping past the lingering legless.

One night we had a guy who passed out cold in his hot beef sandwich. He was slurring away one minute, loudly telling stories no one wanted to hear, and the next minute he was head-down on his order, his right ear lying on the gravy-soaked bread, his right hand in the mashed potatoes, and his mouth slack, his breath sucking the peas back and forth. Glenn was on with me that night, and when we'd exhausted our efforts to wake the guy up, Glenn wondered aloud if the fellow might fancy some dessert. He reached over into the pie cabinet, grabbed the whipped cream, and sprayed a flourish of foamy white on his bald head and put a cherry on top. Then we called the cops to take him away.

"Nice move, kids. Clean him up."

I worked at Millie's all through high school, and over the years I got to know lots of regulars. I had one guy who would come in every weekday morning, precisely at 5:30 a.m., and order four black coffees, half full, lids off. He'd top each cup up with rye from his pocket flask, replace the lids, and head out the door, happy as a clam.

Another guy would show up shortly after him at 6 a.m., just before Joan arrived for the day. He, too, was a creature of habit, with always the exact same order: a plain white fried-egg sandwich and two coffees, one to go. He was Joan's silent nemesis. Funny, because she had no idea. She may have forgotten that once, she'd tried to move him on from his coffee before he was ready—"Get out. I no stay your house, why you stay mine?" His daily revenge was to sit beside the cash with his second coffee, eyes trained on the pool hall door across the street. The minute he saw Joan come out, he'd put his quarter in the jukebox, press D-4, and sit back and wait. Joan walked in that door every weekday morning that summer to the same song—Elton John's "The Bitch Is Back"—and never noticed. As she walked in, this customer would stand up, wink at me, and whistle his way out the door.

There was a French-Canadian trucker who would always order a full-sized raw onion with his sandwich. He'd peel it and eat it like an apple, onion juice squirting every which way, relishing each bite. I guess when you're a long-haul trucker your breath doesn't matter much. He called me

"High Pockets" because my white restaurant supply uniform was always so short. That was Joan's doing. She insisted on my uniforms being *very* short. "Always better tip!" she'd say. How short were they? Well, I certainly couldn't lean over to hear a customer's order. I employed more of a curtsy when serving and removing plates. If the supplier delivered long uniforms, Joan would send them back in a huff. Once, when they didn't get the message, she hacked the order up with a kitchen knife and returned it to the driver. "Now they learn!" she said, arms crossed, satisfied with herself.

Some customers became pals. One day I was complaining about my car to a regular who was a mechanic. John looked a bit like a grizzly bear, with a peak beard that flowed down over his blackened overalls. My car at the time (I went through a lot of junky vehicles) was a Fiat. It was hand-painted with a green-and-yellow racing stripe and held together with Bondo and hope. I think I paid $250 for it. As I poured John his coffee, I grouched that my muffler had fallen off and a new one would be worth more than the car. Later, when I looked out into the parking lot, I saw John under the car. He'd returned with his tool box, jimmying the muffler back on with some wire and brackets. The fix outlasted the car.

I once went with John and his friend to a sports-car racing event. Both of the cars they ran — an old Lotus and a TVR — were pretty beat up, but they had a sponsor nonetheless. It was a condom company. Both cars sported a logo: a cartoon of a man with his foot up the butt of a stork. I was no pit bunny; I was there to work. My job was to hand out "How Not To" pamphlets at the track. Given the range of jokes about rubbers in the pit, it did make some weird sense that my other job revolved around tires. Specifically, the right back tire. My tire. I practiced with my torque wrench for hours until I could change a tire in minutes — still a long way from the Formula One average of 2.6 seconds for all *four* tires, but I felt accomplished.

That mechanical apprenticeship at the track was an unexpected bonus, but the most valuable lessons I got as a waitress were, hands down, about people. Restaurants are the great equalizer. A burger costs the same for the guy in greasy coveralls as it does for the guy in the three-piece suit, though the tip can vary widely. You can tell a lot about people by the way they treat wait staff.

Thirty years later, at a deal closure lunch, I didn't hire someone for a very senior position because of the way she treated a waitress. I had the contract offer in my purse, but decided not give it to her. Her rudeness rang a warning bell: there was no way I was having someone in a senior position infect the company with the unkindness of a caste system.

As an employer, I've found waitstaffing on a résumé a good clue to a great hire. If you see a long stint at a busy restaurant, you'll likely find a pro-active, detail-oriented multi-tasker. Someone who can juggle an armful of hot plates and cold drinks while simultaneously refilling the coffee pot and setting up a high chair will likely ace a complex project — quickly, correctly, and on time. Chances are, they'll be good listeners and clear communicators, too. The mental and verbal ability required to take, order, and deliver a perfectly executed set of meals from a hostile chef to a table of picky eaters just might train a brain better than that second language you've been promising yourself.

And waitstaffing skills are transferable. You'll learn resource management ("I'm sorry, sir, we're all out of liver, but the hot beef is excellent"), how to maximize efficiencies (never go empty-handed in or out of the kitchen), manage expectations and deadlines ("Can I get you a drink while you wait?"), and problem-solving skills ("I'm sorry, sir, but might you have another credit card?"). It's a life-skill mélange of work ethic, diplomacy, and teamwork all rolled into a minimum-wage marathon. Tip well!

THE JOB AT MILLIE'S put money in my pocket and stride in my step. In high school, I felt like I'd started afresh. By my second year at West Hill Collegiate, I was barrelling around town with cool new friends, engaging in all the native Scarberian traditions. We tested our alcohol tolerance in the field on our way to school dances (the first one featured the Stampeders); I had my first kiss in the back seat of a car (Rod Stewart's "Maggie May" was playing); I drove to concerts with my first two eight-tracks blaring — Murray McLauchlan's *Song from the Street* (fate?) and Neil Diamond's *Stones* (they'd both come with the car). Music was quickly becoming all about love. I played flute in the school band, madly crushing on every musician in my row. In my diary there are little hearts over top of seven names in one week: "Eric, Dave, Kevin, Jim, Sandy, Ron and Don [twins] . . . (Squirrel!)"

Much of my Millie's money was spent on gas and car repairs, driving to concerts that I knew my baby-heart crushes might also attend. This carefully orchestrated spontaneity to be where they were failed to result in an actual boyfriend, but it did lead to a very wide musical exposure.

The first big concert I saw was at Maple Leaf Gardens: the Rolling Thunder Revue with Bob Dylan, Robbie Robertson, Ramblin' Jack, and Joan Baez. I had a black-and-white camera and took photos of them all, the size of ants from our seats high in the stands. It was an amazing show—until someone a few aisles behind us threw up and spewed all over the rows in front of him. I escaped the rancid rain until the guy behind me got up to shake off his coat. The music made up for it, though.

I saved the ticket stubs from all the shows I went to. I saw Elton John, Yes, Jethro Tull, Joe Cocker, and every "Cheap Thrills" concert at the Gardens I could afford. I saw Steve Goodman at Convocation Hall, and trolled the Riverboat Coffee House to see John Hammond and Leon Redbone, Ryerson for Long John Baldry, and Varsity Stadium for Chicago. I saw James Taylor, Gordon Lightfoot, Cheech & Chong, Neil Young, and Cat Stevens ("He wasn't very good," my diary reveals).

Music was a big deal in our house growing up. When we were very young, Mum would put on *Night on Bald Mountain* and we'd pretend to be fairies as she stomped around, scaring us into hiding places under the furniture. Mussorgsky still makes me slightly anxious.

Dad loved to sing, especially with his police pal Harry—an exceptional player—at the piano. At Dad's behest I would copy out lyrics to Tom Jones and Engelbert Humperdinck songs, transcribing them line by line from the vinyl. I'd sneak down the stairs and watch him singing "Please Release Me (Let Me Go)," one hand on the piano, the other holding a cigarette and a big glass of rye. It was always a thrill to see him blissed out.

As a teen, I tried on my big brother John's musical choices. John was two years older than me, and at eighteen he looked a lot like Elvis. He had slicked-back hair and a sneery smile, and he and his friends were always fixing up cars in the backyard, their cigarettes rolled up in their black T-shirt sleeves. He didn't listen to Elvis, though. He preferred a "young hoodlum" (Dad's words) from Vancouver named Terry Black and had two vinyl records that he spun endlessly. One was called *The Black Plague* and the other was *Only Sixteen* ("She was too young to fall in love, and I was too young to know"). Yes, Terry was singing directly to me. Loving my brother's music didn't help with our relationship, though. He and his friends roundly shunned me, as big brothers do.

As John veered toward rock and roll, Dad vied with the British tenors, and Mum remained true to the classics, I struck out on my own.

I visited the *Houses of the Holy* with Led Zeppelin, unzipped the Rolling Stones' *Sticky Fingers* album, and marvelled at the paper panties wrapped around Alice Cooper's very scary vinyl. It was a loud collection that concerned my parents, though they were calmed somewhat by mounting evidence that it was folk music that really turned my head. Hippies, free love, and pot. Nothing to worry about there.

The Mariposa Folk Festival on Toronto Island was a yearly ritual. I volunteered with my pals Kevin and Stephen, and we got in free in exchange for a few shifts taking tickets at the gate. I cobbled together a hippy-chick look. It was a backless, fringed, rawhide halter top over a floor-length wraparound patchwork maxi skirt, the perfect thing to wear while helicopter dancing in front of the mainstage.

As volunteers we were allowed backstage, where we ogled performers in the food lines. We were frowned at if we actually approached anyone, but we did manage a few hellos. One year a group of us were sent on a search-and-rescue mission across the grounds, looking for John Prine, who was late for his set. We found him stuck in one of those square, green-mesh garbage cans. The only way to get him out was to tip the whole thing over, which amused him to no end. There was John, covered in paper cups and newspaper, laughing his head off until someone led him gently to the stage. Turns out Laurie Brown, my future co-host at *The NewMusic*, was part of that group of rescuers too, as Laurie and I discovered one day when we found ourselves midway through telling exactly the same story to each other.

Thrilled by the range of musicians that festivals afforded, I ventured out to Winnipeg, Edmonton, and Owen Sound, even driving down to camp out at the twelfth annual Philadelphia Folk Festival in 1973 to see Sonny Terry and Brownie McGhee, Kate McGarrigle, Maria Muldaur, Sippie Wallace, Victoria Spivey, Janis Ian, the Downchild Blues Band, and (who knew?) my future husband, Murray McLauchlan. We didn't manage to get volunteer gigs at the Philadelphia festival, so I couldn't access the backstage parties. But what I wouldn't have given to have been a fly on the wall at a spontaneous guitar pull that transpired that weekend, when Murray, Tom Waits, Loudon Wainwright III, John Prine, Steve Goodman, and

Jim Croce all traded songs and stories sitting around in a hotel room. We campers enjoyed the freewheelin' vibe huddled around fires outside our tents, singing along with whoever brought a guitar. Jim Croce stopped at a campfire a few tents away and we could hear him singing "One Less Set of Footsteps" from across the field. Magical.

My friends and I often hitchhiked around, partly because my thumb was cheaper and usually more reliable than whatever beater car I was driving, and later because I was inspired by my favourite book at the time, Tom Robbins' *Even Cowgirls Get the Blues*. My first extended hitchhiking trip was with my high school friend Pam Pedrick, a tall, blonde athletic star. I know we got at least as far as the Canso Causeway in Cape Breton; but looking at a photo, it's startling to think we made it that far east and back without incident.

Judging from the paraphernalia I have saved in a box, I was a joiner in search of a tribe. Amongst the Girl Guide badges and track ribbons, there are membership cards for organizations like Bakavi (*"To develop an eco-logically sound way of supporting human life"*) and the Christian anti-drug and -alcohol group Toc Alpha (*"Know yourself by self-involvement"*). I also have a cafeteria ID card from a French immersion school I attended at the University of Prince Edward Island, reminding me that I was up for all kinds of exploring not sanctioned by the Toc Alpha crowd. Southern Comfort was the beverage of choice during that summer away from home. Nothing like waking up with a grass stain on your chin to make you re-examine your life choices. Pot was next — but that experiment was literally nipped in the bud when my dad scared me straight.

I'd been at a high school dance. I don't remember what band played, but I do remember the drive home in my little car. I was very stoned, and the normally dead-straight road was unusually hilly that night. It seemed to be undulating like a slow, heavy snake. I white-knuckled it all the way, well under the speed limit, and practically kissed the driveway when I arrived home safely.

I made it to my room, where I should have stayed, but I was desperately hungry. My parents were watching TV in the den, just off the kitchen. There was a big loaf of bread on the counter, so I sawed myself a healthy two-inch hunk and attempted to butter it. The chunks of hard margarine were decidedly uncooperative and kept ripping the bread. No matter. I took a huge bite and attempted to chew but...terminal dry mouth. I had no saliva at all. I reached to put the bread back on the counter, but for some reason I was two feet farther away from the ledge than I'd thought. The bread landed with a soft thud on the floor.

My father turned around, looking back from his chair. "Where have you been?"

(Desperately trying to swallow.) "At the school dance at Laurier."

"Why are your eyes so red?"

"It was smoky in the gym?"

At that point Dad got up and walked over for a closer look, leaning in for the sniff test.

"We're going downtown."

He got his jacket out of the closet and I trailed behind.

Silence in the car.

Once we got to the police station, he leaned across the desk and had a word with the desk sergeant, who gave me a cursory glance, then went back to his work. I was pointed to a chair and told to sit. I sat, coolin' my jets and trying to remember how to breathe, while Dad went over to share a laugh with a few of the officers. Eventually my father returned and took me to a room with a camera in it. I don't think I was fingerprinted, but who knows, I was pretty stoned.

Of course it was all a big scare tactic. There's no official record of my "arrest," but the experience could not have freaked me out more. No wonder my effort, years later, to smoke dope only resulted in paranoia.

Back at home, the chill in the house was like living in a meat locker. The incident wasn't mentioned, and I didn't dare ask when my court date was, but the ordeal had succeeded in pulling the question of what I was going to do with my life sharply into focus. Scorn every opportunity and disappoint my parents? Or get with the program?

Which brings me back to that diary entry: "I don't really know who I am or why."

It reads today as trite and childish, but the decision about what to do after high school was dogging many in my grade thirteen class. My mom was intent on my going to university—I'd be the first one in our family—but I couldn't imagine picking just one field of study, or choosing one career path. Volunteer aid worker? Career waitress? International bon vivant? It all sounded great to me. The world was just too dazzling; I wanted to try everything.

The school guidance counsellor endeavoured to be of service, and called a half dozen of us down to the office one day to discuss our futures. All the kids in the room that afternoon were near the top of the class. Each of the "brainers" had a solid plan in hand. Engineering, Political Science, Computer Studies. Some even had universities chosen and listed in order of preference. I was in wonderment at them all, and not in a charitable way. I was thinking, *Freaks, how could you have so little imagination?* and feeling jealous of them at the same time.

The guidance counsellor hauled out the SVIB-SCII profiler—the vocational aptitude tool of the day—to help me with my life choices and, I suspect, to ensure everyone else's aligned with the tell-all test. We filled out the cardboard cards, carefully marking the little squares with black pencil. The cards were then mailed away to a computer the size of a car, with results to be sent back in two weeks. I still have a copy of my results. Highest occupational skill scores: Army officer, Entertainer, Life Insurance Agent. Hmmm...wide berth there. Lowest occupational skill scores: Computer programmer, Pharmacist, Physicist.

Equally wide!

Well, then. With no obvious career choice at hand, I chose to go backpacking through Europe.

(4)

MY WATERLOO:

GREENED AND GROOMED

"The more that you read, the more things you will know.
The more that you learn, the more places you'll go."
— DR. SEUSS, *I Can Read With My Eyes Shut*

I ARRIVED AT THE University of Waterloo in September of 1976, after bumming around Europe with my friend Liz. Our goal had been to get to as many countries as we could on five dollars a day, which we mostly accomplished. The expense of the "Magic Bus" ride from Amsterdam to Istanbul was offset by the weeks we spent living in a donkey hut behind a restaurant on a nude beach on Mykonos. The nudity was novel, but I was

Restauranteur "Papa Mykonos" on Paradise Beach, Greece.

a prudish sort and it took me a full week to join the rest of the *au naturel*
bathers. I mostly stayed in the shade, waiting tables in exchange for meals,
before I finally got the courage to get the kit off during a volleyball game. I
hoped the sport might be a good distraction. It wasn't. Still, it was a memorable sunburn, and the trip was adventuresome enough to make me feel
ready to buckle down at school.

At UW I'd chosen to major in environmental studies with a minor
in psychology. My first year was spent living in a residence called Dag
Hammarskjöld just a few blocks up the road from campus. It was full of
first-year students, and we spent many evenings working on our Freshman
Fifteen, drinking beer and arguing with the engineering students about the
impact of their undertakings on the planet. Their argument: "We'll fix it
with science." My argument: "We're all going to die and it's your fault!"
No doubt I was insufferable.

My fellow environmental studies students were as free-spirited as my
engineering pals were square. They were the wild-eyed idealists I aspired
to be: Hirsute, corduroy-wearing, dyed-in-the-(humanely harvested)-wool,
vegetarian tree huggers, many of whom had attended alternative schools
in Toronto and seemed to have majored in Challenging Authority. This
might just be my tribe!

At the end of the first year, seven of us moved in together. It was a household of enthusiasts, full of kitchen parties, guitar jams, free-form dance,
and earnest discussions about how to save the world. As well as conventional math and science courses, we environmental studies students took
actual bird courses (we'd meet in the woodlot at 6 a.m. twice a week to
identify birds and trees), volunteered at the local food co-op, and practised
our activism.

"I picketed the sewage treatment plant last night!"

"Excellent! Were you arrested?"

"No."

"Scarred?

"Yes, look!"

"Bonus marks!"

My friend and housemate Joyce and I ran the office of the local grassroots
environmental organization Pollution Probe, selling buttons and posters to
fund anti-nuke campaigns. Another housemate, Phil Weller, volunteered at

the office of W-PIRG (Waterloo Public Interest Research Group), part of the network of consumer activist organizations inspired by Ralph Nader. Phil still works in the environmental field as a respected author and academic in Europe.

The only real challenge with my new tribe was that I was a closet carnivore. Luckily, one of my professors also lived with vegetarians, and we'd meet for burgers—and beer chasers, to cover our meat-murdering tracks.

I would always be an environmental advocate, but by my third year at Waterloo I began to think—however wrongly—that I'd gotten the gist of post-secondary education. Once I knew that with enough time and effort I *could* get a degree, the actual piece of paper didn't hold as much weight for me. (I received two honorary degrees later. I know it's not the same thing, but Mum was happy to see me in hat and gown, so that's what matters.)

Music was becoming a bigger part of my life. I had a weekly radio show on the campus station, CKMS, where I played folk records under the moniker "Amelia Woodstock," and I once made an appearance at the Grad Club Coffee House with my guitar, gamely butchering songs by Joni Mitchell and John Prine in my tentative vibrato. I choose the word "butchering" advisedly. "Tentative vibrato" are words that should never be used in the same sentence as the name John Prine.

Mangling chords at the Grad Club convinced me that I'd never make a living as a musician, though I felt there might be a role for me behind the scenes.

I volunteered on campus, organizing events like "Body Week" and "Energy Week," and inviting guest speakers to the university. When the Feds—the Federation of Students—advertised for a full-time Entertainment/Education programmer, I applied and got the job.

FORMAL CLASSES MAY HAVE been behind me, but school was definitely not out. You might even call my post with the Feds the school of hard knocks; in the course of my job, I was knocked out and maced, my car was torched, and I occasionally took my licks in the press.

In the new full-time paid position (I was paid $9,000 a year), I had a yearly budget of $139,000 with which to entertain the students with concerts, comedy cabarets, speakers, movies, special events, and orientation. The budget was to cover both free events and subsidized tickets for concerts and speakers. For four dollars, students could see two Long John Baldry concert sets with a bus ride to the beer hall and back.

I was required to keep a daily journal in order to justify my existence. The Student Federation had to prove that my paid position was offset by student savings. In my notebook I studiously listed items like: *Saved $1,400 off tent rentals; negotiated $500 off cost of Good Brothers; avoided $75 art direction cost by designing Decemberfest poster (Letraset +$30).* There was a lot of do-it-yourself on the job, blowing up balloons, printing flyers, painting banners, and wandering campus parking lots slipping event notices under windshield wipers.

My knowledge of the actual music business amounted to what most first-time student buyers across the country had—slim to none. At the time, only a handful of colleges and universities in the country had full-time entertainment programmers. Typically, we newbies assumed our positions a month or so before the beginning of the year, which guaranteed that we'd be the most ill-equipped when the competition was the fiercest: Orientation, when ripe young band-booking pullets were just waiting to be plucked by commission-hungry agents.

Orientation is designed to show new students just how much FUN student life can be and to underscore the wisdom of their decision to choose that particular place of higher learning. They needed to become quickly familiar with campus life skills—how to get to class, where to drink after class, what hours the clinic operated—and they also needed to be entertained. Rock concerts in the auditorium, folk music on the green, poetry slams in the pub (they weren't called that then; they were renamed "slams" when poetry got a marketing manager), and for some reason, Morris dancing. What better introduction to student life than flag-waving bearded men with bells on their feet leaping about merrily on the green?

It's a lot to take in for bewildered young adults, so in an effort to be helpful I published the *Little Fed Book*—about the same size and shape as Mao's infamous version, and also red—thinking it was not only a clever play on words but would fit into a shirt pocket for easy reference. Obviously an analogue precursor to the iPhone, the *Little Fed Book* contained maps, phone numbers, directories, discount coupons, and, of course, the orientation entertainment schedule. As I look at it today, our events weren't much different from a modern-day political convention: pancake breakfasts, watermelon football, hayrides, and chants. Hangovers were a given—after all, Kitchener-Waterloo was home to Oktoberfest.

I was pleased with the schedule, even if many of the events lost money. As I've mentioned, booking Orientation was a high-demand undertaking and we college buyers competed head to head—especially those of us who were within sound-check distance of each other. There were about a dozen schools in the same geographical area—Guelph, Conestoga, University of Toronto, York, and all the assorted campuses from Ryerson to Sheridan to Centennial and of course Wilfred Laurier, which was literally up the street from UW. With so many institutions competing for so few bands for events on the same exact days, it was an all-out bidding war during Orientation. Most of us rookie college buyers hadn't a clue how much to pay or even who to call. I began by looking up "Agents" in the Yellow Pages. Once on the phone, we were sitting ducks:

"Hello, I'm calling from the U of W, and I want to book some bands for Orientation."

"How much have you got?"

"Who do you have?"

"Depends on how much you've got."

The agent knows when you're a novice; they're trained to smell fear and taste opportunity. If the agent told us an act had a big hit on Canadian campus radio and was selling out everywhere, how could we argue? There was no Google. *Billboard* magazine was no help locally, and the trade mags of the day were indecipherable to outsiders. There was no alternative but to dive in.

At the end of the first year, it dawned on me that it was ridiculous for educational institutions to be competing with each other on students' dimes. I was convinced we needed to work together and create a learning tool for student buyers. So in 1979, I organized a conference do to just that. But first, a few lessons I learned in my first year as an events programmer:

Lesson 1: Read the Rider

One of the first concerts I booked at UW was Stan Rogers, the dearly departed singer-songwriter from Hamilton who wrote epic stories of Maritime fisher folk. I was a huge fan and wore down the grooves of his first album, *Fogarty's Cove*, at home and at the radio station. He showed up for his afternoon gig driving his own car, with guitar in hand and nary a roadie in sight. At 6'4" Stan was an imposing figure, made more so when he was frowning. He took one look at the stage—an 8-inch wooden platform made from two 4' x 8' risers sitting on top of a little hill on the grass—and sighed.

"Where's the PA?" he inquired, somewhat levelly.

"Didn't you bring it?" I asked.

Stan sighed again.

He put down his guitar, strode back to his car, pulled out his copy of the contract, and pointed to the typed note near the bottom of the first page, which read: "Contractor to supply Sound and Lights."

(Note to self: read the fine print.)

"Don't worry," I said gamely, "I'll call the AV department."

I'm amazed he didn't walk then and there. Happily, the campus pub was open. They had a sound system. Stan waited inside while the bartender came to my aid, rustling up some microphones, speakers, and a baby mixer, and dollied it all out to the field.

While the bartender and I ran cable and tried to figure out which plug went into which hole, I started to fret about an audience. What if you put on a show and nobody came? (Audience attendance would come to be a persistent worry in my life—in months on the road with touring acts, at charity galas, and at my own wedding when guests needed to be transported by barge.)

It was a blisteringly hot day. Showtime was at 2 p.m. and it was almost that, but only a couple dozen students were sitting in front of the risers. Others were strewn about the green, studying, cuddling, playing Frisbee, catching some rays. It was somewhat different from the Woodstockian crowds I'd imagined. I'd thought that if people knew there'd be free music, they'd flock to the stage.

The soundboard was a portable eight-track unit that we set up on a picnic table about thirty feet from the stage, where I now sat, ready to... right! Who would mix? I suppose that would be me.

Stan gamely stepped up to the mic.

"Check one, two, three. Check, Check" — SCREECH! — "$#@%!" There's nothing like feedback to get people's attention. Students sitting on the grass scowled at me, fingers jammed in their ears. Others picked up their books and scattered like it was an afternoon fire drill.

I grabbed every fader on the mixing board and jammed it back to zero. Thank heavens eleven hadn't been invented yet.

Stan glared at me from the middle of the stage, his face beaded with sweat, his lovely bald noggin starting to pink under the scorching rays. He was likely wondering what that idiot college buyer was doing at the board.

I waved helpfully and gave him a big, grinning thumbs-up, hoping to inspire confidence while I grappled with the problem. I figured if I just twiddled the knobs one by one, I could determine which pod was for what and turn off the offending track. It was a painful process, like diffusing a live bomb one input at a time. Any knob might conceal a deadly squeal guaranteed to melt your fillings. In that moment, I developed an enduring respect and gratitude for every capable soundman I'd meet thereafter. Yes, soundman. I never personally encountered a single female sound person. I trust that's changed by now.

Slowly the right cord was coupled with the correct input while Stan patiently strummed, checked, and paced. He, unlike me, was a professional, and eventually he felt comfortable enough to play (or else he just wanted to get it over with). He sounded remarkably good for a man singing through gritted teeth, his baritone voice overcoming the limits of the system and its operator. His songs of privateers Pied-Pipered students out of the buildings and back onto the green. Did I mention the heat? It was far too hot to be performing outside without a roof on the stage (in my defense, the contract did *not* specify a roof). Sweat gathered in Stan's beard. Given the swirl of mic cables, it crossed my mind that the audience might learn something about electrical engineering and water hazards, but we were spared that catastrophe.

At the end of his set (I didn't insist on two) I stood with Stan's cheque in hand, begging forgiveness. He got in his car and sped away. He must have forgiven me eventually, because I booked him again the following year, with his brother Garnet this time, in the pub: with a roof, air conditioning, and cold beer.

Sadly, it was only a few years later that Stan died in a plane fire. It would be fitting to see him awarded a posthumous star on the Walk of Fame one day.

The lessons I learned at Stan's expense helped me build a respectable reputation as a college buyer. I would never again scrimp on production and never knowingly put a musician in a situation where his or her needs weren't fully met.

Harmonium outdoor stage: still no roof!

Lesson 2: Underpromise and Overdeliver

It takes effort (and some luck) to build a decent reputation as a promoter, and in many ways you're only as good as your last show. Horror stories spread like weeds on the industry grapevine, and it's almost impossible to hack down a bad reputation if one takes root. I was determined to hire the A team, overfulfill on the rider (a comprehensive list of requirements specifying everything from power requirements to hospitality), and treat everyone *better* than expected, as circumstances allowed. I had good intentions, but I had lots to learn.

Soon after Orientation, an opportunity arrived to do a real show in a real theatre. The band was CANO (*Coopérative des Artistes de Nouvel-Ontario*), an extraordinary Franco-Ontarian artist collective from Sudbury, originally conceived by André Paiement. André took his life following a bone cancer diagnosis, but the band carried on the vision. As far as I knew, there was no leader, no hierarchy in CANO. The band shared the proceeds from their tours, their publishing income, and the farm where they recorded. At the time it was the only band I knew that operated that way.

October 15, 1978: I'd cavalierly booked CANO for a last-minute show at the campus Humanities Theatre. It was my second month as a buyer and the band's second show in what would be a six-month tour across North America and Europe. Apparently I'd gotten a "great deal" from the agent. (It certainly was great for him. He'd managed the impossible—filling an open Sunday night in a theatre with four days' notice). I set about alerting the student population with all three tools I had at hand: posters, flyers, and the campus radio station. This time, I studied the contract to the letter, scared up a stage crew, hired a piano tuner, and went about executing every detail on the rider the best way I knew how. I wanted everything to be right, even if I knew the show wouldn't sell out on such short notice.

CANO's rider was very specific on hot meals for crew and talent: "No pizza or Kentucky Fried Chicken." Not wanting to disappoint, I spent the day before the show shopping for provisions and baking pies. It never occurred to me to hire a caterer. I was on a budget.

Show day was especially fraught because we couldn't get into the theatre until three that afternoon, and this was a band that typically needed an eight-hour load-in. We had four hours. Doors would open at 7:30 p.m. and I hadn't a clue if anyone would turn up. There hadn't been time to put advance tickets on sale; I was naively counting on a walk-in crowd on a Sunday night from a student population of which many went home on the weekends.

I bounced around the theatre that afternoon like water on a hot skillet, hoping the band would be able to set up and do sound check in half their normal time. I remember someone having to move the piano *after* it was tuned, and holding my breath as pianist Mike Kendel ran his fingers over the keys and then cursed.

Loudly.

In French.

"Omigod, what's wrong?" I asked, thinking I'd have to call the tuner back and have him do it again, which would require another hour and a silent one at that.

"No, it's great!" he enthused. "I hardly ever get to play a piano this good."

Whew.

Everyone worked like demons and we were only half an hour late on the doors. Magically, a crowd of about four hundred had shown up—a little over half full. Even if the show wasn't entirely profitable, it was a masterful musical success. The celestial interplay between Rachel Paiement and violinist Wasyl Kohut, the theatricality of Marcel Aymar, the musicianship of David Burt, John Doerr, Mike Kendel, and Michel Dasti brought on two standing ovations and gushing reviews in all the papers, two in the *Kitchener-Waterloo Record* and one in the campus paper the *Chevron*, whose opening line was: "How can anything that sounds so beautiful come from Sudbury?" (Sorry, Sudbury.)

The CANO show was a seminal moment for me, and the band remembered me ever after (because of the pies, I'll wager). Being hailed as a friend by esteemed musicians is something you should never expect, though it's a treat when it happens. I learned to never book a gig on four days' notice again, no matter how good the deal. But more importantly, I got a revelatory glimpse into the state of the Canadian musical universe and found out just how precarious making a living as a musician in this country could be.

By the time of our show, CANO had released three records, one of which, *Au Nord de Notre Vie*, was a gold-selling record in Canada. I'd naturally assumed that a band with a gold record would be all limos, champagne, and room service, but watching them carefully pack up and stow leftover food after the show, I started to see the real picture. Apparently in Canada you could sell tens of thousands of records, adorn the covers of magazines, tour in theatres to standing ovations, and still not be able to pay the rent.

As it's been said (by Kim Mitchell, I think), and it's mostly true, Canadian musicians are too famous to ride the subway and too poor to hire a car. The more artists I met, the more I became convinced that this just wasn't right. I pledged to learn everything I could about the music business, in the event that one day, if I was ever in a position of influence, I might help to support artistic achievement in a manner more elegant than hand to mouth.

To underscore the point, the second time I booked members of CANO they were part of a pick-up ensemble called the Last Dash for Cash Band. That gig was also the night I was pepper sprayed in the line of duty.

The Waterloo Motor Inn was located on King Street North, a few miles from campus. At the time, the university didn't have a lot of suitable venues for entertainment, so the Federation of Students partnered with the Bingeman brothers, local businessmen who owned the Inn and the Bingeman Roller Rink across town. We were responsible for hiring the band, selling the tickets, and paying for any damages on site. They got the bar. Even with free buses and subsidized tickets, getting students off campus to attend was a gamble, unless the act was very well known.

That night a guy who had watched the whole show demanded his money back because he claimed he didn't like it. When I refused he reached into his pocket, pulled out a spray can, and maced me. Right in the face. It was crazy painful. I thought it was acid—it certainly felt like my face was on fire—and staggered into the washroom to try flushing the substance off with water, which just made it worse. Wasyl Kohut, the band's violinist, came in to help while Susan Rosenberg (a student volunteer who now tours the world with Live Nation) called the cops. Someone had seen the guy run to a room at the hotel.

Once my face simmered down, the cops wanted me to identify the jerk. I stood there like an idiot as they banged on his door, fully expecting to be maced again, but the man was in his underwear, with no can on his person as far as I could see.

It's a toss-up as to whether I'd rather be pepper sprayed or punched, the latter being what happened at an end-of-term Decemberfest dance for the engineering faculty at Bingeman's Roller Rink. We'd booked the Good Brothers, and the place was packed and rowdy. The engineers were celebrating the end of exams by downing buckets of beer from Oktoberfest pitchers and plastic cups.

At one point near the end of the last set, with the band in full throttle and the dance floor packed, I spied a trouble spot from across the room. Five or six patrons were standing on a table, pitchers in hand, bouncing up and down like drunken marionettes. The wooden table looked like a trampoline, bending with the weight. We'd lost a few tables at past events, and the damages had been added to the bill—forty bucks each! Big money considering what we paid the Board of Entertainment staff. (The B. Ent crew, who doubled as security, worked for ten dollars a night and a B. Ent T-shirt.) I could tell the table was about to bust, but before I could think about asking any of the B. Ent crew to intercede, I took off.

I ran across the roller rink floor and got to the table just as it collapsed in front of me. Guys rolled off in all directions, beer splattering high and wide. I was in a full froth myself, out of breath from the sprint.

I grabbed the dude nearest my feet and hauled him up by his T-shirt, his collar jammed up under his ears.

"You have to pay for that table," I demanded.

He stared at me, suddenly focused, and said: "Put. Me. Down."

It was then that I realized his feet were three inches off the floor.

The shock of it—that I'd actually picked him up in a charge of adrenaline—made me drop him, at which point he "dropped" me. Next thing I knew I was looking up into the faces of my B. Ent crew, who were helping me up. The engineers had split, the table was broken, and it was all over. It didn't occur to me to try and find out who the guy was; I accepted that the punch in the face was my fault because I'd provoked him, childhood boxing lessons notwithstanding.

At the end of that first year, I settled down and learned to take things more in stride. By the second year, I'd put on sixty-nine shows and was feeling comfortable in the world of artists, agents, and managers. I certainly didn't get maced or decked again.

Lesson 3: Respect Thy Roadies and Thy Rider
"They're the first to come and the last to leave, working for that minimum wage…"

Jackson Browne's "The Load Out" is a fine homage to road crews everywhere. Roadies are unsung heroes—and compared to most pop musicians, with their relatively short life spans, roadies endure.

They arrive hours before the artist to adapt the stage set-up to locations that range from theatres to outdoor stages to hockey rinks with antiquated electrical systems and boards covering the ice. And they always make it work.

There's a crude roadie credo that goes:

If it's wet, drink it.
If it's dry, smoke it.
If it moves, fuck it.
If it doesn't move, put it in the truck.

I've encountered that breed often enough. But the roadie "genus" I know better is a dedicated bunch of road-hardened professionals. Men (and increasingly women) whose offices simply happen to be constantly on the move. They want their gear to work, so you can't go greeting the first truck like this:

"Can't you just wing it?"

This is a Harry Warr cartoon that I commissioned for the Canadian Entertainment Conference guide the first year we hosted it. It illustrates why the rider is so important and why the story about Van Halen's brown M&M's wasn't a joke. Van Halen's tour manager inserted that infamous clause—to "remove the brown M&M's" from the candy—deep in the band's rider for a reason; the moment he entered a dressing room, he knew whether or not the promoter had respected the rider. Every technical detail, from the stage dimensions to the load-bearing weight of the ceiling points in the roof, must be right—or the show may not go on.

That said, rider requirements can range from the pedestrian to the preposterous. Just for fun, here's a sample of rider requests:

Things to drink: Diet Coke, Classic Coke, Vanilla Coke, NO Coke, Pepsi. Chocolate Yoo-hoo, Jägermeister, acidophilus milk, sugar-free Red Bull, chilled Cristal, tequila ("plus limes + salt"), Stolichnaya vodka, Jack Daniels, Snapple. Warm water, cold water, still water, sparkling water, and full-service English Breakfast tea in china cups (The Who).

Things to eat: Grilled chicken, KFC assorted chicken, NO KFC! One Cornish game hen, one large chicken, and one XL Butterball turkey plucked, thawed, and fully trussed. ("Mr. [Tom] Green refuses to work with frozen game.") Jif creamy peanut butter, Kraft crunchy peanut butter, organic peanut butter, light peanut butter, soy nut butter, almond butter. Snack-sized 3 Musketeers, Beemans Chewing Gum, Juicy Fruit. And my personal favourite: "How about having the condiment fairy drop off a gaggle of new, unopened condiments...We don't want the last few millimetres of sauce that Alice Cooper left in the mustard bottle" (Foo Fighters).

Things to adorn: White flowers (no lilies); lilies, no chrysanthemums, carnations, or daisies (Elton John); black and red roses (Axl Rose); fresh boxer shorts (Barenaked Ladies hated doing laundry). No rugs or carpeting ("Mr. Roth practices martial arts in his dressing room").

Things to play with: One full-sized snooker table (the Rolling Stones); one Sony PlayStation; ribbed Rough Rider condoms (Busta Rhymes). Assortment of adult magazines (Guns N' Roses); mud wrestling ring and wrestlers (Queen). KISS inflatables (KISS).

Things to heal: Registered massage therapist, osteo-podiatrist, chiropractor, ear, nose, and throat specialist. B12, anti-inflammatories, Eucalyptus-infused humidifier, Fisherman's Friend lozenges. Three bottles of oxygen with masks (TLC).

Things to keep you healthy: Ginger root, ginger tea, ginger snaps, half-pint fat-free small curd organic cottage cheese, New Zealand

Manuka honey. Medical doctor on call all day (ZZ Top), wheat grass (Aerosmith).

Things to keep you comfy: Air conditioning in dressing room. No air conditioning in dressing room. Room at precisely 23 degrees Celsius. Hotel room totally blacked: "Please do this test. Turn all the lights out and if you can still see your hand one foot in front of your face, it's not dark enough" (John Travolta). No animals, "anytime." (If there is an animal backstage, Alabama will not perform.)

Things of legend that I've heard of but can't attest to: Seven dwarves (Iggy Pop). Brand new toilet seats (Mary J. Blige and Madonna). Fully stocked koi pond (Eminem). Twelve-foot boa constrictor (Mötley Crüe; Alice Cooper brought his own). Traditional shepherd's pie (Mick Jagger *and* Joe Cocker). Meat adverts in venue covered up (Sir Paul McCartney).

It's not about coddling the talent; it's usually about providing what they need in order to perform at their best. So long as the item doesn't have to be kept alive or flown in from Paris overnight, and doesn't eat too egregiously into the budget, then fine. There are exceptions. If it's a charity gig and you're blanching at the extra grand it will cost to install couches, curtains, and *only white* flowers for Jennifer Lopez, just get on the phone and have a chat. Jenny from the Block is still in there, and last time I saw her she *complained* about the flowers always being white.

Lesson 4: Assume Nothing, Not Even Gender
In those days, most everyone I dealt with—agents, promoters, managers, and roadies—were men. In the late seventies, I think there were about three female college buyers in the entire country, and the only professional female promoter I knew was one half of a husband-and-wife team. Betty and Joe Recchia were promoters in the Kitchener-Waterloo area with whom we at UW both competed and collaborated.

The first time I got an inkling that being a female promoter was "special" was at a Burton Cummings concert at UW's Physical Activities Complex

(PAC). It was a big show for me—the PAC held 5,000 people and, as usual, I was anxious about everything.

On show day I arrived early so I could check on the load-in and make sure our stage crew had shown up on time. Burton's trucks had arrived, and the stacks and cases were rolling in. As I walked on stage, I saw a very large bearded man in a black T-shirt in animated conversation with one of my B. Ent crew.

"Where's your boss?" I heard him say.

"Over there," said my guy, pointing to me.

The bear-like man glanced over at me, then turned back. "No, I mean where's the promoter?"

"Her, over there," the B. Ent dude said, pointing at me again.

Bear man wasn't having it.

"Just tell me who's in charge!" he thundered.

I started to clue in. I wasn't sure if he was annoyed because he thought the loader was an imbecile, or if he just couldn't believe I was the promoter. Perhaps he had never encountered a female member of the species.

I walked over. "How I can I help you, sir?"

"Where the fuck's the coffee?"

Not the last time I'd be expected to get coffee.

The fellow's name was Tiny, and he needed refuelling. They'd been travelling overnight.

Once Tiny's blood sugar was stable and we'd said a proper hello, we got along great. I saw him often over the years, as you do, and he was never combative with me again—in fact, he was rather protective.

Tiny was like a lot of crew guys I've come to know—salt of the earth and dedicated to a rough perfection that ensures that when the lights go down, the show comes up.

Lesson 5: TMI Is Not a Communications Strategy

In my three years as a college buyer at UW, I presented or co-presented scores of acts. Some of them you'd recognize—Tom Waits, J. J. Cale, Harmonium, Eric Andersen, Second City, Teenage Head, Max Webster, Jackie Washington, the Nylons, Valdy, David Wilcox, the Minglewood Band, Dan Hill, Subway Elvis, Kate & Anna McGarrigle, Bob Segarini, Downchild, Ernie Smith and the Roots Revival, and Murray McLauchlan (although I don't remember actually speaking to my future husband then). Some of them have been lost to the vagaries of the music marketplace: the Villains ("We're madder than Madness!"), for example, not to mention a myriad of cover bands—like Harbinger, on whose event poster I earnestly proclaimed: "You've heard Liverpool do the Beatles, now hear Harbinger do Supertramp complete with bizarre special effects!" Suffice it to say I was not destined for a crisp career in advertising. There was a note to self in my journal—*Buy fire extinguisher*—in anticipation, no doubt, of those bizarre special effects. Safety first!

They weren't all successes, of course. As I've said, the investment in my salary was expected to return value for the student fees. As such, my activities were subject to unyielding scrutiny by not one, but two university papers, the *Imprint* and the aforementioned *Chevron*. The *Imprint* was like most college papers, full of impassioned reportage by budding journalists, while the *Chevron* was felt by many to toe the line of the student wing of the CPC(ML)—the Communist Party of Canada (Marxist Leninist).

Both papers were funded by student fees. As I, too, was similarly funded, I thought it my duty to answer any question that was asked. I walked around with my kimono fully open, happy to divulge any fiscal detail the students might require. As a result, we got headlines like "Liverpool Loses" (even though that show was *meant* to be subsidized), and "B. Ent Overbills, Beer Bash Losses," which accused me of "deliberately overcharging the co-sponsors for expenses amounting to $200." Clearing my name required signed affidavits from the other two sponsoring schools. It was a classic headline case of "Axe Murderer Kills 3!"—and then, two weeks later, a tiny boxed correction: "She didn't do it."

I shouldn't complain. The student journalists were learning how to write, just as I was learning how to work the press. They opined that ticket prices were too high or the dance floor was in the wrong place (the reviewer groused that his view was impeded by dancing students), and one decided that the space-rock trio FM's music was too technologically advanced, "making it appear that only drummer Martin Deller is actually working on stage." Imagine.

Eventually, I had only one student paper to parry with. In December, 1978, students voted to withdraw their fees from the *Chevron*. The paper had been ousted from Canadian University Press for "violating staff democracy principles," and had reappeared as the *Free Chevron* for a while, but it lost its campus office in January of 1979.

It was bizarre timing, and this is certainly not a "*J'accuse*" moment, but after the *Chevron* was ousted, a rock was thrown through the window of the Federation office; and shortly after that, I woke up to find the back end of my rusty brown Dodge Dart scorched by fire. Someone had stuck a rag into the gas tank and attempted to light it. Luckily, they'd only succeeded in cutting off the air to the tank, rather than blowing up the car. I admit I was rattled, but it was probably just kids.

There was even a controversy over a band we *didn't* book, the Battered Wives. The Federation of Students' president *wanted* me to book them, which the press caught wind of, and I was only saved from the storm by the band's lack of availability. The papers raged on about it anyway, and in the end I was merely quoted as saying, "I'd rather book a DJ." Fierce talk, Donlon. I had a lot to learn about standing on principle.

I had my chance to take a feminist stance shortly thereafter, but mishandled it when I booked author Shere Hite for a speaking gig, along with feminist comic Robin Tyler. Hite's book, *The Hite Report on Female Sexuality*, was revolutionary but controversial, too, due to her research methodology: 3,000 women voluntarily responding to an essay-based questionnaire. I was delighted to bring her to campus, thinking her visit would open a discussion on female sexuality, sexism, and power. The show, however, was a disaster.

When Hite arrived at Waterloo, the headline in the *Imprint* read: "$2,700 Worth of Sex Talk." Her appearance fee was now public knowledge (that source would have been me, oversharing again), though I'd gamely pointed out in the article that Western University was paying $300 more (a useful distinction, I'd thought, in justifying my existence). Thus, according to the article, "Donlon does not feel Hite is worth the money she is being paid." Oh, dear. What promoter in her right mind would say that, out loud, before the gig with tickets on sale—especially after she'd agreed to the fee? The article went on to say: "However, Donlon added that all speakers today are expensive. She booked Hite because she feels it has been too long since UW featured a female speaker of any calibre." Redeemed (ish).

The headline after Hite's show was "Male Domination Must End"— not a bad start—though the piece went on to point out that Ms. Hite was nearly in tears during her lecture. Which she was. She was heckled by audience members on her methodology and accused of being evasive, "like Nixon on the Frost interviews." Another charged Hite with "exploiting" the audience by charging $3.75 a ticket. Many walked out; some asked for their money back. And one brave fellow stood up during the Q & A and complained that after reading the book, he'd had a "nightmare about the future, when women would have all the power." Poor, dear thing. Though that future appears to be a dream still.

Afterward, those who'd been in the audience kept up the complaints for weeks, gamely hurling letters to the editor and debating appropriate feminist behaviour. As for me, I had no regrets—even if the show did lose money, as was dutifully reported in the press.

READING MY NOTES ON these early days makes me wince; it's like watching my twenty-something self grow up under a public spotlight. But all in all, booking talent was a great adventure. And I have many fond memories.

James Doohan, the actor who played Scotty on *Star Trek*, is one that stands out. His speaking fee was *way* bigger than Ms. Hite's, but on a Trekkie-heaven campus full of engineers, computer studies students, and mathematicians, no one would be rude enough to ask about Scotty's fee. It was an easier gig, too. Scotty would play an episode from *Star Trek*— "The Trouble with Tribbles," for one—and then take a Q & A. A shame he had to play college campuses at all, but given the residuals the actors were allegedly paid on that series, I guess work was work.

I drove to Pearson Airport to pick him up and was about to guide him to the car when he wondered aloud if we had time for a quick beverage. While we were sitting in the airport bar, Dave Broadfoot of the Royal Canadian Air Farce walked by; they recognized each other from a theatre performance they'd done together back in the day. David sat down, Scotty ordered another round, and so we continued. It was entertaining for me on many counts—hanging out with two Canadian celebrities, gaping at the size of the bar bill, and marvelling that Scotty was missing his right middle finger (he'd been shot six times at the Battle of Normandy). Forever after I was intrigued to see how Scotty always hid the missing digit on *Star Trek*. Like Gary Burghoff's Radar O'Reilly on *M*A*S*H*, whose left hand was always behind a clipboard or something, you never saw Scotty's right hand.

By the time we got into the car, I was wondering just how cogent his performance would be. He said a quick hello to the audience, and then caught forty winks while we rolled the episode. He was bright-eyed and bushy-tailed for the Q & A, and no one complained of nightmares after the show.

Harmonium also sticks out in my mind. I was enthralled with their music, and knew that an engagement in English Canada was rare for them at the time. As is still the case with so many French-Canadian artists, Harmonium were superstars in Quebec but relatively unknown outside the province. If the students on campus could just experience them once, I thought, they'd be hooked. *Les deux solitudes*, solved. The band certainly enjoyed the show. I heard afterward that there were some "lingerers" on campus that night; I never did get a hotel bill. I expect there was no shortage of new fans enthusiastic enough to provide a pallet for a handsome Frenchman.

I love this picture because I'm wearing my awesome homemade sandals and harem pants—gathered at the waist and ankle, and slit all the way up both sides. Stylin'!

The photo makes me think, too, about the scores of musicians, roadies, and industry types that I first encountered at Waterloo and still know today. From Ben "Bent" Mink (he insisted on owning a B. Ent crew shirt for obvious reasons) who was in Murray's band the Silver Tractors and went on to make incredible music with k.d. lang, among others; to Donnie "Mr. Downchild" Walsh, Kim Mitchell, the Goods, and scores more in between. It was an extraordinary musical education for me. And in the end, I think I *did* save the students money.

(5)

VANCOUVER-BOUND

"But she's got the urge for going
So I guess she'll have to go."
— JONI MITCHELL, "URGE FOR GOING"

BY MY THIRD YEAR of booking bands, I'd mostly figured out what would work for new students and what was a fair price for talent. But while I could certainly handle the agents, I might still be outbid by competitors — newbie college buyers who would naively overpay. Not a good scenario for us, or a good use of student money.

The only way around it was to summon my inner Sally Field and unite! A Canadian Entertainment Conference (now COCA) for college buyers had been organized years earlier by Joe and Betty Recchia, but was in hiatus when I arrived on the scene.

Given all the mistakes I'd made that might have been prevented with a little inside information, I thought it prudent to share the knowledge. So with the blessing of the Federation president and the Recchias, I undertook to remount and host the CEC in 1980 and 1981. Those conferences led to my next job.

The 1980 CEC brought sixty college and university programmers together at the Waterloo Motor Inn, each delegate paying the princely sum of $70 for a three-day event that showcased nineteen concert performances as well as dozens of speakers on important subjects like Stage Management, Budgeting and Booking, Performing Rights Societies, as well as scintillating ephemera like Withholding Taxes, Splits, and Liabilities.

Organizing the conference meant a ton of unpaid work, but that work was thoroughly satisfying—for me, and for my colleague Susan Rosenberg and the whole B. Ent crew. Once we knew we could do it, we did it again. The second year featured bigger acts with more focused seminars and a better understanding of how we could work together. There were also better parties, at which the redoubtable Tiny saved me from being celebrated, fully clothed, in the pool. On day three Susan and I noticed the attendance rate at the early-morning seminar had plummeted, and so we organized a cart full of Bloody Marys and banged on people's doors, handing them a hair of the dog and insisting they get up and at 'em.

After booking concerts for three years, I was playing with the idea of moving on, but I didn't know what to. I silkscreened a For Sale sign on the back of my CEC shirt and wore it all weekend. Nothing like being obvious. I got a few job offers on the spot—including an oddball serve from someone from the Harlem Globetrotters (the height thing was starting to come in handy)—and one invitation that I accepted.

Rob Hoskins, a West Coast booking agent, had attended the conference. He took a pamphlet that I'd written for the Negotiation Skills panel back to his boss Sam Feldman, president of S. L. Feldman and Associates in Vancouver, a booking and management agency for bands and musicians. The next thing I knew I was on a plane.

Sam wanted an in-house publicity arm for his expanding company. The business risk for the venture would be mine, but I'd start with an initial client list: Sam's management acts—Doug and the Slugs, Trooper, and Headpins. I'd never been a publicist per se, but I thought promoting artists was probably similar to promoting shows. How hard could running my own business be?

I weighed the possibility in the way I always do—by torturing my friends. It was Richard Flohil, an expat British writer, publicist, and music promoter, who convinced me to "Go West." He assured me that I could learn a lot more as a big frog in a small pond than by setting up shop in Toronto. (Now that I think of it, Richard was a publicist in Toronto. Well played, my friend!) It was good advice and it happened fast.

But Vancouver wasn't a small pond at all; it was a thriving musical epicentre. In addition to the success of the more mainstream homegrown heroes like Loverboy, Bryan Adams, Trooper, Prism, Chilliwack, Headpins, and Doug and the Slugs, a potent new punk scene was emerging. D.O.A., with Joe Keithley, led the charge as New Wave bands like Subhumans, Payolas, Skinny Puppy, Strange Advance, 54-40, Images in Vogue, Young Canadians, and Nomeansno crowded the stages. These spikey young upstarts were birthing their own labels and elbowing for position with the reigning rock royalty. The folkier, bluesier side was also hummin', with Powder Blues, Shari Ulrich, Jim Byrnes, Valdy, and Spirit of the West populating the clubs and the festivals. It was a heady time for all levels of the industry, ably assisted by powerhouse managers like Bruce Allen, Sam Feldman, and the emerging Terry McBride.

Video production houses were also surfacing, and the studio business was gaining a stalwart reputation of its own. Little Mountain Sound Studios and Mushroom Studios housed state-of-the-art gear and hosted some of the world's best producers, like Bruce Fairbairn, Jim Vallance, and Bob Rock. The studios, some of which had already built a strong legacy in recording artists such as Led Zeppelin, Diana Ross and the Supremes, Nat King Cole, and Frank Sinatra, now became home to BTO, Heart, and, later, Sarah McLachlan and Tegan and Sara.

It should also be noted, because I certainly noted it when I got there, that studded leathers, sleek cars, and a festive wet-stripper culture was also part of the Vancouver scene. Apparently our "girls" not only had "enormous charm," their gymnastic showbiz innovations were the stuff of legend. Tales of their tall-pole prowess with whipped cream, pillows, and spray hoses spread far and wide, and the town started to build a reputation for putting the "hard" in hard rock. Word was, the title of Bon Jovi's smash album *Slippery When Wet* was not inspired by a cautionary street sign. Produced by Bruce Fairbairn and engineered and mixed by Payolas' Bob Rock at Little Mountain, I understand it was inspired by field trips to the No. 5 Orange strip club in Vancouver. Queensryche, AC/DC, Mötley Crüe, the Cult, Aerosmith, and Metallica were among the many bands drawn by the excellence of Vancouver's producers, studios, and cultural attractions.

This was to be my new stomping grounds.

I met with Sam in Vancouver on a Wednesday. He said that if I could be back in Vancouver to start by a week Monday, he'd clear out a space where I could set up an office. That precipitated the fastest garage sale ever, and less than a fortnight later, I was in Vancouver, open to whatever awaited.

VANCOUVER MIGHT BE SMALL geographically, but it holds two of the biggest music moguls in North America. When I arrived in 1982, Bruce Allen and Sam Feldman were already the reigning musical grandmasters of the West Coast, and their stature on the worldwide stage was beginning to build. In the last quarter-century they have built an entertainment empire that manages world-class talent like Bryan Adams, Diana Krall, and James Taylor; represents more than two hundred artists through its booking agency; and employs over a hundred full-time people under one multi-tentacled, internationally successful company known as A & F Music.

Bruce Allen (the A) and Sam Feldman (the F) were partners, but they did not share an office. When I arrived people couldn't wait to fill me in with stories about their tempestuous relationship. A & F was held together by shared assets and joint finances, but it presented like a bad marriage. The word around town was that it apt to blow at any moment.

I've come to see Bruce and Sam's relationship as somewhat Shakespearean in nature: two competitive overachievers bound in a business relationship that plays out both publicly and privately in act after act. They're sometimes friends, sometimes rivals, keenly aware of each other's artists and whose side of the business is up or down. Still, they appear eternally tethered, their business relationship too intertwined to be rent asunder despite the strength of their powerful personalities.

What they've achieved, both jointly and separately, is extraordinary.

The Bruce Allen talent roster includes Bryan Adams (the biggest-selling Canadian rocker of all time), Michael Bublé, Anne Murray, Jann Arden, and producer Bob Rock. Over the years, he has also managed BTO, Loverboy, Martina McBride and more, as well as sports stars in boxing, curling, and NASCAR.

Sam's management arm, which became Macklam Feldman Management when he joined forces with artist manager Steve Macklam, also guides the careers of some of the world's most revered artists, including Diana Krall, James Taylor, Sarah McLachlan, the Chieftains, Elvis Costello, Bette Midler, and Melody Gardot. Over the years they have also managed Joni Mitchell, Leonard Cohen, and Norah Jones.

The booking agency (now called the Feldman Agency) has been a powerhouse for almost forty years, representing all manner of genres and artists from Rush to The Tragically Hip, from k-os to Nelly Furtado.

It's a testament to their skill and success that A & F operates from Vancouver, not New York or L.A. The world does indeed beat a path to their door. Or, since 1979, when Sam left the building, *doors*, plural.

Sam and Bruce formed their partnership in 1972, when they met while cutting similar paths in the nightclub scene in Vancouver. Both hailed from the Dunbar area of the city. Bruce was a band manager with acts like Crosstown Bus and 5 Man Cargo and was booking nightclubs through his company Bruce Allen Talent. Sam was a graduate of the pool halls and poker dens, a nightclub bouncer before working with bands like Sweet Beaver and Uncle Slug. They met, negotiated, shook hands, and opened their office at 777 Hornby. Their business grew quickly, but so did the friction in the office.

Bruce was known as "The Mouth that Scored." That was the headline on a 1983 *Vancouver Magazine* cover story on Bruce by Les Wiseman. Les called Bruce's rampages a "wondrous thing to behold" and described him this way: "He is tall and when he shouts it is like a Tyrannosaurus Rex bellowing for flesh. He hollers so loud that others in the office voluntarily pull their heads into their shoulders like tortoises and then hurriedly dial concert promoters and record company executives half a continent away for Allen to curse. He turns purple and veins bug out of his forehead and temples. He gets things done."

In the same magazine some years later, in March 1991, Sam's cover story headline (written by Rick Ouston) was "The Emperor of Rock and Roll" and the pull-quote read: "Sam Feldman is a nice guy and a very, very big fish in the small pond of local rock & roll clubs."

Let's just say they had different personalities.

Bruce's style wasn't singular. At the time, yelling was a matter of course in the music business. People who were not naturally good at yelling worked on their form and practiced whenever they could. They'd bark at their secretaries and slam phones and throw product at walls. They'd rant at radio station music directors and swear at promoters, yelling about that idiot not being awake in the middle of the night in France when they needed some information. It was tradition. After all, the music business was founded by fast-talking self-made hitmen and hucksters.

Bruce's forceful personality was working for him. BTO had become a double-platinum act in the U.S. on the strength of massive hits like "Takin' Care of Business" and "Let It Ride." It's nice to hear Bruce speak generously of Randy today, saying that Randy taught him a lot about the business in those days, especially the golden rule of talent management: that artists need a passionate, committed advocate. Which is true, and great managers, as I would come to learn later, are rare.

Meanwhile, Sam was building up the agency side of the partnership, expanding its base of influence, and managing the staff and the business. It was all going along just fine—until BTO broke up, which meant that Bruce was suddenly no longer on the road. The common lore is that it was his day-to-day "bellowing for flesh" that brought things to a head, though Sam could certainly yell too. Sam told me that Bruce's return to the office was akin to "a Green Beret returning home from the war. You can't expect him to work in the corner store." Still, it was an atmosphere that Sam thought was unhealthy for the company.

On the evening of July 31, 1979, Sam called a meeting with the staff and told them he was moving out and taking the agency with him. He told them they were free to stay or leave, and when Bruce walked in the next morning, the office was empty.

Somehow the business relationship survived the split. Sam and Bruce proceeded to build a hugely successful company, albeit each with different artists. Everything they touched didn't turn to gold, of course, but what they shared was a love for the business and a total loyalty to their artists. Somehow that overcame even their competitiveness with each other.

It's ironic that I was introduced to Sam through a pamphlet I'd written on negotiation skills, because it's Sam who's the true negotiator. His quick wit and skilled bedside manner with artists have always been the keys to his success. They say you're judged by the quality of your friends. Well, this is a guy who, for his son's bar mitzvah, had Robin Williams, Billy Crystal, Don Rickles, and Jackie Mason all on tape singing the praises of a kid they'd never met, just because they knew Sam would get a kick out of it—and that they could roast him while doing it.

Sam was my coach. He put the publicity of his bands in my hands, introduced me to club owners, and gave me administration duties on Doug and the Slugs' label, Ritdong Records, even when I hadn't a clue what, for example, a mechanical royalty was. I did well to welcome the challenges he threw my way.

I dove in, doggedly building a business. I hadn't yet met Bruce, though I quickly learned how competitive he was when my new little company was mentioned in the *Westender* and the *Georgia Straight*.

The phone rang. It was Bruce, saying something to the extent of, "If you're so hot, why are you working for Sam? You should be working for me. Come over and you can see for yourself."

I admit I was a little star-struck. Bruce managed Loverboy. I'd been to a party at lead singer Mike Reno's home, and I'd walked around gobsmacked all night. Mike had a huge house near the water with beautifully landscaped lawns and lighting in the trees. There were waistcoated waiters with white towels draped over their arms, serving drinks on trays. Compared to my budget beginnings, this was *The Great Gatsby*.

I was flattered and intrigued at the thought of meeting Bruce, but I knew that even taking the meeting might be construed as disloyal to Sam. Still, I thought I should go, to show my respect at least. And who knew — it might result in a new client or two. They were business partners, after all.

And so, one rainy morning, before our offices were due to open, I drove to Bruce's office in Gastown. It felt like a covert operation, the mist making it seem a little sinister, and I sat for a moment staring at the licence plate on what I knew was Bruce's low-slung Corvette in the parking lot. *UNRULY*, it read. The song playing on CFOX at that very moment was the Police's "Every Breath You Take (I'll Be Watching You)," which suddenly gave me a cold chill. The music world was tight here; there were few secrets.

I made my way up the creaky wooden stairs to Bruce's office in Gastown, where the gold records gleamed on the walls. Bruce was magnanimous. He talked about all the bands he was having roaring success with — Loverboy, Prism, Bryan Adams, and his new signing, Red Rider. He was proud of all "his girls" working in the office. I asked if any of them were co-managers, like Lou Blair with Loverboy? Bruce said no, but that he liked women working for him because they never wanted to *be* managers.

A testament to the times perhaps, but I was not destined to work for Bruce.

Back at Sam's office, I went to confession. I told Sam where I'd been, but that the encounter confirmed that I was in the right place. I mentioned Sting's stalker song playing on the radio, and Sam nodded — a little too deliberately. It was entirely possible that he'd called his friend Don Shafer at CFOX and arranged to have the song play at precisely the time I was heading over the Bruce's. (Just because you're paranoid doesn't mean people aren't following you...)

Thereafter, I assumed my position in the parallel orbits of Sam and Bruce's respective offices. Staff would see each other at various gigs and functions, but seldom intersect. At best we'd nod at each other across the room, like estranged family members — respectful but maintaining a distance. Occasionally, however, the planets would align, or collide — as they did one day when Bruce and I went head to head.

Sam was away from the office, driving back from the Okanagan. The Feldman agents were grinding away, booking anyone who sang into any club they could throughout the Canadian hinterland. It was a typically loud, coffee-guzzling, phone-ringing, telex-humming morning.

Sam's agency office was laid out as one large, open area surrounded by the agents' individual offices, all fronted with glass. Everyone was on display as they worked, and it gave the whole place a sense of theatre. It wasn't unusual to see people letting off steam by kicking back their chairs, stomping into the middle of the room, and letting loose a string of blue invective about this band or that club or about some cheque bouncing, and then storm back into their offices, pick up the phone, and make another call.

"Hey, how's it going in Prince George, my friend? I see you're still open next week..."

On this particular morning, however, the buzz in the office was disrupted by a commotion coming from reception. As the receptionist's voice picked up volume — insisting that "Sam's not here! I don't know when he'll be back!" — I got up to see what was going on.

I saw Bruce was striding past reception and into the open agents' area. He took an immediate left turn into the accountant Harry's office and slammed the door hard. I rushed over and saw Bruce leaning across the desk, bellowing at Harry, who was apparently not giving him what he wanted.

Harry had backed his chair against the wall and I could see he was alarmed. He was a soft-spoken, elderly gentleman who went about the financial business of the company with a mannerly sense of calm. Normally, his office was an oasis amidst the intense energy of the music agents.

I had no idea what Bruce was angry about, but without thinking I pushed through the door and put my hand on his forearm, meaning to steer him out of Harry's office. That got his attention.

Bruce was stunned. So was I. He immediately turned to face me, and as I backed up into the foyer he followed. We were nose to nose. I don't even remember what Bruce was on about; he wasn't yelling *at* me so much as *through* me. His face was getting redder and I could see the veins Les Wiseman would describe in his article. My brain began to disassociate. All I could think was, *I've been here before.*

He was just like my dad.

The more he yelled, the colder I got.

Autopilot.

"Bruce. You can't treat Harry like that. Talk to Sam when he gets back. You should leave."

Maybe the sheer surprise of me trying to push him out of what he likely saw as his own office snapped him out of it. He stopped mid-stream, and looked around. The office was in suspended animation. Agents were craning their necks out their doors, phones in mid-air, watching. Bruce turned, strode past reception, and went down the stairs.

It was all over in an instant, like a sudden storm that had swept by. I felt like I was coming out of a trance.

When Sam got back later that day, he headed straight to Bruce's office. I have no idea what happened there, but I expect it was loud.

As weird as it sounds, I'm appreciative of that moment. Happening as early in my professional life as it did, it made me realize that I could stand up and not be blown over. I know I'd been maced and punched in the line of duty before, but this was different—this was business. Bruce added steel to my armour and I'd need it.

Celebrating Sam's fiftieth birthday. Sam Feldman, me, Diana Krall, and Bruce Allen.

Over the decades Bruce and I have continued to intersect, often at industry functions and charitable undertakings in which he and his many artists have engaged. He's always been gracious, sending flowers and notes when life has been good to me — like my promotion at MuchMusic or being made president at Sony Music Canada.

He's said to have mellowed somewhat over the years. Maybe his climb up Mount Kilimanjaro had something to do with that; or perhaps managing stellar women like Jann Arden and Anne Murray has had a broadening effect (so to speak). Or perhaps we've all just seasoned with the years. I have great respect for what he's achieved and he has always taken my calls (so far). Still, I never pick up the phone to make those calls without taking a deep breath.

Meanwhile, Sam and Bruce opened countless doors for musicians, agents, promoters — and certainly for me in those early days. Sam had organized a spot for me across an outdoor walkway from his offices on West 4th Avenue in Vancouver. My company of one, with the inventive name of Denise Donlon Publicity (DDP), shared space with James O'Mara, a talented photographer and graphic designer who was the coolest dude I'd ever met.

Everything about James was stylish. His European fashion flair, his work with luxury brands, the way he wrote his to-do lists — which looked like they'd been copy-set by an architect. James had already attracted some pretty singular clients and was on his way to world renown. I remember the first time an artist manager named Cliff Jones glided into the office wearing high-top roller skates (no mean feat—we were atop two flights of stairs). Cliff had long blonde hair, a beard, and an earring, all of which made Festus, the foul-mouthed African grey parrot on his shoulder, seem totally reasonable.

There was a laid-back vibe about the West Coast, but it was all business when it came to the music. Sam's office was a revolving door of the who's who of the Vancouver music scene. The parking lot was lined with shiny status symbols. The agents loved their cars. Elaine's BMW, Casey's Saab, Rob's Audi, Shaw's Porsche, and the car I most admired, Sam's yellow 450 Mercedes SL convertible with the tan leather interior. Sam said his only regret about that car was that he couldn't drive it right *into* the restaurant. ("Why should only the valet know how good your car is?" he'd say.) My banged-up Mustang was a tawdry interloper. I was able to trade it in a few years later for a used but flashy white Nissan 300ZX. Only then did I feel like I was fooling some of the people some of the time.

It's the nature of agents to overplay, of course, but even so, my arrival in town had been a tad overhyped by Rob and Sam. At the beginning I was met with a bit of sniffy East Coast/West Coast rivalry–bred resentment. And there was a bewildering array of strange new characters to get to know. Nightclub owners, radio station jocks, newspaper critics, and literally hundreds of musicians in bands I'd never heard of from my small-town perch in southwestern Ontario. This was before any national music service was available, so there really was a great divide between the music scenes of the two coasts. The advantage was that artists could hone their skills locally first, rather than being thrown against a national wall of attention before they were ready.

Even the biggest acts weren't equally known across the country. I remember gazing in wonder at the four (soon to be six) platinum awards for Trooper's *Hot Shots* album, just a few among many gold and platinum album commemorations for Canadian bands that adorned the walls. (It's so great that Trooper has endured for more than forty years. I loved Rick Mercer's ample use of "Raise a Little Hell" and "Here for a Good Time" to celebrate our Canadian troops on *This Hour Has 22 Minutes* and *Rick Mercer Report*.)

My new company got a stroke of luck when my University of Waterloo

chum Susan Rosenberg announced that she was going to spend a year travelling the world. I suggested that she should start by seeing Canada first, and
asked her to drive my Mustang to Vancouver. When she arrived, she decided
to stay, doubling the head count of Denise Donlon Publicity overnight.

Pretty soon Susan and I had a roster of artists and an array of nightclub
clients and one-off jobs arranging publicity shoots and writing bios for
bands. At $50 a pop, a bio was a bargain for those bands. There's a limit
to believable superlatives in bar-band land; the office thesaurus was well
used/thumbed/utilized.

The job with the clubs was to keep their events well publicized by writing and placing print and radio spots. Our office was an envelope-stuffing
assembly line. Most clubs ran live bands five nights a week, along with
special events like karaoke nights, air-guitar competitions, wet T-shirt contests, the ubiquitous Battles of the Bands, and—all the rage for a while—
lip-synching contests.

Sometimes we'd visit up to five club clients in a night, my Mustang,
windshield wipers beating, jammed with helium-filled balloons. I blame
my fear of balloons on that gig. They freakishly pop for no reason. I can't
bear the sound or the smell of them. My son, Duncan, may have been the
only kid growing up in Toronto without balloons at his birthday parties.

The music scene in Vancouver couldn't have been hotter, both with
domestic acts and international touring. I saw everyone from Split Enz to
ZZ Top, Supertramp, the Eagles, and David Bowie. I was amassing a huge
collection of backstage passes, which came very much in handy for one of
our first commissions: working on the Cariboo Hotel.

THE CARIBOO WAS LOOKING for a club redesign, and DDP got the job—
which was astounding, given I knew as much about designing nightclubs
as I did about being a publicist.

John Malton was the man in charge. He must have been a keen sports-
man, because I remember spying a baseball bat behind his desk. Funny how
many music industry offices I would see over the years containing sports
equipment; hockey sticks, cricket bats, golf clubs, putters, and pool cues...

John wanted to recast the club as Coquitlam's premiere live performance space. We decided its novel new name would be Backstage, and we

sketched a new layout that would include a bigger stage and—wait for it—a rock and roll motif.

The plan was to relocate the stage so it was closer to the loading dock and raise it as high as possible without singeing vocalists' hair with the heat from the lights. We also reconfigured the room to allow better sightlines and service flow. Susan and I showed up with drawings and swatches and carpet samples. The carpet samples were sturdy dark weaves flecked with lots of colours to hide the dirt. I laid them out on John's desk. He promptly leaned over, ground out his cigarette on a sample, and then poured beer over it.

"How does it hold up?" he asked.

I was flabbergasted. That sample had a $25 deposit on it! An excellent test, though.

We hung a few dozen "gold records" around the bar (Susan and I made them with spray paint and Letraset) and completed the theme by collaging collections of used backstage passes under glass table rounds. Ahead of our time? Could be Backstage was to the Hard Rock Cafe what Flavor Flav's timepiece was to Apple Watches.

The Backstage's grand opening night was wall-to-wall with the musical elite, and if the number of stolen artifacts and gummy effluvia on the carpet was any indication, the party was a hit. (Happily, I wasn't there to clean it up.) The next morning, I was on a plane to the wilds of Winnipeg and beyond, memorizing the names of the musicians in a band already legendary on the West Coast: Doug and the Slugs.

MY ARRIVAL IN MANITOBA was a Winnipeg cliché: "Portage and Main, fifty below," as Randy Bachman wrote in "Prairie Town." Well, perhaps not quite fifty below, but I remember feeling pretty sorry for myself, hungover and head-down in a stinging hailstorm, fighting the wind on foot while making my way to a record store. I was armed with flapping posters and a satchel full of promo copies of Doug and the Slugs' second album, *Wrap It!* Every record store was a cold call, their addresses sourced from the local Yellow Pages. I would just show up and say, "Could you play this (free!) record in your store?" and "Do you mind if I tape this poster to your window?" We didn't offer payment for placement or free tickets to the show, just made a personal visit to ask for a favour. Typically, bands would rely on the record label to do this kind of advance work, but Sam's philosophy was: "Do it all. If the label happens to do it too, even better."

Winnipeg was only my first stop on the Slugs' Canadian tour. I'd hit stores a week before the show to litter the town with Slug paraphernalia—green plastic slugs, T-shirt slugs, brooch slugs, slug cartoons—hoping to incite *Slugmania!* Advancing Doug and the Slugs gigs took me to big towns and small, from Calgary to Saskatoon, from Portage la Prairie to Dawson City, where of course I touched my lips to the toe in the Sour Toe cocktail at Diamond Tooth Gertie's. The reception to the Slugs in Canada was always congenial. Record stores and radio stations were happy to see someone representing the band, and I started to generate a considerable Rolodex of affable music industry folks.

Advancing their U.S. tour was a different experience altogether. I remember arriving in New York City in my Rent-a-Wreck car after visiting Boston, Poughkeepsie (Pakipsi? Powkeepci? It took ages to find it on the map), and various other small American towns on the eastern seaboard. The Rent-a-Wreck was the cheapest mode of transport I could find, but I'd neglected to check that the locks on the vehicle worked before I drove it off the lot and so spent a restless night in a fleabag hotel in New York, wondering if I'd wake up to find the car trashed and the merchandise gone. Not that any pawn shop might see a goldmine in Doug and the Slugs cut-outs. Sam promised I could upgrade to Budget in the future.

The New York shows were key to a U.S. distribution deal. Sam was trying to convince RCA to release *Wrap It!* It was a strong record, produced by Jim Vallance, who was Bryan Adams' songwriting partner and husband to Rachel Paiement, who I'd met when she was in Waterloo with CANO. The U.S. deal hinged on the Slugs' gigs in April at the famous Bottom Line in New York City. They were to play one night with Ronnie Spector and Charlie Midnight, and then headline on the following night. Regrettably, the Slugs' headline show was cancelled due to a freak weather event. The city was buried in snow, with record winds and below-freezing temperatures. Schools and airports shut down; the Yankee Stadium season opener ball game was cancelled; Broadway shows were shuttered.

It was fascinating to watch the New York media capitalize on a freak weather-ratings bonanza. The evening news had spanking new "SPRING BLIZZARD '82 PARALYZES NYC!" graphics, and intrepid reporters roamed the streets in search of calamity. Mostly they found staunch New Yorkers shrugging their shoulders and resigned to shovelling.

We hearty Canadians set off to enjoy the sudden night off, plowing through the white stuff in search of an open bar. Come to think of it, there were a few New York City adventures with Doug and the Slugs that would end with us staggering down Broadway, singing "New York, New York" at the top of our lungs. Somewhere there's a shot of me in my white leather jumpsuit on top of a pile of green garbage bags after clumsily exiting Sammy's Roumanian Restaurant. I may have had a beverage.

What a joint. Sammy's was frozen in time. The steaks were so mammoth they might well have been mastodon. They sagged over the ends of the plates, competing for space on the table with the gigantic block of ice encasing a bottle of frozen vodka. No wonder Sam loved the place.

John "Wally" Watson, Simon Kendall, Sam Feldman, and me in said jumpsuit.

Happily for the Slugs, the Bottom Line gig was rescheduled and they returned to sell out four shows in two days. RCA released *Wrap It!* stateside, and the first single, "Real Enough," helped propel the record into the Top Thirty in Canada—which was respectable, given that almost everything about the band was as far from Top Forty as you could get.

Because The Slugs were on their own Ritdong label, I got a crash course in how record companies operated. Other than learning on the job, there were few places to get the information besides a somewhat impenetrable tome called *This Business of Music: The Definitive Guide to the Business and Legal Issues of the Music Industry*. A bodice ripper for sure.

The lack of more populist sources meant I spent hours on the phone with people like Vicki Walters from PROCAN (now SOCAN, Society of Composers, Authors and Music Publishers of Canada), who would patiently explain to me the difference between mechanical, synchronization, and performance royalties.

Doug treated me much like his office drudge at first, but with the right application of forelock tugging on my part, we soon got along just fine—and what a gift. He taught me that it's okay to be irreverent, that it's no shame to admit ignorance, and when in doubt to take the risk. As an indie label, we'd never have the resources the majors had, so we had to be inventive.

As rock star lead singers go, Doug Bennett ran a tad against type. He was a riveting entertainer, though you might say his sweaty front-man persona was more circus barker than sex symbol. He would dare the audience to "Get close so you can smell me," prowling into the crowds, sitting on women's laps, tugging men's ties and stealing their hats. There were times when we thought he was dangerously close to taking a punch, but it was that sense of adventure, and the Slugs' buoyant musicianship, that made audiences throng to their shows. John Burton, Richard Baker, Steve Bosely, John (Wally) Watson, and Simon Kendall were always tight enough to make it feel loose.

Doug was an audacious character whose gifts as a showman, singer, writer, graphic designer, ad man, and video maker built a lasting career for the band. He was an all-hands-on-deck kind of guy, one who drew artful storyboards for the Slugs' videos and weird cartoons to use as promotional material to give radio DJs and entertainment writers. His experience as a writer for the *Georgia Straight* taught him how to attract attention, and his slug cartoons were legendary. One favourite was a slug wrapped up in toilet paper, leaving a trail across a map of Canada and the United States for the *Wrap It!* record. The cut line: "Slowly but surely they advance." I still have the T-shirt.

From the beginning, Doug's *Mad Men* approach had been key in building demand for the act. When they couldn't get clubs to book them, they'd produced their own events, like the Beach Blanket Bungle or the Ricky Ricardo Romp, wherein they enlisted themselves as their own warm-up act. When they couldn't get a label to sign them, they'd launched their own. When their first single, "Too Bad," went Top Ten in Canada, Sam Feldman decided to mortgage his house to fund their first full-length record.

Doug was incredibly creative but a stickler for precision, often pushing us and his label distributors—first RCA ("Slug Mates with Dog!" was the headline) and then A&M—in wild directions. He insisted on printing the *Popaganda* album in four different, neon colours, arguing that it would create eye-catching retail displays (which it did) and force the label to ship four times as many copies (which it didn't) so that fans could have a choice between colours and maybe buy them all. (Thirty years later, One Direction would offer four different covers, each featuring one of Louis, Liam, Harry, or Niall, for their 2015 release *Made in the A.M.* I'd hate to be the band member with the most returns...)

The videos were shot on a shoestring, with Doug in the director's chair encouraging the Slugs to showcase their inner burlesque. "Making It Work" is a Keystone Cops–like epic about curing impotence. Doug stars as an aging porn star ("Deep Slug") whose "pecto won't erecto." A vanload of Slugs dressed as doctors arrives with all the tools of the trade—egg beaters, feather dusters, hair dryers, and a plunger—in an effort to "make it work." The video for "Who Knows How (To Make Love Stay)" has the Slugs dressed as cowboys, cross-dressers, hillbillies, millionaires, policemen, and dating game contestants, with cameo impersonations of Groucho Marx, Zorro, Captain Kirk, and Mr. Roarke and Tattoo from *Fantasy Island*. Doug dressed me up as a futuristic space robot, but I got cut (sigh). Twenty frames from stardom...

His long-form twenty-seven-minute promotional video, "The Listening Party," was a sardonic "hand-biting" epic that allowed him to make fun of the record industry while showcasing his skill at video direction. He went on to direct videos with Headpins, Trooper, and Images In Vogue.

Director Doug Bennett "corning around" with Headpins' Darby Mills.

Doug Bennett died from cirrhosis of the liver in October 2004. He succumbed on tour while in Medicine Hat and was airlifted to the Calgary Foothills Hospital. A week later, he was gone. I was honoured to speak at his memorial at the Commodore Club, a sold-out show just like the old days. I hope we did his legacy justice.

AFTER TWO YEARS, VANCOUVER was starting to feel like home. I bought a modest house on a side street near the airport, even though home ownership was risky business at the time. The interest rates were at 18 percent, and I knew someone who'd lost her house because she couldn't keep up the payments and *still* owed a hundred grand on it. Sam offered to co-sign my mortgage, and we had lunch to celebrate. He was in a great mood; I was freaked out.

"Why so sad?" he asked.

"Because I've just made a huge commitment to Vancouver."

"I know," he said, grinning.

Incredible to have that kind of support in a business relationship.

Sam and I had a running joke about my independence. He claims I always made him say, "She works *with* me, not *for* me." I don't know why I was so insistent on that, but apparently I was.

The Slugs brought my old piano from Toronto in the back of their truck and I settled into my small three-bedroom wooden house. The spare room had a revolving door for waifs and strays looking for a place to crash (Old joke: What do you call a musician without a girlfriend? Homeless).

My best girlfriends were two vivacious young women, Diane Tanchek and Dee Lippingwell. Dee was a superb music photographer, capturing live performance shots of people like Rod Stewart, Bruce Springsteen, and Bryan Adams. Diane was an entrepreneur who ran a thriving printing business specializing in rock and roll T-shirts. She had an adorable bearded collie named Dallas who would sit in the passenger seat of her VW Beetle convertible, turning heads everywhere. We'd go on *Thelma and Louise* road trips to see bands with Dallas in the back seat and a six-pack of cold beer in the front. Diane had Coca-Cola labels printed with Velcro closures so we could wrap them around the beer cans. It was a free-flowing, hair-blowin' time, and we had some wild, albeit a tad boozy, adventures.

Diane was Tommy Stewart's girlfriend. Tommy was the drummer of Trooper, and one of his pals was Michael J. Fox. One night I went with them to a Trama show (Tommy's club band when Trooper was off the road). At the time Michael was in *Family Ties*, but was about to start shooting his breakout role as Marty McFly in *Back to the Future*. He grabbed a guitar and practiced his "Johnny B. Goode" performance with that signature strut across the stage. All of us woke up strewn around Diane's living room, not sure who had held whose hair back. It was such a trip to see *Back to the Future* when it came out, just as it's been a thrill to applaud Michael's success, especially his elegant public battle with Parkinson's. He left Vancouver to pursue his star, but he didn't forget his roots. Years later, I ran into Michael and his wife Tracy at a Rolling Stones Clinton Foundation fundraiser in New York City. The room was heaving with stars, but I wandered over and introduced myself. Michael lit up and reminisced with me about those days. What a perfect human being.

I was thriving in Vancouver—gaining respect with colleagues and friends, being invited to musicians' weddings and birthday parties like we all were part of a big rock and roll family.

Even though the agents competed with one another, there was great camaraderie in Sam's office. A & F Music was growing in leaps and bounds, and Sam's Christmas parties were legendary. He loved to roast people, and he and his (then) most senior agent, Shaw Salzberg, would spend days shooting videos, lampooning the business and executing outrageous impersonations of the staff. Sam's imitation of me was bang-on: there he/I was, gabbing on the phone in front of an overflowing ashtray, complete with a big teased wig and a full-length white jumpsuit.

I do appreciate that he could have made a different sartorial choice. That leather jumpsuit was *almost* as goofy as the Playboy outfit I once wore to one of his parties. Even though I was taking on more responsibility and being given every opportunity to grow, that night I was having a momentary huff about assuming subordinate duties just because I was female. Truth be told, my gender had nothing to do with it. I was way out of line. When Sam asked me to help out at the party, I tried to make a point by showing up dressed in a rented Playboy Bunny costume. I know, very *Bridget Jones*. As with Bridget, it sent exactly the wrong message. Sam asked me to serve drinks now that I was dressed for it, even though that had never been part of the plan.

Sam Feldman, "Bunny" Donlon, and Don Shafer

All of this is to say that I was definitely living a rock-and-roll lifestyle. I was smoking and drinking and perming my hair, teasing it as high as it would go (as k.d. lang would say, "The higher the hair, the closer to god"). I paraded around town in my blue vinyl Headpins tour jacket with the fake fur trim, my name on the sleeve and the words "Turn It Loud" emblazoned in big white script on the back.

It took *This Is Spinal Tap* to slap some sense into me and make me reconsider both the jacket and my lifestyle. The movie hit theatres in 1984, and even though it was a satire, I wasn't laughing with the same vigour, or at the same moments, as everyone else in the room. It was a little too close to home. When I walked out of the theatre that night, I turned my jacket inside out and started to seriously consider whether a hard rock world was really the one for me. But before I could make a truly informed decision, I had to gather all the information. And what better way to do that, than to go on tour with Whitesnake.

(6)

THE FEMINIST COMPROMISE

"Don't compromise yourself. You are all you've got."
— JANIS JOPLIN

I WAS STANDING AT the backstage load-in door in Munich. A tall, thin, leather-clad British bloke with long brown hair, a cigarette in one hand and a handful of laminates in the other, had just handed me a backstage pass. I looked down and read: "Whitesnake Slide It In Tour '84, Access All Areas." The photo was of a glossy red mouth, the full lips parted to caress the tip of a tumescent white... Was that a banana? Or perhaps a white snake?

"I'm not wearing that!" I huffed, affronted.

"Well, I guess you're not gettin' backstage then, are yuh, dahlin'?" replied Jimmy, Whitesnake's tour manager.

I did my level best to appear indignant, but he just smiled.

"Oh for gawd's sakes."

I ripped off the backing and slapped it on the inside of my jacket, trying to hide the image.

With a sweep of his arm, Jimmy ushered me in.

I was on the road with a Canadian rock band called Headpins, one of Sam's management acts and therefore one of DDP's most important clients. We were at the beginning of a five-week arena tour with dates in Germany, Sweden, Denmark, and England supporting one of the U.K.'s reigning rock bands, Whitesnake. Headpins would be playing to thousands every night, and were determined to make every minute of this full-blown, pyro-powered tour count.

Slide It In was Whitesnake's fourth record. They were massive across the pond. Their first three records had gone Top Ten in the U.K., and this was their last European jaunt before heading to the United States, where they were determined to break into America. Three years later they did, with "Here I Go Again," a *Billboard* Number One hit and a song already well entrenched in the set list on the tour we were on.

Whitesnake's front line was a wall of flowing hair, black leather, silver studs, and low-slung axes. C'mon, it was magnificent! Guitarist John Sykes and bassist Neil Murray prowled the stage like plundering marauders, John delivering his wheedlin' wheedlin' guitar solos head-back and spread-eagled, topping them off with Townshend-like round-arm flourishes. Jon Lord was a keyboard tour de force, rocking his Hammond B3, and drummer Cozy Powell was a flurry of sticks, thundering in the background. But lead vocalist David Coverdale was the main attraction: Rock God personified.

Gymnastic microphone manoeuvres were a thing at the time. Robert Plant would whip his mic high into the air then deftly catch it to sing, but David used the whole rig like a varsity cheerleader uses batons—bouncing the stand off his knees and thrusting the mic off his crotch. It was phallic as hell. Watching those Whitesnake videos thirty years later takes me right back to the side-stage, to the smell of the sweat and the roar of the crowd. It was exciting, explosive, and LOUD. How loud was it? I remember going to see a Rush show at the Pacific Coliseum in Vancouver shortly after I got back to Canada and wondering what was wrong with the volume.

The tour was a good match for both bands. Sometimes called the "Queen of Canadian Screamers," Darby Mills was Headpins' full-throated female lead singer, athletic in her leg warmers and spandex tights. She and Brian "Too Loud" MacLeod had both been figure skaters in their youth, so leaping off the drum kit and twirling in mid-air came naturally.

You might expect that there was a marked difference between the two bands, given that one had a female lead singer, but aside from stature, there wasn't. On this tour, it was all a variation on a similar theme. Big hair, tight pants, and gobs of swagger, all projecting an air of excess and profligacy.

Headpins was initially formed as a side project for Brian and Ab Bryant, who were on a performance sojourn from their main band, Chilliwack with Bill Henderson. They'd been stalled from performing while they sorted out some legal issues with their label, so Brian and Ab enlisted Darby as lead singer, Bernie Aubin on drums, and Darcy McDonald on keyboards. It was supposed to be a temporary thing, but Headpins took off. The first record, *Turn It Loud*, was a phenomenal debut which sold more than 250,000 copies in Canada, making the band a multi-platinum act. The Whitesnake tour we were on was in support of Headpins' second record, *Line of Fire*. We were hoping that touring with one of the biggest bands in Europe would do what the U.S. dates hadn't yet done — help Headpins reach critical mass.

The U.S. tour dates had been a hot mess, through no fault of the band's. After some Canadian dates with KISS, we'd started down the east coast, the third act on a triple bill with Saga and Quiet Riot. Quiet Riot had a huge hit that year with "Cum On Feel the Noize," but not everyone was feeling vocalist Kevin DuBrow's. We played only two shows, and on the third day woke up to learn that the remaining dates were cancelled. Word was the drummer and Kevin had gotten into a dust-up backstage after the show, which left us and our crew stranded in Florida, while Sam, back in Vancouver, scrambled to arrange new dates.

While we waited we were racking up bills, paying crew wages while the band got by on a slim per diem, money that often reverted back to our tour manager in marathon poker games. One day was spent running around trying to find an emergency dentist when Ab knocked his front tooth out in the shower of our cheap motel. He'd been holding a handrail, but it dislocated from the wall and he smacked himself in the mouth with it. Too bad personal injury lawsuits weren't the rage then; we could have funded some more gigs.

Touring as a working band is all spotlights and gymnastics on stage at night, but during the day it's grungy and bleak—an endurance test of somnolence and flatulence on the bus. There's nothing that can break the illusion of stardom more definitively than the sight of a pasty musician in baggy sweats, folding his smalls behind the spin dry under fluorescent lights.

Time off wasn't doing anyone any good.

Sam did some fancy footwork and pulled together enough club dates for us to make it across the southern United States to hook up with Eddie Money for a few shows. On the way, Headpins sold out Cardi's in Houston, Texas, which was amazing, given the short notice. Cardi's was a signature club, and the band not only set a new house record for the largest crowd since opening night, but also got kudos from legendary promoter Bill Graham, who called Headpins one of the "most professional groups I had the pleasure of working with." It's true. The potential for greatness was there, and Headpins could always deliver a convincing show. But these one-off club dates weren't advancing the cause. Getting the opening slot on the Whitesnake tour in Europe, then, was a stroke of luck. And they treated us like gold.

No matter how good you are, being the opening act can be brutal. The crowd files in late, usually not giving a rat's ass who you are—they paid to see the headliner. Backstage, too, the dynamics between bands can be tricky. If the opening act *does* manage to capture the crowd and grab a great headline—which Headpins often did—they'll piss off the headliners and things can suddenly start to go very wrong. The spotlight fails, a microphone goes dead, or you'll greet the crowd with deafening feedback, none of which, oddly, had been a problem at sound check.

In North America in those days, headlines in print *meant* something. Magazines like *Spin* and *Tiger Beat* sold records. Most major dailies in the country had full-time music columnists. Being on the cover of the *Rolling Stone* was an honour so great, songs were written about it. It was also a time when aspiring music magazine critics—the ones often sent to cover the opening act—made great sport of ripping a band apart.

Inspired trash-talking was a way to make a name for yourself, and being a music critic was a good gig. There was free product (which could be unloaded for cash at the local used record store), free drinks, and maybe even free whatever other incentive was on offer that night. Happily, Headpins did not get ripped apart in the press. Their underdog status was working in their favour, and they'd often wake up to raves in the paper, like this one:

> "MILLS UPSTAGES HEADLINER [BILLY SQUIER] AGAIN."
> —Craig MacInnis, *Calgary Sun*, October 26, 1982

> "STREETHEART PINNED DOWN."
> —Graham Hicks, *Edmonton Sun*, January 2, 1984

> "[PAT] TRAVERS FELLED BY DARBY'S ENERGY"
> —Greg Quill, *Toronto Star*, December 9, 1982

Great fun, but a little awkward when you ran into the headliners in catering. Those hockey arenas could get pretty chilly.

It was trickier when it happened with bands that were friends: Rob Salem in the *Toronto Star* ended his review of a Loverboy show with this: "Opening for Loverboy was Headpins...Mills' high-powered delivery makes Loverboy's Mike Reno look like a wimp." Ouch. At least Loverboy didn't kick the band off the show, as ZZ Top did when Headpins took an encore that bassist Dusty Hill didn't appreciate. It's important to remember the headliner can cut the power at any time; but it should never curb your enthusiasm to blow them off the stage anyway.

Compared to what we'd experienced with headliners in North America, Whitesnake was a dream. The band and crew welcomed us with open arms. Even as press coverage built for Headpins and the crowds started chanting "Headpins, Headpins," we were never in danger of having the "fuck button" pressed on us. As David Coverdale told me later: "The punters paid their money. We'll give them the best show we've got, and that includes you."

Brian "Too Loud" MacLeod, David Coverdale, and Ab Bryant.

Whitesnake's crew, from the lighting designer to the guitar techs, were state-of-the-art road warriors. By the second day out (after we'd been given the once-over), Headpins were awarded full run of their production and were in effect treated as headliners in every way except billing. It was out of respect for Headpins' musicianship, and handy for me, because I continued to run into guys from that crew for years to come. That respect worked wonders when I needed access to artists as a music reporter.

EUROPE DIDN'T APPEAR TO have the same coke scene that North America was enjoying. At least there, I was never asked to venture into some strange U.S. city to score a gram to pay off the lighting guy so we could have a spotlight for Darby.

This tour had more of a smokes-and-booze vibe. It was then that the door to the world of wine opened up just a crack for me, assisted by the late great Jon Lord. He was the first oenophile I had ever met. When everyone else was raging about in the after-hours clubs downing Jägermeister and tequila, I would spy him in a corner with a large glass of red wine, deep in thought as if he were listening to his own personal symphony.

Jon was a social gentleman, though he seemed a little detached on the tour. I suspect that was because he had more of a sideman role in Whitesnake, very different from his long years in Deep Purple, of which he'd been a founding member. On this tour, Jon was free to indulge his own interests.

The European setting was certainly conducive to talking about wine. We motored past endless vineyards, the bundles of sticks stretching along the horizon, leafless and bare at the end of winter. The scenery held little fascination for the Whitesnake crew; they'd travelled these roads too often. Nor were they impressed by the caterer's culinary choices. "Pigs and sticks, pigs and sticks, every fockin' day pigs and sticks," they'd grumble. I thought the spread was opulent, until Jon suggested I try some of what he was having at an after-party. It was a soft, deeply veined Stilton with a drop of fine purple port. It was a gastronomical epiphany. I never thought of "Deep Purple" in quite the same way again.

Me and the late great Jon Lord.

Headpins worked hard, spending their off-time at magazine photo sessions and radio shows, working up a fan base. It didn't always pan out the way we wanted it to, however. When we were invited to perform "live" on Germany's top-rated music television show, *Formula One*, the band braved bizarre circumstances. TV shows were key to selling records in Europe, and because we needed them more than they needed us, we were at the shows' mercy when it came to artistic control.

I remember arriving at one station where we were greeted by a TV crew that spoke perfect English; but, funnily enough, when we balked at lip-syncing or at creative staging ideas — like, say, a decidedly un-heavy-metal neon flower-power backdrop behind a radically slanted stage (dangerous for Darby and Brian, who liked to leap off the drum kit), suddenly no one could speak a word of it. I described being on one such set, in the media release I wrote when I got back to Vancouver, as being "surrounded by eight slats of 'pop art' that could have been rendered by Picasso on acid." When I'd complained about the set, the no-nonsense floor director commanded, "You want you play? Then play. No talk." The band played.

There were a couple of hiccoughs on the tour, too. Whitesnake guitarist Mel Galley, who'd co-written some of the *Slide It In* songs with David, suffered an accident early in the tour that damaged his arm. It left the band short a guitarist, and Whitesnake had a conversation with Brian about filling in on guitar and harmonies. Brian declined the guitar work, but did sing back-up "Snakette" vocals offstage for the remainder of the tour. The tour was also suspended briefly when David fell ill in Ludwigshafen. Band and crew spent the time off either in Munich or Amsterdam. Darby and I temporarily renamed it the "Shop 'Til You Drop Tour," while others engaged in their own favourite pastimes, whatever or with whomever they may have been.

The tour eventually finished up in Stockholm, where both bands played one-upmanship on the other to the delight of 10,000 fans. Brian MacLeod played the riff from "Smoke on the Water" in homage to Coverdale and Lord. The Whitesnake crew got their jollies by littering Headpins' stage with smoke and bombs, detonating explosives mid-song or whenever they felt like it. It was like performing in an active minefield.

Headpins were fairly used to incendiaries. They had toured with flash-pots, smoke, and a "Line of Fire" special effect for their single of the same name. The Line of Fire looked impressive during the performance, though it was nothing more than a long steel pipe with holes drilled in it, hooked up to a propane tank situated just offstage. The crew turned on the tank and lit it from one end, and the flames ran along the stage. The height of the blaze was controlled by the handle on the propane tank.

At first, the pipe was positioned at the lip of the stage, in between the band and the audience. Given the size of some of the stages, though, Ab, Brian, and Darby were sometimes just a foot away from a hot wall of flame which proceeded to burn furiously for the length of the song. Considering how much hairspray and spandex there was onstage, I dreaded a Michael Jackson Pepsi moment—that, too, happened in 1984.

The line of fire was eventually relocated behind the drum kit, but not for safety reasons; there, it provided better access for the crew—and less risk that the song would end as a comedy number. After the band finished the song there would always be some lingering gas in the pipe, and our crew would have to beat the persisting flames out with towels. Search as we might, there were never any black towels; they were always white and looked like "surrender" flags waving behind the band as they moved on to the next song.

The reason for all the pyro on the last dates of the *Slide It In* tour was simple: the Whitesnake crew was leaving Europe immediately afterward. As you might imagine, crossing a border with explosives is never a good idea (this was true even before 9/11), so they were using it all up. And the stage wasn't the only place where pyro people got rid of excess firepower, I learned. I heard stories about "friends" of theirs who'd used up their "stash" in various ways, the most bizarre of which was a fabled booze-soaked soiree on which, apparently, time-delayed detonation fuses were flushed down a hotel toilet, everyone's breath held as they listened for far-off *booms* in the plumbing. I wondered if I might wake up to a foot of water in the lobby one day, but all was high and dry.

What was life like on the road with Whitesnake? Well, you know, what happens on the road stays on the road, and I don't want to get all *Hammer of the Gods* on anyone, but people got up to the sorts of things you'd expect of a testosterone-fuelled rock tour playing encore-driven arena shows to thousands of screaming fans.

Backstage is full of nooks and crannies where there are lots of places for people to explore each other's nooks and crannies, and there'd be the inevitable morning walks of shame through hotel lobbies as ladies tottered out, their tight, sparkly concert clothing a tad obvious in the light of day. I never got the feeling there was anything non-consensual, although more than once I've heard the line (from guys), "Just remember that what they want from you is not the same thing as what you want from them."

You hear stories about groupies being handed down the food chain, from rock star to guitar tech, from gaffer to driver, but I never saw it. Crew members were more likely to be seen with a briefcase than a bra collection on a big tour.

Even as the support act, we had our share of AWOLs and unguents, emergency B12 shots and deadly hangovers throughout the entourage. It was unusual to have two women on the road, but if the presence of either me or Darby tempered the Whitesnake tour in any way, I certainly didn't notice it. Darby and I were working girls, in the actual sense of the word. We didn't expect to be treated differently, and we weren't. As for any compromise I made, wearing that backstage pass was about it.

For all her energy on stage, Darby was conservative on the road. She liked to get to bed early to protect her throat, and she was a picky eater, so late-night drunken dinner parties weren't her thing. In headliner land, David's girlfriend—later, wife—Tawny Kitaen, who would famously cartwheel and caress Coverdale, along with two sports cars, in the video for "Here I Go Again," joined the tour for a while and everything seemed pretty settled over there.

That video is certainly an indication that we were enjoying more innocent times. (In 1984, Madonna's "Like a Virgin" was considered scandalous.) "Here I Go Again" came out three years after our *Slide It In* tour and was in hot and heavy rotation. Compared to the hyper-sexualized booty calls we would see in years to come, the video was tame. Sexy, but not sexist. Yes, Tawny was doing the splits on that Jaguar in a diaphanous nightgown, but she was fully clothed in a gymnastic bodysuit. And she is the one—smiling, in full control—dragging *David* into the backseat. Even so, I remember the lineup outside the MuchMusic editing bay when the video was slow-mo'd to that frame where the guys swore that one of her nipples slipped out.

It's often said that guys get into rock and roll to get laid. I doubt that's universally true for the gals. Not that I would have said no—there was one guy in the Whitesnake entourage that I found pretty fascinating—it's just that no one ever asked. Imagine. Being on the *Slide It In* tour and not getting laid. That's just sad.

Years later, when I was head of MuchMusic, David Coverdale was doing press with Jimmy Page for their *Coverdale/Page* album. Jana Lynne White, with whom I'd co-hosted *The NewMusic*, took a message from me to David when she went to interview them. While the tape rolled, she said: "By the way, Dentist says hello." (Coverdale always called me "Dentist," for some reason. Maybe it was that white leather jumpsuit.)

David said, "Oh, what's she up to, then?"

Jana explained that I was now running MuchMusic.

He said, "She's the boss?!" and looked at Page. "Why didn't I sleep with her when I had the chance?"

Funny! But no need. We were already playing their video in heavy rotation. And besides, David, you know you can only ever sleep your way to the middle.

Jon Lord left Whitesnake in mid-April, about the same time we did. He reunited with Deep Purple until just after the turn of the century, when he began to indulge his orchestral talents in what was essentially another musical lifetime. I was delighted to meet his daughter Sara twenty years later at Sony. She was a smart, feisty manager repping a rock band from the U.K. called Toploader. It was a treat to reminisce about her dad and I liked her immediately, which meant, of course, that Toploader became a bigger priority for us in Canada. That's how it rolls.

WHEN HEADPINS RETURNED TO Canada after the Whitesnake tour, it was not smooth sailing. Our distributor in the U.S., ATCO Records, was in flux. They would eventually transition to a new venture that would be called ATCO-East West, but at that moment we were being ignored. We ventured into the western United States with promises of full label support, but as we got farther south, it was obvious something wasn't right. We saw less product in the stores and fewer reps at shows; more calls went unreturned. Too bad we weren't living in *This Is Spinal Tap*; there should have been an Artie Fufkin to kick.

The gigs weren't perfect, either; especially in L.A., where we were mismatched with a band called the Romantics. Headpins were pelted with beer cans and, for some reason, lit matches, which the audience threw at Darby, trying to set her hair on fire. Not everyone thought the gig was a total loss — there were Playboy Bunnies in the audience that night, and one member of the entourage showed up on the bus with his face covered in a nasty red rash. Impetigo, I think it was.

Sam wisely brought us home, thinking we could better use the time to capitalize on our Canadian success; but that was not to be. To add insult to injury, our Canadian label, Solid Gold Records, went bust. This was brutal for Headpins since, between *Turn It Loud* and *Line of Fire*, they'd sold almost 400,000 records in Canada. But there was no sense in continuing to promote a release with both labels dead.

My next press release for the band, in February of 1985, read:

QUESTION: Can a rock and roll band survive:
- The interruption of a recording session halfway through an album
- An insolvent record company
- A subsequent cash-flow problem
- The sale of their contract to a bank that then sells it to another label??

ANSWER: Absolutely, irrefutably, YES!

I was nothing if not enthusiastic.

While all this was happening with the band, the entire music business was going through some big swings of its own. It was recovering from a four-year slump in the North American markets, even as allegations of payola (the illegal practice of bribing radio stations to play your record) lingered about like a bad smell. But the big change was MTV. By 1984, music videos had become an undeniable part of an artist's success, and Top Forty radio was becoming more pop and R&B-influenced, favouring tracks like Ray Parker Jr.'s "Ghostbusters," Prince's "When Doves Cry," and Tina Turner's "What's Love Got to Do With It." Other than Van Halen's "Jump," hard rock was not on a roll, unless it was served up via big power ballads. Videos had not been Headpins' forte, and the stall on the second record had thrown a wrench into the works.

Still, after five months of negotiations and legal complications, Sam announced Headpins had signed a new deal with MCA, and the band went back into the studio to work on their third album.

By the time the third record, *Head Over Heels*, came out, I had left Vancouver to join MuchMusic. The record went platinum in Canada, but the band never managed to get their arena tour groove back.

Brian MacLeod died in 1992 from a sarcoma that metastasized into bone cancer. He was determined to fight the disease and still make music, even appearing on stage in big golden wigs to cover his dear bald head, but he couldn't win the battle. He left behind a solid songwriting legacy, not only with Chilliwack and Headpins, but in songs co-written with Mike Reno, Bryan Adams, Jermaine Jackson, and Chicago, among others. It's tough to watch videos and interviews with him now. He was so present, and it all comes right back. All those hours on the tour bus — "We're loggin' now!" — breathless from laughing so hard. I miss him.

Thirty years later, Headpins continue to tour, with Darby, Ab, and Bernie Aubin from the original lineup. Whitesnake has just released a special-edition record and a video of a live *Slide It In* show. Sadly, three of them are now gone: Jon Lord, Cozy Powell, and Mel Galley. David Coverdale is still at the helm, though, and very much engaged. When I was announced as president of Sony, he sent me a congratulatory note signed, "Your Obedient Serpent, David."

It was nice to be remembered.

(7)

FINDING MY BIG FEET:

MUCHMUSIC BEGINNINGS

"All the world's a stage and I demand better lighting."
— DAVID LEE ROTH

I WAS ASKED TO join MuchMusic in 1985 by John Martin and Nancy Oliver. John was director of music programming and Nancy was director of music operations (a title she thought made her sound like a singing surgeon). The channel was almost one year old at the time, and John and Nancy were in Vancouver to shoot a Doug and the Slugs special at the York Theatre.

Since the launch of MuchMusic on August 31, 1984, I'd become friendly with Much management. We had mutual interests. I was trying to get my bands on their air and Much was trying to live up to its slogan, "The Nation's Music Station." Because they broadcast daily from their street-front, storefront headquarters on Queen Street East, the outside ambience, the weather, and the characters on the street reflected life in downtown Toronto. In an effort to better represent the entire country, Much sent cameras (okay, usually camera) far and wide to capture regional music news, at first piggy-backing with Mike Campbell, the "cable guy" charged with visiting the distribution companies across the country.

John's job offer was well timed. My promotions company, DDP, was a going concern—i.e., mostly managing to meet its employee payroll of two—but the rock and roll lifestyle was taking its toll. I felt trashed by the travel and the late nights, and was likely in need of a liver transplant.

I was also lonely. Romantically. At twenty-nine, I had a high-spirited social life, but as far as actual boyfriends went, there were no prospects on the horizon. Vancouver was a small town in many ways, and dating within the West Coast music circle could be a little tricky. This was the early eighties after all, and pillow talk about hair products or which brand of control-top pantyhose created a more seamless line under spandex stage pants was just weird.

Much's strategy to gather stories from the road was paying off. The focus on regional reflection helped contribute to the distinctiveness of the channel, and its overall popularity and importance to the Canadian music scene was growing fast. Music videos were in their infancy, but they were already radically changing the way popular music was marketed, promoted, and celebrated.

From the moment MuchMusic was born on August 31, 1984, when J. D. Roberts and Christopher Ward crashed through the cheesy green paper screen bearing fireworks and swirling "M"s and lightning-bolt SCTV-style special effects, music in Canada would never be the same.

The channel was unique in the world. There was no pretense of slickly produced television artifice, none of the "we'll fix it in post!" safety-net mentality of conventional television. Much was live to air, and as a result its mistakes were, too. The audience quickly got the sense that anything could happen and probably would.

Even though it was a newborn, Much was able to launch almost fully formed because it had years of proprietary content to draw on from Citytv video shows like *Toronto Rocks* and *City Limits*—the all-night video and comedy show hosted by Christopher Ward—as well as Much's hip older sister, *The NewMusic*.

The NewMusic provided Much with a five-year-old library of videos, interviews, and music footage courtesy of its original hosts, Jeanne Beker and J. D. Roberts. It had begun as a weekly music news and views show, syndicated across Canada and then in various countries around the world. John Martin had pitched the show to Citytv after being turned down at CBC and Global. Citytv was a natural home.

The original ChumCity MuchMusic gang.

Launched on September 27, 1972, by co-founders Phyllis Switzer, Moses Znaimer, Jerry Grafstein, and Ed Cowan, and bought by CHUM in 1977, Citytv was "News, Movies, Music." The news was local, the movies became famously "Baby Blue," and the music featured concerts, simulcast with CHUM-FM, that were thrillingly live. One of many firsts at Citytv included Canada's first Live-EYE, a microwave news-gathering vehicle that was built in-house and, once retired, mounted on the side of the Citytv building, breaking through the wall, bricks a-flyin'. CHUM Television became an aggressive producer of original programming, with Moses and his believers creating shows and then entire specialty television channels focused on niche programming — FashionTelevision, SexTV, BookTV, Bravo! — of which MuchMusic was the first.

In *The NewMusic*, John Martin had envisioned, and realized, a television version of *Rolling Stone* magazine. Revolutionary for its time, the show dealt *entirely* with music and pop culture, and it quickly gained a strong international reputation for being smart, artist-friendly, and adventurous. Acts were eager for exposure, and hosts were invited everywhere the artists were — on stage, on tour, backstage, and even into bathrooms, where Jeanne famously interviewed British musician Andy Summers of the Police while he was enjoying a bath—under the cover of an increasingly indiscreet layer of bubbles.

John Martin was the ringmaster, working alongside the original team of Nancy Oliver, Anne Howard, Jamie Mandelkau, and Cesare Teodoro. He was an inventive rogue journalist with a penchant for risk-taking and a passion for music, laughter, cigarettes, and beer. Originally from Manchester, England, he brought a wealth of television experience to the show, his most recent gig working as a CBC producer on a TV variety show called *90 Minutes Live* (or, as Peter Gzowski would wryly refer to it, "*90 Minutes to Live*"), on which John booked "strange" musicians like Flo & Eddie or Tom Waits. When the show was cancelled, John found work driving cabs in Toronto until Nancy Oliver managed an introduction into Citytv.

Nancy and John first met when John and his friend John Kastner came bounding down the halls dressed as a rabbit and a pirate respectively, having raided the CBC props department in an effort to meet women. Nancy was not fazed. Her experience with creative personalities had been honed working on *The Hart and Lorne Terrific Hour* with Lorne Michaels—who went on to become the creator and executive producer of *Saturday Night Live*—and writer and director Ron Meraska. When *Hart and Lorne* was cancelled, Moses nabbed Ron for Citytv, and after a short stint with Lorne in L.A., Nancy arrived at Citytv as well. There, she tells me, she found "tons and tons of work, no money, lousy facilities…and [it was] completely hilarious. You really couldn't make it up. I learned a lot as well, and as everyone knows Moses is a clever fellow, so after the bureaucracy of the CBC it was nice to just have to deal with one smart guy with the power to make a decision."

Moses gave *The NewMusic* the green light at an opportune time for John, who was happy to be back in television. His sojourn as a cabbie may have encouraged his hairline to recede, but it in no way dampened his appetite for mischief, and he and Nancy came to be highly complementary production partners. Nancy was organized and reliable, able to pick up the pieces John might have dropped while he was shooting or editing. She was also particularly skilled at creative arbitration, a talent that would come in handy working with and between John and Moses.

Drinks and smokes with Nancy Oliver and John Martin.

The night of the Slugs show when John, Nancy, and I met in Vancouver, I was bummed out because I'd just lost on an offer I'd made on a house. I'd bid $80,000 on a mouldy, moss-covered cottage high on a hill overlooking Deep Cove. I had been musing on the idea of taking a radical break from rock culture, of maybe baking muffins and running a tea shop by the sea. As fate would have it, I was $2,000 short of the curve-in-the-road hippie dream property that would have been worth bajillions now. Tra la. That's how the ball bounces.

John asked me why I was so down in the mouth and when I told him, he grinned and said, "Well, I'm here at the right time then!" and promptly offered me an on-air job at MuchMusic. They were looking for a new host for *RockFlash*, the live hourly update on all the music news of the day. The current host, Jeanne Beker, was off to start a new show called *Fashion Television*.

It was a shake-yer-head kind of proposition. The last thing I'd ever imagined was seeing myself on television. TV personalities were perfectly groomed, self-possessed, supernatural beings with glossy hair, gleaming teeth, and big heads on top of tiny bodies. By contrast, I was an inch over six feet tall, with a slight lisp, a gap in my front teeth, and shaky self-confidence. I could hear that line from Don Henley's "Dirty Laundry" very clearly in my head—"We've got the bubble-headed bleach-blonde who comes on at five"—and I did not relate.

When I protested that I was an unlikely choice, John argued that they weren't looking for models to read prompters; they wanted industry insiders who could bring credibility and connections to the show. He assured me I could be taught the mechanics of television.

"C'mon, honey," said John with his characteristic cackle. "It'll be a giggle!"

"Look at me!" he continued. "If you want to see unconventional, where else would a guy like me have a whole station to run?" He had a point. But he also had to get me past Moses.

I agreed to take a meeting with Moses Znaimer, the visionary who was busy re-imagining television. A week later, John, Nancy, and I met with Moses at a Toronto health food restaurant called the Groaning Board. I think I had a green milkshake.

John pitched Moses an amplified version of my rock and roll pedigree, while Nancy encouraged and embellished. Moses showed vague interest, fastidiously rearranging his food with his fork. John had warned me that Moses could be "prickly" and advised me to just "be yourself" (whatever that was). At length, Moses looked carefully at me, and in a soft, slow, deliberate voice, asked me what I thought about music videos, this new marriage of television and music. I blurted out some half-formed postulation that music was a "hot" medium best enjoyed live, and TV a "cold" medium that could never truly capture the excitement and community of a live show.

Moses stared at me with half-lidded eyes, inscrutable.

Rushing to fill the silence, I babbled on about "art needing to be live to function," which was contextually incorrect (Marshall McLuhan's actual quote was "Art has a live, ongoing function") and hence doubly stupid.

"On the other hand," I ventured, "these music videos seem to be catching on."

After I'd not only been critical of television but misquoted Marshall McLuhan to Moses Znaimer, it was no wonder his next question to me was, "What will you do when it doesn't work out in three months?" (Not *if* it doesn't work out; *when*.)

I remember blurting back: "Well, I'm not *exactly* unemployable."

Provocation is a particular tactic of Moses'. He's adept at posing the precise question that might rattle your chain so he can find out what you're made of, if you're worthy of his time. I, on the other hand, was learning that my inner Donlon had a bit of a hair trigger, which was not necessarily a bad thing for a young lady in a man's business. Meeting provocation with pluck can be a useful combat tactic on the gender battlefield, so long as you're prepared to go the distance. My adventures with Moses were about to begin.

"You've got three months," he said. "If you last that long, I suppose you can stay."

Moses left the table. John and Nancy waited until he was out of earshot, then clapped me on the back. "When can you start? Let's have a beer!"

I flew back to Vancouver and broke the news to Sam. Sam looked at me like I'd lost my mind. Why would I venture into this television unknown instead of sticking with his established and expanding company? He offered to restructure our business relationship, but as hard as it was to disappoint him, I felt I needed to go. There was another reason. After thirty years of marriage, my parents had decided to divorce. I knew that it would be helpful if I was physically closer to them while they worked out their split. Sam graciously accepted the decision and wished me luck, but not before suggesting that, in my new position in Toronto, I might be helpful to his bands.

Sam's star didn't need *me* in order to keep rising, of course. He was a great mentor, and I learned the value of fairness and loyalty in business. He remains a treasured friend.

I wound down DDP, Susan took on the company clients she was interested in keeping, and I was duly roasted at an epic going-away dinner. Shortly thereafter, I pointed my Nissan 300ZX east on the Trans-Canada Highway with my parting gift (a radar detector) newly installed, and a contract in hand as on-air assignment editor of MuchMusic News with a starting salary of thirty-six grand a year (an impressive negotiation, I thought, for an inexperienced anchor). I arrived in Toronto with only one speeding ticket.

IN 1985, MUCHMUSIC'S HEADQUARTERS in Toronto was located at 99 Queen Street East, across from the Moss Park Armoury and in a neighbourhood brimming with pawn shops and shelters. After camping for a month in Richard Flohil's spare room in Cabbagetown, I found a rental space close to the station, and while my new neighbourhood was poor, Toronto's musical talent was rich.

Complementing the success of the early Riverboat days of Joni Mitchell, Neil Young, Gordon Lightfoot, Murray McLauchlan, and Bruce Cockburn,

Toronto was host to a vibrant rock scene that included Rush, Triumph, Toronto, Helix, Kim Mitchell, Gowan, and the marvellously musically and otherwise gender-bending Rough Trade. The Queen Street West scene was a new creative hub for a wide range of artists like Blue Rodeo, Martha and the Muffins, Jane Siberry, the Rheostatics, Mary Margaret O'Hara, and Liberty Silver, and a thriving reggae scene with bands like the Sattalites and Truth and Rights. Clubs like The Edge, the Horseshoe Tavern, and the El Mocambo were in full throttle, and promoters like "the Garys"— Gary Topp and Gary Cormier—brought in bands like the Police and the Talking Heads to fill them up. Up the street from the Horseshoe, amongst booze cans and art galleries, was the Cameron House, which allowed artists like Molly Johnson and Handsome Ned to homestead in the rooms upstairs in exchange for working in the kitchen or behind the bar. It was a supportive scene where art, music, and politics mixed. When I arrived in 1985, the Group of the Year at the Junos was the Parachute Club, a joyful social collective experimenting with a new, groove-based world music mix and whose lead singer, Lorraine Segato, became a great pal. Lorraine Segato has described the Queen Street West scene to me as such:

> The first true "art bar" came into being in 1981 when Herb Tookey, a therapist at the Queen Street Mental Health Centre, bought the Cameron Public House with two partners and reopened it as an art bar and artist rooming house because, "most of my psychiatric clients were artists." By day, elderly war veterans reminisced over draft beer...but at night it transformed into a smoky, sexy bacchanal, offering a hybrid stew of music, theatre, performance art, video, paintings, and an anything-goes sex, drug, and alcohol scene.

The music scene in Toronto was more politically charged than what I'd experienced in Vancouver. It was a time of artful exploration, politics, feminism, and musical camaraderie, where those who created the music were partners in arms with those who would showcase it.

The impact of "The Nation's Music Station" on the Canadian cultural landscape is not to be underestimated. For audiences, it was like having one country-wide radio station that everyone tuned in to, but one that was full of wacky pictures and bizarre characters. You'd hear from viewers in remote areas who grew up with only one local radio station. They'd heard Bryan Adams' "Run to You" on the radio, but the sight of Boy George in "Karma Chameleon" or Prince in his video for "When Doves Cry" beaming into their living rooms 24/7 was a world apart.

As journalist and former *Billboard* magazine Canadian bureau chief Larry LeBlanc wrote to me recently, "MuchMusic was like a breath of fresh air. The channel was absolutely instrumental in building recognizable Canadian mega-stars. Radio broadcasters were still somewhat hostile to the Cancon regulations up to then, but suddenly there were Bryan Adams and Corey Hart being chased down streets... No question that Much can take a bow in the fact that broadcasters and the public began taking great pride in Canadian music on a national scale for probably the first time in history."

It felt like we were part of a creative musical alchemy. For Canadian musicians, MuchMusic was Camelot—not only because the show broadcast music videos, but because they funded them, too.

The CRTC—the Canadian Radio-television and Telecommunications Commission—requires, as a condition of licensing, station owners to invest in Canadian content. When CHUM pitched the CRTC for the MuchMusic licence, it pledged to go beyond just providing on-air exposure and promotion for Canadian acts. Identifying a dearth of supply of Canadian music videos by Canadian acts, CHUM proposed to set aside 5 percent of gross revenues from the new channel to fund VideoFACT (Foundation to Assist Canadian Talent on Video, now known as MuchFACT).

It was a deft move. Videos were an expensive undertaking for Canadian artists, particularly if they were not signed to a major label. VideoFACT would both provide much-needed Canadian content to MuchMusic and, naturally, endear itself to those artists to whom it gave money. Bernie Finkelstein (artist manager and owner of True North Records) was the man in charge of adjudicating the fund for many years, and he did a masterful job.

In its first ten years, VideoFACT funded more than eight hundred music videos, including some early works by artists who would grow to become Canada's most admired: k.d. lang, Celine Dion, Sloan, Sarah McLachlan, Cowboy Junkies, Great Big Sea, Barenaked Ladies, and the Jeff Healey Band, to name a few. VideoFACT also helped to expand genre diversity, and we made a point to push as much of the fund as we could into underrepresented musical areas. When I joined its board, a Canadian R&B and hip-hop scene was starting to emerge; but unlike pop music, so-called "urban music" had little industry infrastructure to rely on. There was no hip-hop–formatted radio station in Canada then, and we were a long way from the likes of Drake, The Weeknd, Deborah Cox, or K'naan being players on the international scene. Among many aided by VideoFACT grants were Maestro Fresh Wes, Michie Mee, the Dream Warriors, k-os, Kardinal Offishall, and Rascalz.

By the time MuchMusic launched in Canada, MTV had been up and running for three years. But Much was no imitator. When CHUM won its licence for the new station, the producers at MuchMusic lost no time in establishing a reputation as the cockier, riskier channel, with a distinctly Canadian sense of humour.

MTV, by comparison, was slick. Their logo was an animation of the MTV flag planted on the moon, and their VJs were cast as stars, equal in wattage to the talent they interviewed.

Much was the opposite of slick. The logo was flat, the graphics were cheesy, and VJs seemed as much a part of the crew as they were stars. That was intentional. Moses and John wanted the audience to believe that the VJs were just like them. There were no scripts, no writers, no teleprompters, no stylists, no researchers, really no nuttin' except for some cameras wheeling around desks.

The studioless space (or "environment," as Moses commanded we call it) was one large room that housed everything: the lights, cameras, and action of master control, as well as the worker bees, the management staff, and the lunchroom. It also served as the makeup and, on occasion, the make-*out* room. It was a revolutionary way of making television and, like many of Moses' ideas, creativity was born from necessity. Until the station moved to its new location at 299 Queen Street West in May 1987, Much didn't have the square footage for a separate office space or a pristine, audio-controlled studio with a separate control room. So they laid it all out for everyone to see — and made a virtue of it.

Much wanted the viewers to see the microphone and camera cables, to hear the blather in the background, to watch people working at their desks or catch a glimpse of an artist hanging out in the background waiting to go on. It was an authentic, rock and roll representation that was unique in the world at the time.

Which is not to say it wasn't unnerving. Most musical guests' experience with television was more...church-like. They were used to the hermetically sealed, whispered, immaculate worlds of the BBC and the CBC.

At Much, lights fell off the grids, microphones went dead, cameras failed, and the signal sometimes went to black. People walked through shots and tripped over cables, and there was always a chance that you might appear more..."spontaneous" to the viewer than you may have liked (especially if you were caught in the background attending to personal hygiene). One of our most cherished moments that became a station ID, was Jim Carrey stopping cold in the middle of his live interview and yelling to the office at large, "Would somebody answer the PHONE!"

Many people think the first video ever played on MuchMusic was Rush's "The Enemy Within," but in fact that was the *second* video. The first video was "Snappy Songs," an early Scopitone video from 1923 featuring African-American singer Eubie Blake. It was a canny choice signifying inclusion, legacy, and cheek, and a marked contrast to MTV's choice of first video, which had been the Buggles' "Video Killed the Radio Star." John was aware that MTV was fighting a PR battle, accused of not supporting videos by black artists until Michael Jackson broke through the barriers, and he intended to make a very different statement.

Blue Rodeo was one of the first examples of just how powerful the new channel could be for homegrown Canadian artists. Their single "Try" had been out at radio stations for a few months, but was getting little traction. Dave Tollington (then head of promotions at Warner Music) bemoaned the situation to John Martin over a beer and re-introduced him to the video. John Martin *loved* the song and personally put the video into heavy rotation. That one move literally broke the band across the country. Blue Rodeo became an enduring success, and Jim Cuddy still hits that note to this day.

When it came to curating the music on the channel, well, Much played whatever it felt like, whatever was good. There were no consultants and there was certainly no payola, although some resourceful record rep might send in a video with a box of doughnuts or a T-shirt every now and then. In the early days there was barely a format. Much played hard rock videos next to world music next to New Wave. There were a few specialty shows like the *Pepsi Power Hour*, *Soul in the City*, and *City Limits*, but mostly it was what we called "videoflow," hosted by three VJs: Christopher Ward,

J. D. Roberts, and Michael Williams. Catherine McClenahan joined for a while as the first female VJ, but eventually a Citytv receptionist named Erica Ehm landed the permanent gig. The shooting day went full tilt for six hours live, seven days a week, and then expanded in later years to eight hours a day. When the broadcast day was over, the whole thing would repeat until the next twenty-four-hour cycle started.

Eventually, as the supply of music videos became plentiful and advertisers started to demand actual demographic analysis of the audience, the station did adopt more Top Forty–like playlists. But in the early days, anyone with a compelling music video was fair game for airplay. In fact, sometimes we played really awful ones (like "Fish Heads" by Barnes and Barnes) just for fun.

JOHN SUGGESTED THAT I spend my first days in the environment, just observing.

"Just find a place to perch," he said. "And then we'll go for lunch."

It was a good strategy, if in fact it was a strategy at all. There was no formal training period, and as for finding a spare chair, good luck with that. People had taken to writing their names on their chairs in magic marker or even duct-taping them to their desks, as it was likely that they would be exchanged for a more decrepit version the minute they got up. I found a black-and-white faux-fur cube just inside the doorway and perched as instructed, watching the cast and crew do their thing.

What I saw was bedlam. It mostly resembled what the channel looked like on air, but was somehow twice as cramped and three times as chaotic — noisier, messier, and more frantic than any viewer could have imagined. I was seeing what the viewers didn't — what happened while the videos played.

Once the VJ finished a "throw" (talking to the audience straight to camera) and the first video in a set began playing, the lights went down and the crew went up — literally. They climbed on desks, stepping on piles of paper and occasionally knocking over drinks and phones to reposition the lights, rearrange a set, or test a microphone. Then they'd hang around smoking or nip outside for a coffee, returning just in time to focus a camera lens before the "and in 3, 2, 1," count to capture the VJ delivering the next throw. There was usually about fifteen minutes before the host was called into service again—the length of time it took to play three videos, a station ID, and two minutes of commercials. No one seemed to mind the chaos, least of all management—in fact, they encouraged it.

As Moses dryly observed to Nancy one day, "You run a very creative establishment..."

Playing casual observer was a good way to begin, even if my first few days at the station were chock full of weirdness. But then, something unusual happened most days at Much.

On day one I was sitting three feet away from Jeanne Beker—the then-host of *RockFlash* whose chair I'd been brought in to fill—as she calmly delivered her throw and gracefully held her smile until the camera light went out. Her delivery was flawless, I thought. But the moment the video rolled, she stood up and yelled, tearing a strip off her producer for not noticing that "My bra strap was showing! For god's sake! I'm doing my job, why isn't *someone* paying attention to what it *looks* like?!"

Now, there would come a day when, as the host of *FashionTelevision*, Jeanne would cheerfully endorse the idea of underwear being outerwear; but not just then. What was more astonishing to me at the time was that she was venting to deaf ears. No one *was* paying attention; everyone had learned to tune everyone else out. I looked over at John, who shrugged, ran his hand through his thinning blonde hair, and lit another cigarette.

Jeanne sighed, rolled her eyes, and shook it off. She was no diva; she was simply seeking the support she needed to present her best work, and she did not disappoint. She went on not only to host *FashionTelevision* for twenty-seven years, but is now a multimedia entrepreneur, a member of the Order of Canada, and a dear friend who charitably donates her time and talents whenever she can.

Day two's adventure was courtesy of Brian Linehan. As-yet unbeknownst to me (having lived on the West Coast), Brian was the king of Citytv celebrity interviews. He had an encyclopaedic knowledge of film stars, and his ability to insert great heaping helpings of that knowledge into his interviews was legendary. His questions were sometimes longer than the answers, and he was always delighted when a Hollywood A-lister looked at him, wide-eyed with wonder, and said, "Brian, how on earth did you *know* that?" He'd smile like the Cheshire Cat. His friend Martin Short impersonated him brilliantly as Brock Linehan on SCTV.

On this, my second day in the environment, I was excited because a bona fide rock star *who I knew personally* was scheduled to arrive at Much to be interviewed. Cozy Powell (the legendary British drummer then with the Jeff Beck Group and Rainbow, and later with Black Sabbath and Emerson, Lake & Powell) had been the drummer on the Whitesnake tour. My great hope was that he'd walk into the environment and greet me with effusive hugs, and everyone would be impressed that the new chick really was connected.

Cozy did indeed bid me a fond hello, then joined me on the faux-fur cube to catch up and wait for his cue. I was pleased to see this did not go unnoticed by the crew; but my little ego trip was short-lived. While they were setting up Cozy's interview, a bellowing commotion was suddenly heard down the hall. Before I knew it, there was a furious Brian Linehan standing over me with an enormous, old-school iron typewriter in his hands. He dropped the thing on my lap and laid into a full-on freak out, something to the effect of, "Animals! How can you live in this pigsty? I've got Hollywood stars and I won't have them walking through this garbage and clutter and newspapers you're all a disgrace should be ashamed of yourselves clean it up!" Then he turned on his heel and stormed off down the hall.

He had stubbed his foot on a pile of old magazines, on top of which had teetered that vintage paperweight. It fell into the middle of the hallway and he'd tripped, headlong, down the corridor. I'm sure he'd meant to throw it on John's desk, but it was really heavy and he only made it as far as the door, where there was nowhere to drop it except on me.

I sat there, open-mouthed, with a twenty-pound typewriter in my lap, while Cozy leaned in and said, "It was quieter on the road."

And just because everything comes in threes, on day three, the building's alarm bells—all of them—started going off during a live broadcast. No one seemed at all perturbed. People finished their phone calls/lipstick applications/catnaps and casually got up. Someone put in a "gap" tape (usually Michael Jackson's "Thriller" because it was the longest video) and, trusting that the emergency would be over in under fourteen minutes, people grabbed their smokes/purses/papers and walked down to the first floor and out the door. John and Nancy sauntered to Emilio's, the bar down the street, to smoke and wait it out, where they were soon joined by assorted floor directors, VJs, and record company promotions people eager to get some one-on-one time with management.

It was a bomb threat and it wasn't the first one. According to police reporter (and voice of Citytv) Mark Dailey, who wandered over to introduce himself and tell me he knew my dad, there was truth to the rumour that threats to the station were racially incited. Turns out there were people in Toronto who were not in favour of the *kinds* of talent that Moses had begun to cast on air.

Toronto was, and remains, one of the most racially diverse cities in North America, and Moses correctly espoused that a channel should look like the audience it broadcast to. The mission was "to broaden the range of voices on Toronto television." Campaigning for diversity made personal sense for Moses — a Montreal Jew born in Tajikistan in 1942 (I think: he doesn't talk about his age) whose outsider, underdog disposition spurred him to challenge convention throughout his media life. Yet it was radical at the time. In the early eighties it seemed that whenever you turned on the news in North America, you were greeted with the same Central Casting scenario: One elder-statesman anchorman paired with one pretty female sidekick, usually blonde; both, invariably, Caucasian.

Citytv aimed to be different, and the station was cast with diversity in mind. One of the more remarkable reporters was Jojo Chintoh. Jojo was from Ghana and he was the first black reporter in Toronto (and I suspect, the country). Citytv's then-director of news programming Stephen Hurlbut recalled to me in an email how the newsroom would get postcards with pictures of gorillas on them telling them to "get that monkey off the air." "We used to get complaints about Jo's English," Stephen told me, "and one day, when I was still a cameraman, Colin Vaughan and I were working together. We were standing in the lobby and Moses came up to us. Jojo, who was only doing freelance piecework at the time, walked by. Moses worried aloud that he couldn't understand him. To which Colin replied, 'You may not be able to understand him, Moses, but there are five hundred thousand people in Toronto who do.'" Jojo was hired as a full-time reporter soon after that.

There was Anne Mroczkowski, whose Scrabble-winning last name was not permitted to be anglicized; Ben Chin, who was a city reporter; Laura DiBattista, an anchor; Dominic Sciullo, a videographer; and meteorologists Harold Hosein and David Onley. David, who battled polio early in his life (and who later became Lieutenant Governor of Ontario), was never asked to hide his crutches nor his scooter from the audience. Citytv became so renowned for hiring diversity that its on-air personalities were often poached by bigger stations, who would swoop in dangling more money and bigger reach.

On-air personalities at City were expected to be experts in their fields, not readers of someone else's copy. Peter Silverman was naturally suited to the investigative consumer advocacy of *Silverman Helps*, given his background as a captain with the British Airborne Forces Association. Airborne was an elite unit with a profound commitment to looking after its men, which explained why Peter always had his camera crew's back. The *Silverman Helps* investigations were not always appreciated by their subjects, and Peter made sure he took the first punch—literally. "The camera person was blind for 180 degrees, and it hurts to get the viewfinder jammed into your eye," he reflected later.

The Citytv sports crew included the wonderful ex-Leaf hockey star Jim McKenny, while Greenpeace warrior Bob Hunter (my hero) presented environmental stories; and our political provocateur was Colin Vaughan (whose son Adam succeeded him on air and then entered politics himself).

After the bomb dogs had completed their sweep and the officers declared everything okay, everyone wandered back inside. I was getting the idea that this was a place where high drama would be a daily occurrence.

I was also getting the idea that I'd made a big mistake. Those first few days at Much were so intense that my dread of being on-air grew. *What in heaven's name am I doing in this madhouse?* I thought. *I'm too old/tall/ugly/ inexperienced to be on TV. I'll be a laughingstock.* Though I should mention—at the risk of being mocked now—that my anxiety was leavened by a somewhat mystical occurrence. I had a vision. I know! Nothing similar had ever happened to me before and nor has it since, but I remember the moment with absolute clarity. At the end of the first week, in the middle of that chaotic landscape, I was struck by a tiny, transcendental flash that I would one day be totally fine, and in control. I don't recall any hubris or ambition, or even what it meant, exactly. It didn't hit me like a bolt of lightning; it was more like a slow-motion surge, and the feeling I got was *Steady. You can do this. You WILL do this.* And then it whooshed away like a receding wave and left me a little stunned.

As Leonard Cohen sang, "There is a crack in everything; that's how the light gets in."

Whatever it was, I was suddenly less afraid. I was ready to work.

WEEK TWO DAWNED AND it was time to assume my position. J. D. Roberts, the charismatic VJ and host of the *Power Hour*, introduced me to the nation. I sat at my station on the *RockFlash* set—which amounted to a desk in the corner in front of a big, square TV, with a decommissioned satellite dish suspended overhead. The dish was painted grey, with a lightening bolt emblazoned over a cartoon drawing of the word "RockFlash" chiselled into a rock. It was very *Flintstones*-esque. On the brick wall behind I'd hung a framed caricature of me drawn by Doug Bennett and signed by all the Slugs wishing "Much Much Much Happiness." The inevitable slug on my shoulder is thinking, "Gee, I never knew Ted Baxter had a sister." Doug's cartoon vision was uncannily true to what I'd chosen to wear for my very first rock report—a baggy yellow shirt and matronly button earrings. My hair was teased into a pseudo-mullet. J. D.'s mullet, on the other hand, was perfect.

Watching the spot now reveals a total deer-in-the-headlights moment. I'm slightly breathless, fiddling with a pencil, physically backing away in my chair from J. D., perched casually on the side of my desk. I'd chosen a story on the Slugs, of course—might as well talk about what I know—and I proceeded to mispronounce Edmonton as "Edmuton." It wouldn't have surprised me if Moses' three-month prediction turned into three-minutes. I was *awful*.

J. D. was a smooth, shining contrast. He could not have known then that one day he would say, "This is John Roberts, CBS News, Reporting from the White House," but his success was inevitable. J. D. had an enviable work ethic, making the most of the time between videos to study the music mags and prepare interview questions, not only organizing himself for the shift he was on, but packing material away like a squirrel for the next one. He worked on his own personal computer (the only one in the operation) and used his time at Much to learn everything he could about broadcasting: how to light an interview, white-balance a camera, and edit his own pieces. I watched him with admiration. His self-taught lessons of *how* it all worked built his storytelling craft and paved his way to interviewing heads of state.

Unlike other more unionized outlets, multitasking was encouraged at Much. It's no wonder the very profession of videographer — I believe Dominic Sciullo was the first — was born at CHUM Television. Videographers were expected to do it all: chase, shoot, edit, and host their own stories, ever on the lookout for a shiny reflective surface so they could shoot themselves delivering their intros to camera.

Once that first painful throw was done, it was full on. My job was to come up with music news six to eight times a day, a fresh item every hour. I wasn't allowed to repeat anything because we expected viewers to watch continuously — *all* eight hours of MuchMusic programming, day in and day out — and many of them did.

It bears mentioning that the sources for such news items were sparse. There were daily hard news feeds, but the information coming over the teletype wasn't exactly rife with the kind of gossipy celebrity coverage there is now. The magazines of the day — *Rolling Stone, Spin*, the *New Musical Express* — were great, but by the time they reached newsstands, the information was a month old or more and little use to me. By the end of the eighties we got a fax machine and then relied on a tip sheet called the "Daily Insider," which sent a dozen or so music-related items and celebrity birthday notices. J. D. would often claim them first. He'd stand at the machine as they rolled in, circling and initialling the items before they were distributed — essentially calling "Mine" — and we'd all steer clear. The only truly useful news-gathering tool for me was the phone. I worked with producer Bruce McNab; he was a master at "rip and read," gathering items from the daily newspapers. But his supply was finite, so the moment each *RockFlash* throw was over, I was calling an ever-widening list of contacts, trying to scare up new information on the hour, every hour.

The news-gathering task became easier as I became known, but the on-air bit didn't. It was difficult to be scrutinized by a pop-culture world obsessed with youth. At twenty-nine, I was ancient by audience standards. Many of the Much staff had either just graduated from college or been invited in off the street. There was a parade of part-timers and hangers-on who courted the spotlight, and Moses would suggest auditions for young people he'd met who had an "interesting look." Indeed, part of the magic of the place was that you could start at reception and end up running a channel. Marcia Martin, for one, started out answering phones when Citytv debuted in 1972 and ended up executive producer of *Fashion Television*, among other shows and channels; and David Kines, who started as an overnight editor on *The NewMusic*, later became vice-president of all the CHUM television music channels.

Like it or not, youth, or the appearance of youth, was an essential part of the music video culture. One minute I felt like the new kid in the candy store and the next like someone's clingy spinster aunt. A ridiculous way for a twenty-nine-year-old to think, I know, but that's how I felt. My on-air presentation certainly needed some work. I'd taken to wearing big, baggy shirts—sometimes with suspenders—and an array of lumpy sweatshirts. One blue sweatshirt, with Benny Goodman on the front, seems (looking cringingly back) to have been a favourite. I shouldn't have worn those outfits to walk the dog in, let alone on the air.

In an effort to upgrade my on-air look, Dennis "Deno" Saunders—one of the original, fun-loving directors at Much—took me in to makeup at Citytv. It was an act of kindness. He wanted to see what might be done about my "heavy-lidded eyes." The makeup artist peered at me over her wing-tipped rhinestone spectacles and soberly suggested plastic surgery. Denno thought that she might find something in her magic makeup bag instead. After that, Denno awarded me a new nickname; "Gila"—as in Gila monster—the heavy-lidded one.

My early *RockFlash* reviews were kinder than I deserved. A full-page *Toronto Star* article by Jonathan Gross that ran on April 12, 1986, bore the headline: "Those Shaky Starts." The article begins with a concession that "The Citytv/MuchMusic idea of easing someone onto the air is five minutes of instruction on how to do a shoulder roll out of a careening Pulse vehicle. It's strictly BYOB (Bring your own Band-aids)." And though he does say that "for the most part Donlon acquits herself as professionally as possible," he points out that "the veejays often use her segment as an excuse to try out some distinctly annoying comic repartee."

I wonder if he meant the time Christopher Ward literally wrapped my head in toilet paper while I was on the phone. It's on an "outtakes" tape, clearly mislabelled because it was *all* broadcast live on air across the nation.

The review continues by saying that the production "looks like an afterthought" and that "Donlon is barely edited and directed and will often make mistakes in the heat of the moment."

I was directed? I'm certain I was never edited.

Maybe he caught the day when Michael Williams and I tried to get Keith Scott (Bryan Adams' guitarist) on the phone from Vancouver—three times in three hours. We'd inserted a still photo of Keith on the screen but nobody could hear him. I kept leaning back behind the big square TV, trying to adjust some knob to no avail, while Michael asked, "Is he using a cell-u-lar phone?" The next hour we tried again—"Can you hear me? Can you hear me now?"—all the while earnestly pledging to the audience, "We'll get him, I promise." Three times we failed, convinced the world would end if we didn't deliver.

Mr. Gross then offered some hope: " . . . Donlon, in time, can't help but benefit from that building's magic osmosis and grow to a major attraction at MuchMusic."

He was right about the building being magic, and though my role was never to be a major on-air attraction at Much, I did get better as time went on. The fun moments started to actually *be* fun instead of mortifying. In one segment, Chris Ward and I are doing *RockFlash* news on the street, after which he reveals that the reason we're the same height is that he's standing on the 6-inch curb while I'm standing on the pavement—in brown stockings and sandals. We came to call this the "basic curb manoeuvre." I put stars on pedestals in this way for years, giving them those precious extra inches so we'd look the same height on camera (and perhaps trying to protect myself from further articles that described me, as one piece did, as an "angular giantess"). The cliché about short stars with big heads is true. To this day, if I'm asked to pose with any diminutive celebrity, I instinctively roll over on one ankle so our heads might end up on the same plane. I'm still being told to "stand up straight."

One of Chris Ward's pals was Mike Myers. From time to time Mike would pop by to practice his emerging character Wayne (later made famous on *Saturday Night Live*'s "Wayne's World"). One day Chris brought him over to the *RockFlash* desk while I was in the middle of delivering a breaking news story about Toronto hard rock band Kick Axe. Chris introduced Mike to me—and the audience—as his friend Wayne, from a band called Bludgeon.

"Wayne" was wearing a black T-shirt under a red-checked lumberjack shirt (a.k.a. Kelowna dinner jacket). It contrasted nicely with his red antler-festooned baseball hat, which held his wig on. Wayne sat beside me as I delivered the news that Kick Axe's guitar player had quit right in the middle of their Canadian tour (Stop the presses!), and then begged to me to ask Kick Axe if he could help them out as their new guitarist—"Only air guitar, eh," but he promised he'd *look* good. I mumbled something about being sure to ask. It was an opportunity for TV comedy magic, totally blown. Watching that tape now, you'd be forgiven for thinking I should never be allowed within twenty feet of a celebrity; but providence didn't seem to agree. One of my earliest live interviews came about quite by accident.

I picked up the phone one day and on the other end was a fellow from Stevie Wonder's entourage. Stevie was in town on his *In Square Circle* tour. The caller said, "Stevie has been watching all day. He wants to come in for an interview." I thought it was a hoax, not only because I knew Much's request for an interview through the label had been turned down, but also because the call came directly through to my line. Then there was that choice of words: "Stevie has been watching."

Really? But it turned out to be true.

"He can be there in an hour or so."

"Of course," I said, still thinking it was a fake call. "Come on down!"

Normally this would have been a job for Michael Williams, who was a soul music aficionado, and would have the expertise to easily interview a legend like Stevie Wonder with little notice. But frantic calls to Michael's house went unanswered, so John elected me to do the interview, if indeed Mr. Wonder showed.

I was petrified. On *RockFlash,* my on-air turns lasted ninety seconds at most. Now I had an hour to study the file before Stevie walked in. I took a deep breath and buckled down.

It was an amazing experience. Despite me jerkily trying to figure out what camera to look into, we settled into a friendly conversation. Stevie Wonder is a genuinely lovely man. I asked him about his process for making videos. He would have to put so much faith into a director's ability to come up with the right images to match his musical intentions, I surmised.

He paused, then leaned in and said, "Can you keep a secret?"

"Sure," I said, looking sideways at the camera. Me and a whole nation of viewers.

"Okay," says Stevie, "I didn't want to bring this up. I was trying to, like, keep this real private but you gotta keep it a secret. *(whispers)* You're, like, really messing my career up, but the truth is, I can *see.*"

It took a full beat before I realized he was joking. I really did think I was the only person he'd *ever* said that to.

Stevie gave me a real gift that day. We connected, and as a result I forgot to worry about myself on air. It didn't matter that I didn't know what camera to look into; what mattered was that I could be a vehicle for *him* to shine. Perhaps my role was to be the support act.

Another early interview experience live on Much was with a playful Iggy Pop. I'm aghast when I watch it now. At one point, Iggy decides to rise up out of his chair, going higher and higher until he makes a *KAPOW!* sound and drops hard back into his seat. "The *Challenger!*" he says triumphantly, laughing like a hyena. I laugh with him, too stunned to react appropriately to a tasteless joke about the crash of the space shuttle, which killed all seven crew members. Good thing the (anti)social media wasn't around then. We would have been thrashed.

In empathy to my younger self, it takes *cojones* to confront bad behaviour, and I still needed to grow a couple.

ATTITUDE, ADRENALINE, ANALYSIS:

THE NEWMUSIC

*"City life is a con, country life is a con, the army is a con, the navy's
a con, cable television is a con! Even rock and roll is a con!"*
— JOE STRUMMER

JOHN SAW SOMETHING IN me that I did not. He not only kept me on, he
insisted that I do more. When *The NewMusic*'s host and producer Daniel
Richler left for CBC's *The Journal*, I was promoted to producer of Citytv's
flagship music show.

The NewMusic ran on television for twenty-nine years and stood proudly
as one of the longest-running television shows in Canadian history. It
was rightfully mourned when, in 2008, it was cancelled by its new owners — CTVglobemedia, who had bought CHUM Limited's properties —
moments before its thirtieth birthday, without even a greatest-hits broadcast
special to bid adieu.

Such a seminal program deserved a better send-off. It seems fitting to
take a moment to briefly encapsulate its legacy now.

When the show launched in 1979, punk was in a full rage. *The NewMusic*
chronicled it all, from the Ramones to D.O.A. to Wayne County & the
Electric Chairs. Jello Biafra of Dead Kennedys explained that their music
was like "screaming with our whole body," and a fan concurred, happily
bragging, "Jello kicked me in the face! He did!" We saw the aftermath of

the Clash's performance at the O'Keefe Centre, where tour manager Kosmo Vinyl is seen counting the trashed chairs and pronouncing: "Fourteen, fifteen, sixteen... There are sixteen rock and roll fans in North America." Henry Rollins of Black Flag told me, "We are never sorry for what we do and what we play," a sentiment no doubt shared by a swaying, sunglass-shrouded Douglas Hart of The Jesus and Mary Chain. He attempted to tell Daniel why he only used two strings on his bass guitar: "That's the two I use. What's the fuckin' point of spending money on another two? It's like two is enough. It's adequate."

Safety pins gave way to hair gel with New Wave, and as the power of music video grew, style and image took a seat upfront. *The NewMusic* captured Duran Duran's fashion sense, the Human League's lipstick, A Flock of Seagulls' hair, Devo's flowerpot hats, and Boy George's, well, everything. And let's not forget Rough Trade. Carole Pope was audacious in every respect. Can you really say "cream my jeans" on television?

Reggae was a favourite at the NewMusic, from Canadians like the aforementioned Satallites and Truth and Rights as well as Leroy Sibbles, Clifton Joseph, and the fabulous dub poet Lillian Allen, to Jamaican acts like Burning Spear, Jimmy Cliff, Toots and the Maytals, and Peter Tosh. Much respect to *The NewMusic* for spending what was likely their entire travel budget to journey to St. Ann, Jamaica, in 1981 for Bob Marley's funeral, recording Rita Marley observing: "He was the people's sacrifice. He was sent for that purpose."

Metal got heavy with Judas Priest and Iron Maiden, rock got harder with Motörhead, Metallica, and Triumph; and Ted Nugent swung about in his loincloth. *The NewMusic* was there to broadcast the incredible footage of fans rioting at the CNE when Alice Cooper pulled a no-show. Alice blamed it on an attack of bronchial asthma, but the cancellation resulted in thirty-one arrests, twelve fans hospitalized, and $25,000 in damages to property. On another episode Twisted Sister's Dee Snider extolled the cathartic virtues of hard rock—"I say a fist going straight up in the air is a lot better than going straight into somebody's face"—and it doesn't get any better than watching Jeanne Beker go face to face with KISS, comparing tongue lengths with Gene Simmons.

Jeanne: "Oh no, you first. Yours has had a lot of exercise." Gene expertly unrolls his prehensile appendage till it extends way past his chin. Then it's Jeanne's turn. Whoa! Even Gene is impressed. "Well! That's fine," he remarks, reverently.

When hip-hop first emerged, *NewMusic* host Laurie Brown had some fun posing questions to fans on the street: What does "def" mean? What does "fly" mean? What does "fresh" mean? Grandmaster Flash, Ice Cube, the Notorious B.I.G., and Snoop Doggy Dog were fast becoming a cultural force. KRS-One brought home the importance of hip-hop as much more than a musical expression, remarking, "A black recording artist can be interviewed on television. Twenty years ago we would have had to come through the back door." We watched the Canadian scene gain strength with Maestro Fresh Wes, Michie Mee, Rascalz, the Dream Warriors, Saukrates, Kardinal Offishall, and Choclair, while another door opened when Run-D.M.C. teamed up with Aerosmith and blurred the lines between rap and rock and roll. And of course there was all the music that couldn't be categorized at all.

The NewMusic had an enduring cultural impact because it covered the music of the day with an analytical eye and a tongue firmly in cheek. We sought to champion musical mavericks as they strode brashly across the room, breaking barriers and sometimes bottles; but we were also unafraid to lampoon music's sometimes bloated self-importance, when it seemed in need of poking with a sharp stick. The show also built a niche for analytical pop-culture television which, sadly, has now largely been abandoned. That the thousands of *NewMusic* tapes aren't now enshrined in a broadcast museum is a crying shame.

John's audacious mission for the show was to be a conduit between the fans and the music, and when I joined, thirteen years after it had launched, we were still following that same guerrilla MO. We manoeuvred hand-held cameras backstage and took fans behind the scenes, shooting what we saw, cockroaches and all. And there *were* cockroaches, not to mention rodents, spit, vomit, urine, graffiti, broken glass, needles, and used condoms strewn about dressing rooms containing cast-off furniture bearing stains of indeterminate origin.

Part of the down-and-dirty approach sprung from the simple fact that we had neither the time nor the money for anything fancy. If ever you asked John for direction on a story, his unfailing response was, "Just shoot the shit out of it," laughing his looney British laugh.

For *The NewMusic* devotees, the show was their record-store clerk. For us, the responsibility to choose artists that we thought worthy of the audience was huge. The amazing thing (among many amazing things) was that we *could* make our own choices. We weren't beholden to anyone except the audience and ourselves. Occasionally we'd get a note from John or Nancy or, even more infrequently, Moses, who operated in a manner that he called "benign neglect," which suited us just fine.

If anything drastic happened, Nancy would look over at John and say, "What do we do now?"

And John would inevitably answer: "Panic?!"

Then you would try and solve the problem with a smile on your face.

John's inspiration for a smart, cheeky show about music grew into an enduring program that was respected around the world, the stewardship of which was a tad daunting for an untested producer.

I BECAME CO-HOST AND producer of *The NewMusic* in 1986, though why John thought I should be the producer of their flagship music show was concerning. Two-minute *RockFlash* hits were a long way from creating a weekly, packaged, purposeful show. I'd never edited anything longer than ninety seconds, my first "field" shoot had been inadequate, and—as an on-air host? I was as different from Daniel Richler as chalk from cheese.

Daniel had been *The NewMusic*'s producer and co-host for three years, and had brought a punkier sense of journalism to the show. He was in his element covering the British music scene, and I remember watching with respect as he jousted with punks on the streets of London, digging into music's pointier edges. He was a skilled interviewer, and we got to see his producer chops shine during his legendarily short-lived interview with Lou Reed in 1986. It didn't go well. Daniel offered question after question but Lou wasn't into it. Eventually Daniel asked him if he'd like to go back to the hotel room. Lou said yes and the whole thing just... ended. It took guts for Daniel to share that moment with the audience and it made me a devotee.

Daniel initiated me into the show by sending me out to interview Burton Cummings. I'd studied up and thought I did a pretty good job, but was caught short when I got back to the station.

Daniel popped the tape in to have a look and promptly inquired, "Where are the re-asks?'

"What's a re-ask?" I asked.

When you work with a single field camera, you are essentially cheating a multi-camera shoot. On a two- or three-camera shoot, as you'd have had with most other TV organizations at the time, there'd be one camera capturing the interview subject and another shooting the interviewer, and if you were *really* fancy you might have a third camera getting a wide shot. We'd see crews about town with up to six people travelling in a pack, which of course we'd sneer at. On our one-camera shoots, we'd shoot the main interview, then beg the artist to "sit in" while we repositioned the camera, lighting, and background to match. Then we'd shoot the interviewer faking the questions all over again: hence the term "re-asks." The artist's job would be to pretend to answer, so we could have the back of his or her head moving before cutting back to the initial shot.

Credible re-asks took skill. If you didn't re-ask the question in exactly the same way, it might not cut with the answer. It was a sorrowful moment in the editing bay when your artist's golden clip ended up on the cutting-room floor because of a poorly re-enacted or forgotten re-ask. Television was very linear back then. Jump cuts were verboten, and the idea of taking a comment out of context was unthinkable. It's laughable now, given the state of "gotcha" journalism and clipped sound bytes.

Chances were, the artists would only hang around long enough to get a couple of nods in, or else they'd do their best to crack you up, making faces or telling profane stories while you calmly pantomimed a range of reactions: *Fascinating. Really? No, do tell!*

Terry David Mulligan was the master re-asker and taught me some Emmy-worthy flourishes beyond the nods: the head tilt, the ear scratch, the chin rub, and, not least, the simple knee-cross manoeuvre—all of which could be mighty convincing.

Without re-asks, my first *NewMusic* interview was unusable. But it did provide a news clip on *RockFlash*, so Burton's time was not totally wasted, thank heavens.

After Daniel departed for the CBC, Laurie Brown and I co-hosted the show with associate producer Michael Rhodes, while Kim Clarke Champniss was enlisted into my spot at *RockFlash*.

Laurie must have wondered *why* this tragically unhip chick was being brought in as producer on *The NewMusic* when her own tenure on the show was already renowned. Let's be honest—Laurie was *way* cooler than I could ever be. She sported a vintage black-leather motorcycle jacket and loved edgy artists: David Bowie and David Byrne, the Jesus and Mary Chain, Bryan Ferry, Kate Bush, and the Cult. She was both *of* the culture and *in* the culture. She sang in a band and had even been cast as a prison guard in Corey Hart's "Sunglasses at Night" video. I had *no* edge. I was a dyed-in-the-wool folkie-cum-rock chick stick figure with permed hair and zero fashion sense. I loved Elton John, Joni Mitchell, Steve Goodman, and, of course, Whitesnake. Laurie might easily have assumed that not only was the producer job her rightful ascension (Laurie continued to produce her own segments), but that the show was going to hell in a handbasket. But John was the boss, he called the shots, and Laurie graciously invited me in.

We worked like demons. We were our own chase producers, researchers, paper editors, and presenters. With the able support of the core *NewMusic* team—Gregg Thurlbeck, John Marshall, and editor Alfred Tonna—we managed to produce the six-segment show week in and week out, with occasional one-hour specials. It was a grinding schedule—perhaps too much for us "older" gals, as an otherwise complimentary *TV Guide* cover story seemed to imply by calling the show "long in the tooth."

Laurie loved poking fun at the improbable, and would always push me to join in. I would have been deeply solemn without her. Once we were shot trapped in space suits as William Shatner's recordings of "Lucy in the Sky With Diamonds" and "Mr. Tambourine Man" were piped into our helmets. Laurie bashed her head inside her helmet, screaming silently in agony. Our outtakes reel at the end of the year typically showed us rolling around on the floor, practically peeing because we were laughing so hard.

IT WAS IMPORTANT THAT we could have some fun, because the competition was becoming fierce. By the second decade of *The NewMusic*, there was a glut of entertainment shows on bigger networks with more resources. *The NewMusic* went from being the only music game in town to having to compete for major stars with CTV, Global, CBC, and, of course, MuchMusic, as well as with all the newspapers, magazines, and radio stations whose musical formats were in line with the stars du jour.

As the demand for artists' time grew, it made it harder for Laurie and I to conduct interviews in the way we wanted, and the show's legacy of legitimacy was beginning to be trumped by networks with larger audience reach. Even our international reach of nineteen countries with over twenty-five million potential viewers via Europe's Sky channel meant little to the decision-makers at the Canadian labels, because their focus was on sales in Canada. The irony was that with the biggest stars, the labels could choose to serve a more mainstream audience, instead of preaching to the converted. A music audience already knew the artist was in town.

One advantage we did have was the one-stop-shopping of CHUM. A single *NewMusic* interview could be used on *RockFlash*, on Much, on Citytv Entertainment News, on *NM* of course, and perhaps, if the artist was big enough and could attempt a few words in French, MusiquePlus.

That competitive bench strength was important because we were demanding broads, and we wanted to call our own shots. What *The NewMusic* didn't ever want was a predictable environment. You needed some pretty potent star power to supersede the surroundings of a hotel couch against bland wallpaper with some plastic flowers on the coffee table.

It was way more fun to shoot in the wild, and luckily many artists preferred that too. We shot in alleyways and basements and in elevator shafts. There were shoots on polo ponies (Stewart Copeland, drummer of the Police), on boats (Donnie Walsh of the Downchild Blues Band), and in cars (Laurie's interview with Thomas Dolby in a borrowed Porsche). Movement created visual interest, so trains, helicopters, automobiles, and tour buses were always a thumbs-up, not to mention the bars, recording studios, barbershops, public parks, shower stalls, and arcades we elbowed our way into.

It wasn't just the location that was important; it was what we did in it. I played pool with Leon Redbone at the Horseshoe Tavern and with Keith Richards at the Squeeze Club. Redbone was a shark; Keith was not. I still have the U.S. five-dollar bill I won from Keith, and a great memory of the interview. Of course I asked him about the rumour that at the end of the world there will only be two things left, cockroaches and Keith Richards. Keith scoffed. "Well, look out cockroach, 'cause I'll eat it!"

I also played a social game with Joni Mitchell, and thereafter hung up the stick. How could I ever beat the pool trifecta of Joni, Leon, and Keef?

Sometimes we had to invent scenarios for the more reluctant quarry. Creative persistence paid off with Hunter S. Thompson. At first we were denied an interview with him because, according to his publicist, Hunter had said: "If I had twenty dollars for every dumb question I was asked..." So we proposed a game of Twenty-Dollar Questions and he went for it. The location was the roof bar of the Plaza Hotel in Toronto. I put a pile of twenty-dollar bills on the table and Hunter was invited to take one for every dumb question I asked. If he thought the question was worthy, he had to put one back. But even though the idea got him there, it didn't play out, and for some reason he kept excusing himself to go to his room. He returned less focussed each time. We deliberated about subtitling his answers in the end.

We did tour bus interviews with everyone from George Jones to Ozzy Osbourne. Tour buses offered an inner-sanctum intimacy, and besides, the artists always had to get somewhere anyway: might as well double your time and do some press. I remember Johnette Napolitano from Concrete Blonde describing an old Twinkie they'd discovered on their bus. As she told it, they'd been detained at the border by sniffer dogs that had found it. Who knows how long it had been there, left by some forgotten band, yet it appeared store-shelf fresh. Johnette claimed that Twinkies were never baked and "chemically evolve" under heat lamps. I, of course, fretted about airing the interview, thinking we'd be sued by Hostess for sure.

Speaking of lawsuits, I took Bruce Dickinson, lead vocalist of Iron Maiden, to the Ontario Science Centre to see if we could make his hair—which was about a foot and a half long—stand up in the Van de Graaff generator (the big silver ball that white-coated technicians use to create lightning bolts and demonstrate electricity to school kids). We were warned about metal on our bodies, but I'd forgotten about the microphones. I'd tucked the cable into the back pocket of my pleated acid-wash jeans (which paired well with my denim shirt and bolo tie). Bruce and I were holding hands during the interview so the current could go from him to me. The machine fired up and as Bruce's hair started going *up up up*, the mic cable in my back pocket started to crackle, shocking me in the ass. "Stop! Stop! Stop!" I yelled to the white coat, gripping Bruce's hand tightly. The technician hit the switch, Bruce's hair dropped, and my ass eventually recovered. Later, as we wandered through the exhibits, Bruce passed an incubator and referred to the newly hatched yellow baby chicks as "Chicken McNuggets." The day before the show went to air, while I was on a week's holiday in Cuba, I sent a panicky fax and asked Gregg Thurlbeck, *The NewMusic*'s associate producer to edit it out, fearing we'd be sued by McDonald's. The response was this:

```
denise donton
c/o Louise Langlois, fiesta representative
hotel marazul

denise: warning, stay in cuba.(stop)  thousands of irate fowl
farmers, rotiseries in hand, await your return at pearson
int'l.(stop) entire city tv building tarred and feathered.(stop)
we have all retreated to swiss chalet in scarborough.(stop)
our telex number is 06-22330. please use code name drumstick.




gregg thurlbeck
the new music
city tv/muchmusic
toronto,canada
return tlx: 06-22330
phone: (416) 367-5757or (416) 591-5757
```

Sometimes the subjects were as odd as the locations. I interviewed Joe Walsh of the Eagles sitting on the trunk of a car at the busy intersection of Yonge and Bloor outside Q107. He was well past his hotel-room chain-saw destruction phase by then: "I don't do that anymore. I switched to a Weed Eater," he said, going on to extol the tool's virtues, especially if you "want to mow your shag rug." He didn't want to talk music, he wanted to talk about the planet—which was fine with me. He'd been alarmed by a documentary he'd just seen on TV. "I saw a hole in the ozone and it was as big as the United States…and it's growing!" he marvelled. At the time I thought he was high (perhaps by "Weed Eater" he'd meant himself?), but it turns out he was right.

One of Laurie's favourite memories is the time she interviewed the Pretenders' Chrissie Hynde in England. Chrissie arrived wearing a "Fuck the Queen" T-shirt. "She thought she should change it before we started rolling," Laurie remembers, "so she simply whipped it off and pulled on another one. [Cameraman] Dave Hurlbut just about fainted." Speaking of nudity, Laurie remembers "standing with the Pogues on a second-floor balcony in Dublin…I was trying to interview a very drunk band when the punters on the ground realized who they were and starting yelling at them…Shane MacGowan proceeded to strip and throw his clothes down to them. Fun."

To me, one of Laurie's best interview questions ever was with Shane, on the occasion of the release of the Pogues' record *Rum, Sodomy & the Lash*. She asked if they had to be in that order. Long pause—he didn't understand. Laurie repeated the question. "*Rum, Sodomy & the Lash*. Does it have to be in that order?" Then Shane lost it. His laugh was a sloppy wet hiss through bad black teeth that sounded like a giant gas leak. The editors played it endlessly. It would have been a meme today for sure.

Jana Lynne White, who took over co-hosting duties after Laurie went to the CBC, recalls going with cameraman Basil Young to interview Sarah McLachlan at her apartment, then at 12th and Granville in Vancouver. As Jana recalls: "Sarah decided to change her outfit for the video shoot and made her wardrobe decision with the bedroom door wide open and her bra-less and beautiful body in full view. My joy was in watching Basil try not to watch, while clearly watching."

Encountering full-frontal nudity went with the territory—for the women. The only such stories I ever heard from the guys were about standing next to a rock star at a urinal. (By the way, I've since figured out that it couldn't *always* have been an accident of timing to be told, "Okay, you can go in now," and to walk in to find the guitar player not quite zipped.)

WE WERE INCREDIBLY LUCKY to spend time with the greatest (and even the not-so-great) musical luminaries; to have unfettered choice in who to cover and who not; to be allowed a point of view; and to make our mistakes in a public playground that really was the world.

We did some serious globetrotting on *The NewMusic*, and many trips were funded by MuchMusic contests, sponsored by advertisers who liked to see the results of their promotions on air. We weren't flying Business. Our trips tended to be middle-row red-eye budget flights, onto which we, dragging kilos of camera gear, herded our contest winners like ducklings. The trade-off for the trip was that before we could go out and film our *NM* stories, we'd spend a day or so shooting the winners "winning." Top of a double-decker bus, check; outside Buckingham Palace, check; alongside a bobby, check; Piccadilly Circus Underground sign, check. Most winners were amiable, thrilled to be wandering around a foreign city, even offering to help carry the gear. But there were also some who you'd rather throw off the bus than shoot waving on it; stories to tell for sure, but let's err on the side of kindness.

We may have travelled on a shoestring, but the mileage was impressive. I went to Hong Kong for the World Music Video Awards (halfway around the world for a thirty-second throw), to Moscow to shoot Scottish band Big Country (where we fuelled our shoots with Tang, boiled eggs, and vodka), and to the red-light district in Amsterdam with Melissa Etheridge—where we were narrowly rescued by police from a knife-wielding mob (literally) of pimps who accused us of filming their girls in the windows. ("It's just B-roll of the signs, Officer!") It was either hand over the tape or be thrown in the canal, gear and all (apparently a broadcast van *had* been pushed into the canal the week before). We handed over the tape.

Our most frequent international destination was the U.K., covering a wide range of gigs. At a Prince's Trust concert, we watched Diana groove in the stands beside a stoic Prince Charles (who did his level best to clap on the two and the four) and then scrummed backstage interviews with the artist royalty, including Elton John, Phil Collins, and Bryan Adams, who signed an autograph for George Harrison's son. The pomp and protocol of that evening was decidedly different from the following night, when Basil and I went deep into the bowels of punkdom at the Town & Country Club, me bribing an arsehole soundman with my per diem for an audio feed ("Did you get a receipt?" "Um, no...") while Basil fought his way to the stage.

Our cameramen were superheroes. Basil is a lovely, fashionable man, whose regard for quality has always shown in his work. That night, he was doused in beer and gobbed on by the crowd for trying to get five minutes of tape from an angry, forgettable band. (In the U.K., the music press had made hype into an art form. Our expectations for the "Next Big Thing" were often unfulfilled). On our way out, two young ladies, one with a mouthful of blood and missing teeth, careened into us before falling forward into the street. "Sod off!" the toothless one spewed when we offered to help, adding blood to the debris on Basil's jacket. It was well after 3 a.m. when we finished and found ourselves sitting on a filthy curb stuffing sodden fish and chips into our mouths with our fingers. Basil was gloomy and spent, almost too hungry to be mad.

"Glamorous, isn't it," he sighed.

That it was.

But the height of glamour for me had to be the Knebworth Festival. It was Woodstockian in scope, and took place about thirty miles north of London on the estate of Knebworth House, once the home of Victorian writer Edward Bulwer-Lytton, who'd famously written the line "The pen is mightier than the sword." I expect the fans who flocked to Knebworth thought the guitar mightier than both pen and sword.

The year we were there, 1990, the festival was billed as the "Best British Concert of All Time" and featured a lineup that included Paul McCartney, Mark Knopfler, Elton John, Robert Plant and Jimmy Page, Cliff Richard, Phil Collins with Genesis, and Pink Floyd.

MTV was the host broadcaster, which meant that cameraman Dave Hurlbut and I were afforded no favours. MTV did not love MuchMusic. We bought shows from them—this concert was among them—but our existence in Canada (which at the time effectively blocked their entrance to the country) was no doubt a thorn in the side of MTV's international aspirations.

Backstage, MTV had set up "MTV World," with trailers and generators and PR runners gently leading stars to their beautifully appointed set to have a nice drink in air-conditioned surroundings before their chat with MTV talent. It was all very civilized and costly.

Dave and I scoffed. Sets? Hardly rock and roll! But truth be told, we were jealous. It was a hot day; we had nowhere to plug in or dump the gear, no audio feed, and no way to get food or water without venturing into the crowd of 120,000 punters. At one point, we went out to gather some B-roll. I hadn't gone more than two hundred yards when I got separated from Dave and stuck in a crush that was so intense, I was literally carried off my feet by the crowd. It was freaking scary but for once I was glad I was six feet tall. At least I could see over people's heads to where we were heaving to. There was a small tree about ten feet away, and I fought my way to it, climbed up, and hung on tight. Eventually the mob eased, and I was able to make my way back to the safety of backstage, sweaty and rattled. I've been wary of crowds ever since.

Dave and I were able to land some interviews, but we didn't feel we'd nailed it without getting David Gilmour. Pink Floyd was closing the show, and we'd been told he "might do something after" (I used to believe that line). So we waited it out side-stage to the very end, at which point the band did a runner, walking off the stage into waiting vehicles and speeding away.

The show was over and the trashed, sunburnt crowd surged toward the exits. Dave and I turned our minds to our own exit strategy. We'd taken the train, then a taxi, to the gig, and were now stranded without a ride.

So we picked up the camera, gear bags, and battery belts, and started humping it all down the gravel road. We were tired and grumpy and had made it about half a mile when we began to grasp that we couldn't walk all the way to London. So we sat down in the grass by the side of the road to consider our options. I put my thumb out and Dave pulled out a flask of bourbon. Hallelujah, brother. Just when we were starting to feel a little more cheerful, Downtown Julie Brown's makeup van sped by, covering us in a cloud of dust.

Eventually we were picked up by a young man in a white, two-seater lorry, who by some miracle recognized me. "You look just like that bird from the Canada show!" (*The NewMusic* was syndicated in Britain.) "I can get you to London," he said, "but there's not much room." We jammed our gear around us on the floor and I sat, hunched over, on Dave's lap, trying to keep as much of my weight off him as I could. My head bounced against the roof until we reached the outskirts of civilization and found a cab to the hotel.

For the whole bumpy drive, the song in my head was Tracy Bonham's "Mother, Mother": "I'm hungry, I'm dirty, I'm losing my mind…everything's fine."

OVER THE SIX AND a half years on *The NewMusic* (four with co-host Laurie Brown and two and a half with Jana Lynne White), plus a couple of years hosting MuchMusic's country show *Outlaws and Heroes*, my back o' the napkin arithmetic indicates I did more than a thousand artist interviews. I'm glad I saved a box of VHS tapes from those days because I can only really remember a few dozen. I'm convinced my brain is analogue; when something new enters my head, something old has got to go. Even in those days, at work, I would walk by someone screening an interview and ask, "What are you working on?" and they'd look up puzzled. "Warren Zevon. It's *your* interview, Denise!" I understood their disbelief; at the time I'd done interview, my brain would have been *full* of all things Zevon, but after…poof!

As much as I loathed being *on* camera, I loved doing the work. I could easily lose track of time in an editing bay, crafting raw material into something fit for air. One time I remember emerging to half-light outside, not sure for a second if it was dusk or dawn. The sight of myself on television was the price to be paid for the privilege of interviewing artists. It's a wonderful feeling when you manage to really *connect* with someone you admire — though that's easier said than done.

An interview is a manufactured construct. It's artifice really, a negotiated transaction between two sides brought together for different — though, ideally, mutually beneficial — reasons. One side has something to promote, and the other sells airtime on his back. One is probed to reveal his deepest feelings, though the other is no shrink. And while the interviewer's goal is to deliver entertainment to the audience, the interviewee can arrive in *any* mood: peevish, combative, hungover, high. She might rather be *anywhere* than right here with you, but she'll put up with the pretence because it's all part of the game.

Your guest will arrive with a handler, usually a publicist, who will insist you focus solely on the movie/record/book being promoted, and who will hover about to ensure the positive is attracted, the negative repelled. If your guest is at all controversial, there may have been an effort beforehand to define the scope of the conversation. The show, or the host, needs to be both powerful and principled to manoeuvre beyond "Take it or leave it."

In-depth long-form celebrity interviews are rare today. We've accepted a faster, soundbite-driven media world and no longer expect our musical stars to also be cultural leaders with something meatier to say. As Don Henley complained to me on *The NewMusic* almost thirty years ago, "God knows we have enough entertainment out there. There are enough musical groups who are just here to entertain, and people have been entertained into a stupor," he said, imploring his fans not to be "sheep" and "bootlickers."

I might mention that Mr. Henley was a tad cranky the day I interviewed him. He sat down, arms crossed and head down, his body language clearly signalling his disinterest. But as the camera rolled, he began to warm up and we managed a smart, engaging interview. When it was done, we got up, shook hands, and he said to the label rep, "That wasn't so bad. Not at all what I expected from MTV."

Ah.

Which brings me to The Art of the Interview. I don't pretend to have mastered it, but just in case the pendulum swings and there is a market for in-depth interviews on music television again, here's a list of some of the things I learned along the way.

The Art of the Interview
1. Make Like a Boy Scout and Be Prepared

There is no greater sin than not doing your homework. Big stars don't suffer fools, and if a slip reveals your ignorance you may not recover.

So, study hard. Be investigative, multi-sourced, and selective in your research. Knowing the subjects' basic biographies and the reason for the chat (new album, book, tour) is a start, but the best interviewers are fully immersed. Study their influences, know the art that inspires them, the politics they admire, the books they read. If you can lay down a big enough base in your own grey matter, the left brain/right brain fun can begin and reward you with questions that will be refreshing for them and entertaining for your audience.

I once studied Carl Jung in preparation for an interview with Sting. Sting is a clever man and I was intimidated, so I had to go deep. Turned out that Jung was a bit of a blind alley, but it certainly changed the dynamic for the better.

Sting had arrived wingy with exhaustion. He'd been on the promo treadmill, doling out half-hour interviews in city after city for days. He walked into the room and said, "You really got a good deal getting me at the end of this day!" then flopped face-first on the couch. We were already rolling, of course, so once he saw the camera was on, he snapped to attention and dutifully rolled out the answers to my questions about the new record. It was an amiable enough conversation but frankly a little boring, and I was starting to fret that I wouldn't end up with anything different from what the guy on Cable 10 was getting. So instead of proceeding in a linear fashion, I blurted out:

"What is the theory of the hundredth monkey?"

Sting started and stopped, taken aback by the question. His eyes darted over to his press agent with a "What the…?" expression, but an autonomic instinct to give a crisp schoolboy response to the headmaster must have kicked in and he said gamely, "What is it? If a hundred monkeys start behaving in a certain way, like opening nuts with a tool, then the whole population of monkeys will start doing it, even though they're millions of hundreds of thousands of miles apart. *(pause)* Why do you ask that? And what has it got to do with me? That's the most *bizarre* question I've ever been asked. What's more bizarre is that I know the answer. Ask me another! It's like a quiz!"

That's when we began to connect. Sometimes it's just one question that cracks open a conversation, risky though it may be.

2. Practise the Art and Understand the Craft

Preparing interview questions is both art *and* craft. Imagine the arc of the interview with a beginning, a middle, and an end. If your first question is "Why did Christie Brinkley leave you?" it will likely be your last. Compose your questions carefully, order them purposefully, then practice them on yourself. Can they be answered with one word? If so, rewrite them ("How did it affect you when..." or "I'm wondering if..."). And don't forsake the reliable, "Why?"

I did manage to get Billy Joel to talk about Christie Brinkley, once. It was a very personal interview, and I was a little astonished at what he was actually revealing. Twenty minutes in, I felt like I should have asked him to lie down so I could take notes, it was that intimate. That was before the cameraman interrupted the interview to tell us there'd been a tape jam.

"What? When did it jam?" I said.

"At the beginning."

"What?!"

Disaster. *Nothing* was on tape. I was crushed. Billy seemed gleeful. I sensed he was already second-guessing what he'd said, and the tape jam was, for him, divine intervention. He agreed to start again, so long as we could have a drink first.

Which we did.

Once lubricated and ready to roll, we were again interrupted, this time by the hotel fire alarm. For sure it was us—the hot camera lights had been on for ages. The firemen piled off the elevator and as they filed past us with their raincoats and axes, Billy gamely threw out, "Hey, we didn't start the fire this time. I had nuttin' to do with it." ("We Didn't Start the Fire" was his hit song at the time.) *That*, we got on camera, which was indeed a life-saving moment—for the cameraman!

3. Listen Up, Buttercup!

As obvious as it sounds, great interviewers *listen*. If your subject is offering up something more interesting than your prepared questions, toss your notes and go with it. But for that, you need to be totally in the moment and fast on your feet.

There's nothing more bush league than watching a host ask a question and then stare at her notes while the subject is answering, only to ask another question completely unrelated to what the subject has just said.

"...and then I murdered my wife."

"Right. And why did you use that particular producer?"

Sometimes your task will be to break through the media training your subject may have had: "Stick to the agenda. Repeat the main message." You see it a lot in sports (remember Tim Robbins' character in *Bull Durham*? "You throw the ball, you catch the ball, you hit the ball...") and in politics. Politicians excel in "deny, deflect, and defend."

For a while it seemed to me that media training had found its zenith in the genre of New Country.

During my time hosting *Outlaws and Heroes*, country artists were suddenly crossing over to the pop charts. Garth Brooks, Clint Black, Dwight Yoakam, and Randy Travis were touring and selling out stadiums. But there was a price to pay. "Getting commercial" was seen as disloyal by hardcore country fans, so New Country artists appeared to have been tutored—all of them, seemingly, by the same Nashville publicist—to ensure they honoured the legends. Try as I might to steer a conversation elsewhere, I was led back to the great country traditionalists like a horse returning to the barn at night.

"And how did you react when your mother died?"

"Well, it was sad, Denise, but once the undertaker had taken her body, we went inside and found a Hank Williams record still there on the turntable. Did you know I was personally related to Hank Williams, Denise? We put it on and don't you know, Hank gave us the comfort we needed to understand she'd be happier in that better place."

Okay, I made that one up, but you get the point. The "Use the names of the greats in your answer" tack comes across as sweet and endearing the first time, but it can get old fast and you start to feel played.

Some artists are masterful at making every interview feel special, no matter how repetitive the questions. I remember Leonard Cohen graciously making the rounds—CBC, CTV, Global, plus radio stations and newspapers—leaving interviewers breathless everywhere he went. He was always asked about writing and he would speak sincerely of his prolonged process, lamenting the claims of others that they were visited by the muse, their job merely to capture the divine on the back of a matchbook. (He may have been thinking of Paul McCartney, who said of writing with John Lennon, "It's just magic." Apparently they'd sit down and say, "Let's write a swimming pool" or "Let's write a car," and amazingly, they would!)

As Leonard said in an interview with me, "When I was writing books people would tell me that there's this magic moment when the characters would take over and write the book themselves. Songwriters have told me that they're just a channel for the mysterious forces that produce songs, but I've never found those mysterious operations to work for me."

Like me, Leonard's examiners would sigh, certain they'd just captured a rare gem—which they had. For someone who cherishes words as Cohen does, the promo tour must have felt like a sausage factory indeed. At least with him, you can count on getting artisanal sausages.

Alone at last.

On the other hand, there's Tom Waits. About his songwriting process, Waits has been quoted as saying: "I think you make yourself an antenna for songs, and songs want to be around you. And then, they bring some other songs around and then they're all sitting around, and they're drinking your beer and they're sleeping on the floor and they are using the phone, they're rude and thankless little fuckers."

The first time I met Tom Waits was when I booked him for a concert at the University of Waterloo, and I've interviewed him a few times over the years. I've never been sure if Waits' persona isn't a character-actor role come to life, though I may have got a glimpse behind the curtain in an interview for his *Bone Machine* record in Cotati, California.

I was travelling with David Hurlbut and the location was down a long dirt road. As we drove along, we noticed more and more fence posts with black vultures perched on them. There were so many vultures we started to think they might be props stapled to the wood, but no, they were real. Fitting for a record featuring murders, suicide, bibles, demons, dogs, and politicians.

We did the interview in what appeared to be a reconfigured chicken shack (Tom liked the echo) with an array of children's toys scattered about: the tiny pianos and wind-up instruments he'd used in the recording. Interviewing Tom Waits is always a unique experience. It's like watching a butterfly fly. In between trying to follow his free-associative narrative and attempting to maintain eye contact, you can end up a little hypnotized. It's quite bewitching.

After we were finished talking, Tom went outside. While Dave packed up his gear, I could hear a voice speaking fast and brash like it belonged to a New York lawyer. Odd. Yet as far as I knew, we were alone out there. I walked outside, looked around, and saw only Tom on the phone. Then I heard his customary growl—"I'll call you back"—as he hung up. Huh. Is the Waitsian character a ruse? If so, he's awesome at it. Or maybe he'd been *playing* a New York lawyer on the phone? Either way, he is, as film critic Eric Hynes has written, "a hot blast of ciggy-smoke hep-cat cool to remind us of the crazy carnival of life."

Well said.

4. *Like a Good Wine, Let It Breathe*

Dead air can be tense. But just like in a Beethoven symphony, the silence can work for you. It can be powerful to let a comment hang in the air, and often the subject will rush in to fill the space with something better than you could ever have imagined.

Chrissie Hynde once gave me gold when I asked her about her challenges as a public figure with strong opinions. She had been taking a beating in the press for some comment or other and I was a sympathetic ear. The less I said, the more she gave:

> You stick your neck out and there's always someone standing there ready to kick you in the head, you know. It doesn't matter what you say — "Oh you're vegetarian, why are you wearing leather shoes?" And you know there's always an answer: "To kick you in the fucking teeth, pal."
>
> (beat)
>
> You know you can't do anything, but people expect you to walk around, they think you're perfect. I mean, I smoke a cigarette. "Oh I thought you were *green*." I mean, *bloody hell*. Oh, sorry I forgot to bring my halo out with me this afternoon.

And on. She was captivating.

And then there was the late Sun Ra, who offered a very singular example of the joy that could be found in silence. Sun Ra was a psychedelic outlier who propounded the term "Afrofuturism" to refer to his style of "cosmic jazz." He also claimed to be from Saturn. Our conversation naturally made its way to the divine.

> SUN RA: People came from somewhere and somewhere is a big question mark.
>
> DD: But we know where you're from.
>
> (I'm thinking, Birmingham.)
>
> SUN RA: Yes, I'm from another dimension.

Then he stopped speaking. I held my breath and waited, but he said no more. The cameraman felt the vibe and stayed motionless too, full stop, on Sun Ra's face. The silence was so long I did not dare break it. When we aired the interview, we added sound effects of birds and crickets to the shot and let it hang there, forever.

I admit that adding crickets was a bit of post-production cheek, so let's be clear: what a great interview should *not* be about is you. *They're* the star; you're just the vehicle. The audience is going to know what you think anyway — probably because your body language will be giving them all the clues they need (your cocked eyebrow, for example, or that odd stabbing motion you're making with your pen).

5. Location, Location, Location

One of the most memorable experiences I ever had was with Ice-T, who took us to Compton in East L.A. He was driving, which was a good thing — it would have been very strange to see me cruising through that hood. It was a few years before the song "Cop Killer" came out, but Ice-T was already a politically charged rapper. The record and video we were there to explore was for a song called "I'm Your Pusher." It had been painted in the press as a pro-drug song, but to me it could not have been more obvious that he was casting *music* as the drug: "You wanna get high? Let the record play."

As we drove past shuttered stores and graffiti, T talked about what it was like growing up in these neighbourhoods and described the self-perpetuating cycle of drugs and poverty: "The best way to keep people poor is to keep them high and uneducated. A nice family, might be a doctor or work in TV or something, and the father can say 'Look, this is [what] the reward of hard work and school is.' But in the neighbourhood you've got uneducated people bringing up uneducated people and the only rewards they can see is the drug dealer, the hustler."

We arrived at a two-storey house with a big white porch and walked up the stairs into a dark living room with unnaturally high humidity. We soon found out why. T's friend was a prodigious collector of lizards and reptiles. There were large, dank terrariums strewn throughout the house. One of the young men there offered to show us his running-shoe collection. We followed him upstairs and stopped in front of a small closet door located under the eaves of the house. Inside were dozens of pairs of perfectly aligned high-top running shoes in every known colour, all in mint condition. As Basil Young was getting a shot of the shoes, a huge green monitor lizard came streaking out of the closet. Both Basil and I almost fell over backwards. That lizard had to have been four feet long and eighty pounds. But the scare didn't end there. In its haste, the lizard knocked over a large semi-automatic gun, which fell down across the shoes.

"Oh, don't worry 'bout that," said our guide, casually tucking the gun back into place behind the door. "It's not loaded. I wondered where that dragon was."

Back in the car I asked T about the way women were portrayed in his work—on album jackets, in videos, all shaking their booties in as little clothing as possible. Was there a fabric shortage in East L.A.? T denied having anything to do with that, saying it wasn't up to him. His girlfriend Darlene was in most of his videos, and he declared that he could barely get her to keep her clothes *on*.

Okay then.

Do what you want, ladies, just make sure it's what *you* want.

6. Be Brave and Challenge Where You Should

I know I said that you should be objective, but there can be extenuating circumstances, especially if the subject deserves to be confronted. Case in point for me was Professor Griff, Public Enemy's "Minister of Information."

Public Enemy was one of the most successful hip-hop acts of the late eighties and nineties. Public Enemy wrote tough, politicized rap and Chuck D, one of the original founders of the group, was a celebrated American voice for racial equality and self-determination. It was he who first referred to rap music as being "black America's CNN."

I was backstage before one of their early shows in Toronto, looking forward to interviewing Chuck D, but it was Professor Griff who arrived instead.

The situation wasn't ideal. We didn't have the main man, and in our search for a quiet spot we ended up in a concrete bathroom crowded against a wall. From the look of the tape, we'd obviously had some audio issues as well. Instead of a hand-held microphone, I'm interviewing Griff with one tiny Lavalier mic. It looks like I'm holding a matchstick up to his mouth.

At one point, I asked Griff about the accusations of misogyny that were starting to heat up around the group.

GRIFF: We don't want women to come out of their role.

DD: Women shouldn't have a role; people are people, male or female.

GRIFF: No that's not true. Women play their certain roles in society. You don't expect women to play a man's role, you understand what I'm saying?

DD: No.

GRIFF: I mean, you don't find your husband doing the dishes and you working on the car.

DD: Yeah, sometimes. What's the problem with that?

GRIFF: There's nothing wrong with that, but it's out of a woman's role. We don't believe our women should do that.

DD: You don't believe that a woman can fix the car while a man does the dishes.

GRIFF: I mean, if it's necessary for her to fix it then yes, but the, [what] we don't want, the *point* is, we don't want women to come out of their *roles,* you understand what I'm saying.

DD: Women shouldn't have a role. People are people male or female.

GRIFF: No, that's not true, we definitely don't believe that. A woman is a woman.

DD: But you're talking about basic equality — *that* is your message. Then equality of the sexes is the same thing.

GRIFF: Women can be women as long as they stay women and men stay men. You understand what I'm saying.

DD: No.

GRIFF: Well then, you better dwell on that. Roll that over in your mind and think about that. If you're a man, be a man, if you're a woman, be a woman, we don't go for this in-between stuff.

Guess I did have to roll it over in my mind. Did we really go from misogyny to homophobia in under two minutes? Later, when the band was accused of homophobic lyrics, singing that "the parts don't fit," or shouting out to James Cagney for beating up "a fagney," it got a little clearer. But it was anti-Semitism that really hit the fan, when Griff was quoted in the *Washington Times* as saying that Jews are responsible "for the majority of wickedness that goes on across the globe." Then people got busy.

The Simon Wiesenthal Center published a statement titled "The new sound in music: bigotry," which said: "What happened to the good old days when the music industry was the voice of positive social change?"

Public Enemy's label, Def Jam, arranged a visit for Chuck D at the Simon Wiesenthal Centre in Los Angeles, where he met with Rabbi Abraham Cooper and a holocaust survivor. Chuck D fired Professor Griff, then rehired him. Sometimes Griff was in the band, sometimes not. Still, I wondered why someone as intelligent and accomplished as Chuck D would let Professor Griff speak for him.

7. Tell The Truth (Public Enemy Part 2)

Be an unbiased witness. That may be an odd statement, coming after what I've just written; but until I was actually making media, I didn't understand how easily the truth could be twisted, how the dog could be wagged. I'd never taken a journalism course and was learning fairness and balance on the job. My media-bias lightbulb moment occurred when I was producing a *NewMusic* segment on bigotry in music, and MuchMusic figured prominently in the story.

The segment was initially sparked by Lenny Kravitz and Living Colour's songs decrying racism in America. Lenny Kravitz's video for "Mr. Cab Driver" illustrated how tough it was for a black man to get a cab in New York City. Living Colour made an even stronger statement with their video for "Funny Vibe," which showed images of ordinary black Americans encountering discrimination everywhere they went—shopping, at work, taking the elevator. There was no mistaking the message when a black man in the video was papered with words like "black," "boy," "nigger," "tar baby," and "spade."

The story I was working on took a U-turn when Public Enemy was banned from Much for anti-Semitic lyrics. Much had banned individual videos before, but never an artist's entire canon. On February 6, 1990, the *Los Angeles Times* reported: "Canada's all-music video station has banned all videos by the rap group Public Enemy, which has been under fire for what is perceived as anti-Semitism in lyrics on its latest record 'Welcome to the Terrordome,' and in past statements by the group's former self-styled 'Minister of Information,' Professor Griff. John Martin, director of music programming for MuchMusic, said: 'We're not comfortable with promoting an act with the kind of anti-Semitism this band promotes. Our position is that we choose not to play their music.'"

Inside the station, there was heated discussion over banning even one video, let alone an entire oeuvre; and Much itself was accused of racism. As John told me in an interview for our *NM* segment: "We made a stand against racism, against people who were anti-Semitic. The band happened to be a black band. I don't see how that makes us racist."

A picket line formed outside the station, with approximately a dozen protesters walking around in a circle chanting, "Don't believe the hype." The leader of the protest wouldn't speak to me, and when I offered him the mic he just continued to chant, "Don't believe the hype," which was too bad. It would have a been a good opportunity for him to expand on the issue as he saw it.

I remember examining the question of journalistic balance in the editing bay when considering which shots of the protest to use. Some were extreme close-ups of the protesters — the signs and the shouting faces. The camera was jostled, and the footage could easily have been edited as depicting an intense, aggressive throng, but when the wide-shot was added — the footage taken from across the street — the protesters were dwarfed by the building, making the protest seem small. I realized how easy it would be to infect the story with editorial bias either way, and began to understand why it's conflicting for journalists to report on a story when they're part of the story. We cut the piece using a combination of shots, with as truthful a representation as possible, but my interest in media literacy was truly sparked.

Media literacy was not a subject widely taught in school, but it should be — especially now that the world is accessed by young people through screens of all sizes, with and without filters. An audience taught to think critically about what it's seeing understands how the images and the messaging can be manipulated and can better participate in the discussion. That is powerful, democratic stuff.

8. Use Your Heart and Your Head

If you're engaged, the audience will be, too. After all, you're there to serve (and yes, sell to) them. Even so, I felt obliged to protect my subject on occasion. Ozzy Osbourne and Eric Clapton were two emotional interviews where I made editorial decisions in deference to the artist. That might seem unconventional now, when getting people to cry on camera seems to be a goal.

Ozzy was difficult to access at the time because he was shaken over the death of a young man who had killed himself, allegedly after listening to Ozzy's song "Suicide Solution." Ozzy hadn't cancelled his tour, but he wasn't doing any media while the furor raged. Our interview requests had been turned down repeatedly by the label, but I'd managed to gain access through an old friend from the Whitesnake tour.

We were invited onto the tour bus. It was difficult to hear Ozzy over the drone of the engines, but it was plain to see that he was a mess. (This was before anyone saw Ozzy bumbling about on reality TV. He was still the Prince Of Darkness then.) He struggled to speak, his nose was running, and his hands were shaking so badly he couldn't work his lighter. He answered as best he could and then I motioned to shut the camera off. We just sat. I didn't feel the need to add to his misery.

In Clapton's case, it started innocently enough. I mentioned I'd seen him at the Prince's Trust earler that year and how I'd marvelled over his performances of "Layla." He lost himself completely in the song, his guitar embodying loss and loneliness like nothing I'd ever heard. He described the song as a desperate cry of rejection; his unrequited love for Pattie Boyd who was then married to George Harrison. Eric eventually married Pattie but it didn't last a decade, though the loss of love was just as strong now as it was then. I wondered aloud that he could be so gifted with talent on one hand, and so unfulfilled on the other. He described therapy sessions, his pattern of going after unattainable people or "If I do get into a successful relationship with someone I sabotage it... I don't know if that's because it's the way it was meant to be because I'm an artist and I have to do it to make the art?... I think that it's the end result of a seriously unfortunate psychological disorder that I may be saddled with for the rest of my life, I don't know."

I asked if music was his outlet for that and he said, "Yeah," swallowing hard and fighting back emotion. I sensed that if I kept prying, the interview would end in tears. I moved on. Guess I'll never be Barbara Walters.

My glimpse into Clapton that day made his song "Tears from Heaven," about his four-year-old son, Conor, who fell from a fifty-third-floor window in New York City, even more heartbreaking.

You can't be a good interviewer without empathy. It allows for a human connection in that contrived circumstance. Conversely, you'll need reptilian skin to endure the times when a connection simply doesn't happen. Sometimes your favourite artists can be your worst interviews, and other times you can walk in ready but ambivalent and enjoy the person so much you can't stop playing their music ever after.

9. Interview Failures: Water Off a Duck

Everyone has interview failures and among mine was Chris Isaak (twice).

Chris was in town to support his massive single "Wicked Game." The video was a racy black-and-white number, masterfully directed by photographer Herb Ritts. It featured our hero, with his movie-star looks, rolling around on the beach with model Helena Christensen. It was a sexy, stunning video and the record was blowing up all over North America. The hype merited an interview, and I planned to ask a few extra questions so that we could include Chris in subsequent *NM* features, like the Elvis Presley special we were compiling for the tenth anniversary of Elvis's death. (Given the perennial lack of funds, the *NM* always worked months ahead, planning features around major rock and roll events and building a library as we went. Our string of "extra" questions started to resemble a Proust questionnaire).

It was a beautiful day and we chose a location outdoors for the interview. Things were going fairly well, I thought, until I offered an opinion about the video. The song had a ballad-like quality that was reminiscent of the King. At the mention of Elvis, Chris stood up, yanked the microphone off his shirt, threw it on the ground, and stormed off. I looked at the record company rep, who was as astonished as I was. We all just sat there, trying to figure out what the hell had just happened. While the rep went off after him, I sat waiting with the cameraman. She returned eventually and said simply, "He's not coming back." Later I found out that just before the interview, he had read some sniffy U.S. article that had slagged him off as an Elvis derivative.

A few days later I got a handwritten postcard in the mail:

8 – JAMES DEAN DENISE —,
IT WAS EARLY... I
THE SNIFFLES... YOU WERE
TALLER THAN ME AND
~~XXXXXXXXXX~~ THE SUN WAS
IN MY EYES... MY
UNDERWEAR WAS MUCH
TOO TIGHT AND MY DOG
ATE MY HOMEWORK.
HOPE YOU GOT
SOMETHING YOU COULD USE
OUT OF OUR INTERVIEW AND
NEXT TIME YOU SEE ME LOOK
FOR A TALL GUY WITH ELEVATOR
SHOES BAGGY SHORTS, DARK 16 OZ
GLASSES, AND A NEW DOG AND DRISTAN
NASEL SPRAY. IM NOT ALWAYS
SUCH A GRUMP – I HAVE
PHOTOGRAPHIC PROOF – A PICTURE OF
ME SMILEING IN 1961. MAKEING YOUR LIFE
A LIVING HELL
Xo CHRIS ISAAK

DENISE DONLON
CITY TV /NEW MUSIC
299 QUEEN ST. W
TORONTO ONTARIO
M5V 129

POSTAL CODE

CANADA

All was forgiven. Until...

I met him again on the set of *Command Performance*, Standard Broadcasting's nationally syndicated radio special (weird that I was allowed to moonlight for a competitive broadcaster, but those were more innocent times). The format of the show included a studio audience and live performances. In between songs, for some reason, Chris refused to walk over and sit with me. I had to practically yell at him from across the room. It was hardly an intimate conversation. My suspicion was that he was ticked off that this was radio, as he certainly looked ready for television. His face and hair were perfect, and he was wearing a country showbiz jacket so flashy that it looked like it was lit from within. We got through it, but it was uncomfortable from the get-go. At least he didn't walk out this time.

Pretty well every *NM* host had someone walk out: Lou Reed on Daniel Richler; Marianne Faithfull on Kim Clarke Champniss ("Is it okay if we stop now? I really can't bear it," she said). Actually, KCC had a couple. In an interview with the Bee Gees, KCC asked an innocent question about backlash. Robin Gibb said: "I resent the idea of people slagging us off, and

I don't want to an interview with someone who does," and then stormed off. Another perfectly fine question by KCC, this one to John Lydon (a.k.a. Johnny Rotten) about the Sex Pistols' setting the stage for punk imaging everywhere, set off Mr. Rotten, who said: "It's nothing to do with image, you damn fool. It's about the songs. End of interview." Even George Stroumboulopoulos wasn't immune. When he asked Sebastian Bach of Skid Row about glam rock, Bach said: "This is over. I don't care, I don't want to talk about Poison. Goodbye." And at a very public press conference, George asked Dr. Dre a perfectly relevant question: "What's the possibility of Suge Knight getting out of prison this summer?" Dr. Dre responded: "I don't like this guy — I don't like this guy." He didn't walk out, though — harder to do at a press conference.

Jana Lynne White's walkout experience was with Tricky, the trip-hop/fusion artist from Britain. As she recalls: "He had just smoked a giant reefer before arriving at MuchMusic for his interview. As soon as he arrived, we hauled him down to the building's basement. After five minutes of getting the lighting right, I gave Tricky my opening question. He blinked, muttered something akin to undecipherable Cockney slang, and stared. I repeated the question. Again, more mumbling, followed by more staring. Then he suddenly stood up, and for the first time spoke clearly: 'I can't even fucking understand the question!' And left. Later, when Tricky played his concert, he publicly apologized to 'the nice lady from MuchMusic who asked him something smart, too smart for my brain after a big blunt!'"

Jeanne Beker's interview with Iggy Pop tops them all. And it's she who walks out.

Jeanne and Iggy are backstage drinking beer and talking after his show, but it starts to go sideways when Iggy sneers at Jeanne's leather boots and manicure.

IGGY: I have more talent —

JEANNE: In certain areas.

IGGY: In any area that you could ever dream of.

JEANNE: How the fuck do you know that? You really are something else.

IGGY: Yeah, in other words, you're about to say I'm a real cunt.

JEANNE: No, I'm not. I'm not saying anything.

IGGY: You just hide it. Yes, you just hide it.

JEANNE: You're really something, man. Okay, that's a wrap.

Jeanne puts her coat on to leave, while Iggy tries half-heartedly to explain that his comments were *honouring* her, but the interview is beyond redemption. No matter, the next time they meet, they get along like a house on fire. That's rock and roll.

The NewMusic always aired the cranky moments. With enough practice the hosts developed a sense of what made good TV. You know you're in the sweet spot when you start editing in your head during the interview, crafting the finished piece even while recording. That's when it feels like magic.

10. Beware the Hubris: Don't Take Advantage and Don't Expect to Be Remembered.

I broke both these rules with Aerosmith. I'd met Steven Tyler a few times before and we'd gotten along swimmingly. So swimmingly, I don't even remember this photo being taken:

So, on the occasion of the release of their album *Pump*, I may have ventured into the interview — with the whole band this time — feeling more cavalier and less prepared than I should have. That said, it's tough to get any depth when you're standing around, pointing a mic at five people when you only really want to talk to one or two. I was also armed with a list of station IDs to collect for Much, as well as a specific question for Laurie. Laurie was working on a feature about hard rock bands buying into the trend of recording big, soaring, hands-up, lighters-lit, sway-back-and-forth-together ballads (Poison's "Every Rose Has Its Thorn," Def Leppard's "Love Bites," Bon Jovi's "Never Say Goodbye," etc.).

The interview was serviceable at best but went downhill fast when I asked the big acoustic ballad question. I don't remember the question word for word, although I'm sure it wasn't, "So are you guys selling out to stay on the charts?" What I do remember is Tom Hamilton glaring, Steven Tyler frowning, and Brad Whitford scowling, shaking his head slowly back and forth. The best I could manage as a next question was akin to, "How's the tour going?"

My fault. I expected our past cordiality to grant latitude, and because it wasn't my question I didn't take the time to properly craft it. I never made that mistake again, and when in the future I *was* remembered warmly by an artist, it was surprising and, I admit, a little thrilling.

Sometimes even when it's bad, it's good. I interviewed Buster Poindexter at X-Ray's, a bar down the street from Much that was co-owned by Dan Aykroyd. It was a bizarre interview. Buster may have had a few and questioned aloud why he was there: "Are we on a particularly hip show or am I casting my pearls before swine?"

I sought to reassure him, of course, and continued on with my questions, but he interrupted and, incredibly, turned, pointed his finger at the camera, and said straight to it: "You viewers are lucky to have this person. You know why? She's sophisticated and she knows how to get the meat out of the man."

Drunk he, proud me.

11. (Because it should always go up to eleven) KEEP ROLLING

I mentioned capturing Sting's bounce on the couch when he arrived wiped out for his interview. We always tried to be rolling, surreptitiously, before and after the interview. It sounds sneaky, but it was just to add colour, and not against the law as we understood it. As long as one person knows a conversation is being recorded...

Even if the publicist interrupted an interview, our rule was to keep rolling. It's much better for the audience to witness an awkward arbitration or a hand in the lens, than to wonder why the screen has suddenly gone black.

Rod Stewart only let his hair down after we'd wrapped. We'd had a sweet but standard conversation, talking about music, aging, and Ronnie Wood's paintings, among other things. Rod shook my hand and said, "Lovely interview. Very, very nice, thank you." While we repositioned for the re-asks, the camera was still rolling. He started reflecting on what he'd said: "You surely wouldn't see me doing this when I'm fifty because it's not possible!" (He's still going at seventy-one.) Then he called Sting a "BASTARD!" (I think he was joking) before telling me what he really thought about Ron's artwork: "He made me look *terrible* in those drawings, and he's my friend!"

One of the joys of being "long in the tooth" was that we were growing up with the artists. Especially the Canadians. In my first interview with k.d. lang—who at the time was just starting out in the "Hanky Panky" days—she picked Basil and me up at the Edmonton airport in her powderblue Meteor and we filmed at her house. It was a little bungalow cheerfully adorned with her inventive visual artistry—including in her fireplace, which she'd turned into a crèche with two painted figurines: Jesus with a mic in his hand, interviewing Elvis Presley. A study on fame.

Years later, in 1990, k.d. herself was famous and we revisited the subject at Beaver Lake in Stanley Park. It was a long walk in with all the gear, but worth it for a natural setting. I'd asked her if she'd ever been "intimidated by people you've worked with." She described singing with Roy Orbison, her nervousness overcome, she said, by the sheer intimacy of singing "Crying" together, the softness of his cheek as they shared the mic.

When the interview was done and the camera was trained on me, we were both a bit goofy. I re-asked the same question about who intimidated her, and this time her answer was, "Just you." It was a struggle to get the work done after that; she was intent on cracking me up. At one point, k.d. says to the camera, "She's really good at these re-asks. She's even better than Connie fuckin' Chung, man!" (Highest praise ever!) When I re-asked a question about a film she'd just shot called *Salmonberries*, in which she played an androgynous Inuit woman, I suggested that people might start saying, "k.d. lang: thespian!" k.d.'s response was, "Careful...!" The exchange was funny, but I knew, too, that there was some seriousness to that caution. On the plane ride home I worried about the tape. k.d. had not come out at that point, and I didn't want to be the one to inadvertently "out" her and betray a trust. I kept the re-ask tape locked in my desk for two years.

When k.d. came out to the *Advocate* two years later, in June 1992, she was one of the first big celebrities to do so—a year before Melissa Etheridge, five years before Ellen, eight years before George Michael. It was a courageous thing, especially with a career to tend to and a Republican President in the White House.

Me and k.d.

I have great admiration for those who wield their celebrity well; the public spotlight is a harsh place. Despite my own discomfort in front of the camera, though, I had come to value what the spotlight could do. I liked having a vehicle to help passionate artists reach bigger audiences, and I liked that *The NewMusic* was a show artists respected because we weren't afraid to tackle bigger issues. Luckily, my time there coincided with an era when musicians were engaged in many social concerns. We were happy to be along for the ride.

(9)

MUSIC + MEANING = MAGIC

"I learned an awful lot from listening to people's music.
And I don't know, have no guarantee, can't prove a damned thing,
but if I didn't believe it, I wouldn't be singing it."
— PETE SEEGER ON MUSIC'S ABILITY TO CHANGE LIVES

I LOVED MY JOB. What's not to love about gallivanting around the world with a backstage pass, covering big musical events, interrogating rock stars, and discovering new music?

As my confidence grew as a producer, so did my affection for speaking with artists who were driven by more than the pursuit of fame. Laurie and Jana were similarly motivated. We loved it when the show could be more *60 Minutes* than *Rolling Stone*, when we could present music in a wider cultural and social context.

It was a time of musical activism. Sting was in the rainforest, R.E.M. were campaigning for Greenpeace, and Little Steven was refusing to play Sun City. There were massive, mobilizing hit songs like "Do They Know It's Christmas?," "Tears Are Not Enough," and "We Are the World." There was Live Aid, Farm Aid, and Sport Aid, and events like the Freddie Mercury Tribute Concert brought attention to the tragedy of HIV/AIDS. There were a few good-humoured pokes at it all (like the "Ramones Aid" video for "Something to Believe In"), but there was undeniably a surge of artists who used their celebrity for good. Peter Gabriel, Bryan Adams, Bono, and Youssou N'Dour were touring with Amnesty International's A Conspiracy of Hope, and at home Blue Rodeo played the Stein Valley Voices for the Wilderness Festival, Murray McLauchlan joined Ian Tyson's Oldman River Concert, Midnight Oil flew to Clayoquot Sound to protest clear-cutting, and Molly Johnson created Kumbaya.

The idea that music could play a significant part in social change wasn't new. There are anti-war songs (Buffy Sainte-Marie's "Universal Soldier"), ecology songs (Marvin Gaye's "Mercy Mercy Me"), protest songs (Pete Seeger singing "We Shall Overcome"), peace songs (John Lennon's "Imagine"), anti-slavery songs (Billie Holiday's "Strange Fruit"), anti-apartheid songs (Stevie Wonder's "It's Wrong"), civil rights songs (Bob Marley's "Get Up, Stand Up"), and hundreds more, sung to demand justice, communicate information, and lift despair; all of them hoping, as Sam Cooke did, that "A Change Is Gonna Come."

When we encountered a song, an artist, or an event that was *about* something, it was irresistible. And so, with artists leading the charge, *The NewMusic* dove deeply into subjects like racism, the environment, violence in music, gender issues, drugs, literacy, and more. Happily, the issue-oriented specials were good for the show, for our brand, *and* for the audience. They underscored our distinction in an increasingly crowded music television marketplace, and because we engaged with the artists in their activist interests, we were seen as partners rather than exploiters and gained access that might otherwise have been limited.

The idea that music television could contribute something beyond entertainment hit home for me when I covered the Nelson Mandela 70th Birthday Tribute in London. It had been more than two decades since I'd written in my diary "I don't really know who I am or why," but it was that concert that told me I was closer to the answer. Music + meaning = magic for me.

IT WAS JUNE 11, 1988, and Basil Young and I were backstage at Wembley Stadium in London. The Mandela event boasted a massive lineup, with more than eighty-three artists on two stages, including Stevie Wonder, Sting, Dire Straits, Whitney Houston, George Michael, Eurythmics, Harry Belafonte, Youssou N'Dour, Chrissie Hynde, Whoopi Goldberg, Jackson Browne, and Miriam Makeba. The host broadcaster was the BBC. Their ballsy embrace of the event was pivotal in helping organizers convince more than sixty-seven broadcasters from around the world to come on board. The concert became one of the biggest consciousness-raising events ever held, even though its messaging was fraught with politics and confusing to some.

I remember asking a young British fellow in the crowd if he knew what the reason for the concert was.

"Gettin' blitzed with the lads," he said.

"Do you know who Nelson Mandela is?" I pressed.

"He's just some guy who got locked up for being a terrorist."

"He got locked up for being a terrorist?" I repeated, hoping for more.

"Piss off!" he said, giving me a stroppy hand gesture and continuing on his way.

Yob.

Mandela had been in prison for twenty-five years. The concert organizers were not overtly calling for his release, even though that was the initial inspiration for Jerry Dammers (of the Specials), a long-time anti-apartheid activist and a founder of Artists Against Apartheid. He had written and released a song in 1984 called "Free Nelson Mandela" and had organized political concerts before, but he was inexperienced as a concert promoter and had lost money. This time, Jerry enlisted veteran producer Tony Hollingsworth to help.

Hollingsworth was well aware that strident political messaging, such as calling for the release of *all* political prisoners in South Africa, would deter international broadcasters from carrying the show. "Dammers damning" South Africa wouldn't fly, especially in the U.K., an ally of South Africa and home of Conservative Prime Minister Margaret Thatcher. So the event was named the Nelson Mandela 70th Birthday Tribute, and artists were advised to be measured in their words.

It was also a time of so-called "benefit burnout," and there was much criticism whenever the promise of a big event wasn't flawlessly fulfilled (stories of food rotting on African docks after Live 8, for example). Stars were even reproached for participating in big charity events for "self-serving" reasons. (A specious argument. It's not for the money — typically, artists on big benefit shows waive personal fees and publishing royalties; nor is it for the publicity — the artists who need the attention are not the ones asked to do the shows.)

With the Mandela tribute, there was controversy over which artists were asked to perform. Why ask apolitical Whitney Houston instead of long-time activist Billy Bragg, for example? But Tony Hollingsworth was interested in the most powerful outcome, and thus in the artists with the biggest draw. He put together a truly historic lineup and put himself, his career, and what money he had on the line.

Even though descriptions of the event deliberately left out the word "apartheid," calling it a "70th Birthday Tribute" and a "Freedom Concert," the organizers still made canny decisions around messaging. Artists performed in front of a massive image of Nelson Mandela, with slogans like "Isolate Apartheid" clearly visible. Some broadcasters saw that as subversive, and set decoration became a more salient consideration in broadcast negotiations of big events from then on.

The event grew to an eleven-and-a-half-hour live concert event sent to a broadcast reach of 500 to 600 million people, though all viewers did not see the entire show. Some broadcasters carried shorter versions with the more political speeches edited out. In Canada, MuchMusic carried the entire event live, thanks to John Martin and, notably, our "Mr. TV," David Kines. The Mandela event was David's international-uplink baptism by fire.

Backstage on show day, Basil and I were unaware of the messaging controversy surrounding the show. Naturally, then, we found it confounding that stars kept responding to my questions about apartheid with little more than birthday wishes for Mandela. I harrumphed away, wondering how so many of them could be so uninformed; but I finally realized something was up when even Stevie Wonder chose his words with obvious care. Though Stevie did say, "We know in very little time, we'll be celebrating the end of apartheid."

Our own messaging choices on *The NewMusic* were unencumbered. I recorded my opening throw outside the South African Embassy in London, in the midst of a street protest where signs read "NO to Apartheid Executions" and organizers were on the sidewalk with petitions for the release of other South African political prisoners. Basil and I did interviews in the Artists Against Apartheid office, and I still use a coffee mug I bought there which bears an image of Mandela behind bars. It reminds me of how far we've come and how far we still have to go.

Painting by Manon Elder from her "HIGHTEA" series.

Meanwhile, backstage at the concert, Basil and I were hard at it. As a proud black man, it was particularly important to him that we cover this event well. With just our camera and a microphone we were a tad underpowered, but in a sea of broadcasters with full crews and sets, lights and cameras on dollies, and logo signage everywhere, we were a nimble anomaly. Basil commandeered a spare electrical outlet behind the BBC set to keep the battery belts charged and we went to work.

In perpetual scrum mode, we approached every artist we saw, rolling as we went. We clipped Peter Gabriel, Tracy Chapman, Midge Ure, Little Steven, Bryan Adams, and tons of others. At one point, two bored BBC crew guys leaned over their riser railing and started to do a loud running commentary: "Ladies and gentlemen, the MuchMusic crew is approaching the artist, the artist is stopping, and...he's leaning in, he's listening... yes...yes, the Canadians have STING! Another GOLD for the Canadians!" They kept it up for a while. It was pretty funny and, given the intensity of the day, quite motivating.

Sting, by the way, made a point of saying, "No one is preaching up here. We're just presenting information." But he was serious about participating. He had flown in that morning and was flying back out to another gig afterward, reportedly against his management's wishes. (Tony Hollingsworth had arranged a clandestine meeting with Sting in a hotel room in Europe and convinced him to appear.) While Sting held the messaging line with us, he made his point in song. When he sang "If You Love Somebody Set Them Free" on stage that day, I heard those lyrics in a whole new way.

At one point Basil said, "Look over there, it's Denzel Washington. We have to get him." He pointed to a handsome man standing alone off to the side, quietly enjoying the parade of stars going by.

"But I don't know anything about him," I protested. Denzel hadn't yet reached the level of stardom he has today, and I wasn't good at winging it. Basil insisted. "Just walk," he said, "I'll fill you in." As we traversed the twenty feet between us and Denzel, Basil became the producer in my ear. He told me that Denzel had just shot *Cry Freedom*, in which he played black activist Stephen Biko, and that he was about to start shooting a movie about Malcolm X. By the time we reached Denzel, I had enough to go on. Denzel was delighted that someone was paying attention to him amongst the musical star power. We got Sir Richard Attenborough next, and his knowledge of apartheid, as *Cry Freedom*'s director, was deep. Now we were getting somewhere.

"Little Steven" Van Zandt was also backstage, and it was his activist passion that we were looking for. "(Ain't Gonna Play) Sun City" had railed against a luxury resort located in Bophuthatswana, a "homeland" that had been created by the South African government to forcibly relocate its black population. The song featured forty-nine artists under the collective "Artists United Against Apartheid," including Lou Reed, Rubén Blades, Bruce Springsteen, Run-D.M.C., Jimmy Cliff, Bob Dylan, and Afrika Bambaataa. It was banned in South Africa and was a Top Ten single in Canada, although it never cracked the Top Twenty in the U.S., likely because it was seen to be critical of Ronald Reagan. MTV played it, though, and it got lots of attention, especially when Daryl Hall publicly called out Queen and Rod Stewart for playing the resort.

Little Steven had been to South Africa to learn about apartheid firsthand, and was embraced by black activists in spite of his Dutch Afrikaner-sounding name. Of his Sun City efforts, he said: "We shut them down for international acts. No one of any significance has played it since the record came out. We made the connection between a cultural boycott and an economic boycott."

Our own willingness to go deeper into the politics of apartheid paid off with Jim Kerr of Simple Minds. At the end of our interview he arranged seats for us to fly with him, Archbishop Desmond Tutu, and Archbishop Trevor Huddleston (president of the Anti-Apartheid Movement and a former priest in South Africa) to Scotland to kick off the beginning of the Nelson Mandela Freedom March from Glasgow to London.

The next morning, Basil and I scrambled to make the early morning flight. I boarded the plane with Basil close behind—or so I thought. Given the importance of the passengers, security was tight, and Basil's camera gear was a bag full of beeping red lights and battery-powered thingamajigs. They held the plane for what seemed like an eternity. I worried that Basil had been detained, but I wasn't allowed off the plane. He eventually boarded with his camera, but without tape or his equipment bag, which authorities had insisted be stowed. We were now unable to interview anyone on the flight (my kingdom for an iPhone!), but the trade-off was that we got to relax for an hour and it was a treat to see how giggly and friendly Desmond Tutu could be, obviously still jazzed by the concert the day before.

In 1980, the City Council of Glasgow had been the first to grant Mandela "the Freedom of the City." It was therefore the perfect place to kick off the 590-mile Freedom March, which ended with a rally in London's Hyde Park at which Desmond Tutu and Trevor Huddleston spoke, Simple Minds sang "Mandela Day," and the whole crowd sang "Nelson Mandela" with The Special A.K.A. and Jerry Dammers. It was a triumphant event, and great to see Dammers to get the recognition he deserved.

The entire Freedom at 70 campaign put added pressure on world governments to take a stand on apartheid and was instrumental in changing the perception of Mandela as a terrorist into an understanding of Mandela as a political prisoner, his actions a rational response to apartheid and his mission to be a leader of peace. Mandela was released from prison on February 11, 1990, and he was elected president of South Africa on May 10, 1994.

The Mandela events were a significant eye-opener for me. I saw firsthand how powerful the cultural zeitgeist could be in communicating information and galvanizing action around an idea. I was energized by the power of popular culture to shift perspectives, especially on human rights issues; grateful to have had such incredible access; and, I believe, journalistically bolder for the experience.

ABOUT THE SAME TIME as I was growing into my activist shoes, Laurie was being sought by *The Journal*. It wasn't the first time the CBC had come after her, but following the birth of her daughter Hadley, she thought it was time to heed the call. According to Laurie's later take: "Making TV with a budget was so much FUN!!! That was actually the big pull (besides the reputation of *The Journal*); it was moving from the City model of making TV with no money, to making the best documentaries in the world on whatever subject I was covering. That was nice."

I was sad to see her go. I admired her ease with artists and her innovative ideas, and we'd grown to be fond friends. One of my favourite Laurie specials was *Musicians as Artists*, which featured Joni Mitchell, Tony Bennett, and Ronnie Wood among a host of others. Laurie wasn't willing to put it to air until she got Miles Davis, and she finally did, at his home in New York City. She returned with a sketch that he'd drawn for her and a story about his gobbing a big green loogey on the floor and then sighing reflectively as he stared at it: "Well there's a piece of me there."

Jana Lynne White was my new co-host. Moses had encountered her while she was working as a creative director at Shane Lunny Productions in Vancouver. Jana had an impressive pedigree in advertising, television hosting, photography, and acting, and she was a strong feminist. I was going to learn a lot from her.

Jana took the lead on a special called *The Big Tease*. It dealt with female objectification, gender issues, and power.

A *NewMusic* sex special? No shortage of material there. Glam Metal bands like Jackl, Mötley Crüe, Warrant, and Poison were pumping out video sexcapades populated by busy ladies washing cars, pillow fighting, mud wrestling, and operating heavy power tools and fire hoses. The fabric shortage continued unabated.

Even the tamer videos were pretty sensational: Aerosmith enlisted Steven Tyler's daughter Liv and actress Alicia Silverstone to doff their Catholic girls school uniforms, don leather pants, and head off on a shoplifting adventure, followed by some healthy exercise on a stripper pole.

As Naomi Wolf told Jana, "Women function as decorative accessories or visual bytes. Young boys think, 'I'm entitled to have my girlfriend look like that,' and girls think, 'I can't be sexual unless I look like Miss July, unless I get breast implants.'"

While directors equated heavy breathing with heavy rotation, hypersexualized images in music videos weren't always a man's idea. Cher straddled a gun turret on the fo'c'sle of the USS *Missouri* in her video for "If I Could Turn Back Time," and most female stars were under pressure to present their sexy model best. Like the exquisite Jann Arden, who was once told: "You know you're twenty-five pounds away from superstardom in the U.S."

The Big Tease special asked artists to explain their choices. Vince Neil from Mötley Crüe defaulted to the "it's art" excuse. Of his solo "Sister of Pain" video, in which he cavorted with a girl robot tightly clad in metal and leather, he said: "As an artist you have to stick with what you feel is right for the video. Now, just to put in a bunch of girls in bathing suits for no reason at all is pretty lame. But if it's part of the song, if it goes along with the theme, then it's okay."

In a separate interview, Concrete Blonde's Johnette Napolitano snorted in response to that, saying: "If I see a Vince Neil video I'm embarrassed. For *him*. It affects his credibility as an artist, because he needs to rely on that. Sorry, Vince. Idiot."

The Kids in the Hall provided a satirical illustration in their video for "Terriers." Bruce McCulloch, performing in a graveyard on a bright sunny day, suddenly stops playing his guitar and turns to the two ladies dressed in black bikinis and veils dancing behind him and says: "You're scantily clad and have nothing to do with the narrative—therefore it's sexist." Then he turns to camera and says: "Wow, that hurt."

According to Tania Natscheff, producer of MuchMusic's *Power 30* (which had replaced the *Pepsi Power Hour*), metal led the wave but hip-hop soon rode it. "It's been a long time since you've seen a metal video put out images like that because it's just not cool anymore," she told us. "The attention is off metal and on to hip-hop, because hip-hop is now the offender."

Dr. Dre, N.W.A, and Biz Markie may have been sincere about pressing societal issues, but the hip-hop video world was less than progressive. The men were portrayed as "playas" and what they were playing with were "hoes and bitches." Shabba Ranks had "A Trailer Load a Girls," 2 Live Crew had them "As Nasty as They Wanna Be," and Snoop Doggy Dog's offering "Can You Control Yo Hoe" included the line: "You've got to put that bitch in her place/Even if it's slapping her in the face."

Thank heavens the ladies fought back with feminist rap. Salt-N-Pepa's "Ain't Nuthin' But A She Thing" showed they were fly, singing about gender-based wage inequality and confidently in control of their own bodies and brains: "Treat me like a sex-object (that ain't smooth) / Underestimate the mind, oh yeah you're a fool..."

Meshell Ndegeocello and Erykah Badu were two more empowered voices included in the *Big Tease* special; single mom Macy Gray, too. Though Gray said she wasn't a feminist...because she didn't accept that women were equal to men. "We're better," she said. And there was also, of course, the Queen.

Right from the beginning, Queen Latifah exuded confidence, saying, "I'm twenty years old and I see a lot of women who are really so unsuccessful and have no ambition, and their only desire is to attain material things but not on their own. They like to go through people. Either they're using their friends or using a man or using their body as a trade for whatever it buys you. That's cheap to me, that's really tacky."

Latifah ran her own label (Flavor Unit Records), and she was in charge. In 1994 she released "U.N.I.T.Y.," a song about disrespect and domestic violence, ending each verse with the line, "Who you calling a bitch?" It won the Grammy for best Rap Solo Performance in 1995.

You can't talk about musical feminists without mentioning Madonna, who had no problem expressing herself to us or anyone else: "People say, 'You have penis envy—you just wish you had a dick.' I say I do—it's in my brain. So if having a dick means having masculinity and being aggressive and having balls or whatever, it's all a state of mind anyway. You don't need the apparatus."

And we can always count on Annie Lennox (who recorded "Sisters Are Doin' It for Themselves" with Aretha Franklin) to offer thoughtful context. As she said to Jana, "I heard a quote from Madonna which I found very interesting. She said she wanted power and isn't that what everyone wants. I really would love to talk to her about that. Because we want power, but it's the quality of our power. Do we want to dominate people with our power? Do we want to be macho with our power? Do we want to be chauvinistic with our power and to what end? This is the ultimate question."

I was, of course, contributing interviews to the special, but I had a lot to learn about feminism myself. I had not yet come around to owning the name. The first time I heard Sarah McLachlan calling herself a "humanist" rather than a feminist, I thought to myself: that's it. I know I disappointed Jana mightily one night by denying the word. She called me on it twenty-three years later.

Jana remembers us being in Moses' office one night—he always held a private party in his executive suite during the MuchMusic Video Awards. I was newly appointed as director of music programming at Much and Jana was arguing with a radio exec about being a feminist. The radio guy told her (while apparently staring at her chest) that there was no way I could be a feminist because if I was, I wouldn't have gotten the MuchMusic job. Jana yelled over to me, "Denise, are you a feminist?" Apparently I yelled back, "I'm a humanist!", an answer that crushed her. I thought I was being clever. I wasn't. Not only that, I'd misrepresented Sarah.

Sarah McLachlan is a trailblazer. In 1997 she, with her friends at Nettwerk Records, launched the groundbreaking Lilith Fair, a festival celebrating female performers. Not only did the first tour gross over $16 million, donating money to women's shelters all over North America, it changed the way women were heard and promoted.

Lilith Fair turned the heads of promoters who'd been resistant to putting even two female artists on the same bill—assuming the show wouldn't sell—and radio programmers who resisted playing female artists back to back on the air. The widely held view was that listeners would tune out.

And about that "humanist" remark. What Sarah had actually said to our cameras was: "Feminism for me is always evolving. I consider myself a humanist first and foremost and I believe that encompasses feminism, the idea that we should all be treated equally and have access to everything that we do, but the same could be said for many minority groups. There's so much inequality on so many levels and that's what I'm striving for as a humanist and a feminist."

Too bad Caitlan Moran's book *How to Be a Woman* wasn't around then. I could have used her advice:

> So here is the quick way of working out if you're a feminist. Put your hand in your pants.
>
> a. Do you have a vagina? and
>
> b. Do you want to be in charge of it?
>
> If you said "yes" to both, then congratulations! You're a feminist.

I improved. In 2000, I received the Woman of the Year Award from Canadian Women in Communications, in part for "cultivating a work environment in which women flourish."

I got the award, but there were many who deserved the credit. It takes vision and determination to achieve balanced representation, and at Much that meant everyone from Moses to Ron Waters, Sarah Crawford, John Martin, Nancy Oliver, David Kines, and many more who bought into a non-traditional workplace and supported diversity and equal opportunity. While I was at MuchMusic and MuchMoreMusic, over half the on-air presenters were women, and 50 percent of program producers were women. The environment was chaotic, but the culture was progressive. Lack of gumption might hold you back, but gender consideration seldom would.

AS I BECAME MORE interested in societal issues, working on the *The NewMusic's* one hour specials provided an incredibly rewarding outlet — and an education.

The NewMusic special called *In Your Face: Violence in Music* was a highlight. It wasn't a new theme — Tipper Gore had made sure the Parents Music Resource Center's version of what needed censoring and stickering reached our attention during the infamous Senate hearings of the eighties. But in the early nineties, there were increasingly more extreme video images aimed at shock value. The "dental horror" genre videos — Green Day's graphic teeth-pulling scenes or the close-ups of Marilyn Manson's dental hardware — were unnerving enough, but there were also themes of violence being explored in hard rock, death metal, outlaw country, and gangsta rap videos. Sometimes the imagery was graphic, as in Mötley Crüe's "You're All I Need" (the first version of which showed a man killing his wife), while others seemed innocuous, like Michael Jackson's "The Way You Make Me Feel," in which Michael stalks a beautiful young woman down a dark street while leering men jeer and crowd her.

Some artists explained, "We're just talking about reality and reality is about death and violence. And unfortunately that's the down side of human existence" (Karl Agell, Corrosion of Conformity). Some were matter of fact: "What I'm writing about is love and the extremes of love and it's news to nobody that extremes of love involve violence" (Nick Cave, regarding his video for "Jack the Ripper"). Chuck D of Public Enemy said he was using his platform to inform: "We live in a violent society from the root." Some had radical notions: "If you really want to boost the economy [in America], the government should have its own channel and they should have executions pay-per-view. They're going to kill the people anyway. I'd pay fifty dollars to watch a guy get the gas chamber" (Henry Rollins, Black Flag). And, some were just…well, you fill in the word. Dave Mustaine from Megadeth (which some called "the thinking man's rock band") said about Tipper Gore: "Well, if she was my wife and she was trying to wreck music for everybody else and my campaign hinged on the fact whether or not she could keep her mouth shut, I'd shut it for her."

The videos could be raw for the sake of raw, like the Prodigy's "Smack My Bitch Up." But there were also important videos and songs that used strong imagery to draw attention to serious issues, from racism and police brutality to domestic violence, misogyny, and sexual abuse.

One gripping a cappella performance we shot was Tori Amos singing "Me and a Gun," a song about her own rape. She looked directly into the camera and calmly sang, "It was me and a gun, and a man on my back, and I sang holy holy as he buttoned down his pants…Yes, I wore a slinky red thing, does that mean I should spread for you, your friends, your father, Mr. Ed."

She told Jana that she wrote the song in a parking lot after seeing the movie *Thelma and Louise*. It reminded her of something that had happened to her.

Jana asked: "I imagine that it's cathartic to write it; I wonder if it continues to be good for you to sing it?"

Tori responded very slowly, carefully: "Each night that I sing it, I go into a trance. And I feel really freed singing it. It's exhausting singing it, but at the same time I can sing it."

Other female artists just got angry. Diamanda Galás said of her "Double-Barrel Prayer" video: "I carry a gun because I do not believe that we [women] are supposed to walk down the street anymore looking invisible. The vermin are on the street. Maybe they were mistreated and all this, but I don't have the time to do a psychological study on everyone who accosts me on the street…Violence is here to stay. I'm just talking about violence to defend your peace."

Sister Souljah said about her video for "The Big Payback by Choice": "There's no excuse for black men or any man to oppress a woman — sometimes when a black man looks at his real enemies, be it the government or white society or white supremacy, you look at it as something that's so hard to fight against and win, so instead of fighting against...You might go home and disrespect a black woman. And it's a weakness and brothers have to start to look at and deal with, so they at least know the difference between their friends and their enemies."

The musical expression of violence as an issue was rife with stereotypes and double standards that needed decoding. Garth Brooks' "The Thunder Rolls" video took a clear stand against domestic violence but was initially banned in the U.S., while the Charlie Daniels Band's song "Simple Man" warned that if someone breaks into Charlie's house, there's always the "twelve-gauge shotgun waiting on the other side." The song was criticized as racist and advocating vigilantism, but went platinum.

You could always count on Ice-T for an interesting take. When I asked him why he wore a large gun made of gold on a chain around his neck, he said, "In our country, my president said that military weapons equals power which equals peace, military strength. And then they take our income taxes every year and they say they're spending it on peace, but they spend it on weapons. So I guess this is a peace symbol."

Daniel Caudeiron, president of the Black Music Association of Canada, said: "The proudest thing that hip-hop could do in the mid-nineties is to actually move from talking about what's been done and how enraged we are about it, but to articulate what *should* be done...You not only can burn things down, but you can build things up. That's the one thing that's missing right now."

As I've reviewed the *NM* special on violence, I was reminded of Devon Martin's "Mr. Metro" video, released in 1990 and partially funded by VideoFact. It was two years before the Rodney King riots in L.A. and the song was inspired by Devon's detention in the U.S., but the video was shot in Toronto. There was no mistaking the plea for police to be more sensitive to the concerns of the black community. Devon was threatened with a defamation suit unless he edited out certain images of Toronto police officers in the video. Devon told us, "It's your responsibility as an artist to be very careful about what you say, because as an artist you have a lot of power." I remember both the tension and the pride in the building as Much chose to stand behind his work and award Devon a MuchMusic Video Award.

In Your Face: Violence in Music was also lauded, winning two awards at the 1993 Yorktown Short Film and Video Festival for myself and co-producer John Marshall.

Still, that *NM* special needs a sequel. I wish there was still a weekly culture show on television that regularly explored the issues and nuances when our vanguard artists — musicians, poets, filmmakers, dancers, authors, and visual artists — take a stand.

ANOTHER NM SPECIAL THAT deserves an update is *Earth to Ground Control*, especially given recent international commitments to combat climate change and the responsibility to meet those targets — voluntary though they may be. The 1987 special was triggered by a video to support the *Greenpeace Rainbow Warriors* compilation, cut to R.E.M.'s "It's the End of the World As We Know It (And I Feel Fine)" and containing footage of dreadful pollution, toxic waste, oil spills, nuclear testing, clear-cutting, whaling, ensnared dolphins, and oil-soaked birds.

Many artists were environmental activists, and that number was growing as news about the deforestation of the rainforest got around. The Grateful Dead announced the Rex Foundation, which funded the Rainforest Action Network, and Sting journeyed to the Brazilian rainforest and set up the Rainforest Foundation Fund after meeting with the Kayapo people whose lands, traditions, and lives were threatened by logging, mining, and damming.

Record labels felt the pressure to examine their own consumptive processes, especially in the manufacturing and distribution of CDs, which is heavily based on petroleum products. Artists pushed for recycled cardboard packaging instead of plastic jewel cases, the use of vegetable-based inks, and the abolishment of the long box and other forms of excess packaging.

We had no trouble filling an hour with interviews with a huge variety of artists, from Midnight Oil to Living Colour to the B-52s. Bruce Hornsby's "Look Out Any Window" was inspired by the dumping of poisonous Kepone into Virginia's James River, and the Parachute Club's "Big Big World," Murray McLauchlan's "Modern Age," and D.O.A.'s "Hole In The Sky" all had strong environmental themes as well.

George Harrison was performing with the Traveling Wilburys at the time and he, too, was passionate about the environment: "In England they're saying, 'We have to try and think of a way to stop them pumping all this crap in the rivers!'...No one's thought of just arresting the bastards! But they're not interested in that because they've all got their hands in each other's pockets." That was the quote I included in the special, but there was lots of gold in that interview. The Traveling Wilburys were in a crazy mood—giddy after doing press all day—and they tried to lighten George up as he continued:

GEORGE HARRISON: Y'know there's more poison poured on golf courses than you can imagine and they tell you on the golf course, they put up signs—"DO NOT LICK YOUR BALLS." They have signs out!

TOM PETTY: It's true.

JEFF LYNNE: I thought it was in case your broke your neck.

Robbie Robertson urged us to consider stewardship and respect of the land versus ownership and defilement. He held up his hands, offering a simple choice: "This is beautiful; this is a mess. Pick one."

We were particularly concerned with representing the First Nations perspective as honourably as we could. Jana suggested we should "Burn with Vern" and asked her friend, Cree elder Vern Harper, if he would welcome us in a sweat lodge ceremony. Vern is a renowned medicine man. Many came to know of Vern more widely when he was sought out by Hurricane Carter after The Hurricane was released from prison.

The sweat was an intense experience and took me, as Van Morrison would say, "into the mystic." We were told to wear something made of a natural fibre that would cover our whole bodies and no jewelry, to fast beforehand with no coffee or tea, and to bring a gift of tobacco. Also, we weren't to be menstruating at the time of the sweat.

It was a sunny summer day as we drove west on the 401 heading for Vern's camp, and I was feeling apprehensive. I was a bit of a claustrophobe, and knew that the heat would be extreme and the tent packed with others. I looked out the window, thinking I would take a mental picture

of the big blue sky to secure in my mind's eye, something open and airy
to focus on if it got too much. As I looked across the fields, I noticed a
hawk flying low and straight and pointed it out to Jana: "Quick, look. A
red-tailed hawk." She had lots of time to see it. The hawk was tracking
the car precisely in speed and direction, and it stayed with us, straight
and sure, for miles, until we turned north off the highway. I'd never seen
a bird do that before. Strange.

Eventually we found Vern's camp. There was a small house beside a boisterous little river, and a fire was burning outside a round, squat structure
about five feet high, laden with blankets and tarps covering a wooden frame.
The sweat lodge. A few young men were about and a couple of children.
We offered our present of tobacco and stood around by the fire. Two of
the men were fire keepers, lifting heavy round rocks of varying sizes from
a wheelbarrow and into the sacred flame, rearranging them with a shovel
and a pitchfork so they could heat uniformly.

Vern said a blessing and there was a sweet-grass smudge. Then we bent
down, crawled into the lodge, and settled on the ground. There were about
eight of us, I think, Jana and I the only non–First Nations. There were two
children of about eight and ten years old, and the rest were bare-chested
men of varying ages.

When we were all sitting cross-legged in the circle around the fire pit, the
fire keepers brought in the stones and arranged them in the centre, within
inches of our feet. The rocks glowed with heat, glistening and sometimes
popping loudly, making me jump. Vern smiled at me in gentle amusement
like he would at a child. I sat up straight, my head against the roof, trying
to keep my face as far away from the heat as I could. Soon Vern signalled
for the flap to be closed and we were in darkness, save for the red veins of
the rocks and the embers in the pit. Vern had explained that there would
be four rounds, for fire, water, wind, and earth. Each one might last up to
thirty minutes and with each session he would lead prayers for our ances-
tors, for ourselves, for individuals in need, for courage, for compassion, for
peace, for Mother Earth. We were instructed to think of a living person, a
friend or relative that needed our prayers, and then it began.

I tried to focus on Vern's words, some in English, some in Cree, following the rhythm of his voice to find my calm. I counted my breath in and
out, willing my heart and my mind to be still. I tried not to think of the

mounting heat, the crampedness of the lodge, the slight disturbance when someone scratched or shifted or wiped away sweat. I tried to contain my fear that one of the rocks would explode like a bomb. It was soon so hot and close that I found myself hyperventilating. *It's too hot. I can't breathe. I'm going to suffocate. I have to get OUT!* It took serious willpower not to bolt. I managed to focus again on my breathing, listening the rhythm of Vern's words and swaying in place to take myself out of my own head. I had no idea how long we'd been in there when Vern stopped speaking and breathed deeply, the flap suddenly open and the sunlight streaming in. I'd made it through the first round.

Jana and I were drenched, the children were smiling, the men calm and sweaty, Vern calm and cool.

The fire keeper brought in more grandfather and grandmother rocks. *You're kidding,* I thought. *More? It's going to get hotter?* This was no s'mores party 'round a campfire. The hot rocks cracked against each other like molten bowling balls, throwing up sparks as they were positioned in the pit. Then the flap closed again and Vern began anew.

Sweat was salty in my eyes and I was itchy everywhere, but I stopped myself from scratching my burning skin, convinced that my nails would slice it into ribbons. I willed my brain to focus again on Vern's voice, on my breathing, on slowing my heart rate. It started to feel more trancelike in this round but it was still a mighty struggle to keep it together. Eventually, again, the flap opened and the sunlight streamed in — along with more molten stones.

I remember the round where we focused on a friend in need. Thinking about another's suffering made my own anxiety ephemeral in comparison and I had a glimpse into the idea that there might be a healing power around us. Perhaps not a physical healing, but maybe, just maybe, a spiritual one.

The last round was the hottest ever and I was not coping. Just when I thought I couldn't bear another second, heart racing, mind freaking out and urging me to flee, Vern leaned over in the dark, adroitly finding me across the stones. He was handing me something. My focus shifted instantly to the object. I felt what it was. It was a hawk's wing, the base bound with leather and beads — light, yes, as a feather. I held it gently, amazed, my panic calmed.

After the flap was opened for the final time and we emerged into the cool air, we went to the river and poured cold water on our skin. I felt very connected to the natural world. As I handed the wing back to Vern, I remembered the hawk that had paralleled our car and told him about it. He just smiled and nodded.

"Your hawk told me what you needed," he said. "Your spirit guide."

Vern laughed later when I marvelled at the heat and told me the sweat wasn't as hot as usual because there were children with us. Ha!

When Jana interviewed Vern for the environmental special she asked: "Will we save the planet?"

"Yes," he said, "I believe so, but we have a lot of work ahead of us and we have to get spiritually, mentally, and physically in shape. Yes, I believe. I don't believe the creator will allow any nuclear wars, but we have to live in our own garbage. We'll choke on it if we don't do anything about it. So I believe the planet can be saved but we really have to move now. We have to make a conscious effort. All the people have to start being unpolluted within their own lives."

As Greenpeace's Bob Hunter remarked on that show: "People would say concern about the ecology is just a fad. And I say, if it's a fad, it's the last one."

Years later, George Harrison's quote about "just arresting the bastards!" rang in my ears when I got involved as a steward with Lake Ontario Waterkeeper. LOW is part of Robert F. Kennedy, Jr.'s Waterkeeper Alliance organization, which uses the U.S. Clean Water Act to take polluters to court, keeps the bounty when they win, and goes on to fight another battle. In Canada—where there's no such bounty—it's harder than ever to win cases against polluters. As Mark Mattson, head of LOW, said in a recent speech:

> The tools I used to use as an environmental lawyer in the 1990s are all gone today.
>
> I used the federal Fisheries Act to get mercury from coal-fired power plants out of Great Lakes fish. That Act has been gutted.
>
> I used the Navigable Waters Protection Act to defend your right to move freely on Canadian waterways, just as our ancestors did. That Act has been rewritten. The word "Water" isn't even in the title anymore.
>
> I used the Canadian Environmental Assessment Act to protect your right to comment on decisions that affect your future. It no longer applies to most major projects in Canada.

Gord Downie of The Tragically Hip works with Lake Ontario Waterkeeper, as do Joseph Boyden, Edward Burtynsky, Karen Percy Lowe and many others. Artists, authors, actors, athletes, and more, all with a goal to achieve swimmable, fishable, drinkable water in Canada. It's more than a fad. Join us. www.waterkeeper.ca.

THE NEWMUSIC SPECIALS WEREN'T all deadly serious.

One of my favourites was *Rock and Roll Ailments.* Myles Goodwyn was right when April Wine sang "Rock and Roll Is a Vicious Game." We amassed quite a collection of artists complaining about chronic ailments caused by percussive flailing, screaming nodal abuse, fan entanglements, and more.

We talked to Max Weinberg, Bruce Springsteen's drummer, about having to tape his sticks to his hands to combat tendinitis from the nightly four-hour Springsteen sessions. By then, he'd had seven operations. Billy Joel's percussive piano playing has resulted in tennis elbow and arthritis. Pete Townshend suffers from tinnitus, a noise-induced hearing loss that results in permanent ringing in the ears. Ozzy was on a steady regimen of moisturizers, vitamins, and humidifiers for his voice, but when that didn't work he stopped drinking and smoking and got a Lifecycle ("Not that I'm becoming a Buddhist monk or anything," he deflected). Paul Young had wrecked cartilage in both knees from sliding across the stage, not to mention cracked ribs from a fan who hugged him too hard. Simple Minds' Jim Kerr also sustained crowd damage, wrestling with an audience member for the microphone and then popping himself in the mouth with it, knocking out a front tooth. Joe Strummer rolled up his pant leg and showed me a gruesome, suppurating gash on his inside calf, caused by the top of his cowboy boot grinding against his leg. He was touring with the Pogues at the time, and like the late, great Stompin' Tom he had taken to fiercely banging his foot to keep time, further infecting the wound every night. Joe needed medical help.

Carpal tunnel syndrome was a common complaint among guitar players, usually brought on by relentless bar chording on low-slung axes. Mike Rutherford gave up playing his double-necked guitar because it became too heavy, and Joni told me she had to stop playing electric guitar on tour because it was too much for her back, strained by polio as a child.

Then of course there's Rock Neck—a repetitive strain injury common to heavy metal guitarists, often spread virally to head-banging fan populations as well. "Guitar Face" isn't an ailment per se—technically, it's more of a condition.

Nodes are a seriously scary diagnosis, and vocalists apply a retinue of potions, procedures, and prayers before they hit the stage. Singers avoid air conditioning like vampires avoid the sun, and private jets start looking like a bargain compared to the germ swamp on commercial airplanes if you're in the middle of a big tour.

Every promoter has the name of the local star doctor on speed dial. These medical miracle workers are part sorcerer, part shrink. Their job is to console, prescribe, inject, kiss it better, and get your talent onto the stage in time to rescue a half-million-dollar gross. The show must go on.

For the rest of the band, that good old B12 shot is never a bad idea—and while you're at it, might as well get the crew done as well. "Bend over, mates! Swab that, please, Nurse. We don't know where it's been."

EVERY *NM* SPECIAL WAS a learning experience. *Rock and Roll and Reading* was no exception—and not just because of its awesome reading list.

Asking musicians about their literary influences was an original Daniel Richler idea. He was producing a segment for Frontier College, a literacy organization whose origins stretch back to 1899, when volunteers travelled to remote lumber camps and mining communities to help people learn to read. A century later, Frontier College is still working, tutoring "adults in the workplace, homeless street youth, prison inmates, people with disabilities, and newcomers to Canada."

According to Frontier, even today, one in six Canadian adults cannot read the headlines in a newspaper.

Laurie, Jana, and I continued to ask musicians about their literary influences and produced two one-hour *RnRnR* specials after Daniel had left for the CBC.

It was easy to assume that musicians might be strong readers—especially in the eighties, when there was not much to do on the road between gigs. That VHS video library on the tour bus got old pretty quick. We'd often find musicians—especially the lyricists—sitting around backstage with a paperback in hand. These were people who worked with words, so it was no surprise to find a wealth of literary references in pop music and videos.

For example, Eurythmics' song "Sexcrime" was based on George Orwell's book *1984*. Red Rider's third record was called *Neruda*, after poet Pablo Neruda. The Grapes of Wrath's band name is the title of a John Steinbeck novel, the Police song "Don't Stand So Close to Me" references "that book by Nabokov" (*Lolita*), and Tom Petty's video for "Don't Come Around Here No More" features Tom as the Mad Hatter slicing cake from the torso of a confectionary Alice. Books weren't always seen as a benevolent influence, as Michelle Shocked revealed. She told us she was put in a mental hospital by her mother, because, as her doctor said, she was "under the influence of literature."

The reading special opened doors previously closed, too. We got the first interview we'd ever scored with Rush's media-shy Neil Peart because I'd asked to talk about books. Neil, an author himself, filled an entire tape without stopping, listing scores of influential authors—well past Ayn Rand at that point.

After the special aired, *NewMusic* viewers wrote in requesting a reading list, which we dutifully compiled, photocopied, and mailed out. It's still an intriguing list today. Here's a sample:

Jon Bon Jovi: Ernest Hemingway, Charles Bukowski

Eric Clapton: Charles Dickens

MC Hammer: *The Art of the Deal* by Donald Trump

Billy Joel: F. Scott Fitzgerald

Johnette Napolitano (Concrete Blonde): William Faulkner, Flannery O'Connor, Anaïs Nin, Edgar Allan Poe, and Henry Miller

Living Colour: Alice Walker, James Baldwin, and autobiographies of Malcolm X and Miles Davis

Jim Cuddy: Gabriel Garcia Márquez

Tom Cochrane: Pablo Neruda

Pete Townshend: Socrates, W. B. Yeats, and James Joyce

Paul McCartney: Comics

Barenaked Ladies: John Irving

Anthrax: *The Bonfire of the Vanities* by Tom Wolfe

Cyndi Lauper: *A Woman's Worth* by Marianne Williamson

Clint Black: *The Bridges of Madison County* by Robert James Waller

Daniel Lanois: *Collected Poems* by Arthur Rimbaud

Don Henley: *All the Pretty Horses* by Cormac McCarthy

The Dream Warriors: *The Wisdom of Martin Luther King, Jr.* by Alex Ayres

Kris Kristofferson: *Catch-22* by Joseph Heller

Kurt Cobain: *Perfume: The Story of A Murderer* by Patrick Suskind

Madonna: Camille Paglia

Meat Loaf: *Pet Sematary* and *'Salem's Lot* by Stephen King

Natalie Cole: The Bible

Nick Cave: *Lolita* by Vladimir Nabokov

Paddy Moloney (the Chieftains): Brian Keenan

Ron Hynes: *Dracula* by Bram Stoker

Simon Le Bon: *The Man Who Mistook His Wife for a Hat* by Oliver Sacks

Slash: *Fear and Loathing in Las Vegas* by Hunter S. Thompson

Sting: *The Gormenghast Trilogy* by Mervyn Peake

Soul Asylum: *A Confederacy of Dunces* by John Kennedy Toole

Stompin' Tom Connors: *Dialogues* by Plato

A *Morningside* producer heard about the special and asked me to talk about it on the CBC with Peter Gzowski. It was a natural fit; Peter was a great literacy advocate and raised money for Frontier College through his Peter Gzowski Invitational (PGI) Golf Tournaments.

It was an honour to be interviewed on *Morningside*, and I was happy to get up on a dark, chilly morning and drive to the old CBC Radio building on Jarvis Street. Inside it was all warmth and activity, busy producers hammering away on typewriters and yammering away on phones. I was ushered through a maze of messy cubicles into the inner studio sanctum and found myself sitting across from Peter, shy in the presence of "Captain Canada." He nodded at me, stubbed out his cigarette, and, as the red light went on, began a sonorous introduction into the mic that went something like this: "In the literacy business it's seen to be a good idea to have Margaret Atwood or Margaret Laurence or, god forbid, me telling people that reading is a good idea. What you really need is wrestlers and hockey players and musicians." He went on to describe the *RnRnReading* series. I'd brought along a few audio segments for him to play, and we settled into a conversation that was so comfortable I forgot that the whole country might be listening in. I mentioned the reading list and Peter enthused that teachers might find the whole show helpful in their classrooms. Any idea how they could get a hold of it? I don't recall my exact repsonse, but it was basically this:

"Well, if it's for educational use, just give me a ring at the station and we'll send out a copy."

Peter looked at me curiously as I blithely gave out my phone number and the segment wound up.

It wasn't until I got back to the CHUM station on Queen Street that I *really* found out just what a big deal it was to be on CBC *Morningside*.

I was greeted by the front desk receptionist, who looked ready to murder me. She was standing because a technician was under her desk, fiddling with wires. She thrust a big handful of pink message slips at me and said, "Apparently you promised all these people a copy of some tape!" The response had overloaded the switchboard—not for the last time that day.

Morningside was scheduled in the same timeslot all across the country. That meant that the show was time-delayed, starting in Newfoundland and then rolling though five more time zones until it got to the West Coast.

By the time I got to the station the show was in Halifax and moving west. Apparently, it was March Break. Teachers were home from school and every one of them, it seemed, was listening to *Morningside*. No wonder Peter cocked that bemused eyebrow at me when I gaily offered my phone number on air.

There was no way we could handle the hundreds of requests we received that day. Not only did we have no budget for tape stock; who would do the dubbing and the mailing? Happily, John O'Leary at Frontier College came to our aid. He and his staff dubbed tapes and shipped them out the door, while we at MUCH scheduled an airing at midnight and encouraged teachers to tape it as part of our "Cable in the Classroom" initiative. For me, I got a little schooling in the power of certain Canadian media, and Gzowski became a dear friend who shared his love of Canada's North with me on PGI literacy trips where we golfed on frozen lakes.

En route with Gzowski to a PGI in the North.

My other lesson was in giving credit where credit is due. I neglected to mention on the Gzowski interview that the *RnRnR* specials were originally inspired by Daniel. Years later, after a magazine article appeared in which I was erroneously given credit for something I'd never claimed (inventing *The NewMusic*, no less!), Daniel Richler wrote a scathing letter to the publication essentially calling me a "fraud." I'd had nothing to do with the article and I was hurt by his letter. I responded in writing and we got into a little public war of words. We've since made up, thank heavens, but it was a great lesson to *always* endeavour to give credit where it's due. I'm sure I've failed at that, especially in this book, and to everyone I've ever forgotten to thank, I sincerely apologize. We rarely accomplish anything meaningful on our own.

The NewMusic's SPECIAL ON corporate sponsorship was my first venture into the great and not-so-great divide between church and state—but far from my last. Navigating the lines between art and commerce, music and business, integrity and job security was to be a continual balancing act.

The special was inspired by Neil Young's "This Note's for You" video. His lyric "Ain't singing for Pepsi/Ain't singing for Coke" made it very clear where he stood on the idea of music, product placement, and corporate sponsorship: "Makes me look like a joke," he sang.

The video went into heavy rotation at Much the minute it arrived. It contained a Michael Jackson look-alike shooting a Pepsi commercial, a Whitney impersonator singing for Coke, and a Bud beer parody complete with a sunglass-wearing pooch. I can only imagine the conversation Neil surely had with director Julien Temple—likely Neil's manager, Elliot Roberts, was part of it too—about whether they should take it to extremes and shoot the MJ impersonator with his hair on fire. "Hell, yeah!" was obviously the response. It's all in there, with "Whitney" putting out the flames with soda pop. At Much, no one on the programming floor batted an eye about whether a Pepsi or a Coke commercial came on before or after the video, although I'm sure there was a discussion on the sales floor. MTV banned the video initially but reversed their decision and gave it an MTV Video Music Award.

Sponsorship of the arts was certainly nothing new. Some of the greatest artists that ever lived, like Michelangelo and Leonardo da Vinci, were sponsored by big families like the Medicis—not to mention the church, which very often controlled the big business of the day.

But wasn't rock and roll the "devil's music"? Was sponsorship an unholy bargain? Among musicians, it was a hot debate: should you take the money and run, selling your song to a deodorant commercial, or was the very idea antithetical to the nature of rock and roll? Rock and roll was born of rebellion and fuelled by subversion; what was it doing cozying up to the man?

Chrissie Hynde wrote a song called "How Much Did You Get for Your Soul?" and Howard Jones was one of many musicians who joined Neil's chorus, saying, "I hate it. I will not be sponsored by anyone. To me it's like selling a piece of your soul...People that do it, they go down in my esteem so fast. I mean, do you *need* the money that badly? They don't. Because the people that are doing it, they don't need the money, so it's like sheer greed."

There was tobacco on tours, perfume on shelves, beer on buildings. Neil told me he hated the idea of looking up from the stage to see a brewery logo lit up over his head and suggested they should sponsor the "Molson Home for the Homeless" instead. Then he grinned broadly: "I'm starting to like that idea!" he said. In Toronto, Massey Hall was a Labatt Blue venue; what's now the Sony Centre (and, in the interim, the Hummingbird Centre) was . then the O'Keefe Centre; and we cheekily referred to Maple Leaf Gardens as Molson Leaf Gardens. Brewery sponsorships were a way to fund ever more expensive touring undertakings, such as Labatt Breweries' reported $25-million investment in the Rolling Stones' *Steel Wheels* tour in 1989. My promoter friend Rob Bennett, who ran a carefully curated concert business promoting artists like Stephane Grappelli and Van Morrison, told me he was doing his best to adapt. He joked, "I've just bought some plastic garbage cans, some hops and bitters. I should be back in the concert business in a few months."

As for the great corporate sponsorship divide, Michael Jackson (whose lawyers threatened a lawsuit over the video) was clearly on the other side. When Jackson's $15-million Pepsi deal was announced with great fanfare by the president of Pepsi in May 1985, Jackson walked to the podium and said in his whispery speaking voice: "This is a great honour. Thank you, Mr. Enrico and Pepsi Associates. Thank you."

Don Johnson, Lionel Richie, and Tina Turner were also aboard the Pepsi promotional bandwagon, while Whitney Houston, Elton John, David Bowie, and George Michael ("If it was okay for Elvis Presley...") lined up with Coca-Cola. Grace Jones announced her Canada Dry sponsorship deal in Toronto by taking a sip, spewing soda all over her face, and delivering the tag line, "You don't have to be sweet to be good," laughing. There was a lot of pop in pop music.

Michelob had Eric Clapton, Steve Winwood, and Genesis in its spots, as once the Platters, Kool & the Gang, and the Commodores had sung for

Schlitz. The Thompson Twins went with Swatch watches, Aretha Franklin with Amoco gasoline. But it had to be a good match to be effective. k.d. lang would never be the right choice for Schneiders.

Some artists were on the fence: like Robert Palmer, who said, "I don't really see it as evil. After all, if you're a fan of a group and you see something hanging up for some soft drink, you don't think they're all going to drink it. You don't associate them with it particularly. Where on the other hand Michael Jackson makes an advertisement for it, that's going the other way. Mind you, it would be difficult to resist at those prices."

Other artists did more than resist. When Bette Midler declined to sing for a Ford commercial, the ad company hired an impersonator and produced a "sound-alike" commercial. Midler sued Ford and the ad agency Young & Rubicam and won on appeal. The court ruled that she had a "right of publicity" in her voice and ordered $400,000 in damages. It wasn't the $10 million "The Divine Miss M" had sued for, but it set an important precedent.

And, of course, there are the legions of artists who were never asked to sponsor a brand but wished they had been. If you were *going* to get involved, the trick seemed to be to what extent. I'm reminded of that old joke: "We've established what you are, madam, now we're just negotiating the price."

The brand will want it *all*. They'll want the artist to drink, wear, and sleep with the product. It's a wonder tour jackets don't look like Formula One jumpsuits. But it's not without risk. The magic dust that makes someone a star is powerful stuff, until the stars don't stay in alignment. Witness the sponsor exodus away from sports figures like Tiger Woods, Magic Johnson, and Lance Armstrong. Pepsi dropped its sponsorship of Michael Jackson at the end of 1993 when the King of Pop ended his world tour, saying he was addicted to painkillers. It was the same year the child sexual abuse allegations surfaced.

Brand association in songs wasn't new, of course. Car mentions in popular songs were quite common. Commander Cody was gonna drive his pappy to drinkin' if he didn't stop drivin' that Hot Rod Lincoln, Wilson Pickett loved his Mustang Sally, and Prince was coveting a little red Corvette (actually a woman). But times had changed since Janis asked the Lord to buy her a Benz. What was new was that it was becoming less about a simple (and likely non-recompensed) admiration for the brand and more about getting paid.

The difference in the eighties was that when a song mentioning a product moved up the charts, the deals started to happen on the *backs* of the song. The most famous was Run-D.M.C.'s "My Adidas." Adidas wasn't at the table in the beginning, but after they saw sales of their running shoes spike, they did a million-dollar deal with Run-D.M.C. and a clothing line was developed. Once people got a whiff of *that* action, the game was on. Mention the product, shoot the video, and wait for the FedEx truck to arrive bearing free product and maybe a cheque. It was a gamble, of course; there was no guarantee the truck would arrive.

Booze was a big one. We saw videos with shots of Cristal, Hennessy, and Rémy Martin. Snoop was "sippin on Tanqueray" in "G Funk (Intro)," and Busta Rhymes collaborated with Sean Combs (a.k.a. P. Diddy, a.k.a. Puff Daddy) on "Pass the Courvoisier." Then the trend shifted from showing off someone else's brand to pumping up thine own. Combs used his brand power to launch and market Cîroc vodka in the U.S.; Jermaine Dupri became a partner in 3 Vodka and Snoop Dog in Landry Cognac; and Pharrell Williams went for the ladies' market with strawberry and peach Q Qream. It was all spoofed in a *30 Rock* episode where Jack Donaghy, played by Alec Baldwin, enlists real-life rapper Ghostface Killah to do a commercial to help him unload his terrible Donaghy Estate Sparkling Wine.

According to Agenda Inc., a San Francisco–based marketing company, 59 different brands had been mentioned 645 times in the songs that made it into the top twenty on the *Billboard* 100 chart in the first half of 2004. The biggest brand name-dropper was Kanye West, who that year mentioned nineteen brands in four singles. And he was just getting started.

As product placement started to become prominent in music videos, it created the "church and state" friction I mentioned earlier. MuchMusic depended on advertisers, and there was concern that this was the beginning of a trend that would shift advertisers from buying commercial airtime (i.e. money to the stations) versus paying to place product directly in the video (i.e. money to the artists). It was a discussion complicated by the fact that music videos were essentially advertisements in the first place, and there was a sidebar issue, when the product was booze, about marketing alcohol to underage viewers.

"Thou shalt have no logos higher than thine own" became a commandment after Moses noticed musicians arriving at the station sporting big

Roots logos on their chests. (Roots would cleverly invite visiting stars to their Toronto showroom an hour or two before their appearance at the station.) Roots wasn't an advertiser with Much. Moses would insist: "How can we convince them to pay for it when you give it away for free?"

Excellent point.

When I was head of Much, I can't remember ever refusing to play a video because of the product placement, but by then product logos were often pixelated out before the video was delivered for television.

Expectations around product placement eventually simmered down. Deals for artist-named perfumes and clothing lines were brokered up front, and the "integrity" stigma mostly melted away. As Neil Young said to me a few years later: "Yup. I think we lost that one, the corporate sponsorship battle, but what a great fight it was." There are always associations that feel like a stretch — take the Canadian Country Music Association's Kraft Cheez Whiz Fans' Choice Award (2003-2007), for example — but sponsorship is now an accepted part of funding an expensive music show and nobody blinks an eye.

I'm someone who greets sponsors with open arms for charitable endeavours, where without good partners, good works may not happen. But it's got to be a sincere, symbiotic pairing. Our *NewMusic* special gave me a valuable lesson on corporate sponsorship, and it was only the beginning. Later at Much, I would learn about protecting the integrity of the brand. At Sony, when the bottom fell out of CD sales, we looked to sponsor partnerships to extend our marketing reach. But at CBC, I protested advertising on radio until the day I was "restructured." No regrets. It's still the right play.

WORK-LIFE BALANCE IS AN EXTREME SPORT

"You live and learn. At any rate, you live."
— DOUGLAS ADAMS, *MOSTLY HARMLESS:*
HITCHHIKER'S GUIDE TO THE GALAXY BOOK 5

I WAS FINDING RELEVANCE and reward in my work—and I was obsessed with working hard and performing well—but that didn't mean I wasn't keeping a weather eye out for love. It had been almost five years since I'd moved east from Vancouver, and I still hadn't found what I was looking for in that department, until my boss intervened.

One Saturday night, I got a call from John Martin. He asked if I would come over to his apartment to talk about the show.

This was odd. John had never asked for a meeting at home; he barely asked for one at work. My first reaction was paranoia—I'd obviously done something wrong. He said he was making his famous spaghetti sauce and would I pop by around seven? *The NewMusic* was on at eight and the opportunity to avoid seeing myself on TV was a no-brainer, so off I went. When I got there, John's friend Murray McLauchlan was sitting on the couch, glass of red wine in hand. Of course I knew who he was; I'd done some of my best helicopter dancing to his performances at Mariposa back in the day, and I'd thrust a microphone in his face while he was exiting the stage after winning Juno awards. But we'd never been properly introduced. I had an inkling that he might be fun—the last time I'd seen Murray in person, he and John were walking across Queen Street with giant papier mâché fish on their heads to take their spots in a Caribana parade.

After dinner, John flicked around the channels before settling on Katharine Hepburn and Humphrey Bogart in *The African Queen*. I asked John what he wanted to discuss, but he waved off the question. Nothing, really; he'd forgotten. Fine by me. I'd had a glass of wine by then and didn't feel like talking shop.

The NewMusic chat had been a ruse. Murray had mentioned something to John about that *NM* girl being kinda cute, and so John, always up for a giggle, happily arranged the meeting.

I kicked off my shoes and settled down on the couch with the boys. Murray offered a foot rub, claiming that he had magic massage hands, and I didn't protest. Murray claims that few things will make a girl fall faster than a foot rub.

Our first real date was at a Japanese restaurant called Nami, and soon after that Murray cooked dinner for me at his house in Cabbagetown. After dinner he offered to read my runes. I thought it was very impressive that someone could be so knowledgeable about science and politics *and* be into the mystic. (Lorraine Segato later gave Murray his nickname, "Murray Many Heads"). He positioned the stones carefully, urging me to think deeply about the questions I was asking so the divine would be revealed. I was smitten. He was totally making it up.

Our early romance seemed to proceed in fits and starts. Some weeks we'd talk every night, followed by others with nary a whisper. I didn't want to be aggressive—he was a celebrated musician after all—but weeks could go by without a call. My friend Karen Gordon explained the concept of "female hours": a woman goes home after a date and counts the hours until the phone rings, while the man hasn't even realized the date is over. What was actually going on was that Murray was struggling with a newly broken heart, not willing to trust feelings that might be in rebound.

Eventually, though, Murray was hanging out regularly at my little apartment in Toronto's west end on Gladstone Avenue—or "HappyRock," as he called it.

A year passed quickly. We were both on the road a lot (absence making the heart grow fonder?) and I mentioned that I had been thinking about buying a house with a friend even though I was a long way from having enough money. Murray, having just done a new publishing deal, said, "Buy a house with me!" I was dubious, but he pushed on: "No strings, just a straightforward business deal. Mutual real estate!" *That sounds safe,* I thought, and soon we'd found a little two-storey fixer-upper south of the Danforth and moved in together.

A year after that, Murray proposed. He'd booked the fireplace table at Fenton's—the very best table, right in the middle of the room. After the wine was poured and we were starting to enjoy a lovely evening out, Murray suddenly got up from his chair, dropped to one knee, and began a heartfelt speech about True Love.

People in the restaurant stopped what they were doing to watch. It was enough that we were both recognizable, even among this banker crowd, but a famous singer proposing on bended knee? Now this was interesting.

Suddenly I was beyond embarrassed. This was simply too intimate a moment for sharing.

"Get up!" I said. And now I'll pause to story check. My version is a little different from his.

Here's how Murray described it in his book, *Getting Out of Here Alive*:

As soon as I slipped the box out of my jacket pocket, the game was up. Denise was hit with an attack of emotional claustrophobia. Just as I was getting down on my knee by her side to present her with the Birks box and say the magic words, she slammed her hand down on the table rather loudly and hissed, "Don't you dare!"

I don't remember the hand slamming. And I'm not sure I "hissed." A forced whisper can sound similar, I suppose. Murray rose, too stunned to continue and sat back down.

"What's the problem?" he said.

"People are staring!" And they were. Especially now.

Waiters hovered with the next course and Murray shooed them away. He was miserable, thinking he'd scared me off. I asked for more time to think. I'd thought we were already committed. After all, we were deeply in real estate together.

Two days later, I said yes. (Murray said it felt like two weeks—female hours in reverse). We were officially engaged.

We got funny reactions from our friends. Ronnie Hawkins said to me, "Murray? That guy could piss off Jesus!" Shelley Ambrose, Peter Gzowski's Executive Assistant at *Morningside*, said to Murray, "You're marrying a VJ? Why?" (Shelley doesn't believe in marriage. I once bought her a fridge magnet that says, "Why should I get married? I haven't done anything wrong!") My mum, though, said that marrying a Scottish pilot was a romantic coincidence, reminiscing about the flyer she'd almost married in London.

It was tough to find a wedding date that worked for our schedules. Murray was putting out his *Swinging on a Star* record and about to start his songwriting series of the same name on CBC Radio. I was travelling my head off with *The NewMusic*. But we managed it on August 11, 1990. We planned a low-key reception of eighty friends and family at Murray's brother Calvin's summer cottage on Stoney Lake. We'd spent some magical time there in our courtin' days, Murray paddling me in a canoe while I rested in the bow on lifejackets and cushions, gazing back at him under the light of the Milky Way.

The morning of the big day, people started to arrive by boat, filling the little wooden island church, St Peter's-on-the-Rock. Prairie Oyster's Joan Besen played the organ as my father walked me down the aisle to where Murray was waiting with his best man, Vezi. Karen Gordon was my maid of honour. During the ceremony a tiny spider lowered itself down a thread and stopped exactly at nose-height between Murray and me. Not sure what it meant—a little small to be a spirit guide—but it got a chuckle from the guests as both of us tilted our heads back to stare at it, cross-eyed.

It had threatened rain all morning, but it turned out to be a lovely day. Much had sent Basil Young to shoot the event for us as a wedding gift and our *NM* editor, the Scorsese-inspired Alfred Tonna, volunteered to edit. Basil and Alfred were certainly close enough to be family, but neither of them knew my actual family and we ended up with more footage of the recognizable than the related. The wedding video is a dramatically edited film that starts in darkness with an impending storm over the lake, accompanied by a *Jaws*-like soundtrack. There are lots of shots of celebrity guests like Tom Cochrane and Molly Johnson and barely a shot of any blood relations. (Mom and Dad both attended even though they'd been divorced for a few years by then. Dad had remarried, and we only had one or two "Ann Landers" moments where one parent threatened not to come if the other was there.) It was hilarious to hear tales of the wedding embellished "on the lake" thereafter. According to the lakevine, Anne Murray, Ronnie Hawkins, and Bono had all been in attendance as well.

First dance: "Stand by Your Man," Tammy Wynette.

NOT LONG AFTER THE wedding I was off travelling again. This time to Oz, which, according to Australian aboriginal lore, led to the birth of our son, Duncan.

The NewMusic had been invited by the Australian Tourism Commission to visit. It was a mutually beneficial arrangement—for two plane tickets and expert guides, they'd get a one-hour special that showcased the beauty and music of Australia, and there was no hint of editorial interference. I *love* Australia. It's the only other place I've ever considered living. It's exotic and familiar at the same time, with many cultural similarities, good and bad, to Canada—from the influences of British colonization (theirs more forced), to the shameful treatment of First Nations peoples, to the way our small populations are dispersed over great geographies.

There was a musical connection as well. Artists like Crowded House and Split Enz (technically New Zealanders but living in Sydney), Midnight Oil,

AC/DC, INXS, and Nick Cave were all amassing Canadian fans, and labels were not immune to the idea that you could build a foothold in Canada as a back-door entry into the U.S. *The NewMusic* happily encouraged them and they returned the favour, offering us vegemite sandwiches at Neil Finn's house, prowling for "shrimps on the barbie" with Paul Hester who, unlike Paul Hogan, found no shrimps, just "snags, chops, and fat," and going fishing with INXS. Australian bands seemed to be up for anything. So were we, although I do not need to bungee jump ever again.

The champion of Aussie attitude was Peter Garrett, the lead singer and frontman of Midnight Oil. The band had toured Canada on the strength of their Number One single in Australia, "Beds Are Burning," a passionate political plea for Australians to reconcile past injustices to aboriginal peoples. The song went to Number Two in Canada, obviously hitting a nerve with us as well.

The Oils toured with aboriginal musicians like Yothu Yindi and Gondwanaland and took on the asbestos mining industry with their *Blue Sky Mining* record. They were uncompromising both ideologically and musically, and the Oils were thrilling to see live. At 6'4", Peter Garrett was aptly described as a "one-man furnace" and was always a great interview. Once, during a conversation in the garden behind his label offices in Sydney, he responded to one of my undoubtedly earnest questions by laughing and saying, "These are serious questions! Not at all what you'd expect on a rock show" — turns to camera — "But don't go away — something light and frothy and irrelevant will come on in a minute."

I told Peter that we'd run into R.E.M.'s Michael Stipe on the street, and he'd been grossed out while swimming on Bondi Beach. He'd come up for a breath of air and was greeted with a floating wad of toilet paper that he sucked into his mouth. Peter responded by giving us a lesson on the lack of sewage treatment into Bondi Bay and strongly advised tourists, straight to camera, *not* to come to Australia because the beaches were polluted. No wonder he ended up as an environment minister.

Despite their "serious business," the Oils were very funny. I remember sitting with Peter and Rob Hirst, drummer and founding member of the band (who had the best biceps in the business, in my opinion). I'd been marvelling at how they'd been together as a band for so long, yet still functioned as a collective. I suggested they might be the only ones.

Peter and Rob thought seriously about it for a moment and then Rob said, "I guess we are. Wait a minute, don't U2 operate as a social-democratic collective?"

Peter replied, laughing: "Yes, provided you do what Bono wants."

Rob: "Wait, were you rolling? Did you get that?"

Peter Garrett is no longer singing for his supper, and since 2004 has been an elected politician for the Australian Labour Party. As well as the environment portfolio, he's been a minister of heritage and education and continues to battle for his beliefs. The Oils played at the closing ceremony of the 2000 Sydney Olympics, and the band wore black shirts on stage with the word "SORRY" printed on them as a message to Australia's aboriginal peoples. The prime minister at the time, John Howard, was in the audience. He had refused to apologize for the government's role in taking aboriginal children from their homes and placing them in residential schools—a story, of course, well known to Canadians. Eight years later, PM Kevin Rudd finally apologized, four months before Prime Minister Stephen Harper did the same in Canada on June 11, 2008.

The opening throw to *The NewMusic* Australia special is a stunning long shot of the Australian coast in the Daintree Rainforest, with me on an outcropping of rock against cashing waves. I'm playing a didgeridoo (a beautiful thing, part art piece, part instrument)—very poorly. To under-score beauty shots of Oz we cross-faded the audio with a recording of a real didge, letting that roll for a few moments until my own, highly discordant performance is revealed. I sound like a gassy cow.

I had no idea then, but playing that ancient instrument had rather momentous consequences. I'd read *The Songlines* by Bruce Chatwin, which describes how aboriginal Australians "sang the land alive," and while there we saw a play about Dreamtime, the Australian aboriginal conception of creation. It struck me as odd that there were no female musicians on stage, and after the performance I asked the didgeridoo musician why.

He said, "In our customs if a woman plays the didgeridoo, she falls pregnant."

I must have looked puzzled.

"It's true and I've seen it done."

I told him that I'd just played a didgeridoo on a big rock for the camera. He just laughed and grinned into the camera in an all-knowing way.

Sure enough, a few weeks after we returned from Australia, I learned I was pregnant.

DUNCAN WAS BORN ON February 8, 1992, at Women's College Hospital, shortly after his mother went into labour on a live national television show. He was seven days early and I wasn't ready. But what new mother is? I still had one tightly scheduled week to go before the due date. I had throws to shoot, edits to complete, a voiceover gig for a dish soap commercial, a *Command Performance* to tape with Bruce Cockburn, and a Cowboy Junkies *Intimate and Interactive* to host, not to mention buying supplies and painting the spare room—yellow.

Murray and I had opted not to know if the baby was a boy or a girl. I figured that after all those months hauling around that extra weight, plus the effort of delivering a human child into the world, I deserved to have a surprise at the end.

On the evening of February 7, I waddled through the front doors of CHUM television to greet Cowboy Junkies. The Canadian alt-rock/country band had reached international attention with their emotive *Trinity Sessions* record, famously recorded live around one Ambisonic microphone. Theirs was an ethereal sound and vibe, and singer Margo Timmins, named by *People* magazine as "one of the most beautiful people in the world," was, too.

I was irritable. The only place I felt comfortable at that point was either in a swimming pool or on all fours. When I got to the station, I didn't know exactly what time it was — my wrists were too swollen to wear a watch — but I knew it was minutes to showtime. Suitably, I was wearing a shroud: a long, black floor-length number, over which ballooned my professionally made-up face. I'd even gone for the fake eyelashes — anything to look presentable in this advanced state — hoping to avoid frightening our young audience. I was a pretty disturbing example of why they should practice safe sex.

As I ploughed belly-first through the crowd of Cowboy Junkies fans pressed against the MuchMusic windows, I felt a distinct and sudden gushy wetness.

What the—?

It couldn't be. Did my water break? It didn't feel like very much, not like the waterworks you see in the baby-training videotapes. Knees squished tight, I shuffled in looking for Nancy Oliver. With two young boys, she was the only mother I knew there. Nancy's skills as a parent had made her well suited to management at The Nation's Music Station. We often acted like kids in a daycare.

"Nancy, I think my water broke. But it wasn't much — really just a trickle. Could that be it?"

"Yes, that's probably it, but we're live in fifteen minutes. How do you feel?" Nancy asked.

"Okaaaay," I said, remembering that my doctor had advised that labour with a first baby could easily take as long as twenty-four hours. His advice was to keep busy.

"It's too late to cancel the show or get anyone else to host," Nancy said. "It'll probably be hours before anything happens. What do you think?"

I *thought* I could make it through ninety minutes of live television; I'd prepared for this show and didn't want all that work to be for naught. Plus I was thinking about the forty dollars I'd spent on my face. I was too frugal to let that go to waste.

As I settled into my chair, I tried to put labour out of my mind. Tom O'Neill, the show's director, had positioned me behind a large black grand piano. Normally *Intimate and Interactive* hosts cruise the environment, so this seating arrangement was obviously intended to hide my bulk. I was grateful for the shield.

The audience was in position and the band were at their instruments, ready to go. My job was to traffic cop; interview the band, guide audience questions, take phone calls, introduce songs, and generally keep the show moving along. There was a basic script that looked something like this:

Intimate and Interactive opening	:15 sec
Cowboy Junkies–specific GFX	:10 sec
Host Intro	:30 sec
CJ Song #1	4.00
Host extro	:10 sec
Host Q&A	2:30
Host throw to commercial	:05 sec
I&I bumper	:05 sec
Commercial	2:00

Repeat for 90 minutes.

The first section went well. The band was beautiful, the mood tranquil, the audience rapt, floating in a little bubble of sonic serenity. Only I was tense. About twenty minutes in, I was suddenly gripped by a spasm, and the first of what were to become increasingly forceful contractions. Thankfully the band was in mid-song so there were no cameras on me. I had a moment to catch my breath and think about what to do.

I looked down at my wrist to get a check of the time, knowing that I'd need to know how far apart this contraction was from what was sure to be the next one.

Damn! No watch. What to do?

I made it through the next song and threw to commercial, at which point the makeup artist came by with some powder and a brush for a quick touch-up.

"Wow," she said. "You're really sweating."

"I'm in labour."

"Yeah, right," she chuckled, walking away.

Hang in there, Donlon, I thought. *Labour can take hours and hours. This show has only an hour more to go. Breathe... follow the rundown... you'll be fine*. But by the time we were back into the third and fourth packs, the labour pains were climbing in intensity and frequency.

I had no idea how far apart the contractions were, so I timed them with the rundown: *PAAAAIIINN!!!*

OKAY we're in the middle of a song — "Black Eyed Man," 3:52 seconds. After that I'll take a phone call, throw to commercial, commercial, bumper, audience question. Okay, looks like I was about ten minutes apart.

Well, that was some information at least.

God help me, why did this *Intimate and Interactive* have to be Cowboy Junkies — the softest, slowest band on the planet? Why couldn't it have been with Metallica or Guns N' Roses? (Though that may have hurried things along). I was desperately trying not to make any noise.

Margo was starting to look a little concerned, and I suspected that the people in the audience were beginning to sense something was up. Perhaps because of how short I was being with the fans.

"What's your question? Next!"

Amazingly, Murray was in the audience that night. Typically, I didn't go to his shows and he didn't come to mine. (There were just too many of them, and we were just too busy. Nor do I weigh in on his records, nor will he tell me how to make television — the secret to a long, happy marriage.) But he was there that night, not letting me out of his sight, and I motioned him over during one of the commercials.

"I'm in labour," I whispered, smiling sweetly. (Okay, I may have hissed.)

Murray, ever calm, took the makeup lady approach: "Don't worry, relax. We've got lots of time, we'll go home after the show and pack a bag and time the contractions..."

"No," I said, "I need to go to the hospital *right after the show!*"

"...And welcome back to MuchMusic's *Intimate and Interactive* with Cowboy Junkies."

While the credits rolled, I headed for the exit leaning on Murray's arm. MuchMusic's head of security *and* HR, Rob Wright, parted the way through the studio crowd and led us out into the parking lot to Murray's car. I thought we'd head straight to the hospital, but Murray was still in "don't panic" mode. It was true that I needed to pack a few things for the hospital. At home, I got my ob-gyn on the phone.

"How far apart are you?" she asked.

"I think about ten minutes."

"Do the contractions feel like they have teeth?" she asked.

Bizarre question, I thought, but apt. "Fangs, actually!"

"Off you go, then," she said. "I'll call ahead for you." On the way to the hospital I felt every bump, every pothole on the road, and begged Murray not to change gears. Every gear shift felt like the baby was pushing through my crotch.

I won't burden you with the gory details, but suffice it to say there was no time for an epidural (even if I'd wanted one), no time to enquire about a warm tub (singer Paul Young had strongly suggested I have a water birth), no time for a sweet-grass ceremony (Robbie Robertson had blessed my big belly at an awards show). The nurse hooked me up to a fetal monitor and the doctor came by and said, "Try and hold off pushing until you're more dilated." He left, hopefully to attend to the woman who was screaming blue bloody murder down the hall. It was an alarming audio backdrop, especially compared to the earlier dulcet tones of Margo Timmins.

I kept telling Murray, "I have to push, I have to push," and he'd say, "The doctor said don't. So don't push, you might hurt the baby."

But I knew it was happening fast. Another nurse came by, took one look, and summoned the doctor back.

"Push!"

I'd gone the distance in a blink. There was no stopping that baby. He had a mind of his own then and still does today. I put a washcloth between my teeth and bore down like a cavewoman. Murray often tells Duncan (who is tired of hearing this story) that he'd wished he had a baseball mitt to catch him, he arrived so quickly.

My theory is that Duncan arrived early because he thought it might be calmer outside than in. The first time I felt him kick had been at an Ozzy Osbourne concert at Budokan theatre in Tokyo, poor wee thing. Okay, maybe it was a prenatal headbang, but he didn't stop thrashing until I tucked in behind a wall to shelter him from the kick drum.

Duncan was born at 1:34 in the morning. The nurse counted his fingers and toes while Murray cut the cord, then put our son in my arms. He was incredible. I gazed down on him, so fresh and pure and alert. What Duncan saw when he looked up was likely more clownish. Between the TV makeup and the false eyelashes now running with mascara, he probably thought his mum was Tammy Faye Bakker.

The nurse who had been attending to the other screaming mother came by and said: "Now, that's da way to have a baby!" I think she was referring less to my speed than to the relative size of mother and child. The tiny lady down the hall deserved every holler. Her 5'1" frame had pushed forth a 13-pound baby. Duncan, at eight pounds, six ounces and begat from a hale six-footer, presented a far less taxing child-to-mother ratio.

I don't mention the nurse's words to fish for praise. If anything, I felt like I was a bystander during the delivery. It's an impressive thing to witness the way your body takes over, snubbing your conscious brain. The concept of "me" was lost; I was running on antediluvian animal instinct. I imagine it's the same no matter if you're in a western hospital bed surrounded by gowned professionals, in a field bearing down in the dirt with a stick in your mouth, or in a *Monty Python* sketch dropping children while doing the washing— "Get that would you, Deirdre?" You are no longer in control. The universe is.

In the next hour my mum came hurtling through the door with a bouquet of flowers, all weepy and proud, and John Martin showed up with a lovely bottle of whiskey. I swear the worst part of the night was not being able to share a glass and toast the little dickens. There was breast feeding to consider.

When everyone had left, I was moved to another room. Duncan was placed in a bassinet beside me and I tried to get some sleep. As any performer will tell you, it's hard to come down after a show, let alone a live show *and* a live baby. I was too high to sleep. I kept looking over at the peaceful little bundle, wondering if it all had really happened. Duncan. Scottish warrior name. Sleeping like an angel, skin so silky and fine. I'll do the best I can for you, little one, I promise.

I awoke to the nurse bringing in a bouquet of flowers from Cowboy Junkies. The note said: "Thanks for waiting." The nurse wondered if I was feeling well enough to let a Citytv cameraman in. Apparently a CP story about the "Littlest Cowboy Junkies Fan" was picked up right across the country with various headlines: "Baby Is Cowboy Junkies Fan," "A Rock and Rolling Baby Boy," "VJ Gives Birth after Closing Show," "Birth Postponed for Cowboy Junkies," "Much Host Almost Has Her Baby On Air." Duncan was well announced.

Whenever I run into Margo now, she asks me how old Duncan is. He's a benchmark of the passing years, and today, at 6'5" with a beard and hair down to his waist, he looks every inch the handsome rock and roller. He's training to be an aircraft maintenance engineer. He's musical and funny and smart, and it's okay for me to brag because I'm his mum!

Duncan, Murray, and me.

THERE'S A POSTSCRIPT TO Duncan's birth story that is a bit of a detour off the chronological track, but worth telling here, I think, because it not only saved a MuchMusic special, it allowed me a unique female bonding moment with the amazing Annie Lennox.

Annie was set to do an *Intimate and Interactive* performance on March 13, 1995, to promote her *Medusa* album (still one of my favourite albums of all time).

It was a tough negotiation from the beginning, and took weeks of lawyering between Much counsel Denise Cooper, myself, and Annie's manager Simon Fuller. Simon is a seriously savvy manager who over time has worked with Annie Lennox, the Spice Girls, and Amy Winehouse, to name a few. He was also the creator of the wildly successful *Idol* franchise. Simon was no slouch.

I and I contract negotiations were often difficult because all parties — artist, label, and broadcaster — wanted to own copyright and creative control. Copyright was tough, because every party had an interest in the production of the show. It was our branding, our cameras, and our production expertise; but there was also the artist's performance, the publishing rights, and the label's tour support, as well as other considerations. Creative control was tougher still. The *I and I* shows were live to air. There was limited ability to "fix it in post." It was a particularly risky undertaking for some artists, who needed to be in a different headspace for a musical performance than they did for an interview. (It didn't work for Beck, for example, who left in the first half of the show and locked himself in his bus while his band vamped on and on, and we pounded on his door.) The Annie Lennox deal got done, but I could tell from the way the negotiation went that there was reluctance on the artist's part and I never felt entirely confident that it would actually happen.

Sure enough, the day before the show, the gear was set up and the band arrived for sound check, but no Annie. The tour manager said she wasn't feeling well. Uh-oh. That didn't bode well. Later that evening, he called to invite me to dinner with the band; perhaps a pre-show conversation would put everyone more at ease.

When I arrived at the Japanese restaurant, Annie wasn't there. I squeezed into a corner of the booth with the band and ordered a sake, my thoughts shifting to how to word the "cancellation due to illness" notice. A while later a small, inconspicuous person slid wordlessly into the booth. Everyone shuffled about to make room while I did a double take. This was Annie Lennox. You could have sat right across from her and never known it was her. She was one of those superstar chameleons, people who can shrink into discreet anonymity and move about unnoticed when they want to.

I laid out the show, describing how we would move performance and interview segments. Annie wanted to know what the audience questions would be. I told her we couldn't guarantee the audience questions but entreated her not to worry—I was hosting and could be a safety net. If she felt any apprehension at all, she just had to catch my eye and I would steer us out into a commercial or song, whatever she needed. I confessed my own shyness around cameras and it became a bit of an *"I'm totally neurotic; No, I'm more neurotic than you"* contest.

Just when it looked like the whole thing was about to go south, I told her the Cowboy Junkies story. Annie was a mum with two young daughters, so I thought she might relate. As we got into the labour and delivery details, I could sense that she was starting to relax.

At that point, I made a hasty retreat, wanting to leave the conversation on a hopeful note. The tour manager promised he'd call me in the morning.

By noon the next day I still hadn't received a call. I gave our publicity manager Sandra Puglieli a heads up to prepare an announcement. By early afternoon, the band showed up for rehearsal. When I asked where Annie was, I got a few shrugs, and I could tell the label was nervous too. Finally, Annie walked in.

"How are you feeling?" I asked.

"Well," she said, "if you can have a baby, I can sing."

It was a fabulous show. The minute the lights found Annie, she was a superstar all the way, miles from the mouse I'd met the night before. She told the audience she was "quite a nervous person," but there was no hint of nerves when she lost herself in the music. She was flawless, theatrical, and charismatic, and the audience dissolved into love puddles on the floor. No one, including me, could quite believe we were all in the same room with her.

She sang "You Have Placed a Chill in My Heart," "Why," "No More 'I Love You's'," "Here Comes the Rain Again," "Train in Vain" — a marvellous, almost gospel reworking of the Clash song — and Neil Young's "Don't Let It Bring You Down," all with a tight band and three beautiful back-up singers.

You could tell at the end that she knew she'd nailed it. While the credits rolled she thanked the audience: "Thank you very very very very very much. You made me feel very comfortable and I was nervous. I'm not used to this interactive shit." When she realized she'd said "shit" on camera, she did it some more: "Shit! Shit! Shit! Shit!" And we took this wild photo:

Afterward there was a party at the BMG offices on the fourth floor of the building across the street. We'd all gathered to have a drink and celebrate when suddenly panic hit the room.

She's stuck in the elevator.

What?

Annie *and* her band. And she's claustrophobic. Emergency services were called, and the firemen arrived and managed to pry open the elevator doors with the jaws of life — at first just wide enough for us to push a bottle of champagne through the doors. The band was singing to cheer each other up, and eventually they were rescued. Remember the singing trick if you're ever stuck somewhere. It has got me through some tight spaces. And while we're at it, don't ever get on elevator with a full bladder. You never know.

(11)

MUCHMUSIC:

AGE OF RELEVANCE

"The less you know, the more you believe."
— "LAST NIGHT ON EARTH," LYRICS BY BONO AND THE EDGE

AFTER DUNCAN WAS BORN, I took a three-month maternity leave and tried to adjust to the joys of motherhood through the jangly-nerve cotton haze of sleep deprivation. I had devoured the *What to Expect When You're Expecting* books, and now shifted to *Your Baby's First Year*, looking for insight into this strange new world. Mostly, I marvelled at how my own mother had managed four children under the age of six with cloth diapers and none of the mod cons we take for granted now.

Duncan's birth spawned a hail of gift baskets, baby wagons, and blue buckets from record companies, colleagues at work, and friends near and far, all of them packed with clothes and toys and music and soothers. It was an orgy of baby ephemera — and almost all of it was adorned with balloons. I was delighted and grateful for every thoughtful gesture, but every arrival triggered my globophobia. CONGRATULATIONS! the things would yell in rubber and foil, bouncing about menacingly on the porch. I'd hand out scissors to the delivery people and drag the bounty in as the balloons flew up, up, and away.

Duncan's birth gave me a chance to consider whether my time as an on-air music journalist had peaked. I was about to turn thirty-six, very likely past my "best-before date" (medically speaking, I was an "elderly" mother at thirty-five—a description I hotly protested) and I no longer thrilled to the idea of scavenging about after midnight in Queen Street clubs, hoping to capture the perfect *bon mot* from a teenaged lead singer with dilated pupils.

The *NM* specials continued to be invigorating, but they were the exception, not the rule, on the show. We didn't have the budgets or the investigative resources to go much deeper than what we were already managing. Motherhood had lent me a new perspective, just as it had for Laurie.

I'd also had a glimpse of a different broadcast world at CBC Radio, having done two stints hosting Peter Gzowski's *Morningside* summer replacement show, *Summerside*. To me, it was a hosting wonderland: smart story producers, connected chase producers, and "greens!"—photocopies on green paper delivered to the door each day containing pre-interview info, backgrounders, and suggested questions on a deliciously wide range of topics, from firefighters in Kuwait to CanLit authors to Saskatchewan relish recipes.

Actually, in my first year doing *Summerside*, I was pregnant with Duncan but told no one. (I was renewing my employment contract at Much at the time, and gender equity aside, negotiating while pregnant wasn't in my interest.) Experiencing morning sickness was also a tad inconvenient. It made me highly sensitive to smell, so walking past the burnt coffee machine or catching a whiff of someone's toasted garlic bagel with peanut butter would send me lurching out of the CBC studio and into the washroom.

Once when I rushed back into the chair to meet the 3, 2, 1 count, I heard a producer remark, "She's good, but she's got the bladder of a gerbil."

The next summer was an even bigger juggle, because Duncan was five months old and for a few weeks I was working both jobs, at CBC and *The NewMusic*. It was a lot to handle and I was no longer a spring chicken. But I had a new co-host at *The NewMusic* to welcome and certainly couldn't leave the show while it was in transition.

Jana and I found our co-host dynamic easily, despite how different she was from me. She was unnervingly gorgeous and had a thoughtful, Earth Mother vibe, which could be a little mesmerizing to someone wound as tightly as I was.

There's been a lot written about balancing career and motherhood, but let me just say this: Work-life balance is an extreme sport. If you're thinking you're doing equal justice to each, you're fooling yourself. You're constantly making choices. Some of them are the right ones. The rest you'll just have to forgive.

While *I* didn't have an actual plan to change anything, other than trifling with the idea of moving back to Vancouver, Moses did. One day he found me at my desk and confided that he was going to replace John Martin. I was shocked but not surprised. John and Moses had not been getting along. They were very different people in terms of management style, and Moses was increasingly vocal about John sometimes working from the Friar and Firkin across the street.

Moses complained about John's "drinking problem." It's true John liked a beer in the afternoon, but I knew he was also out of the office a lot because he was a chain smoker, something he could no longer do at his desk. Gone were the days when we'd emerge from the editing bays in great smelly grey clouds, unconcerned about the clogging effects of nicotine on the machines or the lungs. Many of us thought it was quite nice to pop over to the Friar and have a smoke and catch up with John.

In a more supportive modern environment, there might have been some offer of help, but that wasn't in the cards then. It's not hard to see why Moses, who could be very precise when it came to giving directives, would have clashed with John's "mercurial temperament and guerrilla-management style" (as described on the Citytv website after John's death). Over the years their relationship had become prickly, and Nancy was less and less able to intercede.

Moses told me that he wanted me to take over the reins as director of music programming for MuchMusic, as well as to oversee Entertainment on Citytv News.

This was a problem. John had hired and guided me. We were friends. I did not relish the idea of supplanting him, nor was I sure I wanted the responsibility of managing the entire station. I knew the job was about to get bigger, too, as Moses had his eye on establishing MuchMusic in countries outside Canada, as well as on new CHUM specialty channels to bid for and build at home.

Life was busy enough. Duncan was eight months old; Murray was touring constantly, and when he *was* in town he was recording his weekly CBC radio show, *Swinging On A Star*.

I told Moses I would think about the offer. He looked at me like I was soft in the head. "Why would you need to think about it? It's not every day you get offered a channel."

True. Good point.

"Don't think of it as a channel to be programmed, think of it as an instrument to be played," he said. (This eventually became his tenth commandment.) Wow. That was tantalizing. But I couldn't do it over John's head.

John had known a change was coming. He officially resigned on December 8, 1992, "which ended months of speculation about his status," as Claire Bickley in wrote in the *Toronto Sun*.

"Call me middle-age crazy," John said in the press release announcing his retirement, "but for me, it's time for a change. And I've always fancied the idea of going out at the top."

As Greg Quill wrote of John in the *Toronto Star*: "An affable, street-smart diplomat, he steadfastly resisted pressure to make MuchMusic over in the image of its chart-driven, highly commercial American counterpart, MTV. That resistance has won him critical kudos in Canada and thousands of friends whose music might otherwise have languished outside the mainstream."

To me, John most kindly said, "If it was going to be anyone, I'm glad it's you. You're going to be great." He was genuinely glad for me and told the press so in every interview.

John spent his last day at CHUM celebrating New Year's Eve at Nathan Phillips Square with "40,000 of my closest friends." After midnight, when the mayor had spoken and the revellers had departed, it was done. There was no party for him at the station. He said he didn't want one, but we should have insisted. Later Richard Flohil and *Billboard*'s Larry LeBlanc threw a bash at the El Mocambo, presenting John with a gold record for his many contributions.

John, Murray, and I remained in touch on and off for years after, and I tried to honour his rock and roll spirit in the place — especially in the leeway that he afforded the on-air talent. "VJs were given enormous freedom to be silly," he reminded me, advising that we never lose that.

After leaving Much, John directed an excellent documentary called *The Genius of Lenny Breau*, which won a Gemini Award, as well as another called *Hank & Jimmie: A Story of Country*. He also went to work for a while at BPM, a Canadian dance music channel, but the truth is he never really got his groove back. His marriage faltered, they sold their house, and he saw less of his beautiful son, David. John eventually moved into an apartment over a bar on the Danforth and became increasingly withdrawn. The smoking caught up with him, and in 2005 he was diagnosed with esophageal cancer.

Sadly, he wouldn't let anyone come to see him in palliative care. So Michael Heydon (MuchMusic's creative services producer), David Kines, and I hatched a plan to record good wishes from his friends. We borrowed a camera and a room at the Spoke Club in Toronto and put out a call. His friends and colleagues came in droves. Record company executives, artists, video directors, musicians, drinking buddies, the Queen Street cultural crowd, all of them showed up to tell tall tales and cheer him on. What made it really special was to know that John and David, then eighteen years old, watched the tape together in the hospital.

While John was building his legacy at Much, David was too young to know just what an influential force of nature his dad had been, and to appreciate the great regard in which people held him. We saw his creative, pioneering dad as the "Father of rock video in Canada," which was how CBC described him in their obit.

John died in 2006 at age fifty-seven. As John's friend and Much publicist Bill Bobek told *Billboard* magazine: "John Martin gave me—and millions of others, I'm sure—one of the most creative, exhilarating, and fun-filled rides through the music and music television industries that could ever have been imagined. He did so much for the artists and the fans."

He did. Still today some of John's photos and memorabilia adorn a corner shrine in the Old Nick on the Danforth, one of John's favourite watering holes.

For years after John passed, industry insiders wished that his impact on the Canadian music scene had been properly recognized, but there were few opportunities for posthumous awards in Canada. In 2006, when I was honoured with the Canadian Music Week Humanitarian Spirit Award, I asked CMW's president Neill Dixon if I could use the time allotted for my speech to present a Pioneering Award to John instead. Neil agreed and John's son David accepted the award on stage. It finally felt a little more right.

As I write this, it happens that it's the anniversary of John Martin's death, and in eerie synchronicity many of us have received this photo and note from former Much director Dennis Saunders: "The entertainment/

music landscape has evolved so much in such a short time in so many ways that I wonder if it's even possible for someone to challenge, innovate, and tilt at windmills the way that John did, and bring so many along for the ride."

The late great John Martin.

IN DECEMBER OF 1992, Moses appointed me director of music programming at MuchMusic. Moses was excited about a new regime. He envisioned the next few years as an opportunity for reinvention and expansion. In an interview recorded at a Crystal Award ceremony for Women in Film and Television (WIFT), he told the story this way: "D.D. and I began to get serious about MuchMusic, and I asked her what unique stamp would she would want on her administration and without a moment of hesitation she said, 'Relevance' . . . No question she has delivered on that promise of relevance and she has remembered that rock and roll is about rebellion and having fun, and she's done it with flair and she's done it with grace."

Those kind words from Moses came, I should add, after we'd worked together for a few years. At the beginning, there was rather more flailing than flair.

I was vaulted from an on-air position on a weekly show to running the music direction of an entire channel. Even though I'd worked in a corner of the Much environment every day for seven years, what I knew about sales, marketing, and HR was limited to my experience as a CHUM employee:

"Can I have a bigger tape and travel budget?"

"No. Advertising is down."

"But Much is up!"

"Much is not an island."

That pretty well summed it up.

MuchMusic shared services with the rest of the CHUM Television group, so areas like financial services, technical support, and cable relations were handled centrally, and gains from one channel could be used to build another area. In the time until I was made vice-president/general manager a few years later, I had the opportunity to acquire deeper executive knowledge.

I was looking forward to being at the management table with Ron Waters (president of CHUM Television), Jay Switzer (head of Citytv programming and mentor to David Kines), and David Kirkwood (VP sales and promotions). I also needed to forge a new executive relationship with Moses.

As I look back at my daytimers from those first few months, I note that for some reason the quote "Age and treachery will always overcome youth and skill" is typed and taped on the title page of my 1993 Filofax. It seems rather bleak. I can't remember why I'd printed it out and pasted it there. Perhaps it was a warning to my young self, though I'm not sure I considered myself the young one. What I did know was that I was now expected to act like a grown-up, and that I'd have to come to grips with my tendency to react poorly to being told what to do.

Moses has been called a genius and a visionary, and I suppose, as with Steve Jobs at Apple, meticulousness comes with the territory. Moses saw everything we did as a personal brand extension and expected to deliberate on every aspect, from host presentation to on-air promos to the size of the font on a screen.

Like other managers at CHUM TV, I'd arrive at my desk from time to time to find a pile of paper after Moses had pulled an all-nighter. There'd be newspaper clippings, show reviews, viewer correspondence, and memos carefully inscribed with cryptic notes, arrows, and exclamation points, all in his deliberate penmanship.

Moses didn't get too involved in music programming, aside from the odd memo requesting a Klezmer music specialty show or a karaoke hour, so I could usually fend off the ideas I considered outside the brand. There were musical genres on MuchMusic that I know made him grind his teeth. He told me that we should only ever play "life-affirming" videos. He didn't want an "ugly" channel. Neither did I, per se, but rock and roll was often inspired by life on the edges.

My next few years were a balancing act, trying to find a way to acknowledge Moses' authority while protecting the creative latitude people needed to do their jobs. We did okay. Not because I was particularly adept at "managing up," but because as long as Much was profitable, attentions were turned elsewhere in the realm.

My first order of business was assuming John's chair. Literally. It was bizarre to be sitting at his desk in the corner he'd shared with Nancy Oliver, just four stairs up and fully open to the MuchMusic floor. In any other company, when a new boss comes in, you expect new décor. Had I had that opportunity, I might have asked for a door. I appreciate an open-office concept, but with a live band sound-checking next to your head every afternoon, holding private meetings was a challenge, never mind achieving a linear thought.

Nancy and I were happy office mates. She was in many ways a perfect MuchMusic den mother. She was a model of grace (she actually was a former model), her calm demeanour honed working with John and Moses all those years. I watched in wonder one day as she responded to a VJ tantrum. She pulled out a bottle of bright red nail polish and calmly applied a coat as the VJ ranted on. An excellent tactic. You can't really intercede if you're holding both hands in the air, fingers spread to dry. And she was right: many of the spats that happened in that crazed environment were tempests in a teapot and either died down on their own or became absorbed into the flow. It was a good lesson in macro management. There was no way you could intervene in every drama that was going down at any given moment and still pilot the ship properly.

As a welcome-to-the-job prank, someone anonymously sent me a book titled *Leadership Secrets of Attila the Hun*. I thought it was hilarious and propped it up on the corner of my desk, but Nancy discreetly put it in a drawer. Perhaps she worried that Moses' taste in literature might rub off on me. Moses had an affection for Japanese books, art, culture, and fashion. (At one point there was a Moses fragrance with a photo of himself in a kimono and chonmage hairdo, wielding a sword. The tag said: "Moses. A dynamic fragrance. Avant garde, personable, and intimate. Mysterious and passionate. It is also a richly intellectual experience." The staff referred to it as "Eau de Mo.")

In his office, books by authors like Machiavelli and the sixteenth-century Japanese rōnin warrior Miyamoto Musashi (who wrote on battle strategy and leadership), as well as *The Art of War* by Sun Tzu, were carefully stacked and displayed amongst his other collections of interest. Once, when John returned from a meeting with Moses, Nancy said, "How was it?" John shrugged and said, "Chapter Seven."

Was I an Attila the Hun? I can't imagine it. I was so keen to please in those beginning days that I was flinging yeses about like kisses from a parade float.

I asked Dennis Saunders about it recently over email. Deno was responsible for the three crews on the floor and was a confidant of almost everyone. He and fellow bon-vivant producer Jim Shutsa (the two of them were known as "the Smart Brothers") had been at MuchMusic from the beginning and competed with each other over who could come up with the wildest idea. Case in point was the yearly *Christmas Tree Toss* — or "Flinging Firs," as they called it. The event became quite epic, with pyrotechnics, countdowns, and insider betting. Only Much could devote an entire day of programming to throwing out a tree.

Deno wrote back: "You were between a rock and a hard place. We'd been under the charge of a genial old crazy uncle who let us do what we wanted. We didn't want John looking over our shoulder, but we also knew it was an unsustainable situation — becoming unpredictable and even more loony. People knew it needed more structure and form and a steely hand, there was a general recognition of that. But people wondered if you had the credentials—there were lots of CHUM execs who would have wanted that job. Who you are becomes measured against who you need to be. But you got the benefit of doubt, even though there was lots of apprehension about what was going to happen. They were worried that you'd institute your agenda instead of the agenda of the place. And you did. And it worked."

Thank goodness for the people. MuchMusic abounded with superb producers and staff; "Mr. TV" David Kines, Sheila Sullivan, Neil Staite, Simon Evans, Morgan Fleury, Sherry Greengrass, Michele Geister, Siobhan Grennan, Tania Natscheff, Sandra Halket, Susie Kent, and Margaret Weinrauch Perrotta; live directors Dave Russell, John Keffer, and John Kampilis; music directors John Jones and Craig Halket; and all the camera people able to leap tall buildings in a single bound—Dave Hurlbut, Basil Young, Tony Wannamaker, and Steve Gelder. There are many more, of course, all totally willing to do whatever it took to get us on the air every day. Those were the days, eh?

It was a freewheeling operation with extra levels of unpredictability layered on from both the audience pressed against the windows and the visiting rock and rollers, some of whom rightfully saw it as their job to be disruptive.

Programming MuchMusic in those days was like programming a dozen different radio stations at once. We had specialty shows in many genres— *RapCity*, *the Power 30*, *the Wedge*, *Clip Trip*, *French Kiss*, *Electric Circus*, *Soul in the City*—all trying to serve up what Master T, host of *X-Tendamix*, would call "fresh new vibes." Canadians, we felt, were interested in many types of music, and the programming mix on Much was ambitious, to say the least. We would tinker with it constantly, but trying to find a home for every genre of music on one station was not sustainable.

What we needed was another channel, something that soon became a priority. In the meantime, the music committee members—myself, John Jones, Craig Halket, and the specialty show producers—wrestled with the choices every week.

By the early nineties, MuchMusic was receiving between 80 and 120 new videos in any given week. Of those, we could really only add five or six into regular "videoflow" rotation. Others might play on specialty shows or not at all. For artists and labels, the stakes were high; at times, they even resorted to bribery. There were occasions when videos would arrive with…a box of donuts. (This was Canadian-style payola. No hookers and blow here.)

Food, plus anything that could be emblazoned with a band's name on it, was common currency. There were buttons, posters, yo-yos, hats, T-shirts, mugs, and pens. I still have an Elton John letter-opener and a box of black "Ozzy Rules" tea-light candles. I'm saving them for good.

The promotional items didn't always deliver the intended effect. Once a cold cardboard box was delivered to the boardroom courtesy of a band from the Maritimes. The box was opened to pandemonium. Creeping Crustaceans! A dozen live lobsters were waving their antennae and clacking their claws. They were almost as alarming as the live cow that arrived on a flatbed truck. It had been delivered by the band the Waltons, whose album was called *Lik My Trakter*. It was a pleasant enough cow, remarkably docile under the lights, but there was some fluid dripping from the base of one of its horns, resulting in another hot debate about animal cruelty. We added the video anyway.

Canadian bands had to be creative. They had a fraction of the promotional budgets that American artists did, yet often managed to succeed on talent alone.

Moist's seminal video for "Push" cost about $1,100, and it rocketed into heavy rotation out of the gate, totally holding its own against multi-million-dollar American videos simply because David Usher's performance was so compelling. ('Course, Barenaked Ladies still hold the video budget record for shooting "Be My Yoko Ono" in the Speakers Corner booth for a loonie).

The Pursuit of Happiness' video for "I'm an Adult Now" was shot on a Toronto street corner for five hundred dollars and again, it was Moe Berg's performance that put it into heavy rotation. When the video was remade with a sizeable U.S. budget for a U.S. release, it was nowhere near as compelling. Similarly, Parachute Club's "Rise Up" was another Number One Canadian hit. The $8,000 video was remade and remixed for $100,000 in the U.S. but it never translated. The failure was blamed on the difficulty of marketing a seven-piece band in a year (1983) when the Police, Eurythmics, Michael Jackson, and David Bowie ruled the charts.

Meanwhile, American music video budgets were climbing ever higher. Michael Jackson was the first to break the million-dollar benchmark with "Thriller", and budgets skyrocketed from there. David Fincher teamed up with Madonna for "Express Yourself" for a reported $5 million, and Mark Romanek directed Janet Jackson and her brother in "Scream" for what was said to be $7 million. Big-name directors like Hype Williams, Paul Hunter, and Nigel Dick regularly commanded seven-figure video budgets.

But "the Benjamins" didn't always guarantee artistic brilliance. Nor could they cure a bad song. That said, a bad video hampering a great song would often be reshot. Without Much and MTV, your success was limited. Video was simply that important at the time.

ANOTHER AREA THAT WAS crucial to audience retention was our own on-air talent, an area in which, like all managers of CHUM TV channels, we needed Moses' approval.

When I became director of music programming, original VJs Christopher Ward and John Roberts had left; Christopher to further his songwriting career, and J. D. to be an anchor at CityPulse News. Erica Ehm left a year later to write songs, a book, and to run her record label. There was no shortage of talent wanting to grace our airwaves, however. We continued to cast Much as a dynamic ensemble, with a strong emphasis on diversity. It's quite a list. Wild man Steve Anthony, Master T (who'd been promoted from a Much tape operator), Juliette Powell and Natalie Richard (who were hijacked from MusiquePlus), Sook-Yin Lee, who had sent in a quirky demo of herself playing with squirt guns in a Vancouver back alley, and Rick "the Temp" Campanelli, who won a VJ temp contest and toiled as the Much receptionist until he convinced us to put him on air permanently. Bradford Howe was another temp contest winner. George Lagogianes, Avi Lewis, Glen Baxter, and Lance Chilton were Citytv reporters who often did double duty, as did the "always fabulous" Traci Melchor. Monika Deol's bio was particularly striking—she was born in Punjab, raised on a dairy farm near Winnipeg, moved to the Much news program *FAX* while doubling on Citytv, and then reigned as the star of the dance music show, *Electric Circus*. Namugenyi Kiwanuka was a refugee from Uganda who was introduced to us as "Mary" until I convinced her to celebrate her beautiful Ugandan name on air. There was Terry David Mulligan, the elder statesman with more energy than kids half his age; "Soul Brother" Michael Williams, the musicologist host of *Soul In The City* and *RapCity*; the fearless former editor Bill Welychka, who VJ'd and hosted *Outlaws and Heroes*; Mike Rhodes and Mike Campbell, who travelled the country on Excellent Adventures; Kim

Clarke Champniss, who started at *RockFlash* before moving to *City Limits*; Angela Dohrmann, who left to pursue her acting love; Diego Fuentes, our *Clip Trip* host and another moonlighting actor; Teresa Roncon, who hosted the metal show; intrepid videographers Jennifer Morton and Larissa Gulka; Kathleen Rajsp and Rebecca Rankin, who were hosts of *FAX* before Rebecca left us for VH1; Craig Halket, who was also a gifted music programmer; the outrageous Ed the Sock; the outlandish Nardwuar the Human Serviette; and the hilarious Dan Gallagher who left us all far too soon. (Thanks for bearing with me. Would hate to leave anyone out.)

The Magnificent Eighteen, post-MMVA lean-in, 1994.

They all had their share of supporters and detractors. Monika in particular had many admirers, including Ottawa comedian Tom Green, who duct-taped himself to a pole outside the station to get her attention. It was one of his tamer stunts. At one point Tom and I conferred about a VJ slot, but he was off to pursue adventures south of the border.

We always kept an eye out for new talent, the incoming demo tapes stored in a cardboard box on the floor beside my desk until I could lock myself away and view them all in one big gulp.

Occasionally a superstar would appear, though one of our biggest, George Stroumboulopoulos, didn't come in as a demo. George was introduced to me by John Marshall, who was still a producer on *The NewMusic* (and is now a producer with *Rick Mercer Report*).

George had hosted a talk radio show on an AM sports station called Fan 590 before moving to FM at CFNY, where he hosted a punk show. John convinced me to meet him, and I totally trusted his instincts. (It was John who insisted I come with him to see Rick Mercer when he did his very first one-man show in Toronto. Not a bad eye for talent!) MuchMusic's then director of operations David Kines also knew about George, and had watched him do his live show at CFNY.

John walked in with this pierced dude in a black jacket and the two of them sat down with David and me. My first impression was that George looked a little fierce—until we started talking. He had a gentle self-possession that seemed out of sync with his attitudinal rawness.

We talked about his love of music and motorcycles, about his pet snake and what he fed him. But what won me over was when George spoke about his single mom and the struggles she'd had raising him. The more he talked about her, the more I discovered that George was a feminist born and raised, a guy with a generous heart and many layers. But most notably, he was curious, an essential quality you just can't teach. Plus he practically vibrated with energy. Or maybe that was just his right leg, vigorously bouncing up and down while we chatted.

George was never going to fail the "Why do you want to be a VJ?" question. Too often, the answer to that was:

V.J. HOPEFUL: Because I want to be famous.

DD: Why do you want to be famous?

VJH: Doesn't everybody?

DD: Okay, let's say you get the job and everyone knows who you are. You will be seen as a role model. You will be heard. What will you say?

VJH: Uhmmmm.

DD (nudging helpfully): Do you think you might use your powers for good?

VJH: Oh yes!

DD: How?

VJH: Uhmmmm.

When George was asked "Why do you want to be a VJ?" he said, "I'm not sure I do."

Now I was sure he was perfect. (George, by the way, has certainly used his powers for good, standing as an ambassador to the UN's World Food Programme, travelling to Sudan with War Child and to Canada's North to explore Inuit culture, literacy, and poverty, among other initiatives.)

I sent him up to Moses for approval, apprehensively. I'd already offered George the job.

Moses asked me why I insisted on sending people with piercings and tattoos up to his office. Once, after I'd sent him someone he deemed less than camera-ready, he reminded me he was interested in breaking the stereotype around gorgeous women — "Beautiful women can be smart too!" he would insist. I would argue that he'd already proven that time and again.

George was hired.

George Stroumboulopoulos, David Kines, and me conspiring backstage.

THE CHANNEL WAS INDEED an instrument to be played, but it needed to be played in the key of audience first. My drive for relevance had to be "done delicately," as the Wicked Witch of the West would say. MuchMusic was the meeting place for youth culture and music, but they weren't tuning in looking for more school. They didn't expect to be preached to about the environment or safe sex, about racism or violence or politics; yet these were all topics we tackled. The trick was to speak *with* the audience instead of talking *at* them. Much was one of the first channels to involve the audience directly in the programming of the station, and when we did it right, the viewers dove in. They were eager to engage in the discussion, particularly when the subject was controversial.

Music videos dealt with all the angst, joy, and social issues of the day, often challenging society's status quo. Rarely did a week pass when we were not thrust into an internal debate or even public discussion about whether an artist's video and/or piece of music was a legitimate creative expression, and whether it could or should be shown on national television. As national broadcasters, we were federally licensed and regulated stewards of the public airwaves, expected to reflect "community standards," which often seemed at odds with youth culture and expression.

It was nothing new. From Elvis Presley to Alice Cooper to Madonna, music had always been an agitator. Even Mozart was considered a rebel in his time. And the eighties, of course, saw the Senate hearings in Washington. The PMRC hearings had taken place the year I arrived at MuchMusic to host *RockFlash*, but their influence on how the music business operated was still being felt—certainly by me, as a new programming head—and so they bear a little more discussion here.

In 1985, Tipper Gore (then wife of U.S. vice-president Al Gore), co-founded the Parents Music Resource Center. Tipper and friends were known as the "Washington Wives" because of their relationships to U.S. government officials. The PMRC was concerned about the "explicit sexual language, violence, profanity, the occult, and glorification of drugs and alcohol" proliferating "unchecked" in modern music. They were hoping the hearings would force the Recording Industry Association of America (RIAA) to sticker albums containing explicit material with a warning. It was a hot debate and Frank Zappa, Dee Snider of Twisted Sister, and John Denver famously testified. Frank maintained that such labelling was an affront to civil liberties; Dee Snider argued for the rights of parents to be the responsible arbiters of what was acceptable for their children; and John Denver explained that his song "Rocky Mountain High," which had been misinterpreted as a song about drugs, was in fact about the beauty of nature. He was "strongly opposed to censorship of any kind in our society."

Frank Zappa opened his remarks with a reading of the First Amendment, and then referred to the idea of a ratings system as "the equivalent of treating dandruff with decapitation." Zappa was chastised by Republican senator Slade Gorton of Washington State, who said, "I can only say that I found your statement to be boorish, incredibly and insensitively insulting to the people who were here previously; that you could manage to give the First Amendment of the Constitution of the United States a bad name, if I felt that you had the slightest understanding of it, which I do not." The senator cautioned Zappa that he could be held in contempt and Zappa replied, "Go ahead, I already hold you in contempt."

It was grand theatre. The hearings were widely covered, but were unsuccessful in forcing a rating system.

The RIAA agreed to voluntarily apply Parental Advisory stickers to certain albums. The practice was unpopular, especially when chains like Walmart refused to stock product that contained the advisory. Others argued that the stickers had the opposite effect than intended, and actually increased sales; a sticker just pointed to where the good stuff was. At Much, our "sticker" was a verbal or on-screen warning before the video played: "*The following video contains material that may be offensive to some viewers. Parental discretion is advised.*"

At Much, my wisest and most trusted advisor on matters of appropriate content was Sarah Crawford who, first as head of communications for the music channels and later as VP of public affairs for the corporate parent company, was on my speed dial. Sarah is a charming, unassuming figure. She dressed simply and wore no makeup — an anomaly in itself in our pop culture world — but her intelligence stood out the most. She was a steady hand as we navigated the rapids of public outrage and controversy, always mindful of CRTC regulations and conditions of license while at the same time staying true to our push-the-envelope, politically incorrect, status-quo-challenging youth culture.

Sarah chaired our internal review meetings, the forum where videos that may have contravened broadcast standards were sent for arbitration. The committee was made up of staff who came from all over the building — secretaries, shippers, programmers, management — and also represented as many different genders, religions, races, and sexual persuasions as possible to ensure a range of opinion. We debated sexual content—were those women exploited or emancipated? We deliberated violent imagery—was it an artful commentary on the savagery of society, or was it (as some critics had suggested) a dangerous trigger that would induce young people to rush into the streets with copycatting on their minds?

(No one at Much bought into the cause/effect, monkey see/monkey do argument. We played a truckload of videos with people kissing, and they didn't compel people to suddenly lay a lip lock on each other in the middle of the street.)

We walked a tightrope. When we were seen to be permissive, we were pummelled by the righteous. When we didn't play a video, especially by a popular artist, we were condemned as censors.

Madonna's provocative "Justify My Love" video (1990) attracted incredible public interest and the channel was in the hot seat for even considering it, even though the video did not pass the review committee. It was deemed "too adult" for airplay on Much, yet it stirred debate anyway. Headlines read: "A foretaste of Hell" and "Stop the Music!" Another hot-button video at the time was Mitsou's sexually risqué video "Dis-moi, dis-moi." Interestingly, Mitsou's video was deemed "too adult" for airplay at Much, but fine for MusiquePlus. Les deux solitudes!

Moses, Sarah, and John Martin cooked up an idea to engage with the debate live on air. The show was called *A Question of Taste* and it aired at midnight, Eastern Time. Guests were Mitsou; broadcaster and author Daniel Richler; Desmond Burge, representing the Roman Catholic Archdiocese of Toronto; *NOW* magazine's Michael Hollett; and Sarah herself, who had the unenviable task of defending our right to champion or censure someone's work.

A Question of Taste was hosted, amazingly enough, by me. Amazing to me, that is—because while I remember the controversy and the guests on the show very well, I had totally forgotten that I'd hosted it until reviewing my tapes for this book. Probably for the best. I was deadly serious. I look like I was presiding over a Salem witch trial.

The show prompted a great discussion around sex and violence, art and provocation, censorship and community standards. Audience members who stayed up late to watch and engage with the show got to see the "banned" videos. But what was important was that viewers got a glimpse into the process by which the station's programming decisions were made. Later, we expanded on the idea and began to regularly present a program called *TooMuchForMuch* which asked the question: "Is it possible to watch television critically?"

The range of videos that warranted discussion was enormous. We looked at Ministry's "Just One Fix," starring William S. Burroughs; its graphic depiction of a young man whose body and mind is ravaged by heroin spurred a debate about the efficacy of anti-drug videos and questioned whether rock stars could be good role models. We pondered Dennis Leary's "Asshole," a satirical comment on American redneck culture and one of the most infectious earworms of all time, gave it a thumbs-up, and played the hell out of it. We viewed Wreckx-N-Effect's "Rump Shaker" and earnestly deliberated on whether all those bikini-clad babes dancing enthusiastically on the beach to lyrics like "I don't mind stickin' it to her every single night" was an objectification or celebration of women.

Marilyn Manson was a recurring figure. An artist who manifested himself as an "intentionally ugly anti-Christ self-mutilating Church of Satan cyborg superstar," we wondered if he was acceptable viewing for young people. Marilyn was nonchalant about his own culpability: "It's TV and this is the medium that we're on, so if you want someone to blame, blame yourself."

Much's overall video policy was that videomaking was artistic expression. We'd either play it or not play it, but we wouldn't physically alter it ourselves. To us, that would be akin to telling Picasso that he couldn't paint two eyes on one side of a face. Often, though, the label or artists themselves would re-edit and resubmit. They were accustomed to dealing with varying broadcast standards, standards that differed from province to province (as above), from country to country, and certainly between broadcasters, especially MuchMusic in Canada and MTV in the U.S.

In 1997, Radiohead sent in a video for "Paranoid Android," a world-weary single off their *OK Computer* record. It was a six-minute animated cartoon directed by Magnus Carlsson, loosely inspired by events that Thom Yorke experienced during a night out in L.A. (although I think he imagined that bit about the angel flying the helicopter). In the video, a corpulent male politician wearing a studded black jockstrap and a Zorro-like face mask tries to chop down a metal light standard atop which our cartoon hero is perched. In a bizarre accident of aim, the politician chops off his own legs and arms and falls into the water where he is rescued by two cartoon mermaids. The mermaids are, as you'd expect, topless.

The version of the video that MTV played had the mermaids' breasts pixelated out. At MuchMusic, we weren't bothered by breasts; we were more concerned about the chopping off the arms and legs bit. After much discussion at the standards meeting, we aired the video in its entirety. We got mail, of course, but we were fine with defending our decision.

Thom Yorke himself found the breast pixelation confounding and told us, "You've got a guy, a politician, mutilating himself with an axe—that's fine for the American psyche but oh no, women's breasts!" He shuddered and shook his head.

One night I screwed up big-time on *TooMuchForMuch*. I was hosting a show where the video in question was Nine Inch Nails' "Happiness in Slavery." In it, a man offers his nude body to a mechanized chair that restrains, tortures, and eventually kills him, then churns him out as mincemeat. That night, the *TMFM* guests included a priest from the Archdiocese who was "sickened by the violence" and concerned about our desensitization as a culture. The video's director, Jonathan Reiss, countered that the video was made as a depiction of, and response to, our desensitized culture. BDSM aficionados who dressed for their appearance on the show were happy to point out that the S&M was consensual and the machines were auto-masochistic, therefore it was okay—it was simply the man's personal party of choice and we'd been invited to it.

The video didn't pass. You can find it online—the full director's cut—though the version we received did not have any full-frontal nudity, as I recall. It wasn't the first time there were views that nudity was more offensive than brutality. It was, however, the first time I lost my nerve on air.

Sarah Crawford and I had debated right up to show time whether we should air the whole video or not—late-night time slot or no. But once the unedited version started to play, I got cold feet and stopped it halfway through. The show was intended to discuss broadcast standards, not titillate for the sake of ratings. Someone is seen to die at the end, and I thought we'd be in contravention of our regulatory code even on a show like *TMFM*.

I spent the next week answering blistering (un)fan mail, but I got out alive. I shudder to think what torrent of online haters I would have attracted today.

TMFM was in some ways a modern-day gladiatorial contest, the MuchMusic public square acting as the colosseum, hosting both lions and Christians. Except in our world, it was sometimes the Christians who had the sharpest teeth. Still, the community engagement served us well in the drive for relevance. The process was transparent, the audience knew what we were doing and why, and they had a say even if we disagreed.

THERE WERE MOMENTS, I think, when I took the drive for relevance theme too far—there was, for one example, that riveting special we did on the impact of the GST on the music industry; or, for another, our Free Trade show. Now there were a couple of ratings bonanzas! Not even CPAC would be expected to invite forty music industry execs to a two-hour talk show that debated the impact of NAFTA on the Canadian music industry.

Where I think we *were* bang-on was with our special event programming on events like World AIDS Day and Earth Day, our safe sex PSA campaigns and support for Kids Help Phone, and our bigger undertakings like Kumbaya, our coverage of the federal elections, and our participation in Pride Day.

Kumbaya

As I've mentioned, Kumbaya was singer Molly Johnson's idea. In 1992 Canadian teens and young women were the fastest-growing groups to contract HIV infections, and Molly wanted to combat the notion that AIDS was solely a disease for gay men.

Molly was a force of passion and persuasion. Events of this nature are always more successful when led by a musician, and in the summer of 1993 we held the inaugural Kumbaya event at Ontario Place, to be televised live on Much. It was the first-ever Canadian HIV/AIDS concert broadcast nationally and we took our guidance from author, activist, and saint of kindness June Callwood. Molly convinced more than fifty artists and celebrities to appear, rallying them to raise money and consciousness about this menacing disease that was rife with misinformation and homophobia.

Molly Johnson, June Callwood, and me at Kumbaya.

Molly worked her magic with the entire production. No one got paid, and everything, from the food to the production to the facilities, was donated. Molly's friend Mark Smith was an organizing dervish, as well as the choreographer of the rundown for the show. He and Theresa Dobko wrangled a team of great volunteers who worked with the MuchMusic crew. It's likely that any other TV crew would have looked at the show rundown and run screaming. Even on paper, the sheer number of performers, celebrities, and changeovers was daunting; but it was trickier still to manage, partly because nothing stood still. Not the revolving Ontario Place stage, nor the performer lineup, which spontaneously morphed and flowered like a fecund organism.

That meant hours of bedlam in the production truck as the crew figured out how to mic, light, and shoot whoever appeared on stage in whatever crazy configuration. Mary Margaret O'Hara sang with Blue Rodeo, Lee Aaron with Lost Dakotas, and Andy Kim with Barenaked Ladies. Ashley MacIsaac soloed with the techno group BKS; Triumph guitar hero Rik Emmett took care of business with Randy Bachman and Tom Cochrane; Murray broke our hearts singing "Simple Sorrow"; and an ever-growing celebrity band surrounded Rush guitarist Alex Lifeson in an "I'm not worthy" wave. It was a musical triumph for Molly Johsnon as well. If you've only ever heard Molly sing her jazz oeuvre, you should have heard her that day ripping it up. Janis Joplin would have been proud.

Molly also recruited famous Canadians — authors, athletes, and actors — to introduce the musicians. There was Margaret Atwood, Henry

Czerny, Sandra Shamas, Rebecca Jenkins, Ralph Benmergui, and more. Peter Mansbridge showed up in shorts, which caused a big stir—no one had really seen him stand up on television at that point, let alone glimpsed his knees.

June walked through the crowd, handing out condoms in all colours and flavours, and was straight with the youngsters: "Nobody is safe in this age of AIDS; if you can't be blunt about it at a rock concert, where can you?"

When Maple Leafs hockey great Doug Gilmour arrived, he found Molly backstage and asked: "What do I say? What do I do?" Molly claims I walked up and asked: "Do you have a hockey stick?" He did, in his trunk. Mark Smith handed over a condom and Doug went on stage and showed 'em how it was done. Now that's what you call stickhandling.

The messaging was key. We needed to not only raise money and provide effective information; we wanted to turn fear into compassion. We'd had long conversations with the Much staff who'd appear on-air that day—Natalie Richard, Bill Welychka, Master T, Erica Ehm, and others—about the stance we were taking. Molly and I both agreed that it was about respecting people who were living with HIV/AIDs. We definitely did not want to take the "body bag" approach, the hysterical, mascara-running, pleading-for-money tack typical of many TV telethons. However, two hours into the broadcast, when the phones were *not* ringing, we switched tactics. *Okay, everyone, it's Sally Struthers time. Beg! Let's get those cash registers ringing!* It worked. We raised over $200,000 that day, and more afterward from a calendar that was shot by portrait photographer Andrew MacNaughtan.

The Tragically Hip closed the show with Gord Downie wearing his Save the Humans (said the whale) T-shirt. The show ran hours over time, but no one cared, least of all the broadcaster. Such fluidity of on-air time was a luxury I'd rarely see again.

We worked with Molly to produce four live Kumbaya Festivals, raising money for fifty-three national and three international hospices and AIDS service organizations, as well as many HIV/AIDS awareness initiatives. One of my favourites was an exceptional series of cheeky PSAs (produced and donated through Paul Lavoie at the TAXI agency) that had cartoon dogs humping anything in sight—a pillow, a tree, a man's head—and the admonition, "Wear a condom, dum dum."

After June passed away, Stephen Lewis became Molly's trusted guide, and over the years Molly has raised over a million dollars for HIV/AIDS in Canada. Molly received her Order of Canada in 2007 and continues to be one of those extraordinary people who looks at her snowflake pin and says, "Holy crap! I got things to do!"

The face of HIV/AIDS has changed radically. According to the World Health Organization, 35 million people are now living with AIDS. In Africa, where the Stephen Lewis Foundation does incredible work, grandmothers are living and caring for a whole generation of children who have lost their parents to AIDS. For aboriginal people in Canada, the infection rate is 3.6 times higher than that of other Canadians. Because there are more affordable antiretroviral drugs now available, people tend to think that the crisis is over and we can move on.

We can't.

Vote With a Vengeance

In the leadup to the 1993 federal election we leapt into the political arena, brandishing our naïveté like a sword. I was no poli sci major—what I knew about federal politics could fit into a *Power Hour* promo—but I hoped that together with our on-air crew, the audience, and our musical friends, we might explore the landscape together. If we could find some fun in it, we might encourage politicians to address new issues and open up ways for young people to engage in the democratic process. It wasn't as if our system couldn't use some fresh new ideas! Artists like Madonna were already on board in America, recording PSAs for a non-profit organization called Rock the Vote that worked with MTV.

There were advantages to being election neophytes. Unlike conventional networks that covered politics regularly and were expected to play by the rules, we weren't aware there *were* rules. We had no relationships to protect; we didn't much care if our phone calls were returned the next day. We had videos to play and rockstars to interview, and life would go on. On one hand, it was all very freeing. On the other, it was daunting as hell.

Our first foray into this strange and suited world was the Conservative convention in June. The convention would determine who would succeed Prime Minister Brian Mulroney, whose popularity with the public was falling after two terms. Vying for the position were Kim Campbell, Jean Charest, Jim Edwards, Garth Turner, and Patrick Boyer. We gathered a small production crew and set off to Ottawa intending to bring some "unconventional convention coverage" to the proceedings and aiming to show our viewers how political party leaders get elected.

David Kines found a broadcast truck and booked some satellite time while Dennis Saunders, Jim Shutsa, and I brainstormed a game plan with the VJs.

Mike and Mike of *Mike and Mike's Excellent X-Canada Adventures* somehow convinced the PMO receptionist into giving them a tour of Prime Minister Mulroney's oak-panelled office, before heading over to the Parliamentary library. Like schoolboys looking up dirty words in the dictionary, they wanted to see if Pierre Elliott Trudeau's famous "fuddle duddle" was actually recorded in Hansard (it wasn't). Back at the convention, Steve Anthony ran around inspecting other broadcasters' booths at the convention centre. CTV, CBC, and Global were all massive operations with news-style sets, dolly cameras, and assorted flora, fauna, and craft services tied to satellite trucks. The closest thing we had to a set was a portable Speakers Corner unit plugged in near the convention floor.

Avi Lewis was able to rely on his personal political lineage to play the game his family (he comes from a line of well-known lefties, including his father, Stephen Lewis) had excelled at for years—poking Conservatives. Avi sat down on a concrete step with a youthful-looking Jean Charest and proclaimed: "The best shot you have at being Prime Minister is you're cute! With your collegiate jacket, your curly hair... You're so cute people will forget you're a Tory!"

It was Master T who stole the show—and we almost didn't have him. T was a hugely popular VJ, but he was about as interested in covering politics as a cat is in swimming. It took some work to convince him to go. He protested that he was no "black Peter Jennings," as he put it, but I knew he was a three-paper-a-morning guy and that if he could just be himself, he'd be a natural conduit for issues that concerned young people.

T was assigned to Alberta's "Gentleman Jim" Edwards. T taught Jim how to butterfly dance and then joined Jim's followers dancing to "Sweet Home Alabama" at the candidate's party. That certainly would not have been T's first choice of song, but he got his musical mojo back on track over in Charest's camp when he convinced his supporters to drop their lame leader chant and adapt a Naughty By Nature song instead: "Charest Hey, Ho, Hey, Ho!"

That was an improvement.

It was T's performance with Prime Minister Mulroney at a press scrum that really got people's attention. A political scrum was a little different from what our crew was used to covering at red carpet galas. There were no velvet ropes, just a crush of cameras waiting to pounce on the PM outside the gates of the convention centre. As soon as the prime minister was in sight, the crowds merged, all sharp elbows and hard cameras. T manoeuvred his way through the pack, trying to get the prime minister's attention. He wasn't hard to miss — a styling, dreadlocked 6'5" black man amidst the Ottawa political crowd was a rarity for sure — but the PM pointedly ignored his calls of "Yo, Brian, Whassup? Hey, Mr. Prime Minister, who are you supporting?" As *Globe and Mail* TV critic John Doyle remembered it in his column on Much's 25th Anniversary titled "Lessons from MuchMusic's Glory Days": "Mulroney ignored him, and walked past, a look of disgust on his face. On one of his last days as PM, Mulroney finally encountered a question that left him speechless, and no amount of experience or advice from the back rooms had prepared him for it. As low as his popularity was, it sank even lower at the moment."

"Yo Prime Minister, whassup" made national headlines the next day.

We arrived home from the Conservative convention pumped about our performance. There was a fresh wind blowing for youth involvement and no shortage of musicians wanting to weigh in, especially given what was happening south of the border. Robbie Robertson cited the election of President Bill Clinton as evidence of the increasing power of the youth vote, saying Clinton's appearance on *The Arsenio Hall Show* playing "Heartbreak Hotel" on the saxophone helped young people elect him.

THE LEADERSHIP CONVENTION WAS one thing, but when it came to the federal election, we needed to step up our game. Our naïveté wouldn't be cute for long. I needed some political bench strength. Luckily, I knew just the guy. Matt Zimbel is a Montreal-based musician and leader of the jazz group Manteca. He also has a great sense of humour and a fascination with politics. He and Avi Lewis made an excellent team.

Our other newsroom ace in the hole was Colin Vaughan — the late great political reporter who had once served as an alderman in Toronto. I was forever at his desk pestering him for guidance. "Colin, explain to me why we don't have proportional representation?" Or, "Colin, why would anyone whip their caucus?" Colin would have had way too much fun explaining proroguing.

The day after Matt joined our little production team, the election was officially called. We had five weeks to reinvent election coverage and charged forth. We called our campaign "Vote with a Vengeance." I was never completely happy with that title, thinking at the time it seemed a tad harsh. Given the results, though — the annihilation of the Conservative Party down to two seats — it did seem to fit after the fact.

One decision we made right off the bat was to be as egalitarian as possible. The conventional broadcasters limited their debates to the top three or four parties, but we thought the fringe parties might have some ideas that would appeal to the youth vote. We invited all fourteen federally registered parties to a special event which we called *Intimate and Interactive: A Concert of Politics.*

In order to prime the audience, we served up the people, the politics, and the issues in bite-sized chunks. The most successful were the 90 Second Reckonings and the candidate baseball cards.

The baseball cards were thirty-second graphics interstitials on each candidate, enthusiastically voiced by sports announcer John Gallagher. He was pitch-perfect; he made the candidates all sound like competitive sports stars battling against each other.

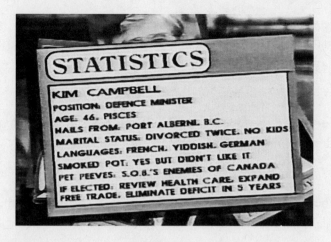

STATISTICS

KIM CAMPBELL
POSITION: DEFENCE MINISTER
AGE: 46. PISCES
HAILS FROM: PORT ALBERNI, B.C.
MARITAL STATUS: DIVORCED TWICE. NO KIDS
LANGUAGES: FRENCH. YIDDISH. GERMAN
SMOKED POT: YES BUT DIDN'T LIKE IT
PET PEEVES: S.O.B.'S ENEMIES OF CANADA
IF ELECTED: REVIEW HEALTH CARE. EXPAND
FREE TRADE. ELIMINATE DEFICIT IN 5 YEARS

It was the TV production values that made it sing.

More meaty were the 90 Second Reckonings produced by Avi and Matt, a series of fast-paced and ferocious musical Coles Notes on a dozen youth issues like jobs, the environment, aboriginal issues, gender equality, education, and the Senate. They hold up pretty well even now. (Sometimes too well. The 90 Second Reckoning I recorded on women's issues cites women's wages at about 70 percent of men's. We're only at about 73 percent today.)

Here's the one on national unity:

National Unity

Quebec the country? Think about it!

Avi: Sometimes English Canada sees Quebec as the spoiled brat of Confederation.

(k.d. lang's "Crying" video)

Avi: But for separatists, it's not a dislike of Canada; it's pride in Quebec.

(Saint-Jean-Baptiste Day march visuals and chanting)

Avi: They say the only way for Quebec to protect its culture and prosper economically is to say:

(Mitsou's "Bye bye mon cowboy")

Avi: Federalists, on the other hand, celebrate and delight in a bilingual Canada. They think Quebec's best chance for prosperity is to stay right here.

(choir singing "O Canada," shot of Parliament Buildings)

Avi: The Tories, the Liberals, the NDP, and the National Party all have the same message for Quebec:

(Tina Turner's "Let's Stay Together")

Avi: The Reform Party has no candidates in Quebec and the Bloc Québécois has no candidates outside Quebec…

(Frankie Goes to Hollywood's "Two Tribes")

Avi: So how do you express yourself…

(Madonna's "Express Yourself")

Avi: On national unity?

GFX: Vote with a vengeance.

Concerns that our coverage might be considered lightweight were relieved by the *Intimate and Interactive: A Concert of Politics* shows. Of the fourteen registered federal parties, we got twelve, with the unsurprising exceptions of the Bloc Québécois and Preston Manning of the Reform Party of Canada. We didn't expect to get the Bloc—there'd be no upside for the party to using campaign time at an English music station—but Preston's absence was disappointing. It was a shame; I think he would have handled himself well. No matter, we commissioned a Preston puppet instead.

Every party's appearance was treated to its own full live *I and I* production and was widely covered by the press. The leaders were surrounded by a youth audience and took questions by phone, fax, and the postmodern soapbox, Speakers Corner. Hosted by our VJs, the leaders were interviewed by our musician pals. We paired Barenaked Ladies lead singer Steven Page with Kim Campbell; Murray McLauchlan gamely sparred with Neil Paterson of the Natural Law Party; Lorraine Segato did a great job with Mel Hurtig of the National Party; and Neil Peart sat down with Jean Chrétien.

Moxy Früvous' drummer Jian Ghomeshi showed some real moxie when he took on NDP leader Audrey McLaughlin. I think Audrey expected a lighter hand. As for Jian, it was the first time he'd ever interviewed anyone and after the show he told me he knew right away he had a future in it. I agreed. He did.

Politicians thought Much was the "cool" place to come, and may have expected little more than a fluffy photo-op, but in fact we were armed and ready.

One of the more entertaining events was with the Natural Law Party. Their yogic-flying campaign PSAs were festooned with fluffy clouds and rainbows and promised an "all-party government and conflict-free politics." Murray's question about their famous "bum bouncing" on mattresses was classic in its restraint: "It strikes me that these people are putting a lot of body English into the idea of 'levitating,' as you say."

Avi pressed Jean Chrétien hard on a timely patronage question, and Chrétien got cranky.

Chrétien: "Shut up, Lewis, I'm talking!" And later, "Listen to me, Lewis" — Avi is trying to interject, waving a news article at Chrétien — "Let me finish. I said very clearly no one is authorized to give a patronage appointment on my behalf!" It was illustrative of how peppery this PM could be.

Chrétien's interview by Rush drummer and lyricist Neil Peart was a coup — both players were a serious get. Neil likes cameras and crowds as much as I like balloons, but astonishingly he agreed. He studied the "Red Book," *Creating Opportunity: The Liberal Plan for Canada,* and probably knew it better than most Liberal party members. Still, it was the first time he'd interviewed *anyone* on camera, let alone a campaign-hardened politician, so we rehearsed it a few days before, sitting at the Friar and Firkin, with me playing Chrétien. Neil was totally ready, but when the moment came to shine, we almost lost him.

On the night of the event, there was big expectation. The studio was full of fans; the Liberal groupies were outside gamely chanting and waving posters. The lights were up, the opening Chrétien baseball card was playing: "*A Capricorn that will replace the GST . . . a 'switch spitter' 'cause he can talk from the left or right side . . .*" The floor director was counting Neil in. He was supposed to walk into his position from the top of the four stairs onto the Much floor while Erica Ehm introduced him. Neil got to the top of the stairs and looked at the crowd, then the cameras, and...

Uh oh, I thought. *He's going to bolt.*

I walked closer and caught his eye, trying to psychically reassure him.

He stood there frozen for what felt to me like long minutes but was really only a few seconds, then took a breath, walked onto the floor, and nailed it. He did not let Chrétien off the hook on AIDS, on helicopters, on handguns, on the GST, on anything.

MuchMusic had become a player in the campaign. Even though none of it was an advertising bonanza for the sales department, our audience numbers remained steady, likely losing as many viewers as we gained during that time.

Election night was the biggest test. Five days out and we still weren't sure if we would go live. We were run ragged from the dozen *I and I*s with the party leaders. As for the traditional election night content with big shiny graphics and results analytics? Um, not so much. We had no electronics system for tabulating or analyzing the votes as they came in, so we just moved in four TV monitors and tuned them to CBC, CTV, Global, and *The Three Stooges,* and referenced their numbers. Our "electoral map" was musician and visual artist Kurt Swinghammer, who stood by with a giant map of Canada and paint brushes and rollers armed with blue, red, and green paint.

We did know how to make live rock and roll television, though, so we defaulted to type. We threw a big party complete with booze and music and celebrities who careened through the halls as we endeavoured to deliver the results.

Our political pundits were Ed the Sock and five youth party delegates playing spin doctor in the corner. Not expecting any visits from the leaders themselves, Matt commissioned fantastic puppets of Kim, Jean, Preston, Audrey, and Lucien Bouchard from an artist friend in Montreal. As the evening went down, Kim and Preston started making deals with each other, and Jean offered Kim a patronage position—all bets were off in puppetland.

Amazingly, a year later, the show won a Gemini for Best News Special Event Coverage from the Academy of Canadian Cinema & Television. I think we won for having the audacity to engage in the first place. Our political programming was widely lauded for its "speak truth to power" approach. Personally, I learned two simple but valuable life lessons. First, you don't have to be an expert to engage in the democratic process; and second, it's right to question authority.

For me growing up, politicians were right up there on a pedestal with parents and police. That had changed for me, and the audience got to challenge authority too. They had a national platform to voice their concerns and offer their opinions about what kind of Canada they wanted to shape—not just inherit. It was heady stuff.

Love Wins

Not much comes close to how proud we all felt in June 1999, when MuchMusic had a float in Toronto's Pride Day parade. Incredibly, we were the first mainstream broadcaster to participate in the festivities, and even then the move was controversial, both inside and outside the station. From the moment we announced our intentions on air, I was forced to carefully consider my personal principles and my responsibilities as a boss.

It all started with Gregory.

Gregory Hewitt was one of a handful of male secretarial assistants who worked in the international sales department in the CHUM-City building. One day he tracked me down and said, "The Toronto Pride Day parade is coming up. Wouldn't it be amazing if Much had a float?"

What a great idea. I started to imagine a massive, musical, colourful float with *Electric Circus* dancers and MuchMusic personalities thumping loudly down Yonge Street, all of us gleefully throwing MM-emblazoned condoms to the adoring crowds. What I couldn't imagine was just how fraught this mission was going to be. Our MuchMusic Pride Day float became a sensational—if somewhat soggy—ideological battleground.

As I've mentioned, reflecting cultural diversity was one of the aspirational values that underscored CHUM Television's reputation as a distinctive broadcaster. The Citytv founders had decided from the very beginning that theirs would be a channel of inclusion.

I should add that diversity is a stated regulatory goal for most Canadian broadcasters. The CRTC requires licensed broadcasters to, "through both programming and employment opportunities, serve the needs and interests of the multicultural and multiracial nature of Canadian society." Not all stations embrace the idea with equal vigour. But the smartest broadcasters know that showcasing diversity is not only the right thing to do, it makes good business sense. Viewers become loyal to stations they can see themselves reflected in.

I brought Gregory's idea to David Kines, Sheila Sullivan, and Sarah Crawford and we were on. There was a lot of excitement in the building and we had a ready team of enthusiasts in the *Electric Circus* crew, who immediately started to plan their costumes. We did not get 100 percent buy-in from everyone, however. I had a number of heated discussions behind closed doors, in which both cultural and religious reasons were cited as excuses for not participating. When I heard, "My priest told me homoscxuality was a sin," I was appalled—but I knew an angry argument wouldn't resolve anything. We had to fight back with kindness. As tough as those discussions were, I coudn't force staff to engage.

It wasn't like the music community was one big happy inclusionary family, either. At Much we applauded artists like Madonna, who for decades had spoken out in support of gay rights; and we called out homophobic lyrics and images on our media literacy show *TooMuchForMuch*. And there was no lack of hateful music out there. In the nineties a number of artists came under fire for homophobic lyrics, dancehall musicians in particular.

Since then, some, such as Beenie Man, have apologized, while others, like Shabba Ranks (whose lyrics included lines like "to kill battyboy would be the greatest fun") were eventually dropped from their labels. Eminem came under fire for the song "Criminal" on *The Marshall Mathers LP*, which was released in 2000. Eminem went on to defend himself, saying that the word "fags" didn't hold homophobic implications for him. A year later, his performance with Elton John at the Grammys was seen as a conciliatory move.

The tide was shifting but progress was slow. TV shows with positive gay portrayals like *Will and Grace* and *Ellen* were beaming into more and more North American living rooms and were key influencers: if you can't see it, you can't be it. But it would be nearly two years until the first same-sex marriages would take place in Canada, in January 2001; and *sixteen* until U.S. President Barack Obama's State of the Union address called gay marriage "a civil right, now legal in states that seven in ten Americans call home." Which made it all the more vital that we take a stand.

We brainstormed with Much communications staff on our slogan for the parade and settled on "Much Comes Out." T-Shirts, tattoo patches, and MuchMusic condoms were quickly ordered, and we mounted an on-air campaign to let our audience know we'd be there. That's when my phone started to ring.

"How dare you tell kids that it's okay to be queer?"

"You better call off that parade or watch out. I know where you park your car."

"Is this that dyke who's running MuchMusic? You won't get away with it. I know where your kid goes to school."

It wasn't one or two calls; it felt like a campaign. It was personal and unnerving. The day before the parade I went to see both Moses and the president of CHUM Television, Ron Waters. I could predict what Moses would say. He'd launched QT (QueerTV) with the brilliant Irshad Manji the year before and he was totally supportive. As for Ron, I knew he was a progressive guy; Ron was one of the first corporate executives I knew of who'd pushed through same-sex benefits in the company health plan. (When I'd gone up to congratulate him, he'd said simply, "It's the right thing to do," like it was no big deal. But it was.)

Still, I hadn't worked closely enough with Ron to be able to predict where he stood on every issue, and I wasn't sure how he would react. But at the very least, as president of CHUM television, he needed to be aware of the security threats. Much wasn't the only CHUM Television station beaming out of 299 Queen Street West, and I was an employee making decisions that could have an impact on everyone.

Ron was incensed at the threatening phone calls and responded unequivocally: "We've got your back." Those four words reinforced the idea that our "Everyone's welcome, Everyone belongs" slogan wasn't just something we wrote on CRTC applications.

I went back down to the floor relieved, reinvigorated, and feeling like I could take on all those homophobic troglodytes with my bare hands.

The preparations in the parking lot were in full swing. The *EC* dancers were comparing costume choices and waving about boas and glitter and the float decorations were fabulous. Yards of garish plastic Astroturf and yellow and red flags had been stapled onto the rented flatbed truck, and two massive papier mâché legs had been mounted, spread-eagled, on either side of a big, round MM logo. All we needed was a sound system and the arrival of our Pride Queen. Gregory, who'd started it all, had suggested that our float queen be Tim Taylor, an assistant who worked in creative services. Tim had been reluctant but eventually agreed.

The morning of the parade, we awoke to pouring rain. It was bucketing down. Undaunted, David Kines procured a wet vac from Canadian Tire and started attacking the watery astroturf on the float while the dancers donned waterproof mascara and practiced their moves on the slippery moving surface.

We had more volunteers than could fit on the float, packed as it was with *EC* dancers, MuchMusic VJs and personnel, and Ashley MacIssac, who performed on violin. Ed the Sock walked behind; neither of us can remember why. It was weird that people could see the man (Steve Kerzner) behind the puppet, but I was glad he was there.

Our Pride Queen Tim was resplendent in a yellow wig, a blue halter top, and a parasol. One of my fondest memories of that day is scavenging for a needle and thread and then attempting some strategic stitchwork to more firmly secure Tim's tits (two green fuzzy tennis balls) into place.

Tucking in Tim's tits.

The sun came out, the parade started, and we danced down Yonge Street in a glittery, giddy celebration of the Human Rainbow. Drenched from water cannons and smeared with confetti and lipstick from fellow revellers, we were happily exhausted, knowing that we'd aced our first-ever "Much Comes Out" Pride Day extravaganza.

The fear that had unnerved me the day before had vanished like a puff of smoke. The power of love in all its colourful, naked, unleashed glory was a triumph over hate.

I knew we'd taken a step forward even when it came to my choice of words. I'd said that I hoped that our audience might grow to be more "tolerant and inclusive" than ever before, but "tolerant" had become a word I disliked. It professes "acceptance," but it's guarded. It only means that we "allow" other points of view. It's paternalistic and passive-aggressive, and nowhere near open-hearted enough.

I'm not "tolerant" of my gay pals—I'm in awe of them. Their stories about struggling with sexuality and with bigotry—whether as bullied teenagers or as guarded adults wary of repercussions at work or with family—are full of sheer courage. My little story of finding the nerve to take part in a parade pales in comparison.

A decade later I thought about that Pride Day parade while driving my son to his first day of high school. He'd been accepted at Rosedale Heights School of the Arts in Toronto, a public school which specializes in drama, visual arts, and music. As we pulled up to the front door, I was charmed by the assortment of young people gathered about on the lawn outside. These weren't denizens of a cliquey institution where you could be shunned if you weren't wearing a little alligator on your shirt. They were a splendid, free-moving ensemble of young people finding and embracing their individuality, certainly in their clothing. There were kohl-eyed Goths dressed in black, dreadlocked hippies in hemp and bamboo, and guitar players in their latest Value Village bargains. There was one skinny young man in a black T-shirt and a tutu who was practicing pirouettes on the lawn. Maybe those kids had seen early Pride Day parades from their strollers. As I came to know Duncan's high school friends, I was delighted by their utter non-judgement of their peers and pals. Lesbian, gay, bi, trans, straight — it's a total non-issue.

Love wins.

MUCH GOES GLOBAL

"Gee Brain, what do you want to do tonight?"
"The same thing we do every night, Pinky…
Try and take over the world!"
— PINKY AND THE BRAIN

The nineties were a powerful time of growth and expansion in the Canadian television landscape. CHUM was on a roll with its radio stations, with the wildly successful Citytv channel in Toronto, and, on the specialty side, with MuchMusic and its interest in MusiquePlus. At the same time, the Canadian broadcast system was consolidating into fewer, more concentrated ownership groups, and the independents were feeling the squeeze. It became increasingly important to have a network of programming outlets in order to operate profitably. As to what to put *on* those programming outlets, you really only had two choices: make inexpensive but popular content your-self, or buy foreign programming and play it back.

Moses preferred to make it. So did we all. And we were good at it, as CHUM's success in international syndication attested. But increasingly in Canada, it was the American shows that drew the biggest audiences, and in order to get some of that action you needed a big wallet and broad audience reach. If you were just buying rights for one independent station in Toronto, you were still competing against the national networks like CTV or Global.

The more consolidated the industry became, the less opportunity there was for independent operators like CHUM, particularly if you didn't also own the pipe—i.e., the distribution system—which, in those times, meant the cable operators. CHUM Television's plan was a three-pronged expansion effort: to extend the reach of homegrown shows like *The NewMusic*, *FashionTelevision, MediaTelevision, MovieTelevision,* and others; to expand the Citytv brand with more local TV stations across the country; and to become a bigger player in the new world of specialty channels.

The CHUM vision for licensing Canadian specialty channels in a regulated universe required that the CRTC buy into the progressive idea of launching as many distinctive channels as audiences and cable operators would welcome.

Moses advocated the "Let my people go" approach. The more the merrier: let the consumer decide, just like at a magazine rack. We would target an underserved segment of interest in the market, cater to it fiercely, and trust that if efficiently operated, it could throw up a modest profit.

While the CHUM team of content producers, executives, lawyers, and regulatory experts explored a multitude of options for new channels—and there were dozens of applications over the years—the one I most wanted was MuchMoreMusic.

MuchMoreMusic

Simply put, MuchMusic was full; the playlist was oversubscribed. With up to a hundred new videos coming in every week, there was a surfeit of choice in a multiplicity of genres. We simply couldn't serve everyone. The ideal was to maintain a wide, eclectic mix, but music fans grouped in tribes: they loved this, they hated that. Jann Arden fans were not likely to sit through a Naughty by Nature video in the hopes that the next one might be Jann.

At its core, Much was about youth, sass, and attitude. Many of our Canadian master-class artists, like Gordon, Anne, Joni, Murray, Celine, Bruce, Robbie, and Leonard, were increasingly finding there was no room at the inn—both on Top Forty radio and in music video land. Some, like Loreena McKennitt, Jane Siberry, Susan Aglukark, and John McDermott, were choosing not to make videos at all. We programmed specialty shows for what was called "adult contemporary" music, but it wasn't enough. I worried that we were headed back to our own musical dark ages, when Canadian singer-songwriters headed south for opportunity.

I think this calls for a tiny bit of Canadian Music history. A Heritage Minute, if you will:

In the fifties and sixties Canada was in a talent free fall, with musicians practically fleeing across the border. Artists like Ian & Sylvia Tyson, Joni, Neil, Leonard, David Clayton-Thomas, Denny Doherty, and Paul Anka all went south. They had to. Canadian records were not abundant on Canadian radio and airplay could be very regional. Aside from a few notable Canadian groups like the Crew Cuts, the Diamonds, and the Four Lads, our charts were full of American rock and roll in the fifties and the British Invasion in the sixties. In Quebec in the fifties, radio stations played French-language covers of British and American hit songs, like César et les Romains' version of Bobby Darin's "Splish Splash" and Les Baronets' "Est-ce que tu m'aimes" cover of the Dave Clark Five's "Do You Love Me." By the seventies, culture-proud French Canada was celebrating homegrown hits by stars like Robert Charlebois, Beau Dommage, and Ginette Reno. In English Canada, music directors complained that Canadian records didn't stack up — that production qualities were poor, and the star quality worse.

Then, from what I can see, five things happened that changed the face of the Canadian music business.

1. In 1967, Canada turned 100. You can't party like a nation without great music, but when we went looking for Canadian songs everybody knew, it was: "What the... Where did everybody go?"

2. In 1968 *RPM* magazine (Walt Grealis and Stan Klees), wanting Canadian music to write about, published a series called "Legislated Radio" that lobbied hard for Canadian content regulations that would force Canadian radio to play Canadian artists.

3. In 1968 Canada elected a swingin', culture-lovin' prime minister. Pierre and Maggie Trudeau loved to dance, and their musical tastes ran wider than the Rolling Stones, so...

4. Pierre appointed Pierre Juneau, a champion of Canadian culture from his days at the National Film Board, as the chair of the CRTC.

5. In 1971, after weeks of lively hearings, the Canadian Content regulations for AM Radio (FM in 1975) were announced, proclaiming that "Canadian broadcasting should be Canadian."

The Cancon regulations required that radio stations play mandated percentages of Canadian music—typically set at 30 percent. Just what constituted Canadian was defined by a new "MAPL" system (Music, Artist, Performance, Lyrics). To make Cancon for radio, you needed two out of four.

Well, didn't that kick up a shitstorm. Broadcasters protested (We'll go broke!), commentators raged (Fascist state!), artists rejoiced (Fuckin' A, eh!)...Well, most of them.

No one went broke. On the contrary, wonderful things happened. Canadian records got heard, radio continued to be profitable, and the MAPL system gave the industry side of the business—the labels, studios, managers, publishers, and promoters—a leg up, too.

I'm oversimplifying, of course. As Larry LeBlanc reminded me, "Prior to the regulations were U.S. breakthroughs by Ian & Sylvia, Gordon Lightfoot, the Guess Who, Anne Murray, and Edward Bear, among others. That creative groundswell, in fact, ended with the regs, only to pick up four years later with Bachman-Turner Overdrive and Rush. Throughout the seventies and eighties labels, in fact, were pulling four and five singles off albums, which was quite damaging to many Canadian artists' careers." The lag is fascinating—and understandable, as supply would have needed to ramp up fast to meet the enforced demand; and it's easy to see, too, how records could have been "burned" with overplay.

But ultimately, the seventies and eighties were a time of great growth. Independent Canadian labels like Anthem (Rush, Kim Mitchell), Aquarius (April Wine, Corey Hart), True North (Bruce Cockburn, Murray McLauchlan, Rough Trade), Daffodil (Crowbar, Klaatu), and Mushroom (Chilliwack, Heart) were flourishing, and GRT Records under Ross Reynolds was signing up a storm (Lighthouse, Dan Hill). Canadian major labels had dozens of direct signings—Deane Cameron at Capitol/EMI had a roster of thirty-five direct signings under his wing at one point. We had exceptional Canadian talent managers: Bruce Allen and Sam Feldman in Vancouver (BTO, Trooper), and in Toronto, Ray Danniels (Rush), Bernie

Finkelstein (Bruce Cockburn), and the late Leonard Rambeau (Anne Murray). Promoters like Norman Perry (Perryscope Productions) in the west, Donald Tarlton (Donald K. Donald) in Quebec, and Michael Cohl (Concert Productions International) in Ontario built the concert market. Michael Cohl and fellow Canadian Arthur Fogel would go on to reinvent international touring as we know it. Today, with Live Nation and AEG Live, it's Canucks who rule the concert world.

Cancon regulations weren't without unintended consequences or controversy. When Bryan Adams was famously denied his MAPL standing on his smash song "Everything I Do, I Do It for You" (on which he had co-writing credits with R.J. "Mutt" Lange and Michael Kamen, who were British and American, respectively) his manager Bruce Allen reacted mightily, lambasting the entire system for promoting "mediocrity."

At the other end of the spectrum, Stompin' Tom (RIP) contended that we could never be Canadian enough. In 1978 he returned his six Junos (by cab) to the office of the Canadian Academy of Recording Arts & Sciences because the awards honoured those "border jumpers" who lived outside the country.

It's good to debate the system. There's always heat around what the "right" percentage numbers should be, the need to support emerging artists versus "burning" the established ones, whether it's even possible to enforce Cancon in digital times, but abolishing Cancon regulations altogether would surely undermine the fertile ground we've gained. It's time for a Canadian content upgrade all around—in music, film, and television— something the Liberal government has recently pledged to do, though it won't be an easy task.

In my time, MuchMusic's Cancon requirements were 30 percent, which, as with radio, was tough at the start, before Canadian videos were plentiful. Later, when Canadian stars made videos of Cancon songs with American directors, their Cancon status on the video could be disqualified. But we didn't complain (too much); we continued to play the big Canadian stars as well as emerging artists. Still, we were running out of room on the channel. I did not want to watch talent wither on the vine due to lack of exposure, not when we'd come so far.

IN 1993, CHUM APPLIED for a MuchMoreMusic licence (among others), but was turned down. CHUM did score a victory with the licensing of Bravo!, but it was disappointing not to be able to mount a channel that I would come to believe we sorely needed.

Maybe this one example (there are many) will make it clear why I cared so much.

That year, Marc Jordan released "Little Lambs" on his *Reckless Valentine* record. It was one of the most heartbreaking videos I've ever seen. The song was inspired by a story of children abused in the 1940s by priests in Quebec; but it captures the grief of mothers anywhere who've been forced to give up their children.

Find the video online, but see if these words don't move you even without the music.

Down the hallways, like a fire
Priests would come drunk with desire
In the silent night I cry,
For the things that they denied.
Say your rosary for me
Get right down upon your knees
Jesus left you all alone,
Little lambs without a home

The video got some airplay at Much, but that song and so many others deserved more concentrated support.

Exacerbating the situation was the threat from south of the border. VH1 — MTV's adult contemporary music video station — was thriving in the States, and if we didn't get a homegrown channel up, the Canadian linkage rules might allow VH1 in — with *no* Canadian content requirements.

In MuchMoreMusic we envisioned a channel that would play a gentler mix of adult contemporary, light rock, classical, soul, jazz, R&B, big band, reggae, and new age. It would be home to our beloved Canadian artists, along with the best from around the world — Elton John, Annie Lennox, Bonnie Raitt, Seal, Sting, Ladysmith Black Mambazo, Ray Charles, Peter Gabriel, and more.

Some thought MuchMoreMusic would be a channel for old farts, but we argued that the psychographics of the music was attitudinal rather than age-based. There were fifty-year-olds who loved No Doubt and twenty-year-olds who loved Sinatra.

The MMM application was filed again on January 11, 1996. We promised thirty-one new full-time jobs and a $17-million commitment to Canadian programming. The competition, we knew, was fierce. Not only was MMM not the only channel CHUM submitted, we were one of forty companies that were after specialty licences that year, of which only twenty-two were ultimately licensed.

MuchMoreMusic application ready for filing.
Left to right: John Jones, Moses Znaimer, me, and David Kines.

A CRTC hearing is a pressure cooker. It's inquisitional in nature, like being a witness on the stand for days, sometimes weeks, on end. We'd cross our fingers for an empathetic commissioner—like courtroom judges, they all had their idiosyncrasies, and theirs was a weighty job. I used to joke that being a CRTC commissioner must have been karmic retribution for some transgression in an earlier life. Once you got through the commissioner's questioning, it was the assistants' turn. They were the ninjas who could unseat the whole thing. They loved to dig in the weeds, looking for detail on infinitesimal numbers, and could drag you under if you weren't sharp.

At the MuchMoreMusic hearing, the presenting CHUM panel was exemplary. It included Sarah, who charmed them with her community standards expertise; David Kines, who brought the programming and technical details; David Kirkwood, who proffered the sales potential; Jay Switzer, the virtuoso who orchestrated the deep business dive on every CHUM application;

regulatory experts Mark Lewis and Peter Miller; CHUM Limited executive VP Fred Sherratt and Ron Waters, who could be counted on to keep us out of trouble; and Moses, who wasn't shy about taking a combative approach on occasion.

I, too, found my groove, singing the praises of Much's considerable contributions to the Canadian cultural landscape thus far, and extolling the virtues our new musical offering would bring should we be granted the licence.

It was an easy case to make. We saw ourselves as an important vehicle for Canadian cultural expression. As we wrote in the application for the MMM licence:

> When Gordon Lightfoot sings about the "Canadian Railroad Trilogy," Joni Mitchell writes about "money riding on the Maple Leafs," Murray McLauchlan sings "Beyond The Timberline," and Barenaked Ladies harmonize about "Jane and St. Clair," we recognize our reality. When Ian Tyson performs "Alberta Bound," Neil Young croons about "a town in north Ontario," Randy Bachman describes his "Prairie Town," the Shuffle Demons perform "Spadina Bus," and the Guess Who sing about "Running Back to Saskatoon," we see ourselves.

Bands like Blue Rodeo, the Rheostatics, and The Tragically Hip — who would come to be called our quintessentially Canadian band — were proudly singing about Canada, and that was important, because with the music videos they made, we really *do see* ourselves: Susan Aglukark in Nunavut, k.d. lang on an Albertan prairie, Great Big Sea in Newfoundland (Oh Yeah!). We hoped MMM would amplify the growth of R&B and soul music in Canada as well. Music videos showed us people and scenery from places in Canada that seldom got exposure, and stereotypes about who we are were both reinforced and dashed. Despite the early predictions about the impact of the music video, video hadn't killed the radio star — it had embellished her.

I concede that my strong Cancon view was, as we would say today, "entitled." When I started at Much, it was the only music video station in the country. We enjoyed strong audiences and didn't fight for every ratings point the way radio, in its crowded markets, had to. Detractors might also say that I could afford to wrap myself in the Cancon flag because I was merely a music programmer, not a station owner. But when it came to licence renewal time, Much was the only station (perhaps in regulation history?) that was *not* asked to increase its Cancon commitment—because we were truly playing to the spirit of the regulations.

It was good to have all that in our back pocket at the hearing; it was actually a pleasure to appear. The team was outstanding, and we retired to the Westin for one (or two) Manhattans (the signature drink of Allan Waters, CHUM's founder). We held then our collective breath during the interventions—both for us and against us. Hearings are a public opportunity for competing broadcasters, industry associations, and interested parties to demand more (or less) of everything: Cancon, closed captioning, tariff increases, et al. And, as in the court system, people might intervene negatively against you, vigorously airing their grievances, and then retire to join you at the bar.

It was a champagne morning (okay, sparkling wine) when we learned that we'd be awarded licences for not only MuchMoreMusic but also Space: The Imagination Station, Star TV, Pulse 24, Canadian Learning Television, and MusiMax in Quebec. Still, the race was not yet won. It's one thing to win a channel; it's quite another to get it up and distributed. There were twenty-two new channels competing with each other for carriage, some of which were owned by the cable operators themselves.

Undaunted, we set MMM's launch date for September 1998 and used the year leading up to that time to lobby everyone in every way we could imagine.

The artists and the labels helped enormously. To create consumer demand, we released a thirty-four-track, star-studded CD (*MuchMoreMusic: Great Music on Television*). It was a rare joint venture with *all* the labels participating, containing the biggest Canadian and international names possible. It was packaged with a fifteen-minute VHS tape of our most beloved Canadian artists singing the praises of the channel.

We pressed the flesh across the country and put on free concerts for cable conventions. At one point, Ron Waters and I were in a meeting with Ted Rogers in his boardroom high up in the clouds, playing him the MMM barker tape. When Bruce Cockburn testified for the channel, Ted leaned over and said with a wink, "I'll bet I know how you got him!" Ron looked at me quizzically. What did he mean? Oh! I got it. He thought I was married to Bruce, not Murray!

But the launch date loomed with no significant carriage. We could create the channel, but in those pre-internet days, without cable operators to carry and distribute the signal, it was like the tree falling in the forest—no one could hear (or see) it. We brazenly told everyone we were committed to launch even without a distributor in place, but I was feeling desperate.

I thought about renting a flatbed truck and a big sound system and asking our musical friends—Anne Murray, Burton Cummings, Gordon Lightfoot, Murray, *and* Bruce—to perform around the clock outside Ted Rogers' house until he gave in. I cornered Phil Lind (Ted's second-in-command) at a cable party and told him I was gathering the musical troops for just such an onslaught. He chuckled and said, "Better not tell Ted." So I went across the room to where Ted was standing with John Tory (currently Mayor of Toronto, but at the time president and CEO of Rogers Media) and told him all about it. Ted looked at me curiously. I'm not sure if he thought I was serious. I was. Our cable relations folks ushered me quietly out of the way and continued their discussions in a more orderly fashion. (In my conceit, I do think it helped.)

The CHUM cable relations team had, of course, been mounting a full-court press for months. At the last minute Rogers came through and added us to their new channel offerings. For sure John Tory was instrumental in that. Shaw Communications came on board next, and we launched MuchMoreMusic on September 30, 1998, to five million Canadian homes.

Left to right: Cam Carpenter, Deane Cameron, Jana Lynne White, Pat Bachynsky, me, John Reid, Ross Reynolds, and Garry Newman.

The launch party was off the charts. Everyone who could be there was: label presidents, promoters, agents, and artists like Robbie Robertson, Anne Murray, Gordon Lightfoot, Molly Johnson, Murray McLauchlan, Chantal Kreviazuk, Tom Cochrane—all hanging out on the cast-off couches we'd bought from Goodwill, newly swathed in cheap shiny fabric. I kept expecting someone to get a spring in the arse or go up in flames from a dropped cigarette, but there were no injuries (other than self-inflicted). The Rankins, Holly Cole, and Chris Isaak performed (and behaved—third time's the charm!). The spirits flowed and we got unprecedented media support, partly, I suspect, because so many of the writers were of an age that they, too, were thirsty for the service.

I loved working on that channel. It felt like *mine* in many ways, a channel I didn't own or inherit but one I'd helped create. I was deeply involved in everything from the station IDs to the set design for *SpeakEasy*, a show where legendary artists would reveal the triumphs and the tragedies of their lives. The show was hosted by Jana Lynne White, who would also be the voice of the channel.

Jana said it beautifully that night to the *Toronto Sun*'s TV critic, Alex Strachan: "We are the first generation to have grown up with rock and roll as the soundtrack to our lives. Rock hasn't become any less relevant to us as we've matured. The master-class artists, the career artists, keep generating new and better material about our lives. It's really the people who are making a life statement who hold my interest."

The launch was a celebration for many and the channel was a joy for years, but no good deed goes unpunished. As I type this, I'm watching a Metallica special on MuchMoreMusic (now called M3) and shaking my head. With all the opportunity to see music these days—on MTV, MTV2, CMT, AUX TV, MuchMusic, MuchLoud, MuchRetro, MuchVibe, not to mention *anywhere* online—why do I need to see Metallica on M3? The spirit of that channel is no more.

TWO YEARS BEFORE, MOSES had been named VP of corporate development at CHUM. He had his eye on more than Canada. World domination? Why not? We all believed that the CHUM brand was distinctive enough to thrive beyond our borders. Might as well get paid for concepts that people were to starting to freely appropriate anyway.

Moses asserted that the "Living Movie" concept—the studioless operating system, the streetfront storefront building, the videography, Speakers Corner—had enough unique character that it could be projected and protected around the world. Moses was hard at work partnering with licence holders for the transfer of the brand "know-how": helping to design and build the operations; educating the staff; and offering access to our original programming.

It was working. Moses was bringing significant royalty fees back to the company and was continuing to press for new opportunities. The CHUMCity International (CCI) corner of the company, led first by Jim Willis then by the irrepressible Stephen Tapp, began to have more prominence in our daily lives.

We were seen as a feisty player, and working with international partners on Much brands in Finland, Argentina, and the U.S. gave me a glimpse into how different cultures worked, which came in handy later at Sony.

Argentina

Soon after I took over as director of music programming at Much, I was on a plane with Moses to South America. In June 1992 he had inked a joint venture deal with Canal Joven for a Spanish-speaking music station in the historic San Telmo district of Buenos Aires. I remember our first late-night business dinner; I was the only woman, surrounded by men in dark suits who were involved in the distribution side of the business. Some of them had arrived with bodyguards, now seated across the room, keeping an eye on the table. I felt like I was in a Scorsese film. It was a typical Argentinian meal, beginning long after I'd normally be in bed, with course after course of red meat on long, sword-like skewers (organ meats first; apparently we were to be served the entire cow from the inside out)—to be washed down with thick red wine. After dinner, Moses suggested we take a picture of the gathering for historical purposes. The men declined. I got the sense that this market didn't operate in quite the same regulated manner as it did in the Great White North.

Our dynamic Argentinian content partner, Ralph Haiek, worked well with David Kines, who was instrumental in setting up the channel. David spoke tech as well as content, and MuchaMusica was on the air in months.

It began simply, with VHS tapes of Canadian programming sent to Buenos Aires, where new Argentinian VJ throws were shot from a location in a converted grocery store and substituted in. Once the studio was in operation, I went down to work with the team. I arrived the day before Enrique Iglesias was due to make an appearance at the station.

Buenos Aires was a bold place in which to begin the international streetfront, storefront outreach. We were warned not to wear flashy watches or jewellery when we visited, nor to walk alone. I was advised that when in a car, I should lock the doors and not open windows at stoplights. I am not a nervous traveller, but on that trip I was overtired from managing a busy station—not to mention having a three-year-old at home—and I was looking forward to getting to the tranquility of the hotel and ordering room service.

I checked into my room, grateful for the bed but too wound up to sleep. Soon, my heart was racing. I was boiling hot and I couldn't breathe. I thought I was having a heart attack. I groped my way into the bathroom. Maybe it was just the blue tint of the lights, but I was convinced I had some freaky disease—I swore I was growing moles all over my body, and that the few I had already had tripled in size. What was going on?

I was having an anxiety attack. I managed to talk myself down eventually. Some brandy from the mini-bar helped, but it was unsettling to be tripped up by your own body. I thought I'd been managing quite well, thank you very much, but adrenaline can only take you so far. There comes a time when you're out of reserves. I'd have to figure out some way to adjust the old work-life balance when I got back.

At the moment, though, there was work to be done. One of my priorities the next day was to get MuchaMusica's front window open. The environment was intended to be open to the street, which was now teeming with Enrique Iglesias fans.

There was huge interest in meeting the handsome offspring of Julio— Enrique's first record had exploded in Spanish-speaking countries. MuchaMusica staff were uneasy about the crowd, so they'd set up an interview location near the back of the studio, away from the fans. That wouldn't do. After some fractured Spanglish negotiations, we reset the location and opened the front window.

If there'd been a decibel meter, it would have red-lined. The moment the crowd saw Enrique, they began screaming and did not stop. The staff was exchanging worried looks, thinking the fans might push right in, but we could not close the window once it had been opened.

The interview went well, assuming that no one actually wanted to hear what was being said. Once the video was playing, security ushered Enrique to the back of the building and eventually the crowds dispersed. Artist management was thrilled at the frenzy (it made good copy) and MuchaMusica's reputation as a fan destination was enshrined.

MuchaMusica was soon a strong contender for viewers and ratings against MTV Latino in Argentina. Theirs was a more pan-Latino channel produced in Miami. It had lots of flash, but there were advantages to being local, especially when it came to reflecting the distinct cultural nuances that existed in South America. There was a lot to learn about international expansion, and sometimes ideas we took for granted had big implications, like Speakers Corner in Colombia.

Colombia

In 1999, CCI's Stephen Tapp and Victor Rodrigues did a format licence deal for Citytv Bogota with Casa Editorial El Tiempo, the publishers of Colombia's national newspaper. Casa Editorial's main shareholders were members of the famous Santos family (Juan Manuel Santos Calderon later became president of Colombia).

Simply put, format deals allowed the licensee to appropriate the "look and feel and operating system" of Citytv/MuchMusic in consultation with Toronto staff. We trained our partners in everything from the lighting and shooting of content to the marketing and philosophical underpinnings of Moses' conceptual approach. It was considered a "perk" to be sent to one of the international locations, although at the time Colombia wasn't at the top of everyone's list, partly due to the activities of FARC (Revolutionary Armed Forces of Colombia), a guerrilla faction operating in the country since the mid-sixties.

I was not involved in Citytv Bogota, so it's not really my story to tell. But I can't resist mentioning two incidents that speak loudly to the "just roll with it" attitude that pervaded Chum's international outreach and gave new meaning to the slogan "Citytv, Everywhere."

In Bogota, it was Speakers Corner (rechristened Citycapsula) that earned the station local respect. It was the first time an average person could get on TV. There were lineups on the street in the first few days, sometimes up to a thousand people waiting to have their say.

David Baker, who was senior director of international development for CHUMCity International, remembers an attack just outside Bogota by about two hundred FARC guerrillas. City sent out a news team to cover the fighting, but the reporter, cameraman, and producer got caught in the crossfire. They were ordered out of the Citytv truck at gunpoint and the truck was stolen. As David recalls:

> Three days later a phone call came in to the switchboard telling them where to find the Citytv truck. Now this *never* happened. When FARC stole a 4 x 4, or any vehicle for that matter, you never saw it again. But the caller said that they appreciated the "loan" of the truck and that they were returning it out of respect. He said they liked Citytv, they had friends working there, and we gave a voice to the "People." For that they were grateful. We wondered, right away, who might those "friends" be?

Citytv "Everywhere."

We also heard a similar story about one of the managers at the station, who was kidnapped while taking a cab ride. They drove him down an alley and looked in his wallet for his ATM card (the practice was to hold hostages for long enough, usually days, to drain their accounts). They saw his Citytv business card and let him go. The reason? The station was good to their employees and stood for balanced journalism and democracy.

Citytv Bogota, by the way, is still on the air.

Finland

Speakers Corner got a slightly different reception in Finland. It was originally positioned behind the station across from the bus depot, and was sometimes confused as a washroom (as opposed to Toronto, where it was sometimes treated as more of a bedroom. The Christmas outtakes tape was always a staff crowd pleaser...).

Jyrki was a MuchMusic International entity that was launched in September 1995. It was a licence deal with Europe's MTV3 (no relation to MTV) channel in Helsinki. It started as a ninety-minute program block, and was an edgy hybrid of both Citytv and MuchMusic.

Like Ralph Haiek in Argentina, Much's content partner in Finland, Marko Kulmala, was proof that to succeed in a global business by focusing on local reflection, you needed the right partners. It helped if they had a sense of humour. It was Marko who insisted the station be named Jyrki, which is a common Finnish name (this, by the way, predated by about twenty years the trend for radio stations in North America to call themselves Bob or Jack). Like me, Marko was also a fan of Ed the Sock. Ed's MO was to speak truth to power, and while he may have caused me to chew a lot of pencils whenever he was live on Much, I never got lead poisoning.

Ed the Sock's Citytv show was on the Jyrki programming schedule and at one point they flew Steve Kerzner (a.k.a. Ed) in to give out an award on Jyrki's music awards show. Steve's jetlag turned to nausea when he landed and spied a full-page ad in the daily paper promising a live Ed the Sock show that very night (Steve was the producer of his own show and knew that more went into its production than most people thought). Not to worry; Jyrki staff promised to guide him through it. Ed found himself on air for a full hour interviewing celebrities he'd never heard of.

"I didn't know an Ismo Alanko from a J. Karjalainen to save my life," Steve told me later. "It was like asking Beyoncé if she was a singer."

"Unlike the Much Music Video Awards," he said, "which was creative chaos, this was just chaos. No cues, no countdowns. I didn't know when I was live or not."

It was always a trip to discover where we aligned culturally and where we diverged at the international stations. Even songs could take on new meaning.

I went with a Jyrki crew to cover a big rock festival held in the midnight sun (a summer day in Finland lasts two months before the sun sets). It was a superb location right on the water. But without the cover of darkness to offer a natural "close" to the main stage, the event took on a Viagra-like vibe of prolonged revelry. The drug of choice was not in pill form, however.

I saw kids staggering around with what looked to be large white plastic Javex bottles tied to their belts. Vodka! I guess you wouldn't want to run out at a multi-day festival where the sun never sets. The Jyrki crew said there were concert staffers, nicknamed "Flippers," who kept an eye out for fans lying face-first in the mud and turned them on their sides so they could sleep it off without suffocating.

Neil Young was the headliner. I knew he was popular in Finland, but the crowd reaction to "Rockin' in the Free World" was over the top. Grown men were crying and clinging to each other. When I asked our Finnish cameraman what was going on, he said, "Russia." Finland and Russia share a long border, and memories of the Winter War of 1939–40 hadn't faded, and no wonder—Russia had annexed huge swaths of Finland's land and wealth, and 12 percent of Finns lost their homes. That's what I still think of now when I hear that song.

Marko was a regular visitor to Canada. He was a fan of Moses' and a big believer in the brand. His attention to detail paid off: in the first year, the show increased its ratings by 50 percent, and the company signed on to another five-year contract. We were tremendously pleased because there were others who simply "borrowed" from the brand as they liked—which was becoming a problem.

News had spread of these radical new ways of making television that was both innovative and inexpensive. The Toronto station was visited by more and more television executives from outside the country, including Lord Marmaduke Hussey, chairman of the BBC; senior executives from NHK in Japan; and Tom Freston and Tony Garland from MTV. Brandon Tartikoff, the powerhouse NBC executive, was quoted as saying, "I can't imagine thinking of television in the same way again." There is a famed Speakers Corner tape with three CBS executives jockeying for position in the tiny booth, saying: "I have seen the future and it is Citytv."

Moses recalls the visit of broadcasting legend Barry Diller, who famously flew in from L.A. on a private jet, spent two hours in Toronto, and returned home the same day. Diller was working for Rupert Murdoch at the time;

Murdoch's Fox had bought six Metromedia stations and was about to start construction on the Fox lot in Hollywood. As Moses tells it: "There was a plan to build conventional TV facilities that would be a template for other stations in the system. [Diller] had engaged a fashionable architect, Richard Meier. We'd met in Los Angeles earlier, but after Diller flew here, the next morning he put all those plans on hold."

Some visitors came by invitation, others not. Moses recalls another "gang from NBC" who didn't announce themselves but stood on the street to have a look. As Moses said in a memo at the time: "As we attempt to license our proprietary concepts in various markets around the world, vigilance is the watchword. Every one of us must take responsibility for the security of our trade secrets." He also tells of seeing CBC president Gérard Veilleux "walk down from his place and stand on the corner to watch Speakers Corner." No harm in that, of course, but Moses got a kick out of a letter he received from a U.S. headhunting firm saying what amounted to: "We hear you're the guy who knows how to run the CBC." Moses wrote back: "Yes I do, but why should I tell you?"

Ultimately it didn't matter how many non-disclosure agreements got signed, how many hands were shaken, or who was watching what was broadcast in plain sight: the unofficial franchise floodgates were clearly open. We started to see elements of Citytv innovations—anchors walking between desks in the newsroom, videographers as reporters, storefront studios—on other airwaves.

According to a June 1996 article in *Canadian Business* by Justin Smallbridge, "Three years ago, for example, a contingent from Chris Craft Inc.'s independent KCOP-TV in Los Angeles visited 299 Queen Street West. The Americans scrutinized the setup, listened attentively to the Znaimer koans repeated by Citytv devotees, then went home to redesign their newsrooms, mobilize their anchors, and wait for a ratings boost. Meanwhile, a CBS-affiliate in Seattle, KIRO-TV, mounted a similar 'unauthorized' bid to ape the Citytv style."

No one blamed Moses for getting pissed. It must have been galling as hell.

MuchMusic USA

1994 was an especially big year for the company's international expansion plans. We were taking on America.

MuchMusic USA was launched on Canada Day in 1994 with partners Rainbow Media Holdings (part of Charles Dolan's Cablevision empire) in a deal negotiated by then CHUM Limited GM Mark Rubenstein.

Two months later at the MMVAs, there was a full contingent of American executives wandering through the Queen Street station to witness the excitement of a MuchLIVE event. The goal was to fire them up to expand our U.S. cable distribution. On hand was a stellar list of Canadian artists from Bryan Adams to Blue Rodeo to Mitsou.

The following morning, our guests picked their way through the alcohol-infused party aftermath to attend a U.S. marketing meeting. Everyone was pumped about the future. I even got a nice memo from Moses: "Last Thursday night's MMVAs and Friday morning's Much in America seminar brought to a triumphant climax a whirlwind of 10th anniversary production and celebration all executed with mastery and flair. Congratulations. I love your ambition."

The media thought that launching Much in the USA was a David and Goliath story, and in terms of size, it was. MTV was in sixty-four countries by 1995, reaching a reported 250 million homes (which also had VH1 and M2) worldwide. We, by contrast, were in the homes of four million cable and satellite subscribers in the U.S. and six million in Canada. Even if you added Finland and Buenos Aires, it all made us little more than an irritating, yet strangely useful, flea. Useful because, with scrappy video channels like us (and, for example, The Box, a national all-request music video service) on the air, MTV could not be accused of monopolistic dealings in its homeland.

Going up against MTV would require herculean strength and resources, but we believed we had a significant marketing advantage — which was, funnily enough, music.

At the time, MTV had begun to play fewer music videos in favour of reality shows like *Singled Out*, *The Real World*, and *The Grind*.

MTV's programming shift was denounced by many, including Bart Simpson, who wrote "I no longer want my MTV" during the opening credits of a *Simpsons* episode. MTV had other music channels, of course — VH1 and later M2, which promised *only* music — but they'd left an opening and we aimed to fill it by offering a loud and proud (though tiny) music alternative.

(By the way, I understood why MTV had moved to long-form programming—it was clearly about viewer retention. The challenge of music videos is their length—they're essentially three-minute short stories, tempting viewers to flip the channel the minute a song they don't like comes on. We weren't above sitcoms at Much, with shows like *The Monkees, Beavis and Butt-Head*, and *The Partridge Family*, but they had to be about music. (The CRTC disagreed with our musical *Partridge Family* argument and we were compelled to remove it from the air.) Personally I thought *The Ren & Stimpy Show* was our bridge too far, although you've got to admit that song at the end, "Happy Happy Joy Joy," was a kicky number.)

There were other music channels operating in America, but I suspect that Much may have been the most irksome, as MTV was not able (yet) to launch in Canada due to our regulatory system.

As Moses said to *Spin* magazine in March of '98, speaking of the MTV map rumoured to adorn Viacom CEO Sumner Redstone's boardroom: "Dozens of countries on it are painted red to represent MTV's market presence, but there's an enormous landmass above the USA coloured white. And the sight of it apparently makes Redstone flagellate the hell out of everyone in the room. There have been days when MTV has wanted to kill us and pull all of our programs."

Even if MTV was playing less music, they were not abandoning their turf. They played hardball with the labels for early exclusivity deals on high-profile new videos. It was a situation we protested vigorously. Music fans set their clocks for new star-powered videos, and it was tough to grow subscribers by serving them the hottest videos lukewarm. The last thing we wanted to do was deprive our Canadian audience of the new stuff.

Our solution was to play the "exclusives" in our country and cover them up on the U.S. feed. Operationally, it was ridiculously cumbersome—forcing us to re-record VJ throws, re-time shows, and re-sequence programming. It got worse when some videos—like new offerings from Oasis and the Red Hot Chili Peppers—were delayed for release in Canada too. As David Kines recalls: "We could sense the mood when an MTV lawyer tried to kill our deal to run an AIDS charity concert called *Red Hot + Rio* with Sting and George Michael. We'd run every Red Hot show over six years. MTV US wasn't even running it but wanted to block our airing anyway."

We believed that music video channels could mirror radio stations in major markets: dozens of channels serving many genres of music, and the more local the better. We put a lot of energy into Much USA, producing more and more programming specifically for the U.S. market. What we didn't do was cover up Canadian music videos in our video flow programming, even if there was no release for the artist in the U.S., which often there wasn't. *Perhaps we could create one*, thought we, hands on our hearts. I loved reverse-engineering Cancon.

We dreamed of the day when we'd have a MuchMusic USA streetfront in New York City, but MTV beat us to it. In 1998, they moved their studios to Times Square. The new studio had windows but was located on the second floor, up from the street and away from the fans—a move we mocked internally, of course; but others noticed that too.

The headline of that *Spin* article in which Moses had mused about Viacom's boardroom map had been titled: "The Great Live North. Like MTV's splashy new format change? Thank Canada's MuchMusic."

MTV president Judy McGrath was quoted as saying, "Imitation is the sincerest form of flattery," a comment she may have regretted when she saw it in print. When the article went on to describe MuchMusic as "the most influential TV network in America," I imagined her reaction was more likely a spit take. Mine certainly would have been. I admired Judy and expect that under different circumstances we might have found some personal camaraderie. There were certainly few other women in the world in similar jobs; it would have been fun to trade battle stories.

(13)

MUCHLIVE

"This ain't no beauty contest. Let's rock and roll!"
— LEVON HELM

IN CANADA WE CONTINUED to work on amplifying the power and distinctiveness of the brand. In other words, going to eleven. One louder. Each evolution of our live performance shows, from *Intimate and Interactive*, *SnowJob* and *SandJob*, and the MuchMusic Video Awards, was growing in size and scope, with bigger stars and larger audiences.

We loved the innovative studio facilities in Toronto, but we were also motivated to get outta town, and because we were hardy Canadians we didn't limit our productions to the fair-weather months. *SnowJob* shows were things of wonder. We shot plucky musicians on wintery stages in British Columbia, Alberta, and Newfoundland, trusting in the weather gods and praying the bands wouldn't get pelted with snowballs (a lesson from Sven Gali's show in Whistler: throwing them back only encourages more), be blown off the stage in high winds (Wilco in Corner Brook), or tempt frostbite (Great Big Sea risked their dangly bits when they took to the freezing stage in shorts and hailed the audience with: "Welcome to the tropical paradise of Newfoundland!"). Marketing pointed out that we might do better with advertisers if we shed the puffy winter jackets, so we shot as much steamy hot tub action as possible. Sponsors no doubt enjoyed the bikinis at *SandJob* 2000 in Florida on MuchMusic USA.

As live outdoor extravaganzas went, though, my personal favourite were the *Electric Circus* dance parties we mounted on Parliament Hill. You could always find the dancers' dressing room by following the trail of glitter and feathers through the House of Commons. We took an immoderate amount of pleasure in knowing that MTV was not dancing on the White House lawn.

My least favourite was our broadcast of Woodstock in 1994. "Two More Days of Peace and Music" was plagued by rain, security issues, and over-crowding and got angrier by the minute. Green Day was pelted with mud on the stage; Nine Inch Nails wrestled each other in mud before they took to the stage; our vehicles were stuck in the mud behind the stage; and at one point I was stranded a mile away carrying thirty pounds of battery belts from the campsite back to the production truck because a twitchy state trooper with his hand on his gun would not let us drive in again once the site was declared a state of emergency. We all lived.

Conceptually, our big musical events were rooted in making the fans an essential part of the show, even though live audiences were always a wild card and required careful crowd control, one thing we never fooled around with.

An early hint that audience engagement might equate with "living dangerously" was when John Martin took Bachman-Turner Overdrive to the Saskatchewan Penitentiary in Prince Albert for a concert. David Kines recalls being "surrounded by prisoners in the middle of the yard when I was handing out MuchMusic pins. Not a great idea in retrospect!"

Both the MuchMusic shooting style and our production teams were held in high regard, and we were asked to record live concerts and DVDs for U.S. bands, as well. One memorable moment was organizing a live *Big Ticket* concert with Van Halen at the Molson Canadian Amphitheatre in Toronto. At the invitation of Ray Danniels (a great manager who always treated me like family) I flew down to Cleveland with director Tom O'Neill to see the band perform, and I wandered through the audience to get a sense of the show and a look at the fans. Crowd shots helped to translate the excitement of a live show to a TV audience. After the show, we met with the band to discuss specifics like camera positions and lighting. At one point, I leaned in (Eddie Van Halen was a little hard of hearing) and said:

"There's only one problem."

"What's that?" Eddie asked.

"Your fans."

"What's the problem?"

"Well, there are a lot of big sweaty guys in ugly shirts. I'm nervous about the close-ups."

"Right . . .," Eddie said, pausing to consider. Then he brightened. "We'll get strippers!"

I thought he was joking, but when the Toronto date came around, there was no shortage of well-endowed ladies in sparkly bras in the first few rows.

And when they said "Jump!" . . .

MuchMusic's true signature style was represented by the shows shot at home on Queen Street West. The Backstreet Boys were the first band that required our closing the streets outside MuchMusic, when they attracted a crowd of over 4,000 screaming fans. After that, street closures became a regular occurrence. Fans would camp out overnight, sometimes for days, hoping to win a coveted wristband and be invited in to personally interact with their idols.

Having bands perform live and then take questions from fans, all on the same show, was a unique concept. And though it was risky, it worked for everyone — including the labels, for whom it paid off in sales. It had to — to take a night off mid-tour to do a TV show was a costly investment in time and lost concert revenue.

Over the years we produced *Intimate and Interactive* and *Live@Much* shows with some the biggest hitmakers on the scene, including No Doubt, Foo Fighters, Sloan, Janet Jackson, Jewel, Sarah McLachlan, the Tea Party, Ricky Martin, Mary J. Blige, 98 Degrees, the Offspring, Britney Spears, Green Day, The Tragically Hip, Jennifer Lopez, Shaggy, Our Lady Peace, *NSYNC, Wyclef Jean, Christina Aguilera, Destiny's Child, Barenaked Ladies, Billy Talent, Evanescence, Coldplay, Meat Loaf, Simple Plan, and tons more. It's a huge list.

Each event required a different vibe; the lighting and set design were tailored to each artist. It was a bit like doing a mini-awards show every month.

It took some years to build the brand, but by 1996–1997 we had more offers than we could program. In 1998 we planned a huge *I and I* with the Spice Girls, and our World Health Organization–dismissing, cannibal-fearing Mayor Mel Lastman sent a letter to the girls begging them on behalf of his granddaughters not to break up before the show (by that time Geri

"Ginger Spice" had left the group). Spice management called me from the U.K., assuming the letter was bogus, but wondering at the letterhead. Had we heard of this "Mayor Lastman"? The manager hoped he wouldn't be breaching any official protocol if he filed it.

The number of fans who came out to see the Spice Girls was estimated at over 6,000, our biggest crowd ever, and it went off without a hitch. The Spice Girls were well acquainted with Much, remembering their previous visit in 1997 when Scary Spice grabbed Master T's face and rubbed it in her ample cleavage. T was rendered momentarily speechless — the look of disbelief on his face was unforgettable.

THE INTERNATIONAL STARS WERE exciting, of course, but the three *I and I*'s that will forever stand out for me, besides the Annie Lennox show, were with Joni Mitchell, Neil Young, and The Tragically Hip. The fact that Joni and Neil had done the show was validation of the highest order, and I believe were a factor, too, in finally convincing The Tragically Hip. We'd worked on big shows before with their (then) manager Jake Gold who produced the biggest outdoor audience ever in Winnipeg for a War Child fundraiser — but this time Jake's standing joke with me was: "The Hip will do an *I and I* the day monkeys fly out of my butt." Not sure about the monkeys, but the day eventually dawned on June 24, 2000. Sook-Yin Lee hosted, and the show was not only transcendent, but patriotic — something we'd come to expect from the charismatic Gord Downie. *Globe and Mail* columnist John Doyle wrote beautifully about the show, which was the same day Stockwell Day was elected leader of the Canadian Alliance Party.

A magnificent moment of Canadian TV was happening at the same time on MuchMusic. The Tragically Hip were doing an *Intimate and Interactive* that went on gloriously for hours. In the pouring rain, hundreds stood outside on Queen Street. Gord Downie, a man with more charisma in his little finger than any political leader and a greater understanding of Canada than all the Alliance candidates, was asked about misconceptions of Canada that he's encountered on the road. "That Canadians aren't patriotic," he said dryly. Then, in one of those spontaneous moments that only happen on

TV, and happen cogently in the electric Much arena, the crowd started singing "O Canada." In salute to a rock 'n' roll band. It was a ragged rendition, but it cut to the heart of this country's culture, a culture alive and well at the corner of Queen and John in downtown Toronto— "ahead by a century" and absent at the Alliance convention in Calgary. It was political and profound and made me thankful for television and the multi-channel universe and the ironies it reveals.

I was blessed to know Gord more fully (perhaps more completely) as a fellow Lake Ontario Waterkeeper steward. His heart is as big as his talent.

IN 1994 JONI WAS promoting *Turbulent Indigo*, the record with her Van Gogh–like self-portrait on the cover. Joni was very involved in the details of the *I and I* negotiation, right down to the colours and sunflowers on the set. It wasn't the easiest contract to hammer out, and in order to close I had to agree to personally host the show. It made sense that she'd want someone familiar; I'd interviewed her in the past and she knew Murray from their Yorkville days. But I was worried about protest from the VJs, and nervous, too, that I was rusty and would do neither the show nor the artist justice. I needn't have worried; Joni carried the show.

Joni was superb: unfiltered, funny, fiercely intelligent, and musically masterful. She had chosen to play solo, just her and an acoustic guitar, which made the performance incredibly intimate. Talk about being "in the moment." Her open tunings, her percussive performance, and her full flavoured voice brought resonance to every note. It would be impossible to be in that room and think anything was missing. Some people in the audience were moved to tears.

She performed nine songs that night, including two new ones, "Sex Kills" and "The Magdalene Laundries," both unknown to the audience, as the new album had not yet dropped.

She told the story of how she came to write "The Magdalene Laundries," which is still for me one of her most moving songs. On first hearing, I thought it was about a residential school in Canada, but it was about a piece of land near Dublin that had been found to contain over one hundred unmarked graves of "fallen women" made to labour as scrub women by the nuns of the Sisters of Our Lady of Charities Magdalene Laundry. It's a story more widely known now, perhaps because of Martin Sixsmith's book *Philomena*, which became a film starring Judi Dench. Yet Joni's four-minute song has a potency beyond those two full-length works.

Someone in the audience asked Joni: "Where does (the) poetry come from?" To which she replied: "I think I'm autistic. Things stick in my craw and they rotate endlessly, and if I don't clear them then I think I'll go mad."

When asked the proverbial "What comes first, music or lyrics?" question, she remarked that if she wrote the music first it was a more challenging puzzle—sometimes even demanding that the lyrics be written in a different language. I remembered her telling me once that she often wrote the lyrics first because if you had to match lyrics to music, you might end up with "Papa don't preach/I'm in trouble...deep." Joni was never one to pull a punch.

She sang "Hejiera," "Cherokee Louise," "Night Ride Home," "Just Like This Train," "Happiness Is the Best Face-Lift"...but I won't attempt to describe them here. As the famous saying goes, "Writing about music is like dancing about architecture."

That show allowed us to bask in the music and marvel at the way Joni's mind worked, her stories adorned with personal musings and little-known facts. When I think back to when I was insisting to Moses that television was a cold medium—well, if it is, then this show was certainly the exception.

The show was appreciated by more than those of us in attendance that night; it won a Gemini Award for Best Performance in a Performing Arts Program or Series.

I've seen Joni on and off over the years and have been blessed to be included at some very special events, from her sixtieth birthday party in a little restaurant up the Sunshine Coast (with uninhibited boa dancing to a local cover band until the wee hours of the night) to the New York opening of the gorgeous ballet *The Fiddle and the Drum*, created for her by Jean Grand-Maître of the Alberta Ballet.

Evenings around Joni require some stamina. She has described herself as "nocturnal," and she'll be just ramping up as we mere mortals are totally spent, having done little but applaud.

One night after she'd been inducted into the Canadian Songwriters Hall of Fame in Toronto, her manager, Sam Feldman, invited a group of us back to the suite. After much drinking, chatting, and smoking, Joni said she wanted to play some new music she was working on. I went into the bedroom to see if we could get the sound system to function for her, and next thing I knew I was sitting on the floor with James Taylor, Herbie Hancock, and Joni, listening to and talking about music. It all seemed pretty normal until I was suddenly self-conscious and feeling totally out of my league. I crept out of the room to let them commune unfettered by a civilian. We need to know our place.

One of my favourite moments with Joni happened in our backyard in Toronto. We were sitting on the bottom step in the garden, me stealing a smoke while Joni kept a lookout. Murray never allowed smoking in the house. "But honey, it's Joni Mitchell," I'd plead. Nope, she has to go outside like everyone else.

I had mentioned to Joni that she shouldn't be alarmed if she spotted any rubber snakes in the garden. We'd been having a problem with skunks and raccoons tearing up the lawn, looking for grubs; I'd returned late from a flight one night to see yards of freshly laid sod curled up like it was just off the truck. The skunks had rolled them up with their noses. We'd tried mothballs and human hair, and a dog wasn't the answer, either. Murray's malamute loved to chase skunks, but they usually got the upper hand.

I'd read somewhere that skunks and raccoons don't like snakes, so I bought a boxful of rubber dime-store snakes in assorted colours and tossed them around. I wasn't sure it would work — those pink and green rubber cobras were hardly biologically accurate — but we were up for trying anything.

I was telling Joni about the battle with the critters when suddenly I saw an actual snake slither across the lawn, from the left to the right, about a foot in front of our toes. It was *huge*: a big yellow serpent about three inches around and at least three feet long with green diamonds on its back. I pulled my feet up and held my breath as it disappeared into the greenery. I got a good look at it, and I've still not been able to find it in any reptile book. Joni just looked at me nonchalantly and remarked, "Oh, you saw it? That's a spirit guide. I see them often," and drew deeply on her cigarette.

The "Hissing of Summer Lawns," indeed.

NEIL YOUNG'S *I and I* — another event I was asked to host during my management years — was an entirely different experience. He tortured me the entire show, in a cheeky, big brother kind of way. Crazy Horse was in the house and they dutifully jammed away in the corner all night, but we got *no* music out of Neil. He walked around with his guitar the whole time, affably answering questions and bantering with the audience. But other than noodling a few notes here and there, he did. not. play. At all. I did my best to convince him, but my entreaties both off camera and on were teased and deflected. "Maybe later," he'd say, wandering over to play with his train set, which had arrived in its own 18-wheeler.

Neil had just bought a partnership in Lionel Trains, the world-famous model train company. He'd always been a fan of trains, growing up beside a railroad track in Omemee, Ontario, and he's a self-described nerd when it comes to technical things. (He'd even devised a digital control switching system for his son Ben, who has cerebral palsy, complete with authentic train sounds for him to enjoy.) Neil had taken to bringing a train set on tour with him, so kids coming backstage with their parents would have something to do.

Watching the show now, and remembering all the times I've seen Neil play live in concert, I get why he didn't perform that day. Performing, for Neil, seems to require a voyage to another plane. If you've seen him in concert, you'll have witnessed how he sinks completely into the music, transported. Switching back and forth from performance mode to interview mode might have been too wide an arc for him to comfortably swing. That's what I think, anyway. Plus, we've known how he feels about cameras in his face ever since Crosby, Stills, Nash & Young's performance at Woodstock. Apparently he told the cameraman: "One of you fuckin' guys comes near me and I'm gonna fuckin' hit you with my guitar." They stayed back.

The *I and I* scenario would have also played into his frustration with seeing his live music on the internet — music that may not have been finished or performed to his satisfaction, yet there it was. So yes, I understood why he didn't play; but it didn't make it any less frustrating at the time. The band was game, the audience was expectant, and live performance was what the show was about!

The set was strewn with candles and Navajo rugs were draped over the pillars, all a good thematic match to Neil's T-shirt, which had a sketch of Geronimo and the phrase, "My heroes have always killed cowboys." But the main feature was that monster train set. It took up most of the environment, with two smoke-spewing trains, mountains, trestles, lots of foliage, and sound effects — train horns and rumbles — which added a significant noise factor to the conversation. That, coupled with the ambient audience noise inside and out, as well as Neil just ambling around the set, sometimes far enough away so as not to hear the questions, made it an unruly couple of hours.

The fans were obsessed with details:

Q: How many guitars?

A: Six or seven on the road.

Q: How many cars?

A: I've kept every car I've ever owned.

"How do you choose which one to drive?" I asked, following up.

"Well, most of them are not working. That narrows it down to one or two... Are we going to get into animals next? Watch out Michael Jackson!"

When might he record with Randy Bachman again? When will he release the long-awaited archival compilations? Answers to those questions and more were "July," delivered with a grin.

When a caller named Ryan struggled (and failed) to compose a question, Neil tried to help.

NEIL: I'll tell you my problem and you tell me your question.

RYAN: Okay, what's your problem?

NEIL: You've been listening to them for thirty years now.

It took me twenty years to look back at that tape, but I have to say it's a rare piece of television that captures many sides of Neil—saucy, serious, and generous to his fans. What they didn't get by way of song, they got by story, and it really was like hanging out in Neil's living room.

Neil talked about the song "My My, Hey Hey (Out of the Blue)," which contains the line "it's better to burn out than to fade away," a phrase Kurt Cobain used in his suicide note. The origins of "rust never sleeps," we learned, came from a recording session with Devo. Mark Mothersbaugh of Devo had a job painting signs for a rust company in Akron, Ohio. Neil said, "Their slogan was 'Rust Never Sleeps' and we haven't talked to the rust company but we're on it (smiles). Most of my songs come from other people's ideas."

He was serious about his advice for aspiring musicians: "If you're a musician and you're worried about music, that is all there is to worry about. I don't think the image makes any difference or what you look like or what the record company thinks you look like. If your music is good and you like your music then nothing can stop you. It's pretty simple — you just have to ignore about 85 percent of what you see."

(Applause)

(Pause)

"It sounds easy, but it's not that easy."

Neil has always taken a strong stand on musical authenticity — his battles with labels are legendary. But another incontrovertible side of Neil is his advocacy. His views are embedded in songs like "Ohio" (police brutality), "Southern Man" (racism), and "The Needle and the Damage Done" (heroin addiction). The *I and I* happened in December 1996. It was a time, like today, of considerable activism and advocacy by Canada's First Nations. The Oka standoff in 1990, and the events in Ipperwash and Gustafsen Lake in 1995, were fresh in people's minds, as were the findings of the Royal Commission on Aboriginal Peoples, tabled mere weeks before the show. It wasn't surprising, then, to get a question from an aboriginal viewer named Jamie in Kamloops who asked what Neil thought about the direction of natives and the roadblocks.

NEIL: Brother, I think you should take a stand. If that's what your heart tells you to do, then you have to take a stand. You have no choice. I think that's where it's at. I think what would be good for all the aboriginal nations around the world (is) if there was a satellite network where all the original peoples could communicate with one another globally in an instantaneous kind of way. I think there would be a lot of big successes from a network for all types of aboriginal nations.

DD: I think that's a great idea, because many of the issues are the same.

NEIL: See that was not my idea, but it's a good idea. (grins)

Almost two decades later, Neil ramped up his level of environmental activism in Canada. He did a series of Honour the Treaties concerts to help raise money for the Athabasca Chipewyan First Nation to fight the expansion of the oil sands on health and environmental grounds. He drove his modified 1959 Lincoln Continental — the "LincVolt" — whose electric engine now runs on cellulosic ethanol, up to Fort McMurray to have a look at the oil sand activity there. Neil compared the site to Hiroshima, calling it an "embarrassment" to Canadians.

It was January 2014. I was at a Massey Hall press conference with Neil, David Suzuki, and Chief Allan Adam of the Athabasca Chipewyan First Nation in Toronto, hoping to grab a one-on-one for the *Zoomer* show I was on at the time. Neil didn't hold back on Prime Minister Stephen Harper: "The blood of these people will be on modern Canada's hands," he said. A statement of action he made to Vancouver's *Georgia Straight* also bears repeating: "We believe that Canada deserves to have the right to clean air, clean water, a clean home, and a clean environment in their Constitution. We demand getting there for all of Canada, and anybody who agrees with us should go for that."

Clean air, clean water, clean environment, enshrined in our Constitution. The brother speaks for me.

WHEN IT CAME TO live shows, there was nothing on television that came close to the MuchMusic Video Awards.

The MMVAs were born out of the ashes of the World Music Video Awards, a global awards show that John Martin had put together with a consortium of music video channels and broadcasters around the world, including Sky Channel in London. It was a grand effort and was beamed to five continents, but it ran for only two years, in 1987 and 1989. In its second and final incarnation Bryan Adams was broadcast live from Moscow, the Fine Young Cannibals from Munich, and k.d. lang and the Stray Cats from Nathan Phillips Square in Toronto. The Bee Gees appeared pre-taped from London, and Whitney Houston presented a Pepsi #1 award to Michael Jackson from Jackson's Neverland Ranch.

The World Music Video Awards were ahead of their time and dogged by challenges. There were language and cultural barriers; the show was expensive to produce; crossed numerous time zones, and each partner was gradually getting swamped by the MTV Video Music Awards.

MTV was extending its global footprint like a giant Pac-Man chomping its way into country after country. MuchMusic was not immune to the pull of its content and had broadcast the awards show since its inception in 1984. In later years, MuchMusic even broadcast live from the red carpet and press room, before and during the show.

I worked the MTV red carpet scrum only once, and that was enough. It was a lesson in humility, jostling for position amidst the crush of kamikaze paparazzi, kettled behind a velvet rope by New York's Finest, and screaming at celebrities for attention. Much was expected to be there, but we weren't granted special treatment among the other international press, despite David Kines' best negotiating, paying a substantial licence fee for the show. MTV was happy to sell us their content, but we knew they weren't necessarily thrilled with *us*, a condition made clear when they threatened to sue us over our use of the letter "M" in the Much logo. We thought they might as well have tried to sue Kermit the Frog—*Sesame Street* characters loved "M"s too—but we did, in the end, adjust our logo, adopting a stylized globe.

What John Martin really wanted to do was a Canadian music video awards show. The birth of the Canadian Music Video Awards (later the MuchMusic Video Awards) was a result of literally thinking outside the box. Moses objected entirely to the idea of mounting a draped-set variety show shot in a black-box theatre, so the gauntlet was thrown to reinvent award shows. That opportunity arose when Pepsi came calling, looking to raise the profile of their upcoming cross-Canada taste challenge train.

The MuchMusic Pepsi Train was a steel-wheeled moving circus that traversed the country in twenty days, leaving Vancouver on June 7, 1990, and giving out awards and hosting live performances in towns and cities across Canada before arriving in Halifax on June 25, 1990, in front of almost 5,000 fans. Artists Maestro Fresh Wes, Blue Rodeo, The Northern Pikes, Jane Siberry, Bruce Cockburn, Barney Bentall, National Velvet, Lee Aaron, 54-40, and the Jeff Healey Band were all aboard. There was a rolling recording studio in a baggage car, and a fully stocked Skyline bar car. Need I say more.

The first stationary MMVAs beamed out of Queen Street West in June 1991. The show was set up, rehearsed, and broadcast in one day—a far cry from the ten days it takes now. Two thousand fans crowded the streets outside, while 1,500 wrist-banded industry folks milled about inside, drinking, talking, tripping over cables, impeding camera shots, and occasionally paying attention to the musicians just inches away, performing live to the nation.

I was a presenter along with Michael Williams, Erica Ehm, Master T, Terry David Mulligan, Ziggy Lorenc, and Steve Anthony. Joining the Crash Test Dummies were live performances from Colin James, Helix, the Grapes of Wrath, the Dream Warriors, Bootsauce, and the Jeff Healey Band. We boasted the world premiere of Air Pirates' "Love Was" video—Ian Thomas' wicked parody of Phil Collins—and John decided to give out an award for "no particular reason" to Bryan Adams.

The morning after was the first of many on which we'd arrive at our desks—having picked our way past roadies tearing down lighting rigs and through the waft of stale beer fumes pervading the halls—to find the party effluvia of crumpled napkins, disposable cups, and half-eaten canapés littering our workspaces. Once I found someone's shoe in my drawer. It was rock and roll, all right.

In 1993, the MMVAs were under my wing. John had invented the party; our task was to grow the concept while keeping the budget and the chaos under control. The team dreamed bigger every year. We'd close down entire city blocks in a week-long set-up of five live stages and broadcast from everywhere—the roof, the streets and the parking lots, and the hallways crowded with industry folk and drunken revellers (often one and the same).

As the show grew, so did the infrastructure and the professionalism of the crew. The meetings expanded—security, local police, fire and safety, operations, production, talent coordination—as did the production team, led by the talented triumvirate of David Kines, Sheila Sullivan, and Neil Staite. That team drew from the entire complement of MuchMusic directors and staff, as well as a cast of characters we borrowed from Citytv operational infrastructure—among them the unflappable John Morrison, Dana

Lee, and Lane Steinhauer, a techno wizard who could fix anything with a soldering iron and some gaffer tape. Security was led by Rob Wright; the sales, marketing, publicity, and communications teams were lead by David Kirkwood, Sarah Crawford, Sandra Puglielli, Dave Caporicci, David Johnson, Michael Heydon, and Susan Arthur. I could go on and on, and I should. It really does take a village. If you look at the MMVAs' website now, it takes a small town!—955 people to put on the show.

It's not an exaggeration to say that MuchMusic pushed the boundaries of live show production, allowing actual fans to engage naturally (they were not rehearsed, told how to dress or when to scream), which was part of the attraction for the artists. We were the ultimate noisy neighbours, closing down John Street, reducing lanes on Queen and Richmond, mounting and coordinating multiple stages, lighting rigs, and control rooms. I'm sure we influenced the price of real estate for cool retail stores (positively) and con-dos (negatively), though we always tried to obey the 11 p.m. sound curfew.

There were lots of production innovations including tents with see-through "crystal roof" canopies so we could get shots from our roof even in the rain. One year we even sprung for a helicopter shot (an expense that we amortized by using the shot over and over again). I'm pretty sure we invented the Fan Choice Award—a hotly contested sponsorship usually won by a salty snack. And I will happily take credit for the awards going gender-neutral in 1997, dropping the "best male" and "best female" qual-ifiers in various categories. As I said to Betsy Powell at the *Toronto Star*: "We don't decide whether or not somebody should be celebrated on their age, ethnicity, or their religion or anything like that so I don't know why sex should be a factor." I thought that one day that the Academy Awards might simply give one award for best actor of any gender, but so far not yet.

Putting on a major show like the star-laden MMVAs is a feat of vision, negotiation, coordination, engineering, and luck. High-wattage stars are always a roller-coaster ride, but when you layer on multiple cameras, stages, and control rooms, along with the weather, a rowdy crowd, and a curfew, "epic" is not hyperbole. We were aware of *all* the things that could wrong, but remained ambitious, if not audacious.

As we grew, we stayed true. We honoured the craft of videomaking as well as the artists. The best video of the year was always Canadian. It was important that our homegrown stars were celebrated with the same intensity as the mounting list of international visitors.

One of my favourite memories, of the Guess Who and Lenny Kravtiz performing "American Woman" together, almost didn't happen.

Randy, Burton, and manager Lorne Saifer were up for it, but Lenny's management was waffling. "It's a totally different song," they protested, pointing out that Lenny's version is in a different key, it's slower, and he doesn't do the guitar solo. They sang the parts to me over the phone. "Listen, Bachman's version is *Dum dah dadadadadaa, da dah,* and Lenny's version is *Bawm kwachakwachakwacha, Bawm Bawm Bawm.*

Hmmm. Methinks thou dost protest too much. It struck me that this would be simple for the musicians to work out, but the decision stalled. Then Lenny's management asked if I could send a recent picture of the Guess Who. Ah. Right. Therein lies the rub. Are the Guess Who hip/young/svelte enough for Lenny?

In the end we had to agree to leave it open to show day, when the musicians had a chance to sit together, which was saying something on a show as complicated as the MMVAs — we needed stage plots weeks ago. Around two in the afternoon, Lenny's tour manager emerged, smiling. We were on. Roadies flew about, consolidating the backline. That night, the music ruled. As it should. Lenny and his band began and then, two minutes in, they changed keys, played a solo, and switched into the Guess Who version. The song went on for five minutes and ended with Burton and Lenny on duelling vocals and the audience pumping their fists in the air.

Classic.

Me, Randy Bachman, Lenny Kravitz, and Burton Cummings.

I remember watching the credits roll on the show that night (credits were always my favourite part—no one died!), marvelling at the magic of this place and all the talented people I was blessed to worked with. I remembered that slow-motion moment in my first week at Much and wondered at the distance I'd travelled, from fighting my fear of being on TV to standing tall in my headset right in the middle of this mad musical circus. They were incredible years of which 1999 was the ultimate.

1999 marked the tenth anniversary of the MMVAs, and it capped off a year of memorable *I and I*'s with Bryan Adams, Blur, S Club 7, Mary J. Blige, and 98 Degrees, and *Live@Much* specials with Lauryn Hill, Cher, Ricky Martin, and Aqua. Our ratings were higher even than one VJ's headgear.

Sook-Yin Lee arrived at those MMVAs dressed all in silver with a large statue of the CN Tower on her head. She is a true original, though the showstopper award went to the Spice Girls' Geri Halliwell, whose red evening gown drew the front pages and officially kicked off the cleavage-baring "Golden Globes" trend. She told Master T she was on the hunt for "a nice Canadian man to fertilize my eggs." Anthony Kiedis of the Red Hot Chili Peppers wore a Ziggy Stardust T-shirt in homage to the undeniable star performer of the night, David Bowie. It was a bright constellation that year: Our Lady Peace opened the show and Britney Spears closed it, while our wranglers manoeuvred Tia Carrere, Sloan, Edwin, Rascalz' Red1, David Usher, Christina Aguilera, and Paul Stanley into place. Bob Ezrin brought his 3-iron in case he didn't make it home before his tee-off time with Alice Cooper the next morning, and when the crowd went crazy screaming for the arrival of the Moffatts, the Barenaked Ladies screamed right back at them.

David Bowie was no stranger to us—over the years he'd done some brilliant *NewMusic* interviews with Avi Lewis and Laurie Brown—but he'd never been performed in the building.

After his sound check, I went back to his green room with Sheila Sullivan to go through some detail with him. He was cordial and warm, shorter than I expected (who wasn't?), and he smelled like he'd just walked out of the shower. As we left, I overheard him remarking to one of his entourage, "This place is chaos. It seems to be run by children!"

It's a sweet memory for me. David Bowie died on January 10, 2016. The loss was profound. For everyone who grew up with him, who's been moved by his music, inspired by his love of art and style, or enchanted by his mind, his death was personal. We felt suddenly closer to our own "scars that can't be seen." He was all that.

NO QUESTION WE WERE part of a Camelot time at MuchMusic. I am immensely grateful to Moses and Ron for allowing us the latitude to "play the instrument" with such experimental licence. I know that kind of freedom is tethered to meeting the bottom line, but I also know how fortunate I was to be able to let my interests in societal issues find a home amidst the business, especially in an institution I didn't own, a company I didn't found.

I was evolving in my thinking about success—personally and in business—coming to believe it must be accompanied by a stronger sense of engagement and commitment. In some ways, those "drive for relevance" programming choices had been selfish—a manifestation of me trying to figure out what it was all *for*. What I was starting to understand was that success had to be grounded in meaning. And if you go looking for meaning, you might just find that sometimes it finds you.

(14)

WAR CHILD

*"If you think you're too small to make a difference,
you've never been in bed with a mosquito."*
— YOGA STUDIO FRIDGE MAGNET

I COULD NEVER HAVE imagined that an engagement in music would
lead me to an amputee camp in Sierra Leone on the west coast of Africa,
shooting a documentary on child soldiers and blood diamonds. Sierra
Leone had just been ranked the worst place in the world to live by the
2000 United Nations Human Development Report. The number-one
country in the world to live was us, Canada. It was a stark contrast. What
was I doing there? Shouldn't I have been at home editing a Madonna special or something?

As a result of all the societal-issue work we were doing at Much, the
station was in hot demand by non-profits and NGOs. Sarah Crawford was
adept at sifting through the requests, and we did a ton of great work with
organizations like Kids Help Phone, the CHUM Christmas Wish, and
CANFAR—the Canadian Foundation for AIDS Research—to name a
few; but we had to be judicious. We couldn't be everything for everybody;
the audience expected us to play some Guns N' Roses videos every now
and then, after all.

Sometimes the right cause just walked through the door. Samantha Nutt
and Eric Hoskins were two young medical doctors who wanted to start
an organization called War Child Canada. Their aim was to help children

affected by war, and they wanted to enlist the spirit and idealism of young people—MuchMusic's audience.

There was something instantly appealing about them, two doctors who had many degrees, spoke several languages, and were brimming with purpose and optimism.

Sam and Eric had spent more than twenty years between them working in some of the most dangerous places in the world: Sudan, Eritrea, Ethiopia, Afghanistan, Somalia, Iraq, and Darfur. Eric was a tall, dark, and serious Pierce Brosnan–lookalike, and Sam was a bubbly blonde slip of a thing who looked more like a babysitter than a medical professional. I quickly learned to introduce her as *Dr.* Samantha Nutt, so that people wouldn't ask her to "please bring us coffee, dear." Her last name wasn't doing her any favours in the *gravitas* department, either.

The more I got to know them, the more impressed I became. Their experiences were miles away from my pedestrian childhood in Scarborough. Eric was a multilingual (including Arabic) Rhodes scholar, the youngest winner of the UN's Pearson Peace Medal, and senior policy advisor to Foreign Minister Lloyd Axworthy. Sam was a Chevening Scholar, which had taken her to the London School of Hygiene and Tropical Medicine and then to Somalia, Burundi, and Liberia. They'd met at McMaster University through their mutual interest in global human rights issues.

Now they were in my office talking about peace, conflict, and social justice as co-founders of War Child Canada. The organization was nothing more than a cell phone in Sam's backpack, but they were compelling. They were passionate about the interconnectedness of foreign policy and public health, the crossover between corporations and munitions, and the impact of war on children caught in the crossfire. These were deeply complex issues, and it was easy to think that nothing would ever fundamentally change. But Sam and Eric didn't see it that way. The more they saw of the injustices and suffering in the world, the more they wanted to do. They knew first-hand how effective the efforts of one person could be. And they knew that MuchMusic spoke to youth often on the brink of engagement. If we could galvanize the attention, energy, and wild-eyed optimism of young people, we really could change the world. Would we help?

It was a persuasive pitch. I remembered my tweenage years and how confusing it all was. Developing a sense of self and figuring out how to fit into the big wide world was part of adolescence. I remember writing my name in school copy books as Denise Donlon, Ellesmere Road, Scarborough, Ontario, Canada, Northern Hemisphere, Earth, The Solar System, The Galaxy, The Universe. You could feel both small and powerful at the same time.

We arranged War Child Canada's first public service announcement on Much, but it wasn't just the audience that engaged. When Sam asked me to go on a trip with them to Sierra Leone, I said yes, even though I had no real idea of where it was.

It had been a while since I'd personally produced any tape, and the idea of getting back into the field was enticing. I offered up my vacation time, and when Ron Waters (who obviously *did* know where Sierra Leone was) wondered why I was heading to such a dangerous place, I insisted that it was important for me to keep my hand in our journalism and he agreed.

Sam reached out to Rascalz, asking them to go on the trip and host the segments. Their celebrity would be the link between this ravaged world and the music television audience. Rascalz were an inspired choice. Red1 and Misfit were influential voices in the Canadian hip-hop scene, and they were principled men. When their *Cash Crop* record was honoured with a Juno award in 1998 for Best Rap Recording, Rascalz refused to accept it. Neither the hip-hop award category nor a musical performance by a hip-hop artist had ever been showcased on the televised portion of the show. The next year, rap was on TV.

Our crew was two women: Tania Natscheff, one of Much's more socially conscious producers, who joined to shoot second camera; and War Child's media director Liz Marshall, who'd also worked at Much and was born to do film work on social issues. When Liz was an eight-year-old girl, she'd written a letter in big block print to Prime Minister Pierre Elliott Trudeau: "I think that our government should get money for the Poor Peolpe Then buying guns and starting wars." She signed it with a big smiley face, and the PM wrote back promising to do what he could. This would be the trip that solidified Liz's commitment to making social issue documentaries.

Sierra Leone was impoverished and broken. Despite the fact that the country was hugely rich in gold, minerals, and diamonds, a history of brutal governments and dictatorships had ravaged the population, and an illegal trade in "blood diamonds"—a term that was very new at the time (and has since been replaced by "conflict diamonds")—fuelled the warlords and rebel groups. Things had deteriorated so badly that commerce had ground to a standstill. There was no functioning economy. By the 1990s government offices were closed, and with no money to pay teachers, schools shut down. Imagine a generation of disaffected young men with nothing to do—no school, no jobs, no hope. They were an easy mark for gangster warlords well resourced with gasoline, drugs, and guns.

One of the worst of the worst was Foday Sankoh, head of the Revolutionary United Front (RUF). He led the civil war that had raged in the country since 1991. Sankoh, who was trained by Gaddafi's militia in Libya, was a brutal rebel soldier who became infamous for kidnapping children and forcing them to mutilate, rape, and kill. Child soldiers—often as young as eight years old—could be made to murder their own families. They were often branded for life psychologically and physically, with the letters RUF carved onto their chests so that they could be identified if they escaped Sankoh's army. Sankoh encouraged his soldiers to pay themselves by looting and stealing what they could before razing the villages. Girls were stolen too and used as porters and wives and sex slaves.

Sankoh's RUF troops were powered by the sale of diamonds, which were mined by forced labour and smuggled out of the country through neighbouring countries like Liberia.

It's incongruous to think that diamonds, so strongly symbolic of love and purity in the western world, could be the cause of so much pain and suffering in Sierra Leone. There, diamonds were not a girl's best friend; diamonds were a guerilla's best friend.

According to the United Nations Development Programme report, as a result of the war, "Conservative estimates suggest that 70,000 people were killed and roughly 2.6 million people, more than half the population, were displaced from their homes. The brutality of the war has been widely recorded; it involved hideous and often macabre atrocities on all sides against civilians, including widespread execution, amputation of limbs, lips and ears, decapitation and gang rape." One theory we heard as to why such brutal tactics were used was that there had been election slogan which read: "The Future Is in Your Hands." The rebels had found an enduringly macabre symbol that the future was, in fact, in theirs.

In May 1999 the UN intervened and a ceasefire was declared under the Lomé Peace Accord. In order to reach an agreement, Sankoh was given amnesty for his war crimes and afforded a government position which gave him control of management of resources and development—the diamond mines.

At the time of our trip in May 2000, there were approximately 11,000 (reports vary) blue helmets in Sierra Leone, but peacekeeping methods had not been wholly effective and the accord didn't hold. Unbeknownst to us, Sankoh's second-in-command in the RUF had refused to disarm, and violence was erupting around Freetown again—right when we were there.

Our War Child/Sierra Leone field party was made up of eight people—Redi and Misfit from Rascalz; their manager Sol Guy; Sam and Eric; videographers Liz Marshall and Tania Natscheff; and myself. We were to arrive at the airport in Freetown from Ghana via helicopter. Lloyd Axworthy, Canada's foreign minister, would meet us at the airport, since he would also be in Sierra Leone, to attend a conference to discuss Canada's role in creating international legislation to stop the use of child soldiers (now called the Optional Protocol to the Convention on the Rights of the Child on the involvement of children in armed conflict).

It was a surreal experience for all of us, especially Rascalz, who had never been to Africa before. It felt like we were in safe hands, though, arriving alongside a hugely respected Canadian politician, and our understanding was that while there still might be fighting going on, the clashes were sporadic and concentrated in the north around the diamond fields, far from us.

Our goal was to visit the amputee camps and the child soldier camps, and interview various NGOs and local journalists in order to tell the stories of those who had been so brutally impacted by the war.

The helicopter ride in was beautiful; the city of Freetown was near the water on a stunningly blue coastline. The mood on board as we drew toward it, though, was sombre. We knew great beauty could exist side by side with dark brutality. We knew we were gazing at the same African coast where for hundreds of years slave-trading ships had departed with their human cargo.

Freetown's history included the *return* of former slaves, as well, and even had a Canadian connection. It had been settled by freed slaves from Halifax, Nova Scotia, in 1792. Aided by the Sierra Leone Company of London, England, 1,192 former slaves—many of whom had escaped from plantations in the southern U.S.—had sailed in fifteen ships to arrive on the western African coast.

Two days earlier, in Ghana, we had been inside an old slave-trading fortress, now known as the Cape Coast Castle, which may very well have been the starting point of that tortuous, two-way journey for some of the Freetown settlers. We were still trying to process the experience.

The castle was surrounded by fishing boats and children playing on the beach, a sharp contrast to the cruelties that had happened inside. Sam, Liz, Tanya, Sol, myself, and a young rapper named Kheaven Brereton (known today as k-os) had walked down the crumbling stairs into the dungeons, stepping out of the blinding sunlight into sudden darkness. Inside the cells it was dank, humid, and alarmingly claustrophobic. Liz worked to adjust the light settings in her cameras as the rest of us tried to come to grips with the fetid surroundings. The rooms were empty, the walls damp and decaying; the floor on which we stood was dark, packed dirt. We were standing on soil that had absorbed the blood of the people who had been held captive here. It was unimaginable to think that these stunted cells could have held up to 1,500 men, women, and children, all of them stolen from their villages. It felt like the shadows of their desperation still clung there. We all felt it.

We, of course, were free to move about—not chained with hundreds of others fighting for space and survival—yet all I wanted to do was *go*, flee this evil place. We turned toward a small wooden door at the end of a long corridor. It was called the "Door to Freedom" though it surely wasn't. It opened to a blast of sunlight onto the beach, where captives would have been forced onto ships, chained, and headed for who knows where.

Sol and I had climbed up on top of the fortress, gulping air. We talked about the stunning resiliency of the people who'd survived. How super-human would you need to be to rise above this abomination?

As we stood on the flat white expanse of the place, we thought—someone should *take this place back*. Imagine a massive concert event right here with successful black musicians and entrepreneurs, doctors and politicians, sports stars and celebrities, all assembled to honour those who'd been stolen, celebrate the triumphs of their progeny, and broadcast it around the world. That would be something.

Red1, Misfit, and Sol land in Freetown.

As our helicopter descended into the Freetown airport, we began to sense there was trouble. We couldn't hear much over the sound of the rotor blades, but we could see a couple of jeeps on the tarmac with a dozen or so armed men in fatigues hanging around, laughing and play-fighting. Some of them had the unsteady gait of drunks. A uniformed man came to the helicopter to greet us, and we were told to grab our backpacks, leave the luggage, and walk quickly and calmly into the airport building. We were also told to hide the cameras; filming was prohibited. We were corralled into a large waiting room, where the drapes were closed and the windows shut. Our passports were collected and then we waited. We didn't know what was going on, but the laughter outside had turned to shouting and we heard the occasional *pop pop* of gunfire. Liz tried to squeeze her video lens through the window to see what was happening, but we were told to sit down and be very quiet. Sam tried to lighten the mood by telling us that if we heard the sound of gunfire when we were in the field, we were to "run in a zigzag pattern." Good to know.

An official explained that ECOMOG—Economic Community of West African States Monitoring Group—soldiers were waiting to return home, probably to Nigeria. Sam added that a year before our arrival, the UN Mission in Sierra Leone (UNAMSIL) had been established to help the Sierra Leone government implement the Lomé Peace Agreement, which included disarmament and reintegration. The number of soldiers operating under UNAMSIL had been increased twice since it was established, but as Sam said, the ECOMOG soldiers weren't reliable. Often they were poor young men from neighbouring countries who were deployed to war-torn regions on the promise of food, a pair of boots, and $25 a month. They could be easily scared and/or bribed. It wasn't the image of the blue helmets I'd come to expect. "Don't worry," she said. "If there has been a change in the safety situation we'll be on top of it."

The arrival of a UN truck was enough to quell the activity on the tarmac, and we rescued our luggage and climbed aboard. Our passports were eventually returned. We were happy to be away from the airport.

On the way in to Freetown we passed a number of makeshift checkpoints. They looked like kids' forts made from rocks and mud, each housing one or two soldiers armed with AK-47s and occasionally a larger fixed-point machine gun. While we showed them our documents, we got a look at the town. There was no mistaking that it had been a battleground: the buildings and walls were pockmarked with gun fire; the ground was covered in rubble.

The first night in Freetown we stayed at a small rundown hotel, which had a crowded outdoor bar populated by customers from all walks of life: NGOs, "working women," and a boorish, drunk diamond merchant showing off a big uncut rock he had in his pocket.

The next day we moved into the UN compound, a large, low-slung former hotel surrounded by UN trucks. We met with the staff to get a safety update, and in the morning we gathered in the parking lot. Our destination was an amputee camp just outside Freetown. Rascalz were late, so Sam went to see where they were. As she got to their door, she smelled something odd yet familiar. When the door opened, a cloud of blue smoke escaped into the hallway. The smell of pot was unmistakable. Sam told them to hurry up and came back to wait with us. When the guys showed up, there was a bigger issue. Misfit was outfitted head to toe in army camouflage fatigues.

Sam said: "You can't wear that. You've got to go and change."

Misfit stood his ground. "But I volunteer for the Canadian army militia. I'm proud to wear this uniform."

Sam was fierce. "You will not go into an amputee camp wearing army clothes. They're a traumatized people. They don't know you're Canadian. We could all get shot at. You either change or we're leaving you here."

Misfit went back to change. I had a moment's doubt as to whether the guys would be a liability here, but we were soon all on the same page.

Our first stop that morning was a sprawling cluster of wooden huts and tents called the Sinan Fakwamu for Tumara Amputee and War Wounded camp. Minister Axworthy was also there.

It was a ramshackle place, sweltering in the heat and grimy with red dust. People were crammed in together in tarp-roofed huts or in tents surrounded by shallow trenches dug for sewage. We met up with a young man named Mucterr who was the chairman of the camp. Mucterr had been a journalist and spoke English. He was also an amputee. When he was captured by the RUF, the rebels cut off his arm "so [he] couldn't write." Then they cut off his ear "so [he] couldn't listen."

Everywhere we looked there was evidence of atrocity, mostly against women and children. There were girls who had been raped repeatedly in the jungle, now taking care of babies who had been fathered by the rebels. There were men with no hands, young girls walking with crutches, their legs having been amputated below the knee or higher; there were tiny children with no arms. We heard stories of how babies would be killed by smacking their heads against a tree.

And yet, we were greeted with smiles and laughter. When we asked young children what they were hoping for, they would often say: "I want to go to school." We found a simple, heart-wrenching sense of hope, despite the all horrors they'd endured.

Redi, Misfit, and Sol were outstanding. Though untrained as journalists, they asked direct, human questions:

What did it feel like?
What do you think of the soldiers who did this to you?
What would you like to happen now?

I watched the way the camp responded to them. Often I'd see Sol playing with the little kids like they were his own. We recorded a young mother sitting with her children as she told Sol how she was forced to watch the amputation of their arms or legs before she, too, was held down across a tree stump and mutilated. Sol was shy about intruding on her grief. He asked her how she felt about us being there filming.

She said: "A lot of video cameras have been coming here and they do this, but I don't see the point of it."

It was a question that many of us were grappling with. We didn't want to objectify the survivors, putting them on display for the media. We were now invested; no longer observers, we were witnesses.

As Redi told me on camera: "It makes me feel sad and depressed. I can't even put it into the words really. It makes things back home irrelevant. I could easily change places with every one of these kids here. They could have been born there, and me here. They have no hate to the people that did this to them. All I see here is just me. Me everywhere."

And then he reflected on his own musical world: "People back home think they're hard core. They think they control the block, but over here a twelve-year-old is packing an M-16 and AK-47. What they're rappin' about is here. And I guarantee half the people who are rappin' about it, and trying to live that life, wouldn't survive in this place. For real."

We talked about the irony of all the gold and diamond bling seen in the music videos. Did those who sported diamond-encrusted dollar-sign necklaces, knuckle rings, or studded teeth have any idea what a blood diamond was? That these symbols of wealth and power could also be rooted in cruelty and enslavement? It was very early in the understanding of what blood diamonds were — eight years before Kanye West released his "Diamonds from Sierra Leone" song.

Sam was busy being a doctor. As we walked through the camps, she would often fall behind, switching from feisty NGO to caring medical professional, dropping to her knees to feel the distended belly of a young child or examine a wound. She didn't have a full kit with her, but she did what she could.

That evening we were invited to attend a reception being held for Lloyd Axworthy by the Honourable Dr. Sama Banya, Minister of Foreign Affairs and International Cooperation. We took the camera and I did an interview with Lloyd about his mission, which was to talk directly to Foday Sankoh and press for the release of the thousands (some estimated as many as 6,000) of girls taken by the rebels. There were three Canadian soldiers at the reception, and they were startled to see MuchMusic filming in Sierra Leone.

"Why not?" I asked. "This story needs to be told. It's been calm for months. The NGOs are here, the UN is here. You are here. It seems safe enough."

"We're only here as observers," they said. "And this is our last night. We're on our way out. You should leave as soon as you can."

That was worrisome, but we had been assured that the fighting was in the north. We were staying in the UN compound, and Canadian authorities knew we were there. We carried on.

Liz was invited to film Lloyd Axworthy's meeting with Foday Sankoh at Sankoh's private compound, up on a hill overlooking Freetown. Liz told us that they were taken into a small room, Sankoh's personal office. Sankoh was wearing colourful robes and a hat, not his uniform. She thought he wanted to give the impression of being a strong African leader.

Liz recalled the experience in a recent email. "It was one of the most chilling experiences. He was a menacing and commanding presence, who clearly had no conscience. He was intimidating. It was beyond chilling just to be in that room."

She described Axworthy as impressive — diplomatic but forceful. He explained that Sankoh was breaking international law pertaining to child combatants and urged him to release the girls. Liz got some footage but was then asked to leave the room and wait outside.

As she wrote to me: "[I was] outside Sankoh's office in the living room. There were two child soldiers standing there guarding his door. They were just kids, maybe fourteen or fifteen years old, dressed in fatigues, holding automatic weapons, and staring at me. I sat on the couch with the camera. There was a TV tuned to the one local community news station. On the TV were amputee survivors, filmed against a simple blue backdrop, talking into the camera, talking about their experiences. I'll never forget it."

She sat there for half an hour before Axworthy's team emerged from the room. There was not much talk in the car. Apparently it didn't go very well; Sankoh hadn't agreed to anything.

The next day we travelled a few miles up the road from the amputee camp and arrived at the St. Michael's Children's Welcome Center. It was a rehabilitation centre for child soldiers, operated by the Family Homes Unit (FHM). There were thirty or forty boys in this camp from what we could see, and we were cautioned against asking them questions about what had happened in the war; the workers didn't want us to stress them unnecessarily. We had to take our time and build some trust if we could.

One of the counsellors told us that a few weeks before, Sankoh had driven up in a jeep, dressed in his military gear and surrounded by his entourage. The boys instantly stood to attention, saluted, and called him "Popay." The camp leaders were devastated, they told us; after he'd left, it felt like they had to start from the beginning all over again.

Tania was shooting B-roll with the small camera and filmed three boys tying a younger boy's hands behind his back. They were playing "war games." She despaired that any amount of healing could remedy the damage that had been done to them.

While some of the boys acted like kids, laughing and goofing around, a few of the older teenagers still felt threatening. They'd surrendered the weapons and the military titles they'd earned in the bush, but theirs was a postured stance with a thousand-yard stare. We weren't in any danger, but I was on my guard, as was Sam.

I admired the work that was being done in that camp; the compassion for kids who had had their childhoods stolen was incredible. But I was finding it hard to rationalize the role of religion. These boys were encouraged to attend services and sing hymns, but how do you replace what they'd known in the jungle—a father-figure warlord who kidnapped them and forced them to commit unspeakable atrocities—with the promise of a mystical and loving father figure they couldn't see? I couldn't help wondering where god had been in the jungle.

It might well take a miracle—in addition to rehab, therapy, vocational training, and a healthy economy—to overcome the challenges the country was facing. Sierra Leone wasn't going to get on its feet tomorrow. Society wouldn't rebuild overnight; the economy would not suddenly rebound. How would rehabilitated child soldiers thrive when they were released into no jobs and few prospects? It was such a difficult mission.

Ultimately, it was the words of the children themselves that offered a glimmer of hope.

Rascalz had introduced themselves and managed to strike up conversations with individual kids. It helped enormously that they were musicians—music can be such a powerful entry point, able to break down cultural barriers and even attitudinal ones. As Sol reflected later, "Art is the greatest bridge, it's the language everyone speaks." Even in town, we watched tough-looking teenagers with mirrored sunglasses be immediately disarmed when they knew Rascalz were Canadian rap stars. At the FHM, the guys gained the trust of a couple of the boys, and we started to film the conversations.

One of Red1's interviews was with a boy of about twelve who had the letters RUF carved into his chest.

"How do they make you fight?" Red1 asked.

"They give you cocaine, to be a wild fighter. If they want to make a fighter out of you, they will give you cocaine. He will abuse you if you don't want to fight. If you fight you will be a second commander. Like me I was a second commander in the bush."

"Why don't you go home to your family?"

"My mother is dead, father dead, the rebels have killed them, so I don't have nowhere else to go. I must stay here."

"How do they go about putting the tattoo on your chest?"

"With a blade," the boy said.

"Just cut it on basically."

"Yes."

Red1 asked the boy if they knew about the amputee camp just down the street. He nodded.

"How do you feel about that?" Red asked.

"I don't feel well. But that is the command they give you. If you don't do that they will kill you," the boy said. "I want to be a new man. Now I am changed, I want me to be a new man, for my future tomorrow. I don't want to be a fighting man again."

"Do you have hope?"

"Yes."

"So do I, my man, so do I."

THE MOST LASTING REVELATION to me, the thing I keep coming back to, was that out of the depths of evil can come the most incredible good.

In the amputee camps themselves, we'd found an astonishing sense of optimism and forgiveness, despite all that they'd endured. They knew child soldiers were living just up the road. They knew that these could be the very same kids who had hacked off their arms and legs, held down their daughters, or shot their mothers. But despite all that, they spoke of love and forgiveness. They accepted that they were victims just like them.

I doubted whether I could be capable of the same forgiveness, let alone of trusting that tomorrow might be better.

I have a photo of Redı on my wall at home. He's standing in the amputee camp holding a little girl who is eight months old. She has been dressed up for the camera, wearing a striped onesie, little red shoes, and impossibly white socks. She's holding onto Red's thumb with her right hand. Her left hand is missing. She would have been a newborn when they held her down and slashed at her arm.

We got up early the next morning so we could shoot B-roll footage of Rascalz on the streets, doing throws to link the footage we'd shot together for air. "Doing a throw" is a deceptively simple way of describing something that can be quite difficult. It usually requires a couple of takes to ensure the performance is good, that people didn't stumble over their words, and to address any camera issues.

In this case, we needed the throws to link the amputee camp to the child soldier camp, and we wanted a shot of Redı and Misfit walking toward the gate and into the child soldier camp.

I'd written fairly basic stuff: "Hi I'm Redı and I'm Misfit and we're in Sierra Leone visiting an amputee camp." What I stupidly didn't expect was that they wouldn't be comfortable saying exactly what I'd written. What happened seems comical now, but it was frustrating at the time. We had so little time and we tended to draw a crowd wherever we went.

Red1/Misfit (walking together toward the camera): "Yo, Canada, I'm Red1 and I'm Misfit and we've been chillin' at the amputee camp."

"What? No, guys, stop please," I said. "You can't say 'chillin' at the amputee camp.'"

"Why not?"

"It sounds disrespectful."

"But we have to be real."

"Well, try and say it in a different way, but like you're talking to your best friend."

"Okay, we'll do it again."

There were a couple more takes, and the guys came through with flying colours. This is what went to air:

MISFIT: We just came from the amputee camp, where we saw that some of the acts of violence on the children there were done by child warriors themselves and we're here now at the rehabilitation centre.

RED1: And this is FHM, and it's a place where kids come and rehabilitate themselves who were forced into fighting wars and then displaced from their families so we're going to go in and meet and greet with some of the families and see what's up — seriously.

MISFIT: Seriousness. What up!

I was scheduled to leave Sierra Leone on May 3 — a day before the rest of the team, because I had a meeting back in Toronto that couldn't be moved. Everyone else was staying to shoot B-roll. Had I known what was brewing just outside town, I would have insisted that everyone else leave, too. But I had no idea. No one did.

I was on a milk-run flight, from Freetown to Liberia, then Ghana to London to Toronto. I was exhausted physically, but didn't fully realize what an emotional toll the trip had been taking until I was aboard the beat-up little plane out of Lungi Airport. I dozed off but woke up with a start, suddenly stung by a chilling question: *What did they do with the hands?*

While you're filming, you focus on the work: capturing footage and interviewing survivors. Get a wide shot, conduct an interview, record a throw. You're trying to stay journalistically objective, editing in your head.

FEARLESS AS POSSIBLE · 295

A degree of detachment is necessary or you'll be unable to perform.

The question that didn't occur to me then came fully to mind now. What *did* they do with the hands? We'd heard terrible accounts from people who said the blades were rusty and dull, that it took an agonizing eternity to saw off their hand or foot. There was one story about a woman who picked up her arm and tried to stick it back on while she was staggering away. I didn't process any of it until I was on the plane. The stories I'd heard played back grotesquely in my dazed half-dream state. I imagined mounds of severed hands and feet; lines of people waiting to be "processed"; a dog running off with a limb...

When I finally got to Heathrow I sat in the lounge and had a very large drink. Then I boarded the next flight and slept all the way to Toronto.

I arrived early enough in the morning to be able to take my son Duncan to school. It all felt shiny and unreal, like I'd returned from a different planet. I was jet-lagged but satisfied that we'd done a good job filming. After I dropped Duncan off, my cell phone rang. It was a man from the Canadian Department of Defence.

"Do you still have people in Sierra Leone?" he asked.

"Yes," I said.

"Do you know where they are?"

"Of course," I said, trying to mentally calculate the time zone and imagine where they'd be. "They should be leaving the UN compound and heading for the airport by now. Is there a problem?"

"There's new fighting there," he said. "The phone lines are down and we just got a report that six foreigners have been killed outside Freetown. It's unconfirmed, but we want to make sure. Do your people have a cell phone? Can you call them and confirm they're okay?"

Cold panic spread through my body and I wanted to throw up. "My people" were seven. It couldn't be just a coincidence, could it?

I spent the morning calling every number I had until finally I got hold of our "fixer" in Freetown, Desmond Kamara, the assistant child protection manager working with the former child combatants at St. Michael's.

"They're okay," he said. He'd just dropped them at the airport. Their flight had to leave early because the airport was being shut down. There were throngs of people, but they had their boarding passes, he said. He was pretty sure they got out.

I thanked him, wished him luck, and called the man back at the Department of Defence, who were able to confirm in a few hours that they were in fact on the plane. The evacuation and the arrival of the British paratroopers made international news. Liz's mom called me and I was so glad to be able to reassure her.

We found out later that the RUF had been advancing on Freetown while we were at the camps. It got bad quickly. Our team got out on May 4 and were home by the time we got the news that five hundred UN peacekeepers were being held hostage by the rebels. On May 6, the RUF had control of the road from Freetown to the airport. On May 8 the place went up. There were reports of a large protest of up to 5,000 people that had converged on Foday Sankoh's house, denouncing him and the rebel troops. Armed rebels fired on the crowd, killing up to nineteen marchers and wounding dozens. The UN had ordered an evacuation of non–Sierra Leonean citizens and British soldiers went in to protect the airport and start an evacuation. UN Secretary-General Kofi Annan called for a rapid response team to help quell the violence. Foday Sankoh was captured on May 17. He was shot in the leg and stripped naked by a mob before he was handed over to government forces.

Foday Sankoh died in 2003 from natural causes while awaiting trial for war crimes. David Crane, chief prosecutor for the Special Court of Sierra Leone, made a statement saying that Sankoh's death from natural causes gave him "a peaceful end that he denied to so many others."

Everyone on that trip was forever changed. Rascalz and their manager Sol Guy tithed proceeds from their next record to War Child for their work in the region, and a few years later Sol produced a television series called *4REAL* that featured young leaders working on social change, education, and poverty initiatives. The show was hosted by celebrities like Cameron Diaz and Joaquin Pheonix, and was distributed in 166 countries and thirty-five languages. Tania continued to work on issue-oriented material at Much, including a sweatshop story with musician Sam Roberts, and Liz started a film company that has produced compelling documentaries focusing on critical international issues, including HIV/AIDS in sub-Saharan Africa, sweatshop labour, water, and animal rights.

For me, the experience was profound. It would take a while to process it all, but certainly the world had been opened a crack. Somewhere in my mind dwelled the feeling that I could no longer confine myself to what was familiar and comfortable.

I continued to document War Child initiatives in other countries, including their work with refugees at the Thai-Burma border and their Access to Justice programming in Northern Uganda following the decades of civil war led by guerrilla warlord Joseph Kony. That time we didn't take musicians; we took four amazing lawyers, Linda Rothstein, Ian Roland, Mike Eizenga, and Sarah O'Grady, as well as videographer/producer Mick Gzowski. They were all incredible, moving experiences. In Iraq, Chantal Kreviazuk and Raine Maida of Our Lady Peace shot the final segment in the War Child–MuchMusic series, which was named *Musicians in the WarZone*. The show reached half a million viewers, a massive audience for social-issue programming on the channel.

As Liz Marshall said: "*Musicians in the WarZone* was award-winning, popular, and effective in reaching a broad youth demographic in Canada — it was undeniably a cutting-edge pioneering effort. No other channel was championing this kind of edgy innovative content with a social justice call-to-action! It was ahead of its time."

(15)

VISIONS OF SPRINGSTEENS
DANCED IN HER HEAD

"Carpe diem."

— FROM BOOK ONE OF HORACE'S *ODES*

IN SEPTEMBER OF 2000, I got a call from an American headhunting firm. These conversations always begin the same way—casual, non-committal, and a little coy: "Would you know anyone who might be interested in the following job prospectus?" While obviously, they're hoping the answer will be: "Why yes, me!"

This time, the call came at an opportune moment. My work-life balance had become what I'd always joked about—an extreme sport—even though there was much to love about life and work. I was surrounded by an excellent team and well lauded. Family life was boisterous and busy. Murray was touring a lot and Duncan, at eight years old, was in full-on extracurricular mode. We appeared to be managing it all well, but I was fooling myself if I thought the pace was sustainable. One of the telltale signs that you should take a break is when you finally do—go, say, on a week's vacation—and immediately get sick. This extreme-sport world doesn't tolerate a break in training.

Heaven knows why I thought being president of a record company might be calmer. A change is as good as a rest?

CHUM was on a roll, having launched Bravo!, Space, MusiMax,

MusiquePlus, CablePulse24, and of course MuchMoreMusic—not to mention local stations in Barrie, Ottawa, and southwestern Ontario. It was a mad, creative time, but it felt like the infrastructure was straining at the seams, especially as we were in the process of submitting applications for more channels. It's sobering to think now how much I would come to miss growth.

The headhunter was calling about a job at Sony Music Canada. They were looking for a new president following the departure of the former president, Rick Camilleri. It was a prestigious position, reporting to Sony Music International, and I had been recommended to the search firm by U.S. artist managers with whom I'd worked at Much.

Would I take a meeting? They would be happy to fly me to New York to meet with Rick Dobbis, president of Sony Music International. I was leery of being seen walking through the doors of Sony Music headquarters; I feared I might be recognized due to my history on air. The last thing I wanted to do was rattle the CHUM chain unnecessarily, especially since I wasn't sure I wanted the job anyway.

"No problem," they said. "There are ways to whisk superstars in and out of the Sony building secretly. We'll have you in and out before anyone knows you were there."

I was already a fan of Sony Music Canada. The company was housed in an innovative, music-centric building built by past president Paul Burger and Quadrangle Architects, on Leslie Street in Toronto. Artists could be signed and recorded in one end of the building and watch their finished product rolling out the door at the other. It was impressive.

I'd recently had an insider's view of it due to an industry luncheon to raise money for music therapy, where I'd been bought at auction to be a temp for a day for an incredible $30,000. It was a staggering number, especially since I'd shown up that morning certain that nobody would bid. Don Oates, senior vice-president of sales at Sony, had saved me from humiliation by bidding furiously against his friend Garry Newman, who was president of Warner. The bid had less to do with what I was worth and more to do with two guys battling for supremacy, of course. Wouldn't be a bad way to start a salary negotiation, though...

Don Oates supervising his "Temp for a Day."

In New York, I was met at the airport by a driver holding a large sign with my name in big block letters. As far as cloak-and-dagger stuff went, it wasn't an impressive start. Luckily it was all clandestine elegance from there.

A sleek black Music Express limo was waiting by the curb, and soon we were cruising toward the Sony offices on Madison Avenue. I was met promptly at the front door and swept into a reserved elevator that opened down the hall from Rick Dobbis' tastefully appointed waiting room.

Rick oversaw a group of far-flung, foreign-speaking company heads— essentially all the Sony Music offices outside of the U.S. and Japan. It was a powerful job. Yet Rick was not at all what I'd expected in a New York record company president. I'd read *Hit Men: Power Brokers and Fast Money Inside the Music Business*. Rick, I'd learned, had sued Clive Davis after he was fired from Arista. He must be one serious s.o.b.! Instead, he was engaged and interested, laughed easily, and was curiously well rounded, happy to talk about politics, culture, books, and especially baseball. His office showcased a collection of gold and platinum albums, signed photographs, and base-ball paraphernalia. (Rick was a Mets fan, he told me, even though his dog was named Dodger.) He couldn't have been more charming. I started to think that if Rick was any indication, this job might be worth considering.

Rick wanted to know about the star system in Canada. What worked and what didn't? What was my relationship with the previous Sony pres-ident like? Did I know Celine? Had I ever met Leonard Cohen? What about this Cancon thing—a help or a hindrance? He was particularly inter-ested in my Blackberry Inter@ctive pager. I was wearing one of the earliest incarnations, which fed one-line texts to the device on my belt (stylin'!). I extolled its time-saving connectivity virtues, and Rick thought he'd have to look further into this newfangled Canadian gadget.

After setting the conversational hook, he started to reel me in. Would I be interested in a little lunch? We went up to the Sony executive suite, where trays of fresh sushi were artfully displayed amongst the fine crystal and linens. Rick greeted fellow execs seated near huge windows overlooking Manhattan. Wow. What a view. It would be tough *not* to feel like a master of the universe dining above some of the highest-priced real estate on the planet.

Rick was a dazzling first date. His years of luring and signing artists had sharpened his skills of seduction. He complimented me on MUCH, telling me how well regarded the service was by artists and managers. He got me talking about myself. "Tell me about your award-winning programming. What are your thoughts on the future of music television? Fascinating. Please continue…"

He knew precisely how to turn a girl's head. It all felt very exclusive and congenial, and the names of the world's musical stars — not to mention dollar signs — were swirling in the air. I could get accustomed to this *real* quick. By the time we finished lunch and he'd tucked me back into the limo, visions of Springsteens danced in my head.

He said he'd call and he did. The next day. I ducked out of the office and called him back from a pay phone on Queen Street West (wouldn't do to be overheard in the office). Nothing like negotiating a big deal on a busy street with swearing street life and garbage trucks loading in the background. My two big questions were: What was the process for signing Canadian acts, and would they be supported in America? And, would I have to release *everything* Sony U.S. put out?

The reason for the first question was obvious. Canadian managers and artists struggled for the affections of the American label heads. Getting a hit in the U.S. was hugely important in that regard — because as far as American labels were concerned, having a hit in Canada was slightly suspect.

I'd heard bona fide Canadian hits being dismissed with comments like, "Of course it's a hit. The stations *have* to play it." There were Americans who saw Cancon less as a boost for homegrown artists and more as thirty protectionist spots on the chart that were denied to them. The perception wasn't helped by one or two Canadian players who painted a ridiculous and condescending picture of Canadian artists as subsidized trough feeders who wouldn't survive on their own.

What I was looking for from Rick was an assurance that Canadian artist signings would be taken seriously and given a shot in the U.S. It was a big ask.

As I'd come to learn, Canada was generally regarded as a branch office by the American recording industry. The power in the global business was in New York, spread among a handful of executives whose views could be highly insular. Canadian label presidents took pride in signing strong domestic artists and skillfully wheeling and dealing with the retail, broadcast, and government brokers in their realm; while some Americans, on the other hand, could be forgiven for regarding the Canadian branches as shipping and marketing mechanisms designed to capitalize on the U.S. company's massive talent investments. In short, sell our records and don't fuck up. What was Canada, after all? In terms of sales size (for English-language records), we were rather like another state, say Texas; but unlike the Lone Star State, we were separated by a pesky border requiring new (and sometimes bilingual) labelling and packaging.

One big North American company would have presented all kinds of efficiencies, but we were not a seamless extension of the American market. For one thing, Quebec had its own language, its own stars, and its own parallel businesses (a constitutional reality not often understood by our industry friends in America). Our sales charts could be quite different too. Big American rock and pop acts and select British acts could sell extremely well in Canada, while other genres, like country and hip-hop, could "underindex," compared to the States.

(There was an expectation for serious Canadian country acts to spend time in Nashville, assimilating styles and session players. As for R&B and hip-hop, we didn't even have a single urban radio station until Flow 93.5 launched in Toronto in 2001, so the chances of a U.S. hip-hop artist selling as well in Canada as they did at home were slim. At the time, MuchMusic essentially bore the broadcast support of hip hop alone.)

For many Canadian artists, a U.S. deal was the Holy Grail. I needed assurance that at Sony, I'd have the bucks and the power to sign the best

Canadian talent and then have the support of the American label to give them a fair shot at making it beyond our borders.

My second question came from a concern that I would have to champion records I might find offensive. MuchMusic had been screening some pretty misogynist videos of late, but the control over whether we aired them or not was always in our hands. Could Canadian record companies veto U.S. releases, I wondered?

Rick had the right answers. He assured me that all Canadian signings would be given proper consideration, and that I could sign whoever I wanted, as far as budgets allowed. As for questionable material, he said that while he couldn't vouch for what they might sign in the future, their legacy spoke volumes. There was certainly no concern with the existing roster. Sony's catalogue was so stellar, most of its artists were referred to by only one name: Streisand, Sinatra, Cash, Ellington, Joplin, Celine, Michael, Mariah, Sade, and on and on. The company had built an impressive and enduring legacy.

I was excited about the prospect of finding, nurturing, and marketing new Canadian artists. When videos arrived at Much, the artists were already fully formed, even the brand-new ones. The songs were written, the records recorded, mixed, and packaged, the artist styled for the video and ready to be widely marketed. The chance to work with raw talent from the very beginning was a rare creative opportunity. I thought of legendary Columbia A&R execs like John Hammond, who discovered Billie Holiday, Aretha Franklin, Bob Dylan, and Bruce Springsteen. (As it turned out, dealing directly with talent was something I would spend less than 5 percent of my working day on — if that.)

"Okay," I said, taking a big breath. "Send me an offer."

A brown manila envelope arrived at home the next day with an offer I couldn't refuse. But there was one more set of meetings to go. I needed to meet Tommy Mottola, CEO of Sony Music, and Don Ienner, president of the largest and most prestigious Sony label, Columbia Records. Though my hiring was Rick's decision and he didn't need their approval, it would be helpful to Canadian artists if these guys warmed to me from the get-go.

I was anxious about meeting Mottola. I read everything I could get my hands on to prepare. Tommy was one of the most renowned record executives in America. Born in the Bronx, he began as an artist himself, then moved through publishing and on to the management of artists, notably Hall and Oates. As chairman and CEO of Sony Music, he'd grown the business from a $1-billion-a-year company to six times that. He worked closely with artists like Michael Jackson, Bruce Springsteen, Billy Joel, and Jennifer Lopez, and was married to Mariah Carey. And he was not only a hit*maker*; he sometimes featured in them. First, he was the subject of "Cherchez la femme" by Dr. Buzzard's Original Savannah Band; then he was referenced in songs by Hall and Oates ("Gino (The Manager)"), Will Smith ("Gettin' Jiggy Wit It" (So So Def Remix)"), The Fugees ("How Many Mics"), Ghostface Killah ("Cherchez La Ghost"), 50 Cent ("Fuck You"), and Lil Wayne ("Spitter"). A streetwise power player, his car was rumoured to have bulletproof windows and he became so iconic he earned a mention in an episode of *The Sopranos*.

Hmmm, interesting! What should I wear?

Rick walked me into Mottola's office on the thirty-second floor. Tommy stood up and we shook hands over his desk. He was wearing a sharp, tailored suit, and his dark hair was slicked back. He was smooth and coiffed, and I thought I could smell money through his cologne. I immediately felt awkward, like a dishevelled kid from the 'burbs. Even his manicure made me nervous. The line from that *My Fair Lady* song popped into my mind: "Oozing charm from every pore..."

I thought I might not like him, but I did. His broad smile and my clear need to make a good impression were a winning combination. He was a rock star, after all.

Tommy's office was subdued and well appointed. The blinds were closed (I'd heard a story that he kept them closed in case his former mentor, ex-CBS president and CEO Walter Yetnikoff, decided to take aim at him through the window—though somehow that didn't seem possible on the thirty-second floor).

"So, Canada. Did you know Camilleri?" he asked.

"Of course," I said. I had often met my predecessor at industry functions over the years, or when he was promoting a high-priority record.

"What's he doing?"

"I don't know. I haven't seen him since he left the company, but I did see a press release suggesting he was going to be a doctor," I offered.

Tommy looked at me sharply, then at Rick.

(I wasn't trying to make a joke; I had seen such a release.)

"I liked him," he said.

I wondered if he'd come to like me. He wished me good luck, and that was that.

Next up was Don Ienner. Now *this* was the executive I should have researched more fully. Donnie could make or break an artist's career in America; he was the ultimate gatekeeper as to what got signed, released, and supported at Columbia.

Don Ienner was a force of nature. He was competitive and combative, a tall, handsome guy who could ignite a room with sheer energy. He was both the youngest and the longest-running president at Columbia. His experience was vast, his mind sharp, and his temper, according to the *Los Angeles Times*, was "legendary." I never felt him to be mean-spirited; he simply saw himself and his artists as the best, and he wanted to be surrounded by the best. He wanted to win. Everything.

Don had lit candles in his office and he was smoking. It felt very inner circle, lighting a cigarette on his couch. He asked me about Murray (who was co-signed to Epic—another Sony label—for *Sweeping the Spotlight Away*, *Day to Day Dust*, and *Boulevard*), and I had a hello for him from Bernie Finkelstein, who had worked with Ienner on Bruce Cockburn. He congratulated Much on taking a run at MTV in the U.S., cannily pointing out, "You know you actually *help* them on the antitrust side, don't you?" I said I thought as much, but surely that was a tactical advantage? There's always room for competition in the good ol' U.S. of A.

We were in and out in ten minutes. I must have passed the audition, as they did mine. What a fun bunch of guys! I thought, channelling my inner Doris Day.

I went home to talk it over with Murray, and we played the Lee Iacocca game where you list all the pluses and minuses. It was certainly an impressive offer on the money and prestige sides, but we knew it would put pressure on the home front with more international travel and added stress while I ramped up in a new position. Murray thought we could handle it and I knew he was proud of me. We'd make it work.

Telling the CHUM folks was brutal. They had been my family for fourteen years. Moses had been a challenging but visionary boss, and I was intensely loyal to the founding Waters family. We'd grown together, taken risks together, gone into regulatory battle together. I knew, though, that people sometimes left CHUM and returned later, armed with new skills and networks, and I was eager to learn.

Moses was incredulous but understanding. The tougher conversation for me was going to be with Ron Waters. I went up to his office with leaden steps. I hoped it wouldn't seem like a betrayal.

I knew I'd be taking Ron off guard. He knew how much I loved CHUM; he wouldn't be expecting a desertion. I levelled with him that I was exhausted by the need to keep running full-out, launching new channels on top of existing ones, and, as Moses would say, "finding creativity in neccssity." Sony was a huge, successful company, and it would be exciting for me to live a little larger, championing projects I believed in. What I did know was that the music stations would be in good hands with David, Sheila, and Neil. We'd built a fine team and my departure would give others a chance to stretch. The transition would be seamless.

Ron offered to match Sony's offer, but I'd already accepted. I hated disappointing him. It's hard to know the right way to handle these situations. If you come to your boss and tell him you're considering another offer, he might think you're playing him. If you accept another job without giving him a chance to counter, it's like you've cheated and the divorce papers are already in the mail. I suppose the only way to approach it is as honestly as possible. Deceit is never good form.

I had the day to tell my closest colleagues, and first up was Sarah Crawford. We'd handled some gut-wrenching issues together as pragmatically as we could, but I knew this conversation would be emotional. We walked outside and down an alley off Queen Street, looking for a quiet spot. We were leaning against a spray-painted wall when I told her.

Sarah was shocked. Her first reaction was priceless: "But you don't know anything about hookers and blow!"

"Actually...," I said, "remember, there was that Whitesnake tour through Europe..."

"Right," she nodded.

We were laughing and crying at the same time. When Joni sang about laughing and crying being the same release, she was right.

David Kines was next. "'Mr. TV" had built an impressive body of broadcasting knowledge since his early days as a videotape editor, and my exit could only mean advancement for him. I had no worries about his leadership, if that's what the decision would be, which happily it was.

The announcement came two days later. The CHUM senior staff assembled in the fourth-floor boardroom while a Green Day *I and I* played on the screens in the background. I remember thinking that would be my last *I and I* as head of the station, and wondered if the song "Good Riddance (Time of Your Life)" might come on to coincide with the announcement that Jay Switzer was about to make. People were stunned. There was hugging and tears—even from some of the men. Moses stuck out his tongue and waggled his fingers in his ears at me. It helped to lighten the moment. Ron handed me two B shares of CHUM stock, so that I would always feel like family, and Marcia Martin, who can be as funny as her sister Andrea, said, "Is that what it takes to get shares in this company? I'm leaving next!"

And I did always feel like family. Years later, I happily accepted Jim Waters' offer to join the CHUM board, ironically just before they sold the company to CTV. It was a sad task to witness the end of a remarkable family legacy.

CHUM TV Girl Power: me, Denise Cooper, Sarah Crawford, and Marcia Martin.

I left with a lifetime of crazy rock and roll stories and an enduring appreciation for everything that freewheeling TV playground had been. Many of us still meet once a year for a big CHUMMY lunch to catch up and reminisce about the old days. We've mostly gone on to other jobs in media, but we all know that the magic of that place—the entrepreneurial creativity of CHUM television and the thrill of flying by the seat of your pants—will never be again. It was a rare adventure and we are all fortunate to have lived it.

THE DAY AFTER THE announcement I was on a plane to the Thai–Burma border to meet up with Dr. Samantha Nutt, along with musician David Usher and his wife Sabrina, on another War Child trip. This time we would be documenting the struggles of thousands of Burmese refugees, who had been fleeing oppressive military regimes, forced labour, and ethnic persecution for decades. It was an early flight and I needed to turn my thoughts to the trip, but the papers had run the news of my joining Sony and my BlackBerry was throbbing. It was awash with good wishes, requests for meetings, and a note from Moses wondering if I was going to get good deals on Sony televisions and when could we talk. I wasn't sure if he was serious. (Emojis didn't exist then.) Labels and artists piled on. It was a head-swelling experience that only succeeded in making me cry. The flight attendant took one look at me and put a double scotch on my tray as he served the morning coffee.

In my journal from that trip, I found this note: *I feel like I've deserted them. Well, I can always go back, but never to that perfect, fine, exciting, creative, meaningful, wondrous, tiring, frustrating, mind-boggling, fantastic job I once had. Oh well, at least I went out before anyone found out I really didn't know what I was doing.*

Astonishing thing, the Imposter Syndrome poking its pugnacious little head through a mountain of congratulatory email. Resilient little beast.

We were on our way to the Umpiem Mai refugee camp on the Thai–Burmese border. Meeting the Burmese refugees who had fled what Amnesty International called "a prison without bars" and trying to bear witness to their immeasurable suffering was incredibly profound. As David said to me, "It was the classic experience where you think things are so important and immediate and so heavy, but if you allow yourself to be pulled out, the world opens up and you suddenly see life through a different lens, one that is less narrow and self-centred. It will change you, and your perspective on the world."

Dr. Samantha Nutt, David Usher, and me.

The trip made for an extreme transition between Much and Sony. I know it sounds trite to compare a conflict zone to a job, but the timeline of those few short weeks made that inevitable. And it *was* helpful to have a wider perspective as I walked into a new job in an industry about to implode.

(16)

WELCOME TO SONY,
THE HONEYMOON IS OVER

*"I can't understand why people are frightened of new ideas.
I'm frightened of the old ones."*
— JOHN CAGE

LITTLE DID I KNOW, when I joined Sony Music Canada in December of 2000, that I was walking into an industry-wide meltdown. The business had been circling the bowl for some months at that point, but few saw the sky falling. After all, the previous year had been brilliant. Worldwide sales in 1999 had reached $38.7 billion U.S.— the highest ever in the recording industry. Turns out, that was the peak. It was downhill from there. My timing could not have been worse.

I'd never worked at a record company, let alone been the president of one, and my learning curve was so steep it was vertical. According to my daytimer, in the first two weeks I analyzed the budget; addressed the troops; found the washroom; reviewed the artist roster; met with HR; responded to dozens of "welcome to the company" calls from fellow international Sony execs and artist managers calling to wish me well, complain about the past, then ask for something; got up to speed on Celine Dion's Vegas plans; vowed to halt cross-border imports; studied the vagaries of Quebec sales; found trust in finance and business affairs; joined an industry pitch to CTV for a Canadian chart show; approved a Ricky Martin promo budget;

travelled the depths of the manufacturing warehouse; tried to memorize the list of distributed labels; scrutinized the release schedule; and endeavoured to make heads or tails out of a tutorial I received from my (departing!) CFO on standard artist payment structure.

The first few days for a CEO are precisely when you must get control of your calendar. Everything from long-ignored HR issues to obscure operations matters will attempt to storm the schedule. Strike while the iron's hot, they'll say. Get her while the door is still open. If you're not careful, you could be hit by the shrapnel of past skirmishes and pressed into service on unresolved issues such as:

- Can employees bring their dogs to work? (Yes. But check if there's someone who's allergic.)

- Should we use more environmentally friendly pesticides on the company lawn? (Sure!)

- Should we open an in-house daycare? (No. What happens when strategic marketing's kid bites health and safety's little darling?)

Business gurus will tell you that great leadership means being able to see the big picture, to clearly communicate the goal, and then to motivate the hearts and minds of those in your organization so they'll follow you over the hill to victory. "Hire and Inspire!" they say. They also say, "Don't sweat the small stuff." But what happens when the landscape is so new that everything seems consequential? When it's so new that you suspect a devil in every unfamiliar detail?

At Much, I'd been at a point where I no longer sweated the small stuff, which left me time to focus on the big stuff like the bomb threat when Madonna visited or the ever-amusing regulatory undertakings. And because I'd come up through the ranks, I could trust my gut. On difficult calls I was seldom challenged.

Sony was very different. Instead of reporting to a family-owned company, I was a cog in a large multinational corporation with so much company jargon that it seemed like a new language. But I soon figured out what bisphenol polycarbonate was (it's the hot goop CDs are made of), how Six Sigma worked (it's a quality-control and efficiencies-measurement system), and what the sales department meant when they talked about "shrinkage." Turns out it's less about cold-water swimming and more about product theft at the store level.

Luckily, when it comes to leadership skills, most gals come well equipped. Anyone who has CEO'd a household knows what it means to organize, prioritize, and energize a team. Women with children excel at motivation and multi-tasking, and I dare say that without a sense of humour mothers would require medication. And moms know that even when you're in charge it's okay to ask questions—people are delighted to impress you with their knowledge at the playground and at work.

For me, the old "fake it 'til you make it" has never worked. The only way I've built any confidence is hour by hour, just like Thomas Edison said: 99 percent perspiration, 1 percent inspiration. And, as a woman, I'm sorry to say, you *do* need to run faster, work harder, jump higher, and learn to thrive sleep-deprived. Remember what was said of Ginger Rogers: "She did everything Fred Astaire did, backwards and in high heels."

There's an early moment of grace in any new job. In those first few days, you actually have time to attend all the departmental meetings and get a sense of what's going on. But when you're in a leadership role, that moment is over quickly. You then have to make some strategic decisions about what your priorities will be, and likely some "blink" judgements on the people you decide to relieve or retain. You can't do any of that well if your calendar is crowded. You must be disciplined about delegation, make time for your own creative thinking, and fiercely control your schedule (one day I may even manage to take my own advice).

Roosevelt's first-100-days approach is now widely accepted as the timeline for establishing new leadership. The company wants inspiration. Walk in with your speech already written. Clearly communicate your vision, set measurable goals, then go get 'em. Attack the priorities, demonstrate some early wins and dig in hard during those next ninety-nine days.

That was my intention, but as John Lennon wrote: "Life is what happens to you when you're busy making other plans."

I was ten working days in when my world flipped upside down. It was a week before Christmas, and I was on the phone with Stu Bondell, head of international business affairs at the New York office. The call was intended to brief me on our various international contracts and build a game plan for addressing outstanding issues. Stu is one of the smartest and, turns out, kindest guys in the business. I'd been nervous about the call, fully expecting to be overwhelmed by legalese, but I had Ian MacKay with me, head of business affairs in Canada, who, along with my new head of finance, Karl Percy, soon became a trusted ally and friend.

We were only a few minutes into the conversation when the front desk interrupted.

"You have a call from a hospital," she said.

I knew Murray was in for an angiogram. I had been expecting a call from him, telling me what time he might be done so I could pick him up.

"That will be Murray. Can you let him know I'll be there in an hour?"

"Okay."

A moment later she buzzed again. "Sorry, they said it was urgent. I tried to get a number for you to call back, but they are insisting they talk to you."

"Okay. Sorry, Stu, could you hold for a moment?"

I picked up the other line and heard the words: "Your husband has had a cardiac episode. We're preparing an emergency surgical team."

I can't remember much more of what was said. Stu and Ian continued the call as I raced to the hospital. On the way I called my mom to pick up Duncan, then called Calvin, Murray's brother, to meet me there.

Within the hour, Murray's immediate family was assembled in the waiting room: his two brothers Calvin and Bill, his sister Sandy, and me. The doctor told us Murray was undergoing open-heart surgery. It seemed impossible. He'd gone straight to the hospital from a karate class, where he was working on his second-degree black belt. He was in strong physical shape. He'd gone off in a great mood.

This was supposed to be routine—"Nothing to worry about, just a simple procedure." Murray's doctor had sent him in largely because Murray was a pilot. In order for pilots to retain their licenses, they are subject to more rigorous medical examinations than the rest of us, and rightly so—you don't want your captain clutching his chest at 10,000 feet.

Around 11 p.m., the heart surgeon walked into the waiting room. R. J. Cusimano is an impressive man—a top-gun cardiovascular surgeon who the nurse had referred to as "The guy who does all the geriatric triples." He was about to go off shift, but had been called to consult on Murray's incident and decided that he'd stay to do the operation himself.

He walked into the waiting room and told us Murray was in ICU, and that the surgery had gone well. Then he asked, "Family?" We all nodded, identifying ourselves as wife, brother, sister, brother. His focus turned to Sandy, Bill, and Calvin.

"Any history of heart disease in your family?"

"No," they all said.

"There is now," he said. "You should all get a stress test as soon as you can."

An hour later we were allowed to see Murray. It was a gruesome sight: tubes in his neck and along his arm and a big ventilator in his mouth, mechanically blowing air—up and down, up and down—into his chest. Cusimano had done a quadruple bypass. He said he only really needed to do one, but once he was in there, he thought he'd "zero time" him. I had always thought that the distinctions of double bypass, triple bypass, and quadruple bypass indicated an increasing severity of the operation, but evidently it's the opening of the chest and the fiddling with the heart that constitute the big stuff. Once you're in, adding another bypass or two is apparently no big deal.

Once we'd looked in on Murray, we stepped outside and were confronted by a wall of freezing rain. Calvin took out a cigarette and handed me one.

"Stress test?" he offered.

Calvin's droll humour. So perfect. I took it.

By the next day, Murray was off the ventilator but was still in ICU. No visitors were allowed except me. I'd called everyone I could think of that would want to know. I wasn't getting a whole lot of answers from the nursing staff, but didn't really know what questions to ask. I was focused on how he was doing, how long it would take to heal, what procedures to follow once he came home.

By day two, December 23, Murray was in the cardiac ward with three other heart patients, all much older than he was. He'd had a busy morning: he'd shuffled halfway to the nurses' station and back before I got there. They want to get heart patients up and walking as soon as they can. Dr. Cusimano swung by, all chipper and full of encouragement. I couldn't stop looking at the surgeon's hands. Those hands had been inside Murray's chest, holding and repairing his actual heart.

Murray was looking better and many of the tubes had been removed. He was blowing into a something called an incentive spirometer, making a ball hover with his breath. Duncan came with me and seemed to handle it all pretty well. Once he was satisfied that he could still give his father a hug, he focused his attention on the beeping machines in the room and then the vending machines down the hall.

As soon as Murray could receive guests, they arrived. Tom Cochrane, Ian Thomas, and Marc Jordan tumbled into the room, guitars in hand and Santa hats on their heads. They sat at the foot of Murray's bed and played and sang.

It was surreal to hear human voices harmonizing in that harsh environment. The guitar sounds echoed off the linoleum floors and swam around the green-washed room, siren songs capturing the attention of everyone on the floor—"What the hell...? Where's that coming from? What's going on?" Nurses stuck their heads in; visitors stood stock-still in the corridors; heart patients staggered toward the room pushing their walkers and dragging their IVs, gawking through the door while their backsides hung out in the hall.

Christmas music. Just a few sweet songs. A warm human gift to remind us that even damaged, cranky hearts can be mended and beat strongly again, full to burstin' with tenderness, friendship, and love.

In a few days Murray was home, with his pills, his post-op instructions, and his red heart-shaped pillow. He was different. He was as weak as a baby but mentally he was ablaze, full of wonder and appreciation, like a kid discovering a shiny stone on the beach. I used to joke that Dr. Cusimano must have fixed the part of his heart that returned phone calls.

As Murray healed, the real story about what happened started to come out. His cardiac trauma had been *caused* by the procedure. The term is "iatrogenic"—a condition caused by interaction with a physician.

It turns out Murray has a left-sided heart. Apparently this is true of about 10 percent of the population, and it means that instead of the coronary artery splitting two ways, left and right, it goes only one way. Murray's angiogram had been conducted in a teaching hospital, and the person who was doing the procedure had tried to force the catheter the wrong way; in doing so, he'd torn the lining of Murray's coronary artery, causing an enormous blood clot to form. That would have killed him had they not gone in.

So Murray didn't have a heart attack. It was a routine procedure that went very wrong.

Murray decided to have a frank conversation with his original doctor. If he levelled with him, Murray would accept what had happened as an accident and move on. Which is what happened and what he did.

Deciding to forgive like that would have been a big decision for anybody, but I think doubly so for an artist. An artistic life is insecure—for many, it's a hardscrabble existence: hand to mouth, feast and famine. There are no pension plans, no medical and dental. A big financial windfall would make any artist's life easier. But Murray chose to act with integrity. He's a man who thinks of principle before money, of honour over opportunity, and that's just one of the reasons I love him.

At the time of Murray's heart incident, he had been writing, recording, and performing for thirty-seven highly successful years. He had twelve Juno awards, three gold records, and his work had been covered by artists like Waylon Jennings and Kris Kristofferson, recorded by Tom Rush and Melanie. His honours—including an Order of Canada—are too many to mention, but above it all he is a terrific father and loving husband and I was so very grateful we didn't lose him.

The first days at Sony had been a whirlwind for sure, but having Murray home from the hospital and recovering well put everything in perspective. The brush with death made our bond stronger, and we knew we could count on each other "in sickness and in health." And I was lucky to have Murray for support. Because life at the new company was about to get truly hairy.

MURRAY AND I COUNTED our blessings over Christmas and managed to find a moment's rest in amongst the family dinners and the New Year's celebrations. A week later I headed back to work, excited about the new job, the artists, and the people at the company, determined to be a force for *good* in the industry.

Sony Music was one of five multinational record companies operating in Canada; the others were Universal, Warner, BMG, and EMI. Sony Music Canada was a significant player due to our strong domestic roster—Celine Dion, Leonard Cohen, Garou, Our Lady Peace, Chantal Kreviazuk, and Amanda Marshall, among others—and because we were the only wholly integrated record company in the country, with recording, manufacturing, printing, and distribution under one roof. Sony was ranked number two in the domestic market at the time.

Our sales force operated as all Canadian major labels did — in ten English-language cities and three French, serving over 1,050 retail, rack, and wholesale accounts like HMV, Sam's, Archambault, and Walmart, not to mention the thousands of outlets like pharmacies, gas stations, and mom-and-pop shops that sold CDs from coast to coast.

We released a ton of product. Before the downturn, the biggest major labels in Canada were releasing upwards of five- to six hundred new titles a year. These new releases were in addition to the thousands of domestic and import titles already available in the catalogue. I was surprised to find that, for some record-store retailers, tracking inventory was rather a mad science. The level of sophistication ranged from modern data management systems to nubby pencils and coffee-stained receipts thrown in a drawer. I was all too familiar with the frustration of artists who'd drive all night to their gig in Moose Jaw and then not be able to find their records in the local store; I'd been there often enough myself on the Doug and the Slugs and Headpins tours. Now I was starting to have some idea of *why* it happened.

Our manufacturing, printing, and distribution plant was busy producing those records seven days a week, putting out product in every genre from classical to jazz, from rock to pop, as well as children's content, fitness DVDs, holiday music, and gifts.

In fact, we were quite good at it. Retail customer surveys rated us number one in the market for fulfillment and turnaround. Our "just in time" shipping operation gave us a competitive edge in controlling inventory and service, and allowed us to keep a tight rein on costs and productivity.

As at any major label, several departments were required to support the product, including promotion and publicity, sales, artists and repertoire (in both French and English), finance, legal, business affairs, licensing, strategic marketing, new media, IT, operations maintenance, engineering, and security. We were also lucky to have a fabulous rapport with Sony/ATV Music Publishing (a separate company that promoted and administered song copyrights), but which also worked out of our building.

At first, juggling the concerns and priorities of all these new departments and personnel — I was responsible for over three hundred people — felt like drinking from a firehose. I had to adapt or drown. As a result, I purposefully focused on building a new skill: the art of compartmentalizing. I don't care if you're the president of a company or a country, you simply cannot lead without compartmentalizing. While I worked through my temporary information overload, I leaned on the experts in the Canadian company. At the same time, I knew, they would also have to learn to trust me. Larry LeBlanc was now the Canadian bureau chief for *Billboard* and reporting on Sony on a regular basis. He recalls, "Sony Canada was seen as a powerful machine with a very strong A&R roster, largely because of the money that Celine Dion brought into the company. But people walked very gingerly around Sony, and the staff was demoralized because of a number of firings that had happened. You were walking into what some people described as a 'culture of fear.'"

For a while I felt a little like Glinda, the Good Witch, peering under the flowers and singing, "Come out, come out, wherever you are!" Slowly, as we got to know each other, there were more smiling faces and fewer furtive glances.

One day I was walking with one of the managers when his assistant ran up with a handful of messages for him and listed the names of people who'd called. "File 'em," the manager said—meaning that she was to throw the messages in the waste basket. He looked back at me, rolling his eyes. I was appalled. I turned to him and said, "Return your calls. Or ask your assistant to redirect them." We did not go the distance together.

I'm judgmental when it comes to arrogance. It was one of the things I always loved about June Callwood—her assertion that "the world needs more kindness." Even if you don't accept that kindness is a winning tactic in the shark tank of corporate culture, it is just good sense to act the way you want to be remembered on the way up—or you'll be kicked twice as hard on the way down.

Besides, I've always felt that the "my way or the highway" approach is the wrong way to lead. We know that it's not the people who are *paid* the most that do the best work; it's the people who feel *valued* the most. That takes effort and empathy, and empathy in particular is seen as a soft and unassertive—female—attribute. When women *do* assert themselves we're seen as aggressive and bitchy anyway, so might as well be "your best self" and get on it with.

There's nothing wrong with being decent, and we certainly shouldn't have to adopt masculine traits or "grow a pair," as I was told to do once.

It's not only inauthentic, it subjugates our femaleness—and surely we've had enough of that.

Humour has worked for me as a leadership tool, even though I've been told that joking with your staff is "unstatesmanlike." I want people to like me; so what? I also want them to enjoy their work environment. I'm not aware that it has ever undermined my authority.

Still, learning to be your best leader self can be confusing when there are so few women role models to emulate. Even though it was right to take that manager down a notch, I immediately felt like I should apologize to him afterward. That may be a gender-based reaction, or perhaps it's just me. I may never shake the wanting-to-please bit.

After I'd been in the new chair for a while, people began to speak out at meetings, taking chances with ideas and owning up to failures, trusting that I wouldn't bite their heads off. I began to feel some positive energy, and thank goodness for that. We were going to need it.

My entrance had coincided (give or take a few months) with the arrival of another newcomer to the music business. Shawn Fanning was a college kid who had just fathered a rambunctious little brawler named Napster. By the time I'd settled in at Sony, the disruptive little dickens had made his presence known. Napster was a kicker and a screamer with a voracious appetite for free music that he loved to share with his friends. He grew big and fast, and by the time he'd reached his terrible twos, he'd made his mark. Napster was David to the industry's Goliath.

UNTIL NAPSTER CAME ON the scene, the music world had been a playground for superstar artists, powerful managers, and industry executives who thrived in celebrity culture. CEOs flew first class, dined in swishy restaurants, and indulged their superstar artists. There were extravagant artist launch parties, massive conventions, and company bonuses.

Sign me up! As I've said, I was looking forward to moving from steerage to business. CHUM had been a magical but relentlessly frugal place where standard operating procedure required us to "throw nickels around like manhole covers." I thought I could be quite good at extravagance given a chance, though some of my friends were skeptical. Pegi Cecconi, VP at Anthem Records and more widely known as QOFE (Queen of Fucking

Everything)—it was actually on her business card—was joking with other Canadian presidents that my work ethic was going to ruin it for everybody, but work ethic wasn't the problem.

The first sign that the tides were turning landed on my desk three days after I'd arrived. It was a directive from corporate "disallowing seasonal expenditures." Great! No gifts, no Christmas party. What a terrific way to hit it off with my new staff. I imagined signing my first festive greeting cards to artists as "Scrooge" Donlon.

Napster, on the other hand, wasn't limiting its festive spirit to one season; Napster enjoyed giving the gift of music all year round. No payment required, no returns necessary. And it was the gift that kept on giving, because once consumers cottoned on to the concept that music could be free, why would they shop retail?

Q: How does a business compete with free?

A: By insisting that yours sounds better, looks better, and *is* better! It's the original, artist-approved, real deal!

Sure, let's try that.

It was like shouting into a gathering storm of voices whose rallying cry was the democratization of music. Not only was music free on illegal sites, but it *should* be free, just like on the radio! (Somehow the idea that commercials paid the broadcast bills didn't register.) Paying for music was instantly uncool. *You bought the new Pearl Jam for $20? Idiot. I would've burned it for you for a buck.*

Protest from record companies claiming that downloading was theft and a criminal activity only served to incite a bonfire of the musical vanities. The labels were tarred and feathered as greedy executives who had profited from the business by gouging the customers and screwing the artists. We were under fire from consumers and artists alike. I remember reading the results of some random survey in which record companies topped the list of sectors that people loved to hate. We were number one! Now *there* was a chart-topper to be proud of. Tobacco companies were number two. Record labels were despised *more* than tobacco companies.

In Canada, the hits just kept on coming. It turned out that in terms of illegal file sharing, Canada *was* a significant international territory. We were blessed with a high level of broadband penetration, and as such we were one of the most connected countries in the world. (In 2002, Canada ranked number three for broadband penetration, behind only Korea and Hong Kong.) So when the opportunity to access free music online came along, Canada *overachieved* as a nation. Compared to every other music territory in the world, Canadians were the number-one users of Napster per capita on the planet. You can imagine how well *that* went over at international meetings. Canada already had a significant piracy problem with bootlegged CDs, and this happy Napster statistic served to cast me as a tall Chicken Little (or Typhoid Mary, hard to be sure). Add to that Canada's outdated copyright laws (I think piano rolls were still referenced on the books) and we were certainly not being carried around on anyone's shoulders while marching bands played.

The major labels responded to illegal file sharing through the Recording Industry Association of America (RIAA), which decided to take action through litigation. Napster was an enemy to be killed, a violator of the worst kind, willfully stealing intellectual property and brazenly sharing the spoils. Legally, it was the correct approach. Copyright belonged to the artist, the labels, and the publishers. This *was* theft. If we slapped them with a restraining order and shut the bastards down, everything would go back to normal. Anyway (we told ourselves), there were some monster records coming in the next quarter that would set things right.

Legal action wasn't the only label strategy. We needed to protect our physical product against illegal copying and convince the consumer that the *only* way—the *right* way—to ensure quality and listener satisfaction and to honour the artist was to buy hard goods from the source. So while R&D departments ramped up in digital rights management, labels investigated new ways to protect existing content, explored new revenue opportunities like CD singles and value-added packing, mounted PR campaigns, and endeavoured to launch legal sites of our own.

In the meantime, illegal file-sharing sites had begun to breed like gophers in a wheat field, and soon the RIAA was playing whack-a-mole with both hands. Fans rushed to sites like Gnutella, Grokster, Freenet, and Morpheus, delighting in this new way of discovering, sharing, and consuming music. It didn't matter that the MP3s had shitty quality, took forever to download, and were rife with viruses. It was the convenience of access, the "word-of-mouse" joy, the range of obscure content suddenly available, the guilty little thrill of getting something for nothing, and—not to be underestimated—the righteous satisfaction of "sticking it to the Man." But the novel attraction in that motherlode of free music was personal choice. Suddenly, you could pick and play and own that one song you really wanted. File sharing was simple and revolutionary, and it revealed an Achilles heel.

Unfettered personal choice was a paradigm shift that was out of sync with the industry's long-established business model, even though the idea that labels had been "forcing" customers to pay for an entire record when they only wanted one song was not a forehead-smacking revelation—the business *began* with singles. But ever since the 33 1/3 RPM high-fidelity long-play vinyl record arrived, holding up to twenty minutes of content per side, the LP had been the industry (and hence consumer) choice for decades. Online downloading made the long-play multi-track album seem like an outdated concept virtually overnight. Long-play records were tailor-made for symphonies, full-length operas, or concept albums like Pink Floyd's *The Wall* or the Who's *Tommy*. But those über-narratives were few and far between.

Vinyl preceded other long-playing capabilities. Eight-tracks and cassettes were de rigueur for a time, but they stretched and broke and jammed in your player. They were replaced by shiny, revolutionary compact discs which not only promised to be an indestructible new format, but could contain a whopping seventy-eight minutes of music. Nature abhors a vacuum and we filled 'er up. Surely more was more! But not any more.

What the audience was telling us was that they wanted *choice*. Free music services revealed that the industry was failing two basic tenets of Business 101: "The customer is always right" and "Give the customer what s/he wants." Album tracks were selected and sequenced and offered in one particular way. The ability to access individual songs, to discover and curate and build personal playlists in unique combinations no compilation department could ever hope to imagine or achieve, seemed an irresistible orgy of digital choice, miles past the mix tape.

The online music sites revealed that our business had operated unlike any other business (with the possible exception of bubble gum cards, where you bought the whole deck to try to get the collectible card you wanted). The free music sites gave people a way to peer inside the plastic, and consumers were no longer content to treat music like a game of chance.

The industry norm was to require artists to produce multi-track offerings, despite the mounting evidence that customers might not want the whole record. To change the model would tear a hole in the fabric of our universe, because the profit structure was set up to support a multi-song product that may or may not contain a radio hit. I should mention that other industry players were complicit in the long-play multi-track format, too. More tracks made more money. Creators were paid for every track, even if only one single sold the album. More pennies to apportion to the artists, the publishers, the labels, the producers, and all the copyright holders.

As sad a statement as this may be, most recording artists never experience what it's like to have a hit. Hit songs are a delicate alchemy that require a rare combination of talent, timing, tenacity, and luck. There are extraordinary talents who write wonderful songs that never get heard, while on the other hand, even the most gifted artists can struggle to produce an entire album of excellence. But the album format required at least ten songs, so co-writers could be called in, or the artists would consider covering others' material. Sometimes musicians would emerge from the studio with more songs than needed. Then a new struggle would begin, with the label arguing for their favourites while the artists fought valiantly for every one of their babies. They'd laboured hard recording them all—but too many songs on a record can weary the listener. Showbiz 101: Leave them wanting more.

Our business could have pushed harder to offer more product choices: not only singles, but doubles and triples. Mini EPs with holograms, red ones, square ones, and extra-chunky, smoky bacon-flavoured ones (thank you, Malcolm Gladwell). Over the years there had been some inventive expressions, but those albums with zippers or paper panties or even boxed sets often meant specialized packaging, non-standard sizing, or unusual shipping containers, all of which would add extra cost to a product that some consumers protested was overpriced already. Bricks-and-mortar retailers were change-resistant when it came to inventive packaging, arguing that it was expensive to rebuild their racks to stock product of varying sizes and shapes. Even efforts like CD singles, which had worked in some parts of Europe, came and went with a whimper in North America.

All that said, I love a full-length CD. I'm one of those people who still buys physical CDs, in *addition* to full albums online. Same for hard-copy books as well as e-books. Physical product versus digital product is a sweet luxury of choice. And I *want* to hear ten songs. I'll listen to twenty back to back if I love the artist. It's how my generation has been conditioned to listen to music.

Most of my favourite records are the ones I've forced myself to listen to in full, lying on the floor, headphones on; immersed in the total experience. It's that deep-dive perseverance through tougher, more artistic material — tracks that could never have been singles — that's given me enduring personal classics like Joni's *Mingus*, or the Beatles' *White Album*, or Thelonious Monk's *Monk in Tokyo* (over which I've spent many happy moments pondering, "Did he *mean* to play that?").

I instinctively bristle at the glib accusation that "there's only one good song on that record" because it usually refers to the single being played *on the radio*. We like it because we know it. Repeat listening is a proven formula for building audience because it builds *familiarity*. It's why we have Top Forty radio in the first place.

Just because it's the single doesn't mean it's the best song on the record; it's just the most radio-friendly, ergo commercially-driven, track. "Don't bore us, get to the chorus!" was a phrase I heard a lot. Top Forty radio's essential mission is to build audience for advertisers. By the time the chosen single has made it to radio it's been A&R'd, vetted, mixed, and remixed, possibly even focus-grouped to appeal to the widest possible demographic. Thou must avoid tune-out at any cost.

I know, I'm not the future and all this ranting underscores my age. My generation curates and collects. Our shelves are jammed with hard goods, bending and groaning under the weight. Kids these days (yes, I meant to say that) discover, listen, comment, and share. More song-oriented than artist-oriented, they collect music in bits and bytes, accessing it online in streams; more like renters, really, than buyers. They don't need to build walls of Ikea shelving because once loved, music can be as easily discarded as an old T-shirt or else stored in the iCloud, quickly accessed if needed again. Yes, there are still collectors — vinyl is making a mini-resurgence — but the days of "the bigger the speakers, the cooler the co-ed" are over.

File-sharing sites created more than a paradigm shift; security issues arose when songs started to appear on the sites when they hadn't even been released yet. Metallica's ironically titled "I Disappear" was splattered all over the net before it was finished, pre-empting its timed release as part of the *Mission: Impossible II* soundtrack. Then it was Madonna's "Music" that got scooped and shared before its official launch. One stolen song was galling enough, but when Metallica realized that their whole catalogue was available for free, they took action and sued. The backlash was brutal, with angry blogging, parody videos, and *SNL* skits. Many artists did not want to risk alienating their fans and kept their heads down. Some spoke out.

Charlie Rose hosted a discussion between Metallica's Lars Ulrich and Public Enemy's Chuck D. Lars insisted that Metallica's battle with Napster was about control of property, not money. Chuck D took a "power to the people" stance, arguing that the internet expanded opportunities for musicians who couldn't get a label deal and would thrive in this new world. Lou Reed stated simply: "Artists, like anyone else, should be paid for their work."

I thought B. B. King's attitude was one of the most sanguine: "It is a good way to promote your music," he told journalist Pat Casey, "but copyright and things of that sort are something that will have to be worked out and they will be worked out. I remember when they didn't want you to have a VCR, but they worked it out and I think for the best. Smart people always get together and work it out."

Problem was, the smart people weren't working it out *quickly* enough. The RIAA sued, the label presidents went to Washington, the legal system was slow to respond, the techs tested glitchy DRM (digital rights management) software, and the pirate sites proliferated. The publicity around the Napster court case only boosted its notoriety and strengthened its appeal. At its height, Napster had close to 80 million users. The fans had tasted freedom and they weren't going back. The genie was out of the bottle, the fat lady had sung, our business model was broken.

AND THEN THE RIAA did something I didn't see coming. They widened the circle of villainy to include the fans. That was a PR battle the labels couldn't win.

The RIAA was aiming at music *uploaders* (versus the downloaders), but individual infringers were an imprecise target because the internet service providers would not divulge the names of their subscribers due to privacy concerns. As a result, when the RIAA laid 261 copyright infringement charges in September 2003, unusual suspects were unearthed. One of them was a twelve-year-old girl named Brianna. The press had a field day citing one of the songs she'd infringed: "If You're Happy and You Know It (Clap Your Hands)." Turns out she had been sharing Mariah Carey and Christina Aguilera as well—among the thousand other songs she'd enjoyed. But her mom didn't think her daughter was doing anything wrong; after all, she'd paid Kazaa a $29.95 service charge.

Another press-worthy example was a surprised seventy-one-year-old Texan. He'd been unaware of any musical infringement. His online activity had been perpetrated by his grandkids.

Canada was under pressure from IFPI (the International Federation of the Phonographic Industry) to sue users as well, and the Canadian Recording Industry Association (CRIA—of which Sony was a member) threatened lawsuits in February of 2004. The CRIA had IP addresses of twenty-nine uploaders and wanted their ISPs to turn over their names, but needed legal permission. When the request went to court, a judge named Konrad Von Finckenstein ruled against the labels in a bizarre decision that turned jurisprudence on its ear, essentially saying that downloading was legal because of a (controversial) Canadian blank-tape levy. The CRIA appealed and the decision was eventually overturned, but by then industry members had reasoned correctly that suing customers was killing our chances to win the bigger war—which was copyright reform. Canada became one of the few countries in the world that chose *not* to sue uploaders.

The lawsuits that did proceed resulted in the recording industry being further demonized—Canadian labels included. At this point the industry was also working to educate consumers and sway public opinion back in its favour with public awareness campaigns.

Our anti-piracy campaigns had three strategic prongs: Fear, Empathy, and Gratitude. The Fear strategy linked copyright infringement with scary criminal activity. You wouldn't steal a handbag, so why steal music? Piracy is a crime. You can click but you can't hide.

The Empathy approach pointed out that piracy is not a victimless crime. Artists were being hurt; people just like you were losing their jobs.

The Gratitude angle thanked people for buying physical CDs. In addition to the anti-piracy warnings printed on pre-recorded music, little cards were inserted into jewel cases, thanking people for their purchase as they fluttered to the floor.

One of the cheekier efforts was Canadian. It was a PSA created by Moontaxi Media for its Puretracks online music store (a legal Canadian site) and supported by the CRIA. The idea was to let parents know that if their kids were surfing illegal peer-to-peer music sites, they might as well be surfing porn and were one click away from computer crashes, viral infections, and probably STDs. The video featured young Johnny on the computer, while just behind him on his bed a film crew was shooting a porno. Mom walks in to tell Johnny that his lunch is ready, oblivious to the danger. Incredibly the video starred Ron Jeremy, an actual porn star.

There were also public policy issues. While the industry was working on better digital rights management applications and copy-protecting releases (which some artists protested because they limited the fan's use and were often faulty), there were many questions to answer — and the answers varied from country to country.

How many times should a CD, once purchased, be allowed to be copied? Once for personal use? Once plus once again for a mobile device? Should it be available for personal use on any device consumers owned, easily transferable from their computer to their MP3 device, their car, their arm while they're jogging through the park? What if you shared an earbud with a friend? I joke, but the debates were complex and endless. Often, too, they felt moot. The faster new DRM tools were invented, the faster they were hacked.

It was a fight on many fronts, but it was a losing battle. One indicator was the increase in CD-R sales. At the time, the best way to store your downloaded music was to record it onto blank, recordable CDs. In 1999, 45 million CD-Rs were sold; in 2000, it was 95 million. By mid-2001, Canadians were buying three blank CD-Rs for every one pre-recorded CD. Yup. The ratio was *three to one.*

Six months into the job, it was clear that the record business was in a bleak downward spiral. Record companies everywhere were cutting costs, reducing spending, and laying off staff.

Yet we were all still attending to our day-to-day business: signing, nurturing, and developing artists; marketing records; manufacturing and distributing product; and pouring on the coals to invent new business models.

There were, of course, people at the labels who were pumped about all the fantastic opportunities this new technology could bring: faster distribution, direct audience interaction, and a world not saddled by manufacturing and shipping costs.

Notwithstanding the potential in a new business model, though, the labels were behind the eight ball. The criticisms were coming from all and sundry, some deserved, some not so much:

1. You were ostriches. You should have embraced the future and banded together to launch your own music site.
You're right, except that U.S. antitrust regulations (sensible prophylactic legislation meant to prevent monopolistic practices) stopped us from "colluding" with competitive labels to launch a viable legal alternative of our own. We had to divide in order to conquer. So Sony buddied up with Universal and launched an online music store called Pressplay, while Warner, BMG, and EMI mounted a joint venture called MusicNet. But the sites were hobbled by two significant flaws. First, people don't search for music by label. No one's first reaction to a new song is, "I love that song. I wonder what label they're signed to?" With the exception of highly specialized labels like Solitudes or maybe Putumayo, few people care what label something is on. And second, fans want *all* their music to be available in one spot. Without an ocean of content from all five labels and the independents, the new sites weren't competitive with the free illegal sites that offered everything. Not to mention the fact that we were asking consumers to pay for music they could easily find elsewhere for free.

2. You were risk averse.
Not true. Record companies were always gamblers at heart. We bet on artists and singles all the time. And when we won, we won big. The model in the old days was that the earnings from the top few superstars paid for the losses on everyone else. It's still the model.

Organizationally, major labels were like most big businesses—pyramidal, hierarchical structures. It's why we courted nimble, streetwise independent labels, incorporating their bright shiny ideas into the corporate culture. But as the business started to crumble, the indies played harder to get and began to spurn the advances of the majors. When I pursued an indie label in Canada, I suddenly felt like I was sporting a bad comb-over.

We knew that digital distribution was disruptive, but also presented heaven-sent, cost-saving efficiencies. We knew that if we didn't embrace the future we would be today's Classifieds to tomorrow's Craigslist. There were efforts to buy our way forward, as BMG did with Napster and Universal with MP3.com, but it wasn't the whole solution.

3. You were dinosaurs, slow and lumbering under your own weight.

Guilty, your honour, with an explanation. While it's true we lawyered up and lobbied and legislated, the stumbling block—and it was a big one—in making deals with legitimate online music distribution companies was all about the money, honey. We were bound to ensure that content creators were compensated, but no one knew how much was fair. Getting paid fairly is *still* the issue on so many fronts.

Existing contracts didn't chart digital territory. Royalties and publishing rights and producer points in the physical world were painstakingly argued, point by point, in contracts the size of *War and Peace*, but this new online world was the Wild Wild West. No one wanted to be the first to make a deal in case they shot themselves in the foot, underestimating the enormity of this new frontier.

Where was the trust, you might ask? Trust had hitched a ride on the first coach outta there long ago. (The seeds may have been planted in Tin Pan Alley, or when Alan Lomax or John A. Lomax held credits on songs they collected and recorded but did not write, like Lead Belly (Huddie Ledbetter)'s "Goodnight Irene," a song Ledbetter himself reportedly learned from his uncles, and the royalties from which were reported to be in the millions.)

In the modern music business, you'd be foolish to walk into a deal without your legal gunslingers in tow, not only to negotiate the deal on the table, but to anticipate where you *might* need rights in a world of changing delivery systems—like in Hollywood, where the "In all media throughout the universe and in perpetuity" language unspooled like the opening screen in *Star Wars*. The age of digital distribution put content creators on their guard, suspicious, nervous, waiting for someone else to draw first, even while the response called for swift action.

The intricacies of copyright are too complex for this book, but I want to make the point that sometimes doing the *right* thing is not the easy thing.

When someone downloads a song for $0.99, that dollar must eventually be divided between dozens of rights holders (including Apple and other online sites, which typically keep the first third). Keeping track of all those pennies requires some serious back-office accounting, not to mention international royalty collectives that monitor use and chase payment. In a penny business a percent of anything requires huge consideration, and the early negotiations were steely-eyed and fraught.

You may think I'm exaggerating. I mean, how hard can it be to carve up the payments on a song? It depends on the song. Here's a quick (but not exhaustive or necessarily in order) list of rights payable to the people or organizations who'd be in line for compensation.

Who Gets Paid
1. Songwriter/composer: One person or many people, depending on who wrote what and sometimes even who was in the room.

2. Publisher: Publishing company which administers the songs for the songwriter.

3. Performers: Singer or singers and musicians on the song, including feature performers and studio musicians.

4. Master rights holder: Usually the label, which owns the recording of the song.

5. Producer: Big-name record producers (and mixers) who can be awarded percentage points of sales (and writing credits), as well as their fee.

6. Beats provider: The person who created the beat track that underscores the rhythm of the work, especially in hip-hop tracks.

7. Synchronization rights: Money earned if the song is used in a TV show/commercial/film/DVD/ring tone/video game, etc.

8. Mechanical rights: Money collected when the song is reproduced or transferred to other formats, e.g. CDs, MP3s, or streaming.

9. Performance royalties: Paid to an organization like SOCAN in Canada, which tracks, collects, and distributes the royalties when

a song is broadcast or performed live in public. (Note: there are separate performance royalties collectives for songwriters/publishers, performers, and sound recording rights holders.)

10. Print rights: Sheet music or song lyrics quoted in a book.

11. And, (because it should always go to eleven): Sampling, i.e. other copyright: if a sample of someone else's song is used in a new work, the number of people needing to be paid can increase exponentially.

Sampling is a big subject and the compensations required for the use of other musicians' work—like when Vanilla Ice sampled the Queen/David Bowie riff from "Under Pressure" in his song "Ice Ice Baby"—is a hot debate. There's no simple formula, and what constitutes fair payment takes into consideration how substantial the use is and what is called "fair dealing" in Canada. How original is the sample? How recognizable? How long? How often is it used in the song? Is it an homage to the original creator or does it parody? Answers to all affect the compensation in the industry, and hopefully the artist who is sampled approves the use.

4. All your eggs were in one basket.
Right! Back to the litany of woes. It's true; record companies were not well diversified. Labels sold recorded music. When that music was suddenly available for free, there was incentive to share in the other offshoots of the brand the labels had helped to build. An artist's livelihood comes from a variety of sources, including touring revenues, publishing, merchandise sales, books, and sponsorship deals. Labels didn't make any money off touring, even though they paid to support the tour in order to sell more CDs; labels didn't share in T-shirt sales, even though the marketing of the artist was part and parcel of creating a demand for the merchandise. There was even a position that labels should share in management fees because the record company folks often helped to guide careers.

When the business began to tank, there was an urgency to engage in "360 deals," utopian arrangements captured in one-page agreements in which the artist and label (and others) acted as true partners, sharing everything equally.

360 deals were slow off the mark. The rights holders were not always thrilled at the idea of signing over a chunk of their ancillary rights. And it's not surprising that music business lawyers wouldn't love the idea. Who would rush into a new world of one-page contracts when you got paid by the hour to negotiate? We all wanted simpler agreements, but let's be clear: A record contract is intensely negotiated. The managers were in the room, the lawyers were in the room, the artist was represented in the room. Negotiations could be so protracted that the artist's advance could be spent on the lawyer's new kitchen before the contract was even signed.

The labels took the heat for being the bad guys. Fine. The labels were not blameless. That said…

5. Be careful when divorcing the beast; you might end up in bed with a bigger, scarier beast.

With the rights holders playing chicken, the free music sites multiplying like rabbits, and sales targets for physical product falling like dead ducks, it took an outsider to supply the solution.

It was Apple that rode up on its white steed. In 2003, Apple launched iTunes with all five major labels on board; a one-stop, multi-functional online site that was fan-friendly, widely populated, and highly innovative. Apple sold 70 million songs in its first year and is now the largest digital music retailer in the world.

All hail Apple!!

It was thrilling to watch digital sales becoming more robust, gaining ground against illegal sites around the world. Today, after a decade of doom, the record business is finally starting to turn around, showing emerging signs of growth. But who is Apple's shining knight campaigning for, ultimately? Consider that iTunes and now Apple Music puts a *lot* of money and power in one place, and they're not shy about wielding that power; nor about making sure the pipe is paid first.

Apple typically deducts approximately $0.30 (depending on the deal) on a $0.99 download before it pays out. Yes, they have distribution and operational costs, but they are certainly profiting. Apple, Google, Microsoft, the cable companies, and the telcos—they're all companies of which music is merely one product, and often a sideline among an array of offerings.

An example which I think underscores the commodity point happened in June of 2015, when Apple got a swift kick from Taylor Swift. Apple told artists that while it was offering its new streaming service, Apple Music, for free, the artists wouldn't be paid for the first three months. Taylor Swift threatened to withhold her latest record, *1989*, telling Apple: "We don't ask you for free phones. Please don't ask us to provide you with our music for no compensation." She and her 59 million fans caused a commotion and Apple immediately caved. Apple's senior vice president of internet software and services, Eddy Cue, sent out the following on social media:

> *@cue: We hear you @taylorswift13 and indie artists. Love, Apple* (Eddy Cue)

> *@cue: #AppleMusic will pay artist for streaming, even during customer's free trial period.*

Nice to know that artists can still lead change.

WHILE SOME POINTED THE finger solely at illegal file sharing for everything that was wrong with the music business, there were more hands besides the labels in that mix: the managers who did the deals, the lawyers who advised the managers, the big box stores that used music as loss leaders to sell fridges, the record clubs that offered ten CDs for a penny, the consultants, the bean counters, the downloaders, the uploaders, the quarterly targets that truncated artist development, the boy bands that charged children $500 for a concert ticket, the culture of celebrity, antiquated copyright legislation, Auto-Tune, catalogue prices, videos that defaulted to T. & A., reality TV shows that made music a contest, Topcon, Ticketmaster, Clear Channel, and sure, let's throw Tipper Gore and the PMRC in there too.

I'm immensely fond of my colleagues in the music business, still busting their butts to make great music, but I learned a few things while at the helm of a (then) sinking ship.

- A successful negotiation is one in which *both sides* win.

- Crisis begets opportunity. Don't take your foot off the gas when you're going up a hill.

- Do well by doing good.

- Believe.

THERE WERE MORE BUSINESS challenges on the way, but I still found great joy in the job and the music was easy to believe in. I was blessed to work with three of the biggest artists in the Sony music world: Leonard Cohen, Celine Dion, and Garou, all of whom were expected to deliver big records.

Leonard was first up. He was working on his new record when I arrived and we were anxious to hear new music. It had been ten years since his last studio release.

On May 27, 2001, I was flying to Los Angeles with our head of business affairs, Ian MacKay. I was cramming on the plane: listening to, reading, and re-reading everything I had on Leonard Cohen.

The purpose of the trip was to hear his new record. Leonard had been working in Los Angeles with his recording partner Sharon Robinson for many months, and the label executives were eager to hear the results.

Leonard was (and is) an icon, revered not only in Canada but around the world. His music sold extremely well, particularly in places like Scandinavia—where I expect his poetic virtuosity helped to pass the long, dark days—and in Poland, where Leonard had outcharted Michael Jackson. There were big sales forecasts on this record and Ian and I would be the first executives in the world to hear it.

My job at this juncture was to listen to the record and discuss marketing plans with Leonard. We were hoping he'd agree to support the release with listening parties, videos, and an international press tour, followed by a worldwide concert tour. It was a lot to ask, given that Leonard had been in a period of retreat at the Mount Baldy Zen Center. But might as well try and grasp the ultimate.

We were staying at a modest hotel on the beach in Santa Monica, very close to Leonard's house and the recording studio where he and Sharon worked. We were expecting to meet him at the studio in the early afternoon. He would call me with directions that morning.

Around noon, the phone rang. It was Leonard.

"Good morning," he said. "We'll need to postpone our meeting for a few days."

"Oh dear," I said. "That's going to be difficult. I've only got today. I have to fly to Nevada tomorrow, and then I'm due back in Toronto. What's the problem?"

"It's a bank holiday here," he said, "and the sound engineer is unavailable."

"What about Sharon?" I asked. She was credited as co-writer and producer; certainly she would be able to operate the mixing board.

"She's not available either," said Leonard.

My mind went immediately to its default position: paranoia. Either the record isn't finished or he's disinclined to let me hear it first; maybe he'd rather go up the chain to Don Ienner or Tommy Mottola.

"Do you have a listening copy?" I asked. "On CD?"

"Yes," said Leonard. "Do you have a CD player?"

I glanced quickly round the room. "I think so," I said, spying a tiny radio beside the bed. "Hang on a moment while I check."

I went over to the little black box on the bedside table. It was a cheap alarm clock with a built-in CD player.

"There's a CD player in the room," I said, "but I'm not sure the sound quality is going to be very good."

Leonard responded gracefully. "Well, that's the way most people listen to music. Let's try."

I probably should have just called around and booked a studio for a few hours, but it seemed the plan was now set, so I ordered a massive cheese plate from room service and set out wine.

Ian popped over with a corkscrew, and sometime around mid-afternoon there was a knock on the door. There was Leonard, smartly dressed in a suit jacket and hat, cool in the heat. He smiled in greeting, hand extended in hello.

I invited him to sit in the only chair in the room, while I quickly looked around for a place to perch. Ian was leaning against the bureau, Leonard was in the chair, so the only place for me was the bed.

I offered Leonard the two bottles of wine I'd picked up at the airport in Toronto. They were Canadian.

"No matter," said he. "I am a patriot."

Over the next hour we, like the Walrus and the Carpenter, talked of many things. I asked after his friend Mordecai Richler, who we'd heard was ill in Montreal, and we reminisced about the time Leonard had arrived with Irving Layton at Much and they'd sung the banana song ("Yes! We have no bananas!") together live on air during our interview. It was lovely to revel in our Canadian connections. We polished off one bottle of wine and started on another.

At this point, I asked Leonard if he'd brought the record with him.

"Why yes," he said. "I suppose we should listen."

He handed me the CD and I walked around the bed to the tiny player. I'd tested the machine earlier, so I knew it functioned. I inserted the disc into the tray, pressed play, and got back on the bed to listen.

The first song started. "In My Secret Life." Hmmm. Not loud enough. I adjusted the volume to the highest level and started the CD again.

I still couldn't hear it properly.

"Maybe if the speakers were pointed more toward us," I suggested.

I tried to pick up the little machine to reposition it to face us, but it was screwed to the end table.

Of course it was.

"Well, we'll just have to listen really hard," I said.

I pushed play again and resettled back on the bed. Nope, the volume was just too low and the sound of the surf outside was creating a white ambient noise.

"Perhaps if we get closer," Leonard said.

He walked over to the space between the bed and the wall, closest to the CD player. There was about a foot and a half of space.

"Let's see if we can push the bed over," I suggested, "unless it's been nailed down too."

We managed to shove the bed over about a foot, and the three of us sat on the floor, side by side, our feet under the bed, backs against the wall.

I reached over and pushed play again. Better.

The songs were recorded with minimal instrumentation. They were intimate, like listening to someone breathe. The slow drum track, then the synthesizer, and then the harmonies drifted in.

Even in those challenging listening conditions I was captivated.

It was easy to enthuse: the lyrics, the simple, melodious mix, the elegance of Sharon's vocals merging with Leonard's hypnotic alpha tones. Even if I couldn't hear all the instrumental nuances, I knew it was special. Hallelujah, indeed.

Having an artist present you with a new work can be awkward. The artist is proud; the label is anxious to hear a hit. You both desperately want it to be great, and sometimes...it isn't. And then it gets uncomfortable fast.

That wasn't the case here. The only uncomfortable thing for us was our positions. (Not *Various*, just cramped.) I loved what we heard. It helped that I was an honest admirer of his work, and Leonard seemed pleased with what I had to say.

Then, about the fourth song in, I got the giggles.

That broke the spell. Leonard looked at me sideways. Literally.

I rushed to explain.

"Sorry, Leonard! It's not the music. It's this. I mean, just look at us. This is a playback session for a brilliant new record, and we're squished on the floor, half in the bag, listening on a 'close and play.' No one would believe it."

Leonard smiled and agreed it was a little unusual. We hunkered down to hear the rest of the tracks and ate all of the cheese.

It was an exceptional record.

By the end of the evening, when Leonard had said goodbye and strolled down the hall with a tip of his hat, I did a little Trudeau pirouette. Ian and I were thrilled. We'd agreed on so much. Leonard would embark on an international press tour and shoot a video for the first single (I was going to send a selection of director reels to him right away). We'd had great fun dreaming up a wild list of people who might write a liner note (Mordecai? Bono? The Dalai Lama?). He promised to consider a concert tour or perhaps a series of residencies, where he could sell out theatres for multiple nights in some of the world's finest cities.

It was an exhilarating day. Leonard had delivered a superb record and the international countries would get the promotion they needed. This was a wonderful way to start a new working relationship.

I popped a quick email to Leonard's (then) manager Kelley Lynch, letting her know the scope of what we'd discussed, and went to bed pumped about everything, including my star-crossed life.

The next morning, I was greeted with an email from Kelley, which basically said, "Leonard really enjoyed his meeting with you yesterday, but he wanted you to know that he's changed his mind."

"On what?" I wrote back.

"On everything."

My plane had just landed in Las Vegas. The parallel with this business being up one minute and down the next was not lost on me.

When I got back to Toronto we started working on a new plan around a small but efficient promo window. Leonard created his own artwork and liner notes, and it was a finely crafted package. The promotion tools included a video shot at Moshe Safdie's Habitat 67 in Montreal by Canadian director Floria Sigismondi, known for her unconventional work with David Bowie and Marilyn Manson. Leonard is shot in black and white as a mysterious visitor who wanders the Habitat and seems to be stalking a somewhat bored alien family with massive egg-shaped heads. It was nothing if not artful.

Ten New Songs was reverently and enthusiastically received. It hit Number One, as expected, in Poland and Norway, and went platinum in Canada, though I wished it had been as strong a chart topper in the U.S.

(17)

THE JOY OF DOWNSIZING

*"The most common way people give up their power
is by thinking they don't have any."*
— ALICE WALKER

IT SHOULD COME AS no surprise that, as president of a for-profit company, my preoccupation was with the bottom line. Sony Music Canada had a history of healthy percentages due to strong A&R and clever organizational practices, and was unique in that we also manufactured and distributed our product instead of outsourcing those services. But this was now a business under siege. Over the four years that I was there, the overall retail value of music in Canada decreased by CAN$228 million.

Every company was cutting costs. There were some obvious cuts at first. The aforementioned Christmas presents; the travel budgets and hospitality; the incidentals and office supplies. There were hiring freezes and percentage cuts across all departments. All the usual things any company in a downturn would address. But no sooner had we completed one round of cuts than the state of the business would demand another. There's no arguing with the thin red line. It wasn't long before we were cutting into the muscle of the organization.

Downsizing is unpleasant work. Laying people off is soul-sucking. Despite all the preparation that goes into the actual act — creative thinking, reorganization, crunching numbers, and the inevitable preparation of severance packages and counselling services, there's just no getting around that it's a shitty job, and even shittier for the people on the receiving end.

If you've seen the Jason Reitman movie *Up in the Air*, it's like that, except that unlike George Clooney, we didn't fly to give bad news to strangers. We went face to face with co-workers, people we liked and respected. Nothing prepares you for sitting down with a colleague and telling them they no longer have a job. Oh, there are lots of ways to phrase it — "The position has been declared redundant"; "We're refocusing operational direction"; "We're restructuring your department" — but the words don't really matter. They're in shock. They're thinking about their families, their debts, their futures. Sometimes there are tears, sometimes anger, sometimes mute silence. HR will guide the conversation efficiently, professionally, but it's always an aching, rotten moment.

What I wasn't prepared for were the compassionate reactions. There were times when people would ask me if *I* was okay in the middle of their own restructuring. It's hard not to cry. More often than not, I kept it steady. I suspected that keeping my own grip in that moment would help the people I was talking to keep theirs. I found out later that I was right.

Those that remained picked up and carried on, sad for their friends and co-workers, grateful they'd dodged a bullet for the time being, sometimes carrying survivor's guilt. The atmosphere was sombre, but the crumbling state of the business was no secret. The other labels were going through the same thing.

Every quarter, I hosted a president's breakfast with the entire staff in order to update our forecasts, celebrate the hits, and mourn the misses. We shared information about the measures we were taking to find new revenue and encouraged participation across the board. Good ideas would come from all corners of the company.

The staff knew the state of play without the detail. The people that worked the DVD lines, ran the printing presses, and loaded the trucks could divine the health of the business by the product they touched every day. They knew precisely how much product was going out. I gave them every number and the executive team answered all the questions they could, but I couldn't answer the biggest one, the only one that mattered:

Q: When will we recover?

A: How long is a piece of string?

There were moments when I felt shattered and spent, when it was hard to find the energy to lead with the vigour people deserved. Staff didn't want to see me dragging my ass in the door. They wanted leadership. They wanted their innovations recognized and their efforts encouraged. They wanted to believe we would weather this storm. I wondered if perhaps a more seasoned record company executive could have handled the situation better, yet I knew that every president of every label was in the same boat. So, I would give myself a pep talk in the car and stride through the front door trying to look optimistic and statesmanlike—even though at times I felt inauthentic and delusional, a bit like Monty Python's legless black knight taunting John Cleese's King Arthur: "It's just a flesh wound!"

We found strength as an executive team. We had a dedicated, creative group of managers and we pledged that even if we couldn't directly control every crisis, we could at least control our own attitudes.

To hell with that poll that rated us behind tobacco companies. We were proud of our work, our artists, and the quality of our product. We knew what an incredible gift music could be to lift people up. We released great records and worked them hard, but we also used the power of music to contribute in a way that was good for the company and good for us. We released CDs that raised money for breast cancer research, for kids in trouble, and for victims of war. We found ways to keep morale as buoyant as possible. A good thing, too, because in the midst of our own troubles, suddenly the world was viciously wrenched into a new fearful reality.

ON SEPTEMBER 6, 2001, I was flying from a Sony Music International meeting in London to Calgary for the Canadian Country Music Awards. In a rare synchronicity of schedules, Murray would also be in Calgary, and we'd arranged for my mum to look after Duncan for a few days.

On the flight I was thinking about our release schedule for the next few weeks (I could never sleep on planes). There was lots to be energized about—Bob Dylan's *Love and Theft* was to be released on September 11 and Macy Gray's *The Id* on September 19; Michael Jackson's *Invincible* was due at the end of October; and we had a new single from Destiny's Child ready to go. In my immediate world, Celine was in the studio, and I had just presented Leonard's *Ten New Songs* at the Sony Music International meeting.

It had been almost nine months since I'd started with the company, and career-wise, things were encouraging. Rick was complimentary about my getting the lay of the land quickly, and I was enjoying the camaraderie of my fellow presidents, even if I had few female confidantes.

At Sony, I was the only female managing director of an international territory in the company. During those directors' meetings, I sat at the table with about two dozen men—the heads of the U.K., Spain, France, Italy, Germany, Australia, South America, and so on. There were female product managers, but I was often the only woman in the room who wasn't cleaning ashtrays or slipping in with an urgent message for their boss.

In Canada, I was often asked by the press what it was like to be a woman in the music business. I remember that, just as often, I'd deflect the question—usually to my height, positing that being 6'1" made up for any gender inequalities. The truth was, I wasn't aware of ever being treated differently, and I wouldn't have whined about it if I was. I was certainly not shy about participating; there were no "Lean In" issues here. I was leaning so far across the table my feet were practically off the ground. (My friend Sarah suggested this book should have been called *Lean Over: A Life in the Music Business*, though that might have sent the wrong message...)

I do remember being warned about gender bias early on at MuchMusic by John Martin's friend Jo Bergman. Jo was a trailblazer—all five-foot-nothing of her. She had toured with the Rolling Stones and was then the VP of video at Warner Brothers in L.A.

I met her in 1987 at the Matador Club in Toronto on a shoot for k.d. lang's "Turn Me Round" video. She asked me how it was going, how I was coping with the sexism.

"Sexism? You mean in music videos?"

"No," Jo said. "The sexism you encounter as a female executive in this business."

I told her that I hadn't experienced any.

She looked at me with incredulity. "Don't fool yourself," she said. "You'll never be one of them. No matter how well you think you're doing you'll never be in the boy's club. They might let you come to meetings, but until you can stand beside them in the men's room and pee standing up, you'll never be a full member." (So to speak.) Those words of caution were the closest I think I ever came to being mentored by a woman other than my mother, and Jo's words came back to me as I waited for meetings in the record company hallways in New York.

In New York, there were two very senior women at the company—Polly Anthony, president of Epic Records, and Michele Anthony (no relation), Sony EVP and Tommy Mottola's right hand. Neither were in my regular orbit, though, and they were rarely at our international meetings.

It would never have occurred to me to ask Michele or Polly Anthony to mentor me because they were women. It would have been like asking them to help me do up my shoes. "Mentoring" wasn't a word anyone used. In our business, women were more likely to be competitive with each other. On Polly's radar, my position was tied to the success or failure of Epic Records in Canada. Is it a hit or not? If not, why not? Hits meant power and that's what it was all about. How to get it, how to wield it, how to keep it.

Polly had it. She was fierce and feisty and she had to be, going head to head with some of the brashest boys in the business. She was an unflinching supporter of Epic artists like Michael Jackson, Jennifer Lopez, and Shakira. She'd won the respect of industry legends inside the company and out, including competitors like the legendary Doug Morris, then CEO at Universal, who she beat out to sign Macy Gray.

The New York ladies were not there to balance gender inequalities, and I certainly didn't expect them to treat me any differently than they would any other managing director. But as the president of a label, I hoped Polly felt she had the power to take a stand against misogynist content when it crossed her desk. I got a glimpse of her spirit when she gleefully championed Macy Gray's "Sexual Revolution" from *The Id*. I'd just seen the video at the meeting in London. I saw it as a jubilant emancipation anthem and was excited to work it.

Polly died young at fifty-nine from pancreatic cancer. From what I saw, she wielded her power well. I, on the other hand, often felt conflicted about power. I admired it, but I was also distrustful of it. I'd seen enough abuse of it, especially in my documentary travels. As a record company executive, I had to examine my own feelings around sexual power, in particular. There were women in business who used their "feminine wiles" as a way to further their ambitions, and I had to guard against rolling my eyes when I'd see a young lady pressing the "girls" into service in meetings filled with men. Mostly I hoped they weren't the only tools in their kit.

I thought about my own culpability in exploiting sexuality at MuchMusic, and took some comfort in the way we'd explored gender roles in our media literacy programming, from Jana's *The Big Tease* to the special MuchMusic had produced the year before I left, *Eve of the Millennium*. There was a vast range of female images on offer in music videos — school girls, vixens, baby dolls, porn stars, goddesses, moms, earth mothers, and hoes and bitches — and an equally wide array of prominent figures to weigh in, like Madonna, Sheryl Crow, the Indigo Girls, Lauryn Hill, Alanis Morissette, Janet Jackson, and, of course, Eve herself.

On the one hand, the nineties had felt like an empowering time for women; but there was a big difference between choice and control. How much "Girl Power" did the Spice Girls really have in the way they were contrived and marketed? How authentic was TLC's message of self-esteem if they themselves were styled to model-like perfection in their video for "Unpretty"? Comments from young women viewers were promising — they were quite discerning about what they thought was authentic versus manipulated.

Yet if I'd been able to look into the future in search of more progress, I'm sure I would have been discouraged by what I saw. If there'd been a Future-Fast-Forward function on my seatback TV screen on that plane in 2001, it would have shown the same "sex sells" scenes in 2013 and beyond that we were watching a decade before, except with faster editing and more double-sided dress tape.

My Future-Fast-Forward function (you gotta love business class) would show me Miley Cyrus on a wrecking ball, Patrice Roberts' "Ah Feeling Mehself," and Robin Thicke, T.I., and Pharrell Williams teaming up for the song "Blurred Lines," though you could argue they're setting very *clear* lines. The men in the explicit version of that video are all nattily dressed, while the women dance around them topless. Artful? Okay — it was directed by a woman — but I'm just not sure it's mining anything new.

How about the next offering on my FFF screen, Jennifer Lopez and Iggy Azalea's "Booty" video? The vid itself is athletic, wet, and unambiguous. The reaction on social media, though — the scope of which *is* new in the twenty-tens — is more complicated. The Australian singer Brody Dalle takes to something called Twitter and says: "JLo and iggy azalea have lost their heads up each other's big butts." Brody is immediately flamed, called out

FEARLESS AS POSSIBLE · 345

for "slut shaming," but she defends herself, this time on Facebook: "How is spreading your bottom apart and singing 'give him what he asks for' empowering at all?... Now if the words were 'I'll give you what I want,' I could back that."

Jennifer Lopez is a smart, successful career woman. If anyone has the power to control her own imaging, surely it's she. Still, it bears repeating. Do what you want ladies, as long as it's what *you* want.

Hang on, my Future-Fast-Forward function has a news feature. There's Beyoncé performing in front of the word "FEMINIST," Emma Watson making a speech to the UN, and Justin Trudeau being elected Prime Minister of Canada. Trudeau has just declared gender parity in his cabinet.

"Why?" asks the press.

"Because it's 2015," the new PM responds.

That's encouraging. Women certainly need to be put on the map — literally. Up to this point (the FFF channel has a neat Statistical Sidebar option), the number of women versus men elected to political office in Canada has been stuck at around the 20-percent mark (which, in 2014, ranked us at number 54 on the world scale — lower than the Islamic Republic of Mauritania).

I trust that our new female MPs are being paid as well as the men, though the Statistical Sidebar tells me that in 2015 women are still making close to thirty cents less on the dollar than men. Numbers haven't improved much in the executive suite, either, where in 2015 only 20.8 percent of board seats are held by women and only 6 percent of board chairs are female. Appears our gender equity numbers in business remain a market failure. I will continue my pilgrimages to thank the Famous Five Bronzes every single time I visit Ottawa.

Let's see what Beyoncé is doing in front of the "F" word. Ah, she's performing on the *MTV Video Music Awards*. Words by the powerful Nigerian writer Chimamanda Ngozi Adichie appear on screen behind her, ending with "FEMINIST." Also encouraging. But there goes social media again. Feminists tweet that she's taking credit for other women's work. Annie Lennox is calling it "tokenism." Heavens, we can be harsh on each other. I always like the idea that if someone takes a positive first step, we should applaud it and encourage her to take two more.

I wished my Future-Fast-Forward screen had a modern version of *TooMuchForMuch*. It would be amazing to see Beyoncé and JLo, Annie Lennox, Caitlin Moran, Gloria Steinem, and... What about Madonna? Is she still making music in 2015? Yes she is! Go Madge.

Oh look. There's Emma Watson addressing the UN. Turn that up.

I think it is right that I am paid the same as my male counterparts. I think it is right that I should be able to make decisions about my own body. I think it is right that women be involved on my behalf in the policy and the decisions that will affect my life. I think it is right that socially, I am afforded the same respect as men. But sadly, I can say that there is no one country in the world where all women can expect to receive these rights. No country in the world can yet say that they have achieved gender equality. These rights, I consider to be human rights...

Well done, Emma. I'm applauding you from my seat. Emma is standing up for those under attack, those who live in places where girls are barred from going to school, married off before they've hit puberty, risk being raped while simply walking to get water, are used as a weapon of war.

Incredibly, Ms. Watson's speech is also followed by a malicious social media barrage—this time threatening her with death and rape. Wow. It's jarring to see that a tool with the potential for powerful democratic connectivity can be so hateful at the same time. This feels like an assault aimed at *all* women. Don't people in the future understand that women's rights benefit men too? Doesn't anyone remember Margaret Mead, who said: "Every time we liberate a woman, we liberate a man"?

Okay, obviously there was no Future-Fast-Forward function on that airplane screen back in 2001. I could muse about our feminist progress another time—it was certainly a two-step forward, one-step-back scenario. What I was probably *really* doing on that flight was trying to get some sleep.

I WAS LOOKING FORWARD to seeing Murray in Calgary—a rare grown-up weekend together while Duncan was in good hands with my mum. Murray was an awesome husband and father. We split things up as best we could and thank heavens my mum could step in from time to time to help. Usually, it was my job to drop Duncan off at school and Murray's to pick him up. I tried not to think about the picture I was presenting to my son, me the nagging harridan—"Get dressed, where are your mitts, hurry, hurry, get in the car!"—arriving in the hallway halfway through the national anthem, while after school Murray arrived like a popsicle-bearing action hero ready to squire him away to soccer practice. I tried not to be jealous. I'd have to work on being more fun in the morning.

I remember Moses saying to me, shortly after Duncan was born: "You need a wife." At the time, I thought it was a bizarre thing to say; but what I've learned is that if and when women manage to make it—despite the odds—to the top job or the elected position, we need superstar support. I'm blessed to have had that with my extended family.

Still, there were sacrifices—of quality time spent with them, most of all. I told myself the trade-off was that Duncan had a happier mom who felt fulfilled, though I wasn't sure I always believed it. Like many working women, I was a guilt-ridden mom. Happily, Duncan is now a wonderful, smart young adult and completely his own person, despite our efforts to shape him in one way or another. I'm convinced that children come out fully formed. All we can really do as parents is love them, teach by example, build their confidence, and let go.

I keep referring to work-life balance as an extreme sport. It is. It's a sport that requires dedicated teamwork, and you will do your best but I doubt you can consistently win. Balance may be impossible to achieve—for us mortals, anyway.

"Balance" assumes that you are managing everything perfectly at the same time. But balance can only be achieved *over* time; we often make one choice at the expense of another. I know I haven't made all the right choices. I've had to work to forgive myself when I've failed, and to remind myself to be grateful that I've *had* choices in the first place. Too many women don't.

Another thing I'd learned: success in work and life would always mean different things for different people. For me, I figured that if I could raise my son, cherish my relationships, serve the company well, *and* make a positive contribution, that would be success. Maybe I could even learn to sleep on planes.

I landed in Calgary charged up about the weekend and jazzed about promoting the new Macy Gray emancipation anthem that Polly had delivered in London. In the Sony world, there was no ambiguity about the meaning of success. Success meant delivering the hits.

It was an enjoyable weekend at the CCMAs. I caught up with lots of people I knew, spent some time with gold-selling country artist Adam Gregory, who'd just turned sixteen years old, and had some fun at the conference interviewing Bruce Allen, who was managing Martina McBride. (When I told Bruce on stage that we were determined to break Adam with or without Nashville, he said, "You must be jet-lagged." And he was right—on both counts). On the morning of September 11, I got up early to head to the airport. Murray was catching a later flight. My plane was in line on the runway for an extraordinarily long time. People were just starting to grumble when the pilot announced that we were going to turn back.

"There has been an incident in New York," he said, but offered no further information.

I turned my phone on and called a pal in the Citytv newsroom who told me that a plane had crashed into the World Trade Center. He had no time to explain. We turned back, disembarked and were ushered into the Calgary airport, where we saw people crowding around the TV screens, watching in horror as the second plane hit. Bruce was there with Anne Murray, trying to figure out how to get her to Toronto. Others were racing to rental car counters to grab whatever vehicles were still available. We soon realized we were all stuck.

I returned to the hotel and walked into the restaurant to find Murray. The people having breakfast were still blissfully unaware, and Murray was surprised to see me there with my luggage—until I told him what had happened. Luckily he still had a room, and I got busy trying to account for the Sony Canada staff; we had people on the road in New York with contest winners. Some fretful hours were spent trying to account for everyone, but finally we did. My mum was fine to take care of Duncan, so Murray and I sat in the hotel room for the rest of the day, glued to the TV, stunned at the unspeakable horror unfolding.

The next day, the planes still weren't moving, but the phone was ringing. Actor and singer-songwriter Tom Jackson and country artist Paul Brandt were organizing a concert to benefit the victims in New York City.

Tom asked Murray if he would perform. On day three the concert was mounted and I was asked to host a small part, which I was grateful to do. On day four air space was still closed, but I was able to hitch a ride on a turbo-prop plane that SOCAN CEO André LeBel had commandeered to get his people back to Toronto.

The terrible impact of 9/11 on the pysche of the world was overwhelming and just beginning. We would all be forever changed in unfathomable ways. In the recording industry, as the price of oil and gold went up, spending on travel and entertainment went down. Tours were cancelled and releases delayed. Big-heartland, stars-and-stripes, yellow-ribbon songs appeared on the charts and a lot of song lyrics took on new meaning.

Clear Channel radio programmers were sharing a list of 165 tracks with "questionable lyrics." It included songs all the way from "Shot Down in Flames" by AC/DC to "Learn to Fly" by the Foo Fighters to "Knockin' on Heaven's Door" by Bob Dylan. Led Zeppelin's "Stairway to Heaven" was on the list, as was "Great Balls of Fire" by Jerry Lee Lewis, "Free Fallin'" by Tom Petty, and apparently anything by Rage Against the Machine. It was not an outright ban (Clear Channel later insisted the list was "not an effort initiated by management" but by their programmers), but it certainly gave a clear indication of the mood of the times.

On the political stage, it looked increasingly like the U.S. would retaliate. There were strong pro-peace sentiments among artists, but "pro-peace" was often interpreted as "against the soldiers" and thus anti-American. A star with a strong point of view was treading on sensitive ground. The backlash endured by the Dixie Chicks, when Natalie Maines voiced her opinion about President George W. Bush following the 2003 invasion of Iraq, is a case in point.

On March 10, 2003, Natalie told an audience in London, England: "We do not want this war, this violence, and we're ashamed that the president of the United States is from Texas" (as the Chicks themselves were). The British crowd cheered, but in America there were CD-bulldozing protest parties. The band received threats of death if Natalie didn't "shut up and sing." Natalie apologized, but it wasn't enough. The incident triggered a heated discussion about free speech. Artists like Bruce Springsteen, Madonna, and Merle Haggard rushed to the Dixie Chicks' defence, while others, like Toby Keith, raged against them.

The girls were certainly not anti-the-troops. Their song "Travelin' Soldier"—a moving song about a love affair between a girl and a soldier who doesn't return home—had been a Number One hit on the country charts, but we watched as the Chicks' newest single, a superb cover of Fleetwood Mac's "Landslide," mimic its own title and drop from the Top Ten to Number 43 in a week.

Three years later, the Dixie Chicks released a fascinating documentary called *Shut Up and Sing* that chronicled the backlash and their courage in the face of it. The cover of *Entertainment Weekly* became part of the film's poster art: the naked Dixie Chicks with the words "Traitors," "Hero," "Peace," "Boycott," "Dixie Sluts," and "Saddam's Angels" written on their bodies. It was sweet victory in 2006 when the band put out one of their biggest records ever, *Taking the Long Way*, which won five Grammys in 2007, including Album of the Year and Song of the Year for the single "Not Ready to Make Nice." The country music community, however, was not quite ready. The Chicks lost to Rascal Flatts for Top Vocal Group at the Country Music Association Awards and the "Not Ready to Make Nice" video lost twice at the 2007 Country Music Television Awards.

"Not Ready to Make Nice" still gives me goosebumps. It's one of the bravest, most personal fuck-you protest songs you'll ever hear. The power comes from a singular story, but it captures the anger and dignity of any woman who's had to rise to battle hostility. I was proud to be the Canadian president of a label that supported the Dixie Chicks wholeheartedly, and the bonus for us was that the band ended up spending more time in Canada.

At a press conference the Dixie Chicks did in Toronto on August 7, 2003, instead of the framed gold and platinum albums we typically gave artists, I'd had shadow boxes made containing the Canadian flag and a soapstone sculpture of a polar bear. The Inuit name for polar bear is *nanuk*, meaning "worthy of great respect," and in the Inuit culture bears symbolize strength and reincarnation. I thought it was a fitting symbol, given the fire and ice these women had walked through, and the band was delighted. I'm still rocking my "Free Natalie" T-shirt.

Canada's non-engagement in the Iraq war began to test U.S.–Canada relations. A headline in *Billboard* for a piece by Larry LeBlanc on April 12, 2003, read: "Canada Considers Anti-War Fallout: Music Execs Wonder if Opposition Will Affect U.S. Relationships." Larry was asking key questions. There had been warnings about economic retaliations and "repercussions" hinted by then–U.S. Ambassador to Canada Paul Cellucci. Artist managers worried that their ability to move freely across the border might be jeopardized. For my part, I was wondering if I would run afoul of my U.S. bosses, since we were about to release a charity record called *Peace Songs*.

THE IDEA FOR A peace songs record was sparked by a conversation with my War Child friends. Doctors Samantha Nutt and Eric Hoskins were worried about the impact of war on women and children. At dinner one night, we reminisced about some of the great flower-power songs written in years gone by, like Marvin Gaye's "What's Going On" or Hal David and Burt Bacharach's "What the World Needs Now Is Love," and wondered what those songs might sound like today. The next day, with the support of the Sony executive team, work began on a new CD collection of "the greatest peace songs ever written" to raise money to help innocents caught in the crossfire.

"Clearing the repertoire" for a compilation CD requires consent by artists, publishers, and competitive label groups, so it generally helps to partner with another label. Lisa Zbitnew at BMG loved the idea, and so we had two strong labels pulling in the same direction.

The project started to generate a momentum all its own. Dozens of artists climbed on board to record and donate new tracks. Yet the project would not have gained the traction it did without Raine Maida, of Our Lady Peace, and Chantal Kreviazuk—both Sony artists, committed champions of the project, and friends of War Child.

Raine and Chantal's trip to Iraq for the War Child documentary had taken place in January of 2001, the tenth anniversary of the Gulf War. Their objective was to draw attention to the impact of a decade of UN sanctions on children in the region.

Their trip had hazardous timing. Iraq had been calling for easement of the sanctions while simultaneously thwarting efforts of UN weapons inspectors. The sabre-rattling heated up while they were there, and a U.S. declaration of war seemed very possible. At Sony Canada, everyone was terribly anxious when we lost contact with Chantal and Raine for two days, and I feigned calm as an American colleague wondered why two of our biggest stars—both with impending album release dates in the U.S.—were in Iraq.

Thankfully, they were okay. They arrived home a few days later with strong views about the efficacy of sanctions (UNICEF was estimating that over 500,000 children had died as a direct result of them), decrying their impact on civilians.

As I've mentioned, that trip was filmed as the final part of MuchMusic's *Musicians in the WarZone* special. Even though I was no longer with MuchMusic at the time, I "inserted myself into the edit," partly to help if I could, but also to ensure that I had the backs of our two Sony stars. I didn't want Chantal and Raine to be painted as "anti-American," and I butted heads with the producers, who wanted to use stronger language than I thought wise. We were able to agree, but it was an interesting position for me to be in. I was wearing a different hat, no longer having authority in a place and on a project in which I was used to having it, and trying to do the right thing without compromising ideologies.

Chantal Kreviazuk covered Bob Marley's "Redemption Song" for the *Peace Songs* record and Our Lady Peace recorded John Lennon's "Imagine." Jarvis Church brought in K'naan (then a young unknown rapper and spoken-word artist) and recorded "One" by U2. Gord Downie recorded

"If I Had a Hammer" by Pete Seeger and Lee Hays, Barenaked Ladies did Bruce Cockburn's "Lovers in a Dangerous Time," and Celine Dion sent her recording of Corey Hart's "Prayer." Others sent their own theme-perfect music. Jann Arden gave us "Fighting for the World"; Leonard Cohen, "Anthem"; and k-os, "Livin' in a World Corrupt." The songs kept coming until we had a double album on our hands.

There was a flurry of activity at Sony, with company volunteers fuelled by pizza and purpose working after hours clearing publishing rights, arranging studio time, and designing artwork, not to mention handling all the little details—like shipping tapes across the Atlantic for Bryan Adams, whose guitar player, Keith Scott, was on a different continent, or coordinating Elvis Costello's recording sessions in L.A. for "Everybody's Crying Mercy."

The lead single came when Raine Maida inspired Avril Lavigne (who was riding high with "Sk8r Boi") with stories about his trip to Iraq. She went into the studio in London to record Dylan's "Knockin' on Heaven's Door"; Dylan approved the use immediately. Then, in fortuitous synchronicity, we learned that War Child UK was working on a similar record called *Hope*. They had enlisted artists like Paul McCartney, Moby, and David Bowie, and we agreed to share tracks.

Peace Songs was a grand mission, but it wasn't without its drama. The bigger the artist, the more freaked out the manager. As I've mentioned, the political climate in the U.S. was very tense. Freedom fries, anyone?

Managers worried that their artists would be construed as "anti-war" in the U.S.—a career-limiting move—and every aspect of *Peace Songs* became closely examined and debated. How would the record be marketed? What would the cover art look like? Which other artists were in? Where was the money going, exactly?

Hours were spent on the phone, cajoling and calming artist managers. We were very clear on the record being a pro-peace collection, not an anti-war polemic. But maintaining an even keel required some peacekeeping negotiations of our own, as there were artists, like Bruce Cockburn, who didn't want their punches pulled.

A few weeks into the project, Bernie Finkelstein called me with the exciting news that Bruce Cockburn was going to re-record his own "It's Going Down Slow" with new lyrics.

That was concerning. I remembered lyrics to that song exactly. I'd played that record to death when I was sixteen years old, trying to learn the guitar parts. The lyrics were:

God damn the hands of glory
That hold the mighty firebrand high
Close the book and end the story
Of how so many men have died
Let the world retain in memory
That mighty tongues tell mighty lies
And if mankind must have an enemy
Let it be his warlike pride
Let it be his warlike pride

He'd written those words thirty years before, but within the context of Bush's declaration of war against Iraq, they could be construed as a bullish indictment of the president. And if Bruce thought they needed to be *more* pointed . . . this was the guy who'd written "If I had a rocket launcher/some son of a bitch would die"!

I fretted, thinking managers would pull their artists' tracks, the record would be considered seditious, and I would be fired. Bernie calmed me down, saying simply: "Denise, you can never go wrong siding with Bruce Cockburn." Right. Let it fly.

I have good friends who would call me chicken-shit for sticking to my guns (as it were) and insisting on a pro-peace record rather than using the opportunity to make an anti-war statement. Others might say I was abusing my power as a record company executive. But I knew from my experience at Much that using your powers for good *is* good business. And I also knew that this project was good for another bottom line besides profit: company morale. That was something beyond valuable in the middle of our overall industry upheaval.

Still, I may have been putting my own job on the line. You might imagine that within the walls of Sony New York — chock full of strong personalities like Tommy Mottola, Don Ienner, and Rick Dobbis — there might be some contrasting personal views about the U.S. declaring war on Iraq.

I needn't have worried. What I saw from the company was impeccable. From Bruce Springsteen to Bob Dylan, Columbia and Epic both had deep history with politically engaged artists. They rode a full range, from Montgomery Gentry's right-wing "Hell Yeah" to System of a Down's anti-war statement "Boom." The latter's video captured pro-peace rallies around the world and had animated caricatures of George Bush, Tony Blair, and Saddam Hussein riding missiles. It was a great comfort to be at home with label executives who had their artists' backs.

Peace Songs ended up being a double album with thirty-one tracks, the lion's share of which were newly recorded. Incredibly, the project was conceived, produced, marketed, manufactured, and in stores in under six weeks. Sony sales VP Don Oates convinced retailers to step up with prominent store placement, and MuchMusic offered free airtime and ran PSAs. Avril's cover of "Knockin' on Heaven's Door" was a hit. The record went gold and Sony Canada cut War Child a $100,000 cheque based on orders on the initial shipment. To my knowledge, *Peace Songs*, which would go on to generate approximately $350,000, was the first benefit album to put money in the hands of a charity before the CD had even hit the shelves.

Sam and Eric got back on a plane to distribute medicines and supplies and arrived in Baghdad on the day the statue of Saddam Hussein fell in Firdos Square and were met at the hospital in Karbala by doctors who had tears of gratitude in their eyes.

Peace Songs goes gold. Left to right: Duncan Coutts, Jesse Colburn, Avril Lavigne, Liam Titcomb, Jim Creeggan, Raine Maida, Evan Taubenfeld, Chantal Kreviazuk, Jeremy Taggart, Sam Nutt, Eric Hoskins, Kevin Hearn, Lisa Zbitnew, Ed Robertson, Steven Page, Harvey Wolfe, me, and Tyler Stewart.

There was no profit for Sony in the *Peace Songs* project, but what we got back in staff spirit was invaluable. A glow of pride permeated the halls and reminded us all of how powerful we could be when we pulled together in challenging times. I hadn't yet heard the term "corporate social responsibility," but I certainly saw how positive corporate governance could pay off.

The very best people, the ones you want on your team, make considered choices about what kind of work they want and what set of values they want to be associated with. Courageous community engagement can enhance a company's reputation and promote stakeholder and employee buy-in and loyalty. You will do well by doing good.

Peace Songs WAS ONE project that buoyed us in a trying time, but the hits to the business just kept on coming—sometimes, from places you'd least expect. In the spring and summer of 2003, SARS (Severe acute respiratory syndrome) landed in Toronto, hitting us with another round of negative economic impact. Concerts and promo tours were cancelled, tourism dried up, and retail took a hit as people stayed indoors. We were indebted to concert promoter Michael Cohl, who staged a massive Canada Rocks! event (a.k.a. SARSstock) with the Rolling Stones to let the world know that it was safe to come back to Toronto.

Sony's biggest act on the bill was AC/DC, who put on a thunderous performance and reminded me again of how tall I am. I am, as usual, over on one ankle and crouching in this shot.

Crouching hard with AC/DC.

One of the impacts of SARS on our business was the delay of a planned installation of our first DVD production line, when Japanese technicians who were set to install the new machinery delayed their visit. It may sound small, but the addition of a DVD-making machine to our production facilities was important to the company. It was seen as a sign of hope that our manufacturing business (and the jobs that went with it) wasn't going to be outsourced (yet). When our Japanese friends did finally arrive months later, we greeted them with a three-day power blackout.

Our first reaction to the massive power outage on August 14, 2003 was fear that it might be a terrorist attack: we promptly sent our staff home. Information was sketchy at first, and New York Mayor Michael Bloomberg initially adopted the "Blame Canada" approach. As it turned out, the outage was caused by a grid failure that affected 50 million people across Ontario and the northeastern United States.

We had a situation. With no electricity to power the twelve CD machines in the manufacturing warehouse, the polycarbonate resin used to make the plastic discs was hardening fast. Our head of manufacturing (and excellent centre-fielder) Vic Macina was at a conference in the U.S. When we were finally able to get him on the phone, he asked, "How long has the power had been out?"

"Four hours."

"We're approaching critical," he said.

If the machines didn't maintain a certain temperature, the entire apparatus would turn into a solid block of hardened junk, like cement setting in a barrel. I thought there might be a little screw under each machine that you could turn to empty the barrels — like replacing your oil in the car — but no such luck.

When night fell, I walked through the empty building with a flashlight. My footsteps echoed off the silent machines and the thousands of CDs and special products stacked, row after row, waiting to be shipped. I had an eerie feeling that I was looking at the future: the death knell of our manufacturing business having arrived sooner rather than later.

In our area of Toronto, the power failure lasted three days, and as it turned out, we were lucky to escape irreparable damage to the machines. All in all, it had been one hell of a summer.

ALL THROUGH THE FIRST decade of the millennium, the global recording industry continued to decline. In Canada we were increasingly concerned with the three Rs—retail, rights, and radio. At retail, the drop in sales of physical product brought closures, buyouts, and bankruptcies as stores like A&B Sound, Records on Wheels, CD Plus, Tower Records, and Sam the Record Man (not to mention hundreds of small independent outlets) closed their doors. And to add insult to injury, the government wasn't helping when it came to the second "R," rights.

Remember how I mentioned that per capita, Canadians were number one when it came to illegal downloading? That wasn't all. In 2004, Canada was again named to the Special 301 "Watch List" by the U.S. government for its lack of action on copyright reform. We joined other "problem countries" like Azerbaijan, Bulgaria, Tajikistan, Uzbekistan, and Turkmenistan. "Canastan," as we came to be known in my meetings, was not a signatory to the WIPO (World Intellectual Property Organization) treaty. We'd ratified in 1998, but we never signed. Kind of like a musical Kyoto.

As well, in a howler of poor timing (for us), at radio, a new "old" format sprouted up in Canada. It was the dawn of Bob and Jack (and Joe and Dave, et al.), playing hit music from the sixties, seventies, eighties, and nineties. These stations did nothing for new artists. We thought that if there was an upside, we might sell more back catalogue—but nope, no increase there. Audiences liked to listen, but they weren't motivated to buy music they probably already owned in multiple formats.

Now more than ever, the major labels needed to diversify our business. We chased new digital revenue opportunities for song licensing and ringtones. We did deals with content aggregators and digital delivery systems. We looked beyond music to car manufacturers and educators to sell our CD manufacturing services for owner manuals and CD-ROMs. Our in-house fulfillment operation meant an exciting launch of CelineDion.com and other merchandising sites for our artists (Celine fans were keen shoppers!). We augmented our physical product with value-added bonus tracks and videos, and our strategic marketing department, led by the determined Therese Garnett, sought new partners everywhere. We put CDs in beer cases, coupons in popcorn, and prizes in Tim Hortons "Roll Up the Rim" coffee cups. We would have put coffee and donuts *in* the CDs if we could.

There was even a *Love* compilation CD marketed with heat-activated K-Y Jelly. (Love to love you, baby!)

We were wide open to ideas from anywhere and staff were putting the pedal to the metal, wearing their "Sony Big Thinker" ball caps to brainstorming sessions. One of my favourite ideas to come from one of those meetings was musically enhanced greeting cards. We never did make those, but I admit to feeling a little smug the first time I saw musical greeting cards flooding the shelves, even though they weren't offered by a record label.

As harsh as the business climate was, we were certainly not taking our foot off the gas, especially when it came to the music.

(18)

HITS AND MISSES

"...the highest duty of the writer, the composer, the artist is to remain true to himself and to let the chips fall where they may."
— JOHN F. KENNEDY

THANK HEAVENS FOR THE music. The music was the joy. Every day new tracks (now watermarked, numbered, and copy protected) were delivered to the company from around the world, some of them from brand-new developing artists gaining a foothold in distant lands and some from established stars readying new album releases. Hearing new music was always exciting, and a hit still had the power to dramatically improve the bottom line.

Meanwhile, the worldwide plan for Celine Dion's next record centred on the heart of entertainment America—Las Vegas.

WHEN I ARRIVED AT Sony, Celine was on a career hiatus. She was caring for her manager and husband René Angélil, who was recovering from throat cancer, and hoping to start a family. Her sabbatical also meant they'd had time to imagine the next adventure—and what a bold adventure it turned out to be. They were about to bet it all on Vegas.

At thirty-two, Celine was not only one of the biggest-selling artists in the company, she was one of the most accomplished stars on the planet. The youngest of fourteen siblings born in Charlemagne, Quebec, by 2001 she had sold over 140 million albums, dominated music charts in both French and English, was one of the highest-grossing tour performers in the world, and had already won more than a thousand awards. Basically, everything that could be won, she'd won. Celine owes her success to her multi-octave prowess, the love and guidance of her manager husband, the support of her family, the adoration of her fans, and her own superhuman dedication to discipline and excellence.

Celine and René are also big-hearted people and sincere philanthropists, giving time and money to a wealth of causes. Celine is a Goodwill Ambassador to the UN and is President of Honor of the Foundation Against Cystic Fibrosis, which she chose to support after her niece, Karine Menard, died of the disease at age sixteen.

Despite Celine's incredible success, there are those who mock her. The whole idea is bizarre when you stop to think about it. What's the opposite of *schadenfreude*? Perhaps it's *mudita*, the Buddhist word for "sympathetic joy," or happiness in another's good fortune. That would be what her legions of fans hold for Celine. For them, all the chest pounding, female impersonating, schmaltzy *SNL* lampooning just encourages them to love her more. And she loves them back. I've watched her sign autographs for hours, and Celine's unbreakable rule when she's choosing material to record is that the songs must provoke an emotional reaction, because she knows that if she feels it, her fans will too. Celine is quoted as saying in Carl Wilson's book *Let's Talk about Love*, "I'm not cool. That's okay." She doesn't care, and that makes her fearless.

Celine has managed to protect and control her incredible career better than most, partly because René was an extraordinary manager (he was a student of managers like Colonel Tom Parker and Brian Epstein, and studied the lives of legendary stars), and partly because Celine is so intensely family-oriented. Even in the bizarro world of Las Vegas, she and René managed to create a family-centric sanctuary, shielding themselves rather well from the twisted, celebrity-obsessed tabloid culture that fells so many.

Like that of any superstar, Celine's inner circle was closely knit, and one of the first things I had to do was to infiltrate Team Celine, which was easier said than done. Their focus was on Vegas, but their strong Canadian roots remained. Vito Luprano, A&R director of Celine's recordings, worked in the Sony Quebec office; and Dave Platel, who ran their management

362 · DENISE DONLON

company Five Star Feeling, operated out of a Toronto office that was so close we could hit it with a 3-iron.

In any entertainment company—music, sports, movies—having a close relationship with the biggest stars is currency. As a result, friendships are often overhyped and one's status in the firmament can be oversold. As a newbie, I was certainly not in the driver's seat—the release of Celine's seventh English-language album, *A New Day Has Come*, would take the concentrated effort of dozens of experts in Canada and the U.S. I could have been easily sidelined, but Dave and Vito were excellent guides and René welcomed me warmly onto the team. (Warmly is an understatement. René loved hot peppers, and once I told him I did too the heat was on at every meal.)

A New Day Has Come would be no ordinary record. The international release would coincide with a TV special, a DVD, a merchandising operation, and a Las Vegas show. Every aspect was paired with selected sponsors and partners, and each required a precise rollout, carefully coordinated with the whole.

The idea for the Vegas show had been inspired by Celine and René's visit to a Cirque du Soleil production of *O* at the Bellagio. The show was pure acrobatic magic on water, and sparked their sense of wonder and imagination. Celine had found the answer to her "What's next?"

René was already well along in his conversations with the creator of *O*—fellow Quebecker Franco Dragone—about what would eventually become a new benchmark in live entertainment. He told me about their vision for Celine—a production extravaganza, massive in imagination and investment. It would set a new height in showbiz spectacle, and most importantly, the show would allow the world to come to Celine.

Rene insisted I see the show that had inspired their vision: "Unless you come to Vegas and see *O*, you will not understand how big we are thinking."

I'd never been to Vegas before and was a little saucer-eyed on my way downtown. Coloured lights, the Eiffel Tower, a sphinx! It was just like in the movies, except hotter.

Ian MacKay and I lined up at the reservation desk at Caesars Palace. There was a furrowed-brow moment when the clerk searched in vain for our names. Then she suddenly brightened and guided us to the velvet-roped VIP area.

"Ah yes, here we are. Your suite is ready."

Suite? I'd booked a room.

I fumbled for my credit card thinking about all the artist demos the price of this suite would surely cost, when the clerk raised her hand in gentle protest. "No thank you, Madame. Your card is not necessary. Monsieur Angélil would like you to have the *full* experience."

The full experience? The mind reeled.

Ian and I were ushered to our rooms, he exiting the elevator at a lower floor as I continued my ascent to the top. When we got to the top floor, the bellman opened the brass-handled double doors to the penthouse. This was no suite. This was a country. Wall-to-wall windows overlooked the city. The living room had a sunken theatre, and the dining area had seating for twenty-four. There was a kitchen, pantry, and bar; a valet's quarters, a nanny suite, and multiple bedrooms with at least five bathrooms offering full-sized Aveda toiletries. I was going to need a bigger suitcase.

The bellman inquired as to whether I would like a maid sent up to unpack my bag.

"Ah, no thank you, I'll be fine," I said, glancing down at my carry-on. I was pretty sure I could manage to hang one suit jacket without injuring myself. I still had an hour before dinner, so I grabbed my goggles and bathing suit and headed down to do some laps circling the immense golden statue of Caesar. Someone had obviously neglected to install the private pool in my suite.

Later, Ian and I headed to the Bellagio. René was right. *O* was incredible. In, out, and on water, the show was exquisitely staged, ethereal, funny, and breathtaking. There were fantastically costumed acrobats diving into pools, a flying piano, a man who walked on water reading a flaming newspaper. Dragone was a genius. His custom-built production was beyond anything that Cirque du Soleil or Celine Dion could have mounted on a travelling tour staged in a different city every night.

Plans were already underway to build a new custom-designed theatre for Celine, and René was working on a multitude of sponsorships, including Caesars Palace, AEG Live, Air Canada, Chrysler, and Coty. René sketched his vision for the operation on a paper placemat, with intersecting lines connecting and circling the players. It was an elaborate game plan.

Back in the land of the label, every territory had a special request to help them market the record in their respective countries. Would Celine be willing to travel to promote the record? Would she do interviews, contests? Would she record different language versions of the single? What about bonus tracks, EPKs (electronic press kits), and press junkets? When could we schedule a day to shoot the video? Every request was weighed, accepted or declined, and then folded into the master plan.

The setup was flawless, and when *A New Day Has Come* was released in March 2002, the record was a monster hit, debuting at Number One in seventeen countries. (Artists will talk about the joy of hearing their song on the radio, but there's nothing quite like seeing a mega-hit be added to station after station, building across time zones until it's circled the world.) Celine had other releases while I was at Sony, the French-language album *1 fille & 4 types* in 2003 and the *Miracle* book, album, and DVD collaboration with photographer Anne Geddes, but for me nothing was as magical as *A New Day Has Come*.

When the Vegas show opened at the Colosseum at Caesars Palace on March 25, 2003, it set a new bar for blockbuster entertainment. All the Sony brass came out, even though our company was in the midst of enormous changes and there were strong rumours of a merger. Even Tommy Mottola—who had departed the company a few months earlier—was in attendance. While we were walking to the after-party, I remember he took me aside and said, "Stay in Canada where it's safe. It's a snake pit down here." I appreciated his advice but it was an intriguing remark, considering his buyout had been reported in the media to be $20 million, plus another $100 million to start a new imprint. I wasn't privy to the figure, but I imagined that in the corporate ledgers the amount may have stuck out like that bulge that slides through a python after dinner.

"A New Day" was a jaw-dropping triumph. On a raked stage 120 feet wide, with live musicians and forty-eight dancers from all over the world, a "flying orchestra," and the largest 3D screen in North America, Celine sang, danced, and even flew among the playful Cirque acrobats. The music, the lighting, and that screen brought to life fantastical worlds: a Roman temple, a heavenly starscape, an enchanted tree, and even Frank Sinatra for a "live" duet. It was a magnificent fusion of magic, beauty, and love, inspired by and for Celine. A lesser artist might have been engulfed by the sheer extravagance, but she soared above it all, the archetypal entertainer.

The show sold out night after night, easily recouping the $100-million cost of the custom-built 4,000-seat Coliseum theatre, and attracting thousands of new visitors to Las Vegas every week. Celine was called a "one-woman economic stimulus package." Her three-year contract was extended to five, and over the first run it grossed more than $400 million in ticket sales, not to mention the incredible boost it gave to Vegas with what was spent by visitors on hotels, food, and gambling. Ol' Blue Eyes would surely have doffed his hat.

The Coliseum later became a showcase for other stars looking for a high-class residency, from Shania Twain to Bette Midler to Mariah Carey. Even Pavarotti performed there. But no one came close to the drawing power of Celine. She and René achieved extraordinary heights. At Celine's first concert after René's death in January 2016, the evening began with the following words from Celine: "I understood that my career was his masterpiece, his song, his symphony. The idea of leaving it unfinished would have hurt him terribly. I realized that if he ever left us, I would have to continue without him, for him."

And she will. With her three boys at her side, her heart will go on.

WHILE CELINE TRIUMPHED IN Vegas, her team turned their focus to Pierre Garand—better known as Garou. Garou was a dreamboat with a powerful rumbly voice and a cheeky charm well suited to his nickname, which, loosely translated, means "wolf." He'd been a singer in a blues band, but his charisma convinced Luc Plamondon to cast him as Quasimodo in the musical *Notre-Dame de Paris*. That was it. Garou's voice spawned three Number One hits in Quebec and he became a star in France.

To me, what made Garou extraordinary was his selfless drive to entertain. He was like a French Bruce Springsteen, working *for* the audience, wooing them, teasing them, toiling to ensure that every single member of the crowd had the best collective experience possible. It's rare to see that.

I remember having the honour of awarding Garou with his first commemorative plaque for selling one million records at the Bercy Arena in Paris. I'd had little to do with Garou's success so far, but it was a privilege I couldn't refuse as president of the Canadian company.

I rehearsed a French script that I'd written on the plane and joined

Olivier Montfort, managing director of Sony France, at the arena to present the plaque at the press conference. I thought I was making a decent effort with my best "Monsieur and Madame Thibault" high school French, but Garou interrupted with a "Permettez-moi?" and proceeded to clown around pretending to be my translator. I had trouble following what he was saying but I didn't care. The press loved it and that's what mattered.

Garou charmed the socks off everyone he met, including Jeremy Irons, who was at the boozy after-party. Mr. Irons cornered me with purpose, saying, "That man has a GOD. GIVEN. VOICE. You must protect it!" He underlined each word with his right index finger, poking me in the chest. "A GOD. GIVEN. VOICE!" he repeated. I promised to do my best.

I was amused and unscathed, but on my return I imagined Murray asking, "Honey, where did those marks on your décolletage come from?"

"Oh, I ran into Scar from *The Lion King* at the after-party..."

I know: flying to Paris, drinking champagne with movie stars. If it makes you feel any better, I headed back to the airport and was greeted by the same flight crew that had flown me over.

"Back already, Ms. Donlon?" they asked.

Life in the fast lane.

Mario Lefevre, moi, and Garou in Paris.

SONY MUSIC CANADA'S DOMESTIC roster was impressive. Between the English and French arms of the company, we had more than two dozen active Canadian artists. Many of them, like Celine, Leonard, Garou, Our Lady Peace, Chantal Kreviazuk, Amanda Marshall, 54-40, and the

Philosopher Kings were well on their way long before I arrived. We also worked with Tom Wilson, Colin Linden, and teenaged country crooner Adam Gregory. On the French A&R side were Lara Fabian, Patricia Kaas, Lili Fatale, and Jorane, among others. The Canadian company was working hard to maximize the success of our artists in Canada, of course, but as always we wanted them to conquer America and beyond.

In order for a Sony Canada signing to succeed in America, it had to be blessed by Rick Dobbis internationally and championed in the U.S. by either Polly Anthony at Epic or Don Ienner at Columbia. Happily, Donnie Ienner was already a fan of both Our Lady Peace and Chantal.

Watching Donnie get excited about a record was infectious. I'd been with the company for about five business days when I had my second meeting with him in his office in New York. He played me the first single from his new signing, Train's "Drops of Jupiter." He could barely sit down he was so energized, and you didn't need big ears to tell it was going to be a smash. I promised him (with no practical knowledge of how it might be accomplished) that I'd bring him a Number One in Canada. Thank heavens, the song delivered.

That said, a huge hit is still rare. Records stall for all kinds of reasons. Timing, chemistry, inept stewardship, in-house competition, poor management, born under a bad sign, or "They're just not into you." Even when the record is solid, the star has power, and the campaign is carefully coordinated, the failure rate is enormous. And even when you've triumphed in one country, achievement in another is not assured.

Success in America is next to impossible without a champion in the U.S. company. That champion has to be invested egotistically and monetarily. They need to feel their ass is on the line. The best guarantee of that is if they've signed an artist personally.

Canadians have been signing deals south of the border for some time. Many of our best-known Canadian artists through the decades, from Joni Mitchell, Neil Young, and Gordon Lightfoot to Shania Twain and Justin Bieber, have all been signed to U.S. labels. Others started on Canadian independent labels and then signed south, like k.d. lang, who went from Bumstead to Sire; Diana Krall, who started with Justin Time but switched to Verve; and Michael Bublé, who self-released before singing to 143/Reprise. As Canadians we're proud of our international stars and we keep birthing new ones, but we're not keeping *all* the business at home.

Fast-forwarding once more to the end of 2015, an astounding seven out of ten songs on *Billboard*'s Top Ten were from five Canadian artists.

As Mike Doherty wrote in *Maclean's* magazine, "The week of Dec. 5, 2015, is surely destined to be a Heritage Minute: seven of the songs on the Ten: The triumphantly apologetic Justin Bieber sat at No. 2, No. 4, and No. 5 simultaneously; Drake's ubiquitous Hotline Bling was at No. 3, The Weeknd's The Hills at No. 6, Shawn Mendes's clap-along Stitches at No. 7, and Alessia Cara's disaffected teen anthem, Here, at No. 10 (it hit No. 8 the following week). All are from Ontario... But just how Canadian are its roots? All five artists are signed directly to various of Universal Music's U.S. divisions, and only distributed via Universal Canada (The Weeknd is signed to both)."

Why do I care?

Because I'm a cheerleading, pom-pom-waving Canadian cultural nationalist. When it comes to talent, Canada is an Arts Nation—we punch above our weight. So why shouldn't we keep more of the business and the money here in Canada too? Sign it, record it, release it to the world, recoup a bigger royalty and reinvest in new talent. And it's not just the commerce; it's the content. If you're signed and managed in the U.S., you'll likely be working with American producers and writers, which can't help make what we hear less "ours." I understand that music is a global business and that, as with Hollywood or Silicon Valley, the centres are elsewhere—but it's not like we lack the infrastructure we once did, north of the 49th.

Perhaps (as has been suggested) I'm just looking through old eyes. In my time there were six major labels in Canada; now there are three. The majors were once signing dozens of Canadian acts each; now they're signing a small handful. But if Justin Bieber can be discovered on YouTube and end up signed to Usher's label, or if Magic!, The Weeknd, and Drake (whose affection for "the 6ix" is unmistakable) can be finding fertile ground in Canada and proudly hoisting their hometowns to the world, then why should I quibble with who they're signed to?

I *am* thrilled that great Canadian talents are ruling the international charts and showing off Canada's rich diversity. It's now a time when artistic success can be thrust onto the world stage from anywhere. When I was president of Sony Music Canada, there were firmer geographical borders around success; when Canadian records were hits in Canada, they were dogged by the question, "When's the U.S. release date?"

The question was sad because it implied that being successful in Canada wasn't enough. Yet it was also understandable. Musicians want the biggest audience possible, and they can bump their heads on the career ceiling pretty quickly in Canada. Our geography is vast and our population small, and there's only so many times you can play Medicine Hat. The size and speed of the market create an imbalance of fame to fortune. Canadian artists can return home from the Juno Awards with an armful of statues to an eviction notice on the door. It also seems part of our Canadian psyche to seek validation from south of the border.

I thought I could bust down any barriers to success with great Canadian talent and sheer force of will. I still think I had the right attitude. If you don't believe you'd take a bullet for your artists, you shouldn't ante up. We were keen to engage the U.S. early and co-sign the deal, so that the artist might enjoy the best of both worlds. Still, you don't go knocking on that door without a hit song burning a hole in your pocket.

Mike Roth was Sony Canada's A&R director. He was a veteran at the company, but retained his boyish enthusiasm for great music, and he had a deft bedside manner when artists needed motivation or to be talked off a ledge. An A&R director's special skill is to smooth the interface between art and commerce. They know the artist and the producer, they've been inside the sessions, they understand what the label needs most—a single that works on radio.

The best part of any day was when Mike popped his head into the office and said, "Want to hear a song?" There's nothing like hearing a hit record for the first time, especially in a beautifully appointed, state-of-the-art recording studio. It's exciting and nerve-racking, especially if the artist is present. Time slows as the engineer cues up the track, pushes up the fader, and lets it roll.

A hit feels exciting and new, yet familiar at the same time. You know it when you hear it and especially when you feel it. It's organic and intimate, partly because playback is always blisteringly loud. Your body resonates like an extra speaker and your brain starts to anticipate the changes. You may very well be helpless when it's over, suspended in silence. And it's Pavlovian. Once you've had that experience you start to crave it again immediately. That's what it felt like to me, anyway.

When the track goes to radio, that's when the promotions team kicks in, trying to keep everything in motion like that plate spinner on *The Ed Sullivan Show*. You have to build on every ad, deliver a great video, trot out the artist, meet and greet and spin away until the song gets enough critical mass to enter, then climb the charts. Everything needs to work in perfect harmony or your single might stall.

A stalled single is frightening. If a single starts to slide, even a point or two, alarm bells go off. It's all hands to the wheel. A two-week slide and a record's bullet can become an anchor. A failed single can sink a record, possibly even a career. If the second single doesn't perform, tour dates get shaky and calls go unreturned; suddenly everyone is in a meeting. As Rick wryly said, "A hit has many fathers; a miss is an orphan."

It wasn't always the case. There was a time when artist development could take years. A surprising number of the most enduring artists have never had a Number One song on the *Billboard* Top Forty chart. That list includes Led Zeppelin, Bob Marley, the Who, Van Morrison, Johnny Cash, the Grateful Dead, Rush, and Bruce Springsteen.

It's likely that our most treasured icons may never have succeeded in today's environment. Bonnie Raitt didn't have a hit single until her sixth record. Bob Dylan has never had a Number One single (though the Byrds had one singing his "Mr. Tambourine Man"), yet Columbia stood by him record after record as he built his audience. There are new ways to build careers today, of course, but I can't imagine seeing Bob Dylan as a judge on *The X Factor*.

As an industry we were demanding bigger returns in shorter timelines and investing more in superstar producers and stylists to get them. When the music is driven by the need to fit radio formats, it can't help becoming formulaic, yet audiences still thirst for the real. When someone as authentic as Adele comes along, the collective sigh of appreciation is heard at the cash register. As esteemed industry analyst Bob Lefsetz said of her in his newsletter, "The Lefsetz Letter," "We knew it was something special. We knew we were witnessing the rebirth of what once was."

I could never stand it when we didn't get the traction we needed to propel it up the charts. It was a tremendous waste of work and commitment to lose a record in that way, and the consequences were too dire — more so for the artist.

But it never feels like that at the beginning.

At the beginning it's exhilarating.

CHANTAL KREVIAZUK HAD ALREADY had a big hit internationally with a cover of "Leaving on a Jet Plane," and we were rooting for her to achieve the same with one of her own songs. Chantal is extraordinary both as a performer and a songwriter, and she's been hugely successful writing and co-writing songs for Britney Spears, Avril Lavigne, Kelly Clarkson, and Drake, among others.

Happily, Sony U.S. was committed, and the first single, "In This Life," from *What If It All Means Something* went gold in Canada and made the Top Twenty on the Adult Contemporary charts in America.

Meanwhile Our Lady Peace was recording their fifth album with producer Bob Rock at his studio in Maui. OLP had both solid management in Canada, with Coalition Music, and a strong relationship with Columbia in New York. The record was called *Gravity*, and the first single, "Somewhere Out There," was a monster hit. The album was released in Australia, Asia, the U.K., and Europe, and went gold in the U.S. and double platinum in Canada.

When I arrived, Amanda Marshall was out of her deal with Epic, but given her powerhouse strength as a live performer, her proven multiplatinum status in Canada, and her success in the U.S. with songs like "Birmingham," I thought we could ignite new champions south of the border at Columbia.

Superstar producers Peter Asher and Billy Mann came on board, and when we gathered in the studio for a playback of "Marry Me" — a melodic ache of a song, expertly produced, and beautifully sung and written by Amanda — I knew she'd delivered a great record.

We shot an edgy video for the first single and title track, "Everybody's Got a Story," and Much put it in heavy rotation. Rick got behind the record internationally and Amanda delivered powerful showcase performances in London and New York. We also shot a full-length live concert performance DVD to show her incredible stage presence to the territories she wouldn't be touring. The record got airplay in Australia and the U.K., went platinum in Canada, and won a Juno for Single of the Year; but sadly, we never got the traction we needed in America. That wasn't Amanda's fault—she delivered in talent and drive—and I pushed so hard I may have endangered my relationships within the company. But you can't always get what you want. Sometimes the planets just won't align no matter what you do.

While I was president of the company we announced signings of singer-songwriters Liam Titcomb, Tom Barlow, and Jeremy Fisher; classical cellist Denise Djokic; rockers the Trews; rappers Kyprios and Project Wyze; and Aselin Debison, whose performance as a child had brought a room full of striking Cape Breton miners to tears. There were also a few co-signings, including Graph Nobel with the U.S. and Marilou with Sony France.

I admit I was personally drawn to artists who had something to say, and often the song that moved me most wasn't the radio-friendly single. I loved songs that could hit you between the ears, as well as in the heart, the feet, and the groin. Was it too much to want art *and* commerce? The business could feel so "anti-art" at times; you had to trust that the drive to create would be solace enough when the going got rough. But I also understood that this was a world that thrived on hits and star power, and that's what my business side aimed to deliver.

LIAM TITCOMB WAS A tall, handsome sixteen-year-old actor and singer-songwriter with an artistry beyond his years and who reminded me of a young Jackson Browne. Mike Roth had been checking in with him since he was fourteen. We knew he was a strong player and performer, but we needed to know that he had strong writing chops as well.

For me, the answer to that question was a song called "Rose of Jericho," about a sweet, blonde light of a girl who had been abused as a child.

You know she swears he had the bluest eyes
Before he took her in the middle of the night
She's just an angel, caught in the undertow
She ended up on the dark side of the road

Liam explained that a rose of Jericho is a desert plant, like a tumbleweed, which can roll through parched land for years and then flower with exuberance when given water. I was blown away by the metaphor. If this was the beginning, there was no telling where he could go from here.

"Rose of Jericho" was too dark to be a first single, so we led with a more upbeat song, "Sad Eyes," which hit the Top Ten on the Adult Contemporary charts.

That was the case for Tom Barlow and Jeremy Fisher as well. The song that put me over the top for Tom Barlow was "Married By Elvis," a bouncy dance-hall-infused song about gay marriage.

> They want to drive down to Vegas
> Get married by Elvis
> Get drunk on champagne and get legally laid
> They'll cherish the kisses
> As missus and missus
> Now is that so terribly strange

That track would be ripe for release in America today. Timing. The first single we released in 2003 was "Walk Away," an empathetic song about young people dealing with depression, gang violence, and domestic abuse.

> Doesn't matter that you're lying in the gutter
> It doesn't matter that your brain's all cluttered
> It doesn't matter that you're covered in scars
> You're never in the gutter with your eyes on the stars.

People's reactions to the song were profound: Tom was told that his song stopped people from committing suicide. Imagine writing a song that actually saved lives. Tom was up for three Junos that year for Song of the Year, Album of the Year, and Best New Artist.

Jeremy Fisher was reminiscent of an early Bob Dylan. He had an impressive dedication to his craft; by the time we met, he'd already racked up over 7,400 kilometres riding his bike, busking, and sleeping in farmers' fields across Canada and the western United States on his "One Less Tour Bus" tour. His manager, "Parkside" Mike Renaud, had sent us Jeremy's independent album, *Back Porch Spirituals*, and we flew him in for a live audition. It didn't seem right to ask him to ride.

Jeremy sang alone on the Sony sound stage, with just an acoustic guitar. He was a powerfully percussive player, and as the last notes faded on his third song, "Fall for Anything," our lawyer Judy Naiberg leaned over to me and whispered, "Do you want me to prepare the execution copies now?"

"Let's sign him before he leaves the building," I whispered back.

Is the world so big, it makes you feel small
Is the hole you dig, deep enough at all
The graveyard is full my grandma used to say
If you don't stand for something you will fall for anything

When we inked the deal, Jeremy wore a shirt that read "CASH" in big letters. I loved his sense of humour. Once again, the first single was a more radio-friendly track called "High School."

It wasn't all folk singers. Kyprios was a hip-hop poet, a clever rapper with a hyper-animated performance style. Described as Everlast meets Lenny Bruce meets Leonard Cohen, Kyprios was intense. He won the first slam poetry contest he ever entered, in New York no less, after delivering an incendiary spoken-word piece about racism entitled "Hate":

Do you know what I am? I am hate. I put the scars on your back, I
    put you in the oven, I dropped the bomb on your country and I
    put those words on your tongue.
You want to stop me? You're too fucking stupid to stop me. I'll even
    tell you how to stop me and I bet you can't.
Well what are you waiting for? Give me some love.

It was tough to watch but important to hear and I trusted his heart.

The song we went with was called "This Is My Hit," a cocky choice for a first single, given that the lyrics take shots at both hip-hop culture and radio.

Don't believe everything you hear, kid, trust me
Analyze
Gotta question, ask it
Or be a market pitch for a specific demographic
Fourteen and a girl, you're the number one target in the world

Question even me, gonna believe a catch or hook?
Have I got substance? I dunno take a look

"This Is My Hit" went immediately into heavy rotation at MuchMusic
and MusiquePlus, but we were unsuccessful in America. Call me crazy, but
perhaps that had something to do with the fact that Epic U.S. had just
signed another white Canadian hip-hop solo act whose name started with
a "K." Kazzer had a great shot with his song "Pedal to the Metal" and is
still performing, though he's now known as the Redlight King.

Two of Sony's strongest domestic acts when I arrived were the Philosopher
Kings and Prozzäk, whose members criss-crossed on each others' projects.
They were taking a break from recording to concentrate on producing, and
they were off to a great start. Gerald Eaton and bandmate Brian West —
a.k.a. Track and Field Productions — co-produced Nelly Furtado's massive
record *Whoa, Nelly!*, as well as K'Naan's *The Dusty Foot Philosopher*, at the
time. Gerald's solo persona was called Jarvis Church, and he delivered a terrific record called *Shake It Off*. Gerald is a true talent, a Grammy-nominated
producer, and a captivating live performer.

We also loved working with the Trews. Lead singer Colin MacDonald
was as Ready to GO! as any young rocker — they spent over 200 days
on the road in 2003 — and Jack Syperek's Jim Morrison swagger would
hold up anywhere in the world. The U.K. took a keen interest and we
rallied round, made videos, and celebrated at the Junos. Their record
Den of Thieves went gold in Canada and The Trews are still rocking on
all over North America.

Classical was represented too. The Canadian company was already well
regarded internationally due to our Glenn Gould catalogue, but the opportunity to sign a new Canadian classical artist was irresistible. Denise Djokic
was a sixteen-year-old cellist from the Maritimes who'd won the use of a
$3-million Stradivarius from an anonymous donor through the Canada
Council for the Arts. We enlisted the aid of Peter Gelb, then head of Sony
Classical in New York (now general manager of the Metropolitan Opera
in New York), for his help with repertoire and promotion, and the multi-
talented Stephan Moccio — who wrote "A New Day Has Come" for Celine
Dion (and later co-wrote and co-produced The Weeknd's Number One hit
"Earned It (Fifty Shades Of Grey)") — produced her record.

Within three months of signing, Denise was invited to appear on the Grammys, performing a one-minute solo cello Bach piece that would lead into Train's massive hit, "Drops of Jupiter." Imagine being sixteen years old and playing solo on a broadcast to millions, not to mention with the biggest musical superstars on the planet sitting in the audience. I was a ball of nerves, but when the spotlight hit Denise, she had the focus of a master.

Denise wasn't the youngest artist we signed; there was Aselin Debison, the doe-eyed eight-year-old with the enchanting voice who'd moved the tough Cape Breton miners to tears. For a young girl, Aselin certainly attracted some powerhouse people. Prime Minister Jean Chrétien called Aselin "the next Celine Dion," and she sang for Queen Elizabeth II at the Toronto celebrations of her Golden Jubilee. We enlisted Peter Asher to record her first album and shot a PBS special in Cape Breton (where striking workers continued to be a theme — we arrived to find that all the crab boats we'd hoped to film in the background were chained together in a blockade in the harbour). Amazing to think that Aselin was already a world traveller promoting the recording at twelve years old.

For the reasons I've outlined, we wanted all of our records to be successful outside of Canada and were relentless in the pursuit. There may have been moments when I pushed too hard. I remember curling the hair of our VP International, David Toomey, who had just joined the Canadian company from the New York office. We'd imported him in advance of big international records coming from Celine, Leonard, Chantal, and Our Lady Peace, staffing up so they would have the best support outside Canada.

Dave was walking by my office and caught me in full froth on the phone, pacing behind my desk, arguing loudly.

I had a full-page trade ad in my hand. It had been placed by a Canadian law firm and trumpeted six acts the firm had just secured to U.S. major label recording agreements, including Three Days Grace (Jive), Billy Talent (Atlantic), and Sam Roberts (Universal). None were affiliated with Sony U.S., but it still made me crazy.

It was obvious I was in a lather, so after the call Dave ducked his head in and asked me who I had been talking to.

"Don Ienner," I sighed.

Dave went white. Nobody yelled when they were talking with Ienner.

I imagined Dave wondering if there was still time to get his old job back. Obviously the head of the Canadian company was certifiable.

The conversation had begun with a discussion on a release date for one of our signings, but had developed into an existential lament for all domestically signed Canadian artists who weren't finding the love south of the border. I think the only reason Donnie didn't hang up on me was because he knew I was passionate about the artists and that, like him, I wanted to win. On the other hand, as I joked later to Dave, his attitude to me may have been more like that scene in *Casablanca* between Peter Lorre's Ugarte and Humphrey Bogart's Rick.

Ugarte: "You despise me, don't you?"

Rick: "If I gave you any thought at all, I probably would."

The music business is a one-percent game. For every hit there are hundreds of misses. Artists don't blame themselves (at least publicly); they need their egos to survive another day. But I blamed myself, even though I'd only been in the job a short while. Overall the Canadian roster was performing beautifully—with Our Lady Peace, Garou, Celine, and Leonard, we were supporting multimillion-selling artists, and there was no question we were managing the company well in every other aspect. But not being able to launch a *new* blazing superstar from inside Canada right away was frustrating.

Granted, I was impatient. And there was a toll to pay in this high-powered world. I was gaining weight and sneaking cigarettes and having crazy dreams about my teeth falling out by the handful. All of those things, I knew, were about control. Even if I wasn't consciously avaricious about my own power, I took it hard when I couldn't make someone else's dreams come true.

Still, I'd do it again. I may not have known when to quit at times, but you have to believe in your artists. If you don't believe, you cannot win. Go big or go home.

And wear a mouthguard.

IT WAS ONE THING to have to come out swinging, looking for wins in an embattled business. But it was something else when you had to go head to head with a beloved artist, like I had to do with Leonard Cohen.

Compilation albums were a reliable profit centre for most record companies before new digital technologies made music available in any combination a consumer might want. This was an area I knew about. At CHUM we'd made a lot of MuchMusic moola with branded compilation series based on genres and shows: *MuchDance*, *X-Tendamix*, and the blockbuster *Big Shiny Tunes*, which became the bestselling Canadian album series ever, selling more than five million copies.

At Sony, our crème de la crème compilation series was *The Essentials*. It had excellent brand integrity, with well-curated collections like *The Essential Tony Bennett* and *The Essential Michael Jackson*. Now we wanted an *Essentials* from Leonard Cohen.

Leonard had already had a number of compilations released in different territories, including the 1975 *The Best of Leonard Cohen* and, my favourite, the 1980 German release *Liebesträume — Leonard Cohen Singt Seine Schönsten Lieder* (which, when I put it through an online translator, came up as: "Dear Dreams — Leonard Cohen Sings His Nicest Songs").

Leonard wasn't interested in working on another compilation. I pleaded, of course: he could remaster the tracks, remix anything he wanted. I promised the moon and stars, and he eventually agreed.

We were generally aligned on what Leonard chose as his essential tracks; but when the final master arrived, "So Long, Marianne" was missing.

I called his manager—still Kelley Lynch at that time—and asked her why it wasn't included. Surely this was an oversight?

"Leonard isn't so keen on that song," she said.

"Really? I can't believe it. It's one of his most beloved songs!"

"He doesn't like it and he won't change his mind, I've already tried."

This was a problem. And it was a problem for the whole company. When I sent the track listing sans "Marianne" out to the international division, the reaction was predictable. Some countries were not even willing to release it without the song, fearing backlash from fans and critics. How can you call it an *Essentials* record without one of the most essential songs?

I began to wheedle and whine at Kelley. Soon Leonard was on the line. His view was that the song "was never as good in reality as it was in memory."

I disagreed, but it's tough to argue with an artist about one of his songs. It's too subjective. It's like arguing about funny.

"That joke's funny."

"No, it isn't."

End of argument.

I suggested that his fans would be disappointed. He countered that his fans would understand. Leonard has deep regard for his fans and often converses on fan sites directly. He would ask them himself, he said, and he did.

Some fans sided with Leonard, while others agreed that an *Essentials* record without "Marianne" would be incomplete.

He still wouldn't budge. I hated to bring up the point that at the time, most artist contracts didn't stipulate that the artist's permission is required to compile; but we were quickly running into manufacturing deadlines and we needed that song.

The next time we talked, I had no choice but to convey the message: "Leonard, you know we can put it out without your blessing."

That did it. The poet was pissed. I literally had to hold the phone away from my ear. He wasn't just angry at me—it was every publisher, every label executive, every corporate suit who profited from artistic work but disrespected the talent.

True artists will go to the wall for their work and so they should. I was crushed but I had to fight back.

"Leonard," I said, "I have always respected your work. Even in the MuchMusic days when I used to interview you, I'd read everything you'd ever written, cherished every song you ever wrote." It was true. I placed Leonard on an artistic pedestal so high it had its own lighting. And cherubs. "I hate to disappoint you, but I have no choice."

Leonard replied: "Denise, if you insist on this course, if you insist on going against my wishes and including this song when I have asked you not to, then go ahead. But you need to know that you will forever hold a much smaller place in my heart."

I could barely breathe.

"Leonard," I said, "I'm very sorry, but that's a risk I have to take."

I put the phone down totally shattered. At home, I sat around for hours, miserable.

The next day I emailed Kelley to let her know that we would be including "Marianne" on the record. I described the call and told her how shaken I was. Later that afternoon I got an email from Leonard:

Sept 5, 2002
Subject: Marianne
Dear Denise,

Kelley passed your letter on to me. I hope you don't mind.
Your place in my heart is as secure as ever.
That conversation was "just business."
I kind of enjoyed it.
I rarely get a chance to argue with anyone.
I'm sorry if I hurt your feelings,
and I sincerely apologize.
I have to answer to my superiors just as you must answer to yours.
The Master Song or So Long Marianne —
nothing really hangs on this issue.
These are all very tiny matters
and have no weight at all in the butchershop
we call the world.
All that matters here is the heart.
So let's keep ours open.

Your old friend,
Leonard

The album came out with "So Long, Marianne" and went on to sell gold or platinum in countries that included the Netherlands, Australia, Poland, and, of course, Canada. And today, Leonard is selling out arena-sized crowds all over the world, adored on the scale he should be, and still singing "So Long, Marianne."

I KNOW HOW LUCKY I am to have worked with great artists; to have gotten a glimpse into their inner worlds. It's reassuring to know that they are not like us. True artists — the icons, the legends, and those aspiring to be so — are different, a little alien. And they have to be.

An artist's path demands time alone, honing the craft, whatever that might be — writing, dancing, painting, inventing, exploring — hopefully finding inspiration in creative solitude. They create because they have to. They may even see themselves as freaks, absorbing what's around them, even raging against a hostile world while looking for love like the rest of us. Their work involves taking personal risks; they mine their vulnerability and hold up a mirror. Their art compels us to think differently about the world; it helps us to make some sense of it, perhaps to feel less alone, offering some insight into what it means to be human.

It's a tough road. Artists can be uncompromising perfectionists. Rarely have I seen a legend come off stage and say, "Wow, I was great!" James Taylor still does two-hour sound checks before a show even though he's played those songs probably thousands of times. I've heard Neil Peart complain that he flubbed a fill, though I doubt a single one of the ten thousand air drummers in the audience caught it. And if you beg to differ with the artist and argue that they were brilliant, they'll appreciate your encouragement, but secretly think you're an idiot.

It's a life of judgement. With every new song, performance, and public appearance they're saying, "Here's my work, what do you think? Do you like it? Do you like *me*?" Artists can avoid the tabloids at the grocery store or resolve never to read a review, but they are their work. And for every hundred rave reviews, it's the one bad one that they'll remember and take to heart.

Our most revered musical stars lead a yin-and-yang existence, a push-and-pull friction of performance and isolation, of external validation and inner self-doubt. They're required to be introverts to create their work and extroverts to sell it.

The business is commercial and inherently anti-art. The goal is hit records and sold-out tours, requiring artists to put themselves on parade at concerts and awards shows and red carpets. Success means being "owned" by the public and fame creates a bull's eye for the stalkerazzi and the anti-social media. It's a paradox that artists need thin skin to create their work and a thick skin to promote it. Some separate the artist from the performer by taking on an alternative persona, like Lady Gaga or Alice Cooper or David Bowie.

(For Murray, for a while, it was a hat. He'd put it on and say "I'm going out to be *him*." Then he'd come home and say, "Fuck the fame," take off the hat, and resume his "Murray Many Heads" life as the father, naturalist, pilot, scientist, handyman, and Renaissance man that I love.)

Artists can build defences, but the barriers between the person and the performer are permeable. Marilyn Monroe's Norma Jean was always there. Those in the inner circle do their best to buffer and buoy, but mega-fame demands a life that is increasingly cocooned, shrouded by tinted windows and bodyguards.

The constant shifting between private, public, and performance isn't easy. Take a small example—the backstage meet-and-greets after the show, where artists are penned in a room to pose with fans, contest winners, and industry folk. Some artists are good at it—just another performance—and some so awkward it's painful to watch. I've seen songs added to charts because the radio music director had enjoyed meeting the artist after a show, and I've seen songs (and at least one career) sink because the artist came across as a jerk. Even the biggest stars are compelled to engage. It's part of what Joni describes in "Free Man in Paris": "Stoking the star-maker machinery / Behind the popular song."

It's a business where success is tough to achieve and tougher to maintain. Sustaining the applause might be the hardest thing of all. The artists I worry about are the celestials, the ones who find themselves alone in their hotel rooms, maybe a little high, trying to avoid the crash after the show. One minute they're in the spotlight as crowds scream their name, and then a few hours later, they're alone with the walls closing in. It's no wonder we see so many train wrecks. The 27 Club has far too many members.

Whenever I hear of an artist in trouble, I immediately think about who their manager is and pray they've got a good one or, preferably, a great one. Someone once said, "Managers take the blame, the artists take the glory," but truthfully, a great manager can make all the difference.

It takes a lot of things to make a manager great. For starters, their business gifts have to be every bit as powerful as their clients' musical ones. Great managers are naturally entrepreneurial, organized, inspirational, and loyal to their artists' vision above everyone else. All the while, a great manager knows best how to run interference when there are challenges, so that their artists can remain true to their mission and not get ground down by the machinery.

Look at the Jacksons. Janet's career had for a strong period been guided by the talented Roger Davies. (Proof that Roger is one of the best managers in the business comes with a glance at his roster, a wealth of one-name ladies like Tina, Sade, Cher, and Pink.) I'm sure his phone rings in the middle of the night, like the phones of all managers. But who did Michael Jackson ultimately call? His doctor.

Great managers know how to say no.

I've been asked more than once to go into management, but I'd seen enough to know it wasn't for me. Not only did I not want to be called in the middle of the night when the party was over, I knew I wouldn't be strong enough for two.

I'm content with having been close enough to the artists I've worked with to share the same air, to applaud their successes and lament with them their frustrations, then hand them back into more capable hands and hope they thrive.

(19)

A YEAR OF RUMBLINGS

"Tomorrow is never what it's supposed to be"
— BOB DYLAN, "DON'T FALL APART ON ME TONIGHT"

IN 2003, BIG CHANGE was afoot.

On January 9, Sony announced that Tommy Mottola had left the company to start a new venture. The following day Sir Howard Stringer, Chairman and CEO of Sony Corporation of America, announced that Andy Lack was the new CEO of Sony Music Entertainment. Andy was an interesting choice. He'd been a newsman and then a broadcaster, coming to us from his role as COO and president of NBCUniversal.

Talk of a merger swirled. But there was always talk — though usually at other companies. Pairings between EMI and Warner had been on again, off again, as had talks of a joint venture between Time Warner and Bertelsmann Music Group (BMG), though regulatory or monetary concerns had often silenced the chatter. Few in the ranks put much stock in the rumours; there was enough to worry about in the day-to-day business.

But in November 2003, the merger of Sony Music and BMG was officially announced. There was rampant speculation as to what the impact would be and to whom. First of all, a merger was expensive; according to reports, the cost of this one was around $400 million. And there would be, inevitably, massive cuts in staff and artist rosters. Beauty pageants all over the world were about to begin.

Sony Canada was acknowledged as a well-run company — bench-marked in the top five against the other international markets — but market conditions continued to be awful everywhere. Inflation was down, unemployment was up, retail closures and bankruptcies were rampant. We were fighting for every sale. With the merger looming, the staff kept their heads up and pushed forward even though no one's position was secure.

The question everyone was asking was, "Who's on first?" The major players all knew one other, some had previously worked with each other, and all were connected to significant artists. Donnie had worked at one point for Clive Davis over at RCA. Clive had formerly been president of Columbia Records and was legendary for his work at Arista, signing dozens of artists including Whitney Houston, Aretha Franklin, and Alicia Keys, as well as L.A. Reid (who built his label LaFace with Clive), Pink, TLC, and Usher. L.A. Reid was now running Arista. Then there was Michele Anthony at Sony and Polly Anthony, who ran Epic and worked with Shakira, Macy Gray, and Pearl Jam. We knew Michael Smellie at BMG was to report to Andy Lack, while Don Ienner had recently been promoted by Andy to Chair of Sony Music, but you'd need a program to keep track of the players.

Rick brought Andy Lack to Toronto to see our operation and meet the staff at a town hall meeting. The executive team did us proud, giving Andy an excellent rundown of the Canadian business, and my position with the company was renewed immediately thereafter. That was a sign of security for me at least, and we continued on.

In August 2004, we received news from Rick Dobbis that he was leaving. He had been an inspiring, cool-headed leader during a trans-formative time, and it was a sad moment for his team internationally. When a similar announcement was made about Bob Bowlin, Sony Music International's chairman and advisor, I started to wonder anew about my own future at the company. When the people directly above you exit, it doesn't bode well. The merger, combined with the state of the business, meant massive personnel changes on both sides of the company. A dozen years later, when I look back at who is still with Sony today, it's sobering.

2004 post-Grammy party. Left to right: Will Botwin, Frank Welzer, Andrew Lack, me, Beyoncé, Bob Bowlin, Rick Dobbis, Michele Anthony, Don Ienner, Mathew Knowles, and Sir Howard Stringer.

This photo says so much: It was taken with Beyoncé in L.A. at a post-Grammy party in 2004. *All* the executives in that photo are gone. Bob Bowlin and Rick Dobbis left in 2004; Will Botwin in 2005; Andy Lack, Don Ienner, and Michele Anthony all left in 2006; and Frank Welzer, head of Sony Music Latin America, retired in 2009 after thirty-seven years at the company. Sir Howard Stringer retired as chairman of the Sony board in 2013. Even Mathew Knowles, Beyoncé's father, is no longer managing his daughter's affairs. The only person still with the company in that shot is Queen Bey. That speaks volumes.

I'm no longer in the picture either.

Before the merger, there were two presidents in Canada—both women. Lisa Zbitnew was president of BMG Canada, and she and I were co-operating in preparing plans for the merged Canadian operations, knowing full well only one of us would be left standing. We'd always gotten along well, but it was cautious work as we weighed each other's executive teams.

Those left standing, we knew, should be the A team; the ones who we felt were best able to grow the company moving forward. But any corporate merger is not a simple formula. You cut costs and eliminate duplication, but it's also an opportunity to re-organize. Performance, track records, and relationships count. Some people play better with others; some people make more money than others, and savings were the bottom line.

There were unique considerations for Sony Music Canada, including our building, which gave us tremendous operating efficiencies. At the end of the day, I campaigned for what I believed best for the Canadian company, even if they were strategies that would likely not satisfy the expectations of the merger overall. It was a personal risk, and I knew it, but I could only present what I thought was right.

I started seeing more executives from BMG visiting Canada. At my first meeting, I was asked by a gentleman: "Do you have a problem with authority?"

"Only if I don't respect it," I said.

It was an honest answer, though not the most politic. I thought about all the times when I'd had to speak my truth to power and how I'd come to most respect those who welcomed differing views.

I don't regret those moments. I believe you must choose principles over personal power, even if it results in being thrown under the bus. I'd also read somewhere that when a culture of "yes" becomes a culture of "no," it's time to go.

I was advised of a time and date when the decision as to who would run the merged company would be made. I was at my desk, waiting for a call. When the phone rang I wasn't surprised to hear that it wasn't me. I knew I'd played a hand in deciding my future.

It was all very amicable. There was no rush for me to leave; I was asked to help transition, but no one wants to be a lame duck president. The new commander-in-chief should take charge right away. I prepared a note to staff, acknowledging their many achievements, thanking them for their support, and singing Lisa's praises. I was confident that her enormous experience would serve the company well through the merger. I pushed "send" on the memo and sat quietly, enjoying my presidential office for the last time.

I enjoyed my four years at Sony, despite how tough the business was. It was a privilege to serve the artists, the people, and the company. I felt that I was retiring from the field with honour.

Staff streamed through the door, concern on their faces for me and, understandably, for themselves. It was a bit like a funeral procession, with friends and colleagues offering condolences, expressing incredulity, promising to stay in touch. It was an emotional afternoon. When managers and artists found out, it was sadder still. They'd have to build new relationships with the new president; I hoped she would champion them as vigorously as I'd tried to.

The company offered to pay for a farewell party, but I declined—they'd treated me well. Instead, I threw a Freedom Fest party at our house instead, where a crush of industry friends came ready to celebrate. Given the state of the business, they considered an exit from the recording industry a win. I would have time to calmly consider my next adventure. But the head can't always control what the heart feels.

I WATCHED THE BUSINESS with interest for years after I left Sony. Out of the ashes of the traditional record business, a golden age had been promised. It was the circle of life, after all. In pop culture nothing lasts forever (well, except Keith Richards).

There's much to love in the new music world. The "democratization of music" has allowed artists to reach out to find their fans and build communities without the hierarchies and infrastructure that many saw as obstacles to their success. Digital distribution, instant access to global markets, and a plethora of new (and legal) downloading, streaming, and connectivity offerings have been revolutionary tools. Suddenly there is room for everyone on the digital store shelves—emerging artists, obscure genres, collector catalogues; superstars, too. There's a wealth of new expression, an abundance of choice, and a myriad of options for exposing music. But it's increasingly evident that artists might die of exposure if exhaustion doesn't kill them first.

For emerging artists, the sparkly new tools imply that the middlemen are no longer required, which in some ways is true. But what I'm seeing is that the DIY trade-off burdens the artist with busy-ness. Independent musicians are not only required to create world-class content, but also to be their own marketers, salesmen, accountants, data-processers, distributors, and customer service departments. They're hustlers, managing their websites and updating their fans on social media, signing autographs and selling merchandise after the show, tying ribbons on the collector-edition vinyl that they'll pop in the mail on their way to couch-surf a contest winner who crowdfunded their recording on Sellaband or PledgeMusic.

As Donna Summer sang, "She works hard for the money."

It's fantastic to have so many options to fuel a career; I'm just not convinced all this grinding serves the art. I'd rather the artist be putting in her ten thousand hours in creative pursuit, not living her life chained to Twitter, serving up hourly musings lest her fans flock off.

That said, I applaud those artists who are grabbing the new social media marketing tools with both hands. Tom Wilson, who I worked with at Sony, is one of those. Tom is an inspired musician and visual artist, a larger-than-life character I can best describe as a friendly, hairy, musical Hagrid. He Instagrams and tweets from the road to build support for all three of his touring entities — Blackie and the Rodeo Kings, Lee Harvey Osmond, and Junkhouse. Aided by his painter's eye and his co-manager daughter Maddy and Allen Moy, their efforts will surely build his relationship with his fans.

I'd always loved my spontaneous marketing meetings with Tom — he was already a Mad Man at heart. If Tom was in the Sony building and saw me at my desk, he'd just barge through the door, bristling with excitement and big ideas. What about a huge picture of his "ugly mug" (as he put it) projected onto the abandoned grain silos on the Lake Ontario shoreline? Or in the sky, like the Bat-Signal — or on the moon!

Many of Tom's enthusiasms could not be realized for one boring corporate reason or another. I hated it when an audacious idea limped out the door because it didn't meet a marketing cost-benefits analysis (or risked a lawsuit). He told me laughingly that I'd once said in frustration, "Tom, you're the closest to my heart but the farthest from my wallet."

Tom didn't sell records on a Michael Jackson scale, but I loved that Sony Canada had him and his Blackie and the Rodeo Kings bandmate, bluesman Colin Linden, on the label. They make solid records and work hard to promote them. They have to, in this new topsy-turvy world. Where once you toured to promote the sale of a CD, now music is given away free to build a touring base. Good thing they're both great live performers, because a concert tour is still a sacred place where people will pay to commune.

The biggest challenge for content creators, now more than ever, is, How do you get paid? The answer is, Any and every way you can. Through touring, merchandising, songwriting royalties, streaming payments, sponsorship deals, endorsements, crowdfunding: whatever it takes.

As Robert Levine said in his book *Free Ride*: "It has never been easier to distribute a creative work. At the same time, it's never been harder to get paid for it."

The new models are both a blessing and a curse. Streaming is seen as a saviour of the business. There are over five hundred licensed digital music services operating worldwide, including Apple Music, Pandora, and Spotify. In terms of features and customization, they're as different from terrestrial radio as the car was from the horse and buggy. But there are also big differences in how creators are compensated. Where once the royalties from a hit song at radio could pay for your house, the royalties from a streaming source barely pay the interest on the mortgage.

There are certainly people getting rich — iTunes is now the largest music retailer in the world — but it's not necessarily the ones who make the music, and the artists are pushing back.

In November of 2014, Taylor Swift removed her songs from Spotify, complaining that the per-steaming royalty rates were too low (between $0.006 and $0.008 per stream). Pharrell was very *un*Happy with his cheque from Pandora. Apparently, the combined publisher and writer royalties from 43 million streams of "Happy" over three months were just $2,700. That kind of coin is not going to keep him in fashion forward hats.

If the superstars are upset, imagine what it's like for everyone else.

And believe it or not, in Canada, it's ten times worse. A coalition called #IStandForMusic, representing approximately one hundred music organizations, is campaigning for an appeal of a 2014 decision by the Canadian Copyright Board on Tariff 8 — which set streaming rates for services like Spotify and Pandora at less than 10 percent of comparable rates in the U.S. Talk about hitting a sour note. It's especially surprising because it took the copyright board six years to come to that decision, a lifetime in the digital age. Barenaked Ladies used to sing about what they'd do with a million dollars; according to #IStandForMusic, in Canada's streaming world they'd need 9,216 plays to buy a bowl of Kraft Dinner, 3 million plays to afford the llama, 5 million plays for the ottoman, and 4 billion plays for the house to put them in.

The silver lining is that the streaming sites are legal, they're paying, and they're growing. But herculean efforts are still required to ensure the creators are fairly compensated for their work.

Of course there are other ways to get paid, like YouTube, which pays creators on an ad-based model. But YouTube — for which music is a main driver — is also in the crosshairs. According to the IFPI, "Services like YouTube have some 900 million users. And yet they pay a tiny portion of the revenues earned by music rights holders — only four per cent of industry revenues globally in 2015." Q Prime manager Peter Mensch has called

YouTube "the devil," and according to an article written by Debbie Harry for the *Guardian*: "The official video for Blondie's 'Heart of Glass' on YouTube has been viewed 49 million times. There are over a million other Blondie videos on YouTube, most of them from unofficial accounts, garnering a combined hundreds of millions of views. Yet none of us in Blondie will receive a fair amount of royalties from these millions of plays." In June 2016, 180 artists—including U2, Paul McCartney, and The Black Keys—aligned, demanding reform of the Digital Millennium Copyright Act and asking for fair treatment against copyright infringement. We'll see how that goes.

Artists still get paid on traditional media, but given all the shiny new toys, it's clear that commercial radio will lose ground as music's main marketing driver. Whether revenues from new services will ever make up for the shortfall between start and scale (when consumers adopt streaming services more widely and royalty rates are fairer) is the question. I hope the artists can last that long.

Today's world is complicated for artists. One might wish for an easier time. I wonder if the benefactor model might work now? Mozart enjoyed the patronage of Archbishop Sigismund von Schrattenbach and Beethoven had Archduke Rudolph. Mark Zuckerberg might enjoy a live-in rapper—perhaps 50 Cent, who recently filed for bankruptcy, would be interested? Or Kanye West, who I see has reached out to both Zuckerberg and Google's Larry Page for help. Maybe Bill and Melinda Gates could offer sanctuary to Sinéad O'Connor, or the Koch brothers could entice Ted Nugent from his shooting range to prowl their Manhattan penthouse.

It's fun to muse, and yes there are many entrepreneurial options for those willing to do the work, but *superstar* success today still requires a dedicated support structure that includes managers, publishers, distributors, and labels.

The three remaining major labels—Universal, Warner, and Sony—are now leaner versions of themselves. It took over a dozen years, but the business is finally turning around. In 2016, the IFPI reported that for the first time, digital revenues outstripped the sales of physical product in 2015, and the global revenues for recorded music improved by 3.2 percent. That figure might be considered a rounding error in any other business, but this is an industry that has been praying to the heavens for *any* sign in the right direction since the turn of the century.

A return to health will bring new opportunities, but to be a true success, the system has to work for more than the established superstars—because the notion of the starving artist has never been truer.

In the past decade, there's already been a huge erosion of our musical bedrock. Since 2006, the number of active artists in Canada has fallen by nearly *fifty* percent—"potentially depriving Canadians," as the Canadian Independent Recording Artists Association memorably put it, "of the next Glenn Gould or Bryan Adams or Arcade Fire."

I pray the remaining artists, songwriters, and performers can hang in there while we're in these "shifting model" waters. It's well documented that there are tremendous economic benefits to investing in culture. That said, there are those that say we don't owe anyone a living. But even if we only think selfishly about it, we should vigorously support artistic endeavour because our lives are so beautifully enriched by it.

As Nietzsche put it, "Life without music is simply an error, exhausting, an exile."

(20)

BURNING OFF A NON-COMPETE

"We make a living by what we get, we make a life by what we give."
— APPARENTLY NOT A QUOTE BY WINSTON CHURCHILL,
THOUGH EVERYONE THINKS IT IS (INCLUDING MY MOTHER)

THE DAY I LEFT Sony, I found myself standing in the kitchen in the middle of the afternoon with my car keys in my hand, slightly high from office affection and a little stupefied, off-balance at being home in the middle of a workday afternoon. I was firmly in the moment, except my mind was cottony, muddled, dislocated. I'd lost something. My drive? My identity? I couldn't put my finger on it.

Murray came up from his office. "What are you doing here?"

"I'm out."

"Great! Now we get you back." Murray reached for a bottle of wine. "Let's celebrate."

Murray was right; there *was* something to celebrate.

Now I could double down on being a mum, a wife, a daughter, a friend. We raised a glass. Cheers, honey, thank you, and here's to the next adventure.

The evening was fun, but waking up the next morning was discombobulating. I suppose it's the same for anyone who's been mergered out/restructured/sacked/outsourced/screwed over/voluntarily retired/taken the package or even quit:

Alarm goes off (forgot to unset it), wake up, roll out of bed, wander into the bathroom, turn on the light, and...stop.

First thought: *Whoa. I don't have to get up. I'm unemployed.*

Second thought: *Woo hoo!*

Third thought: *Fuck. Now what?*

Back to bed.

Rationalizing: *It's a gift! You manifested it yourself. There was nothing more you could do.*

Insecurity: *I'm nothing without a title. I should have fought harder to keep it.*

Spiralling: *This sucks. Do something normal. Make a cup of tea.*

Pep talk: *Remember what Mum says: "The world is your oyster." Reinvent. Do what you want!*

What do I want?

Too big a question.

I reached for my BlackBerry. My Sony address was hopping. I scrolled the torrent of emails; it was like a scab I couldn't stop picking. Flowers arrived (silver lining: "Happy Golden Parachute" balloons weren't a thing), friends phoned, they couldn't wait to see me, it had been too long.

I'm blessed, I'm buoyed.

I'm up, I'm down.

I'm fine, I'm numb.

I crave forward motion.

- Make a list (check)

- Buy new BlackBerry

- Exercise

- Read a book

- Take a cooking course

- Organize basement

- Make a will

- Lose 30 pounds

- Sweep the forest

- Figure out what I want to be when I grow up

I was on autopilot. Twice I found myself driving in the direction of the office without realizing it. (There is something very satisfying about a big, screaming U-turn.) *Turn on the radio.* No good — my brain was trained to assign a chart number before it could enjoy a melody. *Perhaps some retail therapy?* Rogers store. New phone, nice! *Home.* Swearing at the computer. Sony told me I could take my computer, but it was suddenly mocking me with the blue screen of death. Planned obsolescence? Doubtful. I'm an electronic glitch magnet. My family won't let me touch theirs. My kingdom for an IT department!

My dead computer triggered something.

Something else had died.

My social standing. My self-worth.

My imposter demon crept in and sat heavily on my chest, sucking the air out of the room.

I thought of that time I was flying to New York for a meeting. A uniformed, mustachioed U.S. customs official looked down at my passport and said flatly, "Purpose of travel?"

"Business meetings."

"What do you do?"

"I'm the president of Sony Music Canada."

He looked up from his desk and straight at me. "Do you have a business card?"

"Of course," I said, digging in my purse.

He took my card, studied it, and looked at me again. Up and down this time. Pointedly.

Then he puffed a little air through his lips and said, "Really?"

I should have been righteous, indignant. Instead, I felt weak and exposed, certain that he was right to be skeptical.

It's usually women who admit to imposter syndrome. Tina Fey, Emma Watson, Kate Winslet, Jodie Foster, and even Nobel Prize–winning, dearly departed Maya Angelou, who said, "I have written eleven books, but each time I think, 'Uh oh, they're going to find out now. I've run a game on everybody, and they're going to find me out.'" Lately, more men are owning up to it. In his commencement speech at the University of the Arts in 2012, bestselling author Neil Gaiman shared his fear that one day a man with a clipboard would come knocking at his door and say, "It's all over, you've been found out."

Been there. Bought the T-shirt.

Imposter syndrome is a pernicious stalker, always there. It lurks in corporate boardrooms and in television studios, and it especially loves a podium. No matter the validation, or how many dear ones protest that I'm deserving, I can't shake it. It's just a matter of time.

People are skeptical. I *look* confident. That's probably the height. Funny that the thing that made me so self-conscious as a teenager became an asset when I became an adult. I can stand up straight, take a deep breath, and stride into a room. I can look confident even if I don't feel it.

And I've been able to *talk* myself into confidence on occasion. I remember a motorcycle driving test I took. Even though I only wanted to drive my Vespa on city streets to yoga class, I had to pass the same speed tests the Harley boys did. It was an incredibly hot day — almost 40 degrees Celsius — and people were woozy in the heat. There had already been three crashes that afternoon on the backlot during the testing, and an ambulance had to be called. I almost backed out, becoming more anxious as the day went on, but as I was walking to the testing area I saw a poster of industrialist Henry Ford on the wall. It said: "If you think you can, you can. If you think you can't, you can't." I stopped, stared at it, and got a grip. Then walked to the track chanting to myself like the Little Engine that Could. *I think I can, I think I can, I think I can*...And I did.

I don't know why I've adopted this imposter troll — maybe it's as textbook as lingering father issues — but so far, the only way I know how to subdue it has been to bury it with busy. Work. Harder, faster, backwards, and yes, even in high heels.

Maybe imposter syndrome helps to keep you humble. Worrying a fear to death has helped me to avoid making mistakes because I'll have run every conceivable disaster scenario in my head already. I know we're *entitled* to make those mistakes — to fail — but knowing that doesn't seem to help in the moment. Mistakes just prove the theory that we're not worthy.

Women are further complicated by their gender. In researching their book *The Confidence Code*, television journalists Katty Kay and Claire Shipman learned that when dealing with failure, men are more inclined to blame the circumstances and not themselves, while women go straight to "internal attribution." In her book *Lean In*, Sheryl Sandberg cites an internal study done by Hewlett-Packard which found that men apply for a job when they feel they meet 60 percent of the job requirements, whereas women will apply only if they feel they meet them all.

Perhaps it has something to do with the way we're judged even when we get the job. Ambitious men are applauded; ambitious women are bossy. It's hard to hear. Duncan once told me as I hurried him to get ready for school that he thought I was intimidating. He was about six. I was totally taken aback. Intimidating? Had I learned that at work? I thought I was just a goof with a title.

The difference for me now was that I *had* no title. I sat there, a little freaked out, contemplating my next move, talking to myself like I would my young son.

"Focus on the positive, Donlon. You're an experienced executive, with energy and opportunity. Look—you're an award-winning rabbit! A Woman of the Year! A Woman of Vision! A Trailblazer! You're in the Broadcasting Hall of Fame, for heaven's sakes! You're a Woman of Influence! It says so right in the paper. Oh gawd. How am I going to give *that* speech next week?

"C'mon. You have your health, your family, and your friends. Take a breath. Choose your next path with joy and try to accept that that caustic little imposter demon is a part of you. It's going to heckle you when you try new things and harass you when you fail, but you will—just like the song says—'pick yourself up, dust yourself off, start all over again.' But first you should strangle that little sucker."

Okay! Good talk. Same time tomorrow?

I didn't know what was going to happen next, what my next adventure would be. I didn't even know how to respond to the inevitable party question: "What do you do?"

"I'm a...*former* executive?"

"I'm a...*recovering* broadcaster?"

"I...*used* to be important?"

Amazingly, while I looked for an answer that didn't feel awkward, a gift found me—a tiny perfect snowflake.

I MAY HAVE BEEN unemployed, but there was no lack of things to do. The next few weeks were filled with a meeting of the Canadian Music Council (which I co-chaired with Rosaire Archambault and Bill Henderson); a trip to Vancouver for Doug Bennett's memorial; the writing of that "Women of Influence" speech (was I still a woman of influence?); an invitation to attend a women's CEO summit (same question); and just for fun, agitating for change in Ottawa.

Free from any corporate conflicts of interest, I threw my hat in and helped independent label manager Graham Stairs with the newly formed Music Industry Coalition (MIC), a lobby group whose aim was to get government support for new, modern copyright legislation and to press for continued funding for Canadian music.

The MIC was an impressive group of twenty-three organizations representing over 4,600 Canadians working in every area of the music industry. It was impressive partly because we'd gotten together in the first place. Songwriters, broadcasters, publishers, labels, and performers can sometimes be on opposite ends of an issue. (*Raise Cancon! Lower Cancon! Gatekeeper! Trough feeder! Pay me! Play me! Pay me more!*) But this mission was important enough that most of us agreed to stick to the two main points: funding for the arts and copyright.

Joined by a brave troupe of artists — Jim Cuddy, Tom Cochrane, Bruce Cockburn, Gilles Valiquette, Pierre Lapointe, Keshia Chanté — we descended on Parliament Hill.

We met with Members of Parliament from all parties, as well as with ministers, senior officials, and the Prime Minister's Office. We were well armed, presenting not only our case but some happy solutions. I'd learned to never go to Ottawa without offering an opportunity for elected officials to win, but the more politicos we met, the less I thought anyone would adopt "I Promise to Reform Canada's Antiquated Copyright Laws!" as their catchy campaign slogan.

On the flight back to Toronto, I was seated next to Bernie Finkelstein, owner of True North Records. He was as frustrated as I was. We vented all the way home (misery loves company). What was the point of working like a dog when no one seemed to care? Maybe I should join an ashram...

When I got home I grabbed the mail on the way in and plunked my overnight bag on the stairs. Duncan was home.

"Hi, Mom," he called from upstairs.

"Hi, honey," I answered with fake cheer.

"Someone delivered something for you. It's on the counter."

As I went to plug in the kettle, I saw a registered mail envelope. It was from Rideau Hall. Strange that it was addressed to me. I was used to seeing mail from the Governor General's office addressed to Murray, who had received an Order of Canada, Canada's highest civilian honour, in 1993.

I opened the letter and burst into tears.

Duncan came down the stairs and softly asked. "Are you okay, Mom?" It's scary to see your mom cry. "Did something bad happen?"

"No, honey, it's good!"

Then I hugged him hard.

If there's anything that might have a chance of overriding the imposter syndrome, at least temporarily, it's that little white snowflake. For a moment, you feel like every cause you took up, every scar you sustained, was worth it.

In those days you were not allowed to tell anyone until the list was announced, and even then you weren't allowed to wear the pin until you were properly inducted by the governor general at Rideau Hall. I told Murray, of course, and I couldn't wait to tell my mum. She, being a mad monarchist, was going to bust her boiler keeping that secret until it was announced.

The new Order of Canada inductees were announced in February 2005 and in September that year, Murray, my mum, Duncan and I travelled to Rideau Hall in Ottawa for the ceremony. It was an experience I'll never forget—a lesson in pride and humility in equal measure. The room was full of overachievers who nodded in recognition when someone said that when they got the letter, their first thought was that there must have been a mistake. (Interesting there's a Zen saying, "No snowflake ever falls in the wrong place.")

At the induction ceremony, though, as each laureate's citation is read, it's obvious why he or she been so honoured. Some are well-known names — Murray was inducted alongside one of his heroes, O. B. Philp, founder of Canada's legendary Snowbirds—but most are people you've never heard of, their contributions all the more commendable because they're selflessly below the public radar.

The motto of the Order of Canada is *Desiderantes meliorem patriam* — "They desire a better country"—and whatever doubts I may sometimes have about myself, I know that to be true.

That snowflake had landed on me at exactly the right time. I too resolved to earn it.

Busting mom's buttons at Rideau Hall. Left to right: Duncan McLauchlan, Murray McLauchlan, Governor General Adrienne Clarkson, me, and Mavis Churchill (Mom.)

AS I ENDEAVOUR TO recount both the tilts and triumphs of my life so far, I'm noticing a bit of a pattern. And it's a cliché to boot. Whenever one door closed on a corporate job, a gate would open and I'd be nudged into some compelling charitable effort, like a pinball flipped off a lever to "Try again!—but with meaning this time."

It may have the aura of selfless do-gooding, but as most volunteers know, humanitarian work can be really quite selfish. The truth is, it feels good to give. It's a fact that has actually been proven by neuroscientists. The pleasure centres in our brains get lit up by altruistic actions, and it's very rewarding.

And if I'm really honest with myself, my own motivations may be baser than that. Maybe I just need to get my head out of my own butt from time to time. Eve Ensler, author of *The Vagina Monologues*, wrote something in her book *In the Body of the World* that rang true for me, the essence of which was: "Turn self-obsession into service." It's good advice, and sometimes all it takes to do that is to answer the call. Literally. Answer the phone when you're asked to help and say yes.

When I got back from the lobbying mission in Ottawa, Christmas was around the corner. I finally had time to do it right and reverted to the full-on blow-out traditions I'd learned from my mum. I shopped and cooked and decorated the house, and made Christmas puddings as gifts (complete with McLauchlan "Pudding Song" lyrics about Shelagh Rogers' singed schnauzer) from Mum's olde English recipe. The walls of the house were dripping wet for five whole days from the twenty-two puddings steaming on top of the stove. It was very festive.

On Boxing Day, I was basking in the Christmas afterglow when the phone rang. It was Tom Cochrane.

"Hey Den, have you seen what's happened? We've got to do something."

I turned on the TV and saw some of the initial footage of the massive tsunami that hit coastlines from Thailand to East Africa. We learned later that the devastation was the result of a 9.0 magnitude earthquake in the Indian Ocean off the coast of Sumatra.

I'll admit, my first thought was not to leap into action. We didn't know yet the extent of the damage or what the world's reaction was going to be. When musicians engage on a big scale, it's usually when governments fail to, but Tom was right to be on it right away.

"We've got to respond as a country and I need you," he said. "I've already got Alex, and Kathy is on board too. Who should we call next?"

Kathy Cochrane, Tom's wife, is a superb organizer, and Rush's guitarist Alex Lifeson had been watching the tsunami coverage on TV with his grandchild in his lap when Tom called. A woman had just described how her child had been ripped from her arms in a torrent of water and it struck Alex to the heart. He had no reservations. Nor did Jim Cuddy. Or Murray. Or Ed Robertson. From there it steamrolled.

The next call was the CBC, who threw their resources behind a televised benefit. We all agreed that the event needed to be a multi-genre, multi-starred, all-Canadian response that would include not just musicians, but hockey players and authors, dancers and comedians, TV personalities and cultural icons. CBC's talent team dove in and the show hosted more than 150 performers — more than we needed — and had to turn people down days before the event. Anne Murray performed with Bryan Adams; Rush joined musical forces with Ed Robertson and Bubbles from *Trailer Park Boys*; and Ron MacLean appeared with Don Cherry sans the sparring. We had Margaret Atwood, Shaye, Haydain Neale, John McDermott, Austin Clarke, Gordon Pinsent, Luba Goy, Tie Domi, Scott Thompson, Gil Moore, Chris Murphy of Sloan, and Murray's band Lunch at Allen's, with Ian Thomas, Marc Jordan and Cindy Church — the list was enormous. It was the biggest assembly of Canadian talent in one place since "Tears Are Not Enough."

In just over a week, *Canada for Asia* was on the air. Canadians were hugely generous—donations totalled more than $4 million. But I can't say it was all peace, love, and altruism behind the scenes. We must have forgotten to hang up the "Leave Your Egos at the Door" sign; not for the talent, but for the politicos. There were demands for acknowledgement that far overreached the contribution. One elected official asked to be included in the credits for arranging free pizza. In protest I asked that my name be pulled altogether, thinking it would set an example. We knew who did what. That was probably a dumb move, but whatever.

Things quieted down somewhat for a while. We headed off on a lovely family vacation, and following that I volunteered to produce "Rock the Walk," a fundraiser for Canada's Walk of Fame. It was a boisterous event that included Tom Green swinging increasingly heavy poultry (a trussed and tethered Cornish hen followed by a chicken, then a turkey) around his head, while musicians dove to shield their instruments from wet flecks of flying fowl.

I was enjoying my "time off" but my family was getting jittery. Murray teased Duncan, saying that if I didn't take a real job soon I would make *them* my new project. (Many a true word is spoken in jest.) Luckily the phone kept ringing. In May, I got a call asking if it was true that Bob Geldof wanted to mount a twentieth-anniversary Live Aid concert. (I didn't know; Geldof wasn't calling me!) It turns out it was true. This concert would be held on

July 2, 2005, days before the G8 summit at Gleneagles, Scotland, and would be called Live 8. Geldof's plan was to send a loud, noisy message to the leaders of Canada, France, Germany, Italy, Japan, Russia, the U.S., and the U.K. demanding increased aid, debt forgiveness, fair trade, and justice for Africa.

Canada's Prime Minister Paul Martin would be attending the G8 summit. At the time the foreign aid standard for rich countries was 0.7 percent of GDP, a figure that had been proposed in 1969 by then-prime minister Lester Pearson. As was reported in a *Toronto Star* editorial: "Finance Minister Ralph Goodale estimates Ottawa will have to budget $15 billion a year for aid by 2015, instead of $3.6 billion today . . ." Which gives you a sense of how well we were doing and how far we had to go.

I called the biggest promoter I knew: Michael Cohl of (then) the Next Adventure. Cohl is an internationally renowned promoter and theatre impresario who has overseen tours for everyone from Michael Jackson to the Rolling Stones to Pink Floyd. He also happens to be Canadian. He'd already heard from Geldof but hadn't yet committed. A day later, he did.

Michael Cohl and Steve Howard at TNA and Riley O'Connor at (then) House of Blues Concerts were a powerhouse production team. My role was in communications and in helping to organize the efforts of the Canadian NGOs. It was a part I was pleased to play. More than 2,700 organizations worked toward eradicating poverty in Canada, and their networks would be essential in getting the message out and keeping the political pressure on. Gerry Barr, co-chair of the NGO coalition group Make Poverty History, was the official Canadian spokesperson; Jim Rawn at World Vision was instrumental in corralling members of the coalition; and War Child's Eric Hoskins helped to ensure everyone was on message—who knew NGOs could be so competitive?—and that the artists were fully up to speed on the issues and the goal of the event.

There were six weeks to mount a massive concert broadcast event with no budget. The tickets had to be free and no one expected this show to pay for itself in T-shirt sales. The event needed sponsors, the most essential of which was the broadcast partner. CTV's Ivan Fecan and Susanne Boyce came on board to produce live coverage of the Canadian event and include portions of the other concerts happening around the world. Standard Broadcasting, WestJet, and Rogers Wireless came in, as did Holmes Creative, who handled publicity, Pusateri's, who catered backstage, and Dan Aykroyd, who brought cases of Patron Vodka. It was a popular item. Dan sent a number of bottles to our "artist indoctrination" green room, but they all seemed to grow legs. (Don't worry, I'm not looking at you, Mötley Crüe—the Crüe *Carnival of Sins* tour was newly sober, as oxymoronic as that might sound.)

Finding a location was tricky. Hamilton wanted it, as did Toronto, but no venues were available. Senator Jerry Grafstein thought Parliament Hill would make a good location but that was a dead end. I wasn't surprised. What government would want to invite criticism of their foreign aid commitment to their own front lawn?

A large site near the town of Barrie (ninety kilometres north of Toronto) was available and that's where we went. The Molson Park location was a little odd compared to the other major cities where the concerts would be mounted—Tokyo! London! Moscow! Berlin! Barrie!—and no one on the international broadcast quite knew how to refer to us. At one point Will Smith called us "Park Place."

Michael was masterful in pulling together the Canadian lineup from many points of call. Bryan Adams was in, so long as he could play before noon; he had to fly out to another gig that night in Lancaster, Pennsylvania. Sarah McLachlan was in, but she was in the U.S. so played the Philadelphia show. Deep Purple was on Geldof's list and they were able to join us in Barrie. Celine wasn't able to leave Las Vegas, but offered a performance video from there. The lineup was taking shape: The Tragically Hip, Tom Cochrane, Simple Plan, Great Big Sea, Gordon Lightfoot, Blue Rodeo, Jann Arden, African Guitar Summit, Sam Roberts, Barenaked Ladies, K'naan, Mötley Crüe, Run-D.M.C., and Jet. Tom Green and Dan Aykroyd agreed to host, and Neil Young would close the Canadian stage in a Bob Ezrin-orchestrated finale.

We had one press conference in Toronto to announce the show, and another in Ottawa after meeting with MPs who unanimously approved a motion calling on the Liberal government to increase Canada's foreign aid to 0.7 percent. The motion wasn't binding, of course, but we did what we could. The communications side was well in hand, the lead-up to the show well covered. There were the usual complaints that singing for a cause was just a big ego trip for Bono and that "has-been" Bob Geldof.

Rex Murphy was particularly critical of the celebrities rising to the cause. In his *Globe and Mail* column he said: "In the end it will be just one more self-absorbed, pretentious, hollow celebrity shtick, another moment for ex-punk stars and rock maestros in decline to strut before the world's lights and cameras for a moment more."

I'm very fond of Rex but we disagree on this point. *Everyone* is entitled to his or her opinion, rock stars and radio hosts included. Music has been a potent influence on social issues from civil rights to apartheid. So bring on the critics and raise the debate.

Geldof *and* Bono were certainly duelling publicly with Canada's prime minister. Geldof said Paul Martin should "stay home" if he wasn't going to commit Canada to 0.7 percent, which stirred up the pundits anew: "Who does Geldof think he is being rude to our PM?" Experts debated whether finding another $3.4 billion annually was even possible; even if it was, some said, surely there were better ways to use that kind of cash right here at home.

Bono's engagement in Canadian politics wasn't a passing fancy. He and Paul Martin had met about debt relief in the developing world when Martin was finance minister under Jean Chrétien. Bono attended a 2003 Liberal leadership convention where he told the assembled, "The world needs more Canada." In 2004, he praised Martin for increasing Canada's funding commitment to AIDS in Africa, but warned him that he'd be a pain in the ass if Martin didn't follow through. A year later, Bono was on the CBC giving out the PM's phone number, telling Canadians to urge Martin to meet the 0.7 percent target and for Canada to do more.

Tickets for the Canadian Live 8 show were gone in twenty-one minutes and the nine international concerts staged on July 2 would end up featuring more than a thousand musicians. The opener in London was U2 together with Paul McCartney doing "Sgt. Pepper's Lonely Hearts Club Band," and there were other inspired pairings — Youssou N'Dour performed a beautiful duet with Dido; the Black Eyed Peas sang "Get Up, Stand Up" with Rita and Stephen Marley; Sarah McLachlan sang "Angel" with Josh Groban. And Sting sent out an SOS.

On television, the show careered around the world with live performances from Green Day in Berlin; the Pet Shop Boys from Red Square in Moscow; Björk in Tokyo; Andrea Bocelli in Paris; Duran Duran in Rome; Alicia Keys in Philadelphia; and Nelson Mandela in Johannesburg, who took the stage wearing a T-shirt with his prison number, 46664, and telling us that overcoming poverty was not "a gesture of charity" but "an act of justice."

There were lots of great moments in Canada. Tom Cochrane got the crowd going with "Life Is a Highway." Bryan Adams' solo acoustic performance of "All for Love" ended with a line from "Tears Are Not Enough." Deep Purple played "Smoke on the Water." Bruce Cockburn was lyrically right on the money with "Waiting for a Miracle," and Neil Young closed the show with a stage full of musicians who were "Rockin' in the Free World." It was doubly special that Neil was even there—he had suffered a brain aneurysm earlier that year.

Live 8 production with Steve Howard, me, Riley O'Connor, and Michael Cohl.

Backstage, along with War Child's Eric Hoskins and James Orbinski, former president of the Nobel Peace Prize–winning Médecins sans Frontières (nothing like having rock star doctors to talk to rock stars), we spent the day reinforcing the messaging with artists and screening the film clips produced for the show.

One of the films was a stylishly shot PSA with the tagline: "Every 3 seconds a child dies because of extreme poverty." Shot in black and white, the film captured celebrities like Cameron Diaz, Penelope Cruz, Liam Neeson, Usher, Justin Timberlake, George Clooney, and many more snapping their fingers to illustrate what three seconds looked like. It was a powerful moment when broadcasters toggled from city to city, showing millions of people from around the world snapping their fingers, together, in time.

(The concept was inspired, but it wasn't immune to people taking the piss. There's a story that Bono was doing a show in Ireland later on and he stopped to snap his fingers every three seconds, saying, "Every time I snap my fingers, someone dies of poverty." Apparently some wag in the audience yelled back: "Then why don't you stop snapping your fockin' fingers then?")

The Live 8 moment that hit home for me came when Bob Geldof introduced a news clip that had been part of the original Live Aid. Filmed by CBC journalist Brian Stewart and edited by Colin Dean, the footage was shot during the 1984 Ethiopian famine and focused in particular on a little girl named Birhan Woldu who almost died on camera. She became "the face of famine." It was that footage of the children, Geldof told us, that inspired him to launch Live Aid in the first place. Now, twenty years later, Geldof brought Birhan Woldu onto the Live 8 stage in London. She was now "the face of hope," a healthy, confident, accomplished young woman about to take her final college exams in Ethiopia. She held Madonna's hand while the pop star sang "Like a Prayer." (Apparently she'd chosen Madonna because she was the only artist she'd heard of.) It was a stunning moment, though Geldof's linking Birhan's miraculous transformation directly to Live Aid was a stretch. Her survival was more likely attributable to Brian Stewart who, realizing the severity of young Birhan's condition while they were filming, had alerted a nurse, who then gave her rehydration aid. Brian found Birhan and her family years later and has been contributing to her education ever since.

Four days after Live 8, on July 6, the thirty-first G8 summit was underway in Scotland. At the end of the summit, the leaders announced that aid to Africa would be doubled and that $40 billion of the debt owed to the IMF and World Bank by the poorest African counties was cancelled. It was a grand gesture and a signal of good intentions (although it's debatable how much can be credited *directly* to pressure from Live 8 — announcements like these are generally negotiated well in advance). But the needle hasn't moved much in the decade since.

According to 2014 OECD figures, some countries, like the U.K., Sweden, and Norway, have achieved their 0.7 percent target. Sweden and Norway have exceeded theirs, at 1.1 percent and 0.99 percent, respectively. By comparison, the U.S. is at 0.19 percent, and since 2013 Canada has dropped 10 percent to 0.24 percent. We are not making poverty history.

But that doesn't mean we shouldn't keep trying.

Maybe a big honking rock concert won't change the world, but what it *will* do is put the issues front and centre for a time. Once the spark is lit, the onus is on us to keep the pressure on. There will always be cynics, but a sadder notion still is the idea that we shouldn't try.

AFTER LIVE 8 MURRAY said, "You said you'd take some time off. It's been nine months, three charity events, and you haven't stopped yet." He was right. What a gift it would be to take a summer off—that hadn't happened since I was eleven. I would have time to bask in the sun, read for pleasure, cook for my friends (even relaxation has a list!), and, as it happened, to care for my mother.

My mum was then seventy-nine years old, running a B&B where she served a Welsh pastry called tiddy oggie. "People come from miles around for my tiddies!" she'd say. She was fit as a fiddle. I'd call her to find out what she was up to, and she'd say things like, "I'm laying bricks in the driveway!" She was unstoppable until she suffered a bowel infarction. She was in emergency for three days until her surgery, the complications from which almost killed her. I sat with her in the dark throughout that first terrible post-op night, using the light from my BlackBerry to monitor the time until she could receive another shot of morphine. She begged and begged me to end her life; the pain was too much. She was in hospital for two months, and her recovery was further complicated by contracting the MRSA superbug. Every day as I walked to the hospital I pleaded and made deals with whichever higher power would listen, so that we wouldn't lose her.

Her surgical wound was massive and infected, measuring ten inches down her abdomen and six inches across. The nurses had to change her dressings every day and it looked like something you'd see in war footage. The battle metaphor was not lost on us. Over the weeks she got weaker; she was losing the fight against the infection. I tried to always be there for the changes, so she could squeeze my hand while she tried not to cry. Her pain medication was increased, but it was beginning to impact her kidneys and we feared they would shut down. It was a terrible ordeal.

Weeks passed and I thought we would certainly lose her. I was in constant touch with my army of angels—four medical professional girlfriends who helped to translate the information I was getting from the doctors and guided me on what questions to ask. I am grateful for our medical system, but patients really do need an advocate. One day, a wound specialist visited and remarked that it was a shame the hospital didn't have another "vac machine"; they only had one and it was in use. A vac machine would mean they would only have to change the dressings every two days, lessening the ordeal and giving Mum a better chance to heal.

"Why can't we get her one?" I asked.

"They're expensive," the specialist said.

"How much is it?"

"About twenty-five thousand dollars."

"Could it get here faster if I bought one and donated it to the hospital?"

"Are you serious?" she said.

"Deadly," I responded.

She left the room to make a phone call. When she returned, she said, "It will be here tomorrow. You don't have to pay for it."

I'm convinced that machine saved my mother's life. We watched it vacuum the infection out of her abdomen, filling up the receptacle hour by hour, day by day. The nurses were finally able to lower the dosage of her pain medication, and she was eventually released with home care and a portable unit.

It took a year for my mother's wound to fully heal. She required another surgery and wasn't rid of the MRSA for many months after that (don't get her started on hand-washing in hospitals!), but she's eighty-nine now and we're blessed to have her with us.

"Ragged Girl" makes good. Mom at eighty.

I may be secular when it comes to religion but I'm grateful when somehow the universe provides. It would have been impossible to be at the hospital day and night had I been beholden to a big job.

Fortuitously, five years later, I had time again when my friend Pegi was diagnosed with Stage 4 lung cancer. (Pegi had long given up smoking, though she now enjoyed Nicorette. "Smoke?" she'd inquire after dinner, offering up a piece of gum.) She was told to get her affairs in order.

Pegi is a tenacious fighter. She is, after all, the Queen of Fucking Everything. Her email to her friends said: "It's going to be a long fight, but I hate losing." And she didn't. Pegi's friends rallied around her, taking her to the hospital for treatment, supporting her through weight loss, hair loss, and all the pain and indignities cancer patients endure. Pegi fought cancer and won.

Schedules and self-importance melt away when we're reminded of why we're really here—to help one another. It's a privilege to be in a position to help. And when all is said and done, it's the love of your family and friends that really matters in the end. This was a truth I came to better understand through working with a man who lives his life with that fully in mind: Frank Giustra.

IN MAY OF 2006, Sam Feldman called me about producing an event for his friend, movie and (then) mining entrepreneur Frank Giustra. Frank wanted to hold a dinner in Toronto to celebrate his friend former U.S. president Bill Clinton's sixtieth birthday and raise funds for the Clinton Global Initiative (CGI).

My mum was on the mend, and I was, as they say in the theatre world, "between engagements," so I had the time. But I wanted to know more about the initiative. A moment online led me to the CGI website where I found what looked to be the Holy Grail of NGOs, a charitable organization whose mandate was to "create and implement innovative solutions to the world's most pressing challenges."

The CGI looked wholly innovative, an organization with bold philanthropic objectives that were supported by solid business practices and led by a charismatic world leader. It held a conference, I learned, every year in New York City around the time of the General Assembly of the United

Nations—in fact, later that year Frank would wangle me an invite, and I'd have the chance to see it for myself.

It was an incredible gathering. I was, as my friend Graham Greene would say, "walking in some tall corn." At any moment I could be twenty feet away from some of the most boldface people on the planet: Archbishop Desmond Tutu, Tony Blair, Al Gore, Jane Goodall, Carlos Slim Helú, Ted Turner, Robert Johnson, Tony Bennett. Organizations like the World Health Organization were there, as were UNICEF and Médecins Sans Frontières, the Bill and Melinda Gates and Rockefeller Foundations, and the Carnegie Corporation. The president of the World Bank was there, as were the presidents of at least six countries, from Tanzania to Iceland to Norway. Panels were moderated by media elite: Tom Brokaw, Anderson Cooper, and George Stephanopoulos.

It was rarefied air for sure, but it was no boondoggle. Attendees were expected to make a commitment, complete with written objectives, implementation strategy, and the metrics by which the project's success would be measured. Sir Richard Branson's commitment had made headlines the year before, when he pledged to invest all profits—an estimated $3 billion—from his travel companies over the next ten years to fight climate change. The first two CGI conferences, held in 2005 and 2006, brought in $9.3 billion in pledges.

I wondered, as I looked around, how different this organization might be from the ground-up collaborative approach of my War Child friends, who were guided by humility and the deep insight of their local partners. Would this be a big money, big power, top-down strategy instead?

I was dubious when I saw heads of massive brands in attendance, like Walmart's Lee Scott, PepsiCo's Indra Nooyi, and executives from GE, Cisco, Nike, and others. Their first priority is profit, not public interest. Big corporations are powerful. Their lobbyists not only shape government; some would argue they're the ones in charge. Of course there are corporate objectives with altruistic motivations, but we also know that to be seen to do good can be camouflage for corporate misdeeds.

I listened hard and came away convinced by the CGI's approach—that the solution to some of the world's biggest problems needed public, political, *and* private cooperation. Corporations were there because they'd stated intentions to move forward in positive ways. The CGI commitment process could be a useful tool to keep intentions honest. It *is* possible to profit without ravaging the earth, polluting your surroundings, or exploiting your workforce. We live in hope.

The conference attendees weren't all bigwigs. I saw moments of alchemy between the powerful and the seemingly powerless. In one meeting a nurse stood up and asked for help. She needed medicines delivered along an African road that was controlled by bandits. A mining company executive whose trucks travelled that same road was in the audience, and he stood up and offered safe passage. Their spontaneous collaboration could solve a safety and cold train problem (medicines needed to be kept refrigerated to work) and save lives without having to spend a dime.

There was also some serious star power in attendance. Angelina Jolie and Brad Pitt were representing the Jolie-Pitt Foundation. Angelina spoke about her experiences as a UN Refugee Agency Special Envoy, meeting a child beggar in Syria who sold tissues on the street. He was bandaging the infested wounds of a man who had been tortured and burned because of his religious beliefs and was now a refugee living on the Syrian streets. Jolie was moved by the child's compassion for his friend and also his abilities as a tiny caregiver. She asked him if he could imagine a future as a doctor, but the concept was foreign to him because, well, *he had to sell tissues on the street*. When she said to the CGI crowd, "We have to help them be doctors," she won the hearts of the room.

Brad offered up $3 million for a Katrina rebuild project. "If there's anyone who understands the repercussions of climate change," he said, "it's the people of the Gulf Coast." His donation was immediately matched by another conference participant. Later that afternoon, I saw them with their heads together at a table, drawing up their commitment.

The casual conversations I fell into were serendipitous—like the one I had with an elegant African-American woman who asked me to watch her purse while she went to get a cup of coffee. She told me about her plan to build a hospital for women and children in Kenya. I told her I doubted she would have trouble generating the money—she was enthralling. "Oh the money's no problem, dear," she said. "Michael's going to help." Michael? Turns out she was Michael Jordan's mum. A few years later I saw that she'd done it. Another chance encounter happened a few hours later, at a working lunch on global health. My seatmate was a slightly hectic, beautifully dressed woman who'd dropped into the empty chair beside me. She joined the discussion without missing a beat, and after the session she told me about an idea she had for a "global harmonic convergence moment" where everyone in the world would sing or play the same note at the same time. "Call me," she said. "Maybe we should work together." I looked down at her card; it was fashion designer Donna Karan. Huh. It was like that.

For sure there was a lot of wealth and power in the room, but it didn't strike me as a crowd who believed that "he who dies with the most toys wins." It felt more like an Andrew Carnegie vibe. Carnegie once wrote, "The man who dies rich, dies disgraced."

It was certainly that way with Frank Giustra. He was a Vancouver-based entrepreneur who had made his riches in mining, the market, and movies. He knew many wealthy people who believed that the accumulation of wealth would bring them happiness, and he was hoping to convince them otherwise by showing them that parting with their money was a better way to that. Frank had been inspired by the work Bill Clinton was doing around the world and pledged $100 million to the Clinton Giustra Sustainable Growth Initiative (now called the Clinton Giustra Enterprise Partnership, or CGEP). He further committed half of all his future earnings to development work, and is focused on poverty alleviation through economic development.

The income disparity between rich nations and poor nations is staggering. In January 2016, an Oxfam report announced that 1 percent of people own half of the world's wealth. It's not only difficult to get your head around that statistic, it's alarming to realize there's only one outcome to extreme inequality, and that's ever more friction and instability in the world.

Frank writes a series of articles for the *Huffington Post* and tweets at #DearRichPeople, imploring them to give more of their wealth to the betterment of humankind. I was about to see just how good he was at that, working with him on two extraordinary fundraising events in Toronto: a sixtieth birthday event for Bill Clinton, which raised $21 million in one night, and a CGSGI event which raised another $16 million two years later.

"I'm in," I told Sam. "When is it?"

"September 9."

That would give us only four months. Normally planning for an event as big as the one envisioned would start at least eight months in advance; a year would be ideal. And to further stack the deck, the date was smack dab in the middle of the Toronto International Film Festival. Production gear would be at a premium; there wouldn't be a red carpet to rent for miles. Luckily we would need a blue one — the Clinton Foundation colour.

Frank would mastermind the vision and lean on his friends for donations; Sam would use his connections to broker talent; and I would produce the event itself. As far as formal credits went, Frank didn't want one, asking to be listed only as a member of the advisory board. When I asked him why, he said, "To be meaningful, philanthropy must come from the desire to do good, not recognition."

The first time I actually met Frank was when he and another FOB (Friend of Bill), Tim Phillips, flew in to do a walk-through of the venue for the event, the Royal York Hotel. The Royal York was good choice, given its experience hosting dignitaries, celebrities, and royalty — Queen Elizabeth II.

By the end of the tour, Tim seemed satisfied and said, "Well, it's obvious you've done this before."

"Well, no, actually," I responded.

Frank shot me a concerned look. Tim peered at Frank.

"Don't worry," I backpedalled. "I've produced other things."

Frank still looked worried.

"I've done award shows like the MMVAs. Last year I was a co-producer on the Live 8 event. How hard can a dinner be?" I said.

They relaxed, but I shouldn't have. Not only did we have a pounding deadline, but the level of talent, security, and politics was beyond anything I could have imagined for a charity event for six hundred people. Frank was the definition of a Big Thinker.

There was no *How to Run a Charity Gala* handbook that I knew of, but that was probably a good thing. If we'd followed normal procedure, the event would have been a nice dinner with a brand-name entertainer. Instead, it was a star-studded philanthropic extravaganza that guests still talk about to this day and that raised a fortune to help people in need.

I certainly learned a thing or three along the way.

Fundraising Gala Tip #1: Build a Great Team

I called my friend Shelley Ambrose, who'd just returned to Toronto from working with the Canadian Consulate in New York, with then Consul General Pamela Wallin. Shelley is an organizing dervish. When people say "If you want something done, give it to a busy person," they mean Shelley.

We discussed the event in her kitchen over a glass of wine, and I asked her to join as associate producer. She was hesitant, not wanting to commit to a four-month project while she was busy scouting her own next adventure.

"Oh come on," I pleaded. "It's one night. I mean, really, how hard can it be? It's just a dinner."

Over the next few months, Shelley would mock me repeatedly with that line.

Justina Klein was the next on board. She was in Toronto to launch her own event-planning company after having worked with the Raptors, Live Nation, and the Air Canada Centre, among others. Frank had described her as "buttoned down." That was appealing. Justina turned out to be a methodical marvel, able to track all the bits and bobs on spreadsheets she'd manufacture out of thin air. And there was no end of details to track on our critical path: hotels, private planes, pace cars, production grids, security schedules, budgets, seating arrangements, and all the myriad minutiae that very, very important people come to expect. As the scale of the event and the level of talent grew, we three gals started calling it "the Oscars without the staff." In many ways, it *was* just like an awards show; even without the TV cameras, there was no shortage of rock-star expectations.

As we got closer to the date, the folks who worked at the Clinton Foundation kicked in. Eric Nonacs, Hannah Richert, Courtney O'Donnell, and Sasha Blaes were smart, multi-tasking, results-obsessed BlackBerry addicts who worked at a level of proficiency that a former president of the United States might expect. We were going to get along just fine.

Event Tip #2: Lean on Your Friends

The talent bar was high. After all, this was a sixtieth birthday party for WJC, a sax-playing, music-loving world leader whose daughter Chelsea was named after a Joni Mitchell song. Sam, Frank, and I brainstormed on an all-star list of entertainers who would deliver on three important counts:

they would wow Clinton, they'd be politically and ideologically onside, and the guests would adore them.

My relationships at Sony and MuchMusic could get me past the receptionist, but it was Sam's Rolodex and Frank's friendship with the former president that really cranked up the star power.

Any event will always collect a bag of "no"s first. Sting was booked at a film festival; Paul Newman had a theatre commitment; Sheryl Crow was on tour with John Mayer; Bette Midler was shooting a movie; the Dixie Chicks were in Oakland; Diana Krall and Elvis Costello couldn't do it but would donate their Steinway for the auction; Shania sent her regrets; Jackson Browne sent his on my voicemail (I saved that for a while); and on and on.

As with any event, we needed a ringer, a name with which to answer the inevitable first question: "Who else is in?"

Billy Crystal was the first to commit.

You simply cannot get a better first-in than Billy Crystal. He's a movie star, writer, director, playwright, eight-time host of the Academy Awards, and of course, a comic genius. His name on the bill signalled an event of the highest order.

Then came the exquisite Sarah McLachlan. What about Josh Groban? They'd sung "Angel" together at Live 8 and the song would be a great thematic nod to the foundation. Was he available? Yes! Josh was in.

When James Taylor said yes, I was astonished. I thought James was a more private philanthropist like Bruce Springsteen, who often donated money on the condition of anonymity. This was big.

We already had a great lineup, but Frank wanted it to be over the top. Who would emcee? Someone suggested Kevin Spacey. He was in a play in London but had that night off. He was in! We just had to make the flights work. Who would lead "Happy Birthday"? What could be more perfect than a sax tribute from The Big Man himself? Clarence Clemons said yes and so did Sharon Riley & Faith Chorale. A show's got to have soul. R&B queen Jully Black? Yes! What about country? Tim McGraw! Rock and roll? Jon Bon Jovi! At this point there were so many artists, we'd need a musical director to keep the trains running on time. Paul Shaffer? Who better — and he's Canadian!

Now I'm making the talent booking sound easy. But big stars are not sitting by the phone waiting to be asked to do something for nothing. It took two and a half months of outreach, waiting, cajoling, waiting, nail biting, waiting, wheedling, and more waiting, interspersed with moments of sheer elation when we got a "yes."

Event Tip #3: Go Big or Go Home

The next challenge was to sell the tables. Shelley and I built a save-the-date mailing list that included everyone we knew who could write a cheque, but Frank set the bar a tad high for our modest circles. People in Toronto were used to paying anywhere from $5,000 to $25,000 for a gala table, but the highest price for a table at Frank's party was $200,000 (upped to $300,000 at the next year's event). Frank was an arm-bending force of nature, and his mining, prospecting, and banking friends anted up. The pressure was on to pull off an extra-extraordinary event while keeping the costs down. Guests could rightly expect a decent meal for $20,000 a plate, but we were not about to waste money on ice sculptures.

Event Tip #4: Green Your Event

For the Clinton gala, things had to be in line with the values of the foundation. Our goal was to create environmental elegance. Green initiatives had luckily come a long way since Woody Harrelson turned up on a red carpet well intentioned but rumpled in his hemp tuxedo, and I had recently been re-schooled in all things green while working with the intrepid Michael de Pencier, a publisher, eco-investor, and co-founder of the Green Living Show. We arranged plantable take-home centrepieces, printed our communications on FSC paper, and offset our power consumption with Bullfrog Power (a concept that intrigued Tom Cruise to no end and amused John Travolta's people when I insisted on knowing *exactly* what plane he was going to fly to the second event so we could calculate the emissions). Fortunately the Royal York had a hip chef who had his own apiary and herb garden on the roof of the hotel and didn't look at us like we were eco-maniacs when we insisted on an organic, 100-Mile Diet dinner. And sourcing VQA organic wines provided Justina, Shelley, and I with a bleary food-and-beverage tasting one afternoon. All work and no play...

Event Tip #5: Start on Time, End on Time

Typically, a gala will have one or two musical performances. We had eight.

Plus a superstar comedian, a superstar emcee, and a superstar keynote speaker—the 42nd president of the United States—none of whom was accustomed to being told to "Hurry up!" We were beginning to doubt that the event could be stage-managed efficiently. What a roster like that really needed was a revolving stage, but there was neither time nor room to build one.

It was handy that Shelley and I had experience in television and radio production. We knew about pacing and about preparing your guests, and we also knew how to be strict about timing. Every speaker thinks two minutes is five. Musicians will talk in between songs, comedians will keep going as long as there's a laugh. If this event wasn't choreographed like a fine ballet, we'd need to serve a second meal—with bacon and eggs.

Event Tip #6: Surround Yourself with Excellence

This event required a triple-A production wizard and we had it in Grant McAree. The entertainers were donating their time, but they expected flawless support. In his real life, Grant tour-manages artists like Diana Krall and Norah Jones. He was a marvel of grace under pressure, flawlessly stickhandling the technical needs of the show while appreciating that we were watching every penny. In the final weeks, we staffed up with Rich Bruggeman, Lesley Sharpe, Michelle Levy, and a small army of overqualified volunteers.

Our volunteers were well acquainted with high-powered charity events, having attended many of them. We had a national columnist stuffing envelopes; an HR specialist running reception; a vice-president, an executive director, and a publisher working the rope line (where guests would have their picture taken with WJC); a high school principal overseeing the auction; and an assortment of well-titled executives wrangling artists. No matter their rank in civilian life, Justina commandeered those volunteers like a drill sergeant. She also ran the security meetings. There were seven different levels of security—mostly men—comprised of the U.S. Secret Service, the RCMP, the OPP, the Metro Toronto Police Service, hotel security, our hired event security, and assorted personal bodyguards. You've gotta love a gal in charge.

Event Tip #7: Communicate Seamlessly

Media planning and communications is normally an entire arm of an operation—how to get it, spin it, and use it to thank your sponsors. As for publicity, we didn't want it. Press were allowed in for former president Clinton's speech and were ushered out immediately after. It was part of what made the night special—people could let their hair down and not fret about being on the front page of the tabloids the next morning.

Turns out, the thing we thought would be the easiest—the programs and press releases—required endless revisions and tiers of approval. Apparently the Clinton Foundation had more going on in their world than just us. We'd threaten and whine, passing along messages from our frantic suppliers, like our patient-to-a-fault graphic designer Bill Douglas: "I can no longer guarantee the ink will dry in time on your program." Or the audiovisual suppliers: "The editor has refused to work two all-nighters in a row." The film for the CGSGI gala came down to the wire because we were holding out for Morgan Freeman. He agreed to do the narration, but all he had was a two-hour window in L.A. Filmmaker Johnny Boston found a studio and the voice-over was recorded remotely, guided over the phone. Mr. Freeman was in and out in twenty minutes. Yes, the ultimate voice of gravitas *is* a one-take wonder.

Meanwhile, I had a deadline issue of my own. I was a new member to the CHUM board and the company was in the midst of selling. It was a clandestine affair, and we were sequestered in boardrooms flanked by lawyers and bankers. Frank was accustomed to sending and receiving answers at any hour, but between his intermittent BlackBerry reception in Africa and me in a mergers and acquisitions lockdown in Toronto, connections were sporadic. I'd race back to the office at night and get the work done, but explaining why I was incommunicado for hours in the middle of the day was delicate—the emergency dental work excuse was wearing thin. I couldn't tell Frank I was occupied by a massive media deal. If anyone knew what was about to go down, I'd be in Martha Stewart insider-trading land. Later, when the CHUM sale was announced and I could tell him what had really been going on, Frank may even have been impressed.

Event Tip #8: Tiny Lootbags that Don't Tick
Even rich people love a present. Our event gifts for the birthday were "Clinton Foundation"–logoed tchotchkes from Birks. They were

Canadian (then), matched the event (blue), and were small enough that guests didn't need a linebacker to carry them to their cars at the end of the evening. They also came beautifully wrapped. Who knew that would be a problem? The sniffer dogs did — they came with the RCMP. If they barked the wrong way, we'd have to unwrap and rewrap all 625 gifts on the afternoon of the show. No one had time for that. Never have I wanted to please a canine more. The Secret Service joked that it was a good thing the gifts weren't watches — apparently packages that tick are disconcerting.

Chanel had sent over goodies that required volunteers to attend a tissue-placement session in which they were instructed in the delicate art of gift bag assembly: "With thumb and two fingers, lightly pluck up a tissue. Wave it once, then twice in the air, to fully puff the tissue before placing it gently deep into the bag." We loved the products, but the three-finger air swoosh became our secret signal for high maintenance, and it was always a giggle to see Justina or Shelley with one hand on the phone and the other in the air waving their imaginary tissues.

Event Tip #9: Give Everyone a Chance to Play

At any corporate table of ten, it's likely nine of them are guests and haven't yet put their hands in their pockets. It's important to offer everyone a way to contribute (raffles, balloon surprises, keys that unlock mystery doors, silent auctions, bodybuilders at the exits to flip people over and shake them out...). You should at least be getting the cost of the food and booze from each guest. As the wonderful Jack Rabinovitch says every year at the Scotiabank Giller Prize gala: "For the price of a good dinner in this town, you can buy all the nominated books." It's a great line and effective in its support of Canadian literature.

We had a live auction. The trend in galas at the time was to create "unattainable experiences" — something you couldn't possibly buy in a store — and we wanted to surpass our guests' expectations. We all leaned on our friends for donations, but it was the Clinton Foundation staff who pulled off the most phenomenal auction items, many of which were offered by Friends of Bill, some of whom were in the room. Here's just a partial list:

Trips: Carnegie Hall with Paul Newman; front row at New York Fashion Week.

Sports: Flight school with Michael Jordan; golf with Wayne Gretzky; opening pitch at a New York Mets game.

Music: Go backstage with U2 in Hawaii; meet Barbra Streisand in Malibu; attend a Rolling Stones concert in New York City to be filmed by Martin Scorsese.

And, the ultimate life-changing experience: Travel with Clinton and Giustra to Africa to witness some of the work of the Clinton Foundation.

That last item sold twice. No wonder the event raised the amount that it did.

Event Tip #10: The Devil's in the Details

Suddenly it was the night before. In the last few weeks, we'd moved the production office to the site, and the place was full of people hauling boxes, photocopying, printing schedules, checking flight details, and reconfiguring tables.

Shelley and I were working the script (draft seventeen) and tweaking the rundown when Sam called and asked me to join him and his wife Janet, Billy Crystal, Billy's wife Janice, and his manager David Steinberg for dinner.

"Impossible," I said.

"You've got to eat," he said. "We'll be here till 11 p.m. Come on over and at least have a drink and say hello."

At 10 p.m. we signed off on the script and sent everyone home — they'd need to be fresh. I scanned through Billy's script one more time. It was blisteringly funny, but there was a problem. There was one joke that I thought wouldn't work. Best to tell him in person, I guess. I'd swing by the restaurant on the way home and finish my calls in the car.

I was still on overdrive and talking (too loudly) on the phone when I walked through the restaurant toward the back corner. Sam shot me a look (Cell phone? Really? Hang up!) as he motioned the waiter to pull over another chair.

Sam introduced me, but before any further pleasantries could transpire, I turned to Mr. Crystal and launched in, horns a' blaring.

"Hi, Billy, nice to meet you," I said. "We have to rewrite part of your script."

Sudden silence. All eyes on me, forks held in suspended animation.

His manager glared at me like I'd just passed wind at the table. His thought bubble read: *Who is this broad and how dare she mess with Billy's script?*

"Oh. Sorry. I mean . . . It's just that . . . One of your jokes doesn't work."

Death stares round the table. Sam wondering whether he could reach me from there.

I groped around, trying not to lead with my chin. "See, Kevin Spacey already has an exchange-rate joke and he's on before you." This was a hedge; that wasn't the real problem with the joke. But my attempt at diplomacy went over like screen doors in a submarine. I could hear my watch ticking. This was improving by the second.

I rushed on, explaining that Billy's script, which was of course brilliant! and hilarious!, had begun by riffing on why President Clinton would choose Canada of all places to celebrate his birthday and there was a line that said: "We are here for Bill's sixtieth in Canada. I'm not sure why; with the exchange rate here, he's seventy-four."

The problem was that the math was backwards. The actual exchange rate (a figure not unknown to the bankers in the room) would have made the president younger, not older (which was the way Spacey told it). "That's great that you caught it," Billy said. "I'll send you a new line in the morning."

"Fantastic," I said and finally stopped for air.

The storm clouds cleared, the dog barked, and everyone laughed. After answering, "So what's Spacey's material like?" to the best of my ability, we spent the next hour talking about what a great show it was going to be.

Event Tip #11: Showtime!: Expect the Unexpected
Show day dawned and we were up and at 'em at the crack of dawn. Grant was working miracles. Sound and lights had been loaded in overnight and were going up by the time we arrived. To say we were pressed for time was

an understatement. We had about three hours in the afternoon to sound-check and rehearse Kevin Spacey, Billy Crystal, and nine different musical performances. Everyone wanted more time; everybody was important and everything was urgent. I ran interference with managers and artists, chatting them up, calming them down, crossing my fingers that there wouldn't be flight delays or tardy sniffer dogs.

Meanwhile, the seating arrangement kept changing because last-minute VIPs were being added, including Hillary Clinton—*She's coming, no she's not, yes she is, Chelsea's coming too*—which meant a re-alignment of all the Secret Service positions. (They're very precise in terms of their sight lines.) Even so, it was fairly normal day-of-show stuff.

What wasn't normal was that Tim McGraw's road manager was in the production office insisting we boot Jon Bon Jovi and his wife from Tim's table. Apparently the two men had some bizarre sports rivalry. We re-arranged the tables, but we needn't have bothered—McGraw wouldn't sit down anyway. While Jon was performing, Tim paced around backstage, waiting to confront him. I was actually worried that he'd take a swing. After Jon's performance they went out to the loading dock. I sent security, but was told later that Jon's wife had stepped in and sorted them out.

Kevin Spacey arrived mid-afternoon, and he had an issue. He'd read his script on the plane and insisted on it being drastically shortened. We knew it was way too long and had already tried to cut it, but the Foundation wasn't budging on a word. Kevin sighed, ordered a G&T and went off to work it.

Then we had a communications issue. The walkie-talkies had been acting up all day. Eight channels had been assigned to different streams—production, stage, hotel, volunteers, etc.—but reception was becoming increasingly garbled. I heard a male voice announce they were tarping the stage because it looked like rain. Rain? We were indoors! Turns out it was the production manager for a Virgin Festival concert on Centre Island. The town was so busy, radio frequencies were bleeding every which way. We had no choice but to confine ourselves to two of the clearer channels—a big difference from eight. Now people had to relay information face to face. I pitied the girls in heels and thanked goodness the Secret Service had their own comms.

Just when it looked like our finely tuned schedule was about to unravel at the seams, it all came together like a fine soufflé.

The cars drove up, the lights went on, the dogs sniffed, the bars opened, the photographers flashed, our "lounge pianist" Stephan Moccio tinkled the keys in the reception, the VVIPs got their photo moment with the president in the rope line, and the doors to the banquet room swung open to a beautifully set room. The night had begun.

Kevin Spacey found a way to deal with the reams of Foundation information he'd been given to read: he'd do impersonations of different Hollywood characters. He wanted to start with Johnny Carson, and I nabbed Rick Mercer out of the crowd to be Ed McMahon. Rick welcomed everyone with a bang-up "Heeeeeeeere's Johnny!" Shaffer zoomed in with the Carson theme song and we were off to the races.

I have to say that there's never been a greater gift to a show flow than Paul Shaffer and his Letterman band. They can roll with anything. Paul would get a spontaneous idea to embellish a moment, play one bar of a song, and the band would pick up on it instantly. I understand there's a Paul Shaffer Drive in Thunder Bay beside the community auditorium. He should get the whole highway.

"Johnny Carson" riffed on the U.S. relationship with Canada, reminded the Americans that Canadians kicked their "arses" in the war of 1812, and did the age joke: "The single most important reason why President Clinton is celebrating his birthday in Canada is because with the exchange rate, turning sixty is actually like turning fifty-two in the United States." Then he rolled out a stellar cast of characters. He impersonated President Clinton reading from his biography *My Life*. As Christopher Walken, he described the work of the Clinton Foundation. Jack Lemmon detailed its HIV/AIDS program. Katharine Hepburn stammered through the CGI's plans on obesity. Marlon Brando talked about the success of their programs and begged for Doritos. Buddy Hackett thanked everyone who put the show together. Jimmy Stewart acknowledged the table sponsors and Walter Matthau took the media sponsors.

Spacey was a triumph and never complained, even when I had to lean on him several times throughout the night to calm an unruly room.

"Just climb up there and tell them to quiet down!"

Josh Groban was followed by Tim McGraw, who did three songs instead of two. (If I'd had a hook…) And then Billy Crystal took the stage, targeting the president and ad-libbing all the way through. He recalled the good old days before WJC was sixty, when "We thought Condoleezza Rice was a Cajun dish, Al Jazeera was a jazz musician, and Dick Cheney hadn't shot his first friend yet." WJC was laughing so hard he was crying.

During dinner, people were out of their chairs, doing the most animated version of square dance meet-and-greets I'd ever seen. When everyone in the room is a somebody, it's tricky to know who to talk to and for how long, because of who else you might be missing. Guests were glad-handing with the president, taking photos with Jon Bon Jovi, chatting with Billy Crystal. It was a star-studded swarm.

Rick Mercer sent me an email halfway through that said, "You guys did a fucking amazing job. The room is on fire."

Ha! I thought it was my *hair* that was on fire.

Nelson Mandela sent effusive birthday greetings by video to the "spritely young man of sixty," and then the president took the stage. Clinton talked about the interconnectivity of everyone on the planet. He cited what he saw as the most significant scientific event during his presidency: the sequencing of the human genome, which proved that genetically, we are 99.9 percent the same.

"The idea that our differences are more important than our common humanity is at the core of every single problem we have in the world today," he said. "What I'm hammering home is that our differences make life more interesting but our common humanity matters more. Anyone that doesn't believe it has committed a philosophical and humanitarian heresy."

Clinton was at his oratorical best, out of office and relaxed. The whole of his speech had a jazz musicality to it. He tuned up slowly, feeling the room, thanking people individually; then he laid down his written notes and addressed us directly, building the rhythm with facts and figures, illustrating the challenges the world was facing and then leading into the chorus, telling us what we could do together to surmount them. He scatted about, adding a few jokes and flourishes, and then he hit the high note with a big finish, landing squarely on the "ask." Except it didn't feel like an ask, because the crowd had already been won. They were ready to give.

When auctioneer Christian Kolberg took the stage, the room really *was* on fire. Auctioneering is a science. Kolberg had studied the items, knew who was in the audience, and had an expert understanding of how to build excitement and empty pockets. At one point he was actually standing on a table, egging on duelling bidders. New auction items appeared spontaneously. Kevin Spacey offered himself as a personal tour guide to his Eugene O'Neill play in London, complete with flights that he'd secured from another guest he'd just met in the room.

Once the auction was over and Josh Groban joined Sarah McLachlan for "Angel," people were mush. Jully Black sang "I Travelled," a song about triumph over adversity. Jon Bon Jovi covered "It's Only Make Believe," a Conway Twitty song he'd sung for the president at his fiftieth birthday party and pledged to sing again every ten years for the next hundred years. James Taylor, accompanied by Boston Symphony Orchestra cellist Owen Young, sang "Fire and Rain." Sharon Riley & Faith Chorale then flowed onto the stage to join James in "Shower the People."

Then it was time for the surprise birthday moment. Clarence Clemons took the stage unannounced, playing "Happy Birthday" on his saxophone, and a blue cupcake tower was wheeled out, sparklers ablaze.

As all the performers joined James Taylor in "How Sweet It Is (To Be Loved by You)," the audience crowded the stage, while we scrambled to add the totals. I handed a note up to Kevin, who announced that we'd raised $20 million. It was a gobsmacking amount even to this crowd.

The event had run late, but nobody cared, and no one wanted to leave. That was a detail we'd overlooked. Had we been on time, people could have retired to the hotel bars, but they were long closed and everyone wanted to know where the after-party was.

Eventually, the last of the guests were ushered out and the load-out began. I went up to the artist's floors to check that all was secure.

The elevator doors opened to an unusual sight. The large lobby table was covered in miniature booze bottles — the mini-bars from the entire floor had been raided. In a suite at the end of the hall, a party was raging. The place was packed: Billy and Kevin were trading jokes, Clarence and Sarah were laughing, James Taylor had gotten out of bed because his room was next door, Frank and Sam were hosting (Sam was ordering food), and even the Secret Service had joined in, finally off duty because the former president was wheels up.

It had all the makings of a legendary party but I was done. I asked one of the Secret Service guys if he had the key to Mr. Clinton's suite. I had no energy to go to the front desk and I'd been planning on crashing in it after he'd left — no sense in paying for a room no one was using.

"You're in it," he said.

"What?" Oh great. The party was *in my room*!

I left them to it and crashed with Shelley.

Me, WJC, and Shelley Ambrose.

The next morning, the ballroom looked a little like the day after Woodstock—except instead of mud, it was blue icing. Shelley, Justina, Lesley, Michelle, and I gathered for a quick post-mortem fuelled by left-over cupcakes and coffee.

There seemed to be quite a few people missing their flights that morning, but otherwise it was kudos all around. Emails were flying from guests and artist management, reliving moments and raving on about the evening. Shelley and I went off to tabulate final receipts and prepare the press release. Turns out, in the heat of the auction, we'd made a million-dollar rounding error. To be safe, we'd rounded *down*; the actual figure was $21 million. The event had raised twenty-one million dollars in one night. It's still a record in this town.

Event Tip #12: THANK YOU, THANK YOU, THANK YOU
The high from the night lasted throughout the weeks of follow-ups, thank-yous, accounting, and auction fulfillment that still had to be done. It was cheerful work and people couldn't stop reliving the night. I was imagining all the good work that would be done for the Clinton Foundation's HIV/AIDS initiatives with the money raised. Frank, however, was just getting started. He wanted to do it all again, and a year and a half later we did.

THE SECOND EVENT WAS just as mind-blowing. Since it was a similar undertaking to pull it all off, though, I'll relive just one story from that night. I've chosen it because I remember it with such fondness and because it gave me a glimpse into the heart of a singularly sweet, talented soul: Robin Williams.

This time, the evening started behind schedule, because WJC arrived late. At first it wasn't a problem; the guests were buzzed about the event and mingled about happily. In the ballroom sound checking were Norah Jones, Shakira, and Wyclef, and in the green room with Frank were Tom Cruise, Elton John and David Furnish, David's mum and dad, Burton Cummings, Eugene Levy, John Travolta and Kelly Preston, and Robin Williams. Once the former president joined them there, no one wanted to leave, but we had to break it up. There was work to do. The highest-priced VVIP tables had been promised a private hello and photo-op.

They were waiting in another room and getting antsy.

Now as you might expect, *all* of the places where a current or former American president is apt to go will have been properly inspected and mapped by the Secret Service, with ingresses and egresses secured and travel time noted. If all had gone to plan, Clinton would have been walking through an empty corridor to the VVIP room; but because they were late, the corridor was jammed with well-heeled guests when he arrived.

I needed to clear the way. I walked into the middle of the room and began.

"Ladies and gentlemen, if I could have your attention. President Clinton has arrived (murmur of excitement) and needs to walk through this room to get to that room just over there. I know that many of you are looking forward to saying hello, but he needs to do a little work first. So if you'll just stand back so we can clear a path, that would be appreciated."

As I delivered my little speech (which had no effect at all), Robin Williams had edged over to see what was up and immediately engaged, ordering people about by pretending to be the Gestapo.

"Uhnt you vill all schtep back! Uhnt you vill not reach out to touch za Pres-ee-dent, Uhnt you vill avehrt your eyes!" It was hilarious. I wish I could remember it all. It was that rapid-fire rush of spontaneous comedic improvisation that only Robin Williams could do, but it just made the crush worse as more people rushed over to see what was happening.

I crossed my arms like a stern schoolmarm and said, "Are ya done?"

Robin backed away bowing his head, pretending to be chastised. "Sorry, excuse me, ma'am, pardon me..."

I turned back to the task at hand, flapping my arms like a goose trying to herd a *bigger* crowd of people into the corners. "As I was saying, if you would please clear this area—"

And Robin leapt back into it. "Uhnt you vill stand BACK against za valls...no zudden movements...you vill not reeeeach into your jackets..."

He was irrepressible. As much as I loved riffing with Robin Williams, I was at a loss for what to do. Frank texted me from the green room. *We're on our way.* Uh oh. They'll be walking into a wall of people. Just then, the Secret Service expertly deployed, parting the crowd like the Red Sea, two steps ahead, behind, and around the president. Robin stepped back, clicked his heels, and saluted as Clinton was whisked into the VVIP photo room. The crowd melted away.

"You were a great help." I said to Robin. He just laughed.

A few weeks after the event, I answered the door to a FedEx parcel. It was a signed movie script from Robin, with a note thanking me for being an "unsung hero." Incredible. I mean, who does that? I wondered how many other people he'd uplifted in a similar way.

It was heartbreaking to hear of his death. RIP Robin.

One of the best performance photographs I've ever seen of Robin Williams was from onstage that night. We'd lit the walls with gobo-projected words like "Sustainable" and "Impactful" that described the CGSGI mission. Robin is caught in the throes of an outrageous joke, and the words glowing on the wall, seemingly bursting from his body, say "High Impact." To me it perfectly captures so much of his life force.

The incredible Robin Williams.

The ending to that evening remains warm and clear in my memory. As Elton played "Rocket Man," "Don't Let the Sun Go Down on Me," and "Tiny Dancer" to the enraptured guests, I gazed over the room. There was no question in my mind that we'd been involved in something extraordinary. The words that shone on the walls of the ballroom took on a new resonance. Collaborative. Transparent. Innovative. Effective. I had no doubt Frank would steward the money the events had raised in all of those ways. You can see the results at http://cgepartnership.com. As I type he's on the Greek island of Lesbos helping Syrian refugees, having raised

$5 million ($500,000 of which was his own) to build a refugee centre for the International Rescue Committee.

For a girl who grew up wearing used clothing, it felt surreal to be in a room where people could raise their hand and donate a million dollars (or three) just like that. For those of us who don't "roll like that," that's okay. We can do the work instead.

I appreciate that working with celebrities in fancy ballrooms is worlds away from where the real work is — on the ground in humanitarian crisis situations. But it all has value, and I'm blessed to have been able to weave some good work into the corporate jobs I've held. Was I trying to wash my hands clean from a profit-centric corporate world? I doubt it. I like money. Hopefully I've been frugal enough that I might even avoid being a burden to the family one day.

But I also recognize that money for money's sake is offensive, that celebrity for celebrity's sake is hollow, that the modern world is fuelled by power junkies and greed. I for one could certainly stand to be reminded — repeatedly — that the riches we should really care about are those that are inspired by the heart, that come from service to others.

I resolved to think more mindfully about what I really wanted to do with my life. In what ways could I be of service? As it turned out, I was to become an actual public servant, and soon found myself on that grassy knoll outside the CBC station in Sydney, in front of two hundred protesters.

(21)

OVER MY DEAD BODY:

LIFE AT THE CBC

"We realize the importance of our voice when we are silenced."
— MALALA YOUSAFZAI

ON APRIL 8, 2009, I was in Cape Breton with Andrew Cochrane, managing director of CBC's eastern stations in Nova Scotia, New Brunswick, and PEI. I was visiting CBC radio stations across the country to deliver the news about the latest round of cuts. The CBC was facing a $171-million shortfall. Resources would be reduced, shows would be cancelled, jobs would be lost. The mood was as gloomy as the maritime sky.

The Sydney, Nova Scotia, station employed about a dozen people, each of them well known in town. Their kids played together, they shopped at the same stores—they would naturally have shared their worries among friends. It was their neighbours who lined the street to show support for their beloved Sydney station and to greet me—CBC Radio management from head office in Toronto.

Part of the reason for my visit was to ensure I had an understanding of each regional station, community by community. We needed more than just numbers on a page to make the best of a bad situation. This was my first face-to-face meeting with the Sydney staff. They had no reason to trust me. I was an outsider, a "former VJ" (as one headline crowed), probably bent on "dumbing down" or, worse, commercializing radio.

There wasn't a street protest at every station I visited, although at one there were staff members who chose to walk around wearing black armbands. But inside it was the same: a reluctant gathering of taciturn faces and crossed arms. They'd been through cuts before. My weak offerings of coffee and Timbits did little to warm the atmosphere. I did my best to smile, shake hands, and compliment their programming. I listened as often as I could to local stations across the country from a computer on my desk in Toronto. Eavesdropping on shows beaming from Iqaluit or Winnipeg or Victoria was one of the joys of my job; it reminded me of why I was there.

Staff did their best to be civil, but they wanted the numbers. What would be the impact *here*? How many jobs? Would the station be closed? Who else was being cut? It was human nature to hope that some *other* department in the corporation might take the brunt of the cuts and so spare them. Radio eyed TV, drama sniffed at sports, news looked sideways at comedy. Children's programming was often in the crosshairs. After all, kids can watch the same thing twenty times and not get bored — why spend any money there at all? And of course, if programming was taking a cut, management better be taking a bigger one. And *Qu'est-ce qui se passe avec le French?* Were francophone resources being hit as hard as the anglophones'?

The news for Sydney was that the radio station would not be shut down, but it would be shrunk. A dozen positions were estimated to be on the block between the two stations in Halifax and Sydney. It would be painful.

I did my PowerPoint, staff peppered me with questions, and Andrew saved me when I was out of my depth with the local specifics. Andrew was a smart, approachable manager who was open to any question, but we didn't have all the answers yet. We did not know which jobs would be cut on which shows, who would bump whom in the union seniority shuffle, or how many positions could be saved by early retirement options.

As the staff returned to their work, I ventured outside to get a sense of the mood on the hill. The placard-waving crowd was being addressed by a man with a bullhorn, who I surmised was the local Liberal politician. He was delivering what sounded like a campaign stump speech: "If the Liberals were in power, we would guarantee stable funding for the CBC."

That got my attention.

I walked over to the man, meaning to whisper in his ear a reminder that the last $400-million cut was made by Liberal hands.

The man lowered his bullhorn, looked at me, and said, "Who are you?"

"I'm Denise. I'm head of CBC Radio," I replied.

"Well then, be my guest," he said, handing me the bullhorn and gesturing to the crowd.

I don't remember exactly what I said to the assembled, but it was similar to what I'd told the CBC staff inside. First, that the Sydney station would not be closed. The crowd cheered and I had their attention. There would, however, be cuts. I talked about how deeply distressing it was for all of us, that we'd looked under every rock to try and spare cuts to programming and people. I pointed out (as if it might be some consolation) that national radio shows would be affected too, that we would have to cut music, drama, and sports programming as well. I urged them to continue to listen, and that their stories, their concerns, their local issues would still be reflected on programs, even if it had to be on a broader regional show. I told them how proud we were of the content this local station produced, and that I was very glad they were there. It would be a dreadful day indeed if no one had come to show their support for the CBC.

Cutting staff and programming at small stations was a tough message to deliver but we had no choice. In radio, there was precious little to cut besides programming and people. Those legends of largesse I'd heard before I joined the CBC were fairy tales. Aside from the bricks and mortar, the studios, and the transmitters themselves, our budget *was* people—over 80 percent of it, in fact.

CBC English radio provides a considerable public service. At the time of that trip to Nova Scotia in 2009, there were thirty-seven stations in Canada, with thirty-two local morning shows and twenty-seven afternoon shows. Every year we produced more than 65,000 hours of highly rated, often award-winning content. In the three years before I arrived in 2008, CBC Radio programs had won more than a hundred major international and national awards, including Broadcaster of the Year at the International Radio Program Awards in New York. Our content was exchanged with other public broadcasters like the BBC, the Australian Broadcasting Corporation, and Radio Netherlands Worldwide, not to mention the distribution of CBC Radio programming to more than one hundred cities in the United States.

It's a lot to be proud of and it all sounds very grand, but the reality is, if you peeked through the window at one of the smaller stations, you'd see empty desks. Many were shaved as close to the bone as you could get, while still remaining on air. If you cut two jobs in Gander, Newfoundland, you'd literally shut down the station. In La Ronge, Saskatchewan, there was one guy. He had the key to the door and was also an announcer and operator.

Like many small stations, CBC Sydney had a mighty connection to the community. Its morning show, *Information Morning*, was number one in the market and had a whopping thirty share, which means that a third of all radio-listening in the morning was tuned to it. Robust listenership was what you'd find in practically every region with a local CBC Radio service. I was already a believer, but the more I saw first-hand, the more I saw the small stations as remote lighthouses, resolutely pulsing with vital information. They were key to a strong, reflective CBC, and I believed deeply that their lights had to be kept on.

What I didn't tell the crowd that day was just how close some stations had come to being gutted. In my mind's eye, I could clearly picture those ugly numbers costing small stations resources across the country; their headcounts tallied, their real estate assessed. Small stations were one of many "no sacred cow" options that had to be considered by a corporation facing such drastic cuts.

It was crushing for me to be gazing at yet another bleak list. The cold numbers gave no hint of the people or the cultural loss to Canadians locally and nationally. I fervently believed in the value of CBC to Canada, and it was likely that passion that saved my ass on that grassy knoll.

Small stations would close over my dead body.

IT WAS RICHARD STURSBERG, executive vice-president of CBC English services, who had wooed me for two months to join the CBC. There had been no mention of cuts, and there was no need for one—the impact of the global economic crisis hadn't yet been felt by the Canadian broadcast industry. But by the end of September 2008, when I joined the team, I felt an astounding sense of déjà vu. I'd been in this movie before.

Once again I had walked into a corporation that within months was putting in place fiduciary measures, instituting hiring controls, freezing discretionary spending, and pulling back on projects and contracts. The recession fuelled by the subprime mortgage crisis in the U.S. was about to reach the Great White North, affecting every industry in a way that hadn't been seen since the Great Depression.

Richard's first call had been in the summer of 2008. I had just packed the last box on the second event for the Clinton Giustra Sustainable Growth Initiative. The plaques had been awarded, the thank yous sent, and the millions raised were beginning their work in far-off lands. I was at our little cottage, happily puttering, swimming, spending time with Duncan and Murray, hosting our friends, grounding myself on the water. I wasn't thinking hard about my next adventure yet; I assumed I'd have plenty of time to do that in the fall. But when the time came, I promised myself, I'd look for something small. Something that would feed my soul for a change instead of me feeding it; something that made a meaningful contribution. Something in a growth industry, for sure.

I answered the phone in my bathing suit, standing barefoot on a warm mound of black-and-pink granite.

The CBC? Heavens, no. I'm flattered, and thank you for calling, but no. Sorry.

The position of executive director of CBC English radio was available because, under Richard, there were no longer separate VPs of radio and television; there was now one VP of English services (Richard) who managed both content streams. The former radio VP, Jane Chalmers, had retired, and its current manager, Jennifer McGuire, was moving from radio to run news, leaving an opening for the executive director (later GM) of radio.

I loved the CBC, but the Corporation wasn't an obvious job consideration. It was the opposite of small, and over the years I had heard from friends who worked there of tough unions and evil management, of government animosity and withering cutbacks. Hard labour. Bread and water.

As a listener and as a Canadian, though, I had sympathetic ears. I'd fallen hard for the CBC over twenty years ago, when twice I'd been privileged to sit in as a guest host for a vacationing Peter Gzowski. I'd loved hosting morning radio. I'd thought then that if I was lucky, one day I'd end up in a host's chair. Maybe when I was old, I'd thought then, — fifty, maybe.

There'd been a close call when I was in my early forties. Shortly after Peter retired, I was presented with a co-hosting opportunity on a new show that would replace *Morningside*. As flattering as the offer was, I turned it down. I was happy at MuchMusic, and I hadn't yet determined on which side of the desk I was meant to sit — the management side or the creative side. (I still don't know. Perhaps I was meant to paddle with a foot in two canoes.)

Richard himself was also a consideration. He was a controversial leader at the CBC. His ideas about "popularizing" Canadian prime-time television were seen by some as a contradiction of the CBC's mandate. Richard was not overly fond of the word "mandate." He hadn't come up through the ranks at the CBC, but he was well versed in the broadcasting and communications industries, having served federally as an assistant deputy minister to broadcasting and culture in the early nineties, then working in distribution with the satellite company Star Choice Communications before chairing the Canadian Television Fund. His job prior to joining the CBC was as head of Telefilm Canada, where he had stated a determination to increase audiences, a mission he sought to continue at the CBC.

Stursberg's arrival coincided with the 2004 National Hockey League lockout — which wasn't his fault — followed by a Canadian Media Guild lockout (which represented 85 percent of the CBC workforce) in the summer of 2005 — which many argued was. (Richard and three other CBC managers, the "Gang of Four," had not come to a new agreement with the union over issues around contract workers, a more flexible workforce, and seniority-bumping procedures.) I expected he would be a challenging boss, but that wouldn't be a first.

Richard wouldn't take no for an answer, and I agreed to at least think about it. So much for mindlessly whiling away the summer. Then he suggested we meet for lunch. Somehow it always starts with lunch . . .

Richard proposed we meet at the Spoke Club, the downtown Toronto members-only club frequented by local arts and letters intelligentsia. We said our hellos at the bar and meeted and greeted our way to the table. It seemed that anyone Richard didn't know, I did. *I'm not getting any better at clandestine meetings,* I thought.

We talked about mutual acquaintances, of the collapse of the music industry and its implications on other creative industries, and then moved on to public broadcasting. I was pleased to discover how passionately he spoke about ensuring the success of the CBC both in television and radio. We compared favourite shows and hosts, then brainstormed a little about expanding into underserved markets, me thinking of Fort McMurray, he of Hamilton. It was a pleasant lunch and then I said no again.

Richard is a persuasive fellow. He said he was used to people saying no to the CBC; he aimed to rebrand it as the place where the boldest, smartest people clambered to work.

In the end I did accept the job, but not before much fretting and dithering. I canvassed my friends and ex-CBCers (most of whom told me to run in the opposite direction), tortured my husband (who listened patiently but steadfastly refused to tell me what to do), and made no end of "pros and cons" lists. In the end, I didn't accept the position because Richard wore me down (which he joked about in his book *The Tower of Babble: Sins, Secrets and Successes Inside the CBC,* published after he left the Corporation). I accepted because I believe in public broadcasting. I accepted because I wanted to honour the snowflake on my lapel, and I accepted because the words of my dearly departed friend Peter Gzowski rang in my head. He'd said of the CBC, "If it falters, no one will build it again." And that scared the pants off me.

Before I agreed, I reviewed the Canadian Broadcasting Act. I knew that the CBC had to be in for some strategic change, and I wanted to ensure my own beliefs were aligned with its stated mission, which was in part to "present a wide range of programming that informs, enlightens, and entertains"; to "contribute to shared national consciousness and identity"; to be "distinctively Canadian [and] reflect Canada and its regions"; and to "actively contribute to the flow and exchange of cultural expression." I could certainly salute all that. I saw the CBC as fundamental to our democracy, vital to our cultural expression, and key to our values as a nation.

Richard had enticed me further with talk of a bright future of expansion and aggressive digital development. He was looking forward to a modern reorganization of the physical space in Toronto, one that would result in new real estate money and the opportunity to evolve as a content company. He expected that my experience in exploring new business at Sony would be advantageous to rolling out radio content on multimedia platforms. He also wanted to bring more business rigour to the tasks of growing audiences at radio, to which my experience in commercial broadcasting at CHUM might prove helpful.

I was excited by the opportunity to help grow a beloved cultural institution, especially one that had a $1-billion government appropriation. Compared to my collapse-of-an-industry experience at Sony, I expected the CBC's parliamentary appropriation might help to mitigate any immediate turbulence caused by disruptive technological changes and allow us to serve the audience in bold new ways, all of which would be executed with smart planning, precision, and, ideally, applause from appreciative Canadians. A girl can dream.

What I didn't expect was that my experience in "managing efficiencies" (that euphemistic term for laying people off) would be called upon so early.

ON SEPTEMBER 30, 2008, my institutional training began. Unlike at Sony Music Canada, I was no longer in charge, but part of a team in a somewhat more labyrinthine structure. That would take some getting used to. The CBC is a crown corporation and subject to layers of oversight from a variety of stakeholders, including the president, the board, and, especially, the audience, who are never shy about sharing their views on how the CBC should be run. The CBC was also operating in a landscape in which significant changes in technology, distribution, and media consolidation were occurring at light speed. And, as I quickly came to appreciate, we were about to be hit by an economic recession. Once again, so much for the honeymoon.

During the first few weeks I was briefed by individual department heads, their thick organizational decks mounting up in piles on my desk. Ah, the decks. Like many crown corporations, the CBC loves a deck. My new colleagues would arrive bearing executive summaries, their graphs and charts straining against large bullnose clips. I began to notice them in teetering bundles in other offices, their contents taunting bustling managers who had few minutes to spare.

Any notion I may have had that the CBC was full of sleepy bureaucrats was dashed. The place was hopping. I used to think I was pretty good at time management, but here it was the executive assistants who excelled. Meetings jockeyed for position based on seniority, urgency, and departmental priority. The EAs were air-traffic controllers, scheduling inbound appointments, lining up meetings on the runway, finding ten minutes here, half an hour there, while new issues circled overhead. The place wasn't sleepy by any stretch, but it was more bureaucratic than I was used to. Apparently I just couldn't lay down an edict and expect everyone to heave to; I needed consensus before radio priorities could be fuelled and readied for takeoff— which required more meetings.

In no time, I became like every other CBC executive, arriving breathless to boardrooms juggling a laptop, the relevant deck, and a buzzing BlackBerry. Most everyone typed as they walked, head down, nipping through elevator doors and pirouetting around mail trolleys, the most agile slipping into one meeting on their way to the next. "Walk with me," we'd say, instead of "Hello."

One of my favourite moments was when the jovial Scott Moore, newly anointed head of sports, burst into a meeting room a few minutes late, stopped in his tracks, and roared: "MEETINGS AREN'T WORK!" My first encounter with Scott was when I had been positioned in (not so) playful opposition at an off-site leadership meeting organized by the CBC President, Hubert Lacroix. We were assigned to debating teams. The subject: "CBC should not be in professional sports." I was to argue *for* the statement. Excellent! How to win friends and influence people. Sports was the advertising and brand backbone of CBC Television. As I presented my seditious arguments, Scott jumped up from his seat in the audience and, in Don Cherry–like fury, tore off his sweater and bellowed "Never!" to cheers. It was comical then, but it's a shame his "Never!" was not prophetic. Hockey is now at Rogers, where Scott is today.

I enjoyed the people, and in many ways the CBC felt like home right away. A number of Much personalities were now there. I'd worked with George Stroumboulopoulos and Sook-Yin Lee at Much. I'd met Steven Sabados and Chris Hyndman—who now had a popular lifestyles show on

CBC—in the Citytv makeup room, where Chris would refresh my face while Steven did the same to the studio. Shelagh Rogers and Stuart McLean were mutual Gzowski pals. Peter Mansbridge's wife Cynthia Dale and I were in a quilting group (aptly named The Noisy Nine). I'd hung out with Rick Mercer in Newfoundland, and I knew Jian Ghomeshi from his Moxy Früvous days. I was looking forward to meeting some of the most talented producers and journalists in the land—Anna Maria Tremonti, Carol Off, Michael Enright, Rex Murphy, Eleanor Wachtel, Bob McDonald, Andy Barrie, and so many others.

But it wasn't just the people; it was the public service piece. In many ways, I had acted like a public broadcaster when I'd worked at a private one. I had been glued to my car seat by CBC radio programming more than once. I remember one morning in October 1995 when I sat in the CHUM parking lot as Gzowski spoke to a woman in Saskatchewan who had just plowed a big "NO" in her farm field so that people in planes would know where she stood on sovereignty. I was so moved, I walked into my office and announced to MuchMusic that we were packing up and going to Montreal to try and deconstruct the Quebec referendum for young people. And so we did.

Having an ingrained sense of public service was going to come in very handy. It was a value that would see many of us through tough terrain.

As head of radio, there was no *end* of matters on which to get up to speed. Some expected, many not. The Radio 2 music service had just been relaunched to howls from the classical community; the CBC Radio Orchestra arrangement was about to end; a virtual music library was about to be tested; the Massey Lectures were about to start for another year; the CBC's Journalistic Standards and Practices bible was scheduled for an update; and a digital *Metro Morning* pilot was being considered. My calendar was already chock-a-block with regular weekly and bi-weekly meetings, plus there were a few new ones: a confab to address the aforementioned budget freeze and hiring controls, a CRTC command performance in Ottawa to "explain" Radio 2, and a looming CRTC licence renewal hearing, among other things.

Sometimes the worries that kept me up at night were wholly unforeseen, like transmission infrastructure and coverage. I know…fascinating! But I mention this issue specifically because in many ways it's a metaphor for the challenges that affect the entire CBC: how to continue to provide quality service to Canadians, manage dwindling resources, and stickhandle government relations (or not), all while simultaneously embracing a digital future.

There are approximately five hundred Radio One and Radio 2 transmitters (and more for television and French services) sending CBC/Radio-Canada signals across the country twenty-four hours a day, seven days a week. The towers are decades old. Some are rusty and past their best-before date and some are in remote, hard-to-reach areas. They were erected between 1974 and 1984, when the government made a capital investment grant to the CBC to ensure that every town or city with a population of five hundred people or more would have access to the public broadcaster. It took over a decade to erect the transmitters across the country, and I've come to think of them as fine a unifying idea as Sir John A. Macdonald's railroad.

When I arrived, there was no new money to repair or relocate them, and the cost to distribute our signals on this aging infrastructure was about to grow exponentially. I can hear you thinking, *What about using satellite or digital distribution?* I assure you those options were fully explored, but they weren't the solution for remote areas in need of targeted *local* information. At the time there were no cost-effective technological solutions in reach and there were few buyers for the old towers anyway. What we needed was an injection of cash.

I ordered a blown-up map of the transmitter infrastructure and put it up on my wall. It was impressive. Little tiny triangles were dotted across the country, from the craggy coastlines of Newfoundland and Labrador in the east and British Columbia in the west to the vast reaches of the Canadian North, where I imagined the CBC radio waves washing across the snow.

As I fixated on the map, I thought about a photo I'd seen recently of Prime Minister Stephen Harper, all flush in his parka, on yet another trip to the North. He had made more trips to the Arctic than any other PM before him; he was staking claim to Canadian sovereignty. As new waterways opened up due to melting ice, his presence was a signal to other nations that the North was part of Canada. Hmmm. If sovereignty was his focus, I thought, what better manifestation of Canadian ownership than the CBC transmitter towers?

There was a great tradition of early explorers planting flags to establish their territory. Weren't the big steel transmitters, which had been sending

Canadian voices in French, English, and eight aboriginal languages throughout the land for decades, exactly like those flags? Wouldn't the prime minister see the value in keeping them humming? Surely it would be cheaper than mounting gun turrets through the Northwest Passage and less messy than hand-to-hand combat with the Russians and the Danes, who were busy mapping the ocean floor around the North Pole, supposedly rich with oil and gas reserves.

Nothing ventured, nothing gained, I thought, and rang John Agnew, the managing director of CBC North, to gather more information on our northern services, then sat down to compose a letter.

"Dear Prime Minister Harper," I typed. "Enclosed please find a map of the CBC Radio-Canada transmission infrastructure. You will find that many of our radio transmitters are scattered throughout our Great White North where they are beaming signals carrying Canadian content in both official and eight aboriginal languages. . ."

I hadn't licked the envelope before I received a phone call from a pleasant gentleman from our corporate offices in Ottawa. He welcomed me to the company and hoped I was enjoying myself so far. He wondered if I knew that the CBC had an office in Ottawa that handled communications with the PMO. It was a congenial call but its intent was clear: *Please stand down. We have people for that.*

I hung up the phone and glanced suspiciously around my office. Was it wired? A bug in the phone? Under the lampshade? Couldn't be. I'd just paid five bucks for that lamp at the *Air Farce* props auction. I must be paranoid. I was, however, getting a sense that there were limits to the power of my new office.

Richard disavowed me of any fanciful notions of getting money from the government for transmitters or anything else. What we needed to do was to decide which transmitters we could afford to fix and which ones we'd simply have to let fall down. This, to me, was unacceptable. Would decisions be based on size of population served? Remoteness of location? Distinctness of market? You couldn't just say that a community of less than a thousand people had to lump it. Those were typically the remote communities that needed coverage the most.

The transmission infrastructure and coverage puzzle was fascinating and confounding. It was my first foray into debating the complex definition of "public service." (Happily the senior executive team took the position later that radio coverage to small communities was a manifestation of CBC's mandate despite the significant operational costs.) I appreciated the learning curve, especially working with the smart folks in operations. But the job was also frustrating. Getting traction to either fix an old problem or present a new solution sometimes felt like trying to turn an ocean liner with no power steering. I just hoped that I wouldn't end up rearranging the deck chairs on the *Titanic*.

AS THE WEATHER GOT colder that year, an undercurrent of gloom began seeping in. Advertising revenue continued to underperform. At first there was hope that with the proper controls, and some good luck in the hockey playoffs, we could recover. But that hope was fleeting. The U.S. subprime mortgage crisis was impacting the entire world: the financial world braced for insolvencies, businesses got the jitters, consumers curbed their spending, advertisers pulled back the reins, and sales forecasts continued their descent. Personally, I was starting to feel like Bill Murray in *Groundhog Day*.

We made it to Christmas with some optimism that revenue might recover, but January brought finality to the sinking fiscal news. No broadcasters were hitting their targets. The headlines blared: "Rogers Cuts Back" and "Layoffs at CTV" (the *Hollywood Reporter*), "Global to lay off staff, cancel local newscast" (CP), and "Networks float idea of shutting smaller stations" (the *Globe and Mail*).

CBC's government appropriation meant we were inoculated against, but not immune to, the vagaries of the marketplace. (The budget for CBC/Radio-Canada in 2008–2009 was $1.6 billion, of which $989 million was our operating appropriation from the government.) Other revenue came from program sales, real estate, specialty services, and television and digital ad revenue. Between 20 and 25 percent of CBC Radio-Canada's overall budget was based on advertising revenue (depending on which era was being measured).

By January of 2009, the advertising sales shortfall was $70 million on the English side alone. By February, adding insult to injury, the Leafs were firmly out of a playoff spot. When a Canadian team doesn't make the playoffs, viewership of *Hockey Night in Canada* goes into a nosedive—sometimes as much as 30 percent. Given that approximately half of the ad revenue for English services was associated with hockey, cheering for the Leafs makes sense.

Hubert Lacroix had been pressing the Harper government for bridge financing, but they turned us down. That was the last straw. The senior executive team assembled in the boardroom to hear the now inescapable verdict: CBC/Radio-Canada was facing a $171-million shortfall.

The cuts would be widespread, through French and English services, national and regional stations, radio and television, corporate and management. No area would be spared. The early estimate for English services was the loss of 393 jobs—*if* we could manage to sell certain real estate assets and *if* we could recover some of the advertising losses.

Finance had been working the numbers hard. All manner of scenarios were presented. Every department was looking at nasty numbers, but for me, the ones that seemed most egregious were those aligned with radio and regions.

I could feel my adrenaline starting to rise. It was hard to believe I was up on my hind legs already. I wasn't even sure who to fight. I pledged to myself that there would be no scorched earth under my watch. If we had to cut we would do it in a way that might enable new growth one day.

Richard had talked about small stations before I'd agreed to join the CBC. There didn't seem to be any consistent rationale for why some places had a local radio service and others didn't. He questioned the wisdom of having four stations in Newfoundland, a province of about half a million people, and none in Hamilton, a city with a similar population. He flirted with the idea of opening a new station there. The fact that we didn't have a frequency in Hamilton (even if one opened up, it would be competitive and expensive to win) didn't seem to be an issue.

Still, the idea of launching a new station was thrilling. The CBC hadn't opened a new local station in decades, and there were service disparities everywhere you looked. There were no local stations in Lethbridge, Kingston, or London, or in places like Fort McMurray that were growing in leaps and bounds. We knew that six million Canadians were living in cities with a population of more than 50,000 people, none of which had their own local stations. They listened to other people's weather, traffic, city hall coverage, local tragedies and triumphs. There was a definite need for new regional services, but surely, I thought, they wouldn't come at the cost of existing stations.

What I didn't know at the time was that Richard had floated the idea of closing small radio stations to the CBC board. Savings at small stations could be redistributed to other more strategic areas, he'd argued. It wasn't just the savings in headcount; the real estate could be sold as well. He was getting little traction. Richard was accustomed to resistance from the board, but I don't think he expected resistance from his new head of radio as well.

Let me be clear about my relationship with Richard. I liked him even though we disagreed. He's a highly intelligent individual with a spirited sense of humour. In *The Tower of Babble* he describes himself as "arrogant" and "truculent." Others have described him as "a bad man" (*The Walrus*), a "one-man wrecking ball" (Antonia Zerbisias, the *Toronto Star*), "A lightning rod for disgruntlement" (John Doyle, the *Globe and Mail*), all of which are quotes on the jacket of his book. He was a strong leader and the CBC needs strong leaders, for better or worse. He will chart a path—even if he's singular in his ardour for it—and charge the hill. He appreciates candour and likes to surround himself with bright people who will challenge him. He would urge us to "Be bold! Take risks!" I remember he quite rightly asked us to "Celebrate failure!" One wit at the table responded, "We can't even celebrate our successes, how are we going to celebrate our failures?"

He was patient with me. A few months into the job, I arrived for my bi-weekly meeting and vented about the depth of the cuts to radio. I argued how strategically wrong it was to cripple a service that was threadbare already. I pointed out that closing stations would hurt us at licence renewal. I contended that serving underserved communities was one of the biggest reasons we merited government appropriation in the first place and moaned that we would be seen as untrustworthy stewards and punished. I predicted revolt from radio staff who wouldn't accept being "cut to support TV." (Many felt that because this funding crisis was market-driven and radio was non-commercial, therefore only television should be cut. It wasn't radio's fault.) I reminded him that radio was chock full of value—just pennies per minute per Canadian to produce versus television. Radio doubles your time! Why force me to cut the service for which people will march in the streets?

If that wasn't enough, I even waded into the unspeakable territory that was better left unsaid: the French-English funding share. How were the resources divided? Was it fair? It certainly wasn't representational. How was I supposed to walk into small stations, where there were employees on the French *and* English services sides, and make a larger cut to the English than the French, especially when English services was serving more people? I asked Richard why Hubert wasn't addressing this issue. He was the first francophone president in years—he was the only one who *could* fix it if indeed it was broken. (CBC has increasingly been moving to a "one company" model. In the 2014/2015 CBC/Radio-Canada annual report, English Services operating expenses are listed at $939,164,000 and French Services at $683,670,000, ie: approximately 58 percent vs 42 percent.)

Richard nodded and commiserated and let me have my say. He was also discreet. I was unaware that he'd already pressed Hubert on the French-English split until I read it in his book.

Richard wasn't shy of controversy or fearful of anyone, including small-town MPs, the CRTC, or the president of CBC—which is probably obvious judging from the end result: Richard was dismissed in 2010. Richard relishes a good argument and will have it with his superiors as well as his subordinates. He would listen and you *could* win. Good to know.

What helped to win the day for small stations (aside from strong support from the president and the board) was simple truth and straight numbers. Local radio programming is key to attracting the largest possible Canadian audiences, and Richard liked big numbers.

Local morning shows are CBC Radio's prime time. In my time there, twenty out of twenty-three local morning shows across the country were in the top three in their markets. A solid morning show floats the ratings boat for the rest of the day. If you have a strong *Metro Morning* in Toronto or *Early Edition* in Vancouver, your audience share will remain higher for the CBC throughout the day. There was not a single case where this wasn't true. The corollary was also true. In a city like London or Kingston, which was without a local CBC Radio station, the overall share was lower. If we cut a local station, we would lose listeners to the national shows as well.

The Radio One programming day played like a big accordion, starting with local programming in the mornings, then moving to national programming with shows like *The Current* and *Q*, then back to local, and so on until "drive time," when listeners wanted updates on their local community on their way home from work, before the nationally broadcast *As It Happens*. The schedule breathed in and out of local and national stories, arts and culture, reflecting small communities and the North to the rest of Canada and back. It was and is, as has been said, our "cultural glue." As one regional managing director put it: "We should be local till it hurts."

Some stations were located in politically sensitive areas. CBC stations in cities like Sudbury, with big nickel, or in New Brunswick, with big oil, provide necessary journalistic independence. Northern stations were particularly valued because there were few alternatives, and let's just say that *every* station in Newfoundland and Labrador was capable of rousing a ruckus with MPs of any stripe if their local station was in danger of being closed. Even at a government level, my sense was that the politicians might complain about the CBC as a whole, but local stations were the thing you just didn't touch.

Small stations made a compelling case for public funding especially when there wasn't a big enough population to make a business case for private commercial interests to operate. A public broadcaster's first concern wasn't about profit—providing returns to their shareholders—it was about providing service to the community. Local CBC stations delivered actual "survival information" to audiences that may have had no other option. Survival information in private radio is weather, traffic, and breaking news. Survival information at CBC might mean actual survival. CBC Radio in Yellowknife may not alert you to gridlock on Franklin Avenue, but it could tell you the depth of the ice on Frame Lake so you could avoid crashing through and dying.

It's true that producing one big national morning show instead of making twenty local morning shows would have been a cost-saving measure—and I fear that one day it may come to pass—but it would render the overall service less relevant to Canadians.

The more I learned about local stations, the firmer became my resolve to keep them open. My position was that we should serve the underserved, and what I often said was: "You don't know until you go."

Richard's position was that we should serve the biggest numbers of Canadians possible. What he often said was: "You can't be a public broadcaster without a public."

We were both right.

IN ANY CRISIS THERE is opportunity. I was excited about a local service extension plan that would not only retain the existing stations, but build new ones. In the CBC Radio executive office, we had a small team, all of whom were key players in setting strategy and generous with filling the gaps in my institutional knowledge. Chris Boyce was director of programming; Havoc Franklin worked with the regions; Chris Straw headed up program development; and Ted Kennedy was radio's chief of staff. Ted advised me that years ago there had been a plan to expand local radio to fifteen new markets. There had been no increase in our radio service since the early seventies, and the population changes since then had been massive. We dusted it off and dug in.

You could be excused for thinking we were tilting at windmills. How could we possibly build new stations while we were cutting existing ones? The answer was, the new stations would work differently. They'd take advantage of new technologies; they'd be smaller and tighter; they'd share program efficiencies with larger stations and build new workflow models. Their journalists would be tri-medial (radio, TV, digital) and, ideally, develop local partnerships with community organizations. We hoped that piloting these new stations would provide insight into new ways of working with a smaller staff at the existing stations while we weathered the cuts.

That said, the fate of the small stations was just one of the areas to consider in radio's overall budget cut. The national radio shows would be hit too, and we worried about a diminished journalistic ability to cover and contextualize important stories for the audience, of losing our newest diverse hires, and of the impact on morale. It was daunting to face this challenge so early on in my time there, but I gulped back the fear of making bad choices due to institutional ignorance and tempered it with the hope that fresh eyes might bring some new perspective.

I know there are those who think a 10-percent budget cut might be easy to find. There are those who think that the CBC is fat. That it's over-resourced and lazy. It's a story competitors particularly love to spread and I've heard politicians practically spit the words "$1 billion in subsidy" like it was poison on their tongues. Secretly, I'd been hoping that some of that story might turn out to be true. A nice juicy bit of fat would have come in handy. But no such luck. In my tiny tenure at CBC thus far, I'd had a moment to look under the hood at radio. My private sector background had given me some expectation of what I should see, but I was astonished at what I found. Or didn't find. We were running on fumes.

Contrary to my intention to be visible — open-door policy and all that — much of my first few months was spent hunkered down behind closed doors with spreadsheets, research documents, and calculators. The process needed to be deep and consultative, so managing directors came in from across the country and gathered with the heads of arts, current affairs, music, and digital, ready to engage but also primed to fight for their constituencies.

The job was to get everyone's input, then land the tough decisions. The problem was too big to waste time fighting across media lines or programming genres, but there *were* inter-company resentments. The one I heard most was the complaint I cautioned Richard about: that radio was being cut to solve TV's problems. The most colourful descriptor I heard was "It's like a poodle giving a transfusion to a gorilla."

Radio folks would walk through the atrium shaking their heads at a splashy sound stage newly erected for TV's coverage of an election night or a massive *Battle of the Blades* banner, wondering why there was no money for a *Quirks & Quarks* promotional T-shirt or a *Sunday Edition* coffee mug. TV shows got flashy launches and photo-emblazoned trucks. Radio was the Cinderella stepsister with rumpled fleece and sensible shoes, carrying her bicycle into the subway.

When I arrived, the atrium of the CBC building in Toronto was festooned with the faces of television hosts. There were photos of Peter Mansbridge, Rick Mercer, George Stroumboulopoulos, and Chris and Steven. All lovely people on shows worth promoting, but the only image of a radio host was of dearly departed Barbara Frum in the Barbara Frum Atrium (and she of course had hosted *The Journal* on television as well.) It took two persistent years before I got a flight of radio show signage on the main floor, and then it was only on the elevator doors. The atrium took longer.

One argument was that radio didn't need big promotional dollars. Richard referred to us as "tiny perfect radio" and the "sheltered workshop," meaning that because CBC Radio was non-commercial, it didn't have to compete with private radio stations for ad dollars. The truth was that Radio One *did* compare itself with private radio stations in terms of audiences, and we did extremely well.

I'm not intending to turn this into a story of a fight between radio and television — the media streams work well together. But it's worth remembering that in the past, radio had had its own VP, who'd attended board meetings alongside the TV VP. As I've said, the structure had changed before I arrived. Richard represented all of English services, and I presented to the board at their pleasure. In Richard's book, he said: "The raison d'être for merging CBC English services under one person was the challenge of creating a content company...to move away from being a radio and a TV company to becoming a company focused on particular genres...a news company, a music company, a sports company, and a talk company. To get there all of the assets had to be integrated in a single structure."

And so, my job was to convince radio folks that we were all in it together. We already shared services like finance, HR, legal counsel, technology, business development, and communications, and now radio, TV, and digital also shared a vice-president.

In March 2009, Richard convened a live CBC staff town hall meeting to explain the severity of our financial situation and the impact on our operating budget. It was held in the Glenn Gould Studio in Toronto and streamed to CBC employees across the country.

He relayed the good news first: audience numbers were up. Radio One was enjoying record numbers; Radio 2 was building traction with younger audiences, and CBC TV was celebrating its highest audience numbers in the decade. Audiences were responding well to shows in the prime time schedule like *Dragons' Den*, *Little Mosque on the Prairie*, *The Nature of Things*, *Rick Mercer Report*, and *The National*. *The Fifth Estate* was enjoying bigger audiences in its new time slot on Friday night. He expressed his delight that CBC TV had finally beat Global's share of available audience in prime time — with Canadian shows! But if Richard was expecting a "We Beat Global" chant to spontaneously erupt in the crowd, he was disappointed. Many in the audience didn't share the same glee at besting the private stations — they were more concerned with what they saw as program distinction and quality. There was also grumbling that CBC TV — whose head of network programming was Kirstine

Stewart—had brought in two American shows, *Jeopardy!* and *Wheel of Fortune*, as prime-time lead-ins.

When Richard got to the bad news—that our estimated ad sales could be down by as much as 24 percent by end of year—the crowd started to shift and mutter. They knew what that meant. More cuts. Richard removed his jacket and rolled up his sleeves. It was more a reaction to temperature than tempers, but it was interpreted by some as a provocative gesture and the mood became abruptly acrimonious.

I was sitting in the front row of the Glenn Gould Studio with the rest of the management team. I had never been to an all-staff assembly and hadn't met most of the people in the room, but I felt I couldn't just sit there and watch things get ugly. A communications manager urged me to get up. I took the microphone, then a slow breath, and turned to face the audience with an appeal to solidarity. I reminded everyone that this current threat to our financial resources was coming from external economic forces. As tough as the situation was, we could not allow ourselves to be fractionalized internally. We could not be at odds with each other when now more than ever we had to find ways to face these difficult times together. I asked them to remember what Peter Gzowski had told me—"If it falters, no one will build it again"—and hoped everyone would keep the faith.

It did help cool the room, and the meeting ended shortly afterward; but as I made my way to the public lobby, I saw that the fight wasn't over. A handful of angry producers and journalists, including *Fifth Estate* reporter Gillian Findlay and producer Neil Docherty, were engaged in a loud argument with Richard. I knew how they felt. I, too, anguished about the future of the service and the brand. I feared the cuts would impair our ability to be good journalists and impact our service to Canadians. I couldn't imagine the wrath that might have erupted had small station closures been announced at that town hall meeting. But what could we do? We had to try to make the best choices in a bad situation and work harder to find new ways to shore ourselves up.

I arrived back at my office feeling nervous. I worried that my little speech had cast me irrevocably on the side of management (which I was) and not on the side of the content creators (which I also was). When I opened my email, I was grateful to see a note from Michael Enright.

From: Michael Enright
Date: 9/8/2009
Subject: del gratis

DD: I know that thank-you's to senior management are as rare as a beer salesman at a Baptist picnic, but here's one. Your efforts at staving off what I think would have been a PR disaster are most gratefully appreciated. You responded with alacrity, understanding and good sense... In the next weeks we can proceed and turn out a product that will make us all proud.

Cheers,
Enright

Michael had been through many administrations and to get a thumbs-up from him meant a lot. It gave me more confidence to trust my instincts.

AFTER RICHARD'S TOWN HALL meeting, we continued working on the numbers, adjusting in increments as the sales figures landed. We finished the fiscal year in a slightly better position than forecast. Hubert Lacroix made a presentation to the treasury board that detailed the magnitude of the budgetary challenge and we were spared *another* 5-percent cut. The government allowed CBC to sell off a real estate asset and the company offered a voluntary early retirement incentive, but eventually the notices of redundancy had to be issued.

At radio we still had a 9-percent cut to administer. It was significant. We froze hiring, slimmed staff across the board, cancelled shows including *The Point*, *The Inside Track*, and *In the Key of Charles*, and put *Outfront* on a repeat pattern, hoping to re-engage first-person documentary programming in the future. Positions at current affairs shows like *The Current*, *As It Happens*, and *The Sunday Edition* were cut. We reduced drama production and added a block of repeat programming in the afternoons. At Radio 2 we made a whopping 50-percent cut to the budget for the live concerts we recorded across the country. We protected our services in the North and in regions we reduced staff and shrunk the length of local noon-time shows to an hour, but there were no closures of small stations.

Television made cuts, too. They cut episodes on some of their biggest shows, including *This Hour Has 22 Minutes* and *Little Mosque on the Prairie,* and daytime shows like *Steven and Chris* were put on hiatus. The promotions budget was cut; program repeats were increased, equipment updates stalled. The news department was particularly challenged by their reductions. They were in the midst of a massive reorganization for which they needed *more* staff, not less. I admired Jennifer McGuire and the CBC News team, who somehow managed the cuts without a mutiny.

The news segments that were delivered to radio at the top of the hour weren't my department (the overall radio current affairs shows were), but I was concerned. Investigative journalism in particular is courageous work that requires significant talent, resources, legal support, and moral courage. It's more than daily reporting; it's the kind of deep work documented in the Oscar-winning movie *Spotlight,* about the *Boston Globe's* reporting on predator priests.

The delivery of fair and balanced information is vital to democracy, never more so than today. Too many news services operate like sensationalist entertainment outlets, their reporters becoming faux-martyr grandstanders—the breathless cub reporter ducking for cover at a late-night street protest, the rain-soaked weatherman yelling from a windy street in the path of a hurricane. Serious journalists don't put themselves in harm's way as a ratings gambit—they're in pursuit of truth. When I watch Susan Ormiston reporting on the refugee crisis from Syria, or Nahlah Ayed on conflict in the Middle East, or Adrienne Arsenault reporting on Ebola from Sierra Leone, I worry. These women are sharp and experienced, but CBC's shrinking financial situation has meant that foreign news bureau resources have had to be reorganized at the same time that journalistic work is becoming increasingly more dangerous. CBC takes great care to ensure their journalists are prepared, ensuring that they train for hostile environments and, if the situation calls for it, travel with risk specialists. Yet we know that every year scores of journalists are murdered, imprisoned, or "disappeared" all over the world. Insurgents and tyrants know that the capture of a journalist garners more world attention than the death of traditional combatants. Being a member of the press in a war zone has lost the protective immunity it once had.

Two weeks after I started at CBC, Mellissa Fung, a CBC reporter for *The National*, was kidnapped while on assignment in Kabul. I was enormously impressed to see the level of organization and support of the team at the CBC (led by then CBC News publisher John Cruickshank) as they worked for her release. She was held for twenty-eight days in a dark hole, sexually assaulted, and finally released on November 8, 2008. She went on to write a book called *Under an Afghan Sky*.

Investigating stories at home can also be hazardous. It took Radio-Canada's *Enquête* five years to uncover the massive story of corruption in Quebec's construction industry. Journalists faced intimidation but they persevered. *The Fifth Estate* has brought us countless programs that have opened our eyes, from the Karlheinz Schreiber–Brian Mulroney Airbus dealings to the International Emmy Award–winning documentary *Made in Bangladesh*. One of the last shows journalist Linden MacIntyre brought us from *The Fifth Estate* was *Silence of the Labs*, which documented the Harper government's firing and muzzling of Canadian scientists and closing of research institutes across the country. We know about these things because the CBC supported those journalists and CBC lawyers backed them up (counsel Daniel Henry, in particular, worked to change Canadian laws for greater public access to information for all journalists). That support ensured that the public broadcaster could operate in the public interest and speak truth to the powerful, often for the powerless.

Cutting too deeply puts the truth at risk. Investigative content is costly. Not allowing journalists and producers in news and current affairs the time and resources to do their work results in a rip-and-read mentality that is prone to error. As budgets at newspapers and commercial news organizations are increasingly challenged, it makes funding the public broadcaster even more essential.

News was a significant contributor to radio's hourly programming, and we were certainly all in it together. Once the radio plan was set, Chris Boyce, Ted Kennedy, and I travelled to stations across the country to talk to staff. We described the mission to operate as one content company, detailed how the decisions were made, and underscored our intention that despite the cuts we would continue to serve Canadians with world-class content and deliver it in new ways. The announcements were met with stoic resignation, frustration, and sometimes tears. We commended staff on their exemplary work: I encouraged them to "keep the faith."

We addressed the public too, inviting stakeholders, local politicians, and people from community organizations to gatherings where people could hear first-hand from senior radio management. One encounter I remember fondly was in Saskatchewan. There were about two dozen people in the room, and at the end of the session I asked if there were any more questions. There was a tiny elderly lady who had sat through it all but hadn't said a word. I asked her if there was anything she wanted to add.

"Are you cancelling *Birdline*?" she asked.

Birdline? I looked at the station manager for help. She whispered, "It's a weekly call-in show." Like the weekly gardening shows that run regionally, *Birdline* was a segment in their local noon-hour programming, where callers described the birds in their backyards, sometimes whistling their songs to be identified by a guest ornithologist.

"*Birdline* should be fine," I said.

The lady nodded, put her hanky in her purse, and stood up to leave.

Thank heavens we still had a *Birdline* somewhere in the country. I loved that there was still a place for whimsy at the Canadian Broadcasting Corporation.

(22)

STUCK IN THE MIDDLE WITH YOU

*"While money can't buy happiness, it certainly lets
you choose your own form of misery."*
— GROUCHO MARX

THE CUTS TOOK SOME months to be fully realized. I'd been told that
reductions at the CBC felt like death by a thousand cuts, but I didn't realize they were also applied in slow motion.

We knew which shows would be affected, but we didn't yet know which
individuals would be terminated, which was precisely what staff wanted
to know. There was a complex union seniority process to follow. It could
possibly mean that the job was lost in Halifax but the person who walked
out the door was the fresh face in Sydney we'd just taken on. A shrinking workforce made reaching our diversity goals tougher to achieve, but a
diverse work force was not an objective that could be parked.

Diversity is especially important for a public broadcaster servicing an
increasingly multicultural Canada. That it was good public policy *and*
good business was proven conclusively by the success of CBC Radio's
Metro Morning. Starting in 2001, station manager Susan Marjetti led the
charge, insisting the show *sound* like Toronto looked—Canada's most
diverse city. Every aspect of Toronto's drive show programming, from
the guests to the music to the public affairs coverage, was put through
a diversity lens. At first there was trepidation about the change in programming, and worry that they'd lose their loyal, older, whiter audience

while courting a new diverse one. But instead, the audience grew. *Metro Morning* became the number one morning radio show in Canada's biggest radio market for the first time in December 2003, an achievement it has repeated over *eighty-five* times since then. When long-time *Metro Morning* host Andy Barrie retired in 2010, turning over his chair to Matt Galloway, a convoy of taxicabs representing all manner of Toronto's cultural diaspora circled the building in homage.

Diverse reflection in programming won't happen just because we wish for it, just as a vibrant and peaceful Canadian mosaic won't happen unless we actively work at it. CBC hired people from different cultural and racial backgrounds, but we also needed to know how to measure diversity in our programming. I suggested a page out of the Cancon MAPL book, in which a points system could be assigned for guests/hosts/director/principle characters/staff on programs. Richard embraced the idea with enthusiasm. Christine Wilson, executive director of network programming at CBC TV, ably championed the project and soon developed a new diversity programming system called ECHOSS. We hoped it might one day become the industry standard.

There is progress in the media. We are seeing a much wider range of characters on television and in movies, and somewhat less stereotyping. I thought back to twenty years ago when MuchMusic's host of *Clip Trip*, Diego Fuentes, asked me for time off to play a part in a new Canadian TV series.

"How long will you need?" I asked.

"Only a few weeks. I'm Hispanic, so I'm playing a gangster—as usual. I should be killed off by the end of the first episode."

When Graham Greene's performance in *Dances with Wolves* was nominated for an Oscar, he said to me, "I loved playing Kicking Bird, but when do I get to play a Jewish lawyer?"

Twenty-seven years later Graham was cast as Shylock in Stratford's *Merchant of Venice*.

Today on television we see Latinos as star detectives, there is an African-American female president, singers in wheelchairs, and a transgender reality show. More, please. The more we choose "empathy over antipathy," and the more we learn to celebrate our differences rather than discriminate against them, the better off we all will be.

DIVERSITY GOALS WERE JUST one of many areas that risked compromise in CBC's effort to do more with less. Something had to happen to stop the bleeding, or quality and service would be cut to the point where no one would care. I feared the day when people would no longer march in the streets for CBC. If radio became a revenue generator, it might have more defences of its own against the next wave of cuts (and sadly, they did seem to come in waves).

Commercializing Radio One is often where that conversation starts—an idea that gets kicked around like a sad, deflated ball whenever money is tight, which is constantly. I'm against commercializing radio and I'll tell you why. But first, it bears mentioning that CBC Radio had carried advertising until 1974.

In 1975, the CRTC (then helmed by Pierre Juneau) gave approval for CBC Radio to become non-commercial. It was generally held that the service could henceforth focus purely on public-interest programming. At the time, advertising revenue was not seen as a big loss; the radio service was only bringing in about $2 million of it annually—which was, according to internal lore, less than it cost to go out and get it.

Part of the reason sales had been so low was that CBC Radio's numbers were in the toilet. It needed a revolution and it got one under the stewardship of the intrepid Margaret Lyons. Margaret is long retired now, but I was delighted to meet her at the fortieth anniversary gathering for *As It Happens*. Margaret brought a much-needed attitudinal change to CBC Radio. She wanted it to sound less ponderous and more personable. New shows like *The Sunday Edition* (called *Sunday Morning* then), *Quirks & Quarks*, and *This Country in the Morning* (which became *Morningside*) told Canadian stories with warmth, intelligence, and humour. *As It Happens*, which was created by Mark Starowicz (who created, among many other successes in television documentary, *Canada: A People's History*) is still on the air almost fifty years later, as adept at covering politics and current affairs as it is in charging around the world in search of bad puns and cheese-rolling competitions. Margaret led the change CBC Radio needed, and its numbers climbed ever after. Ironically, that same success today makes it a prime target for commercialization.

I was wholeheartedly against putting commercials on CBC Radio, even though it was suggested by some marketers that if we did we could bring in $50 to $100 million a year from Radio One alone. But in a "shared services" situation, there can be no guarantee that radio would be allowed to keep the money; it would likely go into the overall content company coffers against the entire operating budget and be dispersed against the Corporation's strategic priorities. But the bigger argument for me was that advertising would ultimately result in the loss of distinctive programming and lead to our eventual annihilation. I know that sounds alarmist and doomsday, but here's why I believed (and still believe) it.

Radio One has a large, loyal, well-educated, largely affluent audience. Because the service is both national and regional, I knew we could sell both national and local ads. But I also knew we wouldn't then be raking in all those millions right away. There would be a getting-to-know-you phase when advertisers would want to pay the least amount of money for the most exposure, and there would certainly be some audience decline as listeners reacted to the interruptions (research says that "commercial-free" is always among the top three reasons why people like CBC Radio).

Different radio shows would sell at different rates, depending on the location of the station, the time of day, the type of content, and who was listening. Morning is prime time for radio, as is the afternoon drive. Morning shows on CBC Radio are local, and the shows would attract local advertisers. Salespeople would be hired (or commissioned) to manage the inventory, which would mean increased cost (or a cut of the revenue). As for the national radio shows, straight sponsorship of shows ("*The Current* is brought to you by Intrepid Insurance") is easily a perception problem when you're in the middle of an investigative feature on insurance companies. Another important consideration (and here's where the rubber meets the road): was a spot on a current affairs show like *The Sunday Edition* or *As It Happens* worth the same as one on *Q* or *The Debaters* or *This Is That*? No, because the show demographics and audience numbers vary. Younger-skewing audiences are more attractive to advertisers. Producers on shows that generate less advertising revenue would be under pressure to adjust their content to attract more twenty-five to thirty-four-year-old females because they're seen to have the biggest buying power. I expect show producers would be asked to "lighten up": fewer stories about sad human rights violations or complex government issues, please. Perhaps more lifestyle programming, top ten lists, comedy, maybe a reality radio show! Oh, and with twelve commercials an hour, please get to the point more quickly and in shorter segments and sound bites. Pretty soon it would sound like everything else on the radio. Reliance on advertising leads to indistinct programming. "We stray from public service when we aim to attract private money"—I'm not sure who said that, but it bears repeating.

Even if advertising was a runaway hit, there could easily be unintended consequences. Elected officials might decide that the Corporation didn't need as much government funding after all, especially to fund radio that didn't sound so different from what private radio was offering (the populist CBC TV programming conundrum in a nutshell) and cut the appropriation further.

Aha! you say. *The National* takes advertising and so does the CBC News Network. True. And they do an excellent job. Nonetheless, news is a competitive arena and, as we see in the U.S., increasingly prone to showbiz tactics to attract viewers. When you chase the money, the market rules, not the mandate. The CBC's brand distinction must be that it serves the public, not private or political interests, and it must remain crystal clear in that mission.

I'm sure there were some who thought I was being hysterical; obdurate, at best. Why shouldn't we consider ads if the alternative was laying people off and closing stations? Didn't I say that I wanted to protect programs and people? It's not that I wasn't open to discussion. There just wasn't a scenario that I didn't see heading to the same conclusion: CBC Radio would lose its program distinctiveness, private broadcasters would complain about unfair competition using tax dollars, the government could argue that CBC no longer served its mandate, the funding would be cut further and . . . Game over.

And by the way, who says that those estimated millions are achievable? There's the market and the regulator to consider. In May of 2013, I sighed on the sidelines as CBC Radio 2 and Éspace Musique (Radio 2's French-language counterpart) were granted permission to air advertising in CBC's licence renewal.

The decision was called "crazy" by a dissenting CRTC member, Tom Pentefountas, who wrote: "This crazy pursuit—and I emphasize the term—will destroy the very exemplary trademark character that these services enjoy among Canadians." To me, the ruling was a hobbling hat trick. It allowed

CBC Radio 2 to sell only four minutes of commercials an hour (versus the standard twelve), required proof that it was not infringing on private broadcasters' revenues (good luck with that), and placed conditions on the content it could play, asking it to commit to a minimum number of "distinct selections" per month.

It was a classic case of "Stuck in the Middle with You." Ad revenue is determined by the size and demographics of the audience. It's quite simple: you want big money, you play the hits. In order to significantly increase its audience and thereby make itself attractive to advertisers, Radio 2 would have to change its music mix (again) and gravitate to sounding like every other Top Forty station...which is, of course, why the CRTC put those conditions on the music mix in the first place. Dizzy yet?

As it turns out, neither service was close to achieving their revenue estimates. When new cuts were announced by the CBC in 2014, $13 million of an overall $130-million shortfall was blamed on the failure of Radio 2 and Éspace Musique — now rebranded as Ici Musique — to meet advertising revenue targets.

A public broadcaster that depends on commercial advertising is ever a conflicted construct. How can the CBC offer distinct programming that serves its mandate and distinguishes itself from the private broadcasters (by offering what they don't), and still attract big commercial revenues? How can the CBC be truly cost-efficient when it must serve the underserved by operating in small markets? (If there was a business case for "for-profit" broadcasters in those markets, they'd be there.) Even the government appropriation (your tax dollars) to the CBC is a prickly pact. CBC journalists hold the government's feet to the fire with one hand, while relying on their budgetary goodwill on the other. They're like the dog that bites the hand that feeds it. But CBC's relationship to the government *must* be arm's length and independent, otherwise it would be Radio Pravda or Korean Central TV.

For the CBC to be properly funded without selling commercials — as many believe should be the case — the government would either have to up its funding or the money would have to come from somewhere else. Either way, it's a big nut.

For months I have felt a great, self-imposed pressure to present the solution to CBC's funding dilemma in this book. After all, I've been inside, and so should have a better understanding of what's to be done. To that end, I've spent many hours going around in circles trying to square the mandate (which needs an urgent update) with the money (least amount for biggest return), and then trying to figure out how it should best be funded. Ultimately, two things have happened. First, my editor has wisely insisted that we "'spare the reader" (as she'd suggested similarly elsewhere: "I appreciate that it's well researched, Denise, but no one wants to read twelve pages on how the CRTC works." She used to be fun!); and second, I've accepted that I have not found the perfect solution. There is no plausible silver bullet, and many of the alternative funding ideas are either politically impractical or lose their veracity when you get down to the detail. A workable scenario will require a cobble of smart ideas, each very carefully modelled against market conditions and actual numbers.

Nonetheless, at the risk of both oversimplifying and incurring the exasperation of my editor, here are three of the alternative funding ideas most often proposed:

1. In exchange for CBC being wholly non-commercial (advertising revenue would revert to the private broadcasters), the CBC should receive 100 percent of the Canadian Media Fund. Intriguing, but even *if* the numbers worked (and as CBC wrestles with the loss of hockey ad revenue, they soon might), the private broadcasters wouldn't let their CMF funding go willingly without due consideration for their own Cancon commitments. (The timing is especially poor while foreign providers like Netflix offer their services in Canada, hauling out what some estimate to be more than CAN\$515 million annually, but are not required to invest in Canadian production.)

2. Adopt the funding mechanisms used by other public broadcasters, such as the BBC in the U.K., Yle in Finland, ZDF in Germany, RAI in Italy, or DRS in Switzerland, which collect television licence fees from the sale of appliances and/or usage of television signals. (Australia's ABC is most like the CBC, but they, too, are dealing with a \$300-million funding cut.) Let's just say that new consumer "taxes" in whatever guise are a tough sell.

Similarly, requiring Canadian distributors to add a CBC sur-
charge to their subscription rate card is a big ask. (CBC has tried
this route; it was part of a failed "value for signal" bid in 2012.)

3. If not a tax, a donation. Perhaps CBC Radio could become like
National Public Radio in the U.S. Not a bad idea, if it wasn't
grievously hampered by scale. Canada simply does not have the
population base to make charitable donations from "Listeners
Like You" a robust option. I like a tote bag as much as anyone,
but at best we'd make a dime on the dollar compared to what
NPR takes in.

Indeed, "explore alternative funding models" was just one suggestion
contained in a July 2015 Senate report called "Time for Change: The CBC/
Radio-Canada in the Twenty-First Century." I was pleased to see the report
acknowledge that Canada needs its national public broadcaster and that
"broadcasting is a public good." There were twenty-two recommendations
in all, including that the CBC divest itself of real estate, archive its content, reflect regions, and "examine the costs and benefits of commercial
advertising." Many of the recommendations contained in the Senate report
were already underway, which is, I expect, why the CBC's comment on the
report was: "Frankly, we were hoping for more."

The Senate committee made programming recommendations as well,
suggesting that the CBC present "Canadian history and nature documentaries and high-quality comedy and drama" as well as Canadian film, arts
performances (ballet, opera, symphony, theatre), quiz shows, and amateur
sport. I agree that the CBC should air arts programs and celebrations of culture like the Scotiabank Giller Prize and the Governor General's Performing
Arts Awards. The challenge is that sporting events, arts performances, and
theatre productions are some of *the* most expensive programs to produce
and promote (because they're typically one-offs), and do not attract huge
audiences. I wish it were otherwise, but they just don't. Unless it's a long-running contest. *Battle of the Pointe Shoes*.

The biggest audiences are watching American dramas, big sporting
events (hockey, Olympics), national news (especially in times of crisis),
contests ("shiny-floor shows"), and reality-TV series. And the reason we

see so *many* people battling alligators, selling out their adulterous spouses, and competing to stay on the island is that non-scripted programming is among the cheapest to produce.

The question for the CBC, ever and always, is: What is the right programming mix? And that's followed quickly by: Where's the money coming from?

Senator Art Eggleton — the one senator who broke from the Senate report pack — suggested that the per-capita money the CBC receives from taxpayers should be raised from $29 to $40 and adjusted for inflation, and that the CBC should "get out of the commercial advertising business altogether." At $29 per capita, the CBC is one of the lowest-funded public broadcasters in the world, third from the bottom, and well below the average funding for public broadcasters, which is estimated at $82 per capita.

By the way (and because I'm so firmly on the pulpit at the moment), it should be noted that even at $29 per person, the CBC is the deal of the century. For that you get over thirty services including radio, television, and online programming services in English, French, and eight aboriginal languages delivered in five-and-a-half time zones coast to coast to coast. You get news and information from foreign correspondents as well as regional current affairs and arts programming; you can time-shift and podcast your head off and lose yourself in on-demand world-class content 24/7 if you want to. Oh, and it's no small accomplishment to be "distinct" while cuddled up beside the biggest media producer on the planet.

WHILE I WAS AT the CBC, no one was walking around waiting for money to suddenly appear. And so we explored new ways to generate revenue for ourselves, from selling content internationally to monetizing niche content on new websites we built for books, music, and comedy.

There was concern from staff that advertising on our digital content was a slippery slope to the day when *all* our radio content was online — and, therefore, commercialized; but we pushed on. Happily, the audience didn't object — they were used to seeing ads on the internet.

We put banner ads and pop-up boxes on the site, and embedded commercials and promos in our music streams and podcasts. We sought sponsorship for big radio initiatives like *Song Quest* and *Canada Reads*. The digital ad dollar (or should I say penny) universe was in its early stages then, but perhaps in the future it would make a significant revenue contribution.

We looked at other public broadcaster funding models, explored content co-productions, and brainstormed with futurists and noted capitalists, including one fun-filled morning with a Dragon from the Den. We looked at selling tickets to live recordings and music festivals and investigated commissioning more Canadian independent radio production, but unlike TV, where content is funded by an assortment of funding envelopes, licensing fees, and tax credits, a similar system does not exist to fund independent Canadian radio programs. (That could be addressed. If the result was more excellent programming like Terry O'Reilly's *Under the Influence*, we'd all be the better for it.)

There is huge interest in our radio content internationally, and that sales initiative was well underway. Shows like *As It Happens*, *Q*, *The Vinyl Cafe*, *WireTap*, *Ideas*, *Spark*, *Quirks & Quarks*, *The Sunday Edition*, *Tapestry*, and *Dispatches*, as well as broadcasts of the Massey Lectures, are sold through Public Radio International, American Public Media, and Public Radio Exchange, and carried on SiriusXM satellite radio. When I arrived, *As It Happens* was being distributed to more than one hundred North American stations. We pledged to push *Q* to that many cities in a year and we achieved that goal in nine months.

Outside North America, CBC Radio content was also well received. We shared content with BBC, ABC, and Radio New Zealand, among others. Some of our live recordings of classical music concerts were broadcast regularly throughout Europe via a partnership/exchange agreement with the European Broadcasting Union. While we were chuffed to know how much our Canadian content was valued by audiences internationally, other public radio stations were tight for funding too, so program sales didn't net a lot of cash. Still, we persisted—every penny counted.

There were other content-bundling ideas. Ted Kennedy proposed starting a radio "news wheel" service that would curate and syndicate our radio news and current affairs content. We piloted a schedule and Ted set out to see if there were any buyers. There were nibbles, but not enough to cover the costs.

We thought about weather. Weather is big business. We've all grown used to seeing graphic headlines that practically screech: "RUN FOR YOUR LIVES!" I see that CBC National News has now outsourced weather to the Weather Network, but at the time we wondered if extra funding might result from the government if we were officially Canada's Emergency Broadcast Network, like ABC in Australia.

I suspect Canadians already think that CBC *is* Canada's Emergency Broadcast System. It is not, although CBC does excellent work in times of crisis. I saw CBC staff in action in the spring of 2011 while travelling with Johnny Michel, managing director of CBC stations in British Columbia. We were driving along Highway 16 (also known as the "Highway of Tears" due to the unsolved disappearances of young aboriginal women) from Prince George to Prince Rupert. The smell of smoke hung in the air, and as we drove we often didn't know if we were heading into or away from a major fire. Our cell phones were in and out of range and CBC Radio was our only safety net. The station provided updated information as to where and in what direction the fires were burning and relayed information from local emergency services. As it happened, we were unexpectedly waylaid, not by fire but by debris. A large grey rock suddenly crashed through the windshield, having bounced off a passing hay truck. Johnny was covered in glass and had a big stone in his lap, but luckily he wasn't hurt. We traded the car for a five-hour bus ride into Prince Rupert (executive travel at its finest!) while the fire crisis continued unabated. When we arrived in Prince Rupert, the smoke was dense and the staff had little time to meet—they were working full out, relaying fire updates to the B.C. interior.

What I'd learned from my contact in Australia was that being the Emergency Broadcast Network took an emotional and physical toll on their staff. They were broadcasters, after all, not emergency rescue operators. But as I watched the fire devastation in Northern Alberta in the spring of 2016, I wondered what might have happened if we *had* managed to launch a new service in Fort McMurray.

I mention the EBN story simply as an example of the number of rocks we turned over trying to figure out how to fund all the imperatives set out in the Broadcasting Act. And since we'd never have enough for everything, the question of how to spend what money we did have was all the more confounding.

As Richard put it succinctly in his book: "A plan for the future of the CBC also needed to resolve the contradictions of the Corporation itself. The tensions and uncertainties—whether the CBC was a vehicle for popular culture or the higher arts, small towns or large ones, popular music or classical, advertising or ad-free, need to be explicitly addressed and resolved one way or another. Until it was absolutely clear what the CBC was about and how it wanted to move forward, it would be impossible to produce a sensible or coherent approach. The CBC needed a plan with teeth."

Wisdom teeth, I think he meant.

There was no sense hanging about waiting for a new mandate. We pushed on, dedicated to delivering service to Canadians whenever and wherever they wanted it in whatever way we could afford it.

IF CONTENT WAS KING,
CONTEXT WOULD BE QUEEN

"I get so much information, I haven't a clue what's going on!"
— RON JAMES

BESIDES CUTTING JOBS, SEARCHING for money, and growing digital delivery, my main focus as general manager was the CBC English radio stations — Radio One (talk), Radio 2 (music), and Radio 3 (online music); to grow audiences; and to support President Hubert Lacroix's strategic vision of the time: "People, Programs, Pushing Forward."

Radio One

Happily, Radio One was in solid shape. Its bouquet of programming offerings, from current affairs to comedy, from science shows to drama series, was robust and well received. The brand integrity was strong and our core audience was intensely engaged. Morning shows across the country were consistently in the number one, two, or three top-rated positions. We were enjoying historic share numbers of Canadian audiences. Incredibly, Radio One was capturing 65 percent of all talk-radio listeners and we were confident that the days of radio weren't numbered. As I've heard Andy Barrie say: "Humans are genetically wired to the sound of the human voice, and radio is here to stay."

Despite the success of the service, we did have a significant challenge: attracting and retaining younger listeners. Radio One's audience was steadily growing older. That was fine; so was Canada's population. But younger listeners and new Canadians were not gravitating to the service the way they had in the past. We needed to woo new listeners without disenfranchising the existing audience, and we needed to do that in the face of increased competition from both new and traditional sources and a general softening in radio listening globally. Oh, and with no money.

Millennials are as good as lost to traditional broadcasters. They're not impressed by the rigid one-to-many model of over-the-air media. They're not content to listen passively or to wait patiently for their favourite show to appear. They consume content in bite-sized, time-shifted, self-controlled chunks on mobile devices and laptops, tablets and phones, and soon, I expect, subcutaneous chips. They're multi-tasking maniacs. Social media plays a huge role in determining what they want to watch, listen to, and comment on. As digital guru Don Tapscott told us, "Community trumps content."

That didn't mean we were about to give up on content. What it meant was that we had to retain an unblinking focus on excellence as we engaged community. If listeners could choose to listen to any radio station in the world—dial-in news from Asia, current affairs from Moscow, drama from the BBC—or stream any music they wanted from an ocean of choice, why would they choose to listen to CBC Radio?

For me, the key came down to one word: context. They used to say "content is king"; but when you could get headlines from anywhere, who could you turn to, to make sense of it all? Our answer: the CBC. In a world of choice, what had emerged was a filtering and contextual failure, and we saw *that* as Radio One's opportunity. If content was king, context would be queen. We would amplify relevance and deepen meaning for the audience in the programs we offered. We would apply the highest quality standards to inform, enlighten, and entertain. We would protect our journalism and strive to be the most trusted, unbiased, relevant Canadian source. And we would continue to be excellent. "Good" wasn't good enough for the public broadcaster. While others raced to the bottom, we would race to the top.

My new mantra became: In a world of choice, why us?

We resolved to extend Radio One's broadcast leadership into the digital world so that when our listeners wanted even greater context on a story, or to engage with a like-minded community, they could do so online.

Our radio program development plan became what we called a

"360-degree approach," requiring concepts for new shows (piloted for the summer season) to include multi-platform applications and interactive technologies; existing shows, meanwhile, would adopt new social media tools to engage with their audiences.

It wasn't just a question of moving audio to online—we needed to embrace the correct and most efficient tools. Content is not agnostic; it must fit the device. For example, audio content travelled better online when it came with pictures.

One of the most effective ways to enhance our digital radio content, we found, was to add video. Chris Boyce and the Q producers were already there; the radio studio was wired with cameras. That video-added value was proven conclusively by Jian Ghomeshi's astounding interview with Billy Bob Thornton.

I'm wincing to use it as an example now, given everything that has transpired around Jian Ghomeshi, but it remains a convincing illustration of how visuals can heighten the dissemination of information.

Billy Bob had arrived for his interview on Q with members of his band, the Boxmasters. Jian read his introduction: "While Billy Bob Thornton's name is most often linked to his cinematic endeavours, the Boxmasters is anything but a diversion from the silver screen. He's always intended to make music and he just got sidetracked. These days, music is a major priority in his life and it's something he's obviously embracing."

Billy Bob's reaction to the intro was to become instantly irritable and uncommunicative. He insisted there had been a communication with Q's producers not to mention his acting career. To my knowledge there had not. On the contrary, CBC producers fight hard to ensure the journalistic integrity of their shows; an agreement to not mention a key piece of information about a guest would have been extremely unlikely.

Here's a snippet of how the conversation went:

JG: Billy Bob, you guys formed in the last couple of years, right?

BB: I don't know what you're talking about.

JG: How so?

BB: I don't know what you mean by that.

JG: Well, when did the band form?

BB: I'm not sure what that means.

JG: Oh…Well…when did you guys start playing together?

Silence. Billy Bob was looking away and frowning.

It went downhill from there. Billy Bob deflected and obfuscated, Ghomeshi struggled, the Boxmasters squirmed, and the interview got crankier and more uncomfortable by the minute. It was riveting.

Ghomeshi's *audio* interview with Billy Bob was instant news. I was in New Brunswick at the time and my phone was crowded with messages asking if I'd heard it. When the *video* footage was uploaded to the *Q* site, it went viral. It became the number one most-viewed video on YouTube and had audiences in the U.S., Britain, Pakistan, Kazakhstan, and beyond. The interview was a mesmerizing, slow-motion train wreck. The segment went on to garner over 3.5 million views. There's no question it was compelling content, but the story would not have travelled so far if it had only been audio.

Together, the radio teams achieved a lot, including the goal of attracting younger listeners. We were able to positively adjust the mean age of our audience to a healthy, sustainable fifty-two years old. (Coincidentally, I was fifty-two at the time, and feeling quite robust.) We didn't lose our core audience in the process and we had attained historic audience numbers — growing our share by a full point. Every Radio One objective required focused teamwork and engagement from producers, talent, managers, and staff from many departments throughout the CBC. We were under pressure to deliver while our resources shrunk, but the joy was in working with smart, dedicated, principled people day in and day out.

Radio 2

The growth potential of Radio 2, the channel dedicated to music, presented a more serious challenge. Over the years, the channel had focused on classical music, resulting in a very peculiar audience demographic. Half of Radio 2's audience was over sixty-five. That wasn't a problem in itself — CBC wasn't ageist — but they were, as is said, not getting any younger. Radio 2's audience was growing older at *twenty times the national average*. It wasn't that our "silver tsunami" was aging more speedily than other humans like some fifties sci-fi movie, it was that there were so few younger audience members tuning in to Radio 2 that they weren't there to help spread out the demo. As a result, the average age of listeners had increased twenty years in twenty years. It was the same audience growing older every year. If the service did not succeed in attracting younger listeners, the audience would essentially die off. Radio 2 needed to engage younger, more diverse audiences to be relevant to more Canadians.

The month before I arrived at CBC, Radio 2 had just been relaunched to address this challenge, as well as a second one: its mission to serve *all* musical genres. Based on the results of a massive arts and culture study and consultations with over 325 industry groups, orchestras, cultural leaders, arts writers, and the CBC board of directors (it was a two-inch deck!), the new R2 was launched with a camel of a schedule unlike anything I'd ever seen.

It was a block genre schedule, starting with singer-songwriters in the early morning, flipping to classical mid-morning, followed by a blend of easy listening, then a more aggressive drive mix in the late afternoon, with various jazz and special-interest shows in the evening. No other modern music station demanded that their audience follow them from Verdi to Valdy.

That said, the reasoning behind the schedule was bang on — to celebrate Canadian music in all its genres — but it was impossible to please everyone with only one station. (Shades of MuchMusic's programming dilemma, but with the added classical conundrum.) The launch brought cheers from Canadian singer-songwriters and outrage from classical music fans and opera lovers (classical was removed from the mornings, but still took up the bulk of the afternoon). Within days of my arrival I was being cornered by classical music lovers everywhere I went. At the ballet, beautifully dressed ladies and gentlemen demanded an explanation; my mum's friends swarmed me at dinners; my cottage neighbours called from their kayaks; even Bryan Adams' opera aficionado father shared his views on the phone with vigour. I offered to come over to people's houses and hook up the four new digital classical music streams myself, but there were no takers.

We weren't about to make a change to the schedule again — the relaunch had been two years in the planning — but we could definitely fine-tune the one that had just launched. The goal was to make Radio 2 the "most powerful force in Canadian music." While the privates sold ads, we would sell music.

To do that, the service needed a targeted promotional campaign, some announcer training, and some "tweaking" of the music mix in terms of song selection, formatting, and genre transitions.

The station was playing a lot of "discovery" music in support of emerging Canadian artists, which I loved, but I also understood that it's demanding for an audience to listen to music they've never heard before for too long. We humans love the familiar—it's why playing the hits works on commercial radio. We needed to find the right mix of familiar and discovery in order to dial our audience numbers up. Music programming is a craft that private broadcasters invest millions of dollars in, wanting to know within seconds if a song is resonating, to learn what makes listeners tune in and out. We would have to borrow some of that knowledge—not to make Radio 2 a "hits" station by any means, but to take advantage of the tricks of the trade where they were useful in terms of audience retention.

Instead of programming hit after hit, we would see if we could increase the appeal of new, unfamiliar songs by providing superlative "intramusic" and "intrapersonal" talk. Intramusic talk provided information about the artists and intrapersonal talk focused on enlightening the audience on ways to listen. Some of our established hosts, like Tom Allen, who has a master's degree in music performance from Yale and is a writer as well an accomplished trombonist, were especially good at it. It was, in a way, a revamp of an early FM style that had disappeared from commercial radio.

Unlike Tom, many of the new R2 hosts were in the announcer chair for the first time. It was an accomplished ensemble of working musicians, including acclaimed mezzo-soprano Julie Nesrallah, alternative hip-hop artist Rich Terfry (a.k.a. Buck 65), the handsome Tom Power, who played in a band called the Dardanelles, and the wonderful jazz singer-songwriter Molly Johnson. Laurie Brown, host of *The Signal* and my former co-host on *The NewMusic*, is an accomplished broadcaster, but she too had done time in a pop band, and you can't get more of a musician than Randy Bachman. His show *Vinyl Tap* would grow to become one of the hits of the service. The schedule was rounded out by *A Propos* host Jim Corcoran, one of Quebec's leading singer-songwriters; *Saturday Night Blues* host Holger Petersen, who owned and ran his own label, Stony Plain Records; jazz musician and vocalist Tim Tamashiro; and George Stroumboulopoulos, who plays the piano and in his earliest days on air was a radio DJ.

The new Radio 2 hosts had naturally good radio voices, but more than that they were curious and musically accomplished. They were used to talking to audiences in their live shows, but addressing a crowd from a stage is different from the tight, entertaining, informative storytelling chops needed on the radio, when talking to one person—the listener.

The first performance meetings seemed set to take a page from arms-crossed, shoelace-examining love-in of the funding-cuts town halls. Performers can be resistant to coaching, but once we got started, it was useful and generally appreciated. Everyone wanted to be great.

And we needed to be great quickly. We were about to launch some new promotions.

TO MY SURPRISE, THE CBC had never sponsored a national tour. In commercial radio, telling your audience they could win tickets to see U2 was a huge advantage. We dove in and were able to secure both Leonard Cohen and Diana Krall tours right away.

Another bit of fun that garnered us a lot of attention was the Obama 49 contest. The idea was to introduce new U.S. president Barack Obama to Canada through our music, and the audience engaged with fervour, arguing, voting, and sometimes sending essays defending their choices. In the end number one was Rush, number two was Gordon Lightfoot, number three k.d. lang, number four Leonard Cohen, number five Stan Rogers, and so on. Glenn Gould and Oscar Peterson were in there, too. We compiled an iPod with the playlist for President Obama. There were some naysayers, of course—why hadn't we celebrated a Republican president in the same way?—but overall, it was a smash.

The Great Canadian Song Quest was another promotion that resonated with the listeners. When I found out that Gordon Lightfoot's "Canadian Railroad Trilogy" had originally been commissioned by the CBC, we thought we ought to revive that tradition. Listeners vied for their favourite places across the country and then voted on which artists would best capture them in song. It was a solid marketing initiative for the station and the audience engaged mightily. The Quest ended with a concert and an iTunes compilation of thirteen new songs celebrating the country's musical legacy, including tracks by Joel Plaskett (the Cabot Trail), Hey Rosetta! (Gros Morne National Park), Hawksley Workman (Algonquin Park), and Lucie Idlout (Iqaluit).

We pushed hard with communications to launch a new attention-grabbing advertising campaign. We couldn't afford to be safe. One TV spot that I thought was stunning featured a bored young man listening to his iPod on the streetcar. When he tunes into Radio 2 his entire experience changes, and he finds himself on stage having grown wings and entertaining thousands of adoring fans. The song in the spot was from K'naan, who was, at the time, virtually unknown. I loved his song "Wavin' Flag," and thought, *Hey, why not give a struggling new Canadian artist a leg up?* Funny in retrospect, as we subsequently watched the song blow up around the world when its "Celebration Mix" version became Coca-Cola's anthem for the FIFA World Cup.

By the end of the year, we'd succeeded in moving the needle on Radio 2. We'd raised the profile of the service and the audience numbers were starting to move in the right direction. But there was much more work to do.

Radio 3

Radio 3 was a digital music service that had grown out of an abandoned idea for a third broadcast radio network. It was a Webby Award–winning, user-generated site that celebrated Canadian independent music. Radio 3's motto was "Breaking New Sound," and their branding was quirkily Canadian. Radio 3's mascot was Bucky, a proud yet benevolent male deer whose head had been grafted onto the body of a Canada goose. (I suspected that Bucky had not been approved through head office.)

Radio 3 staff were based in Vancouver and were led by the irrepressible Steve Pratt. When I arrived, the site was populated with over 85,000 songs uploaded by more than 19,000 Canadian independent musicians. That number soon crested 100,000. Who knew Canada even *had* that many independent musicians? Radio 3 was at the very fore of building and servicing online music communities, sharing personal playlists, and exuberantly promoting new releases. There were cheeky blogs, live streams, concert calendars, and active links where fans could, and did, purchase music. It was a happy hive of Canadian content and musical patriots, and — bonus! — the Radio 3 community were loyal CBC listeners.

We were learning a lot from Radio 3 about how communities engaged online. Years before Instagram, we were getting photos from Radio 3 fans eager to show their affection by goofing around with the CBC logo (a.k.a. "the exploding pizza"). They made CBC logos out of things like sandwich meat and perogies. They baked it into cookies and fashioned it into stained glass. They knit it into sweaters and ties. There was a photo of one gentleman who had a large CBC logo tattooed in black ink on his forearm (though he may have been a fan of the service in general).

The Radio 3 audience were not only keen enthusiasts, they were young and fiercely Canadian: organically, without (ironically) a regulation in sight. One of my happiest moments was when we were considering how much foreign music we should program on the service. Some thought we should stream more American hits, while others thought we should boldly proclaim the site 100-percent Canadian. It was an internal argument that went round and round until R3's fearless leader Steve said, "Let's ask the users." It was a nail-biter of a weekend. We promised the audience that we would abide by their decision and made the voting process completely transparent. The listeners voted overwhelmingly to make the site 100-percent Canadian. I was so proud.

Radio 3 was instrumental in helping us understand the best ways to engage audiences digitally—hugely valuable when it came to building new content ventures from scratch.

Brave New Waves 2.0

Three new digital content initiatives that we managed to build were CBC Music, CBC Books, and CBC Comedy. There were small advertising revenue projections attached to their builds, which helped in gaining support for the projects within the company, and they had Richard's blessing. He especially liked CBC Books—it was his idea. We were all interested in owning niches in the new digital landscape. It offered us the opportunity to be both a broadcaster and a narrowcaster.

The idea that radio could be, in a sense, "PVRable" was an attractive prospect. Unlike television, radio wasn't an "appointment tune-in" medium. Our core CBC Radio One audience typically turned it on and left it on, even through a wide variety of content—they were that loyal to the brand. The great advantage of digital delivery is that you can super-serve many content niches at once by curating similar genres such as comedy, current affairs, or science shows together.

With podcasts and other online archiving tools, listeners could create a personalized, customized programming schedule as they liked, accessing their favourite shows when *they* wanted to, not when we happened to program them. It was a shift from *our* schedule to *your* schedule.

For CBC Radio, the most obvious niches to compile were areas in which we already excelled.

CBC Music

Our goal for the CBC Music website was that it be recognized as the premier source for Canadian music, offering a full spectrum of genres in partnership with Canadian musicians, creators, and industry stakeholders.

It was a lofty goal, but we were inspired. The timing was right and we had an exceptional team. Advances in technology gave us the tools, and CBC's long-time investment in recorded concerts, interviews, documentaries, and specials on radio and television gave us the content. Even though the traditional music industry was experiencing catastrophic disruption as sales for physical recordings plummeted all over the world, interest in music had never been greater. We would take advantage of this opportunity by creating a musical ecosystem powered by a myriad of on-demand digital and mobile tools with live hosts and highly customized music streams. We would focus on the celebration and discovery of new Canadian talent and take advantage of our terrestrial Radio 2 service as a "Power of the Tower" promotional instrument to the new site.

A strong CBC Music site could also help resolve the Radio 2 challenge of serving all genres of Canadian music with only one terrestrial channel. Online, there could be channels for everyone.

CBC already invested more in recording live music than anyone else in the country. We worked with over three hundred Canadian organizations, funding the recording of (at one point) hundreds of new live concerts every year. An online music site would carry advertising and sponsorships, and we hoped to negotiate new revenue-sharing agreements. One day we might also negotiate new rights that would allow us to unearth the wealth of previously recorded concerts held captive in the vaults by outdated rights agreements.

And we would grow audience. Younger listeners lived online. Getting their attention would be a challenge, but we intended to create a new space where they could gather, listen, watch, and play with connective toys they didn't even know they wanted yet. We'd be a musical Gretzky, but we'd have to do it quickly.

We gathered a dozen of our brightest, most bushy-tailed digital thinkers and set about brainstorming the most mind-blowing music site ever. They were some of the happiest hours I ever spent at the CBC. The group was a machine of bold ideas, imagining endless customizable streams and extraordinary community functionalities, giddy with innovative possibility.

I set about crafting the pitch, and admit I went a little crazy with my penchant for alliteration. Apparently, the music site was brought to you by the letter C. The new site would be Canadian. It would build Community with active music discovery. It would Curate its Content using the best musical navigators in the country. It would Connect artists to audiences and fans with each other. It would be highly Customized with personalized playlists, member pages, and favourite features. It would add Context to the music, with personality and enriched information. It would provide Cohesion, bringing music together from all our media lines and allowing music Content to be accessed seamlessly. It would Celebrate Canadian Creators, becoming a musical Catalyst and a meeting place for Canadians to engage with musicians. We would Communicate our support for homegrown music to the world and make Ca$h while we did it. With revenue from paid downloads, premium subscriptions, advertising, syndications, ticket sales, and merchandise, we would Compensate the Content Creators! I cobbled together thirteen Cs! Lucky 13.

Functionally, Radio 3 had its detractors, because it didn't operate on CBC's digital mainframe. Its success was considered unscalable by some, even though the site had already enabled many of the features we needed to launch at CBC Music. I played offence at head office, hoping the build could continue in Vancouver, not content to wait behind larger revenue-generating departments like CBC Sports or News. Richard was onside conceptually. He liked innovation, but he also needed to ensure that all the moving parts worked together.

The team forged ahead. We determined which social media functions were essential to the launch and which we could add later. We decided we would offer web radio channels for a dozen genres of music to start, including classical, jazz, singer-songwriter, alternative, hip-hop, electronic, and world beat; we would add new genres and streams as we built up steam.

There would be fan pages on which to commune and build personal play-lists, contests, "Buy" buttons, and a ticket hub for special CBC music events. At Radio 2, we began to add video to some of our live concert recordings. We started to roll out high-impact signature events, beginning with a much-lauded Hip Hop Summit in Toronto, celebrating twenty-five years of Canadian urban music and featuring K'naan, Michie Mee, Kardinal Offishall, the Dream Warriors, Maestro Fresh Wes, and Choclair. We began the many conversations with rights holders.

I hosted a Music Day for a wide range of industry experts, musicians, promoters, labels, publishers, programmers, and of course Apple, hoping the new site would be the answer to some of their challenges as well. We'd be dead in the water if we didn't have the support of the industry. Given the rights negotiations that the site would require, we would need everyone on board. (That would be no small feat. When I walked Richard through the list of rights and agreements negotiations required, he said, "It's like having bees in your head!")

I saw the music site as a boon for everyone, and certainly for classical music. The R2 changes had stirred up a ruckus not only with fans, but with some industry players, as well. As an example, after seventy years CBC had ended their funding relations with the CBC Radio Orchestra based in Vancouver. We were the last public broadcaster in North America to fund an orchestra, but ending the relationship was still a difficult decision that got some bumpy public play. As a peace offering Mark Steinmetz, CBC's director of music, and I guaranteed some future concert recordings and access to rehearsal space, but the sore spots still chafed.

As it happened, the next meeting of Orchestras Canada—where we wanted to announce our plans for the CBC music site—was in Vancouver. Mark was dubious we would be welcomed. He was not eager to enter the lion's den again, having endured the wrath of audiences and orchestras during the Radio 2 launch. But I—ever the wide-eyed idealist—was hoping that they would see the new site as helpful. Essentially, we would build the site and they could populate it. It would be one large gathering-place where the entire classical community could interact, promote their content, celebrate their triumphs, and serve their regional audiences. A classical Radio 3.

Mark and I rehearsed the presentation on the plane and then again at breakfast before the meeting. The gathering was eerily quiet as I made my way to the podium. I wondered if it wouldn't have been a good idea to put up some chicken wire: conductors have good arms on them. I pressed play on the PowerPoint and started talking. Once the presentation was over, there was silence. Crickets. I looked at Mark. He was holding his breath. I looked for an exit.

Then, one person started clapping. It was Erika Beatty, then head of Symphony Nova Scotia. Erika was a progressive leader bent on reinventing her programs and her audiences. Her clap grew into applause. We were saved.

It turned into a great meeting. We found common ground in the challenges before us: negotiating rights with musicians' unions and attracting younger audiences. We kicked around some amusing conundrums, like whether it was a good idea to allow tweeting from the concert hall to help spread the word. We concluded our presentation wearing neither tar nor feathers and flew home with renewed energy to be a force for good in the classical community.

CBC Music launched after I left. It didn't have every bell and whistle that we'd originally conceived, but it was up and running. God speed to them.

CBC Books
Compared to the music site, the book portal was a snap. Richard found us the initial seed money, even though the revenue projections were tiny. The Canadian literary world was undergoing some of the same massive shifts in distribution that the music industry had gone through a decade earlier. They welcomed a new place where the love of reading could be championed.

Publishers knew the power of CBC Radio to sell books. Shows like Eleanor Wachtel's *Writers and Company* and Shelagh Rogers' *The Next Chapter* had legions of stalwart fans. Regional radio shows across the country interviewed local authors regularly, and we had our own CBC Literary Awards in fiction, non-fiction, and poetry, which were long-lasting though relatively unknown. And of course there was *Canada Reads*, one of the country's most popular and influential literary events. As with the Scotiabank Giller Prize, the winning book invariably becomes a bestseller. Lawrence Hill has publicly acknowledged the stunning impact *Canada Reads* had on *The Book of Negroes* when it won in 2009. Incredibly, he won again in 2016 with *The Illegal*.

The Books team was as excited as the Music team and planned an ambitious site that would aggregate our content and build robust community around it. In phase one we would curate our own deep database of radio and television, audio and video interviews with authors, and *Quill and Quire* magazine's archive of reviews. We would add functionality for the audience with contests, reviews, book clubs, and social media. I wanted a *What's My Line?*-type section where famous Canadians uploaded photos of their bookshelves and we had to guess whose home library it was. I suppose if I'd had a better title, like "Shelfies" (actually, can I ™ that right now?), it might have met with more enthusiasm...

We launched phase one to applause from the book community in the CBC atrium and soon after live-streamed radio's *Canada Reads* competition to over twenty-two countries. It was deeply satisfying to be able to share CanLit with the world, and its success helped to open a door for me to ask Jack Rabinovitch to consider bringing the Scotiabank Giller Prize back to the CBC.

CBC Comedy

CBC Comedy was piloted next. Someone said that "Laughter is the sound of understanding." So if anyone's wondering why comedy should be in CBC's "mandate"...What more need be said? Canadians are especially good at comedy and it's a fine export. From Mike Myers to Martin Short, from Samantha Bee to the king of *SNL* Lorne Michaels, it's nice that we can help our American friends find the funny. We all need a good laugh.

CBC Radio has had a rich history of funny business, from the early days of the thirties and forties with *The Happy Gang* and *Wayne and Shuster*, through *The Royal Canadian Air Farce* starting in the seventies and *The Dead Dog Café Radio Hour* in the nineties, to today's *The Irrelevant Show* and *Laugh Out Loud*. We were delighted when Steve Patterson's *The Debaters* made it to TV—albeit for one season. Television, for its part, had hit the magic number of one million viewers with its shows *This Hour Has 22 Minutes* and *Rick Mercer Report*.

Pat Kelly and Peter Oldring's *This Is That*—a hilarious parody of the CBC itself—was one of the newest comedy shows on radio. The show not only bit the hand that fed it, but swilled it around and spat it out on your foot, grinning all the while. Many listeners have been conned into thinking its comedic take on current affairs shows was real. They wrote and phoned in outrage over a Montana town that changed its name to Banff, Alberta, Canada; expressed concern for sixty-eight people lost in a corn maze; and were indignant that a man had been an unpaid intern his whole working life.

The Comedy website was originally envisioned as a user-generated model. Comedians uploaded their work, vying for a top spot as voted by the public; happily, the comics were paid for their pleasure. Jeff Ulster was the wizard behind the curtain and the early testing he did with material from radio's *Laugh Out Loud* show met enthusiastic response. It was originally called CBC Punchline and evolved into CBC Comedy. Go for the laughs!

CBC Radio App

The CBC Radio app was a marvellous digital success story. The Radio 3 team in Vancouver initially led the way. To me, they were like the overnight elves in the workshop, leaving beta versions in development to play with in the morning. Steve Billinger, head of CBC digital strategy and business development, brought Apple in and powered it forward. It was early in the app development world and Apple was enthused about working with a brand as strong as CBC, especially at a time when only 800,000 people in Canada owned iPhones. The CBC Radio app hit number one in the News category on the first day of launch and by day five reached number five overall, having been downloaded by 15,000 Canadians. By year's end, Apple voted the CBC Radio as one of the top ten apps of the year.

In the six months following the app's launch, Radio One's podcast downloads increased from 600,000 per week to a million per week. Research showed that one-quarter of all podcasts then downloaded in Canada were CBC Radio's. It was like having a brand-new radio station and was a strong affirmation that smart digital strategies could both super-serve existing audiences and attract (and, we hoped, retain) new users.

ALL OF THIS NEW digital activity served to underscore to me that, at the end of the day, it's the content that matters. Yes, a modern CBC must serve Canadians via new distribution methods and on new devices, but as Apple knew so well, it was the content that compelled people to engage, and ours had to continue to be exceptional. As exciting as it was to introduce new digital offerings and offer new ways to put the "public" in "public broadcaster" with user-generated content, none of it would matter if the programming suffered. So while we were cutting in some areas and repositioning in others, we held our breath over the summer for the 2010 BBM (Bureau of Broadcast Measurement) fall ratings book, when our audience numbers on the main service — CBC Radio One — would be measured.

THE SUMMER OF 2010 at the CBC was particularly memorable. There was a G20 conference, new summer radio shows, and a sudden change in management.

The G20 gathering of the world leaders was happening right across the street from our headquarters in Toronto, and the CBC's contingency planning was impressive. Led by operational Yoda master Fred Mattocks, every possible impact on the staff, the building, and our ability to broadcast was considered and all contingencies tested, from the simplest (protesters interrupting traffic), to the most alarming (a catastrophic event, wherein the CBC building would be reduced to a smoking black hole). Given how the G20 actually unfolded, from the kettling of protesters to the secret laws enacted to search and detain, I was grateful for every contingency and comforted that the CBC was in such capable hands.

Ruth Abernethy's Glenn Gould sculpture dons a gas mask.

The summer of 2010 also debuted eight new shows on CBC Radio One, including the aforementioned *This Is That*; a Jann Arden vehicle called *Being Jann*; *Promised Land*, which told the stories of new Canadians; and David Suzuki's *The Bottom Line*, chosen from a lively jury process led by Chris Straw and Chris Boyce in the programming department. If the new summer shows resonated strongly with the audience, as had *White Coat, Black Art,* and *Age of Persuasion,* they would end up on the full schedule.

The summer is a good time to experiment, for obvious reasons. But when September arrives and the audience returns to their more regular routines, it's all hands on deck. The staff had been going full out, doing more with less, and I hoped they'd be rewarded with good ratings in the big fall book.

And were they ever. Even with reduced staff, the new repeat schedule, and a new audience-measuring device (BBM had moved from manual ratings books to PPMs—"electronic people meters") our combined share had grown to 14.7 percent for Radio One. It was another historic high. It was doubly exciting because we were bucking the trend. Research was showing that, overall, Canadians were listening to less radio and spending more time online. At that year's International Radio Program Awards at the New York Festivals, CBC radio and news programming won an astounding seventeen awards, including CBC Radio winning the coveted Broadcaster of the Year award (the Best in the World!) for the fourth time. Gold and silver award winners included *The Current, Ideas, Afghanada, Sunday Edition,* and *Q.* I could barely see Anna Maria Tremonti across the CBC table, there was so much hardware on it. It was a stupendous achievement for a broadcaster under fire, and validation that radio staff was still churning out exemplary programming. I ran around the Toronto building with cupcakes and congratulations, hoping that our lead would hold to the next ratings book, and the one after that.

CBC's hardware haul at the New York Festivals.

What hadn't held was Richard's relationship with Hubert Lacroix.

(24)

FUTURE-READY

"Always forgive your enemies; nothing annoys them so much."
——OSCAR WILDE

IN AUGUST 2010, RICHARD was suddenly just...gone.

We knew Richard had been feisty at board meetings—he was not a shy man. But it seemed that he and Hubert were becoming less able to hide their irritation with each other as they sought to determine new direction for the Corporation. As Richard wrote in *Tower of Babble*, "Things were getting worse all around...We were working at complete cross-purposes. Bain was frustrated. The board was frustrated. The president was frustrated. I was frustrated." Richard wanted the aforementioned "plan with teeth": clear direction on the mandate issues—commercial or non-commercial, high art or pop culture, big stations or small stations, etc. Hubert was president of a crown corporation and wanted due process. The Corporation had engaged Bain & Company, a team of outside consultants, to help set future strategy for the CBC. Richard was not a fan. The exercise was time-consuming and executives were grumbling. I'd been through a similar process at Sony, when McKinsey & Company was trying to make business sense of the merging of two multinationals. I was reminded of the wry comment I'd heard from my Sony boss Rick Dobbis at the time: "They borrow your watch so they can tell you the time."

Still, there was naught to do but play ball. Maybe they *could* provide a remedy for what was described as the "schizophrenia" of the Corporation—the endless tug of war between money and mandate, stretched over a muddy programming puddle in the middle. As long as the CBC was dependent on advertising, it compelled the broadcaster to present popular programing on television that would attract big audiences, but at what cost to the brand?

Richard didn't buy the argument that popular meant poor quality. His vision was to make the CBC 100-percent Canadian in prime time, filling the schedule with well-crafted Canadian shows that "people like to watch." Richard wanted to solve what he saw as the utter market failure of the English-language television system, which was that Canadians preferred to watch foreign shows instead of their own. At the time, the list of top twenty TV shows in Canada were *all* American — *Grey's Anatomy*, *The Amazing Race*, *Entertainment Tonight*, and *Glee*. The numbers showed that we celebrated American television entertainment culture before our own, and it was a sad state specific to English-speaking Canada. Quebec enjoyed a robust homegrown star system sprung from a desire to protect its language and culture. Chart-topping shows like the long-running *Virginie*, *Tout Le Monde en Parle*, and *Yamaska* were must-tunes for legions of French-Canadian viewers.

There were lots of reasons for the imbalance, including the size of market versus the cost of production, our proximity to the largest pop culture producer in the world, and Canada's simultaneous substitution system (where Canadian TV stations buy broadcast rights to American shows and air them at the same time as the American transmission, but substitute Canadian advertising for the American ads).

Richard believed that CBC could produce English-language programs that were both distinctive *and* popular. And he largely succeeded. Shows like *Little Mosque on the Prairie*, *Republic of Doyle*, *Battle of the Blades*, and the Canadian adaptation of *Dragons' Den* regularly attracted audiences of a million people. It was his "Tim Hortons versus Starbucks" approach — more populist, less elitist. Whether these shows were entirely "distinct" or properly served the mandate to "inform, enlighten, and entertain" was a lively argument. For me, programs had to pass the "click" test. If you were clicking through channels and didn't know right away that what you were watching was on CBC, then it wasn't distinct enough. I enjoy watching a Canadian series shot in St. John's, Newfoundland, or in Indian Head, Saskatchewan, but I also wanted more arts programming produced in bold new ways. Why can't ballet be shot with the intensity of a figure skating commercial?

Richard found the endless tug of war exasperating, precisely at a time when CBC needed bold, clear direction. Suddenly Richard was no longer seen prowling the halls. It all felt a little too quiet.

NEWS OF RICHARD'S DEPARTURE was met with mixed reactions. Some said good riddance, while others respected his bullish vision to reinvent Canadian prime time. You couldn't argue with success over six years. The television audience market share had increased 34 percent overall. Press reports wondered if dismissal was the reward for success at the CBC. It wouldn't be the first time or the last when that question was pondered as the back door closed on a colleague.

Hubert Lacroix said in a short news release: "It was an opportune time to ensure alignment of the senior team on the future of the public broadcaster." The statement was debated in the halls. Did it mean that the course we were on in English television was out of alignment? But Hubert confirmed the current path when he named Kirstine Stewart, then head of English TV programming, as interim EVP. The money was in television and consistency was important while the search for Richard's replacement was on. Kirstine had been in charge of specialty channels at Alliance Atlantis before Richard recruited her to the CBC, and she'd brought *Being Erica* and *Little Mosque on the Prairie*, among other shows, to the TV schedule. I didn't know her well—she was seldom at the weekly executive meetings (though the network programming office was always represented)—but I did remember reading more than once that a fortune teller had foretold that her future was to be prime minister.

Hubert informed staff there would be a wide executive search for the new EVP of English Services in both official languages. I got a call asking if I would consider applying for the position. I had television experience and I was a senior executive in the company. I thought about it, but what I really thought about was radio. Radio needed a fearless champion at the executive table and while I certainly had my fear*ful* moments, I was fortified by the importance of the mission and the value CBC Radio held for Canadian listeners. I was proud of CBC Radio's success, I enjoyed the culture of the service and its feisty folks, and it was exciting to be working on the new multimedia digital initiatives, building to the future. At work and at home, I had enough on my plate.

I decided not to put my hat in the ring. I pledged to salute and support the next EVP and hoped the committee would recruit someone exceptional. Looking back, I realize I should have been thinking more strategically. I made a Career 101 error.

If you are ever considered for advancement in a company, you should always engage. Even if you go through the interview process and aren't awarded the new position, you'll have had a chance to strut your stuff. It's also helpful to the company for overall succession planning, to get a clearer sense of the vocational aspirations of their employees. You'd think I would have learned at Sony that in the corporate world, ambition rules. But at the time, career advancement wasn't my main motivation. Stewardship of CBC Radio was. Turns out career advancement wasn't in my future either. Six months after the new EVP was announced, I was restructured.

In January 2011, Kirstine Stewart was officially named EVP, English Services. At the time, the CBC was in admirable shape and the media lines were playing nicely together. Radio was a valued partner in some of the big company-wide initiatives such as Live Right Now and One Million Acts of Green (championed by Julie Bristow, executive director of factual entertainment). Radio producers found ways to integrate promotional support for TV on air and online, and had been particularly supportive around FIFA, an event that dovetailed beautifully with our diversity initiatives.

TV's audience share was up and before Richard left it had once again been named Media Player of the Year by *Marketing* magazine. New shows like *The Lang and O'Leary Exchange* and *Power and Politics* were doing well. News was delivering more live, breaking news across media lines, and *The National*'s numbers were growing. Kirstine promised to get rid of *Jeopardy* and *Wheel of Fortune*.

On the radio front, current affairs shows were going full throttle, handling a very busy news cycle with the Arab Spring, the federal budget, a royal wedding, and the earthquake and tsunami in Japan. Radio launched a solid summer lineup, including a spirited new drama, *Backbenchers*, by playwright (and two-term Dartmouth MP) Wendy Lill, and veteran CBCer Brent Bambury's Saturday-morning *Day 6*. And, to my delight, the local service extension project finally got some traction.

It was exciting to see that initiative as a cornerstone in Hubert Lacroix's "Strategy 2015" five-year plan. Ted Kennedy, myself, and others on the radio team had been pushing the service-extension rock uphill for two years, piloting new workflow assumptions in Cranbrook, Nanaimo, and Kingston, honing the business case, and strategizing about which locations when. The project had expanded beyond radio to involving tri-medial reporters equipped with light digital technology, which meant the initiative was no longer squarely on the radio table but now in the capable hands of the news department's Heaton Dyer, who would steer it through all the departments and the rest of the way home. (The first local digital-only CBC service was launched in Kitchener-Waterloo in 2013, and the plan has continued to evolve, with service extensions now in Kamloops, Saskatoon, Hamilton, and Quebec.)

There were, of course, new challenges to the budget. CBC TV, like other broadcasters, was required by August 2011 to make the expensive conversion from over-the-air transmitters to digital. And there was the persistent worry was that the Corporation would lose *Hockey Night in Canada*.

Soon after Ms. Stewart assumed her new executive vice-president position, we did what helpful CBCers do and briefed her on radio strategies and priorities. My intent was to be reassuring; radio wasn't a problem child. Chris Boyce and I scheduled a tour of the radio programs in the Toronto building to introduce Kirstine to as many of the hosts and producers of our iconic national shows—like *Cross Country Checkup*, *As It Happens*, *The Current*, *The Sunday Edition*, and *Q*—as time would allow. We had only a short window in her schedule, but I assumed we'd have more time down the road. I'd also had the chance, a few months before, to spend an early hour with her in the control room of the *St. John's Morning Show*. We'd watched two radio staff manning the three-and-a-half hour show—one on-air host and an operator who sourced and played back audio stings and interviews, managed the call-in phones, cued her host, and monitored the front door for guests, all at the same time. I hoped the octopus agility required to keep the show on the air had made an impression. You don't know till you go, after all.

But in March, I started to feel the ground shift. Kirstine implemented a new reporting structure that meant the regional stations would now report to CBC News editor-in-chief Jennifer McGuire. Previously, regional managing directors had shared reporting "dotted" lines to radio, to TV, and to news. On paper, this was a cleaner structure, but to me it seemed that radio's position in the company structure had diminished.

I tried not to take it personally. I knew from a business point of view that the moves toward a "modern content company" would involve consolidation. It didn't serve to dwell on personal politics. Moreover, it was suddenly the politics of the nation that had everyone's attention.

On March 22, Jim Flaherty tabled the 2011 Conservative budget. On March 25, a non-confidence vote won in the House. On March 26, Governor General David Johnston dissolved parliament and an election was called. On May 2 the Conservatives won a big majority and on June 2 the forty-first Canadian parliament convened.

These were three mega-months for the media; everyone from the news department to our radio current affairs teams were working flat-out to keep Canadians informed. The executive team was also looking at Ottawa, expecting that CBC/Radio-Canada would be called to appear at its CRTC licence renewal hearing in the fall.

I was oddly excited about the appearance, knowing from experience that it would bring an opportunity to acknowledge our successes and present future strategies. No hearing is complete without interveners, and we dove in to encourage participation. I sent out over a hundred letters to high-profile Canadian cultural leaders and artists asking for letters of support, and was chuffed by the speed and level of support we were receiving back.

On June 8, Kirstine hosted the TV fall launch, announcing the season's lineup to the gathered press with CBC TV stars in attendance. Select radio hosts had been asked to join as well — Carol Off, Anna Maria Tremonti, and Jian Ghomeshi among them. I knew they'd gone to some trouble to attend. They'd adjusted their schedules, moved interviews around, dressed up, spent time in hair and makeup. During the event, Kirstine gave a shout-out to radio from the stage, acknowledging Jian Ghomeshi. While the crowd applauded Ghomeshi, I watched the other radio hosts stand a little taller in anticipation of hearing their own names, but they were not announced. After the event, I got an earful from Carol Off and Anna Maria Tremonti. They were insulted — not just for themselves, but for the disrespect they felt it implied to radio.

I took it up with Kirstine. I hoped she would appreciate the feedback, perhaps schedule some one-on-one time with radio hosts... But that's not how it went. Her leadership style was different from Richard's.

Two weeks later, on June 22, I was in Ottawa, having been asked to attend a CBC board meeting with Kirstine Stewart and Jennifer McGuire. Also attending were Sylvain Lafrance, executive vice-president of French services, and Alain Saulnier, managing director of news and current affairs in French services, Jennifer's counterpart at Radio-Canada. Jennifer was there to report on the results of the recent News Balance Study commissioned by the Corporation, and I was expecting to take questions on radio current affairs programming and to describe the processes radio undertakes to ensure journalistic fairness and balance.

It wasn't unusual for executives to be asked to appear so soon after a federal election, nor was it unusual for CBC/Radio-Canada to conduct independent analyses of its news content to (as is described on the CBC website) "assess our news content and services in terms of breadth and depth, impartiality, credibility, accuracy, fairness, and balance..." The previous study of the federal election (2009) had "found no indication of partiality in the network's coverage. They also found that all political parties represented in the House of Commons were treated equitably and that no bias was evident."

Radio-Canada presented the results of a similar independent study conducted for their news department (by the Centre d'études sur les médias), which said in part, "There is likely no bias in the Radio-Canada teams' attention to the different parties in the running." Alain and Sylvain defended their journalistic coverage as balanced and fair. That said, it was a feisty meeting.

Alain recounts the meeting in his personal diary in his book *Losing Our Voice: Radio-Canada Under Siege*: "Presentation to the board in Ottawa on equity and balance. Was 'skinned alive' by P. Gingras about biased coverage of Harper and by R. Racine on the election night coverage. A tough moment."

Next, it was English Services' turn. It was an animated discussion. I remember speaking to all the ways in which we worked to ensure fairness and balance in radio programming, from the diversity in voices to the range of opinions to adherence to the Corporation's recently updated Journalistic Standards and Practices bible, and came away thinking that both Jennifer and I had represented the journalistic rigour of CBC English services well.

The next day, on June 23, it was announced that after thirty-three years, Sylvain Lafrance was leaving Radio-Canada. He would stay on until October to ensure a smooth transition. (Alain was handed his walking papers in February 2012.)

On July 6, 2011, I went to attend my biweekly meeting with Kirstine. She greeted me on her way out the door. There was another body sitting in her office: Human Resources. That was a shocker. The HR rep began to inform me of the contents of the envelope in her hand, but I asked her to stop. She looked like she was about to cry, and I knew that if she did I would too. I was not escorted from the building. I went to my office, shut down my computer, and collected my purse. I took my Charlie Pachter print off the wall. Staff loved that painting. I'd hung it as a comment on what happens to the CBC when funding is continually cut. It's a painting of a skeletal moose. The caption reads: "So I guess that's it then."

I left the building and drove home feeling angry and a little dazed, but one thing I was very clear about—I knew I would never regret standing up for all I believed the CBC to be.

The note to staff announced Chris Boyce's new role as executive director as part of a "restructuring" in English Radio Services (the radio GM position had been eliminated) and thanked me for my support of CBC and the values of public broadcasting, adding that I was leaving CBC Radio "more than ready to meet the future."

We'd had the highest ratings share in the history of CBC Radio and had surpassed our internal targets. The audience demos were healthy, and our multiplatform advances were bringing exceptional results in audience engagement. The new book portal had been successfully launched and the digital music strategy was well in hand. The service extension plan was alive and every small station was still standing. Twenty of twenty-two morning shows were in the top three; nine of them held the number one spot. I felt indeed, that radio was future-ready.

I headed to the cottage and waded through volumes of email, from people at small stations to big stars at TV, through blurry eyes. Friends arrived. They brought wine and pie and comfort food. Murray offered food for thought. "One day people will know how much you saved," he said.

It took a while to shake off my anger. I dragged my hurt around like Jacob Marley's chains for way longer than I should have, but I learned to let it go. It was too heavy to wear and it didn't suit me. I've tried to focus instead on gratitude. To the smart, funny friends I made at the CBC who are still in my life, and to the colleagues I can still hear on the radio and watch on TV, I'm applauding you from here.

CANADIANS DESERVE
A STRONG CBC

"Don't it always seem to go, that you don't
know what you've got til it's gone."
—JONI MITCHELL, "BIG YELLOW TAXI"

IT WAS TOUGH TO watch CBC from the sidelines. The Corporation seemed to lurch from one upheaval to another, while the cuts came in waves. The 2012 budget contained reductions of another $115 million over three years. In April 2013, Kirstine Stewart left to run Twitter Canada and later became Twitter's VP of media for North America. (She left Twitter North America in 2016.) In September, Heather Conway, the Art Gallery of Ontario's chief business officer, was named EVP of English Services and was greeted with the loss of *Hockey Night in Canada*. In October, Conservative Minister of Canadian Heritage James Moore announced a second five-year term as president for Hubert Lacroix. In April 2014, Hubert Lacroix announced another 657 job cuts over two years to cover a further $130-million loss to the budget, of which 334 full-time jobs and $82 million would come from English services. This time it would mean a significant reduction in the sports department; fewer original TV series; the cancellation of radio drama; reductions in overseas news bureaus; and a further decrease in live music recording. In-house documentary production was gutted, regional supper-hour news production was reduced, and late-night news was lost in the North. Respected CBC journalists Alison Smith and Nancy Wilson announced their retirement, and investigative journalist and Scotiabank Giller Prize–winning author Linden MacIntyre tied his departure directly to the cuts. He knew what the impact would be on young producers and reporters and wanted Canadians to get the message that these job cuts were not meaningless. On top of that, in June of 2014 there was another announcement of an estimated 1,000 to 1,500 job cuts by 2020.

Employees were pushing back, some openly challenging the president and the CBC board to do more to fight the funding crisis. That same June, at a presentation called "A space for us all" to unveil CBC/Radio-Canada's 2015-2020 strategic plan, a representative from the Canadian Media Guild suggested Hubert Lacroix should "protest and resign." Also that month, a group of former board members, including Robert Rabinovitch (president from 1999–2007) and Guylaine Saucier (chair from 1995–2000), sent a letter to CBC board chair Rémi Racine, which read in part:

> We call upon you to clearly and publicly inform the government that these cuts will effectively eviscerate the CBC/Radio-Canada and will ultimately bring about the demise of this important and valued national public service.

In November protesters marched in the streets in Montreal, Quebec City, and New Brunswick, and a letter of resignation was presented to Lacroix demanding his signature at the CBC Annual General meeting in Montreal. The following fall, on October 29, 2015, CBC/Radio-Canada's two largest unions, the Canadian Media Guild and the Syndicat des communications de Radio-Canada, issued a statement on the CMG's website that called for Hubert Lacroix and the CBC board to step down. Isabelle Montpetit, president of the Syndicat, told the *Toronto Star* simply: "We concluded that [Lacroix and the board] no longer have legitimacy."

Hubert Lacroix's 2014–15 *annus horribilus* was exacerbated by the news that he had wrongly claimed $30,000 in "living-related expenses," which he promptly repaid and apologized for. It was embarrassing for a president who had pledged transparency throughout his tenure. More transparency questions erupted when Peter Mansbridge and Rex Murphy were scrutinized over speaking fees, followed by controversies around Amanda Lang and then Evan Solomon over alleged conflicts of interest. The controversies and relentless cost-cutting were surely taking a toll on morale.

But none of it was in the same league as the shocking sexual abuse allegations against CBC Radio host Jian Ghomeshi.

The news rolled out with an announcement that Ghomeshi was taking an indefinite leave of absence. I, like many, thought he was taking time off to mourn the death of his father. But two days later, CBC announced that their relationship had "come to an end." Then came the infamous Facebook posting, a 1,500-word piece from Ghomeshi protesting his dismissal and admitting to "rough consensual sex." At first his post was met with tremendous support, receiving approximately 100,000 "likes," as people on social media decried the CBC for firing him. "The CBC has no business in the bedrooms of the nation" was the revised Pierre Trudeau quote.

But when the accusations of sexual assault began to surface, the tide turned. Ghomeshi's PR firm left him, as did his agent and manager, his book publisher, and the musical artist he managed, Lights. Ghomeshi filed a $50-million, then $55-million, lawsuit against the CBC. A month later, the suit was withdrawn. (He filed a grievance through the Canadian Media Guild in accordance with their collective agreement.) Then came formal charges. On October 1, 2015, Ghomeshi pleaded not guilty to five charges: four charges of sexual assault and one of overcoming resistance by choking.

When the allegations first surfaced, I was glued to the news coverage like everyone else and shocked by what I saw. Friends, family, and the media began to call, but I had little to say. I was not aware of any complaints of violent conduct toward, or sexual harassment of, women by Ghomeshi. Moreover, I was curled up in a ball, wrestling with what to do.

This felt personal to me—for two reasons. One, I'd been head of CBC Radio for three years. Who were the women? Did it happen under my watch? If it did, why didn't I know? Murray couldn't understand why I was taking it all so terribly to heart; but there was a second reason. The sexual assault allegations that were coming forth from an increasing number of women brought back a dreadful memory of my own that I had submerged for forty-five years. I had to talk to my mother before I could open up to my husband. I needed to tell her first about what had happened to me when I was fourteen.

I was sexually assaulted by a man that was known to our family. It happened in the front seat of his car. He had offered me a ride somewhere. At first I was flattered by his attention, but it got bad fast. I remember how hard it was to kick when my pants had been pulled around my knees, but I was lucky. I had the strength to fight him off. And no, I don't want to talk about it anymore. It was traumatic then, and it's hard to write about it now. I can still smell the upholstery.

Mum was upset to hear what had happened. She wanted to know why I didn't tell her then. "Your father would have dealt with him," she said.

"I didn't want there to be trouble," I said. I'd thought it was my fault.

About ten days after the Ghomeshi scandal broke, I sent a note to a few dozen close friends and family which told of my assault and said, in part:

> I didn't think I could read another word about Jian Ghomeshi, but here I am writing. To show my support for the women and to share what I know as a former executive at the CBC.
>
> This is what I know. When I first walked through the doors at CBC in Toronto I remember being impressed with the level of employee support. There were signs in bathrooms and public space advising staff that if they felt stressed or overwhelmed support was available. There was a number to call, people to talk to, sexual harassment policies were clear.
>
> It certainly felt like a workplace that empowered women; the number of women in management was over 50 percent, the place was booming with smart, strong women. My overall sense was that people took "respect in the workplace" seriously, yet we hear now that a young female producer at Q says she left, rather than file a complaint. I wish that young woman had knocked on my door. If I had heard the words "Hate Fuck" in the workplace, I'm sure I would have reacted like a mother bear.
>
> People are wondering if Jian's "star" status protected him. It's true he and the show were held in high regard by the audience and by the Corporation. But so are many "star" radio personalities hosting respected shows created by talented producers and staff. This story feels so personal to so many because he was the smart, suave, trusted voice on the radio, and radio is a very intimate medium. We thought

we knew him. I've read that the CBC is conducting an investigation into whether their policies and practices can be improved. That's clearly the right thing to do.

I hope that women who have the courage to come forward are treated with grace and respect by everyone. I know how gut-wrenching it would be to "tell," let alone formally accuse someone of sexual harassment or assault. This story has brought my own event fully forward.

For my sisters, I wish you strength in speaking your truth and stamina on the journey. May you receive buckets of love from your family and friends, and eventually find peace. At the very least, perhaps this dreadful situation will result in stronger support for victims of violence, that it will heighten our vigilance and deepen our compassion.

Yours,
Denise

I received many tender and supportive responses to my note, but I also got responses that were unexpected and deeply disturbing. Women friends, some of whom I'd known well for many years, shared their own stories of sexual assault. One woman told me that she had been raped as a teenager and never told anyone. Her attacker went on to rape and murder another woman. The man was imprisoned for murder, but she lives not only with the horror of her own rape, but with the guilt that because she didn't tell, another woman died.

It's the walking wounded out there.

Former *Toronto Star* reporter Antonia Zerbisias started the Twitter hashtag #BeenRapedNeverReported with Sue Montgomery, a journalist friend in Montreal. Both women had been raped and never told. The hashtag went viral, trending worldwide. Within days there were over eight million participants on the site, testifying and telling their stories. Women were feeling a shift from "victim blaming" to "victim empowerment."

For a moment.

Then came the trial in February 2016.

The trial was to hear five criminal charges brought by three women relating to four separate events. Every day, Ghomeshi and his lawyer Marie

Henein travelled a gauntlet of cameras and protesters on their way to the courtroom. In court, Ghomeshi did not speak. As the complainants brought forward their testimony one by one, the focus began to turn on the "reliability and credibility of the complainants," and on March 24, 2016, Judge William B. Horkins acquitted Jian Ghomeshi of all charges.

In his decision, Judge Horkins referred to the witnesses' testimony in language that included the following: "a failure to take the oath seriously"; "wilful carelessness with the truth"; "inconsistencies"; "proceeded to consciously suppress relevant and material information"; "flirtatious emails"; "an undisclosed evidence of a continued relationship"; and "possible collusion." "Put simply," he wrote, "the volume of serious deficiencies in the evidence leaves the court with a reasonable doubt." He also wrote: "My conclusion that the evidence in this case raises a reasonable doubt is not the same as deciding in any positive way that these events never happened."

Horkins' verdict was met with outrage and so-called "hashtag activism." The judge was accused of "victim blaming," the lawyer of "betraying all women," and protesters marched to police headquarters.

(An assault charge brought by former *Q* producer Kathryn Borel was withdrawn by the Crown on May 11, 2016, when Ghomeshi signed a peace bond, apologizing to her for his behaviour in the workplace, causing another wave of reaction.)

Many questions arose and were debated in the news and in social media. Why weren't the complainants better prepared? Had they been failed by the system? Why was the focus so heavily on what happened *after* the alleged assaults rather than on what happened *during*? Is there a difference between law and justice? If the complainants had told "the truth, the whole truth and nothing but the truth," would the verdict have been different? Will this trial and other high-profile cases deter women from coming forward in the future?

I wrestled with the questions and debated the answers with my friends—some of whom are lawyers, and some of whom are women who have been hurt and even raped. There was a wide range of opinion and expertise, and little consensus. I examined my own feelings as much as I could bear to. When I was assaulted, I did not tell. And I'd had no reason to assume I would not be believed, especially by my father, who had seen too much of the damage done by those who abused power and privilege. But even so, telling isn't the same as bringing formal charges.

In court, the complainant's credibility is examined, her private life is exposed, and she must relive the trauma of an experience she's tried hard to forget. Cross-examination has spanned the distance from "What were you wearing?" to "Why couldn't you just keep your knees together?" — a question Alberta Court judge Robin Camp actually asked a nineteen-year-old woman in a sexual assault case in 2014. (A formal inquiry has been called to determine whether Judge Camp, who was promoted in the interim to the Federal Court by Peter MacKay, should remain on the bench. He is currently not hearing cases.)

There is much that is right about our system of justice. The burden of proof is high, and people who are charged are given the presumption of innocence until proven guilty. That is as it should be. People have a right to a fair trial and the evidence must be tested as a caution against false accusations. But there is also something very wrong. I'm not surprised when women tell me they don't trust the system. They point to alarming numbers in sexual assault cases. According to an analysis of Statistics Canada data by University of Ottawa professor Holly Johnson, in Canada in 2012, out of 1,000 incidents of sexual assault, thirty-three were reported, twelve resulted in charges, six went to trial, and three resulted in convictions. How is that not a fail?

High-profile cases of sexual assault have brought a shift in the conversation and we must continue to ensure that our judicial system is the best it can be. Women and men who find the courage to report must be treated with respect and all the actors in the system, from the police to the bench, must be sensitized to the many human ways people react to sexual assault. I doubt there's a "normal" for anyone. (And by the way, the word "victim" should never be equally applied either—I certainly don't see myself as a victim.)

If we in North America don't protect the vulnerable with the laws and procedures we've so painstakingly developed, how can we ever be credible in reaching out to help women who have no voice, no protections at all?

THE CBC WILL WEATHER this scandal. And now, with the renewed funding of $675 million over five years which the Liberal government has promised, there is hope it may even thrive as it further evolves as a modern public broadcaster.

There are those who think the CBC needs to be blown up and built again. It could certainly be blown up, but Gzowski was right; rebuilding it would never happen. There are simply too many economic, ideological, and competitive forces that would defer it, derail it, or delay it to the point where we'd forget why we even needed a Canadian public broadcaster in the first place.

Let's remember that the CBC was created initially to "foster a national spirit and interpret national citizenship" and to "guard against" the flood of foreign content coming our way. That was in 1928. Has it succeeded? Not entirely. Who could have predicted the torrent of content that's now available? Actor Eric Peterson has described Canada as an "occupied country" when it comes to English Canada's consumption of American pop culture and news. He's not wrong.

The CBC needs to be strong and free. I'll even accept "As Canadian as possible under the circumstances," but we need to deal with it properly now. That includes an urgent mandate review and an update to the Broadcasting Act. We need to reset the governance from the president to the board, and determine a new funding mechanism (commercial or not) that would enable it to meet a clear, redefined mission with excellence.

Otherwise, just get it over with. Put up the colour bars and walk away. Maybe one day the institution will be visited by prospecting historians looking for answers as to where Canada went.

R. B. Bennett and Mackenzie King showed leadership thinking in the creation of public broadcasting in Canada and we need leadership thinking now, as we ponder what national spirit and citizenship Canada will be celebrating on our 200th anniversary. The question remains:

Q: Why should Canadians invest in a strong public broadcaster?

A: Because we deserve it.

We deserve to live in a thriving democracy of informed, engaged citizens who value inclusion and diversity. We deserve quality information: news and current affairs coverage that is fair and balanced, that doesn't insult our intelligence, that investigates matters of interest to Canadians and demands accountability. We deserve an innovative creative culture where the arts matter, where we're encouraged to think differently. We deserve a place to wrestle with our concerns and explore our shared values. We deserve to have a gathering place to tell our own compelling stories through our own unique lens. We deserve a public forum where we can celebrate our triumphs and share our humanity, where we can laugh together or mourn as a nation. We deserve a place to imagine our future together. We deserve a strong CBC.

(26)

THE ZOOMER:

MY WAY OR THE HIGHWAY

"We can disagree without being disagreeable."
— BARACK OBAMA

CONRAD LOVED IT WHEN I quoted Obama.

On October 7, 2013, a new television show called *The Zoomer* debuted on Moses Znaimer's VisionTV. Imagined as a weekly current affairs and lifestyle show (*Television for Boomers with Zip!*), it was co-hosted by Lord Black of Crossharbour—and me.

"What's it like working with Conrad Black?" everyone asked, handily replacing the "What are you doing now?" question I normally got when out and about.

"Fascinating," I'd say. "No surprise we are seldom on the same side of an issue, but I didn't expect him to be so generous."

"Yeah, he can afford to be..." Some people can't resist a little snark.

"I mean generous of spirit. He's charming with the crew and curious about the guests. He treats the show like it's a clever cocktail party with cameras."

Which is what we wanted the show to feel like. And what it was—at the beginning, at least.

Over the years after I'd left MuchMusic, Moses and I had spoken about me joining his growing Zoomer empire. Since 2008, Moses had been building an impressive media company aimed at the fifty-plus (soon to be forty-five-plus) audience, which he saw as a growing legion, a demographic typically ignored by traditional media and advertisers. "Zoomers" had time on their hands, money in their pockets, enthusiasm in their hearts and…elsewhere (as Moses liked to point out). By 2012, ZoomerMedia included television, radio, print, digital media, conferences, and trade shows, and was affiliated with CARP (Canadian Association of Retired Persons), an advocacy group with more than fifty-five chapters in Canada, of which Moses was president.

At our earliest conversation about his "new vision for aging," I was fifty-one. According to Moses, I was the "perfect Zoomer"—I lived enthusiastically, I travelled, I practiced yoga, I drove a Vespa! Problem was, I didn't feel Zoomer-like in the least. I aspired to be younger, not older, and I wasn't sure I was aligned with all of Moses' wide-ranging views. His interest was flattering but I went off to join the CBC.

Four years later, when my time at the CBC ended, Moses sent me his mission statement for a new ZoomerMedia television show:

> The ZoomerDaily (title tbc) will be our flagship program of analysis, commentary, and new ideas; leavened by humour, satire, musical performances, as well as the usual passing parade of Politicians, Pundits, Authors, Actors, Cooks, and Causes. The show will constitute our "take" on the world from a Zoomer point of view. It will pose the following questions: What's going on? What does it mean to me? What is to be done?

The concept was intriguing: a current affairs show that combined culture and lifestyle and was targeted to an underserved demographic. What would it actually look like? I sat down at my dining-room table armed with the daily newspapers, assorted websites and magazines (including *Zoomer* magazine, of course), a massive sheet of white paper, Post-it notes, and coloured markers. I set out to craft the perfect show.

Six hours later, I pushed back from the table, energized. Moses was right—there was no shortage of content about, or of interest to, Zoomers. I'd meant to imagine one show, but I'd written three, laid out in real time like a TV rundown, segment by segment, complete with headlines, bumpers, and commercials.

It was April of 2012, and Madonna, at fifty-four, had a new record; it was the one hundredth anniversary of the sinking of the *Titanic*; and *60 Minutes* anchor Mike Wallace had just passed away. Feature guests could include Linden MacIntyre, who'd just released his new novel, *Why Men Lie*, and Jeanne Beker, who was in the news because *Fashion Television* had been just been cancelled after twenty-seven years. For music, we could have Gordon Pinsent, Blue Rodeo's Greg Keelor, and Travis Good of the Sadies do a music performance from their record *Down and Out in Upalong* ("Upalong" being what Newfoundlanders used to call Canada). Maybe Gordon would tell that funny story about the marijuana cookie he'd eaten by mistake at a recording session, which could lead into an update on the latest in medical marijuana.

There was a rise in STDs in retirement homes and many current affairs stories in the papers were perfect for Zoomer panel discussions on topics like:

- Canada's lack of planning to deal with dementia

- Should senior drivers require mandatory testing?

- A "Who's Zoomin' Who?" segment on Canada's fighter jets

There'd be inspirational quotes and fun bumpers with health tidbits called "Fruit and Fibre" (not all my ideas were keepers), as well as gardening and cooking segments. A "ConZoomer" panel would test the latest products (like those walk-in bathtubs), and we'd have a "Zoomerang" for audience polls and feedback.

There was a wealth of in-house talent at the Zoomerplex. There was Suzanne Boyd, *Zoomer* magazine editor and political junkie; consumer advocate Dale Goldhawk; Dr. Zach Levine for health and wellness; David Cravit, author of *Beyond Age Rage*; Libby Znaimer, vice-president of news and information at Classical 96.3FM and AM740; and the redoubtable Susan Eng, then executive vice-president of CARP, for all the important advocacy issues. And conveniently, there was a bible. Moses had been deep in the subject of aging for years, philosophizing on issues that ranged from alternative medicines to dying with dignity, all of which were all published in his monthly column in *Zoomer* magazine.

The chance to build something totally new doesn't come along that often. If *this* was anything like the show Moses had in mind, it was a show I would love to help create. I'd missed producing shows while I'd been in management, and it had been two decades since I'd been an on-air personality—maybe I was past worrying about what I looked like on TV. The creative angel on one shoulder joined forces with my devil ego on the other, elbowing my insecurities aside. "You'll be back on the A-list!" they whispered. "You'll be asked to *host* galas again, instead of running them!"

Still, I wondered about working with Moses again. I knew him to be an exacting boss; but he was also an innovator, a legend in the TV world.

What could possibly go wrong?

I ROLLED UP MY idea board with the coloured sticky notes and went down to the Zoomerplex for a brainstorming session with Moses and his production team.

Moses seemed delighted with what I'd laid out and his excitement was infectious. He would cost this show and get back to me. I left the rundown template with him and went my merry way. There was no timeline for next steps and I had lots to do. I was off to film in Northern Uganda with War Child and had committed to volunteering with Lake Ontario Waterkeeper for their first Toronto gala, as well as to head a twentieth-anniversary committee of the Governor General's Performing Arts Awards. There were also actual paying job opportunities to consider. I was grateful that the phone still rang.

Five months later, an email from Moses popped up in my inbox. He'd just had an exciting meeting with Conrad Black! He was imagining a Rachel Maddow-meets-Charlie Rose–type pairing.

What the what!? This was not only a surprise, but a different show altogether. We'd talked about comedian co-hosts. What was Moses thinking?

Conrad had been all over the papers that summer, having returned to Canada from his stay in Florida at the Coleman Correctional Institute and then the Federal Correction Institution in Miami as a "guest of the American people." I thought Conrad and I would be oil and water. I certainly didn't see him as a lifestyle host and I was no Rachel Maddow—she was in a political commentary league of her own. No, I wanted the show I'd sketched out. Anyway, it was too late; I had a lovely job offer in the book world. But Moses was never a man to take no for an answer.

He said that the idea of the original show was still on but that it could start as a weekly instead of a daily, and he extolled Conrad's virtues as a co-host. He would not only contribute fascinating conversation, said Moses—and there was no question Conrad had an exceptional intellect and strong opinions—but his notoriety would generate huge interest. I listened, I pondered. I consulted Murray and my good friend Matt Zimbel, a musician, artistic director, and broadcast executive. I'd worked with Matt on our political coverage at MuchMusic and he had run MusiMax in Montreal, so he knew Moses well.

Both Matt and Murray were readers of Conrad's books. (I had *A Matter of Principle* on my Kindle, finding its dictionary function handy when stumbling over words like "fissiparous.") Matt was cautiously enthusiastic and I knew Murray respected the manner in which Conrad had conducted himself throughout his trial and because "he took his punishment like a man" (versus begging forgiveness on Oprah's couch, as was the fashion).

Lord Black had served thirty-seven months for three counts of mail fraud and one count of obstruction of justice as head of Hollinger Inc. I was certainly no expert on his guilt or innocence (the court proceedings were lengthy and understood by few but legal scholars), but he'd done his time and he did it well, assisting fellow prisoners with letters and appeals, among other things. He maintained his innocence, and appeared to have come through a transformative time in his life with grace. I certainly believed in reinvention. We agreed to shoot a pilot.

The next conversation was with Conrad, Moses, MZTV VP of original programming and operations John Moutsatsos-Thornton, and Matt Zimbel, who'd flown in from Montreal. Conrad was congenial and attentive while I walked him through my Post-it note rundown.

It was a stimulating conversation and we settled on a smart dinner-party vibe. There'd be boldface guests. There'd be wine on set! There'd be pitted prunes on the table! (Matt's idea. If anyone engaged in a filibuster, I could disarmingly offer, "Pitted prune?" as a way to truncate a rant.) We thought about feature interview guests, some of whom we managed to book during the season. On Conrad's list were Brian Mulroney, Donald Trump, Nigel Farage, Boris Johnson, and Dame Edna. On mine were Gordon Lightfoot, Karen Kain, Bob Ezrin, and Joseph Boyden. Divergent lists, but I expected there'd be few Venn diagram moments when we'd be keen to interview the same person.

I started to think seriously about Conrad as an on-air personality. Would he be as animated on television as he was in person? Would we get along even if we took opposite views? And most importantly, how would the audience respond?

At one point I asked Conrad: "Can you be any fun?"

"What do you mean?" he said, leaning back in his chair.

"Well," I said, "people will tune in initially because they'll want to see you. You're a polarizing guy. But I think they'll *stay* if the show has some useful information and some laughs."

Conrad raised an eyebrow.

Matt and John joined in. We had thrown around an idea for a sketch while we were waiting for Conrad to arrive.

"Let's say we shoot a skit where I go into a bank to ask for a loan. The bank clerk asks, 'Do you have any collateral?' I say, 'Why yes,' and turn to reveal you walking into the frame."

Conrad smiled. "I believe I can manage that."

I drove home feeling like this had the makings of a wild adventure. Matt agreed to come back to Toronto to co-produce a pilot. Much would be revealed in that process, but I needed to make a decision now.

I liked the idea of returning to broadcasting, and the fact that there were few media outlets that would be banging down the door to hire on-air hosts in their fifties was not lost on me. But the show would be an unknown entity with a controversial co-host—a "convicted felon" at that (good thing my father wasn't around to add his two cents). Conrad was intriguing to say the least, and it would be fascinating to hear from someone who'd been through such a transformative time. There was a vulnerability to him that I hadn't expected. My bigger worry was holding my own in our on-air conversations; I'd need my wits about me, not to mention a dictionary. It was a weekly show, so I'd have lots of time to prepare; I hoped that what I lacked in IQ, I might make up in EQ.

I decided to go for it.

MATT AND I MOVED into a boardroom at the Zoomerplex and got to work shooting a pilot. A temporary set was constructed with the artful design sense of ZoomerMedia's Bill Mantas and Matt, using one of Moses' key symbols—an antique Predicta TV.

One crucial element of the piloting process was to see how well Conrad would perform as an interviewer. He suggested that Margaret Atwood might sit for a pilot interview and she graciously agreed.

It was a lovely talk. We learned that Conrad and Margaret are co-owners of a cow that got auctioned off when the Kingston Penitentiary farm was closed and that they were both, as Conrad put it, "somewhat scandalized by prison conditions in this country."

"We are scandalized," Margaret agreed.

It was not a surprising view given Conrad's recent past, but reassuring to hear how comfortable he was with referencing it.

As on any television show with two hosts, camaraderie is important. I knew that there'd be time to get a sense of the chemistry during the pilot process. We shot two panel discussions, one on "Radical Longevity"—there was no lack of new science or wacky ideas exploring the idea of living to be 150 years old—and another on a subject we thought would offer Conrad a perfect platform to show off his love of history: the recent surge of historical films. Fortuitously, there happened to be a bumper crop of historically based movies in theatres at the time, from *Lincoln* to *Hyde Park on Hudson* to *Argo*—solid Zoomer films and a slam dunk for Conrad. He'd be in his element, addressing the curious inaccuracies of Hollywood. I mean, why *would* a brilliant director like Steven Spielberg find it necessary to fiddle with the facts on the life of Abraham Lincoln? We debated the accuracy of *Hyde Park on Hudson*'s portrayal of a love affair between Franklin Delano Roosevelt and his sixth cousin Margaret "Daisy" Suckley (a hand job in the car? Really?), supposedly based on letters between them. Conrad of course had written a book about FDR and complained that the film took "scurrilous liberties" with the facts, and then played an ace: "Well, I happen to *own* some of those letters…" Okay, then!

We were jubilant after the "Hollywood History" taping. The conversation had been fast, funny, and…perspicacious. And the team was becoming friendly at work and, on occasion, socially.

One evening, Murray and I were invited to dinner with Conrad and Barbara Amiel at their house. For some reason we assumed it would be a small gathering of six or eight people—like the dinner parties we hosted at our house. But this was no small gathering. It was a special dinner for friends who had stood by Conrad during his trial. The guest list was notable, the ambience elegant. We were met by trays of wine and sparkling water held aloft by well-appointed catering staff, one of whom whisked our own proffered bottle away.

Murray and I were chatting with Conrad while dozens of guests mingled in the sumptuous living room. A waiter came by and offered a tray of lobster canapés. When I looked up to thank him, I came face to face with a dear friend of ours.

"Hubert!" I gushed (I may have squealed).

"Hubert!" echoed Murray.

The tinkly cocktail conversation seemed suddenly quieter. I looked around and saw amused eyes upon us. Murray and I chuckled about it later. "Goodness, darling—try and refrain from hugging the help."

That Conrad and I lived in different worlds was brought home even more sharply shortly thereafter, when he, Matt, John, and I gathered in his sumptuous library to refine the list of luminary interviews we would chase for the show. Ever the Canadian enthusiast (it was a pretty American list), I suggested we might be able to get Rush. The band was in the news with their recent induction into the Rock and Roll Hall of Fame.

"Excellent idea," said Conrad. "He's been very supportive."

"Who?" I said, rather surprised. "Geddy? Alex?"

Conrad stared at me. "No, Rush! Rush Limbaugh!"

Right. (Far right, actually.)

We would come to know that library well; Moses insisted that Conrad's "TalkBlack" editorials be shot there. "TalkBlack" was a series of Conrad's personal perspectives that would end every episode of *The Zoomer*. Moses wanted sweeping shots of the library. The camera would come to rest on Conrad, who would deliver his essays straight to the audience. It was a scene straight out of *Downton Abbey*. All that was missing were a tumbler of cognac, a roaring fire, and dogs at the master's feet, although Barbara's two Hungarian kuvaszoks did wander in on occasion.

Matt and I thought it would be useful for the audience to see a more approachable side of Conrad. Matt wrote a series of short sketches called "Five Fun Things to Do with Conrad Black" that included yoga, afternoons in the park, and taking public transportation.

In the public transportation sketch, Conrad and I board a Toronto streetcar. Conrad comes up the stairs behind me and I point to the cash box and say, "The money goes here; no tipping." Conrad's line (which he delivered beautifully) is, "Where's the business class?" The driver's beaming smile as he closed the door was priceless.

In the yoga sketch, I'm twisting on a mat while Conrad is sitting cross-legged in a business suit and bare feet while being instructed to breathe deeply and focus on the "third eye." I lean over and whisper, "You might want to loosen your tie." In another sketch, I'm reading Conrad's *National Post* column aloud while Conrad patiently corrects my pronunciation. I put down the paper and remark, "You know, these are very different big words than the ones Stephen Lewis uses."

But my all-time favourite was "American Justice System," starring Conrad and McLean Greaves, ZoomerMedia's then VP of digital media. Mclean (who has sadly passed away since) was a handsome black man with fashion-forward spectacles and gorgeous dreadlocks. He's sitting on a park bench in the sun reading *A Matter of Principle*. Conrad walks into the shot and sits down beside him. McLean glances over, a quizzical look on his face, then checks the book jacket to confirm that yes, indeed, his bench-mate is the author himself. He puts his book down and says to Conrad, "You know, you're not the first black to have problems with the American justice system." Fist bump!

Matt and I were delighted with the content for the pilot. The co-hosts were getting along well, and we were having some fun. There were a ton of production decisions to make, all of which required Moses' input and approval, but the process was giving us a sense of what he liked and what he didn't, and we still felt we had lots of room for creativity and collaboration. My assumption was that once the pilot was approved, we'd be left to run.

The sizzle reel — the sales tape produced for a U.S. TV buyers' conference — was an early warning signal about editorial control that I did not heed. Cut from the two pilots we'd shot and entitled "Lord Have Mercy, Black Is Back!" it trumpeted Conrad at his exuberant best, with short clips of him saying "Rubbish!" and "We're just chumps!" and "[They're] treating us like bumboys!" underscored by bold gold graphic words like "Lord!" and "Mercy!" cut to grand orchestral music (Gustav Holst's *The Planets*, Opus 32). The tape included the TTC sketch and a clip with *Zoomer* magazine's Suzanne Boyd about sex toys for seniors from an interview that I'd done, but generally it was all Conrad all the time. I was less concerned about my lack of face time than by my feeling that the tape was edited in a sensationalist sales style that didn't represent the ambience of the show I thought we were making.

Moses pointed out that it was just a U.S. sales tape, designed to "get people talking." It *had* to be extreme. Not to worry; I was included—as copy—in the print version (the photo used was only of Conrad): "In every episode Lord Black will conduct a feature interview with some of the world's Greats, and close with an editorial. "TalkBlack" segments will feature his views on issues that really get under his skin—ageism, pension reform, the U.S. justice system, prison reform, gun control, and the world's financial crisis. Co-host Denise Donlon will conduct "The Zoomer Roundtable," a lively discussion of current affairs, health, wealth, and new ideas, enlivened by humour, cooking, and live performances."

At that point I didn't have a contract and there were months to go before we'd actually be making the show for air (Matt and I would eventually sign on as co-producers; Moses was the executive producer). The launch date was eight months away (then anticipated to be September 2013), and there were lots of ideas still floating around. So while Moses investigated U.S. distribution, Matt returned to Montreal to work on his documentaries and I went off for two months with Murray to write. We'd always dreamed of "living like locals" in Italy. Ten weeks, off-season, first in Lecce, then in an Airbnb high on a hill just south of Florence. It was heaven, and gave us ample time to determine whether the stories told of a good bottle of Italian wine for three euros are true. They are!

As I'd expected, news of the sales sizzle reel wasn't confined to the TV world. The press responded with interest. On January 30, 2013, the *Globe and Mail* ran a Brian Gable cartoon that depicted a dowdy production assistant placing a studded mediaeval mace on each of the hosts' chairs. The caption read: "Conrad Black to launch new talk show. Interviewing format anticipated to be...spirited."

THE FIRST EPISODE OF *The Zoomer* aired on October 7, 2013, and it was shot while the paint was literally drying on the walls.

The subject was longevity, with a pre-panel taping on assisted dying. Conrad's interview with Brian Mulroney was already in the can, as was his "TalkBlack" editorial on the U.S. justice system. We'd booked Molly Johnson to perform live. The wine was poured, the set was packed, and the crew were enthusiastic despite their lack of sleep.

There were some technical issues—the tiny new digital cameras offered beautiful images but were a nightmare to focus, and there were some marathon post-production editing sessions dealing with crashes, glitches, and endless changes. But it was a new show and we were all rolling with it. Plus, the unique upside to filming at the Zoomerplex was the presence of a creative multi-tasking team. Where else would the carpenter who built *The Zoomer*'s roundtable during the day operate the Steadicam at night?

Moses was deeply engaged. How tight the shots, how fast the edits, how big the fonts, which music to use, which guests to invite, what topic to discuss, what comments would go to air—all of it required the approval of the executive producer. I understood. It was his show on his channel. I'd expected him to be keenly involved—at the beginning.

ONE OF OUR EARLIEST shows was on ageism in Hollywood. The show opened the same way every week, with a mysterious half-lit over-the-shoulder shot of Moses typing an email of direction (à la *Charlie's Angels'* Bosley telling the Angels what to do). This one read: "To Conrad, Denise. Subject: This week's assignment: *In 2006, a famous Oscar-winning actress said that in Hollywood 40 is the new 100. But since then several major motion pictures have been made starring actors in their 60s, 70s, and even 80s. Are the old new? Or, is this a temporary anomaly from an industry still fixated on 'youth'?"*

Our guest lineup for the panel discussion on Hollywood was stellar: actors Mary Walsh, Wendy Crewson, and Walter Borden; director Ruba Nadda; film critic Richard Crouse; and Zoomer program buyer Beverley Shenken. The rest of the episode promised to be just as exciting: Blue Rodeo would perform live in the studio, and we had astronaut Chris Hadfield lined up for Conrad's feature interview and author Joseph Boyden lined up for mine.

The interview with Joseph, a celebrated writer of First Nations heritage and dear friend, had been booked for weeks; his new novel *The Orenda* was a natural for an author's segment. It had been planned as a pre-taped sit-down interview with me, but when there were no cameras available for the one-on-one (my first feature interview didn't air until the twelfth show), Joseph reworked his schedule and agreed to join the roundtable instead.

As it happened, Conrad was writing a book on the history of Canada, and his "TalkBlack" editorial that day was on Canada's First Nations. He began by saying, "There are rays of hope for the native people," which was great, but I was concerned about other language that followed, especially when he referred to First Nations people "as heirs of a Stone Age civilization" and "victims of a genetic predisposition to alcoholism."

Moses and I argued hard about running it. I lost. Moses wanted "heat."

I believe he got it on that show. During the roundtable discussion on *The Orenda* there was a feisty interchange between Joseph and Conrad, but it was Mary Walsh who really dialed it up.

The conversation started with Joseph describing the rich cultures of First Nations in Canada and the destructive influence begun with the arrival of the French and English. Conrad pointed out that there'd already been a "really terrible degree of violence between the tribes and the bands," and that the "Iroquois massacred the Huron with regularity."

Joseph reminded him that it had been a violent time everywhere — "the Spanish Inquisition was going on at the same time over in Europe" — and argued that the Huron population was decimated "through disease that the French brought." "Not deliberately, of course," he added, when Conrad protested.

Conrad argued that "they hadn't really mastered the wheel, though... it was a primitive culture"; to which Joseph retorted: "They didn't need the wheel; they mastered the canoe." Conrad conceded that the canoe was "magnificent" and asked that Joseph didn't "misunderstand his remarks as being hostile to the people." Joseph said, "When I hear the words 'primitive' and 'First Nation' [together], of course my hackles are going to rise."

At this point I attempted to describe the failure of our educational system to school us properly in all the First Nations' contributions to Canada — the medicine, the democracy, the art, the environmental stewardship. I pointed out that we would have lost the War of 1812 had Canada's indigenous peoples not interceded.

Joseph added that "Canadians too often believe that 1867 came along and suddenly there was a country," but that in fact there were very complex groups of societies in North America before that. Conrad remarked that "it was an under-populated continent," to which Joseph protested that "a lot of archaeologists argue that it was as populous as Europe was, and it was the advent of diseases brought in—"

And that's when Mary Walsh could hold back no more, diving in with vigour: "But who would say it was 'underpopulated'? And who's making these decisions? Is it some high power? Is it a 'lordly' decision that you're making, Conrad, that it's underpopulated?...I mean, every question you ask—although you right after it say, 'Of course I'm not being, in any way... I'm not questioning anything'—you're questioning! Everything! Every single question you asked was offensive to me and I am not—"

Conrad looked straight at Mary and asked levelly, "Are you going to subside soon?" To which she responded: "No! No, I'm not."

It was gripping television.

While the audience milled around for autographs after the show, Conrad, ever curious, asked for Joseph's email address to continue the conversation later. I was hopeful that the words "Stone Age" might not appear in reference to First Nations people in Conrad's forthcoming book *Rise to*

Greatness: The History of Canada from the Vikings to the Present, but . . . you can't have everything.

To my mind, that show delivered what Moses had said he wanted — smart, animated conversation, laughter, music, celebrity, and controversy — but he wanted more of the latter. Over the next months the table got more crowded, the guests more adversarial, the camera framing more extreme, and the editing more intense. It became increasingly obvious that I had little editorial control.

Moses wanted a show that "will have everybody talking about it," and at Moses' station Moses' editorial stance ruled. "I don't make a fetish out of balance," he said. Final cut would always be his.

THE FINAL STRAW FOR me was when *The Zoomer* aired Conrad Black's interview with Mayor Rob Ford. It was December 9, 2013, and everybody was definitely talking about it. Mayor Ford was in scandalous full glory, putting Toronto on the international map for all the wrong reasons. On November 5, 2013, after months of denying that a video showing him allegedly smoking drugs existed, and in the midst of apologies for public drunkenness and under police surveillance, Ford admitted he smoked crack "probably in one of my drunken stupors" and apologized. Two days later, a video showing Ford in an angry, vulgar rant surfaced, and two weeks later he retaliated against former staffers who'd complained to police that he was consorting with a woman they believed to be an "escort or a prostitute." He insisted that the woman was a friend, not a prostitute, and added, in reference to a separate accusation that he'd said "I want to eat your pussy" to a former female staffer, "I'm happily married. I've got more than enough to eat at home." (Matt was driving when he heard that comment and almost ran into a pole.) For many it was the last straw of many straws. Four days later he was stripped of his executive and budgetary powers by Toronto City Council.

In the month before the *Zoomer* taping, Ford was making headline news practically every day; giving him more air time was not high on my agenda. I was not present for the taping of the interview (nor was Matt), nor did I edit it. As it happened, it almost got the show and Rob Ford sued by *Toronto Star* reporter Daniel Dale.

Rob Ford told Conrad: "Daniel Dale is in my backyard taking pictures. I have little kids. He's taking pictures of little kids, I don't want to say that word but you start thinking what this guy is all about..." Dale maintained that Ford had implied that he was a pedophile and served Ford, ZoomerMedia, and VisionTV with libel notices and threatened a lawsuit against Ford and ZoomerMedia if Ford didn't apologize "publicly, abjectly, unreservedly, and completely." At first Ford protested and stood by what he said. Then he apologized. The threat of legal action was dropped.

ZoomerMedia's response was: "We are pleased to see that Mayor Ford has responded to the libel allegations by Mr. Dale by offering a full apology and retraction of his comments. We have always believed that this was primarily a matter between Mr. Dale and Mr. Ford. However, we sincerely regret the part ZoomerMedia played in broadcasting the offending words spoken by Mr. Ford, and apologize for that. We can confirm that those words will never again be broadcast on any of our television outlets or websites."

For a show on a channel whose beginnings were in religious programming, it felt to me like an unholy mess. That interview was my tipping point. It underscored that this was not the show that I had imagined at my dining room table fifteen months earlier. Moses was determined to be a hands-on owner with an editorial point of view, and that was his prerogative. But I could not be a submissive producer, supporting editorial decisions that were not mine. This was not my first rodeo, after all, and at the end of the day it was my face on the show.

I RESIGNED FROM *The Zoomer*. Life is too short to waste time on things that don't serve you, I had to remind myself—ironically, given that Moses's Zoomer philosophy is about living long and living well. Not only was I not using my powers for good, I felt I had little power at all. Still, I count my lucky stars that I am *able* to make a conscious choice about what kind of work I do.

The Zoomer is still on the air. It now appears to be a monthly show hosted by Moses' sister Libby Znaimer or Faith Goldy, formerly with the now-defunct Sun News Network—a channel that was colloquially called "Fox News North." I hope it's making Moses happy.

Do I have regrets about my time on *The Zoomer*? Yes, and you might think this slight in the scheme of things, but one regret was that I wasn't able to influence Conrad's stance on climate change. During the taping of a roundtable on the environment (which, despite my strong opposition, gave equal time to climate-change "skeptics"), we discussed the latest report by the Intergovernmental Panel on Climate Change, which said that scientists were "95 percent certain" that humans are the main clause of climate change. Conrad called the reports "statistical skulduggery." Lost that round.

The Zoomer experience was a footnote, really: eighteen months in my life. But it was an important footnote, because it reminded me that, as I go into my third act, in order to be happy, I have to engage in work that is true to me, that makes a positive contribution, and to be as fearless as possible *whatever* the circumstances.

So bring it on — I'm finally ready.

(EPILOGUE)

I REST MY HANDBAG

"The purpose of our lives is to be happy."
— THE DALAI LAMA

WELL. THIS BOOK TURNED out differently than the one I *thought* I was writing. I didn't intend to belabour the "tales of woe" career adventures that are now crowding the last half of it. (If I had, I might have called it "Peaked Early" and offered it up as a case study to HR professionals.)

No. My intention was to have some fun — to write a light, swashbuckling tale of celebrity adventures (well, as many as those unfortunate confidentiality clauses would allow) in an attempt to a) outrace my wonky monkey memory, and b) offer Duncan an opportunity to read about what happened on that Whitesnake tour (if he ever felt the need).

Even though "Johnny Cash told me never to drop names," I was going to describe the time I danced at Diana Krall's wedding with Steve Buscemi (all knees and elbows), at Elton John's house, or when I was being pressed into service as an "Iron Maiden" for Harry Belafonte (his stage shirt had fluffy sleeves and three snaps that fastened at the crotch). I was going to tell tall tales of The North — in Pond Inlet with Hunk Snow, Barney Bentall, and Mike Stevens feasting on maktaq (note: always bring a nutsack) or golfing for literacy using an *usuk*, a frozen walrus penal bone, as a putter on Frame Lake in Yellowknife (another note: never, ever take the first dog sled run — huskies are explosive poopers). I was going to tell fashion forage stories like the trip to Whitehorse, where I bought some ancient trade beads used by the Hudson Bay Company, then worried that they might be an offensive appropriation. When I earnestly asked Buffy Sainte-Marie if it was ok for me to wear them as a bracelet, she considered for a moment and said, "That's a good question, let me ask you one... Do they match your outfit?" (Magnificent *and* mischievous!) Or that time at the Governor General's Performing Arts Awards when Neil Peart overheard Shelley Ambrose and I competing for who spent the least at Value Village on our gala dresses. (Shelley won that year — $19.00). "Next year you'll be saying, 'I got mine in a dumpster!'" he said.

I also intended to tell more serious stories, but the book was simply too long to fully recount the War Child trips to Northern Uganda or the Thai-Burmese border or other far-flung places.

Turns out, this book was wilful. It kept wandering off on different tacks, wanting to dwell on Canadian cultural industries, on lessons learned and on the "inside baseball" of life as a lady in leadership roles. And I had to surrender, because a) profligate name dropping is as unsatisfying as asking those VJ hopefuls why they wanted to be famous, and b) because only in the writing could I begin to know what I actually wanted to write about.

When I was approached by Sarah MacLachlan (the publisher, not the singer nor Murray's daughter) I didn't know if I had a book in me, let alone if I could write. Sarah advised me to "Just write! Let's see what happens." And so I did. And I soon found out what Salman Rushdie meant when he said, "It just requires so much of you, and most of the time you feel dumb." Totally. I mean, I've always respected authors, but now I'm in fawning awe of them. I've heard of writers who would rather write than eat. That is *so* not me. For me, writing was an exercise both fattening (sitting is the new smoking) and arduous (for someone who carries an imposter demon around in her fanny pack).

I took to putting encouraging phrases on my computer, like "The ass will not kick itself" when I needed to be nagged; or "Kindness, Kindness, Kindness" when I was feeling vengeful; and "Faster, Funnier, Donlon!" when I fell down rabbit holes and felt utterly lost. I had a tendency to overwrite (course, you know that by now). Murray hit the nail on the head when I asked him to read a chapter. "You know how you write?" he said. "*Then the rock star was struck on the head with a piece of falling lavatory ice. But first, let me tell you everything I know about aviation history...*" He wasn't exaggerating. I did spend a good part of a week writing about the history of the Avro Arrow as an example of misguided government action, not to mention examining Dorothy's character in *The Wizard of Oz* as a feminist archetype.

I overwrote because I didn't want the book to be an "unearned memoir." I'm no Oprah or Aung San Suu Kyi or Malala Yousafzai, for heaven's sake. My adventures have been small in the grand scheme of things. But I've come to appreciate that even if the scale of our lives vary enormously, we're all on some sort of hero's journey, grappling with life's obstacles and opportunities, encountering our tyrants and allies, and hopefully, one day, coming to terms with all the forky-tail decisions we made along the road.

I realize now that writing has been essential to my journey. It seems that my path has been about facing the fear and about trying to convince myself that I wasn't, in fact, a "slovenly bitch" or a "clumsy clod" or a "dunce." I'm insecure, yes, flawed and often fearful. But I've tried to walk with truth and to write with as much courage as I can muster.

Publishing a book has been part of trying to "break on through to the other side" — to where the confidence lies, even though I know that I'm setting myself up for judgement, throwing out opinions that may not be shared, relating events that people may not like or even recall in the same way. So if my ego has tricked me into assuming more credit than I deserve, recounting a memory that is mistaken, or neglecting to mention someone who let me stand on their shoulders, I beg your forgiveness. I hope you can forgive my mistakes as well.

Confidence, I have heard, arrives magically for women at age fifty. Fifty was supposed to be when we forgive ourselves our questionable choices, embrace our wobbly bits, accept that we're enough, and begin to live large with new-found self-assurance. Fifty was supposed to be when we no longer gave a damn about what other people thought. Huh.

I remember the morning of my fiftieth birthday. I walked into the bathroom, turned on the light, and blinked expectantly at my reflection, hoping to find my swagger. My first thought was, *I'm exhausted.* The second was, *Fuck. I need to get my eyes done.* Which I promptly went and did. Happy birthday to me. The Gila Monster was finally tamed, and I could watch TV again without holding my eyelids up with both hands. The gift of confidence, however, had not yet arrived.

What did arrive, was a sudden frustrating loss of nouns, and those crazy covers-on/covers-off hot-flash power surges (Murray complaining, "It's like sleeping next to a roast!"). I have to say, the whole "bursting into flames every twenty minutes" thing is irritating—especially at work. Nothing undermines an air of authority quite like having to put down your laser pointer during a meeting in order to strip down to your camisole. Trust me, they look at you differently in your underwear, no matter how tastefully appointed. Still I was willing to go with it—if the return was not giving a damn.

But no, confidence didn't arrive at fifty. But another gift did, as good or better—joy, laughter, and a little bit of wisdom outside of the workplace. I found my tribe. Nine wonderful warrior women (a.k.a. The Tuscany Girls) who travelled together to Italy to celebrate that big 5-0 with two glorious weeks of art, food, wine, and laughter—the kind that had tears running down our legs. The wisdom came in truly believing that life really is about the friendships you have (these gals and more), the people you love, and the contributions you make.

So, while much of this book has been about corporate life, it's helped me to learn that we shouldn't struggle so hard to find value in things that don't serve us. I learned to guard against losing my objectivity with deluded relativism (it's nice once you get in!) and acknowledge that I wasn't willing to do anything to keep the corner office (looking for love in the business world is like looking for love in all the wrong places). The right place to start looking for love is surely with oneself. Not your egotistical grasping self, but your true self; the kind one, the compassionate one, the authentic self. The self that is present when you're outdoors in nature or moved by great art, when you're singing out loud or caring deeply for another.

And I learned that it's one thing to *write* sweet words about kindness and compassion; it's quite another to honour them—to endeavour to leave a positive footprint in this beautiful, chaotic, and sometimes ugly world.

Murray and I have just celebrated twenty-five years of marriage. We've had amazing adventures—in Africa and Asia and Europe (me driving a tank, while he flew an F-16), performing together—once (I was the Scarecrow, he the Lion in a rendition of *The Wizard of Oz*), even laughing (eventually) about me breaking his nose. (He snuck up on me when I was naked in a hotel bathroom in Nashville, putting on mascara. It was an accident! I was trained by my brothers to be skittish.) We don't mix our careers with our marriage; we focus on life. We enjoy our little island paradise at the lake (running water *and* electricity!), my sacred place, and try to be good partners and parents. Duncan is twenty-four now. I want to kayak with him more, lose less at Scrabble (don't ever bet money, he's good), and toast him topping the tree year after year with the old tin star. We look forward to celebrating Murray's beautiful daughter, when she earns her Ph.D. for her thesis on the effect of climate change on people living with disabilities, and to many more years with my lovely mum.

I'm not sure what's next for me. But if you hear that I'm considering another corporate job that requires me to lay off people, feel free to talk me off the ledge. I'm definitely going to keep looking for that confidence. It hasn't arrived yet, but I think I can see it from here.

As Murray sings, "The second half of life, is where the fun begins" (though I have to admit, I had a fair bit of fun in the first half).

> The second half of life is where the fun begins
> You've come to terms with who you are
> Made peace with who you've been
> The most important time you spend
> Might not be from nine to five
> The big wide world just waits for you
> In the second half of life.

NOTES

Chapter 1: Be a Donlon!

The opening quote is from a T-shirt I saw a young man wearing as he walked down the street in my old neighbourhood. I wasn't sure it if was cocky hubris, or a simple matter-of-fact. Still don't know!

Chapter 2: Tall, Flat, and Bullied

The opening quote from Winston Churchill can be found at http://www.brainyquote.com/quotes/quotes/w/winstonchu103788.html.

For more information on the Esher Place Shaftesbury Home school for girls, see http://www.childrenshomes.org.uk/EsherSH/.

For more information on Britain in the 1930s, see Juliet Gardiner, *The Thirties: An Intimate History of Britain, London, U.K.: HarperPress, 2010.*

For more information on Borstals, the reformatories for young offenders in the U.K., see http://www.politics.co.uk/reference/young-offender-institutions and http://www.dailymail.co.uk/news/article-2121843/Brutal-exercise-hard-work-strict-education--topped-bit-musical-theatre-The-days-Borstals-knocked-yobs-shape.html.

I first saw the term "misheightened" on Twitter, written by author Stacey May Fowles.

Chapter 3: Millie's, Music, and Marijuana

The opening quote is something my friend Shelley Ambrose, publisher of *The Walrus*, says all the time. She also says "I rest my handbag," which became another chapter opener. Thanks, Shelley!

The quotation from Bakavi's mandate, "To develop an ecologically sound way of supporting human life," is taken from the back of my Bakavi membership card. It goes on to say: "To encourage life-based pursuits. These would include: interpersonal relations, creativity, co-ordination, appreciation and spiritual, intellectual and psychic development." We were busy!

The motto "Know yourself by self-involvement" is written on the back of my Toc Alpha membership card, which expired on December 31, 1976 and entitled me to "All privileges of TOC ALPHA." Not sure I took advantage of everything . . .

Chapter 4: My Waterloo: Green and Groomed

The opening quote is from Dr. Seuss, *I Can Read With My Eyes Shut* (New York: Random House Books for Young Readers, 1978).

For the list of rider requirements and especially "Things of Legend I'd Heard of But Can't Attest To," I got contributions from friends, drew from personal experience, and did some research on the website The Smoking Gun (http://www.thesmokinggun.com/backstage/rb/tina-turner).

The history of the *Imprint* and the *Chevron* can be found at Howard Fluxgold, "Waterloo's students oust campus paper," *Globe and Mail*, December 12, 1978.

Information on Shere Hite was based on general research and specifically two articles from the time: Jon Shaw, "Fed Sponsored Lecture, $2,700 Worth of Sex Talk," *Imprint*, February 1979; and Anne McNeilly, "Male Domination Must End, U.S. Author Says," *Kitchener-Waterloo Record*, February 16, 1979.

Chapter 5: Vancouver Bound

The opening quote is from Joni Mitchell's song "Urge for Going," *Second Fret Sets*, 1966–1968, released in 1968 on Reprise Records.

The quote from the article on Bruce Allen is by Les Wiseman, "The Mouth that Scored," *Vancouver Magazine*, 1983.

The quote from the article on Sam Feldman is by Rick Ouston, "The Emperor of Rock and Roll," *Vancouver Magazine*, March 1991.

Larry Leblanc did a great interview with Bruce Allen and Sam Feldman, available at http://www.celebrityaccess.com/news/profile.html?id=441. I also found a video interview of me interviewing Bruce at Canadian Music Week: https://www.youtube.com/watch?v=toTzfhGTFSg.

Chapter 6: The Feminist Compromise

The opening quote from Janis Joplin can be found at http://www.brainyquote.com/quotes/quotes/j/janisjopli163010.html.

Cardi's was a signature club, and the band not only set a new house record for the largest crowd since opening night, but also got kudos from legendary promoter Bill Graham, who called Headpins one of the "most professional groups I had the pleasure of working with."

Rob Salem's review of Headpins opening for Loverboy is from "Fans Cheer Loverboy's 'Hunk Rock,'" *Toronto Star*, August 24, 1983.

Chapter 7: Finding My Big Feet: MuchMusic Beginnings

The opening words of David Lee Roth's (which he said to me while we were adjusting his interview lights) can also be found at http://i95rock.com/the-top-ten-quotes-from-the-most-quotable-man-in-rock-diamond-david-lee-roth.

Photo of the original Citytv MuchMusic gang: (Sitting, front and centre) John Martin. (Kneeling) Michael Heydon, Moses Znaimer, Jim Shutsa, Jeanne Beker, Nancy Smith, Jay

Switzer, Elise Orenstein, Ron Waters. (Standing) Sherry Greengrass, Sandy Carroll, Peggy Rennie, Greg Mandziuk, Dennis Saunders, Simon Evans, Christopher Ward, Anne Howard, Brian Neal, Bob Segarini, Dave Johnson, J. D. Roberts, John Gunn, Annette Falcone, Cathy Hahn, Nancy Oliver, Joan Paley, Gail Goldman, Mary-Jo Bennett, Mike Proudfoot, Kathy Porter, Dave Kirkwood, Peter Whittington, Dennis Fitz-Gerald, Jay Levine. From the 1995 Much Handbook. Photo by Dimo Safari.

Lorraine Segato's recollection of the Queen Street West scene was related to me by email.

Martin Short as Brock Linehan can been seen at https://www.youtube.com/watch?v= 3dCEUErRzWE.

Peter Silverman's memories of *Silverman Helps* were related to me by email.

Jonathan Gross, "Those Shaky Starts," *Toronto Star*, April 12, 1986.

Chapter 8: Attitude, Adrenalin, Analysis: *The NewMusic*

The opening quote from Joe Strummer was captured on *The NewMusic* in May 1984.

Interview conversations excerpted here are transcribed from a box of VHS tapes of *The NewMusic* during my time there from 1986 to 1993 (found amongst the spiders in my basement), as well as from recordings in the MuchMusic archival library. Thank you to CTV/Bell Globe Media for graciously allowing me access to their treasure trove of tape, and to Heather Middleton for her prodigious tracking skills.

The quote from Jello Biafra of Dead Kennedys is from *The NewMusic* special *In Your Face: Violence in Music*, which aired in 1992.

The section on *The NewMusic* covering Bob Marley's funeral was recalled to me in an email by Bill Bobek, the MuchMusic publicist who orchestrated the trip.

Watch the coverage of fans rioting at the CNE when Alice Cooper pulled a no-show here: https://vimeo.com/102038547.

The Tom Waits quote on songs can be found at http://performingsongwriter.com/ tom-waits-quotes-quips/.

Eric Hynes, "Six Ways of Looking at Tom Waits, Character Actor," *Phoenix New Times*, October 4, 2012.

Professor Griff's quote in the *Washington Times* was found at https://en.wikipedia.org/wiki/ Professor_Griff.

A report on the Simon Wiesenthal Center's published statement, "The New Sound in Music: Bigotry," can be found at http://www.upi.com/Archives/1989/09/22/ Wiesenthal-ad-charges-bigotry-in-lyrics/8070622440000/.

The February 6, 1990 *Los Angeles Times* report on MuchMusic's ban on all videos by Public Enemy can be found at http://articles.latimes.com/1990-01-03/entertainment/ ca-72_1_professor-griff.

Chapter 9: Music + Meaning = Magic

The Pete Seeger quote is from a *NewMusic* interview conducted by Jeanne Beker (date unknown).

The NewMusic special *The Big Tease* aired on Citytv on November 20 and 21, 1993.

Sarah McLachlan on feminism is from a MuchMusic interview recorded in Toronto on August 21 or 22, 1999.

Caitlan Moran, *How to Be a Woman* (New York: Harper Perennial, 2012), p. 65.

The NewMusic special *In Your Face: Violence in Music* aired on Citytv on November 21, 1992.

The NM special *Earth to Ground Control* aired on Citytv on November 17, 1990.

The excerpted speech by Mark Mattson, founder of Lake Ontario Waterkeeper, was given at the LOW gala in 2014 at the Palais Royale in Toronto.

The NM special *Rock and Roll Ailments* aired on Citytv on August 7, 1989.

The NM special *Rock and Roll and Reading* aired on Citytv on April 20, 1991.

For Neil Peart's current recommended reading list, visit http://www.neilpeart.net/book_club/ and https://www.nypl.org/blog/2012/11/05/neil-peart-reading-list.

The NM special *Corporate Sponsorship* aired on Citytv on November 26, 1988.

The Agenda Inc. findings are quoted in several sources. Here's one that mentions these particular stats: http://articles.baltimoresun.com/2004-08-22/entertainment/0408240461_1_brand-cadillac-songs.

Chapter 10: Work-Life Balance Is an Extreme Sport

The opening quote is from Douglas Adams, *Mostly Harmless: Hitchhiker's Guide to the Galaxy* #5 (New York: Pan MacMillan, 2009).

Murray McLauchlan, *Getting Out of Here Alive: The Ballad of Murray McLauchlan* (Toronto: Viking Penguin, 1998), p. 370.

Much Down Under aired on MuchMusic in July 1991.

Cowboy Junkies' *Intimate and Interactive* aired on MuchMusic on February 7, 1992.

Annie Lennox's *Intimate and Interactive* aired on MuchMusic on March 13, 1995. You can view it at https://www.youtube.com/watch?v=q_kVjrjcSC4.

Joni Mitchell's *Intimate and Interactive* aired on MuchMusic on September 23, 1994. You can view it at https://www.youtube.com/watch?v=2Wn2qaUhtxM.

Chapter 11: MuchMusic: Age of Relevance

The opening quote is from U2's song "Last Night on Earth," which was released on the album *Pop*, Island Records, July 1, 1997.

Claire Bickley, "Martin, CITY Split," *Toronto Sun*, December 9, 1992.

The tribute to John Martin is by Greg Quill, "MuchMusic Creator Moves to New Things," *Toronto Star*, December 9, 1992.

The PMRC hearings can be found in full at https://www.youtube.com/watch?v=d65BxvSNa20&feature=youtube.

A Question of Taste aired on MuchMusic in 1991. The whole show is available (as I type) on YouTube at https://www.youtube/1xBO_m678_E.

The *TooMuchForMuch* episode on Marilyn Manson ("intentionally ugly anti-Christ self-mutilating Church of Satan cyborg superstar"), hosted by Avi Lewis, is currently available at https://youtube/oL9CjWlowWM.

The first *Kumbaya* was aired live on MuchMusic on September 5, 1993. Watch highlights here: https://www.youtube.com/watch?v=bEMb72Kd_OY.

MuchMusic's *Vote with a Vengeance* election coverage aired live on MuchMusic on October 25, 1993.

Much Comes Out aired live on MuchMusic on Sunday June 27, 1999 as part of Lesbian and Gay Pride Week, June 21–27, 1999.

Chapter 12: Much Goes Global

The *Pinky and the Brain* quote can be found at https://en.wikiquote.org/wiki/Pinky_and_the_Brain.

The CRTC's 1994 licensing decisions can be found at http://www.crtc.gc.ca/eng/archive/1994/DB94-287.htm.

David Baker sent the Bogota story and photo to me in an email. (No idea who took the photo — we'd have to ask FARQ.)

Moses Znaimer's comments on Barry Diller and CBC president Gérard Veilleux were related to me in a phone call on the morning of September 20, 2015.

Justin Smallbridge, "Think Global, Act Loco," *Canadian Business*, June 1996. Available at http://justinsmallbridge.com/clips/19960601CBcitytv.html.

Moses Znaimer's comments on Barry Diller's visit and Viacom CEO Sumner Redstone's boardroom were reported in an article by Roger D. Friedman, "The Great Live North. Like MTV's Splashy New Format Change? Thank Canada's MuchMusic," *Spin Magazine*, March 1998.

R. Serge Denisoff, *Inside MTV* (Piscataway, NJ: Transaction Publishers, 1988), p. 163.

Chapter 13: MuchLIVE

Levon Helm's quote is something he often said before a live show.

The review of The Tragically Hip's *Intimate and Interactive* show is from John Doyle, "When Much Mattered. Lessons from MuchMusic's Glory Days," *Globe and Mail*, August 31, 2009.

Neil Young's *Intimate and Interactive* (called "Neil TV") aired on MuchMusic in 1996 and appears (at the moment) in six parts on YouTube: https://www.youtube.com/watch?v= vXdhVWLit54&list=RDvXdhVWLit54#t=38.

Neil Young's statement on the environment was published in an article by Charlie Smith, "Neil Young Talks about Tarsands, Constitution, and First Nations Before Blue Dot Show in Vancouver," *Georgia Straight*, November 9, 2014. Available at http://www.straight.com/ music/767036/neil-young-talks-about-tarsands-constitution-and-first-nations-blue-dot- show-vancouver.

The line "scars that can't be seen" is from David Bowie's "Lazarus" on the album *Blackstar*, which was released on January 8, 2016, on Columbia Records.

Chapter 14: War Child

The MuchMusic War Child special *Musicians in the War Zone* aired in the fall of 2001. It can be viewed at https://www.youtube.com/watch?v=aLX3HK6eJTY.

For more information on the war in Sierra Leone, visit http://web.undp.org/evaluation/ documents/thematic/conflict/SierraLeone.pdf and http://articles.philly.com/2000-11-15/ news/25612803_1_unamsil-revolutionary-united-front-peacekeeping-effort.

For more history on the Ghanaian slave trade, visit http://www.ghanaweb.com/ GhanaHomePage/history/slave-trade.php.

Chapter 15: Visions of Springsteens Danced in Her Head

The opening quote is from Book One of Horace's *Odes*.

Fredric Dannen, *Hit Men: Power Brokers and Fast Money Inside the Music Business* (New York: Vintage, 1991).

Chuck Philips, "Passion for Music Drives Columbia Chief to Make Plenty of Industry Noise," *Los Angeles Times*, January 29, 2001. Available at http://articles.latimes.com/2001/ jan/29/business/fi-18445.

Chapter 16: Welcome to Sony, the Honeymoon Is Over

The quote from composer John Cage is available at http://www.52composers.com/cage.html.

Statistics on global music sales in 1991 can be found at http://www.ifpi.org/content/library/ worldsales2000.pdf.

The quote by Bob Thaves on Fred Astaire can be found at http://www.gingerrogers.com/ about/quotes.html.

Canada's ranking for broadband penetration in 2001 is available at https://www.itu.int/osg/ spu/ni/promotebroadband/casestudies/canada.pdf.

That Canadians were the number one users of Napster per capita on the planet was a figure quoted by members of CRIA (Canadian Recording Industry Association) at the time.

The phrase "extra-chunky, smoky bacon-flavoured ones" is a nod to Malcolm Gladwell's TED Talk, "Choice, Happiness and Spaghetti Sauce," which can be viewed at https://www.ted.com/talks/malcolm_gladwell_on_spaghetti_sauce/transcript?language=en.

For the article reporting on the backlash against Metallica when they sued Napster, see http://betanews.com/2000/04/13/metallica-sues-napster-universities-fans/.

Charlie Rose's interview with Lars Ulrich and Chuck D can be viewed at https://www.youtube.com/watch?v=1OIqtHBbDWA.

Lou Reed's statement that "Artists, like anyone else, should be paid for their work" was published in an article by Jane Martinson, "We Can Work It Out, Says MP3," *Guardian*, May 4, 2000. Available at https://www.theguardian.com/media/2000/may/04/mondaymediasection.business.

B. B. King's interview with Pat Casey can be viewed at https://news.google.com/newspapers?nid=1298&dat=20000914&id=IzEzAAAAIBAJ&sjid=iQgGAAAAIBAJ&pg=6704,4125578&hl=en.

The statistics on Napster's users were found at https://en.wikipedia.org/wiki/Napster.

The story of the twelve-year-old girl named Brianna, the seventy-two-year-old grandfather named Derwood Pickle, and the Massachusetts grandmother named Sarah Ward, all of whom were charged with copyright infringement by the RIAA, can be found at https://www.eff.org/files/filenode/riaa_at_four.pdf.

The quote from the RIAA spokesperson is available at http://www.mp3newswire.net/stories/2003/Brianna_LaHara.html.

The story of the CRIA trial to sue uploaders can be found at http://www.theglobeandmail.com/technology/cria-again-pursues-file-swappers-in-court/article1117122/.

The stats on the number of Canadians buying blank CD-Rs can be found at https://www.ic.gc.ca/eic/site/ippd-dppi.nsf/eng/ip01114.html.

A good reading of the complex story of the songwriting credits on "Goodnight Irene" is given by NPR Music, currently available at http://www.npr.org/2000/08/19/147729367/-goodnight-irene, and Dave Marsh's thoughts at http://www.counterpunch.org/2002/07/20/alan-lomax/

The stats on Apple's song sales in its first year can be found at https://en.wikipedia.org/wiki/ITunes_Store#Music.

A breakdown of Apple's cut on a $0.99 song purchase on iTunes is available at http://appleinsider.com/articles/07/04/23/itunes_store_a_greater_cash_crop_than_apple_implies.

Coverage of Taylor Swift's fight with Apple over the company's offering free streaming of artists' songs can be found at http://time.com/3940500/apple-music-taylor-swift-release/ and http://money.cnn.com/2015/06/21/media/taylor-swift-1989-apple-music/. Bob Lefsetz also has some fun with the story: http://lefsetz.com/wordpress/2015/06/22/eddy-cue-caves/.

Chapter 17: The Joy of Downsizing

The Alice Walker quote can be found at https://en.wikiquote.org/wiki/Alice_Walker.

The statistics on the number of women versus men elected to political office in Canada is available at http://www.ipu.org/pdf/publications/wmnmap14_en.pdf.

The statistics on Canadian women's versus men's pay, as well as the number of women with board seats and board chairs, are available at http://www.canadianwomen.org/facts-about-the-gender-wage-gap-in-canada; http://www.swc-cfc.gc.ca/initiatives/wldp/wb-ca/rep-rap-en.html; and https://hillnotes.wordpress.com/2015/03/05/womens-representation-on-corporate-boards-in-canada/.

Emma Watson's UN speech can be viewed at https://www.youtube.com/watch?v=p-iFl4qhBsE.

Margaret Mead's quote "Every time we liberate a woman, we liberate a man" can be found at http://www.nywici.org/features/blogs/aloud/womens-history-month-profile-margaret-mead.

Clear Channel's list of songs with "questionable lyrics" can be found at http://www.slate.com/articles/news_and_politics/chatterbox/2001/09/its_the_end_of_the_world_as_clear_channel_knows_it.html.

Martie Maguire, "The Dixie Chicks Come Clean," *Entertainment Weekly*, May 2, 2003.

Larry LeBlanc, "Canada Considers Anti-War Fallout: Music Execs Wonder if Opposition Will Affect U.S. Relationships," *Billboard*, April 12, 2003.

Raine Maida and Chantal Kreviazuk's trip to Iraq was part of MuchMusic's *Musicians in the War Zone* and can be viewed at https://www.youtube.com/watch?v=aLX3HK6eJTY.

UNICEF's estimate that over 500,000 children died as a direct result of sanctions has been widely quoted. Please see https://www.theguardian.com/theguardian/2000/mar/04/weekend7.weekend9; http://www.commondreams.org/headlines/072100-03.htm; and

http://news.bbc.co.uk/2/hi/middle_east/418625.stm. The number is controversial, as this article shows: https://www.thenation.com/article/hard-look-iraq-sanctions/.

That Canada made the United States' Special 301 Watch List of intellectual property rights "problem countries" can be found at http://www.keionline.org/sites/default/files/ustr_special301_2004.pdf and http://www.michaelgeist.ca/2011/05/ustr-watch-list-canada/.

Chapter 18: Hits and Misses

The opening quote is from President John F. Kennedy's 1963 Convocation address during the ground-breaking ceremony of the Robert Frost Library at Amherst College. You can read the entire speech at https://www.amherst.edu/amherst-story/magazine/issues/20032004_FallWinter/poet_president.

Celine Dion's sales have surpassed 200 million albums worldwide, and in 2016 she received the Billboard Lifetime Achievement Award: http://www.billboard.com/articles/news/bbma/7356823/celine-dion-icon-award-perform-2016-billboard-music-awards.

Carl Wilson, *Let's Talk About Love: A Journey to the End of Taste* (London and New York: Continuum International Publishing Group, 2008).

The information on Tommy Mottola's buyout from Sony can be found at http://www.hollywoodreporter.com/news/tommy-mottola-mariah-carey-life-417617.

Information on Las Vegas's Coliseum theatre can be found at https://en.wikipedia.org/wiki/The_Colosseum_at_Caesars_Palace.

Las Vegas is still betting on Celine: http://www.newsweek.com/can-celine-dion-save-las-vegas-66205.

Mike Doherty, "What Canadian Pop Moment?" *Maclean's*, January 2, 2016. Available at http://www.macleans.ca/culture/arts/what-canadian-pop-moment/.

Bob Leftsetz's comment on Adele in "The Leftsetz Letter" can be found at leftsetz.com/wordpress/2011/08/17/adele-at-the-greek/.

Leonard Cohen kindly gave me his blessing to reprint his email and the story.

Chapter 19: A Year of Rumblings

The opening quote by Bob Dylan is from the song "Don't Fall Apart on Me Tonight," which was released on his album *Infidels* on October 27, 1983, on Columbia Records.

The cost of the Sony–BMG Canada merger of around $400 million and the impact expected at the time can be found at http://articles.latimes.com/2004/jul/20/business/fi-sonybmg20.

Ed Christman, "Sony/ATV Chairman Blasts Payouts from Internet Radio," *Billboard*, December 11, 2014. Available at http://www.billboard.com/articles/6405565/sony-atv-chairman-pandora-payouts.

The CIRAA statistics on artists active in Canada in 2006 can be found at https://openparliament.ca/committees/canadian-heritage/41-2/21/zachary-leighton-2/only/.

Robert Levine, *Free Ride: How Digital Parasites Are Destroying the Culture Business, and How the Culture Business Can Fight Back* (New York: Anchor, 2012).

Information on Taylor Swift, Pharrell Williams, and Rosanne Cash's issues with Spotify is available, respectively, at http://time.com/3554438/taylor-swift-spotify/; http://www.businessinsider.com/pharrell-made-only-2700-in-songwriter-royalties-from-43-million-plays-of-happy-on-pandora-2014-12; and http://mashable.com/2014/02/07/rosanne-cash/#ApDgVfLY7Eqy.

You can read more about the #IStandForMusic protest at http://musiccanada.com/news/artists-music-companies-support-resound-application-for-judicial-review-of-copyright-board-tariff-8-decision/.

Mark Savage, "Metallica Manager: 'YouTube Is the Devil,'" BBC News, April 18, 2016. Available at http://www.bbc.com/news/entertainment-arts-36072736.

Nelly Furtado, "YouTube Pays More than Nothing. That Doesn't Make It Fair," *Guardian*, May 2, 2016. Available at https://www.theguardian.com/music/musicblog/2016/may/02/nelly-furtado-youtube-artist-royalties-fair-pay.

Debbie Harry, "Music Matters. YouTube Should Pay Musicians Fairly," *Guardian*, April 26, 2016. Available at: http://www.theguardian.com/music/musicblog/2016/apr/26/debbie-harry-youtube-royalties?CMP=share_btn_link.

The IFPI's 2016 global music report can be found at http://ifpi.org/news/IFPI-GLOBAL-MUSIC-REPORT-2016.

The CIRAA's statistics on the 50-percent decline of active Canadian artists since 2006 can be found at https://openparliament.ca/committees/canadian-heritage/41-2/21/zachary-leighton-2/?page=1.

There's an interesting back story on the quote from Nietzsche: http://harpers.org/blog/2010/09/reconsidering-nietzsche-six-questions-for-julian-young/.

Chapter 20: Burning Off a Non-Compete

The quote attributed to Winston Churchill can be found at http://www.winstonchurchill.org/resources/quotations/135-quotes-falsely-attributed.

Maya Angelou's quote referring to imposter syndrome can be found at http://www.learning-mind.com/imposter-syndrome/.

Neil Gaiman's commencement speech at the University of the Arts in 2012 can be viewed at http://www.uarts.edu/neil-gaiman-keynote-address-2012.

Sheryl Sandberg, *Lean In: Women, Work, and the Will to Lead* (New York: Knopf, 2013), p. 61.

The line "pick yourself up, dust yourself off, start all over again" is from the song "Pick Yourself Up," composed in 1936 by Jerome Kern and written by Dorothy Fields. The song was written for the Ginger Rogers and Fred Astaire film *Swing Time*.

Eve Ensler, *In the Body of the World: A Memoir of Cancer and Connection* (Toronto: Random House Canada, 2013), p. 175.

The statistic on Canada doubling its foreign aid is from a June 25, 2005 *Toronto Star* editorial titled "Canada Can Afford Aid to the Poorest." Bob Geldof's comment that Paul Martin should "stay home" if he wasn't going to commit Canada to 0.7 percent is also quoted in this editorial.

Rex Murphy, "Let Us Excori8 Live 8," *Globe and Mail*, June 25, 2005.

CBC journalist Brian Stewart's documentary on the 1984 famine in Ethiopia can be viewed at https://www.youtube.com/watch?v=tFPr-zAXNuc and https://www.youtube.com/watch?v=uS-QWEq76zs.

The 2014 OECD figures are available at http://www.oecd.org/dac/stats/documentupload/ODA%202014%20Tables%20and%20Charts.pdf.

For more information on the Clinton Foundation and the Clinton Global Initiative, visit https://www.clintonfoundation.org/clinton-global-initiative.

Sir Richard Branson's pledge to invest all profits from his travel companies over ten years—an estimated $3 billion—to fight climate change is available at https://www. clintonfoundation.org/main/news-and-media/press-releases-and-statements/press-release-clinton-global-initiative-surpasses-previous-year-s-total-5-7-bill.html.

Totals of funds raised at the first two CGI conferences can be found at https://www. clintonfoundation.org/main/clinton-foundation-blog.html/2012/09/21/clinton-global-initiative-milestones.

Andrew Carnegie's quote "The man who dies rich, dies disgraced" can be found at http:// www.pbs.org/wgbh/amex/carnegie/filmmore/description.html.

Frank Giustra's $100 million pledge to the Clinton Giustra Sustainable Growth Initiative (now called the Clinton Giustra Enterprise Partnership, or CGEP) is documented at https:// www.clintonfoundation.org/main/news-and-media/press-releases-and-statements/press-release-president-clinton-and-business-leaders-launch-sustainable-developm.html.

The January 2016 Oxfam report is available at http://www.oxfam.org.uk/media-centre/press-releases/2016/01/62-people-own-same-as-half-world-says-oxfam-inequality-report-davos-world-economic-forum.

For more information on the Clinton Giustra Enterprise Partnership, see http://cgepartnership. com/.

Tim McGraw's football feud with Jon Bon Jovi can be found at http://www.people.com/people/article/0,,750286,00.html.

Chapter 21: Over My Dead Body: Life at the CBC

The full text of Malala's speech to the UN is available at https://secure.aworldatschool.org/page/content/the-text-of-malala-yousafzais-speech-at-the-united-nations/.

Richard Stursberg, *The Tower of Babble: Sins, Secrets and Successes Inside the CBC* (Vancouver, B.C.: Douglas & McIntyre, 2012), pages. 215, 225–26, 258, 261–62, and 289.

For more information on the Canadian Broadcasting Act, see http://laws-lois.justice.gc.ca/eng/acts/b-9.01/page-1.html.

The 2008–2009 CBC/Radio-Canada budget is available at http://www.cbc.radio-canada.ca/_files/cbcrc/documents/financial-reports/2008-2009-ar.pdf.

For a recent example of how having the Leafs in the playoffs affects ratings, see http://www. huffingtonpost.ca/2016/04/12/rogers-feeling-the-sting-of-all-seven-canadian-teams-missing-nhl-playoffs_n_9671502.html.

The 2015–2016 CBC/Radio-Canada annual report is available at http://www.cbc.radio-canada.ca/site/annual-reports/2014-2015/_documents/annual-report-2014-2015.pdf.

Michael Enright kindly gave me his blessing to reprint his email.

Mellissa Fung, *Under an Afghan Sky: A Memoir of Captivity* (Toronto: HarperCollins Publishers, 2011).

Chapter 22: Stuck in the Middle with You

The opening quote from Groucho Marx can be found at http://www.quotes.thinkexist.com/quotation/while_money_can-t_buy_happiness-it_certainly_lets/166852.html.

The line "empathy over antipathy" is a quote from Mark Riley at Mallard Digital: http://www.mallarddigital.com/about-us.html.

The history of the CRTC's approval for CBC Radio to become non-commercial was drawn from Richard Stursberg's *The Tower of Babble: Sins, Secrets and Successes Inside the CBC* (Vancouver, B.C.: Douglas & McIntyre, 2012), p. 217.

A reference to the quote from CRTC member Tom Pentefountas can be found in an article by journalist (and author of the book *Saving the CBC*) Wade Rowland at http://www.waderowland.com/crtc-decision-cbc-licence-renewal-allows-advertising-on-cbc-radio-2/.

The statistics on the cuts to the CBC announced in 2014 can be found at http://www.cbc.radio-canada.ca/en/media-centre/2014/04/10s/.

John Erhlichman, "Why Netflix's Canadian Sales May Top Half a Billion Dollars a Year," BNN.com, April 18, 2016. Available at http://beta.bnn.ca/why-netflix-s-canadian-sales-may-top-half-a-billion-dollars-a-year-1.473874.

Reports of the Australian Broadcasting Corporation's $300-million funding cut can be found at http://www.smh.com.au/federal-politics/political-news/abc-and-sbs-facing-200300-million-shared-cuts-over-five-years-20141111-11kecn.html.

The July 2015 Senate report called "Time for Change" can be accessed at http://www.parl.gc.ca/Content/SEN/Committee/412/trcm/rep/rep14jul15-e.pdf.

CBC's comment on the July 2015 Senate report "Time for Change" ("Frankly, we were hoping for more") can be found at http://www.cbc.ca/radio/asithappens/as-it-happens-monday-edition-1.3160387/senate-report-says-time-for-change-at-the-cbc-1.3160870.

The quote from Senator Art Eggleton can be found at http://www.theglobeandmail.com/opinion/heres-a-better-senate-plan-for-a-vibrant-cbc/article25593281/.

The global public broadcaster funding chart is available at http://wevotecbc.ca/2014/10/30/cbc-funding-is-approximately-29-per-capita-down-from-33-per-capita-prior-to-the-harper-cuts/.

Kate Taylor also wrote an excellent article about it in the Globe and Mail titled "CBC Plan Needs Sober Second Thought," July 25, 2015.

Richard Stursberg's quote regarding the CBC's need for "a plan with teeth" is taken from *The Tower of Babble*, p. 289.

Chapter 23: If Content Was King, Context Would Be Queen

Jian Ghomeshi's interview with Billy Bob Thornton on *Q* can be viewed at https://www.youtube.com/watch?v=IJWS6qyy7bw.

For more information the growth of Radio One, please see CBC's 2010–2011 Annual Report: http://www.cbc.radio-canada.ca/_files/cbcrc/documents/financial-reports/2010-2011-ar.pdf.

Chapter 24: Future-ready

The opening quote from Oscar Wilde can be found at http://www.brainyquote.com/quotes/quotes/o/oscarwilde105222.html.

Richard Stursberg's comment on Hubert Lacroix can be found in *The Tower of Babble*, p. 307.

Hubert Lacroix's comment on Richard Stursberg's departure from the CBC can be found in Guy Dixon, "Top CBC Executive Leaves Broadcaster," *Globe and Mail*, August 6, 2010. Available at http://www.theglobeandmail.com/arts/television/top-cbc-executive-leaves-broadcaster/article1212869/.

David Akin, "CBC Axes Exec, Despite Ratings Success," *Toronto Sun*, August 9, 2010. Available at http://www.torontosun.com/news/canada/2010/08/08/14962161.html.

On journalistic transparency and accuracy at the CBC, see http://www.public-value.cbc.radio-canada.ca/story/10/.

CBC/Radio-Canada's study of its news coverage of the 2009 federal election, which "found no indication of partiality in the network's coverage," can be viewed at http://www.public-value.cbc.radio-canada.ca/story/10/. The study also found that "all political parties represented in the House of Commons were treated equitably and that no bias was evident."

The description of the CBC/Radio-Canada board meeting described by Alain Saulnier can be found in his book, *Losing Our Voice: Radio-Canada Under Siege*, (Toronto: Dundurn, 2012), p. 158.

Chapter 25: Canadians Deserve a Strong CBC

The opening quote is from Joni Mitchell's "Big Yellow Taxi," which was originally released on her 1970 album *Ladies of the Canyon* on Reprise Records.

The CBC job cuts announcement is available at http://www.cbc.ca/news/canada/cbc-to-cut-657-jobs-will-no-longer-compete-for-professional-sports-rights-1.2605504.

Linden MacIntyre, "Why I Left the CBC and Its Toxic Atmosphere," *Huffington Post*, January 22, 2015. Available at http://www.huffingtonpost.ca/linden-macintyre/ghomeshi-cbc-macintyre_b_6204668.html.

The June 2014 announcement of an estimated 1,000 to 1,500 job cuts by 2020 is available at http://www.theglobeandmail.com/arts/television/cbc-plans-massive-staff-cuts-as-it-shifts-to-mobile-first-strategy/article19354305/.

The Canadian Media Guild's reaction to the CBC's 2015–2020 strategic plan is available at http://www.friends.ca/news-item/12205, http://www.friends.ca/news-item/12198, http://www.friends.ca/news-item/12190, and http://news.nationalpost.com/news/canada/cbc-cutting-back-evening-news-in-house-production-in-shift-towards-digital.

The Canadian Media Guild and the Syndicat des communications de Radio-Canada's statement calling for Hubert Lacroix and the CBC board to step down is available at http://www.cmg.ca/en/2015/10/29/lack-of-confidence-in-the-cbcradio-canada-president-and-board/#sthash.18CugUKa.dpuf.

Isabelle Montpetit's comment on Hubert Lacroix and the CBC board can be found at http://www.thestar.com/news/gta/2015/10/29/cbc-president-and-board-must-go-union.html.

Hubert Lacroix's living-related expenses controversy: http://www.cbc.ca/news/politics/hubert-lacroix-apologizes-for-30k-expenses-error-1.2552238 and http://www.cbc.ca/news/politics/cbc-president-hubert-lacroix-repays-30k-in-expenses-1.2546300.

Information on the Jian Ghomeshi scandal can be found at http://www.cbc.ca/news/canada/jian-ghomeshi-s-55m-lawsuit-against-cbc-being-withdrawn-1.2849523.

Judge Horkins' ruling in the Ghomeshi trial can be found at http://www.cbc.ca/news/canada/toronto/horkins-decision-ghomeshi-1.3505808.

Reaction to Judge Horkins' verdict in the Jian Ghomeshi trial is available at http://www.huffingtonpost.ca/2016/03/24/ibelievesurvivors-jian-ghomeshi_n_9539294.html.

Kathryn Borel's statement following the end of the Ghomeshi trail can be found at http://www.cbc.ca/news/kathryn-borel-statement-jian-ghomeshi-case-1.3577280.

The call for a formal inquiry on Alberta Court judge Robin Camp is available at http://www.cbc.ca/news/politics/judge-robin-camp-judicial-inquiry-1.3697014 and http://globalnews.ca/news/2612649/looming-inquiry-into-federal-judge-exposes-flaws-with-canadas-judicial-appointment-process/.

The analysis of Statistics Canada data by University of Ottawa professor Holly Johnson can be found at http://www.cbc.ca/news/canada/toronto/ghomeshi-trial-sexual-assault-chill-1.3441059.

That the CBC was created initially to "foster a national spirit and interpret national citizenship" and to "guard against" the flood of foreign content coming our way is documented at http://www.thecanadianencyclopedia.ca/en/article/canadian-broadcasting-corporation/.

Actor Eric Peterson's description of Canada as an "occupied country" when it comes to English Canada's consumption of American pop culture and news can be found at http://www.cbc.ca/radio/q/schedule-for-friday-jan-23-1.2952210/eric-peterson-on-why-canadian-culture-should-stay-canadian-1.2952217.

Chapter 26: The Zoomer: My Way or The Highway

The opening quote from Barack Obama can be found at http://thinkprogress.org/politics/2008/12/18/33898/obama-defend-warren/.

The email from Moses Znaimer is used with permission.

Conrad Black's interview with Margaret Atwood can be viewed at http://www.thezoomertv.com/videos/conversation-with-conrad-extended-margaret-atwood-interview/.

The Zoomer TTC skit can be viewed at https://www.youtube.com/watch?v=fKCYwoiN6W8.

The Zoomer yoga skit can be viewed at https://www.youtube.com/watch?v=89PkBu78ciY.

The Zoomer American justice system skit can be viewed at https://www.youtube.com/watch?v=Vy-PHI5KUes.

Conrad Black's interview with Brian Mulroney can be viewed at http://www.thezoomertv. com/videos/conrad-black-vs-brian-mulroney/.

The Zoomer Ageism in Hollywood segment can be viewed at http://www.thezoomertv.com/ videos/episode-5-zoomer-films/.

The Zoomer panel on First Nations with Joseph Boyden can be viewed at http://www. thezoomertv.com/videos/episode-5-zoomer-films/.

Conrad Black's interview with Rob Ford can be viewed at https://www.youtube.com/ watch?v=AUTdbRTWONg.

Daniel Dale, "Rob Ford: Daniel Dale Tells Us Why He Is Taking Legal Action — I Am Serving the Mayor of Toronto with a Libel Notice. Here's Why," *Toronto Star*, December 12, 2013. Available at https://www.thestar.com/news/city_hall/2013/12/12/rob_ford_daniel_dale_ tells_us_why_hes_taking_legal_action.html.

Rob Ford's apology to Daniel Dale is available at http://www.cbc.ca/news/canada/toronto/ rob-ford-apologizes-again-daniel-dale-drops-lawsuit-1.2469456.

ZoomerMedia's response to Rob Ford's apology to Daniel Dale can be found at http://www. zoomerradio.ca/news/latest-news/zoomermedia-apology-on-airing-of-ford-comments- accepted-by-toronto-star-reporter-daniel-dale/.

Conrad Black, "Trust Scientists, Not Shamans," *Huffington Post*, October 12, 2011. Available at http://www.huffingtonpost.ca/conrad-black/global-warming-science_b_1007166.html.

Epilogue: I Rest My Handbag

The quote from the Dalai Lama can be found at http://www.brainyquote.com/quotes/ quotes/d/dalailama132971.html.

"Johnny Cash told me to never drop names" is an old Nashville joke, usually made before bruising one's toes by shamelessly name-dropping.

The Salman Rushdie quote is from Jack Livings, "Interviews: Salman Rushdie, The Art of Fiction No. 186," *The Paris Review*, Summer 2015 No. 174. Available at http://www. theparisreview.org/interviews/5531/the-art-of-fiction-no-186-salman-rushdie.

PERMISSIONS

Every reasonable effort has been made to trace ownership of copyright materials. The publisher will gladly rectify any inadvertent errors of omissions in credits in future editions.

Lyrics

Page 246: "Little Lambs"
Written by Marc Jordan and Steve MacKinnon
82 Margaux Music (SOCAN)
Used by permission.

Page 354: "It's Going Down Slow"
Written by Bruce Cockburn
Published by Rotten Kiddies Music LLC (BMI)
All rights reserved. Used by permission.

Page 372: "Rose of Jericho"
Written by Liam Titcomb
Published by Sony/ATV Music Publishing Canada (SOCAN)
All rights reserved. Used by permission.

Page 373: "Married By Elvis"
Written by Tom Barlow and Mladen Alexander
Published by Thinktank Fish Tunes (SOCAN) / 369 Productions (SOCAN)
Used by permission.

Page 373: "Walk Away"
Written by Tom Barlow, Mladen Alexander
Published by Thinktank Fish Tunes (SOCAN) / 369 Productions (SOCAN)
Used by permission.

Page 374: "Fall For Anything"
Written by Jeremy Binns
Published by Jeremy Fisher Music Inc. (SOCAN) / Sony/ATV Music Publishing Canada (SOCAN)
All rights reserved. Used by permission.

Page 374: "Hate"
Written by D. Coles
Published by Spit Shine Music (SOCAN)
Used by permission

Page 374–75: "This Is My Hit"
Written by D. Coles and Tawgs Salter
Published by Spit Shine Music (SOCAN)
Used by permission.

Page 524: "The Second Half of Life"
Lyrics and music by Murray McLauchlan
Administered by Sony/ATV Music (SOCAN)
Used by permission.

Excerpts

The excerpt from John Doyle's column on pages 265–66 appears by permission of the *Globe and Mail*.

Photographs and Illustrations

Pages 53 and 65: Photograph by John Bast.

Page 58: Courtesy of Harry Warr.

Page 76: Courtesy of Janet York.

Page 83: Photograph by David Little.

Pages 92 and 93: Courtesy of Darby Mills.

Pages 102, 121, 122, 216, 218, 230, 231, 250, and 277 : From the MuchMusic archives, courtesy of Archival/Bell Media.

Page 104: Courtesy of Brigitte Cavanagh.

Page 116: Caricature by Doug Bennett.

Page 130: Photograph by Marko Shark. From the MuchMusic archives, courtesy of Archival/Bell Media.

Page 134: Photograph by Lee Silversides, Island Records.

Page 161: The painting by Manon Elder is from Manon's High Tea series featuring twenty-two Canadian women. Used by permission. See http://www.manonelder.com/projects/hightea/.

Page 193: Photograph by David Hurlbut.

Page 200: Photograph by Andrew McNaughtan.

Pages 202 and 271: Photographs by Barry Roden. From the MuchMusic archives, courtesy of Archival/Bell Media.

Pages 225 and 406: Photographs by Andrew McNaughtan.

Pages 238 and 239: Photographs by Mima Agozzino and Justin Stockwood. From the MuchMusic archives, courtesy of Archival/Bell Media.

Page 266: Courtesy of Thom Ryder.

Pages 277 and 279: Photograph by David Leyes. From the MuchMusic archives, courtesy of Archival/Bell Media.

Page 293: Courtesy of Liz Marshall.

Page 309: Courtesy of Sabrina Usher.

Page 400: Courtesy of Rideau Hall.

Page 425 and 427: Photographs by Barry Roden.

Page 430: The photo of Robin Williams is courtesy of Barry Roden and used by kind permission of Robin Williams' estate.

Page 434: Courtesy of CBC Sydney.

Page 493: Courtesy of Charlie Pachter.

Page 514: Photograph by Yuri Dojc, courtesy Zoomer Media.

All other photographs and images were provided by the author.

MuchMusic/M3 Photographers: Barry Roden, Mark O'Neill, Craig Samuel, James Pattyn, Alex Urosevic, and Greg Henkenhaf. From the MuchMusic archives, courtesy of Archival/Bell Media.

ACKNOWLEDGEMENTS

I know, I know, I'm the queen of lists. I've been trying to quit, though now is actually the appropriate time to thank the heroes and sheroes who have guided me along this bookish path.

Love always to my darling Murray for your endless reassurances as I waffled and whined, and to my beloved Duncan who was hushed far too often while I wrestled with words in the next room. Loving thanks also to my courageous mother and my stalwart brothers who sanctioned their stories, and to my dear late father who taught me to stand tall and push back.

To Sarah MacLachlan, President and Publisher at House of Anansi Press, thank you for believing I had something worth committing to paper, and thank you to my editor—the fearless Janie Yoon—without whom this book would have been an unstructured, indulgent disaster, and to copy-editor Melanie Little, who got my jokes and nipped and tucked my errors.

Heartfelt thank-yous to every generous first reader who offered their criticisms and corrections—especially my enthusiastic friends Shelley Ambrose and Douglas Knight, who gamely plowed through the whole thing and buoyed me up.

Thank you to Susan Stephan and Lee Perkins for their eyes on our childhood; and to Aeriel Rogers, Sam Feldman, Janet York, Susan Rosenberg, John MacLachlan Gray, and Darby Mills for weighing in on our adventures from Waterloo to Whitesnake.

Thank you to Sarah Crawford, Ron Waters, Moses Znaimer, David Kines, Denise Cooper, Bill Bobek, Dennis Saunders, Nancy Oliver, Jay Switzer, Stephen Tapp, Laurie Brown, Jana Lynne White, Steve Kerzner, Stephen and David Hurlbut, Jeanne Beker, George Stroumboulopoulos,

Molly Johnson, Gregory Hewitt, Adam Vaughan, Carol Love, Pegi Cecconi, and Neil Peart for their notes and nods through the Citytv/MuchMusic years, and to Heather Middleton who treasures the archives in the MuchMusic library.

My deep appreciation to Samantha Nutt, Frank Giustra, Sol Guy, Liz Marshall, Molly Johnson, Mark Mattson, Ilana Landsberg-Lewis, Linda Rothstein, Ian Roland, Mike Eizenga, John Monahan, and Michael Charles for your leadership in using your powers for good.

A low bow of gratitude to those who helped to adjust the tuning on the Sony years: Rick Dobbis, Ian MacKay, Richard Pfohl, Billy Mann, Graham Henderson, Karl Percy, Deane Cameron, Larry Leblanc, Gillian Howard, and Don Oates. And, of course, to Leonard Cohen, who gave his blessings.

Thank you to those who helped me serve the CBC sections: Ted Kennedy, Chris Boyce, Eva Czigler, Carol Off, Anna Maria Tremonti, Eleanor Wachtel, Jennifer McGuire, Fred Mattocks, Mary Lynk, Mark Steinmetz, and Richard Stursberg. Thank you to Matt Zimbel, my comrade in arms at *The Zoomer* (and otherwise), and to everyone who cheered along the way, including Jack Rabinovitch, Alan Doyle, Michael Hollett, Ray Danniels, Scott Carmichael, and all the musical friends who professed that they couldn't "wait to read it."

To the dear ones who might have wished to be included in this book but weren't, I beg your forgiveness, and for those who were included but wish they weren't, I beg your forbearance. Thank you to those who shared differing opinions; and to those who may have different versions of events, I look forward to their telling! To the wise legal eyes that helped me make better choices: Daniel Henry, Brian MacLeod, and Peter Howard, I am in your debt.

My eternal affection to the mighty Tuscany Girls: Shelley Ambrose, Lorraine Segato, Gillian Howard, Janet Beed, Leanne "Skippy" Stepnow, Shelly (other) Woods, Susan Willmot, and Sam Nutt, for their wisdom, their laughter, and their joyful appreciation of the goddess Athena.

And finally, thank you to the artists who capture our souls and help us to feel, to question, and to empathize; long may you reign. As Bob Marley sang: "One love, one heart."

INDEX

Please note: Page numbers in italics refer to photographs; subentries are arranged in chronological order. Parenthetical glosses have been provided only where necessary to identify artists or individual persons. Numerical entries are alphabetized as if spelled out (e.g., "50 Cent" as "Fifty Cent"; "U2" as "U Two"), with the exception of CBC Radio 2 and Radio 3. Only selected songs and albums have been indexed.

DENISE DONLON is one of Canada's most successful broadcasters and corporate leaders. She has been a co-host and producer of *The NewMusic*, Director of Programming and VP/General Manager of MuchMusic/Citytv, President of Sony Music Canada, General Manager and Executive Director of CBC English Radio, and co-producer and co-host of *The Zoomer*. She has also devoted herself to numerous charitable initiatives, working with organization such as War Child Canada, MusiCounts, and the Clinton Giustra Enterprise Partnership. She sits on a number of boards and has been honoured with the Humanitarian Spirit Award and the Trailblazer Award at Canadian Music Week, Woman of the Year from Canadian Women in Communications, Woman of Vision from Wired Women, and was inducted in the Broadcast Hall of Fame. She is a Fellow of the Royal Conservatory of Music and a Member of the Order of Canada. She lives in Toronto with her husband, Murray McLauchlan, and their son, Duncan.